Contents

Directory of Maps

Insiders' Guide®
Charleston

Help Us Keep This Guide Up to Date

Every effort has been made by the authors and editors to make this guide as accurate and useful as possible. However, many things can change after a guide is published—establishments close, phone numbers change, hiking trails are rerouted, facilities come under new management, etc.

We would love to hear from you concerning your experiences with this guide and how you feel it could be made better and be kept up to date. While we may not be able to respond to all comments and suggestions, we'll take them to heart and we'll also make certain to share them with the authors. Please send your comments and suggestions to the following address:

The Globe Pequot Press
Reader Response/Editorial Department
P.O. Box 480
Guilford, CT 06437

Or you may e-mail us at: editorial@globe-pequot.com

Thanks for your input, and happy travels!

Insiders' Guide® Series

Insiders' Guide®
to Charleston

*Including Mt. Pleasant, Summerville,
Kiawah, and Other Islands*

Seventh Edition

By J. Michael McLaughlin
and
Lee Davis Todman

Guilford, Connecticut
An imprint of The Globe Pequot Press

The prices and rates listed in this guidebook were confirmed at press time. We recommend, however, that you call establishments before traveling to obtain current information.

Cover illustration: IndexStock
Maps by Trapper Badovinac

ISBN 0-7627-1060-8

Manufactured in the United States of America
Seventh Edition/First Printing

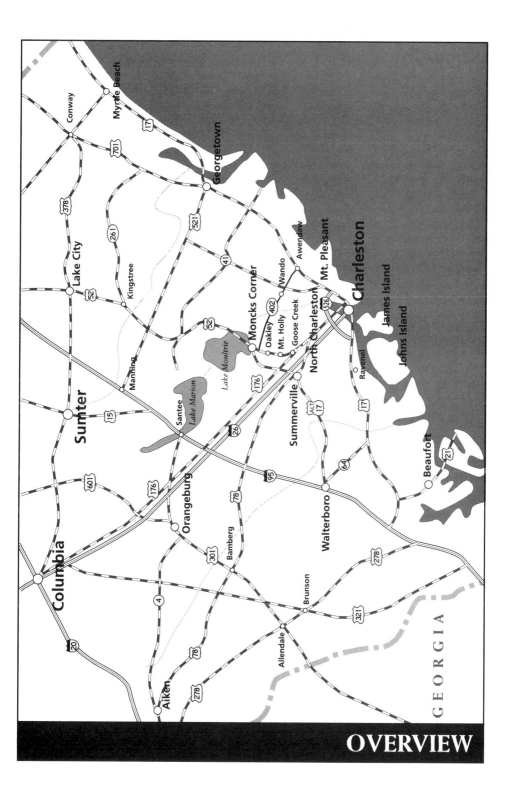

OVERVIEW

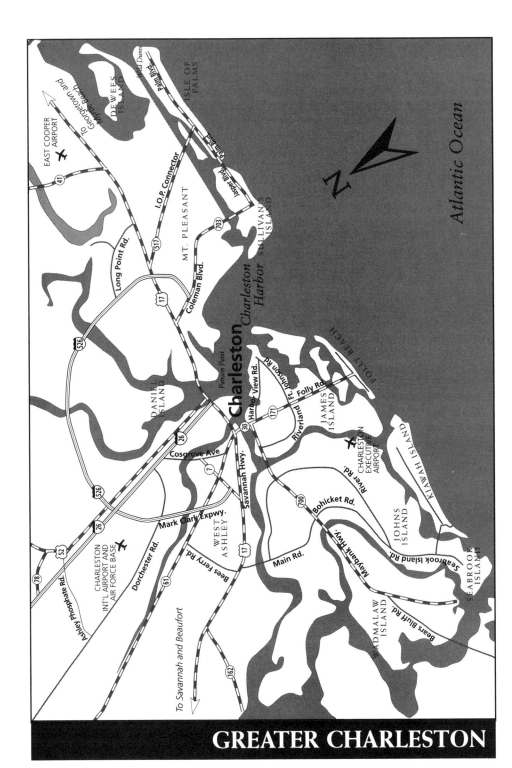

GREATER CHARLESTON

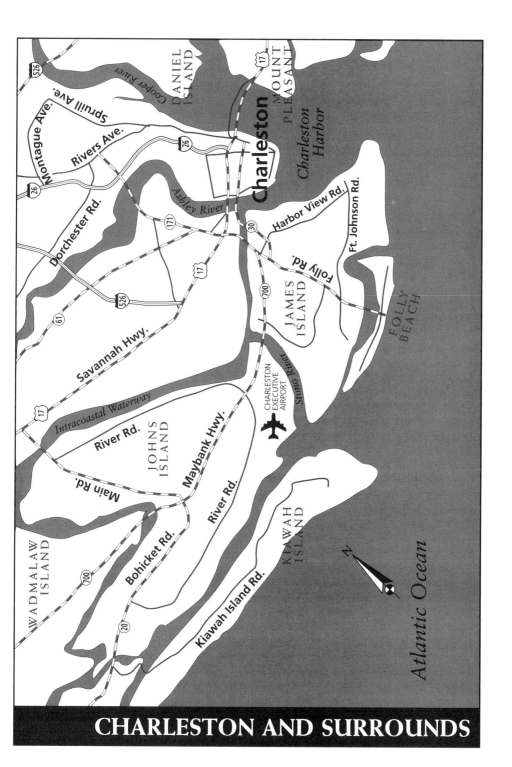

CHARLESTON AND SURROUNDS

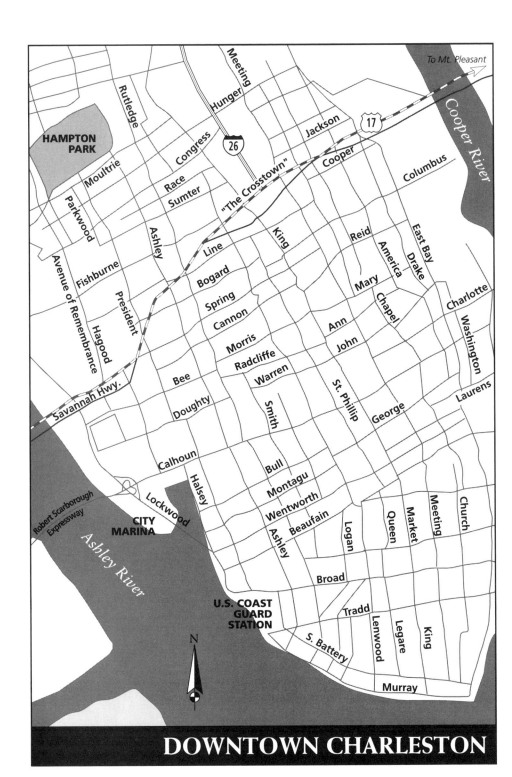

DOWNTOWN CHARLESTON

Preface

Welcome to Greater Charleston, where three South Carolina counties (Charleston, Berkeley, and Dorchester) blend together and create the scenic backdrop for a unique and wonderful lifestyle.

This is a land of history, the home of Revolutionary statesmen. This is a city of gallantry, glory, folly, and pain—where democracy was nurtured and secession proclaimed. This is where, very early on, beauty was deemed as important as survival, whatever the cost. Pride was encouraged. Families were sacrosanct, and God was dutifully acknowledged in mind and matter.

The socio-political passions and turbulent economies that made Charleston such a fascinating place 200 years ago are still very much with us today. Only now the canvas is larger, the paintbrush wider. And Charleston's colorful story just gets bolder as the years go by.

One of the reasons Charleston seems so timeless has to do with geography. The historic Peninsula (the heart of Charleston's identity) is bound by two rivers, the Ashley and the Cooper. Despite whatever else those rivers have meant to Charleston and its people over time, the waters effectively impounded the 18th-century city. This watery restraint forced all real growth and change northward—pushing it upward, spilling it over onto neighboring lands. Even today, neighborhoods that were built "east Cooper" or "west Ashley" always carry the unspoken phrase "of the Peninsula" and bear indirect witness to the old city's powerful presence.

The natural containment of the Ashley and Cooper Rivers (effectively protecting the Peninsula from change) had an accomplice in the Lowcountry itself. The southeastern third of South Carolina is physically low, close to sea level, prone to swampland, marsh, and innumerable shallow creeks and streams. The land was hostile toward early settlers and planters, and it was costly to railroad builders and almost every other developer. It didn't welcome growth and it resists change to this day.

So in many ways Charleston was isolated and remained something of a cultural island while America pushed westward into its destiny. Charleston and its captive Peninsula effectively stayed behind, surrounded by its many coastal distractions.

As it has for eons, the endless marsh still seems to change color every day. And unspoiled beaches can still be caught playing tag with a restless (occasionally punishing) sea. Charlestonians still know that not far away they can find dark and mysterious swamps that, in certain moonlight, whisper primordial secrets in the native tongue of an ancient higher power.

If this is isolation, then it's splendid isolation. This is the Lowcountry: a place, a people, a unique perspective on the world.

Is it any wonder we love living here?

Acknowledgments

For their input, expertise, and assistance in many forms, we thank all who helped with the production of this book. These include the research departments at the Avery Research Center for African American History and Culture, the Charleston County Public Library, Historic Charleston Foundation, and the Public Affairs office of the 437th Airlift Wing at Charleston Air Force Base.

So much of living here is a visual delight. We'd like to thank David Berry, Tommy Ford, John Meffert, and Bill Struhs for their photography and energetic view of our city's many charms. Gracious thanks go, as well, to the various Lowcountry attractions whose staffs helped provide us with images enhancing our descriptions for this book.

Mike would like to thank Rick Burton and the Greater Charleston Concierge Association for their support, enthusiasm, and groundwork in gaining access to so many great dining establishments and Lowcountry attractions. Ken Kochersperger's diligent fact checking and gracious phone work were a great help along the way. Mike also thanks the pair of doves who built a nest on his office windowsill and raised a new family to go out into the world. They gave him daily lessons in patience and a fresh perspective on projects of long duration. Lee would like to thank her brother, Hugh Davis, for being the final authority on all things sporty. She would also like to lovingly pat her dog, Battle, who adjusted to her changing work patterns and stoically endured almost criminal neglect. Mike and Lee would like to thank Mike Mrlik for his phone follow-through as well as footwork on the streets of Charleston and his good company on various fact-finding missions. They would also like to thank Bailey Williams for his encouragement and perseverance for the duration of the extended process. Nancy Thomas lent her maternal insight into Childcare and Kidstuff. Her perspective gave added depth to many other chapters as well.

Our thanks go to Erika Serviss for editing this book and working with us on a schedule that was amazingly career-friendly for all concerned. Thanks go to The Globe Pequot Press for recognizing the value of the Insiders' Guide series and opting to bring it to the people in markets all over the country where the information can be used and appreciated.

We also appreciate the time and information shared by the employees of Trident agencies such as the Charleston County Community Education Program, Charleston County Park and Recreation Commission, Charleston Metro Chamber of Commerce, South Carolina Wildlife and Marine Resources Department, and the Summerville Chamber of Commerce.

Special acknowledgment again goes to the keen eye and sharp scissors of the RPD/JHD Clipping Service, whose constant watch for "Insider info" saved us miles of walking and weeks of laborious research.

—Lee Davis Todman and J. Michael McLaughlin

How to Use This Book

This guide is made up of data-packed chapters that provide the kind of practical information you need to enjoy the Greater Charleston area. The early chapters of this book are generally focused on tourism, history, and attractions. This information is useful to visitors (and residents alike) who want to know more about the city and its surrounds. The latter chapters are especially helpful to newcomers who have decided to make the Lowcountry their permanent home.

If you are planning a visit or move to Charleston, surf the chapters to make contacts ahead of time. If you are already here, or on your way to the city, flip to the Getting Here, Getting Around chapter to determine the best route to your desired destinations or to one of our accommodations chapters for information on lodging (hotels and motels, bed and breakfast and atmospheric inns, or vacation and beach rentals). And if you have arrived and are carrying the book around as a reference tool, just zip to a particular chapter to find the best or closest restaurants, entertainment, recreation, lodging, kidstuff, and attractions. There's even an index at the back of the book so you can pinpoint a specific place quickly and easily.

We have worked to create chapters that stand alone but are cross-referenced so that you can easily set your own pace and schedule for getting to know Charleston. You decide when to immerse yourself in the history and culture of the community and when to make more immediate decisions about where to eat, where to sleep, what to do at night, and where to shop until sunset. Our job is to coordinate the information and organize it clearly so that your time is more enjoyable.

With this seventh edition of the *Insiders' Guide to Charleston*, we hope to again provide a multidimensional view of this area through description, our personal impressions, and some of our preferences. We include addresses and general directions as well as phone numbers so you can make specific plans.

Up front, we've provided area maps to help you get your bearings here in the Lowcountry. We give you brief Insiders' Tips for quick insights and more lengthy Close-ups with information that is particularly interesting, unusual, and distinctly Charlestonian.

In many of our chapters we've included quick reference information such as potentially confusing highway designations, emergency and healthcare phone numbers, and convenient parking garages. Of course, you'll want to use our price codes in the restaurants and accommodations chapters. These are designated at the beginning of the chapter.

Our Lowcountry Daytrips chapter is designed to help you branch out from our immediate area, and a chapter called Kidstuff is offered as a collection of some of our favorite ways to show your children a healthy good time. The former is heavily peppered with historical references (because so much of the Lowcountry is all the more interesting when understood in the context of its past). The latter is a subjective overview of venues and activities that have afforded us hours of fun with children we know.

You will notice that throughout the guide we refer to four main general areas—downtown Charleston, east of the Cooper (River), and west of the Ashley (River). Downtown includes the peninsula and the area slightly north; east of the Cooper includes Mt. Pleasant, Sullivan's Island, and Isle of Palms; west of the Ashley refers to the area just across the Ashley River bridges. We've separated the western islands, James, Johns, Folly, Kiawah, and Seabrook Islands, as a fourth area.

Within chapters such as Restaurants, Nightlife, Hotels and Motels, Parks and Recreation, Healthcare, and Neighborhoods, expect to find geographical subcategories for your convenience. Further, Shopping is organized to benefit two broad categories of readers. We start with a rundown for tourists and visitors who want to explore the major shopping venues downtown. We organize the shopping opportunities by merchandise categories. Then we direct newcomers and residents who seek the convenience of shopping in the outlying areas, again, according to merchandise categories.

Area Overview

Charleston

Mt. Pleasant

Sullivan's Island

Isle of Palms

North Charleston

Berkeley County

Dorchester County

West Ashley

James Island and
Johns Island

Folly Beach

Kiawah Island

Seabrook Island

Here's an overview of Charleston and its surrounding areas. This chapter is arranged in the geographical order you will see again and again, and offers some information that will help provide a peek at what's here now to see and enjoy.

Charleston

Exactly 768 miles from New York City, 590 miles from Miami and almost 2,500 miles from Los Angeles, Charleston remains an undeniably livable city for those fortunate enough to call it home. It's a city of unhurried grace and distinct Southern charm blessed with an uncanny number of historic structures, many of which have been transformed into handsome offices, restaurants, stores, and homes.

Charleston is the second largest city in South Carolina (Greenville takes first place). The city's estimated 1999 population was 100,122. The city's Standard Metropolitan Statistical Area encompasses three counties: Charleston, Berkeley, and Dorchester. This is sometimes called the "Tri-County Area" or the "Trident Area," and in 1999 this population was estimated at 552,803. Projected population growth for the Charleston metro area predicts 619,500 people by the year 2015.

Charleston has a warm climate. In January, the average temperature is 55 degrees; in July, it's 82 on the average. But it's prudent to note that summertime temperatures can peak above the 100-degree mark. And the humidity, which is considerable in the Lowcountry during any season, makes the hot seem hotter and the cold seem colder. Spring in Charleston, however, more than compensates for any discomfort during the other seasons. Many consider it the best time of year in the area; days are warm, nights barely chilled, and the whole world appears to be dripping in wisteria vines and azalea blossoms.

A 1999 business survey concluded that the Charleston economy continues to be sound and growing. The economic boom is most evident in the vast, newly connected lands of Daniel Island and Cainhoy. Just to the east and north of peninsular Charleston, these areas were annexed in 1991 into the city of Charleston. Daniel Island, which is 4,500 acres, is now being developed as a planned, environmentally sensitive community (see our Neighborhoods chapter).

Charleston also offers a wealth of job opportunities. Throughout the area in the banner year of 1997, the Charleston Regional Development Alliance was responsible for securing more than 4,585 new jobs, including those at the Nucor steel plant and Mikasa, a manufacturer of tabletop products. Since then new employment opportunities continue to accrue at a steady rate.

More than eight million tons of cargo pass through the Port of Charleston every year. As the largest cargo port on the Southeast Atlantic and Gulf coasts (the fourth largest container port nationwide), the port directly and indirectly employs an estimated 17,000 people.

Throughout history, Charleston has stood as the cultural capital of the South. The performing arts are well represented here with a symphony orchestra, community theater groups, and several ballet companies. The Gibbes Museum of Art and numerous art galleries display the city's impressive appreciation for visual pleasures. The abundant

Charleston Vital Statistics

Most of these facts and figures pertaining to Charleston and South Carolina are covered in much greater detail in the following pages of this Insiders' Guide to Charleston. However, here's an at-a-glance overview of the area for first-timers and international visitors—plus a quick reference for those in a big hurry.

Charleston Mayor: Joseph P. Riley, Jr. (D)   **South Carolina Governor:** Jim Hodges (D)

Population: City of Charleston: 100,122 (in 1998)
Metro Area: 552,803 (1999 estimate)
South Carolina: 3,885,736 (1999 estimate)

Area (sq. miles): City of Charleston: 88.14 square miles
business district: 7.6 square miles
South Carolina: 31,113 square miles

Nickname/Motto : "The Holy City."
Translation of Latin motto from the city's official seal: Aedes Mora Juraque Curat, "She guards her buildings, her customs, and her laws."

Average Temperatures: July: 82 F
January: 55 F

Average Rainfall: 52 inches per year

City/State Founded: First English Colony of Carolina founded: 1670
Officially separated as Royal Colony of South Carolina: 1729

South Carolina's Major Cities:
Columbia (State Capital), Charleston, Florence, Georgetown, Greenville, Hilton Head, Mt. Pleasant, Myrtle Beach, North Charleston, Spartanburg, Sumter.

Major Colleges/Universities:
Charleston Southern University, College of Charleston, The Citadel, Trident Technical College, Johnson and Wales (culinary institute), Medical University of South Carolina

Important Dates in History:

1670   founding of Charles Towne colony
1680   colony moved to safer location on peninsula
1719   revolt leading to establishment of South Carolina as province of British Crown
1783   newly liberated city changes name to "Charleston"
1822   Denmark Vesey slave uprising
1861   outbreak of War Between the States.
1904   construction of U.S. Navy Yard
1977   debut of Spoleto Festival USA
1989   devastation by Hurricane Hugo

Major Area Employers:

Medical University of South Carolina, Charleston Air Force Base, U.S. Navy, Charleston County School District, CareAlliance Health Services, Robert Bosch Corporation

Famous Sons and Daughters:
Charles C. Pinckney—youngest signer of the U.S. Constitution; John Rutledge—another signer of the U.S. Constitution; John C. Calhoun—Statesman, U.S. Vice President; Edward Rutledge and Arthur Middleton—signers of the Declaration of Independence; Francis Marion, "The Swamp Fox"—Revolutionary War hero; Eliza Lucas Pinckney—entrepreneur of rice/indigo culture; Mary Boykin Chesnut—Civil War diarist; Dubose Heyward—author of *Porgy*; Philip Simmons—world-class wrought iron artisan; Septima Clark—educator and civil rights activist

Major Airports/Interstates: Charleston International Airport; I-26; I-526.

Public Transportation: CARTA (bus system); DASH (downtown area shuttle)

Military Bases:
Charleston Air Force Base (437th Airlift Wing); United States Coast Guard Group Charleston Station; Charleston's NAVELEX (Naval Electronics Engineering Command and NOAA (National Oceanic and Atmospheric Administration) Coastal Services Center

Driving Laws:
Right turn on "Red" permitted; seatbelts must be worn at all times in moving vehicle; headlights must be on when wipers are used; speed limit on State highways is 55 MPH; speed limit on Interstates is 70 in designated limited access areas

Alcohol Laws:
Legal drinking age: 21 years; Blood/alcohol content of 10% or higher is DUI in South Carolina, but .06% to .09% can also be designated DUI at arresting officer's discretion

Daily Newspaper: *The Post and Courier*; daily circulation, 108,927

Sales Tax : 6% City/State sales tax on all non-eatable goods
12% City/State accommodations tax

Broad Street, dominated by the spire of St. Michael's Church, is the traditional heart of Charleston's leagal and business district. PHOTO: COURTESY OF CHARLESTON AREA CONVENTION AND VISITORS BUREAU

examples of architectural preservation, showing the city's longstanding heritage of building excellence and craftsmanship, also bear witness to this esthetic awareness. (See our chapters called The Arts and Architectural Preservation.)

For five consecutive years, Charleston has been recognized in popular tourist magazines as one of the top-10 domestic travel destinations. It's even been proclaimed by etiquette guru Marjabelle Young Stewart as the "most mannerly" city in America. We hope that will turn out to be your experience as well.

Mt. Pleasant

Anyone who crosses the new Cooper River bridge into Mt. Pleasant will never forget the journey (see the Close-up, "A View to a Thrill," in our Getting Here, Getting Around chapter). Directly across the Cooper River from Charleston, Mt. Pleasant dates its founding to 1680. The original heart of Mt. Pleasant is the area known as the Old Village. It is designated a National Register Historic District with gracious homes from both the colonial and antebellum periods. Today, the city carefully preserves its rich heritage and small-town appeal. The 1999 estimated population for Mt. Pleasant was 44,785 (a 48.7% jump from the 1990 Census figures).

The population numbers for this thriving community certainly make it qualify as a "city." But, as the name implies, the "town" of Mt. Pleasant is an apt description for the state of mind and the attitude of the businesses you'll find there. Although it serves as a major bedroom community to the Charleston Peninsula, it's still a viable community unto itself.

The days when Mt. Pleasant residents were dependent on the Peninsula for primary shopping, dining, and entertainment venues are gone. Mt. Pleasant's new $40 million Towne Centre is clear proof of that with its fifteen separate buildings housing 60 tenants within 425,000 sq. ft. of upscale shopping space.

Patriots Point, the world's largest naval and maritime museum complex, is Mt. Pleasant's biggest attraction. It is dominated by the aircraft carrier *Yorktown*, World War II's famous "Fighting Lady." You can also board tour boats at Patriots Point to visit Fort Sumter National Monument, where the Civil War began (see our Attractions chapter).

Adjacent to Patriots Point is Patriots Point Links, one of the area's most popular public golf courses. The 18-hole, par 72 layout provides spectacular views of Charleston Harbor and the Peninsula's skyline (see our Golf chapter). The Mt. Pleasant/Isle of Palms Visitor Center at the corner of U.S. Highway 17 and McGrath Darby Boulevard is a good place to start when exploring Mt. Pleasant.

Sullivan's Island

South of Mt. Pleasant and across the Intracoastal Waterway, Sullivan's Island is one of Mt. Pleasant's three true barrier islands (Isle of Palms and the private island of Dewees are the other two). Access to the island is via the Ben Sawyer Causeway (S.C. Highway 703) from Mt. Pleasant or via the Isle of Palms Connector (S.C. Highway 517) through the Isle of Palms.

Largely a quiet, residential island of old and new beach houses, the island's 1999 permanent population was about 1,800. There is also a smattering of charming 19th-century "summer homes" that have somehow managed to survive the hurricanes and changing fashions of vacation architecture. The few restaurants and pubs on the island are crowded along Middle Street and create something of a strip for strollers who might want to "pub hop" during the evening hours.

Sullivan's Island is the site of old Fort Moultrie and its accompanying interpretation center, which is operated by the National Park Service. There you can trace the fort's 171-year history from the American Revolution through World War II (see Forts in our Attractions chapter).

Another interesting by-product of Sullivan's Island's military days is the fine old row of "quarters" (not far from the lighthouse) that date back to World War I. Still standing at attention along a quiet side street is a handsome line of large frame houses that once served as "officers' row" for the garrison at Fort Moultrie. Now private homes, these former examples of elite military housing speak eloquently of another time from the island's (and our country's) past.

Isle of Palms

As the years have gone by, the Isle of Palms has grown increasingly popular as a resort and residential island. In 1999, the year-round population was about 5,000, but when you add the seasonal renters and the day visitors, the island can host thousands of additional people on any given summer day. Its proximity to Charleston is one of the reasons; its six miles of wide, sparkling beach is another attraction.

Those who are here for the short term can enjoy a wide range of accommodations from one end of the island to the other. And the island has a full complement of shops, restaurants, goods, and services to make life very comfortable.

World-famous Wild Dunes resort, at the northeast end of the island, offers fine restaurants, conference facilities, a fitness center, multiple tennis courts, and two championship Tom Fazio-designed golf courses. Wild Dunes is a busy destination all year long (see our Neighborhoods and Vacation and Beach Rentals chapters). The Wild Dunes Yacht Harbor is one of the finest marinas on the Eastern Seaboard. Maybe best of all, Wild Dunes is still only 15 miles from downtown Charleston, offering visitors the chance to enjoy the best of both worlds.

> **Insiders' Tip**
>
> Here is a statistic that says a great deal about the development "styles" of the resort barrier islands of Kiawah and Seabrook: over the past decade, Kiawah's population growth has been well over 40%, while Seabrook's population has only grown by 11%. Some people are attracted to a "resort destination" image while others prefer the "quiet residential" atmosphere. Both have great appeal.

North Charleston

North Charleston, only incorporated in 1972, is geographically the third-largest city in South Carolina, with a population of 84,000. Its reputation as the hub of the Lowcountry is justified; it's clearly the business and transportation center for the lower half of the state. The international airport and the Amtrak station are here. Also, Interstate 26 and the Mark Clark Expressway (Interstate 526) make getting anywhere in the Lowcountry a snap (see our Getting Here, Getting Around chapter).

One of North Charleston's main attractions is the Charleston Area Convention Center Complex, which includes the 14,000-seat Coliseum and the 2,250-seat Performing Arts Center. These state-of-the-art venues draw crowds from all over the area and host a wide variety of events ranging from Broadway shows to major rock concerts and ice shows. It's also the home of the South Carolina Stingrays, our local ice hockey team (see our Spectator Sports chapter).

Not only does the area have more than 4,795 hotel rooms, but the rates are also generally lower than those found elsewhere in the Lowcountry (especially downtown Charleston). This makes North Charleston a favorite haunt for business types and convention travelers. If you're arriving via I-26, you may want to stop at the North Charleston Visitor Center just across from the Coliseum. You'll find plenty of area information there.

Berkeley County

In the 1980s, Berkeley County, just north of Charleston County, was the fastest-growing county in all of South Carolina. The boom came when major new industrial concerns invested more than $1.7 billion in the county economy.

The greatest concentration of population and residential and commercial development has been in the southern portion of the county near Moncks Corner. Berkeley's central town, however, remains Goose Creek. Other county towns include Hanahan and Moncks Corner. Total population of these towns is more than 46,000, according to latest estimates.

Currently, industrial development is concentrated along U.S. Highway 52 north of Goose Creek and on the island formed by the Cooper River and the Black River and its tributary branches. The major Berkeley County employers are Santee Cooper (electric utility), Bayer Corp. (manufacturing) and Nucor Steel.

Much of the northern portion of Berkeley County is still productive, cultivated farmland. Most of the eastern portion of the county and large areas of the west remain in beautiful pine forests—one of the county's most distinctive features.

Dorchester County

Dorchester's $127 million in economic development during 1997 largely came from the expansion of existing industries. The major employers in Dorchester County include the Robert Bosch Corp. (anti-lock braking systems), Industrial Products, Inc. (industrial textiles), Lieber Correctional Institute and Giant Cement Co.

Although St. George, with its 1999 population of about 1,900, is the county seat, the part of Dorchester County currently seeing the greatest amount of economic growth is Summerville. With a 1999 population of 24,875 the town's healthy mix of retail, commercial, and tourist-related businesses along with light manufacturing concerns seems to be attracting both newcomers and business investors.

For a historical perspective on Summerville and a brief driving tour of the town's historic homes, see our Lowcountry Daytrips chapter.

West Ashley

The City of Charleston annexed its first West Ashley tract in 1960, and the area has been growing ever since. The population doubled from 1960 to 1990 and was approaching 60,000 at last count.

West Ashley is a patchwork of old and new neighborhoods and businesses that line the major traffic arteries (U.S. Highway 17 S. and S.C. Highway 61). Many of the older neighborhoods have graceful old live oaks and spacious, well-tended lawns. In fact, there's a new movement afoot to do some strategic planning aimed at preserving this "village" atmosphere—especially in the area surrounding the foot of the Ashley River

Bridge. And please note, the local residents don't live in West Ashley or at West Ashley, they simply "live West Ashley."

West Ashley is home to Charles Towne Landing State Historic Site, a nature/historic theme park on the site of the original English settlement. It also claims the beautiful Ashley River Road, which leads to Drayton Hall, Magnolia Gardens, and Middleton Place (see Historic Plantations in our Attractions chapter). You'll find Charleston's largest shopping center—Citadel Mall, with 100 tenants—in West Ashley. And the area has the "Automile," a strip of new and used car dealerships along Savannah Highway (U.S. 17 S.) and one of the major engines of the local economy.

By far, the largest employer West Ashley (you'll get used to saying it that way) is Bon Secours St. Francis Hospital, which relocated to a new facility in December 1996 (see our Healthcare chapter). This huge, 32-acre medical complex added 875 new jobs to the area economy, and many other spin-off businesses have followed suit. Another major employer is Dillard's, a department store chain.

James Island and Johns Island

Geographically, James Island, which lies due west of the Charleston Peninsula, is less rural than Johns Island. It is essentially a bedroom community for Charleston with small shopping strips scattered along the main roads of Maybank Highway and Folly Road.

What remains of James Island's rural character may be threatened by the easy access now made possible by the James Island Expressway (S.C. Highway 30). This increasingly busy roadway connecting the island to the Peninsula is fueling rapid development—especially along Folly Road toward Folly Beach. The remaining tracts of farmland are likely victims of rising land values and are prime targets for real estate developers.

While Johns Island may be still agricultural in appearance, change is in the air. A 1997

Wrought-iron gates are classically Charlestonian. PHOTO: DAVID C. BERRY

Charleston Harbor gives visitors and residents cooling sea breezes and easy access to the Atlantic.

study shows that Johns Island is home to more than half of the nearly 2,000 people employed on the resort islands of Kiawah and Seabrook (plus most of the 400 more who work there during the busy season). Some say this is a preview of the island's future. Forecasters predict that Johns Island will continue to be developed into another bedroom community for Charleston, much like James Island is today.

Folly Beach

This eccentric and diverse beach town likes to call itself "the edge of America." Only 10 minutes from historic Charleston, this is a tourist's world: one where there's plenty to see and do.

First of all, there's the beach—Folly's claim to fame. It runs almost 6 miles along the Atlantic side of the island. Folly has had serious erosion problems in the past; the beach was "renourished" a few years ago by mechanically pumping millions of cubic yards of sand back onto the shore, and there's talk about needing to do it again. But there's still plenty of sand, sun, fun, and (yes) folly to go around.

The island has a year-round population of 1,708, according to a 1999 head count. But the population swells enormously on any summer day, when the hoards of beach lovers (young and old) come out to play. Employment opportunities are almost exclusively limited to the tourist trade.

Crabbing, sunning, surfing, swimming, surf fishing, biking, waterskiing, and sailing are going on. You name it, Folly Beach has got it. Folly touts its 1,000-foot fishing pier, finished in 1995, complete with snack bar, tackle shop, and full-service seafood restaurant. The pier is reminiscent of the old days when beach pavilions were all the rage for dance bands and swing music. (For more on area piers, see our Hunting and Fishing chapter.)

Although there are walk-throughs along the beach that lead from Arctic and Ashley avenues to the surf for day visitors, it's best to go to the west end of the island and visit Folly Beach County Park. Admission is $5 a vehicle, but once you're inside you've got restrooms, showers, drinking water, ample parking, and probably the best open vistas on the island. (See our Parks and Recreation chapter.)

You'll find many reasonable short-term accommodations at Folly Beach (see our Hotels and Motels chapter). There are also seasonal rentals and a lot of interesting full-time residents on the island. It is Charleston's truly original beach playground.

Kiawah Island

Only 21 miles from Charleston is Kiawah Island, renowned for its natural beauty and environmentally responsible development. The endless acres of marsh, the 10 miles of pristine Atlantic beach, the thick forests, and abundant wildlife are only the beginning. Amongst all this are championship golf, first-rate tennis, exclusive shopping, and fine dining. Like the beach itself, the opportunities for enjoyment here go on and on.

Golfers have a selection of courses to play. They can choose from Turtle Point by Jack Nicklaus, Cougar Point by Gary Player, Tom Fazio's Osprey Point, and the famed Ocean Course by Pete Dye (site of the memorable 1991 Ryder Cup). (See our Golf chapter for more details.) In November 1997, the Ocean Course hosted the 43rd World Cup of Golf with teams from 32 nations competing. Televised in more than 80 countries, this was the world's most watched golf tournament to date. On Kiawah, tennis buffs have two complete tennis centers with fully staffed pro shops, extensive instructional facilities, and a zoned practice court with an automated ball machine.

The island's accommodations are all outstanding. Some guests prefer being pampered at the Kiawah Inn. Others prefer the privacy of furnished villas or cottages conveniently scattered around the island. Bear in mind that Kiawah Island is a private community with access limited to property owners, guests of the resort, or designated rental agencies. Full-time residents number 1,017 according to a 1999 estimate, but seasonal visitors swell this number to more than 7,000. (See our Neighborhoods and Vacation and Beach Rentals chapters.) Public access to the beach is available at Beachwalker County Park at the west end of the island.

Seabrook Island

Seabrook Island is on the Atlantic shore just 22 miles south of Charleston. It is unique in that it is totally private and completely owned by its residents. Entry to the island is controlled by a security gate for the privacy of residents and guests. The beauty of the island is striking. Visitors can enjoy 3.5 miles of unspoiled beach along the Atlantic and the banks of the Edisto River, which flows into the ocean at Seabrook.

The Club at Seabrook offers championship golf courses: Crooked Oaks, designed by Robert Trent Jones Sr., and Ocean Winds, designed by Willard Byrd. A beach club, a tennis center, and a beautiful Island House Club with restaurants, bar lounges, and a golf pro shop are here. Also unique to Seabrook is its equestrian center.

The island has more than 450 villas available for rent as well as more than 1,055 permanent residents whose homes are situated along the beach, marshes, lakes, and golf courses.

Bohicket Marina, just outside the Seabrook Island gate, is a superb marina and an attractive shopping area. Two hundred slips are available for all sizes of motor cruisers and sailboats. Boat rentals and charters for deep-sea fishing, crabbing, shrimping, or exploring the miles of ocean creeks are also available. (See our Boating and Watersports chapter.)

Sailboats plying the waters are common sights in the Lowcountry. PHOTO: THOMAS P. FORD

Getting Here, Getting Around

Getting Here by Auto
Getting Here by Air
Getting Here by Other Methods
Getting around the Lowcountry

Visitors to the Trident area who arrive via different modes of transportation are faced with challenges unique to each form. For instance, if you drive, fly, ride the bus, or take the train, how are you going to negotiate the trip into town or—worse yet—out to the fringes? Say you come in on a yacht, or you are a passenger on a cruise ship. What next?

We've answered these questions individually, and the headings identify each transportation mode. It may seem a little lengthy, but we've tried to take you by the hand to lead you each step of the way in the Lowcountry.

Getting Here by Auto

We have tried to give very specific directions and many options for travel into and around Charleston. Our reasoning is both practical and designed for those interested in getting more out of their drive than simply moving from point A to point B. With heavy seasonal traffic (in spring, as many as half a million visitors come to Charleston by car), seemingly constant road and bridge work, and a peculiar system of one-way city streets, getting around Charleston is not always simple on first try.

Also, parking on the Peninsula is always a problem. The city has made strides toward managing the situation to the benefit of both residents and tourists, with restricted parking hours in residential neighborhoods and parking garages for public use. Metered parking spaces are limited but convenient when you find them. To avoid costly tickets, a parking garage is your safest bet.

While there are ways to maximize speed in travel around the Lowcountry, there are other ways to chart your journey to take advantage of the beautiful setting. Here are our suggestions for both, tailored to arrival from the main highways.

Charleston via U.S. Highway 17 N. (Savannah Highway)

To Johns Island, Kiawah, and Seabrook

If you are driving north on Savannah Highway (U.S. Highway 17) and your destination is Kiawah, Seabrook, or Johns Island, the fastest route is to take a right on Main Road. Look for a major intersection with a green sign indicating Kiawah and Seabrook. When you cross Limehouse Bridge, you are on Johns Island. To go to Kiawah or Seabrook, continue to the end of Main Road, which turns into Bohicket Road, and follow the signs. Kiawah will be on your left, and Seabrook will be at the end of the road.

To James Island and Folly Beach

If you want to go to James Island or Folly Beach from U.S. Highway 17, take a right before you reach the Ashley River Bridge at the intersection of Wesley Drive and U.S. 17.

Stay on Wesley until it merges with Folly Road. Cross the Wappoo Bridge and stay on Folly Road to James Island and Folly Beach.

To Downtown Charleston

If your destination is the city, you can take either a panoramic approach or the shortest connection.

The Scenic Route: Should you have the extra minutes and the inclination, turn right at Wesley Drive as if heading to James Island or Folly Beach. Stay on Wesley until it merges with Folly Road, cross the Wappoo Bridge and stay on Folly Road until you see, on your left, the exit for the Robert B. Scarborough Bridge (also called the James Island Expressway or S.C. Highway 30).

In terms of time from Savannah Highway, this will take about 10 minutes longer than the quickest route to Calhoun Street, a main street traversing the Peninsula from east to west. However, the splendid views can make it a nice option when traffic snarls on the Ashley River Bridge (see our Close-up, "A View to a Thrill, Sometimes at a Standstill," in this chapter).

Take a Number

Bombarded by highway designations that seem to be blurring into one another? Confused by well-meaning Lowcountry direction-givers who throw out numbers faster than a lottery-ball machine? Take heart! Below is a brief listing of highways and connectors that are often referred to by locals without the state or U.S. prefixes.

For your information and cross-referencing ease, please note these numbers, with a few of their local incarnations:

U.S. 17 N. (the Crosstown, the Bypass, Georgetown Highway)
U.S. 17 S. (Savannah Highway)
U.S. 52 (Rivers Avenue)
U.S. 78 (Summerville Highway)
S.C. 7 (Sam Rittenberg Boulevard)
S.C. 30 (James Island Expressway)
S.C. 517 (Isle of Palms Connector)
S.C. 700 (Maybank Highway)
S.C. 703 (Coleman, Ben Sawyer, Jasper, and Palm Boulevards)
S.C. 61 (St. Andrews Boulevard, Ashley River Road)
S.C. 171 (Folly Road)
Interstate 526 (Mark Clark Expressway)

Remember, don't be afraid to ask for specifics. When true Insiders are pressed for directions, they can almost always find a way to shepherd you from point A to point B.

The Speedy Route: If you prefer the most direct route downtown, cross the Ashley River Bridge on U.S. Highway 17 and veer right onto Lockwood Drive. You make your next decision at the first stoplight: If you are interested in visiting the medical complexes or the College of Charleston, shops on King Street or the Charleston Visitor Reception and Transportation Center, go left, and the road will actually curve into and become Calhoun Street. King Street intersects Calhoun, and you can turn right or left to park and shop. To find the visitors center, follow the green and white signs that will direct you to upper Meeting Street, an intersecting street that is just one block past King, off Calhoun, on the left.

But if you need to reach the southern portion of the Peninsula, follow the straight arrow at that first stoplight. This will be a continuation of Lockwood Drive. You'll drive past the City Marina and Rice Mill Building, round the corner by the Coast Guard Station, and onto Broad Street. Broad eventually dead-ends at East Bay Street. Take a right on any intersecting street to find addresses referred to as Below Broad.

To the Northern Peninsula

To use U.S. Highway 17 N. to reach the northern Peninsula, cross the Ashley River Bridge in the second from the right lane of the bridge that reads "Lockwood Drive North." Continue straight off the bridge to the traffic light and turn left onto Lockwood Drive North. A Charleston RiverDogs sign pointing left is at this intersection. Continue up Lockwood through the next traffic light, where RiverDogs and Citadel signs direct you around onto Fishburne Street to Riley Park, sports fields and on over to Hagood Avenue. Turn left onto Hagood Avenue at the stop sign, and The Citadel Bulldogs stadium is on the right. To reach The Citadel campus, follow Hagood Avenue until it dead-ends into one of The Citadel entrance gates.

To North Charleston

There are two ways to get to North Charleston. First, you can take a left onto S.C. Highway 7 (Sam Rittenberg Boulevard), follow it until it merges with S.C. Highway 171, then cross the Memorial Bridge (which locals call the North Bridge) into North Charleston. Another option is to take a left from U.S. Highway 17 onto the Mark Clark Expressway (I-526), which will take you by the new Charleston Area Convention Center Complex and the airport, or to I-26 and the commercial districts of North Charleston.

To Mt. Pleasant, Sullivan's Island, Isle of Palms

To reach Mt. Pleasant and other East Cooper areas from U.S. Highway 17 N., take a left onto the Mark Clark Expressway (I-526) and stay on it until it intersects (again) and dead-ends at U.S. 17 N. in Mt. Pleasant. To go to the Isle of Palms, take a left on U.S. 17 N. and after about five miles, look for the Isle of Palms Connector (S.C. Highway 517) exit on the right.

If your destination is Sullivan's Island, take a right on Georgetown Highway (U.S. 17) and follow it until it intersects with Coleman Boulevard. Take a left at the light and follow Coleman (also called Ben Sawyer Boulevard at this point) as it crosses the Ben Sawyer Bridge to Sullivan's Island.

Another way to reach Mt. Pleasant and other East Cooper areas from U.S. 17 is to cross the Ashley River Bridge and the overpass to the Crosstown. You'll see signs for I-26 to the left, but you'll want to stay in the right lane under the signs to Mt. Pleasant. Once on the Silas Pearman Bridge over the Cooper River, negotiate into the right lane. Across the bridge, take the lane marked S.C. Highway 703. You will see the Mt. Pleasant welcome sign on the left as you drive down Coleman Boulevard (S.C. 703). Eventually, this road crosses Shem Creek near the historic Old Village residential area. It later becomes Ben Sawyer Boulevard (still S.C. 703) before it crosses the Ben Sawyer Bridge to Sullivan's Island.

To reach the Isle of Palms, take a left on Jasper Boulevard (also S.C. 703) and drive across Sullivan's Island to Breach Inlet. Cross the bridge over the inlet, and you are on the Isle of Palms. To find Wild Dunes, the largest resort development on the island, follow Palm Boulevard (S.C. 703) and the signs to the Wild Dunes Reception Center.

If you intend to head north on U.S. 17 to reach Mt. Pleasant destinations such as Hobcaw, Towne Centre, Snee Farm, Boone Hall or, eventually, McClellanville and Georgetown, stay left on the Silas Pearman Bridge over the Cooper River and cross the U.S. 17 N. overpass.

Charleston via U.S. Highway 17 S. (from Georgetown, Myrtle Beach)

To Isle of Palms, Sullivan's Island, Mt. Pleasant

If you are headed south on U.S. Highway 17 and want to go to the Isle of Palms or Sullivan's

Island, take a left onto the Isle of Palms Connector (S.C. 517), which goes to the Isle of Palms. At the end of the connector, take a right to go to Sullivan's Island and Mt. Pleasant or a left to go to Wild Dunes.

To North Charleston

If you want to go to North Charleston, take a right onto the Mark Clark Expressway (I-526) off U.S. Highway 17 S. The airport, the Charleston Area Convention Center Complex, and other destinations are clearly marked along the way.

To Downtown Charleston

If you want to drive into the city, it's best to follow U.S. Highway 17 S. to the older, two-lane Grace Memorial Bridge. (Note, however, the new safety regulation that if you are driving a vehicle that weighs more than five tons, you must follow the detour and cross the Silas Pearman Bridge in the reversible lane. If you're uncomfortable with the old bridge, you can opt to go this way in your car.) If you want to go to the southern parts of the Peninsula, we recommend two options after crossing the Grace Bridge. For King Street (its shopping district and the nearby visitor center), stay in the left lane, exit left, and turn right at the stop sign onto King. Another option is to stay in the right lane of U.S. 17 S. and take the Rutledge Avenue exit; then stay on Rutledge Avenue until it intersects with Calhoun Street. Take a left for destinations off the Calhoun route (such as the College of Charleston campus and King Street shopping) or a right to reach the medical complex. You can also stay on King Street or Rutledge Avenue until it dead-ends at Murray Boulevard (The Battery), getting a glimpse of some of the city's more desirable real estate along the way.

If you are looking for The Citadel or points around the school (such as Joseph P. Riley Jr. Park, Hampton Park, and sports fields), stay on the Crosstown until you come to Hagood Avenue and take a right. You will pass sports fields and can drive straight to the back gate of The Citadel. Hampton Park is just outside the front gates of the school.

To West Ashley

If you're going to West Ashley on U.S. Highway 17 S., there are two options. First, you can take a right on the Mark Clark Expressway (I-526) and stay on it until it intersects with Sam Rittenberg Boulevard (near Citadel Mall) and eventually dead-ends at an intersection with U.S. 17. The second option is to stay on U.S. 17 S. until you cross the Grace Memorial Bridge, the Peninsula via the Crosstown, and eventually the Ashley River Bridge.

To Other Points West

For James and Johns Islands, Kiawah, Seabrook, and Folly Beach, stay on the Crosstown (U.S. Highway 17 S.), cross the Ashley River Bridge, then take a left at the first stoplight at the intersection of U.S. Highway 17 and Wesley Drive. Stay on Wesley one block until it merges with Folly Road (S.C. 171). To reach destinations on James Island, Johns Island, Kiawah, or Seabrook, cross the Wappoo Bridge and take the first right onto Maybank Highway (S.C. 700). For other destinations on James Island and for Folly Beach, stay on Folly Road (S.C. 171).

For another route to James, Johns, or the resort islands, while still on the Crosstown take a left at the last light (Lockwood Drive) before crossing the Ashley River Bridge and look for the Folly Beach exit onto the Scarborough Expressway (S.C. Highway 30). This route will take you on a panoramic ride and deposit you on Folly Road on James Island. Take a left to go to Folly Beach or a right to go back toward West Ashley. If you are headed to Johns Island, Kiawah, or Seabrook, take a left on Maybank Highway (S.C. Highway 700) at the last stoplight before the Wappoo Bridge. If you are going to West Ashley or downtown, cross the Wappoo Bridge, and go straight. Then, you may either bear right to access the Ashley River Bridge into town or bear left on Wesley Drive to intersect with U.S. 17.

Charleston via I-26

To North Charleston

For travelers coming in on I-26 from the west, there are several options depending on your desired destination. You will pass through North Charleston on I-26, so check exits for specific locations. To go to the airport or Charleston Area Convention Center Complex, take a right on I-526 (Mark Clark Expressway) and look for signs.

To West Ashley, James Island, Folly Beach

If you want to go to West Ashley, exit right at Cosgrove Avenue, which becomes Sam Rittenberg Boulevard (S.C. 7). Sam Rittenberg forks at the Ashley Landing Shopping Center, and you can either bear to the left on S.C. 171 toward the Ashley River Bridge, or stay to the right on Sam Rittenberg Boulevard. The boulevard is intersected first by S.C. Highway 61, then by U.S. Highway 17. Take a right onto S.C. 61 to go to the many historic gardens and plantations or a left to go to the Charleston Peninsula.

Another option for reaching West Ashley is to stay on the interstate as it winds around to become U.S. 17 S. (the Crosstown), then cross the Ashley River Bridge.

To access James Island and Folly Beach, take the Cosgrove Avenue exit and cross the North Bridge, where Cosgrove becomes Sam Rittenberg Boulevard. Stay left on Sam Rittenberg (S.C. 7) to S.C. 171, which leads to S.C. 61. Follow S.C. 61 to Wesley Drive (at the In & Out Car Wash) and turn right. Cross U.S. 17 on Wesley until it merges with Folly Road (S.C. 171). To reach destinations on James Island, cross the Wappoo Bridge and take the first right onto Maybank Highway (S.C. 700). For other destinations on James Island and for Folly Beach, stay on Folly Road (S.C. 171).

To Johns Island, Kiawah, and Seabrook

To go to these destinations, take a right on I-526 (Mark Clark Expressway), which will eventually merge with U.S. Highway 17 S. Continue on U.S. Highway 17 south of town and turn left onto Main Road at the major intersection with the green sign to Kiawah and Seabrook. Limehouse Bridge leads to Johns Island. To go to Kiawah or Seabrook, continue on Main Road until it becomes Bohicket Road at Maybank Highway (S.C. 700) and follow the signs. Kiawah will be on your left, and Seabrook will be at the end of the road.

To the Northern Peninsula

If you want to go to the Peninsula, here are a couple of options. Take the Meeting Street exit off I-26, turn right on Meeting, and follow the signs to the Charleston Visitor Reception and Transportation Center. Another route is to follow the interstate until it ends at the Crosstown (U.S. Highway 17 S.), then take the Rutledge Avenue exit off the Crosstown. Both streets run south and culminate at The Battery. If you are looking for The Citadel or points around the school, stay on I-26 until it ends at the Crosstown. Look for Hagood Avenue (just before McDonald's), take a right, and drive straight to the back gate of the school.

To Mt. Pleasant, Sullivan's Island, Isle of Palms

If you are heading to East Cooper from the interstate, there are two options. For the first, take I-526 (Mark Clark Expressway) or U.S. Highway 17 N. If you choose to take I-526 to Mt. Pleasant, you'll be treated to beautiful scenery, but watch your speedometer. Radar-equipped patrol cars are common. From I-526, you can go to Sullivan's Island by staying on Georgetown Highway (U.S. 17 S.) until it intersects with Coleman Boulevard (S.C. 703) at the light. Turn left on Coleman (which becomes Ben Sawyer Boulevard) and cross the Ben Sawyer Bridge onto Sullivan's Island.

If you want to go to the Isle of Palms, there are again two possibilities. First, you can take a left onto Jasper Boulevard after crossing the Ben Sawyer Bridge. This will lead to a bridge across Breach Inlet and onto the Isle of Palms. For the other route, take a left onto U.S. 17 N. after exiting from I-526, and then a right after Sweetgrass Shopping Center onto the Isle of Palms Connector (S.C. 517). This route offers direct service and allows you to bypass Sullivan's Island traffic and the inevitable openings of the Ben Sawyer swing bridge. The connector also offers a stupendous view of the island and the sparkling Atlantic Ocean spread before it.

The second East Cooper option from I-26 is to take the Mt. Pleasant exit onto the Silas Pearman Bridge (U.S. 17 N.), which takes you to Mt. Pleasant and the islands. Exit the bridge in the right lane and you will see Mt. Pleasant's welcome sign on the left as you

> **Insiders' Tip**
>
> For those who really want to put on the Ritz, go all out and call Classic Limousine Service, (843) 745-8500, to rent one of its classic Rolls-Royce limos for a very special occasion. Take a spin in the 1966 all-white Silver Shadow or maybe the 1960 Silver Cloud II. Better yet, order up the 1939 Silver Wraith, just like the one Dudley Moore had in *Arthur*. We'll alert the media.

drive along Coleman Boulevard. Eventually, this road crosses Shem Creek at the edge of the historic Old Village residential area. It later becomes Ben Sawyer Boulevard before crossing the Ben Sawyer Bridge to Sullivan's Island. To reach the Isle of Palms, take a left on Jasper Boulevard and drive across Sullivan's Island to Breach Inlet. Cross the bridge over the inlet, and you are on the Isle of Palms. To find Wild Dunes, follow Palm Boulevard (S.C. 703) and the signs to the Wild Dunes Reception Center.

However, if you intend to head north on U.S. 17 to reach Mt. Pleasant destinations such as Hobcaw, Towne Centre, Snee Farm, Boone Hall, or eventually McClellanville and Georgetown, stay left on the Cooper River Bridge (Silas Pearman Bridge), and cross the U.S. 17 N. overpass.

Charleston via I-95

If you are heading north on I-95 (from Savannah), the shortest route to Charleston is via Exit 33. The signs will direct you to Charleston and Beaufort. See "Charleston via US Hwy. 17 N. (Savannah Highway)," above, for further directions into the city. If you are heading south on I-95 (from Fayetteville, North Carolina), the best idea is to take I-26 just past Santee, S.C. (Exit 86). Travel about 50 miles along I-26 to access all Charleston area destinations. (See above "Charleston via I-26.")

Getting Here by Air

Charleston is more accessible than ever by air. The Trident area boasts a full-service international airport with three major carriers taking off and touching down throughout the day. Four national rental-car agencies service the airport, limousine and shuttle services are available, and the terminal has a 1,550-space parking lot for passengers and those seeing them off or picking them up.

There are also four Lowcountry locations serving the needs of private pilots; one location is an auxiliary service of the Charleston International Airport. All are reasonably convenient to the downtown area, and specific amenities are noted below.

Major Airport Service

Charleston International Airport
5500 International Blvd.,
North Charleston
(843) 767-1100; (843) 767-7009

When newcomers need to deal with air travel in the Greater Charleston area, it's good to know a few basic facts: What major airlines serve Charleston International Airport? Who do you call to see if a flight is going to be on time or not? What are some of the route and time factors involved in getting to the airport? And what about ground transportation and parking? Answers to all those questions follow, but first, let's take a look at the historical time line of the area's major airport.

History

In 1928, the City of Charleston leased 782 acres northwest of the city for construction of a municipal airport. A year later, the new airfield was officially opened for business. This facility served Greater Charleston until 1942, when it was turned over to the federal government for military use during World War II (see our Military chapter).

After the war, the city resumed control of operations at the airfield, and in 1949, the first civilian airport terminal was completed. In 1952 the government got involved again, leasing the airfield to begin operations at the new Charleston Air Force Base. Today,

Close-up

A View to a Thrill, Sometimes at a Standstill

First, the good news. The views from many of the beautiful bridges in Greater Charleston are breathtaking. But here's a word of caution: Traffic tends to snarl on them and can screech to hour-long or hours-long halts.

The old Grace Memorial Bridge, which jauntily spans the Cooper River and marshes below, is a thrilling experience—unless you are stopped on its two lanes. With the main culprits being congestion, never-ending repair work, and accidents, predicting traffic jams is a roll of the dice. The newer Silas Pearman Bridge, with one reversible lane leading in and two others leading out of town, suffers the same maladies. The Mark Clark is also congested at peak hours but offers less resistance in terms of road work. Flow on the Ashley River bridges has been greatly eased by the existence of the James Island Expressway, but drivers should be aware that both old Ashley River bridges still open for boat traffic.

On the very bright side, let us boast for a moment about exceptional views of this area made possible by the completion of three major highway projects during the 1990s. On Labor Day weekend 1993, the Robert B. Scarborough (also known as the James Island Expressway), crossing the Ashley River via S.C. Highway 30, was finally opened. The project was 30 years in the planning and cost $125 million to build, but many of us think the bridge is worth every penny in terms of convenience and aesthetics. The expressway is almost 3 miles long, and its 2.14-mile bridge—starting at the intersection of Calhoun Street and Lockwood Drive—extends to Folly Road on James Island. Happy motorists can enjoy a waterfront view of the Peninsula, its skyline punctuated by 18th- and 19th-century church spires, and its harbor dotted with the masts of sailing vessels.

The second treat for the eye is made possible by the Mark Clark Expressway (I-526), connecting North Charleston with Mt. Pleasant. Its bridge affords an interesting view of Charleston, East Cooper, and the nearby Grace Memorial and Silas Pearman bridges. The expressway goes through miles of undeveloped property and Daniel Island, which is currently under development. You may be tempted to stop and snap a quick photograph, but for safety reasons, we wouldn't recommend it.

The third awesome view is from the Isle of Palms Connector (S.C. Highway 517), which rises high above the winding creeks and marsh to a point where, unobstructed by high walls, rails, or wires, the traveler can see miles of gray-white beach and endless deep-blue ocean beyond.

The Cooper River bridges: Enjoy the view, you might be here awhile. PHOTO: THOMAS P. FORD

Charleston is officially designated the "Southeastern Commercial Gateway" for the Air Mobility Command (AMC).

In 1970 the Charleston County Aviation Authority was created, and by 1979 this entity had taken over ownership of the airport. On March 30, 1985, the greatly expanded and modernized present terminal was dedicated as Charleston International Airport.

Today's 280,000-square-foot facility has 10 gates, all served by covered loading bridges. The walking distance from the terminal entrance to the most remote aircraft gate is only about 800 feet. The international area and customs service inspection area have 25,000 square feet of space and process international passengers quickly. If you're interested in business opportunities at Charleston International Airport, contact the Aviation Authority Development Office at (843) 767-7000.

Flight Information

Major airlines serving the Trident's international flight facility include: Continental, (800) 525-0280 (reservations), (800) 335-2247 (baggage); Delta, (800) 221-1212 (reservations), (800) 325-8224 (baggage); and USAirways, (800) 428-4322, (reservations), (800) 371-4771 (baggage).

Commuter airlines serving the Charleston International Airport are COMAIR, (800) 354-9822; Midway Corporate, (800) 446-4392; Trans World Express, (800) 221-2000; and United Express, (800) 241-6522.

The number to call if you want to check an arrival time for an incoming flight is (843) 767-7009. Checking before leaving for the airport can save time and frustration. The airport's information desk always has the most updated flight schedule data available.

Rental Cars/Parking

Chances are, your preferred rental car service has an airport outlet in Charleston. The four national companies that serve the airport are Avis Rent A Car, (800) 331-1212 or (843) 767-7030; Budget, (800) 527-0700 or (843) 767-7051; Hertz Rent A Car, (800) 654-3131 or (843) 767-4552; and National Car Rental, (800) 227-7368 or (843) 767-3078.

The terminal's parking lot accommodates 1,550 cars. Short-term parking rates (for meeting incoming passengers) are 75¢ per half-hour. Parking in the short-term lot (24 hours or less) is $12 a day. There's a separate long-term lot available at $6 a day. All parking areas are clearly marked.

Getting to the Airport

As a simple rule of thumb, plan on allowing at least a half-hour to get to the airport if you're driving from downtown Charleston. Allow even more time during rush hours or on busy holiday travel dates.

Take I-26 west (toward Columbia). Exit off I-26 at Exit 212-B marked "Airport and I-526-Savannah." Continue approximately one mile on I-526 (toward Savannah) and exit at the Montague Avenue exit. A sign will also read, "Trident Research Authority, Coliseum, and Airport." Turn right at the light (at the exit to International Boulevard) and continue approximately a mile and a half to the terminal.

If you are driving south toward the city on I-26, take the Mark Clark Expressway (I-526) exit. The airport exit off this highway is clearly marked, and you'll again head into the terminal area via International Boulevard.

For local residents and those who need ground transportation to the airport from downtown or other locations, there's a central phone number through the Charleston Aviation Authority that will redirect your call to the next available option. Call (800) 750-1311 for this airport limousine pick-up information.

Taxi, Limo, and Shuttle Service from the Airport

Several Charleston area hotels, motels, and bed and breakfast inns offer shuttle service to and from the airport. Check with your reservation agent, your inn's concierge or your hotel for specific details. Near the baggage carousel, you'll find a lighted courtesy board showing several of the area's better hotels, motels, and bed and breakfast inns. The attached phone offers speed-dial service to those places offering airport pickup service.

If you're left to your own resources for transportation into the city, you have a couple of options. Outside the baggage claim area, across the pickup zone, is a small booth offering taxi and limo (van) rides to Lowcountry destinations. Various cab companies, as a service of the Aviation Airport Authority, take turns picking up fares from this booth. Here's the gist: If you are in a great hurry, a taxi will take you immediately at a metered rate of $1.65 a mile for the first three passengers. Additional passengers will pay $10 each. The average ride from the airport to a downtown hotel will be around $19 to $22. If you're willing to wait about 15 minutes, you can catch a shuttle (really a van) with several other passengers at a much-discounted rate of $10 per person.

Passengers heading to the nearby Charleston Air Force Base can catch an immediate taxi for a flat rate of $7. Those going to the former Navy Base can take an immediate taxi for $12. Those heading out to the Naval Weapons Station can expect to pay about $25. A trip for one to Kiawah or Seabrook by taxi is about $50 for the 30-mile journey. Those heading for Wild Dunes can expect to pay about $39 for that 23-mile ride.

If you want private limousine service and make reservations in advance, you can choose from a number of limousine companies available in the Lowcountry (see the "Limousines" listing later in this chapter).

Private Plane Service

Greater Charleston offers four options for private pilots—all convenient and uncongested.

Mercury Air Center
6060 S. Aviation Ave., North Charleston
(843) 746-7600

Just across the runway from the Charleston Air Force Base, off Aviation Avenue at Charleston International Airport, Mercury Air Center's new terminal and service facility offers four long runways, nine instrument approaches, and 24-hour all-weather service. This is your best choice if you want to land a private plane in close proximity to downtown. Mercury Air also offers a wide range of services—from rental cars to limousines to dinner reservations and catering arrangements—along with avionics repair and general maintenance. The maintenance number is (843) 554-9191. Tie-downs range from $25 per night for single engine aircraft to $40 a night (with ramp) for a twin-engine plane. The first night is free with a fuel purchase, and both AV and jet fuel are available.

East Cooper Aviation
700 Airport Rd., Mt. Pleasant
(843) 884-8837

Private pilots have access to the East Cooper area (including Wild Dunes) via the East Cooper Airport in Mt. Pleasant. This facility offers a 3,700-foot runway, tie downs, jet fuel, and AV gas service. Rental cars are available on the premises through Enterprise. The office and terminal are open from 7 AM to 7 PM in the winter, with hours extended to 8 PM after April 1. Helicopters are accommodated on site.

Mercury Air J.Z.I.
2700 Fort Trenholm Rd., Johns Island
(843) 559-2401

Private pilots wanting access closest to Kiawah and Seabrook will most likely want to choose Mercury Air's J.Z.I. airport on Johns Island, 12 miles south of the city. It offers two runways, 5,000-by-150-feet and 4,311-by-150-feet long. The facility offers jet fuel and 100 LL gas. The tie-down rate is $9 per night for a single engine craft and $12 for a twin. First night tie-down fee is waved with the pur-chase of fuel. Rental cars are available on the premises, and limited limousine service to Kiawah and Seabrook is offered. Operating hours are 6 AM to 10 PM.

Pelican Aviation
890 Greyback Rd., Summerville
(843) 851-0970

This facility for private pilots flying into the Summerville area and Berkeley County has a 3,700-foot runway. It offers airplane detailing, general maintenance, and flight training, plus jet fuel and AV gas. Tie downs are $5 per night (with first night waved with purchase of fuel). There's a courtesy car on site for daytime transportation to area resorts and restaurants. The office and terminal are open from 8 AM to 6 PM through the winter and 8 AM to 7 PM after April 1.

> ## Insiders' Tip
> Beware! Many Charleston streets and alleys are one way. With so many interesting distractions vying for your attention, it's easy to miss the signs. So keep a lookout and be careful.

Getting Here by Other Methods

By Bus or Train

If you are arriving or departing by bus, the Greyhound Terminal, 3610 Dorchester Road, (843) 747-5341 or (800) 231-2222, is in North Charleston and is a routine stop for cabs. Call (800) 231-2222 or (843) 744-4247 for rates and schedules.

The Amtrak Train Station, 4565 Gaynor Avenue, (843) 744-8263 or (800) 872-7245, is also in the north area. Amtrak runs on the CSX Railroad lines, and there are two north-bound and two southbound stops each day. Call for ticket prices and train schedules.

By Boat

There is a growing leisure craft and passenger ship industry in Charleston.

Cruise ships dock at the passenger terminal off Concord Street in the Historic District. Daytime walking there is fine if you have the time and the stamina, but we endorse travel by cabs or limousines at night for safety and convenience. (See the subsequent listings for taxis and limousines.)

Private yachts moor (pending availability) at any of several marinas in the Trident area (see our Boating chapter for more information). Cabs or rental cars are the best solution for ground transportation unless you are docked at the City Marina, which is centrally located on the Peninsula near popular destinations and on the DASH route (see more on the DASH system under "Public Transportation," following). The nearby Ashley Marina has easy access via walkway to the City Marina and connecting DASH routes.

Getting around the Lowcountry

Taxis, Limos, and Rental Cars

Taxis can be scarce here in the Lowcountry, especially at odd hours. Because of that, savvy travelers needing cabs should keep a list of taxi phone numbers in their purse or wallet.

The more popular solution is to rent a car from one of the nationally recognized car rental companies, all of which are represented in the area.

Limousines, it seems, are more loosely defined. A limousine can be anything from a stretch Caddy to an airport van. What follows is a list of taxi, limousine services, and rental car options.

Taxis

Checker Taxi
(843) 747-9200

Express Cab
(843) 577-8816

North Area Taxi
(843) 554-7575

Yellow Cab
(843) 577-6565

Limousines

Above and Beyond Limousine Service
(843) 402-0600, (800) 755-8667

Affordable Limo Service
(843) 406-1515, (800) 694-3295

Carey-Parker Limousine
(800) 336-4646

Coastal Limousine
(843) 579-2505

Jennings Limousine
(843) 852-0336

Private Cars
(843) 760-6060, (800) 222-4771

Rental Cars

Avis Rent A Car
(843) 767-7030, (800) 831-2847

Budget
(843) 760-9025, (800) 527-0700

Enterprise Rent A Car
(843) 723-6215, (800) 736-8222

Hertz Rent A Car
(843) 767-4552, (800) 654-3131

National Car Rental
(843) 767-3078, (800) 227-7368

Thrifty Car Rental
(843) 552-7531, (800) 367-2277

Public Transportation

Public bus transportation in the area is a great way to circumvent the city's automobile congestion and parking woes altogether. This service is provided in the Lowcountry by the Charleston Area Rural Transportation Authority (CARTA). Under CARTA's auspices is the Downtown Area Shuttle (DASH), a separate system generally dedicated to the transportation needs of tourists in the downtown area and historic district. Together, CARTA and DASH operate 25 routes linking downtown, West Ashley, North Charleston, and East Cooper plus Charleston International Airport.

While the green DASH trolleys are not considered tour vehicles per se, their turn-of-the-century "antique" trolley look is clearly an eye catcher—and it's one way to quickly identify a DASH vehicle from the more modern-looking (yellow and green) CARTA buses that operate in the metro area. DASH trolleys and metro CARTA buses stop at designated shelters, benches, and trolley stop signs located throughout the city. For safety reasons, drivers are not allowed to pick up passengers at locations other than the designated color-coded stops.

One-way and all-day CARTA and DASH passes are available on board the vehicles. You are expected to have exact change. One-way fare is 75¢, although those with a senior-citizen or Medicare card can ride for 25¢ each way Monday through Friday from 9 AM to 3:30 PM or after 6 PM, and all day Saturday and Sunday. An all-day pass is $2. Transfers

City and County Parking Facilities

Charleston's municipal and county off-street parking system is one of the best solutions to the city's ever-present shortage of parking spaces. In a city planned and built (and rebuilt several times) before automobile congestion was ever an issue, these lots and parking garages are a welcome oasis. In some cases, the city planners have even done a fairly good job of making the garages blend into the historic cityscape. If you're not looking carefully, you might mistake a parking garage for an old warehouse or an office building.

Some facilities near hotels offer special overnight rates for guests with proof of hotel registration. Usually, a hotel key will be convincing enough. Others offer only hourly rates. Here's the general rule for most city-owned parking facilities: It's 75 cents for the first half-hour, 75 cents for the second half-hour, then $1 per hour. The all-day rate is $8. The overnight rate (where offered) is $10 with a hotel registration, and the monthly rate (where available) is $90.

In any case, unless your accommodation provides off-street parking or you want to feed a hungry meter, these parking options may turn out to be your only choices:

Aquarium Garage,
24 Calhoun Street, (843) 579-7679, 1,100 spaces.

Camden Exchange,
John or Hutson Street off Meeting Street, (843) 720-3866, 308 spaces.

Charleston County Health Complex,
21 Courtney Street, (843) 720-7050, 1,640 spaces.

Charleston Place Garage,
off Hasell Street, between Meeting and King Streets, (843) 724-7419, 404 spaces.

Concord-Cumberland Garage,
corner of Concord and Cumberland Streets, (843) 724-7387, 651 spaces.

Cumberland-Meeting Garage,
30 Cumberland Street, (843) 724-7381, 536 spaces (with more under construction).

East Bay-Prioleau Garage,
between Mid-Atlantic and South Atlantic Streets, (843) 724-7403, 339 spaces.

Gaillard Municipal Auditorium Parking,
off Calhoun Street and Alexander, (843) 973-7207, 596 spaces.

George-Society Lot,
off King Street, between George and Society Streets, (843) 724-7384, 152 spaces.

King-Queen Garage,
off Queen Street, corner of King and Queen Streets, (843) 724-6777, 454 spaces.

Liberty-St. Philip Garage,
corner of Liberty and St. Philip Streets, (843) 724-7382, 540 spaces.

Market and Horlbeck,
in the block between Market and Horlbeck Streets, (843) 724-7385, 120 spaces.

are free. Inside the Visitor Reception and Transportation Center and at 13 area Piggly Wiggly (grocery) stores, you can buy a 10-ride pass for $6 or 40 rides for $21. A 31-day pass is sold for $18.

The Visitor Center sells seasonal passes for $40 which are good from Jan 1 through June 30 (for spring) and July 1 through December 31 (for fall). Police, guide, signal, and service dogs are the only pets allowed on board.

To encourage visitors to leave their cars at the Visitor Center garage facilities and parking lots and choose public transportation, a free hour of parking is granted in exchange for a used one-day DASH pass at the checkout booth. Call (843) 724-7420 for more information.

Insiders' Tip
Start early on your trip to the airport. International Boulevard has gained a reputation as a notorious speed trap, so be sure to keep an eye on your speedometer. Many travelers have missed flights thanks to a heavy foot and the ever-vigilant officers.

Bicycling

If you plan on spending time on the Peninsula or out on the beaches, why not park the car and consider renting a bicycle by the hour or day? Now you can even put your bike on a CARTA bus (with their new front-loading bike racks) and enjoy the convenience of public transportation. For in-town, Mt. Pleasant, and Kiawah service, we recommend The Bicycle Shoppe, which offers three locations: 280 Meeting Street, (843) 722-8168; 1768 U.S. Highway 17 N., Mt. Pleasant, (843) 884-7433; and 1 Beachwalker Drive, Kiawah Island, (843) 768-9122 or (888) 271-2453. These folks rent single-speed adult cruisers and hybrids. Another option is Mike's Bikes, 85 Wentworth Street, (843) 723-8025, or on James Island at 915 Folly Road, (843) 795-3322. For delivery and three-day or weekly rental to many of the islands, try Sea Island Cycle, 4053 S. Rhett Avenue, North Charleston, (843) 747-BIKE. Serving Kiawah and Seabrook Islands is Island Bike and Surf Shop, 3665 Bohicket Road, Kiawah Island, (843) 768-1158.

History

Civil War and Subsequent Struggles

Cultural Renaissance and an Economic Boom

Charleston through the '90s

North Charleston

West (of the) Ashley

Built as a "Grand Modell" with cultural roots as diverse as her bounties of thick pine forests and blue-green waters, Charleston is a rich mixture of early English, Irish, French, Spanish, German, Swiss, Santo Domingan, African, Native American, and Caribbean influences.

While each of these cultures left its mark on the city in a unique way, no influence was stronger than that of the British. Archaeologists tell us countless generations of Native Americans lived on and around the land now called Charleston before the first permanent English settlers arrived. But little remains of their occupation outside of the archaeological record in the ground itself. The first English settlers, arriving in the spring of 1670, were adventurers coming to lands granted by King Charles II to eight Lords Proprietors, who claimed ownership of the "Carolinas"—presumably extending from the Atlantic to the shores of the Pacific.

As the settlers navigated into what is now Charleston Harbor, they passed enormous mounds of bleached, white oyster shells at the tip of a peninsula where two rivers met and named the area Oyster Point. Seeking higher ground, the colonists sailed farther up one river to a high bank they called Albemarle Point and established the first crude encampment there. They dutifully named the new settlement Charles Towne for King Charles II. The two rivers, called the Kiawah and Etiwan by local tribes, were renamed the Ashley and Cooper, respectively, in honor of two of the Lords Proprietors. The original settlement area is now a South Carolina state park called Charles Towne Landing State Historic Site (see our Attractions chapter). A decade later, because of their need for protection, the Charles Towne colonists were drawn back to the Oyster Point peninsula between the two rivers—clearly a more defensible location. Here, the foundations of what is now Charleston were first laid.

By 1719 the colonists were tired of being exploited by the proprietary government, and friction ensued. This resulted in the colonists coming under even more discipline from the English crown, which meant forced allegiance to a series of appointed royal governors. This troublesome governmental entity stayed in place for the colonists until the American Revolution.

In 1725 the British sent over a plan for the new settlement called the "Grand Modell," intending to guide the development of 600 prime acres on the peninsula into a proper town. Amazingly, traces of that early English plan are still evident in the plat of today's Charleston Peninsula.

Due to the great success of this busy English port and its merchant-planter aristocracy, the town soon became a small city. To many, the 18th century will always be Charleston's Golden Age. Early travelers to this thriving Colonial port took back to Europe impressive stories about Charles Towne's elegant architecture, wealthy citizenry, and sophisticated lifestyle. Indeed, during these heady, pre-Revolutionary years, rice and indigo from the plantations were sent out to eager markets all over the world. In exchange, hundreds of boatloads of enslaved Africans were brought to Charleston to ensure a cheap labor force to work the land. In stark contrast to this grim exchange, the arts flourished and Charles Towne was considered the brightest jewel in England's Colonial crown.

Many of the seeds of the American Revolution found fertile ground here in the Carolina Lowcountry. Political passions ran high, and once war broke out there were many high-profile Charlestonians deeply involved on both sides of the issue. Actually, the first decisive American victory during the Revolution occurred at the Battle of Fort Sullivan just outside the city. However, at first the war didn't go well. For a while, Charleston fell to the British, and during this time the city suffered the first of its two unseemly "enemy occupations."

Newly liberated after the war, the city became incorporated in 1783 and adopted a new, shortened name: Charleston. As the 19th century dawned, the newly named young city of Charleston experienced an incredible building boom. Today you can still see an extraordinary number of Adam-style buildings from this remarkable period. Among them are the Joseph Manigault House at 350 Meeting Street, built in 1803, and the Nathaniel Russell House at 51 Meeting Street, built in 1808 (see the House Museums section of our Attractions chapter).

As cotton and tobacco were added to the plantation products earning handsome profits in the international marketplace and even more money flowed into its thriving port, Charleston continued to grow. By the early 19th century, Charleston's flourishing middle class of merchant-tradesmen offered services and locally manufactured goods from small, street-front shops. Many of these shops were clustered along what is now King Street.

Some traders sold simple things such as household necessities and fresh produce brought in on wagons from outlying gardens. Others were true artisans in their own right and produced work such as early Charleston-made silver products and locally crafted furniture which are now highly prized on the antiques market today. This flourishing "wagon trade" on upper King Street preceded the retail stores that make up the present shopping district.

Civil War and Subsequent Struggles

In April 1861, Confederate soldiers fired on Fort Sumter in Charleston Harbor, thus signaling the start of the devastating War Between the States. After the city's second "enemy occupation," this time by Federal troops, Charleston was at its lowest ebb. Years of relentless bombardment, sweeping fires, and economic starvation had taken a terrible toll on the once-grand city.

Because Charleston was widely known as the "seat of secession," it is probably true that Charlestonians received especially severe punishment during the Reconstruction years. Recovery was slow to come and sometimes halfhearted. Some say Charleston never did recuperate from the Civil War until the arrival of the Navy Yard in 1904 and the subsequent economic booms of the two world wars.

Fires, earthquakes, hurricanes, yellow fever epidemics, and even the boll weevil threatened Charlestonians' health and wealth during the late 19th and early 20th centuries. In fact, during the immediate post-Civil War period, basic survival—not the notion of luxuries—was foremost on everyone's mind.

After the turn of the century and the arrival of the Navy Yard, things started looking better. Phosphate, an organic fertilizer, was mined along the Ashley River and processed in several local factories. This proved to be a significant new source of income for many old plantation families who still owned phosphate-rich lands. Other landowners converted to timber farming as the South slowly rebuilt a working economy.

It has been observed that in the most difficult of times Charleston citizens were "too poor to paint," but they were also "too proud to whitewash." This inability to modernize maintained an almost timeless feeling throughout the city and actually worked to preserve Charleston's now-legendary cache of historic homes and public buildings.

Many Civil War re-enactors visit the ruins of Fort Sumter and reflect on the history that transpired there.
PHOTO: COURTESY OF CHARLESTON AREA NATIONAL PARK SERVICE

Cultural Renaissance and an Economic Boom

In the 1920s, a kind of artistic renaissance occurred in Charleston. The city's now-quaint architectural backdrop inspired a new generation of artists, writers, poets, and musicians who captured regional and national acclaim. (See our Arts chapter for more about this fascinating period in Charleston's history.)

At the same time, the aesthetic and economic value of Charleston's architectural legacy started to be realized. This was when the city's early preservation ethic was first formulated, and it was kept alive through the especially difficult Depression years of the 1930s. (See our chapter on Architectural Preservation for more information.)

World War II brought another boom to Charleston with the Navy Yard expanding to produce war materials and more job opportunities than Charleston had seen in decades. After the war ended, many workers drawn here by the Navy decided to stay on and settle down. The sea, the mild weather, and a growing business climate kept pulling newcomers to the Lowcountry through the 1950s and '60s.

In the '70s, Charleston's chamber of commerce launched a national advertising campaign based on the simple phrase, "Charleston: America's Best Kept Secret." This, of course, was intended to let this cat out of the bag. And it worked splendidly. With high-profile events like Spoleto Festival USA and the (almost always sold-out) public house tours every spring and fall (see our Annual Events chapter), the message was getting out—Charleston was a beautiful, historic, and highly desirable place to visit.

Charleston through the '90s

Today Charleston's collection of historically significant architecture attracts visitors from around the world, and the city's remarkable preservation ethic is now a model for historic cities all over the industrialized world.

In 1996, an estimated 3 million tourists visited Charleston, each spending about $124 a day here. By 1999 that figure had grown to 3.7 million visitors, infusing Charleston County with an estimated $3.2 billion in tourist dollars.

That should get you up to speed on the history of the Lowcountry's centerpiece, the historic Peninsula. Now, let's take a quick look at the historical backgrounds of the other regions making up the Greater Charleston area.

East (of the) Cooper

Across the Cooper River east of the Peninsula is the land mass often referred to by locals as East Cooper. Actually, this is a grouping of several separate localities, all of which have proper names that further identify them to locals and visitors alike.

Mt. Pleasant

People have been drawn to Mt. Pleasant since the late 17th century, when the lands east of the Cooper River were still wild and uninhabited. In 1680 a large parcel of this land was granted to Florentia O'Sullivan, an Irish-born soldier of fortune who arrived at Charles Towne with the first English settlers in 1670. The land's proximity to the Peninsula was obvious, and local island planters built summer houses (used during warmer months when plantation living was deemed "unhealthy") near the water. One area came to be called the Old Village, and it's still a very desirable Mt. Pleasant address today.

Almost seven miles down what is now U.S. Highway 17 N., Snee Farm was the rural home of Revolutionary patriot Col. Charles Pinckney. Pinckney helped frame the Constitution, and George Washington visited his home in 1791. Today, Snee Farm is officially designated as a historic site (managed by the National Park Service) where visitors get a unique view of how the lives of slaves in the area molded and built a society. (See our Attractions chapter.)

Mt. Pleasant was incorporated as a town in 1837 after apparently drawing its acreage from two villages as well as former plantations on Haddrell's Point. Part of this land was once the property of Andrew Hibben, in whose honor a village street is named.

Shortly before the Civil War, Mt. Pleasant residents met at Renken's Long Room, near the old ferry wharf, and decided to follow Charleston's lead in advocating secession from the Union. Later, during the hard times of Reconstruction, Renken's Long Room housed industrious members of this community in night school and a debating society.

The local economy was based on farming for about a century, and Mt. Pleasant's vegetables were reputed to be among the best in the area. The Old Village was an important link to the mainland and the islands. When mail was transported from the north down the former King's Highway, it was brought to Haddrell's Point, then carried over to Charleston by ferry. Eventually, trolley tracks ran from the south end of Pitt Street to Sullivan's Island, transporting people and goods across what is now the Intracoastal Waterway.

When a bridge spanning the Cooper River opened in 1929, it changed the profile of Mt. Pleasant forever. Shrimping became an important industry in the 1940s, and the picturesque setting of Shem Creek, with its commercial shrimp fleet bobbing at the docks, became a major attraction.

Although some travelers then and now just pass through Mt. Pleasant on their way to the resort islands or heading north to Myrtle Beach, a percentage make the town itself their vacation destination. By the 1970s Mt. Pleasant was booming as a bedroom community for the whole Charleston area, and real estate development here still blossoms. (See our Real Estate and Neighborhoods chapters).

Sullivan's Island

The captain of the *Carolina*, the ship that brought the first English settlers to this area, was Florentia O'Sullivan, and it is for him Sullivan's Island is named. He was a member of the provincial parliament and held the deed to much land east of the Cooper River.

In the early days, Sullivan's Island was covered with pine trees and was used as a strategic point of defense for Lowcountry settlers. This sandy barrier island is only 3 miles long and no more than a quarter-mile wide. Still, it was more than adequate to serve as a defensive buffer for attacks off the Atlantic. In 1706 the Spanish-French fleet lost footing here after a battle at the west end of the island. Here also, the British naval and land forces of Sir Peter Parker were set back in one of the most decisive battles of the American Revolution.

A lesser-known fact about Sullivan's Island is its sad history as a point of debarkation for untold thousands of enslaved Africans before the American Revolution. In the years between 1700 and 1775, the number of slaves off-loaded and "processed" for sale at a now-vanished facility on the island was staggering. Today, a lone marker commemorates this site—only recently acknowledging this uncomfortable fact.

At the northwestern end of Sullivan's Island, you'll find Fort Moultrie, which is a name connected in many ways with Lowcountry history. Gen. William Moultrie rescued the patriots' battle flag here during the Revolution, and 100 years later, Federal commander Maj. Robert Anderson moved his forces from Fort Moultrie to Fort Sumter. Osceola, the famous Seminole Indian chief who was held prisoner at Fort Moultrie until his death, is buried outside the fort. As a young soldier, Edgar Allan Poe was stationed at Fort Moultrie and later wrote an island-inspired story, "The Gold Bug."

Insiders' Tip

Insiders tend to find an even kinder welcome if they show an interest in Lowcountry history. Feel free to ask questions and learn more. Most Lowcountry residents are historians at heart—they grew up with it!

Charlestonians began building summer residences on Sullivan's in the 19th century to escape the heat of the city. As recently as the early part of this century, "moving to the island" meant packing up all the household essentials and making the break for several months. By the end of World War II, a school and a few shops made year-round living possible.

Today most islanders choose to live there full time, and Sullivan's is a favored residential area. Much of the island has been rebuilt since the devastation of Hurricane Hugo but development has been closely monitored so that there is still precious little commercial activity and a relatively subdued lifestyle.

Isle of Palms

Just across the eastern tip of Sullivan's Island and over the bridge across Breach Inlet is the Isle of Palms. While slightly larger than Sullivan's, the Isle of Palms is another classic example of a coastal barrier island. This sandy strip of land is nearly five miles long and a half-mile wide at its midpoint.

Even in the early years, Sullivan's Islanders ventured over to this next island for boat picnics or to fish and shrimp the teeming waters. By the late 19th century, some visitors came regularly by water or the newly built railroad bridge. Records from 1941 indicate that Sullivan's Island had only 25 year-round residents at the time.

After World War II, local businessman J. C. Long, who owned the entire Isle of Palms (and plenty more elsewhere), started selling small vacation homes on the island. During the next three decades, growth was steady. As the Isle of Palms pavilion became, like the Folly Beach pavilion, an entertainment center, the island's reputation for fun and games also grew. Surfers discovered the waves in the 1960s, and the young flocked to the ocean-side strip of eateries and shops to strut their tanned bodies by day and dance from club to club by night.

By the end of the 1970s, the undeveloped northernmost point of the Isle of Palms became Wild Dunes, a self-contained, upscale, planned resort community. Today many Isle of Palms residents are full-timers who call Wild Dunes their permanent home. But there's also a steady stream of short-term visitors who come out to enjoy vacation rentals or just a day's or evening's entertainment.

North Charleston

According to the Smithsonian, a giant, prehistoric condor once flew over land being used for the U.S. Air Force Base in today's North Charleston. Its fossilized remains were found there not far from a much later stone hatchet, a few arrowheads, and human bones that tell us Stone Age humans lived in the area thousands of years ago.

Shortly after the first English colonists put ashore and established Charles Towne in 1670, lands in the north area were granted, sold, and resold. Early on, deer skins, pitch, tar, and turpentine from the north area's abundant pine trees became an important part of the Lowcountry economy.

By the time of the American Revolution, there were probably 60 plantations in the north area successfully raising rice and indigo. Later, regular ferry service was available on the Ashley and Cooper Rivers, making the distance to Charleston easily conquerable. Largely because the plow didn't come into general use here before 1810 and planters neither used fertilizer nor rotated their crops, the soil in the north area was quickly played out. In fact, it was of little use for agriculture after the American Revolution.

Things took an upward turn north of the city in 1830 with the coming of the railroad. In fact, it was the destruction of these tracks and trains that had the most harmful impact on Charleston during the Civil War.

The Important Role of Phosphate

Phosphates used in making fertilizer were discovered and mined along the Ashley River after the Civil War, employing thousands of freedmen during Reconstruction. These freedmen became landowners and formed churches and burial societies that are still in evidence today. Phosphate mining soon encouraged the building of booming fertilizer plants in the north area. These, along with successful lumber companies, provided employment, company housing, and (at last) the basis for a diversified economy not exclusively tied to peninsular Charleston.

What is now North Charleston was also the epicenter of the Great Earthquake of 1886. Although no Richter-scale standard for measuring earthquakes existed at the time,

Close-up

Meet You at "The Four Corners of Law"

The intersection of Meeting and Broad streets is affectionately known in Charleston as "The Four Corners of Law." The old line (mostly used these days by carriage drivers and guides for walking tours) is meant to imply that you can do literally everything legally required in life right here at this one important Charleston intersection.

On the first corner you can get your mail (at the oldest operating post office building in South Carolina). On the second corner you can get married (at St. Michael's Episcopal Church, built in 1761 and the place where the visiting George Washington once worshiped). On the third corner you can pay your taxes (at the Charleston County Court House). And on the fourth corner—if necessary—you can get divorced (at Charleston's City Hall, built in 1801).

This attitude thinly disguises the notorious Charlestonian attitude that, indeed, this intersection is (to locals) the center of the universe. The tongue-in-cheek attitude ranks right up there next to the other one-liner that graciously allows, "The Ashley and Cooper rivers come together at Charleston to form the Atlantic Ocean."

The Four Corners of Law at the intersection of Meeting and Broad Streets is the very heart of the Holy City. PHOTO: DAVID C. BERRY

the tremor that shook the area that hot August night was devastating in many ways. Not only did it take 60 lives and leave thousands homeless, but it also did an estimated $6 million in damage, dealing a major blow to Charleston's priceless architectural treasures. The quake's epicenter was measured near what is now Interstate 26 and Deer Park.

But the greatest catalyst for change in the north area was not of a natural kind. Instead, it was the arrival of the U.S. Navy Yard in 1904. Suddenly land values soared, drainage plans were drawn up, and roads were built. North Charleston was slowly gaining an identity of its own.

The words "North" and "Charleston" were first put together in 1912, according to Ruth W. Cupp, a *News and Courier* writer who compiled a warm, memory-filled history of the area in 1988. The words provided the name for a vast land development plan that included 3,000 residential lots for housing "the labor force of the future." Although this would-be North Charleston real estate development went into foreclosure during the Great Depression, the inertia for a separate municipality continued to build momentum. Workers from the Navy Yard started a savings and loan association—one of the first in the country. Then, West Virginia Pulp and Paper Co. broke ground for a new plant in the area. Things started looking up.

With the coming of World War II, thousands of newcomers settled in the north area as the Navy Yard needed employees to man three shifts working day and night. After the war, private industry and residential communities multiplied quickly. Aviation traffic increased, and an interstate highway was built. Soon the growing pains of a burgeoning city began to call for more political autonomy. The various factions and communities grafted themselves together and formed the city of North Charleston on July 12, 1972.

Residents take pride in the fact that the population center for Greater Charleston, as in the entire Trident area, is in North Charleston. Smart businesses and industries looking for a place to grow are noticing that fact in greater numbers every year.

West (of the) Ashley

Here's another area that pays a kind of allegiance to Charleston's Peninsula through its very name. The neighborhood called West Ashley is, literally, west of peninsular Charleston and across the Ashley River. This was Charleston's primary artery of economic growth following World War II. And like many other similar older growth areas, West Ashley contains its share of urban sprawl. The corridor of U.S. Highway 17 S. (heading toward Savannah) saw Charleston's first planned shopping center (St. Andrews) and the city's first postwar subdivision (Byrnes Downs). Its relative convenience and proximity to peninsular Charleston, along with the new connector highways, make West Ashley neighborhoods a desirable address today.

James Island

The Cusabo Indians, whose name has been translated as "Coosawhatchie River People," lived on James Island four centuries ago and left their archaeological mark ahead of white settlers. It was probably the Kiawah tribe that first blazed a trail from the Stono River to the beach, where its leaders met to make treaties and smoke peace pipes. This path became King's Highway, an important road for European settlers, and what is today's U.S. 17 S.

On the map, the land mass of James Island can be located southwest of the Peninsula. It is bordered by the Stono River, the Intracoastal Waterway, Charleston Harbor, and the Atlantic. Its protective barrier island is Folly Beach. James Island was called Boone's Island in early records, named for the colony's agent, Joseph Boone. Around 1671, James

The first shots of the Civil War are believed to have been fired from James Island onto Fort Sumter.
PHOTO: COURTESY OF CHARLESTON AREA NATIONAL PARK SERVICE

Towne, the second settlement in South Carolina, was officially established on one of this island's creek banks.

In the 19th century, plantations were built along with the village of Secessionville—a summer retreat for plantation owners. It is believed that the first shots of the Civil War were fired from the island's Fort Johnson onto Fort Sumter in 1861 (see the Forts section of our Attractions chapter).

By 1866 all but a handful of dwellings—from stately plantations to gin mills—had been destroyed by the war. The island then became a farming community, where first cotton and then vegetables were the major cash crops. Today there are many businesses and residential areas covering this once sparsely populated land. James Island residents are enthusiastic about the convenient highway connector, S.C. Highway 30, which opened in 1993. It channels traffic directly to and from the Peninsula and has initiated the next chapter of James Island's history.

Johns Island

Larger, more agricultural Johns Island is due west of the Peninsula—past the West Ashley suburban sprawl and James Island. It's technically an island because it is surrounded by the Intracoastal Waterway, the Stono River, the Kiawah River, and Bohicket Creek. Cusabo Indians also inhabited Johns Island before the British arrived. By 1695 there were perhaps 14 white families farming the land, which was also home to wild animals such as buffalo, wolves, and cougars. With the plantation system came the development of Legareville, a summer village of homes built by plantation owners.

Johns Island has developed as a patchwork of natural waterways separated by farmland, residential property, and commercial development. The island has always been something of a breadbasket for the Greater Charleston area.

After the Civil War, when many black families were disenfranchised, Johns Island became a refuge for them. On and around what had once been plantations, little hamlets and church parishes (called "Praise Houses") formed. Small farms and garden operations were soon flourishing—many of which are still in operation today. Tomatoes, strawberries, sweet corn, zucchini, pumpkins, blueberries, and melons are only some of the produce that grows beautifully in the rich Johns Island soil.

Folly Beach

Fun-loving Folly Beach is the geographical barrier island due south of James Island. This 6-mile-long, half-mile-wide sandy stretch of land makes up for its diminutive size with a rich and colorful history embracing both good times and bad.

> ### Insiders' Tip
> Charleston has been the scene of numerous historical firsts. The first regularly scheduled passenger train service in America was established here in 1830.

It is believed that the Bohicket tribe of Cusabo Indians summered on Folly as late as the 17th century. During the Civil War, there were Union batteries at both ends of the island with thousands of men. For many years after the conflict, war-ravaged Folly Beach was described as a "tent city" because of the many temporary dwellings still used for shelter there. More permanent beach houses were built by the turn of the century, and George Gershwin stayed in one during the 1920s while he was writing his famous folk opera, *Porgy and Bess.*

It was the giant pier and pavilion that put Folly on the map. Famous names such as Tommy Dorsey, Artie Shaw, Guy Lombardo, Vaughn Monroe, and the Ink Spots played at Folly's Atlantic Boardwalk in the 1930s. The unique venue and nationally known entertainers drew crowds from the Charleston area and far beyond.

Around 1936 a township form of government was established. Fire destroyed the boardwalk in 1957, but it was reopened in 1960 as the Ocean Plaza. During the next decade, Folly became a mecca for surfers. Drawn to the sizable waves, they congregated around the pier—a popular surfing spot. Again in 1977, fire destroyed this landmark, and eight years later a high-rise hotel (now a Holiday Inn) went up in its place.

Hurricane Hugo scrambled homes and businesses on this island as well, but Folly is once again a popular destination and condos are the newest trend in housing. A handsome new fishing pier lures anglers and sunbathers alike to this quaint and colorful beach community.

Kiawah Island

Kiawah Island is 21 miles from the Peninsula—due west of James Island and Folly Beach—but it has a history and a natural ambiance all its own.

It was home to the Kiawah Indians as early as the 16th century. Europeans arrived in 1688, when the island was granted to Capt. George Rayner by the Lords Proprietors of the Carolina Colony. By 1739 ownership had passed to John Stanyarne, who cleared much of it for growing indigo. In 1807 the title passed to Stanyarne's son-in-law, Arnoldus Vanderhorst.

Vanderhorst was an influential public servant and helped to establish the College of Charleston among other accomplishments. He introduced the planting of cotton on Kiawah and eventually passed the island on to his son. All in all, various members of the Vanderhorst family owned Kiawah Island for the next 180 years.

During the Revolutionary War, British troops occupied the island, and Union forces raised their flag on Kiawah for two years during the Civil War. When the war was over, the Vanderhorsts resumed farming on the island, but ultimately lost the battle with the boll weevil in 1914.

The 10,000-acre island was unoccupied and used as a private hunting reserve between 1952 and 1974 under the ownership of Mr. C.C. Royal of Aiken, South Carolina. Old-timers still talk about the profit turned in '74 when Royal sold the island—which he had purchased for $50,000—to the Kiawah Island Co., a subsidiary of the Kuwait Investment Co., for $17.4 million.

Under Kuwaiti ownership, the island became a world-class luxury golf/tennis resort and residential community. In 1988, when Kiawah once again changed hands, the selling price had jumped to $105 million.

Seabrook Island

Just off the eastern tip of Kiawah—due west of Johns Island—is Seabrook. This barrier island is roughly 2,200 acres in size and located about 22 miles from downtown Charleston.

Like Kiawah, Seabrook has a known archaeological history dating back to approximately 200 B.C. Nomadic bands of Native Americans roamed these lands for thousands of years, leaving shell ring deposits that are still evident today. These piles of shells from edible marine animals were once huge mounds, perhaps 25 to 70 feet in diameter.

In 1666 British subject Lt. Col. Robert Sanford arrived on Seabrook as an explorer in royal service to King Charles II. He described these shell rings as being "discernable a good way out to sea." By 1684 the local Stono Indians were persuaded to cede their lands (for mere beads, cloth, and trinkets) to the proprietary government, which, in turn, sold the property to English settlers.

> ## Insiders' Tip
> Another Charleston first: In 1786 the nation's first golf course, called Harleston Green, was America's earliest golf club, the South Carolina Golf Club. The course has long since been absorbed into the urban landscape, but a proliferation of newer courses has kept the Lowcountry in the swing of things.

The island was used as a staging area for Hessian and British troops during the American Revolutionary years of 1779 and 1780. In 1816 the island was sold to William Seabrook of nearby Edisto Island, hence the present name. Under Seabrook's ownership, the island was used for growing cotton.

At the height of the Civil War, Seabrook sold his island to William Gregg, who tried to re-establish the cotton plantation after the war. He failed and rented the land to Charles Andell of New York City, who, with a group of missionaries, tried to establish schools on the island for newly freed blacks. After Andell's death in 1876, his brother William continued the cotton-growing operation—introducing a new, finer grade of cotton with longer, silkier fibers that became world-famous as "sea island cotton."

After the turn of the century, natural and artificial disasters (such as hurricanes and fires) along with the boll weevil brought an end to Seabrook's highly profitable cotton-growing years. Hardship caused Gregg's widow to sell off Seabrook's oceanfront land to sportsmen for hunting, fishing, and recreation.

In 1939 the Episcopal Diocese of South Carolina rented land on Seabrook to establish a summer camp for underprivileged children. In 1951 about 1,408 acres of land were given to the church, some of which is known today as Camp St. Christopher.

In 1970 the diocese sold about 1,100 acres to private developers who planned the private, residential community that Seabrook Island is today. Eighteen years later, the town of Seabrook was incorporated, and it celebrated a decade of private ownership and self-government in 1997.

Restaurants

Charleston

East Cooper

West Ashley

James, Johns, and Folly Islands, Kiawah, and Seabrook

Believe it or not, you won't have to go very far to find a Charlestonian who will tell you that as recently as 20 years ago there were only a few white tablecloth restaurants in the entire city. That seems incredible today, when there are easily two dozen truly fine dining options to choose from on any given evening out on the town.

Charleston's dining traditions go way back—to England, in fact, where high tea was served in the late afternoon. In Colonial Charles Towne, that habit evolved through the influences of time and climate into a late lunch—usually served at 2 PM or so. This meal was the heaviest of the day.

Before the era of air conditioning and the advent of a more homogenized American lifestyle, Charlestonians held on to this Anglican dining custom for many generations. It moved the effort of meal preparation away from the hottest time of the day and left the shank of the daylight hours essentially uninterrupted for commerce and industry. Until the 1960s (and even later in some cases), schools dismissed their children promptly at 1:50 PM for "two o'clock dinner" and resumed the business of formal education at 8 or so the next morning. Most downtown businesses closed at 1 PM for an hour or so—as did the banks and law offices—so the business owners could saunter home, enjoy 2 PM dinner, and return by early afternoon.

It goes without saying that fine dining was still not neglected in the evening hours—especially where entertaining was concerned. The elegant formal dining rooms of Charleston's famous houses attest to that.

The concept of going out to a restaurant for dinner is a Johnny-come-lately idea to die-hard Charlestonians. That's why there were so few fine restaurants here before the late 1970s.

With the revitalization of our downtown area and the draw of people to all places South, there has been an accompanying influx of outstanding new culinary talent and the interest to match. In fact, Charleston is now home to one of the country's most-respected culinary institutions, Johnson & Wales University. This deepens the talent pool for dining establishments all over the Lowcountry. Now establishments and styles fit almost every whim, while making a true effort to share and preserve the traditional fare of the Lowcountry. We have included information and opinions in this chapter that may help you with your selections.

The list here is not exhaustive but gives, we feel, a fair representation of what is available on the downtown Peninsula, in Mt. Pleasant, on the islands east of the Cooper, and in the areas and islands west of the Ashley River. Eateries are categorized geographically, not by type of food offered. So pin down the location where you want to dine, then dive into the listings to see what is available. Bear in mind that many of the downtown restaurants are housed in old and historic buildings that may not be wheelchair-accessible. If that's an issue for you or your party, it's always good to call ahead.

Whatever your budget, we feel confident you'll find in the following listings the perfect setting for enjoying Lowcountry meals that will augment your stay in the Trident area.

Price Code

The reference guide below should be used to translate the average price ranges of dinner for two persons, minus cocktails, wine, or gratuity. We caution that prices, hours, menus, and means of payment are frequently subject to change, so if you have any doubts about an important issue, call ahead. Since most restaurants will accept cash, traveler's checks, and all major credit cards (but almost never personal checks), we only inform you of those establishments that do not take plastic.

Here are our breakdowns for average entree prices for two and the correlating symbols.

$ . . . . Less than $20
$$ $21–35
$$$ $36–60
$$$$ . . . . More than $61

Charleston

82 Queen $$$
82 Queen St.
(843) 723-7591

This multi-award-winning restaurant has several personalities—one of which is sure to please. Exploring the eleven dining rooms at 82 Queen is an adventure in itself. The grounds include three 18th-century town houses, two inside bars (one full-service and one just for shots), an outside raw bar that is a very popular hangout for the after-work crowd, a partly glassed-in romantic gazebo, and outdoor tables for dining. Lowcountry seafood, beef, lamb, and fowl are specialties of their updated traditional Southern cuisine. Farm fresh herbs and vegetables are locally grown for their kitchen. The wine list includes more than 140 selections. Lunch and dinner are served daily, and reservations are encouraged. (See our Nightlife chapter for more.)

Alice's Fine Foods and Southern Cooking
$, no credit cards
468 - 470 King St.
(843) 853-9366

Near the downtown visitor center on King Street's fast-developing upper region, Alice's is the place for those who like old-fashioned, down-home, no-nonsense Southern cooking. Alice's serves okra soup, Southern-style collard greens, fried chicken, and a delicious macaroni and cheese pie. Lunch and dinner are served daily. Lunch is low-key, comfortable, and popular with the downtown office crowd. You can expect the lunch line (cafeteria-style) to be steady, so come early.

Anson $$$
12 Anson St.
(843) 577-0551

This elegant restaurant on Anson Street is between the Market and the trendy Ansonborough neighborhood. Anson is as well appointed as it is deserving of its reputation for fine food and good service. The nouvelle American menu includes a decadent cashew-crusted grouper in champagne sauce that should not be missed. If you're among those who enjoy steak tartare, Anson's consistently gets rave reviews. Other temptations include outstanding first-course pizzas and Thai chicken with fresh mango and curry rice. When it's time for dessert, look for their dense, moist house-made chocolate cake. Dinner is served nightly; reservations are recommended.

A.W. Shuck's Seafood & Oyster Bar $$
35 Market St.
(843) 723-1151

More than a decade has passed since Shuck's first opened its doors, and a lot has changed in the Market area since then—at Shuck's in particular. What was originally a cozy, popular bar packed with locals has become a bigger, fancier eating establishment where the bar is no longer the major draw. Shuck's features both indoor and outdoor dining. Oyster connoisseurs will be interested to know the mollusks are sold raw or steamed at market price. Beef, fowl, shrimp, grouper, scallops, snapper, and children's plates are all on the menu. A.W. Shuck's is open daily for lunch and dinner. Locals and visitors alike enjoy the abundance of artwork throughout the restaurant by local painter John Doyle.

Baker's Café of Charleston $–$$
214 King St.
(843) 577-2694

Baker's Café is a romantic little gem tucked away in the block below Charleston Place. Much more than a bakery (although what's baked is delicious), it is a sophisticated but comfortable restaurant that's open daily for breakfast and lunch. Sunday brunch at Baker's, lasting until 2:30 PM, is particularly delightful, with unusual dishes such as Eggs Charleston (with a bed of snow crab substituted for the Canadian bacon), mimosas made with freshly squeezed orange juice, and a basket of hot-from-the-oven baked goods. Wine and other spirits also are available. Dress is nicely casual.

Beaumont's Café $$$
12 Cumberland St.
(843) 577-5500

Beaumont's is a delightful and distinctive French restaurant with a nice selection of French and American wines. The atmosphere is light and airy, and the food is quite good. While the menu changes about four times a year to take advantage of seasonal bounty, you can count on such traditional French dishes as the fillet of flounder meunière and bouillabaisse or rack of lamb with beans and grilled tomato. Beaumont's is open for lunch Friday through Sunday and for dinner every day. For wine lovers, they have more than 100 labels on hand.

Blossom Café $$–$$$
171 East Bay St.
(843) 722-9200

Blossom Café is another see-and-be-seen place downtown but offers the bonus of being as affordable or extravagant as your budget allows. The café, open every day, has indoor and outdoor dining, an in-house bakery, a cappuccino bar, and an extensive New American menu with Italian and Mediterranean influences. The menu is the same for lunch, dinner, and late-night dining, featuring pastas, seafood entrees, and gourmet pizzas from the oak-burning oven. An added bonus is free parking just next door.

Bocci's $$–$$$
158 Church St.
(843) 720-2121

This cozy Northern Italian family restaurant near the Market keeps them coming back for more calzones, salads, seafood, and pasta topped with a choice of four fabulous sauces. Mozzarella lovers go for the hand-pulled cheese. Another favorite is scallops wrapped in prosciutto. Try the shrimp and pasta salad too. There is a front-room view looking onto historic Church Street. Bocci's is open every day for lunch and dinner.

Boissons Café $$
42 Ann St.
(843) 853-0120

At a time when French restaurants are fairly scarce in Charleston, it's good to know there's Boissons. This is a small, but very authentic, French café in the best sense of the word. The menu is not extensive or particularly ambitious—but delightfully rich in its attention to detail and Continental finesse. Even the atmosphere is like a Paris café with just the right mix of cabaret and le jazz hot. A small bar completes the scene for a memorable lunch or dinner. Try their sea bass with roasted onions, if it's available, or the lamb loin with shiitake mushrooms. Dessert items change daily, but listen for their wonderful apple tart to be men-

Treat yourself to some of our scrumptious Lowcountry cuisine.
PHOTO: COURTESTY OF CHARLESTON AREA CONVENTION AND VISITORS BUREAU

tioned among your choices. Located not far from the visitor center, this may be a great first introduction to Charleston's many dining options. Dinner is served Tuesday through Saturday, 5:30 PM until whenever; reservations are encouraged.

The Bookstore Café $–$$
412 King St.
(843) 720-8843

Near Marion Square and upper King Street, The Bookstore Café serves breakfast and lunch and sells freshly baked goods. Far enough from the madding crowd, this café offers some serenity along with its daily specials. Menu items include its signature potato casseroles. Specials might be quesadillas, a focaccia sandwich, roast pork, and fried green tomatoes. Take home some rhubarb-raspberry jam and beer bread. The café opens at 9 AM Monday through Friday; Saturday and Sunday hours begin at 8 AM. Closing time is 2 PM every day.

Buca Di Elena $$–$$$
82 Society St.
(843) 958-9060

Located between Meeting and King Streets on Society in what was a mid-19th-century Charleston single house,

here is a charming taste of Sicilian and Neapolitan cuisine. Small, intimate, and personal downstairs (with outdoor seating in warm weather), there's an upstairs bar with piano, too. It matters that the chef is formerly of the famed Algonquin Hotel in Manhattan and knows how to make a memorable evening of authentic southern Italian dining. His special focus is on the food of Naples and that of Sicily. Try any of the veals—Marsala, parmigiana, alla Elena, or alla Romana. All are superb. The seafood dishes are great here, too. Many wines are available by the glass, or you can order one of over 35 of their fine Italian labels. Dinner is served Tuesday through Saturday, and reservations are a good idea.

Carolina's $$$
10 Exchange St.
(843) 724-3800, (888) 486-7673

Carolina's is on the site of old Perdita's, a much-respected restaurant of days gone by. There is little in the decor reminiscent of the establishment's roots, as Carolina's is designed for today. There are three main areas: the noisy, see-and-be-seen front dining section, with its showy wine collection (said to be one of the largest in the Southeast); a central bar with tables on two sides; and a more secluded, traditional dining room to the right of the entrance. The menu is expansive, and the style Nouvelle American with seafood, veal, and lamb—grilled in many instances. One favorite is the sweet potato-crusted filet of flounder with avocado salsa. Their pecan brittle basket with vanilla bean ice cream and fresh fruit barriers is ample for two and a perfect ending. Carolina's is open every day for dinner only, and the dress, while generally casual, edges toward the snazzy side. Reservations are suggested. (See our Nightlife chapter.)

Charleston Grill $$$–$$$$
224 King St. (in Charleston Place)
(843) 577-4522

This is the grande dame restaurant in Orient Express' Charleston Place. In this richly wooded and traditionally decorated eatery, quality is the byword. Service is exuberant for those who demand close attention, and the wine list can compete with any in town. It isn't exactly stuffy, but the atmosphere is definitely upscale. The food is simply superb. Its nightly specials are always as billed, but the regular menu is abundant in attractive choices. Try the young zucchini blossoms stuffed with Maine lobster with fried oysters for starters. And the fresh elk tenderloin over braised apples with fresh crosnes in a coastal huckleberry reduction makes for an exotic entree. Desserts are announced nightly for those with a taste for excess. Live jazz begins at 7 PM and adds a cool balm to the well-orchestrated scene. Dinner is served nightly, and the bar opens at 4 PM. Reservations are welcomed.

Charleston Chops $$$-$$$$
188 East Bay St.
(843) 937-9300

Don't let the name mislead you—this is not your mother's Sunday pork chops. This is an elegant dining experience with possibly the largest list of gourmet specialties in town including a wine list with over 180 choices. Still, it's the place (on East Bay Street, anyway) to go for good prime rib, a thick veal chop, or ginger and lemon grass

seared tuna. Charleston Chops is an excellent source for roasted rack of lamb and succulent seafood, too. If you need to go exotic, try the appetizer list, where you'll find ostrich brochettes, beef tartar, and much more. As for steaks, the beef is 21-day, aged Certified Black Angus—consistently tender and served as ordered. Executive Chef Jeff Gibbs' greatest creations are non-beef specialties, such as garlic and herb-crusted salmon, pan-seared duck, and a mixed grill of wild game. Classical and contemporary tunes from the piano bar will entertain you throughout the evening. Charleston Chops serves dinner Monday through Sunday beginning at 5:30, with the bar opening at 5. Reservations are recommended.

Circa 1886 $$$–$$$$
149 Wentworth St.
(843) 853-7828

When the giant landmark Victorian townhouse on Wentworth Street opened as a high-end B&B, the whole concept for the genre in Charleston expanded upwardly—in more ways than one. Not only would the envelope for luxury accommodations be expanded, an on-site restaurant would be opened of similar caliber for the convenience of the mansion's guests and other discerning diners. Thus, Circa 1886 was born (about a year later), and it seems well worth the wait. Named for the date of the Wentworth Mansion's construction, this small and intimate dining venue in what was once the carriage house offers seasonal cuisine that conceivably might have been served to the home's owner at that time. One favorite on the winter menu is shrimp, oysters, crab, scallops, andouille sausage, and tasso ham in a rice crust with roasted tomato-saffron broth. Or if you're game, try the wild boar chop fricandeau with British runner beans.

Desserts are elaborate and served with the appropriate panache. The lemon mousse crepe with champagne-raspberry sauce makes a pleasant ending. An intimate bar and attentive but unobtrusive service add to the ambiance here—and Circa 1886 provides a quiet evening of fine dining clearly intended to be a cut above the rest of the downtown restaurant crowd. An impressive wine list with more than 280 labels is available. Dinner is served Monday through Saturday from 5:30 to 9:30 PM. Reservations are required.

Doe's Pita Plus $, no credit cards
334 East Bay St.
(843) 577-3179
651 Johnnie Dodds Blvd., Mt. Pleasant
(843) 971-2080
5134 N. Rhett Avenue, North Charleston
(843) 745-0026

Doe's offers healthy fast food that's a hit with the lunch crowd. The fresh-baked pita bread for pocket sandwiches and salads is prepared to order (right there in plain view) while you wait. Although there are several tables and chairs in the front and back, most people think takeout when they think of Doe's. The Tasty Chicken Pocket is very popular—bursting at the pita seams with plums, celery, chicken, green onions, lettuce, tomatoes, and alfalfa sprouts. For variety on the side, sample Doe's ethnic fare such as baba ghanouj, tabouleh, or Lebanese potato salad. Children love the banana and peanut butter pocket and do well in the high-chair stationed in the rear dining area. Nonalcoholic beverages are sold. Doe's is open daily until 8:30 PM Monday through Saturday and until 5 PM on Sundays.

Elliott's on the Square $$$
387 King St.
(843) 724-8888

Just off Marion Square in the Westin Francis Marion Hotel is this convenient option for hotel guests, conventioneers, and locals who know a good thing. As the flagship restaurant for the hotel, you'll find the breakfast and lunch business brisk, the service efficient, and the food good. The focus here is on new American cuisine with a sophisticated nod in the direction of southern favorites—as might be expected. The lobster gnocchi with corn, tarragon, and curry cream sauce is a knockout. Another favorite is the Lowcountry fried oysters with smoky tomato

remoulade and jicama salad. Look for international dishes on the menu, too. Wine is available by the glass or from an extensive list of domestic and imported labels. Dinner service begins at 5:30 PM and is available until 10. The restaurant is open seven days a week. Reservations are recommended.

Fish $$–$$$
442 King St.
(843) 722-3474

As the name implies, this is a small restaurant on upper King Street that's mostly about (but not exclusively dedicated to) seafood. You can count on the fact that none of the seafood brought to table will be more than 36 hours from its native waters. The fun décor is part of the charm. You enter through a courtyard past a fountain and discover an environment that's creative and unusual without being too cute. Don't overlook the risotto-encrusted calamari tossed with cabbage and peppers or the tempura asparagus drizzled with hollandaise. If you're game for it, one of their specialties is the mako shark. Another favorite is their black grouper in beurre blanc sauce. You might like to try the "Captain's Seafood Pot," a traditional steam pot in saffron broth, suitable for two seafood-lovers. The dessert they're all talking about is the mudslide cake. Fish is open for lunch Monday through Friday. Dinner is served Monday through Saturday, 5 to 10 PM.

Fulton Five $$$
5 Fulton St.
(843) 853-5555

Fulton Five is an authentic taste of old Italy tucked away on Fulton Street, just off King Street in the heart of the antiques district. The building looks Old World enough to be European and the al fresco dining experience is definitely continental in feel. A new upstairs dining area adds another perspective on the charms of quaint and narrow Fulton Street. The menu is constantly changing with new and more exciting entrees. But if the following dishes are available, we heartily recommend them. Start with antipasto Spoleto (grilled fresh mozzarella and prosciutto rolled into a romaine leaf with tomato vinaigrette). Next, move to the pumpkin ravioli with a sage and brown butter sauce. Then enjoy the caper-crusted tuna loin with lemon and fennel butter. For a light, sweet touch, order a grapefruit, orange, or tangerine ice made in-house or tiramisu—the perfect finale. A fine selection of Italian and other wines is always on hand. Fulton Five is open only for dinner Monday through Saturday. Reservations are suggested.

Garibaldi's $$$
49 S. Market St.
(843) 723-7153

Garibaldi's is a charming Southern Italian restaurant that has survived, apparently without flinching, the continuous ebb and flow of popularity on Market Street. There is service downstairs, with a small bar and a few romantic outside tables, and there's also a formal dining room upstairs. Try the outstanding, crispy scored flounder, and enjoy any of the five pastas. Another favorite is the American red snapper au poivre. Garibaldi's Italian take on our Lowcountry seafood is worth the trouble of finding parking in the congested Market area. Dinner is served each evening, and reservations are required.

Gaulart & Maliclet (Fast and French) $–$$
98 Broad St.
(843) 577-9797

Tucked neatly into what was once a long, narrow doctor's office with lovely old molding, G&M (called "Fast and French" by locals) is a tiny Parisian-style café serving delicious, contemporary French fare. The counter-style service offers cheese plates, salads, and house specials. The owners (French, of course) know what they are doing and are pleasant while doing it. Some favorites are the curried sesame chicken and the Swiss fondue with French bread. They serve breakfast, lunch, and dinner almost every day except Sunday. No dinner is served on Monday.

Hank's Seafood Restaurant $$$
10 Hayne St
(843) 723-3474

Old-time Charleston Insiders remember a place called Henry's which was part and parcel of this city's colorful "renaissance era" in the 1920s and '30s. It was a seafood joint down in The Market (which was a whole lot rougher in those days) and among other distinctions, old Henry's served liquor throughout Prohibition with (apparently) no interference from the city fathers. Hearty "receipts" for seafood soups and dishes laden with cream and flavor were always offered at Henry's and generations of Charlestonians were raised on it. Hank's is today's reincarnation of that tradition, with a lot of sophistication added to the mix. An old warehouse has been carefully outfitted with a quasi-period-looking fish-house decor without being too cute about it. And several of the old Henry's dishes have been reproduced or improved upon for modern palettes who now flock there from all over the world. This is where she-crab soup is done right (lovingly flavored with crab roe and sherry) and oysters are still served on the half-shell atop beds of crushed ice. Look for some of the old Henry's casseroles, if you like, or try the specialties (like sea scallops or seared tuna). There are several fried seafood platters that feature a variety of old Lowcountry receipts, as well. Spirits are still high and served at Hank's willingly. Reservations are taken from 5 until 10:30 PM, Sunday through Thursday, and until 11:30 PM on Friday and Saturday.

High Cotton $$$
1199 East Bay St.
(843) 724-3815

A relatively recent addition to Charleston's array of fine eateries along the East Bay corridor just north of the Exchange Building is High Cotton. This one is the latest from the Elliott Group (which also brings us Elliott's at the Westin Francis Marion, Slightly North of Broad across the street and Slightly Up the Creek over in Mt. Pleasant). They call this one "an unabashedly masculine and American saloon," but don't look for anything Wild West about it. Instead, there's dark mahogany woodwork, exposed brick walls, lots of alligator skin upholstery, and a hearty menu of meats, game, lobster, and fresh fish. Local dishes include South Carolina squab, rabbit loin, venison, and spit-roasted quail. Fresh seafood is also available—for which out-of-town visitors from inland locations all seem to call. The spirits served and the service rendered are up to the Elliott Group's high standards. Dinner hours are 5:30 to 10 PM, Sunday through Thursday, and 5:30 to 11 PM Friday and Saturday. Their weekend brunch is popular, too. Call for reservations.

Hominy Grill $$
207 Rutledge Ave.
(843) 937-0930
On Rutledge Avenue, within a stroll from the huge MUSC hospital and medical office complex, there's a small but worthwhile café that's anything but institutional. This is a favorite with the medfolk, as you would imagine, so the best time to find a table is off the peak meal rush hours—although breakfast, lunch, and dinner are all offered. The cuisine is contemporary Southern, with several attractively served specials listed daily on their chalkboard menu. Look for some Lowcountry favorites like McClellanville crab cakes with Hoppin' John and pickled cucumber salad. Or, there's a sesame-crusted catfish with sautéed okra, baked cheese grits, and Geechee peanut sauce. Desserts are terrific and their bread-pudding with raisins and caramel sauce is a special treat. Hominy Grill opens for breakfast at 7:30 AM, Monday through Friday. Weekend brunch starts at 9. Dinner is served from 5:30 until 9:30 PM on weekdays, and until 10 on Saturday and Sunday night.

Hyman's Seafood Company $$
215 Meeting St.
(843) 723-6000
A casual, always-crowded seafood dining experience for lunch or dinner, Hyman's offers a large selection of fresh-caught fish and a wide variety of shellfish. A raw bar and lounge are upstairs. Hyman's regularly fries in vegetable oil for those who want traditionally fried seafood. But you can order your fish broiled or blackened. Try the okra soup, even if you have always shied away from the vegetable. The she-crab soup is award-winning. Open every day, the restaurant serves meals all day long. We suggest parking in the Charleston Place garage.

Jack's Café $, no credit cards
41 George St.
(843) 723-5237
The turnaround at Jack's is fast, and the food is as typically American as the no-frills apple or peach cobbler. College of Charleston students, professors, and alumni as well as King Street merchants frequent Jack's for old-fashioned burgers (served in plastic baskets) and milk shakes. The value is definitely part of the draw but so is the vegetable soup (and, in fact, all of the food). People eat at booths, the counter, or around a few tables. It's all very low-key and functional. Takeout service is available. Jack's is open weekdays only for breakfast and lunch.

Jasmine $$$
16 N. Market St.
(843) 853-0006
It's not easy for a relatively small restaurant in a city like Charleston (where there are so many good choices for tourists and locals) to carve out a niche for itself. But Jasmine has managed to do just that. Their menu has what many other menus have—seafood, beef, chops, lamb, and fowl—but the chefs here (literally) bring something unique to the table. They cook with Lowcountry ingredients, but they add something that comes from having studied the cuisines of Asia, Europe, and most of the great dining cities here in America, as well. Try their Gulf oysters baked with lemongrass butter and bread crumbs as an appetizer. A knockout main

dish is their grilled cider-cured pork tenderloin with fresh sauerkraut and potato pancakes and mustard sauce. The spicy barbecue grouper with rice noodle stir fry and sweet and sour eggplant is a hit, too. In-house prepared desserts include a warm, bittersweet chocolate bread pudding and an apple confit torte with cinnamon ice cream and Calvados syrup. Lunch is served Monday through Friday; dinner is Monday through Saturday.

Kaminsky's Most Excellent Café $
78 N. Market St.
(843) 853-8270
1028 Johnnie Dodds Blvd., Mt. Pleasant
(843) 971-7777

Kaminsky's is an A-plus addition to the list of indulge-thyself Peninsula eateries. The surprise is, its just wonderful desserts and the right coffees and spirits to accompany them here. The handsome brick walls of the Market Street location make a backdrop for a nice showcase of art, and the café's intimate size contributes to its appeal. Try an exotic coffee or nonalcoholic drink with a delicious dessert. The milk shakes, for instance, are legendary. Be prepared to face a dilemma: There are 150 other choices. Relax with a beer or glass of wine; both lists are international and impressive. Kaminsky's is open every day from noon to 2 AM. (For more about the Mt. Pleasant location, see the East Cooper section of our Nightlife chapter.)

The Library at Vendue $$$
23 Vendue Range
(843) 723-0485

In the Vendue Inn, this restaurant gives the feel of an old English library but has a progressive menu that changes with the availability of fresh ingredients. One can almost make a meal of The Library's delicious, heavy appetizers: the chilled potato, leek, and caraway soup, for instance. However, seafood, steaks, veal, lamb, and accompaniments (offered à la carte) are prepared in ways that lure diners onward. The pan-seared black grouper crusted in blue crab with citrus ginger

Dijon is a big hit. Save room for great house-made desserts such as the chocolate trifle. Breakfast, lunch, and dinner are served seven days a week. The popular rooftop bar with its delightful views of Charleston Harbor is a great idea for sunset cocktails, and it closes at 10 PM.

Louis's Restaurant & Bar $$$–$$$$
200 Meeting St.
(843) 853-2550

The chef who opened the prestigious Louis's Charleston Grill in Charleston Place struck out on his own in 1998 with this chic and sophisticated option for the high-end dining patron. This is Louis Osteen's colorful showcase for new American-Lowcountry cuisine. The interiors were designed by famed New York restaurant designer Adam Tihany, and the look is high-tech with tongue somewhat in cheek. What matters is Osteen's talent for taking traditional Southern ingredients and recipes and presenting them in surprising new ways. The menu changes often, but his beer-braised rabbit with foie gras-stuffed cabbage for an appetizer is tops. Then there's the aged black Angus strip steak with green peppercorn-Calvados sauce. The seafood entrees are adventuresome with their roasted Chilean sea bass on a bed of melted leeks, shredded oxtails, and leek broth. The desserts are all priced the same and include a cheese selection. Try the vanilla cream cake with lemon curd and blackberry syrup. Louis's is open only for dinner Monday through Sunday. The bar opens early (4 PM) and has its own menu, so there's a select afterwork crowd through the week. Reservations are required.

Magnolias Uptown/Down South $$$
185 East Bay St.
(843) 577-7771

Magnolias tops the list of hot restaurants on the Peninsula. In fact, *Travel & Leisure* called it "the place in downtown Charleston." This is new American-Lowcountry cuisine, and the chef's specialties include spicy shrimp and sausage with tasso gravy over creamy white grits and tomato bisque dotted with generous lumps of fresh crabmeat. The expansive menu will remind you of the restaurant's California, Tex-Mex, and Cajun inspirations, but the atmosphere is strictly refined New South. Enjoy eating in the beautiful dining rooms at Magnolias but also try your hand with Magnolias' recipes at home: Chef Donald Barickman's Magnolias Southern Cuisine is a hot seller cookbook. Lunch and dinner are served daily. Reservations are definitely encouraged.

Marina Variety Store & Restaurant $$
City Marina, 17 Lockwood Dr.
(843) 723-6325

Enjoy good food as well as a magnificent view of the Ashley River at what regulars call "The Variety Store." Offering daily breakfast, lunch, and dinner in a very casual setting, the restaurant serves basic, good food. For instance, you can order eggs, bacon, and toast for breakfast after church and come back for a tuna salad sandwich and cup of vegetable soup after the noon regatta. If you want to return that night, a dinner of fresh fish with red rice and a salad is a distinct possibility. Spirits are available, and children are welcome.

McCrady's Tavern $$$–$$$$
2 Unity Alley
(843) 577-0025

McCrady's has recently experienced a new incarnation that retains much of the old Tavern's charm, but adds new space and sophistication. The dark wood and exposed brick interiors hark back to the days when George Washington supposedly supped here. And the huge fireplaces add their own charm. But the service and—most of all—the cuisine is the reason to go there. Here, fine dining is a major event. McCrady's serves appetizers like house-cured salmon "pastrami" served with toast points and a zesty mustard sauce. There's a lobster and new potato salad, too. For entrees, try the rack of lamb marinated in herbs with thyme-whipped potatoes. But delicious varia-

> # Insiders' Tip
> Check the menu or specials board at Lowcountry eateries for Beaufort Stew (sometimes called Frogmore Stew), a hearty one-dish supper that's a staple meal on the islands. It's smoked sausage, fresh ears of corn and shrimp all boiled together with special spices. This fare is often served at Lowcountry oyster roasts as an alternative menu item.

tions of duck, chicken, beef, pork, and fish are always on the menu. If you're still able, try a dessert like the pear and almond tart or the molten chocolate cake with caramel ice cream. The sommelier's wine list is extensive and impressive. It's open Monday through Saturday for dinner. (See our Nightlife chapter.)

Mellow Mushroom $–$$
309 King St.
(843) 723-7374

Some visitors to Charleston may be familiar with the earlier version of this specialty pizza den that was a big draw in Atlanta when it first opened in the 1970s. Our version is new to the King Street crowd and the College of Charleston kids who weren't around for the "groovy" version in Hot 'lanta. In addition to the specialty pizzas like their "Mega–Veggie" with a garden's worth of fresh non-meat ingredients, their dough is made with spring water. Calzones, hoagies, and salads are on the bill, as well. The location is ideal for students, but MM attracts out-of-towners, too. It's especially popular with late-nighters and lunch-timers from King Street's business district. They're open daily for lunch and dinner and the bar stays open until 2 AM.

Mistral $$–$$$
99 S. Market St.
(843) 722-5708

Mistral is a very cozy, small, and intimate bistro. Live jazz is featured every day except Wednesday for lunch (starting at 11 AM until 4 PM). The music resumes in the evening starting at 9 PM. Lunch and dinner are served in a French Country atmosphere with an emphasis on seafood and sauces. Their house pâté is a favorite with locals. This is understated elegance—a place where you can go light or heavy, from salads to seafood. Don't miss the homemade bread!

My Tho $$$
304 King St.
(843) 965-5091

Named for the executive chef's home village in Vietnam, this is Charleston's first truly upscale Asian-American dining adventure. They specialize in Thai, Vietnamese, and American Fusion cuisine served in an intimate and authentic atmosphere. The lavish décor features rich architectural accents and beautiful objets d'arts. The service is especially accommodating in their willingness to help the uninitiated explore new culinary territory. Try cold Vietnamese spring rolls or sweet and sour Thai shrimp soup as an appetizer. For an entree, go for their Vietnamese rice pancake stuffed with shrimp, lobster, port, sprouts, and more. Exotic sides let you wrap and dip the pancake in multiple adventures in flavor. Live music and dancing complement this international dining experience.

Olde Towne Restaurant $$
229 King St.
(across from Charleston Place)
(843) 723-8170

Owners Spiros Fokas and Steve Ferderigos have been serving authentic Greek lunches and dinners here daily for more than 20 years. The menu includes seafood, salads, Greek chicken, and the ever-popular Steve's Special—a sampler, good for the whole gang. Pictures of classical Greece line the walls, and a grill in the front win-

dow offers a tempting display of chicken being roasted on a turning spit.

O'Reilly's Irish Pub and Seafood Tavern $
288 King St.
(843) 577-0123

Formerly Mike Calder's, O'Reilly's is a sports-friendly pub that pleases its clientele with deli-style food and a colorful atmosphere. Such favorites as chef salads, soups, and club sandwiches are always available. Try the Reuben or the toasted tuna sandwich. O'Reilly's has 5 imports on draft and is popular with the College of Charleston crowd that seems ever-present on King Street at night. O'Reilly's is closed on Sunday. (See our Nightlife chapter.)

The Palmetto Café $$$
130 Market St.
(843) 722-4900

This restaurant is inside the large Charleston Place complex and serves breakfast, lunch, and dinner in a relaxed but upscale café atmosphere. The breakfast buffet on Saturday and Sunday is a very elaborate event with several choices of entree and salad, fresh vegetables and fruits, plus desserts. The garden atmosphere is particularly attractive and convenient to those staying in the hotel or shopping downtown. It falls in the pricier category, but everything is beautifully presented and it is well worth the price on a special occasion (like your first visit to Charleston). For lunch, there's nothing like their chilled red and yellow Johns Island heirloom gazpacho. Follow that with crab cakes served with blackberry, rhubarb, and roasted tomato sauces. This stylish restaurant features optional courtyard dining and is open daily for breakfast and lunch only.

Peninsula Grill $$$–$$$$
Planters Inn, 112 N. Market St.
(843) 723-0700

The restaurant in the Planters Inn is the Peninsula Grill, an elegantly simple and altogether comfortable dining experience that has "extraordinary" written all over it. For instance, half the menu is devoted to the Champagne Bar, which offers an Old World selection of champagnes by the glass and a list of mixed cocktails that reads like a page from Noel Coward's Private Lives. The Champagne Bar Menu includes a full selection of oysters, lobster (fresh from Maine), and other seafood specialties. Try the sautéed jumbo shrimp scampi with lima bean, corn, okra, and tomato gumbo. The steaks, chops, and accompanying side dishes are equally fine, and you're tended to by a courteous and capable staff. As for wine, there's an extensive list—mostly from France and California. Several labels are available by the glass. Peninsula Grill is open Monday through Sunday for dinner only starting at 5:30 PM. Reservations are required. (See our Nightlife chapter.)

Pinckney Café and Espresso $$
18 Pinckney St.
(843) 577-0961
There's nothing quite like Pinckney Café in Charleston. Sure, we have other restaurants in single houses (see the Close-up on single houses in our Architectural Preservation chapter), and you can dine on the porch at those as well. But Pinckney Café is unique. The decor is "less is more," so you can enjoy the changing art exhibits. The menu could be called "new American bistro," as it includes gourmet soups, salads, seafood specials, and a delicious black bean burrito. Cappuccino is a perfect finale, but try the bread pudding with caramel sauce, too. Pinckney Café is open daily for lunch and Wednesday through Saturday for dinner. Seating is limited, so we reccomend that you avoid the peak hours of noon to 1 PM. Reservations aren't required unless you have a party of more than six.

Poogan's Porch $$–$$$
72 Queen St.
(843) 577-2337
Poogan's Porch is in a charming old Charleston house where lunch and dinner can be enjoyed fireside or outside beneath the stars on the porch or patio. Expect casual family dining (including a children's menu) with such Lowcountry favorites as Albertha's she-crab soup, shrimp creole, okra gumbo, seafood specials and even—on the wilder side—an occasional alligator. Lunch and dinner are served seven days a week; reservations are recommended for dinner. Sunday brunch is from 10:30 AM to 2:30 PM.

Robert's of Charleston $$$$
182 East Bay St.
(843) 577-7565,
(800) 977-7565 (outside S.C.)
Starting in 1976, one of the most popular restaurant experiences in Charleston was Robert Dickson's one-man show that married music and fine dining for a delightful evening on the town. He closed in 1994 to lead small tours to Italy and do private catering, but the call of the crowd brought him back in 1998. Reservations are required well in advance for his five-course, prix fixe meal ($70) and a menu that changes seasonally. You might start with scallop mousse in creamed lobster sauce followed by breast of duckling in a mango sauce. Then for your main course, he'll serve beef tenderloin with Béarnaise sauce accompanied by fresh vegetables in interesting combinations. Desserts are very special with Key lime tart plus tropical fruit in guava sauce being just one example. But get this: Your chef is also your entertainment! Robert is an accomplished baritone with a vast repertoire of popular Broadway musicals to his credit. He sings while his guests dine, and his pianist fills in as he slips away to the kitchen between songs and prepares your next course. Your wine is pre-selected from a list of the chef's international favorites. The fare for the entire evening seems pricey, but it's always an unforgettable night. Many patrons are celebrating special occasions, which adds to the electricity of the event. This is a performance that takes place every Thursday through Saturday with a 7:30 PM seating. Don't dare be late.

Saffron $–$$
333 East Bay St.
(843) 722-5588

This is a light and airy restaurant, contemporary in design and good for solo ventures or joining friends. This pitched-roof, modern building is divided into a gourmet product section with imported pastas and olive oils; a full bakery (you'll be seduced by the scent and leave with a loaf of bread); and a dining room with booths and tables scattered about. Popular menu items include the seafood and spinach salads, pasta dishes, and the classic carrot cake. It's open for breakfast, lunch, and dinner seven days a week. Saffron does a Sunday brunch from 10 AM to 2:30 PM.

Saracen Restaurant $$$
141 East Bay St.
(843) 723-6242

Housed in the former Farmers and Exchange Bank, built in 1853, Saracen is worth the trip for its exotic architectural curiosities alone. The building fantastically mixes Gothic, Hindu, Moorish, and Persian styles. But the world-class cuisine is exceptional too. Expect some Asian and Moroccan entrees as well as European dishes. Try the Thai honeyed lamb bisteeya or the honey and sesame-crusted sea bass on beet couscous. Saracen has an upstairs oasis called Charlie's Little Bar that's a delightful place to have pre-dinner cocktails while waiting for your table. (See our Nightlife chapter.) It's open Tuesday through Saturday for dinner only, and reservations are recommended.

Sermet's Corner $$
276 King St.
(843) 853-7775

After the success of his first eatery west of the Ashley, Sermet's creative artist and chef opened a new location on King Street to rave reviews and standing-room-only crowds. The cuisine is Mediterranean-influenced—with spicy pastas and fresh green salads—and it's a refreshing option on the King Street luncheon and dinner scene. Look for their lavender honey and black pepper marinated pork tenderloin with creamy ricotta polenta. The desserts are straight from heaven. In season, there's a rhubarb and raspberry pie that is definitely to die for. Sermet's is open daily from 11 AM to 3 PM for lunch; and they reopen for dinner starting at 5 PM.

Slightly North of Broad $$–$$$
129 East Bay St.
(843) 723-3424

In one of the many 19th-century cotton warehouses that line East Bay Street, there's this trendy option for S.N.O.B. types. Cute name notwithstanding, the folks here are very serious about good food. It's what they call a "maverick Southern kitchen" with multicultural overtones. The sautéed shiitake mushrooms with foie gras mousse filling on a bed of fresh sautéed spinach with a port wine sauce are divine. This restaurant is a favorite of those who want to lunch with friends (Monday through Friday) or have a special evening on the town (any day of the week). Reservations are encouraged.

Sushi Hiro $
298 King St.
(843) 723-3628

Sushi Hiro is a small sushi bar nestled between M. Dumas and Sharky's Pizza on King Street. In addition to à la carte sushi, there is a varied appetizer menu including tofu salad, shrimp tempura, and even soft shell crab. Complete dinners range from chicken or beef teriyaki to a combination sushi plate. If you like your seafood unscathed by the flame, this is the downtown place for Japanese delicacies. In addition to stools around the prep station, there are several freestanding tables for those seeking more privacy. Management does not welcome tank-top-clad patrons. Sushi Hiro is open only during dinner hours, Monday through Saturday.

Taste of India $–$$
273 King St.
(843) 723-8132

Taste of India serves authentic North

Indian food, with a few menu items reflecting Bombay and South Indian cuisine. Natural spices make the difference here in appetizers (for instance, nargisi kabob—deep-fried, herbed, minced lamb patties), curries, vegetables, and even salads. An eight-course lunch buffet is served Monday through Saturday. Dinner is served every day. Sunday brunch includes 13 courses (you heard us right) and starts at noon and is served until 3 PM.

Tommy Condon's
Irish Pub and Seafood Restaurant $–$$
160 Church St.
(843) 577-3818

The most authentic Irish pub in Charleston, Tommy Condon's has live Irish music Wednesday through Sunday and serves a wide variety of imported beers and ales such as Bass and Newcastle Brown. The menu is a mixture of Irish and Lowcountry items including shrimp and grits, seafood jambalaya, and fresh fish of the day. There is a covered deck for outside dining, and patrons are welcome for lunch or dinner any day of the week. The kitchen closes at 10 PM, but the bar stays open until 2 AM. (See our Nightlife chapter.)

Vickery's Bar & Grill $$
15 Beaufain St.
(843) 577-5300
1313 Shrimpboat Ln. (Shem Creek),
Mt. Pleasant
(843) 884-4440

Vickery's Bar & Grill is in the Market Corner, a strip of shops just north of Saks Fifth Avenue and Majestic Square at the downtown end of Beaufain Street, and is as talked about for its unusual bar as for its good food. There's always an eclectic bunch of interesting folks to meet—young professionals and rebels with a cause. The fare here is vaguely Cuban, with a Southern twist. The original Vickery's is in Atlanta and has always earned good reviews there. Grab a booth or a table, inside or out, and order a burger (with piping hot, hand-cut fries) or a delicious seafood entree. Vickery's is open for lunch and dinner seven days a week. Their

new Mt. Pleasant location is attracting the East Cooper after-work crowd. (See our Nightlife chapter.)

Vincenzo's $$
232 Meeting St.
(843) 577-7953

Here is the ole family-owned, lovingly run neighborhood Italian restaurant—the kind many of you from New York may know. But this one's right here in the Lowcountry, and we're the better for it. Nothing is pretentious; there's no phony posturing. It's simple (good) Italian food in a pleasant atmosphere served by an attentive staff that cares about your dining pleasure. There's a good selection of imported Italian wines to complement the menu, which is filled with all your favorite Italian dishes. Expect to find antipasto, fettuccine alfredo, ravioli, lasagna, and veal in a variety of guises. The white pizza is a local favorite (with five grated white cheeses) as is the veal piccata (which comes with a side of spaghetti and homemade tomato sauce). Vincenzo's is open Monday through Saturday for lunch and dinner.

Wild Wing Café $
36 N. Market St.
(843) 722-9464
644 Coleman Blvd., Mt. Pleasant
(843) 971-9464

Wild Wing Café is popular with the younger-than-30 bar crowd, but also has appeal to those of us who have topped out the age group but not our attraction to a good time. Wild Wing serves a wonderful platter of chicken wings (of course), dressed in all kinds of herbs and spices—from the Ginger Wing to the Flying Fajita. There are great dips, sandwiches, and salads as well as buckets of beer for a table packed with thirsty friends. The bar serves a variety of bottled beer and spirits as well as nonalcoholic beverages. Wild Wing is open for lunch and dinner every day. The companion restaurant in Mt. Pleasant has more of the same for the East Cooper crowd.

East Cooper

From all-American to Italian, health food to junk food, there are dozens of restaurants in the East Cooper areas of Mt. Pleasant, Sullivan's Island, and Isle of Palms—enough to suit anyone. Here we highlight some of the local favorites, whether they fall into that category for the food, atmosphere, staff, or all those combined. Remember, this list is not exhaustive. These areas are growing so fast, there are new options opening almost every week. The point is, don't feel you've got to go downtown for a good dining experience. East Cooper can compete with downtown's offerings any day.

Mt. Pleasant

For the most part, Mt. Pleasant's restaurant fare is family-oriented. There are exceptions, of course, for fine dining and special occasions. Here are some of the local favorites.

101 Pitt $$–$$$
101 Pitt St.
(843) 971-0001

Some visitors may recall an upscale restaurant at the Guilds Inn called Supper at Stacks and its downstairs counterpart, Capt. Guild's Café, which are now gone. Taking their place is a new gourmet establishment downstairs at the Inn called 101 Pitt. It is small and intimate—but convenient for inn guests and Mt. Pleasant residents. The creative menu is "new American cuisine" with a Lowcountry flare. Out-of-towners will find tasty seafood dishes like crab cakes with red pepper sauce and fire-roasted corn salsa for starters, and entrees like miso marinated sea bass in sake broth. Those not looking for Neptune's offering will find entrees like peppercorn-crusted beef tenderloin with burgundy demi-glace. The dessert menu changes with delightful seasonal surprises. Hours are Monday through Saturday 5 to 10 PM. Reservations are suggested.

Alex's Restaurant $
302 Coleman Blvd.
(843) 881-7714

Open 24 hours a day, this Alex's is a popular spot for breakfast on the way to the beach or a late-night meal on the way home. Recently, the Sunday lunch crowd has been thick too. The restaurant is large and attractive, and draws locals as well as visitors to the area. You can't beat its standard bacon, eggs, and biscuits with plenty of hot joe. Other Alex's Restaurants are scattered throughout Greater Charleston, especially in the north area.

Bull & Finch Restaurant and Pub $–$$
1324 Theater Dr. (Towne Centre)
(843) 884-6455

This is a mall eatery; but in this case that's not the kiss of death. In fact, this one is quite charming and modeled after the "Cheers" pub of TV fame in Boston. There's a band or singer on hand every night, which is a big plus for the up-front bar. There are 14 English and Irish draft ales and stouts to choose from, plus 16 others (mainly American) in the bottle. Wine and port is available by the glass or the bottle with an international selection. You'll find a very good dinner in the quieter back room. Beef Wellington topped with Portobello mushroom duxelle inside puff pastry is one of the favorites. Another standout is their New Zealand lamb loin chops marinated and drizzled with fresh mint oil. "The Duke's Shepherd Pie" is for die-hard Anglophiles. The pub is open daily for lunch and dinner.

Capriccio $
1034 Chuck Dawley Blvd.
(843) 881-5550

This affordable and friendly Italian restaurant is actually owned by a Frenchman. That's the beauty of the place—it's for those who love to go out several times a month and customers who love to dine well. All the entrees are around $10 and yet the menu reads like an Italian cornucopia. There's a special every day such as vitello (veal) parmigiana topped with mozzarella pomodoro sauce or rigatoni contadina. Try one of the numerous linguini with Capriccio's special gift for sauces. Mussel lovers say these are the best in town. All the dolces (desserts) are $5.50, and they change daily. There are a number of Italian coffees for after-dinner reflection. This is for serious lovers of Italian cuisine. Dinner only is served Monday through Saturday. Reservations are preferred.

Carpentier's Fine Wine and Cheese $
974 Houston Northcutt Blvd.
(843) 884-9386

Insiders know the deli at Carpentier's is a gourmet's delight. Choose from prepared meats, European breads and cheeses, homemade pâté, and daily specials. The distinctive aroma of roasted coffee and fresh-baked cookies and pastries fills the air. A selection of imported beers and fine wines is available, and there are a few small tables for dining in the store. Carpentier's is open from lunchtime to 7 PM, Monday through Saturday.

Coco's $$–$$$
863 Houston Northcutt Blvd.
(843) 881-4949

Charlestonians and frequent visitors to the city's busy restaurant scene were understandably crestfallen when the French restaurant called "Le Midi" burned and was closed. Things looked up, however, when it was learned that chefs Francois Rivalain and Alain Saley (from Le Midi) had found a new home at Coco's in Mt. Pleasant. Here, the menu is a mix of French classical and provincial, the atmosphere is warm and bistro-like and best of all, some of the favorite dishes from Le Midi are revisited here. Try the Le Flounder Alain, for instance, which is pan-fried and topped with a brown butter sauce. Their roasted half duckling with cherry sauce is another big hit. The wine list includes about 30 labels, a dozen of which are available by the glass. Enjoy a leisurely-paced dinner at Coco's—you won't want to hurry this good thing. When it's time for dessert, try the classic mousse au chocolat or the creme

caramel. Neither will disappoint. Dinner is served Monday through Saturday from 5:30 to 10 PM. Reservations are a very good idea.

Eastside Bakery & Café $, no credit cards
1055 Johnny Dodds Blvd.
(843) 881-1260

Eastside serves homemade pastries to eat in or take out and some delicious, healthy nouvelle American lunch items such as unusual soups, salads, and sandwiches. Lunch is served Monday through Saturday.

Fonduely Yours $$
853 Coleman Blvd.
(843) 849-6859

It is safe to say that Fonduely Yours is a one-of-a-kind dining experience in this area. As the name suggests, this restaurant specializes in fondues. Try cheese, vegetable, seafood, teriyaki, and sirloin fondues, and don't miss the chocolate fondue for dessert. The food is tasty and the whole concept is lots of fun. With fondue, you're the chef and you do the cooking right at your table. Dinner is served each evening starting at 5:30 PM.

Gourmet Blend $, no credit cards
354 W. Coleman Blvd.
(843) 849-8949

For a delightful treat, try Gourmet Blend's salads (sometimes shrimp), sandwiches, muffins, and the like while taking advantage of the large selection of fresh-brewed coffees and teas. One exciting plus is that Gourmet Blend has a drive-up window to make it handy for working lunches or pickup meals after work. It's open Monday through Saturday from early morning until late afternoon.

Idlewild $$
976 Houston Northcutt Blvd.
(843) 881-4511

This restaurant offers what the owners call "new American cuisine," and they have a delicious take on fresh seafood, pasta, steaks, salads, and sandwiches. This is a popular choice with local power lunchers for food and a little business. The menu is varied and extensive enough

Courtyard settings and café atmospheres encourage basking in the Lowcountry's mild climate.

PHOTO: FLETCHER NEWBERN

to stay interesting through multiple visits. Don't miss the oyster salad or Portobello mushroom appetizer. The flank steak comes highly recommended too. Idlewild is open for lunch and dinner Monday through Saturday.

J. Bistro $$–$$$
819 Coleman Blvd.
(843) 971-7778

This is one of Mt. Pleasant's most stylish restaurants. *Upwith*, a hip, local tabloid when J. Bistro opened in 1995, rated it the best new restaurant in town when it first hit the scene. Obviously, it's a casual bistro setting, but New American cuisine is served with real flair. There are many evening specials designed to entice—look for their pecan-crusted catfish fillets over creamy grits, topped with spicy hollandaise or the jumbo lump crab salad. J. Bistro is open for dinner Tuesday through Sunday, and there's a wonderful Sunday brunch. Reservations are not accepted. You may have to wait, but it's worth it.

Locklear's Fine Seafood $$
427 Coleman Blvd.
(843) 884-3346
504 Folly Rd., Charleston
(843) 762-2549

Locklear's has been one of the most popular seafood restaurants in Mt. Pleasant

for years. Now there's a James Island location, too. But it's known for the chicken salad plate and she-crab soup as well. It's also considered a bargain. Call ahead for takeout lunch and remember to consider the "Heart Choice" health-conscious items on the menu. Locklear's is open seven days a week for lunch and dinner. Reservations are accepted.

Max & Moritz $$
1920 Houston Northcutt Blvd.
(843) 856-9511

There was a time when Charleston had several good German restaurants, but these days the options are somewhat limited. Happily, there's this cozy neighborhood spot in Mt. Pleasant which offers a touch of Old World, Central European cuisine. There's a wine list with reds and whites from California, Germany, and France to set the mood. Then, try one of their appetizers like the Bavarian liver sausage spread with pickles, tomato wedges, mustard, and good German bread. Next, the wiener schnitzel served with spatzle makes a good choice. Of course, the desserts are hearty and good (if not for the waistline). Try the Black Forest Delight or the Rote Grutze served with French vanilla ice cream. Dinner is served from 5 until 9 PM Tuesday through Thursday. They're open until 10 on week-

82 Queen white chocolate cheesecake with graham cracker crust and a fresh raspberry puree.

end nights. Sunday Brunch is offered from 11:30 AM until 3 PM and dinner follows from 5 until 9 PM.

Melvin's Southern BBQ & Ribs $
925 Houston Northcutt Blvd.
(843) 881-0549
538 Folly Rd., Charleston
(843) 762-0511

The delicious barbecue, cole slaw, onion rings, hamburgers, and vegetables at Melvin's make it a good bet for a quick

meal. This has been a Lowcountry outlet for barbecue for at least 50 years. The prices are quite reasonable too. Melvin's is open Monday through Saturday for lunch and dinner.

Mustard Seed $$
1220 Ben Sawyer Blvd.
(843) 849-0050
1978 Maybank Hwy., Charleston
(843) 762-0072

This simple, yet sophisticated eatery is a big hit with the vegetarian crowd—although they offer seafood, too. And clearly, not everyone who frequents "the Seed" has abandoned meat; they simply enjoy the varied and creative menu offered here. In addition to a regular menu, there's a blackboard with daily specials that shows why there's sometimes a waiting line out the door. The artichoke, spinach, and Parmesan fritters are one example. The huge and authentic Greek salad is another. Desserts are very special, too. Their coconut cream cake and chocolate cream pie are superb. A conservative but adequate wine list keeps customers amused if, in fact, a short wait is necessary. Be patient: it's worth it—and the food is a good value, too. Lunch is Monday through Friday, 11 AM to 2:30 PM. Dinner is served from 5 until 9 PM on weekdays, and until 10 on weekends.

Niko's Café $–$$
1039 Johnnie Dodds Blvd.
(843) 881-8646
In the handy Anna Knapp Plaza is this ethnic offering. Niko's offers full-service Greek dining to enjoy on the premises or on the go. All the favorites are here—rotisserie chicken, gyros, and even Greek-style pizza. This is a favorite of the working-lunch types who want a healthy alternative to fast food. Niko's is open only for lunch Tuesday through Saturday.

R.B.'s Seafood Restaurant and Raw Bar $$
97 Church St.
(843) 881-0466
Another casual spot where diners get a view of Shem Creek, R.B.'s serves oysters, scallops, fish, and shrimp as well as landlubber fare such as hamburgers, steaks, and prime rib. R.B.'s is right on the creek, where shrimp boats dock and boaters cruise to see and be seen. R.B.'s colorful atmosphere makes this a happenin' place for young singles, especially on weekend nights. R.B.'s is open daily from 11:30 AM to 10:30 PM.

Ronnie's $$$
1 Shrimp Boat Ln.
(843) 884-4074
Ronnie's is an upscale seafood and beef restaurant on Shem Creek. Specialties include local seafood, Maine lobster, and king crab. The kids love to watch the crustaceans swim in the giant tank, and adults park themselves, if possible, at a table next to the window for a view of the shrimp boats. Ronnie's is open for dinner every day and serves a nice Sunday brunch as well. On Thursday and Sunday nights, there's even live jazz outside during warm months.

Shem Creek Bar and Grill $$
508 Mill St.
(843) 884-8102
To experience dining out the way the locals enjoy it, go to Shem Creek Bar and Grill (just "Shem Creek" to the regulars) and you'll find yourself surrounded by loyal Lowcountry patrons. (See our Nightlife chapter under East Cooper.) The menu has something for everyone—from burgers and steaks to lobster and grilled seafood specials—and Sloppy John's Oyster Bar is always a temptation. During the warmer months, Shem Creek is the hangout for the boating set, many of whom arrive by power craft. There is casual dining inside and out, with views of the creek from most seats. John and Angie Avinger also own and operate the One-Eyed Parrot and Banana Cabana on the Isle of Palms (see subsequent listing).

Skoogie's $
840 Coleman Blvd.
(843) 884-0172
For quick deli food and terrific milk shakes, stop at Skoogie's. The all-time favorite is a Skoogie hot dog (the best around) with a root beer and a heaping order of fresh-cut french fries. Their fresh-made sandwiches are a higher caliber than the usual fast food fare and the service is fast and friendly. This is a big hit with kids and the pre-teen after-school crowd. But there's a separate area for grown-ups where a cool beer is waiting. Skoogie's is open every day for lunch and is especially popular on good beach days. Dinner is offered but closing is often early—around sundown.

Slightly Up The Creek $$–$$$
130 Mill St.
(843) 884-5005

Monday through Sunday dinner here is an adventure in "maverick Southern dining" and a total delight. Patrons enjoy the fireplace in winter, dockside tie-up in warm months and the great Shem Creek view all year. Menu favorites include Lowcountry Jambalaya, grilled salmon, and sautéed grouper. A "Southern vegetable plate" is an interesting option for the vegetarian crowd—not limited to traditional veggie receipts. There's a honey-glazed pork tenderloin that's fabulous too. The wine list features French, Californian, and even Oregonian vintages. This is also a popular stop for Sunday brunch from 10 AM to 2 PM.

Sticky Fingers $–$$
341 Johnnie Dodds Blvd.
(843) 856-9840
235 Meeting St., Charleston
(843) 853-7427

If you're a parent, the place to go on Tuesday night is Sticky Fingers. This barbecue restaurant has a special menu and room set up just for kids, so the parents can take advantage of the option of dining alone (or not). Any day (or night, for that matter) is great for ordering Sticky Fingers' famous ribs. They come in about every style possible: Tennessee Whiskey, Carolina Sweet, Memphis, and Texas Style, to name a few. The eatery also serves chicken, salads, and sandwiches. It offers a full bar and is open seven days a week for lunch and dinner.

The Trawler Seafood Restaurant $$
100 Church St.
(843) 884-2560

Visitors have been writing home about The Trawler for more than 25 years. In its new incarnation, The Trawler's updated menu features new twists on their seafood, steaks, chicken, crab legs, and lobster. Open every day for lunch and dinner, the restaurant has satisfied a couple of generations of Lowcountry visitors. Sunday brunch is popular with the after-church crowd. The signature crab dip is a

> ## Insiders' Tip
> Health food shoppers have found a proverbial mecca in Earth Fare over in the South Windermere Shopping Center. This large, well-stocked supermarket specializing in natural and organically grown foods, also has an attractive corner cafe equipped with simple tables and booths. You select your meal from a cafeteria-style line or deli and seat yourself. Bringing home the bacon was never so inviting. You don't even have to be a health nut to dine there.

must for starters. Call the number listed during oyster season to find out about roasted oyster specials.

The Wreck of Richard and Charlene
$$, no credit cards
106 Haddrell St.
(843) 884-0052

Tucked between Magwood and Wando seafood companies in the Old Village of Mt. Pleasant, look for the two flags (there's no official sign or designation) to find The Wreck. The restaurant is very unpretentious, and you can arrive by your own boat if you don't mind crawling around on the docks to disembark. You may dine on the deck or screened-in porch if you like that outdoor feeling. Try the shrimp and grits or the lightly fried scallops. Portions come in either Richard's size (large) or Charlene's size (not as large, but plenty), so order according to your appetite. Beer and wine are available. The Wreck is open daily for dinner seven days a week.

Sullivan's Island, Isle of Palms

Patrons often expect tropical, ocean fare when dining on the islands. These restaurants offer that, with a twist of old Charleston thrown in as well.

Atlanticville Restaurant & Café $$
2063 Middle St., Sullivan's Island
(843) 883-9452

Not far from the cluster of businesses, restaurants, and bars across from the island's playground-like park is this small and casual option for new American cuisine. Locals and tourists alike go for the grilled chicken satay with Thai peanut dipping sauce or the calamari appetizer in Asian spices. Along with the seafood, Atlanticville offers a full array of steaks, pork loins, and pastas. On Tuesdays, the menu is delightfully and authentically Thai which is already a local legend. There's a covered deck for outdoor dining and an extensive wine and beer list. It's open seven days a week for dinner only plus a Sunday brunch from 10 AM to 2:30 PM.

The Boathouse at Breach Inlet $$–$$$
101 Palm Blvd., Isle of Palms
(843) 886-8000
The Boathouse on East Bay
549 E. Bay St., Charleston
(843) 577-7171

Right on the infamous stretch of water known as Breach Inlet, with spectacular sunset views, is this unique restaurant. The decor is nautical but nice, and the menu includes pastas, grilled fresh fish, and house specialties such as coastal crab cakes with green Tabasco sauce and fried red onions and the fresh catch of the day. The sides are as interesting as the entrees. Look for stone-ground grits, bleu cheese coleslaw, and collard greens. Landlubbers on the Peninsula have their own Boathouse on East Bay Street serving the same fare. Dinner is served seven days a week.

Long Island Café $$
1515 Palm Blvd., Isle of Palms
(843) 886-8809

Long Island Café became a local favorite soon after its doors opened, and it still has a loyal following. The café's changing menu is always interesting. Their herb-grilled sea scallops, the sesame crusted salmon and its pork loin with ginger-garlic sauce are all popular with patrons. A nice selection of soups, salads, and sandwiches is also available. The management is terrific with children, and sometimes displays kiddie artwork on a wall. Long Island is open every day for lunch and dinner. Its Sunday brunch, where the cheddar, ham, and apple omelet is a favorite, is from 11 AM to 2 PM.

One-Eyed Parrot and Banana Cabana $$
1130 Ocean Blvd., Isle of Palms
(843) 886-4360, (843) 886-4361

The One-Eyed Parrot and the downstairs Banana Cabana are fun restaurants with good food, served oceanside. John and Angie Avinger have stamped their winning sense of style on this eatery. The menus include various versions of shrimp, scallops, oysters, dolphin, tuna, a Bimini stew (a tomato-based seafood and sausage dish) and steamed oysters in season. One favorite is the crab cake, as a sandwich or alone. Seafood aside, Caribbean chicken (baked or fried), steak, salads, and pasta specials are also on the menu. Childen love an early supper outside on the deck at the Cabana. They play with other children and occasionally get the mojo and start dancing right in front of the evening's featured musician. Both restaurants are open daily, but the Banana Cabana serves lunch and dinner. The One-Eyed Parrot is open for dinner only. (See the Sullivan's Island and Isle of Palms section of our Nightlife chapter.)

Sea Biscuit Café $, no credit cards
21 J.C. Long Blvd., Isle of Palms
(843) 886-4079

This is one petite charmer—complete with a tiny front porch, substantial side porch (for dining), and fabulous island fare. The Sea Biscuit, tucked away on one of Isle of Palms' less chaotic streets, serves breakfast or brunch with the house specialty: fabulous biscuits. Try shrimp and gravy with grits and eggs, seafood omelets, quiche, and even

Hank's, a reincarnation of an Old Charleston tradition. PHOTO: WILLIAM STHRUS

eggs Benedict. The café serves a delicious house tea, and children can order a pancake that's a Mickey Mouse look-alike. Get there early or expect a wait. Lunch is served after breakfast Tuesday through Friday; breakfast only is served Saturday and Sunday.

Sea Island Grill $$–$$$
The Boardwalk Inn, Wild Dunes Resort,
5757 Palm Blvd., Isle of Palms
(843) 886-2200

The premier new restaurant at the upscale Wild Dunes Resort is called the Sea Island Grill, formerly The Grill. As the name implies, the cuisine has changed to feature the freshest Lowcountry seafood creatively served up by Chef Enzo Steffenelli who has served up his magic at some of the best seafood restaurants in downtown Charleston during his impressive career. In addition to the wide selection of seafood dishes, entrees include creative presentations of steaks, chops, and poultry. Try the Flounder Boardwalk, crabmeat stuffed flounder filet served on a bed of shrimp and corn succotash and drizzled with herb butter sauce. If you are up to it, finish off with the Ultimate Chocolate Cake for two, a thick slice of a rich, multi-layered chocolate cake made with bittersweet chocolate mousse and raspberry marmalade. The Sea Island Grill is open for breakfast, lunch, and dinner seven days a week. Call ahead for reservations and the required gate pass for entrance in Wild Dunes

Station 22 $$
2205 Middle St., Sullivan's Island
(843) 883-3355

Casual, but not quite flip-flops and a T-shirt, Station 22 offers variety on its menu and island history on its walls, which showcase dozens of photographs of turn-of-the-century Sullivan's Island. Find appetizers like their "world famous" Poblano Chile Pepper, roasted and stuffed with feta, parmesan, and mozzarella cheese. For an entree, try the Portuguese-style mussels with shrimp and sausage on linguini or the daily seafood special. Save room for Uncle William's Brownie Fudge Pie. Open every day for dinner. (See our Nightlife chapter.)

Sullivan's On the Island $$
2019 Middle St., Sullivan's Island
(843) 883-3222

A favorite with the islanders and others in the know, Sullivan's is a family restaurant with affordable, good food. Not fancy, Sullivan's is just what the regulars want—a place to order delicious, traditional specials that include steaks, burgers, shrimp, and grits, or oysters and scallops with a veggie and dessert for less than $12. Dinner is served Monday through Saturday. There is a children's menu, and Sunday brunch is served from 11 AM to 2 PM.

West Ashley

Because the West Ashley area is so widespread and residential in nature, the restaurants tend to be located along the main traffic corridors. Both family restaurants and ethnic favorites are represented here.

California Dreaming Restaurant and Bar
$–$$
1 Ashley Pointe Dr.
(843) 766-1644

You can go to California Dreaming by car or by boat (yes, you can tie up at a dock), and it's always an adventure. The kids pretend it's an old fort (although it isn't), and the views of the Ashley River are mesmerizing. The restaurant and the bar do an incredible, nonstop business year round. The interior is colorfully decorated with flags and divided into two dining levels with seating for 260 (and the place is often full). The little ones are welcome and can order nonalcoholic drinks (such as a blue concoction called a Smurf) and food from a special menu. Patrons really go crazy for the soft, buttery croissants and the house salad (topped with eggs, almonds, ham, and bacon—almost a meal in itself). The twice-baked potato is another big hit. All fish is fresh and local, and the burgers, ribs, and Mexican dishes are popular. A decadent dessert list includes the fabulous house special—apple-walnut cinnamon pie. Lunch and dinner are served every day, and hours are extended on weekend nights. Reservations are suggested. (See our West Ashley section of the Nightlife chapter.)

Chancy's $–$$
1759 Savannah Hwy.
(843) 763-3395

The parking lot here is always jammed with Chancy's regulars who come to drink, watch sports, and enjoy a meal. This restaurant was once voted in a Post and Courier survey as having the best shrimp and buffalo wings in the area. Try their burgers, salads, and any special—from grilled steaks to pork chops. There is a game room, and food is served from lunch until late night, Monday through Saturday.

Easterby's Family Grille $$
2388 Ashley River Rd.
(843) 556-5707
1977 Maybank Hwy.
(843) 762-4890

Easterby's on Ashley River Road (S.C. 61) is a comfortable, affordable place for casual dining and local seafood. It's a popular lunch stop for tourists heading out to the plantations along the highway (see our Attractions chapter). Dinner patrons enjoy the same seafood (fried or not), steaks, and pastas, she-crab soup, catfish stew, shrimp creole, and soft-shell crabs. Spirits are available, and reservations are not necessary unless you're in a large group. Dinner is served nightly until 10 PM.

Emperor's Garden $–$$
874 Orleans Rd.
(843) 556-7212

West Ashley gained a popular eatery with the opening of Emperor's Garden. This Chinese restaurant across from Citadel Mall prepares crispy Peking duck (a participatory dish put together, like crepes, at the table) to perfection, and it stuffs its egg rolls with substantial portions of real ingredients—no mystery meat or imitation soybean product here. Their pot stickers are the real thing, too. Customers come from all over, and children are welcome. Lunch and dinner are served seven days a week.

Kim's Korean and Japanese Steak and Seafood House $$
North Bridge Shopping Center,
1716 S.C. Hwy. 171
(843) 571-5100

Kim's Korean and Japanese Steak and Seafood House offers authentic "table show cooking" for dinner seven days a week. Not only is this a fun experience, but the food is also well prepared and a

A sweating glass of
sparkling iced tea is
a Southern tradition,
and most restaurants
will gladly refill your
glass gratis. Be sure to
let them know, however,
if you are specifically
looking for our
good old-fashioned
sweetened tea.

chrome and glass, and desserts are now the specialty. Not only is the food good and predictable (the menu doesn't change, and favorite specials are repeated), but it's also just five minutes from the city, and parking is no trouble. Connoisseurs of spirits will enjoy the great selections of wine and imported beers here. Regulars are partial to the pita pocket sandwich with gazpacho or black bean soup at lunch. For dinner, try their pasta specials; they have plenty of variations on the theme. There is live jazz on Thursday evenings. The Med Deli is open from late morning to late night every day but Sunday.

delight for the palate. Choose either the beef or pork bulgoki with the spicy Korean sauce, a house favorite. Takeout is available, and reservations are not required.

Liberty Café and Pub $–$$, no credit cards
9 Magnolia Rd.
(843) 571-7255

When Liberty Café opened its doors a number of years ago, the neighbors were right to applaud. This friendly restaurant was most welcome along the busy Savannah Highway business corridor. Since those days, the reputation has spread, and people now come from all around with their families in tow to eat tasty, affordable food in a cozy café setting. Try the big burgers, wood-grilled entrees, or a particular favorite: the mussels with angel-hair pasta. Beer and wine are available, and Liberty serves from late morning to late in the evening, Monday through Saturday. (See our West Ashley section of the Nightlife chapter.)

Mediterranean Delicatessen & Café $–$$
90 Folly Rd.
(843) 766-0323

Talk about your neighborhood magnets. The Med Deli, as locals call it, is a real draw for West Ashley and downtown diners. It has a high-tech look with lots of

Melting Pot $–$$
946 Orleans Rd.
(843) 763-4110

Just across from Citadel Mall, Melting Pot is a wonderful source for takeout or eat-in Greek and American food. Try a simple Greek salad (big enough to count as lunch) or order the sampler for a crash course in ethnic cooking, but always save room for the outstanding desserts. There's a small but interesting grocery section too. Melting Pot is open all day Monday through Saturday.

Miyabi Japanese Steak House $$
1870 Sam Rittenberg Blvd.
(843) 571-6025

This Japanese steak and seafood restaurant rates high on the family entertainment scale because of the hibachi style of tableside preparation and the knife-juggling Japanese chefs. Meals include a light soup, salad, and entree, and the food is consistently good. If you have never experienced this form of dining, be advised you may be sharing grill and dining space with strangers. Try the steak and shrimp for a sample of what the hibachi does for surf and turf. Try the sushi bar if you like yours untouched by the flame. Dinner and drinks are served seven nights a week, and early-bird specials are common. Call for reservations.

Outback Steakhouse $$
1890 Sam Rittenberg Blvd.
(843) 763-8999
715 Johnnie Dodds Blvd., Mt. Pleasant
(843) 849-9456

This steakhouse so dominates the mini-mall it occupies that the mall itself has taken on the Outback name with locals. And for good reason: This Aussie-style beef and barbecue restaurant and bar is a standing-room-only watering hole for young up-and-comers. The huge bloomin' onion is the signature side dish, and it comes with a secret sauce that kicks like a kangaroo. Kids are welcome, and dinner is served seven days a week. There's another location in Mt. Pleasant so East Cooper types can dine "down under" and never cross a bridge.

Penachio's $
2447 Ashley River Rd.
(843) 556-1855

This is a delightful little Italian restaurant specializing in pasta and seafood dinners that include salad and garlic bread. There are specials Monday through Thursday, and our favorite entree is Mediterranean shrimp with sautéed black olives, mushrooms, tomatoes, and feta cheese. Dinner and cocktails are available Monday through Saturday starting at 4 PM. Their "Missing Links Piano and Sports Bar" draws the ballgame crowd. Look for the white lights in the trees out front—that's Penachio's. Seating is limited, so reservations are recommended.

Piccadilly Cafeteria $
Citadel Mall, 2070 Sam Rittenberg Blvd.
(843) 571-6700

This is a big ole mall cafeteria like you remember from the 1950s. The values are hard to beat, even if you're cooking at home. There's always a wide variety of foods to choose from, and the employees are always very kind. Try the eggplant casserole if it's on the menu the day you stop in. Piccadilly is open late morning through dinner every day of the week.

Reeve's Bar-B-Que $, no credit cards
2004 Ashley River Rd.
(843) 763-5798

Reeve's Bar-B-Que serves tasty Southern meals featuring ribs, chicken, fried catfish, country-style steak (that means pounded, floured, and fried), barbecue with various sauces and, of course, spirits. Reeve's luncheon buffet is always a daily favorite—as is its breakfast buffet on weekends. It's open Tuesday through Sunday, late morning to late evening. The catering operation is open seven days a week.

Sweetgrass Café $$
1124 Sam Rittenberg Blvd.
(843) 766-2800

Here's a café that focuses on Lowcountry cooking—plain and simple. Located in Orange Grove Plaza, convenient to the vast West Ashley crowd, this family-oriented restaurant serves appetizers, soups, salads, sandwiches, egg dishes, pastas, main courses, and specials. The simplicity comes from the fact that all entrees are prix fixe, and we're talking around $15 here! Choose from Lowcountry shrimp and grits, Carolina catfish with spicy crawfish, or pecan crusted pork loin with pear and port sauce, to name just a few. All the favorite side dishes are here, as well. The pecan pie could shame your

Charleston's shrimp fleet uses sweeping nets to scoop up the tasty bounty. PHOTO: THOMAS P. FORD

mother. Sweetgrass is open Monday for lunch only, Tuesday through Saturday for lunch and dinner.

T-Bonz Gill & Grill $–$$
1668 S.C. Hwy. 171
(843) 556-2478
80 N. Market St.
(843) 577-2511
1028 Johnnie Dodds Blvd., Mt. Pleasant
(843) 971-7777

Another vibrant, happening spot with several locations throughout the city, T-Bonz serves a wonderful filet mignon (when you say rare, they take you at your word) as well as fresh gourmet burgers and even seafood. There's plenty of beer on tap including T-Bonz' own custom-brewed ales. The Mt. Pleasant location has its own brewpub. Photographs of regular customers and Western paraphernalia adorn the walls, and you can't miss the enormous painting of the renegade cowboys on horseback. Regular customers order side veggies (sautéed and delicious) and feel comfortable having the kids along. Takeout is another option. They're ropin' em in for lunch and dinner seven days a week.

Trotter's Restaurant $$
2008 Savannah Hwy.
(843) 571-1000

Trotter's Restaurant, in the Town and Country Inn, is a good find for an all-out buffet—breakfast and lunch as well as weekend seafood spreads. Sunday brunch is popular with the after-church crowd. The buffet table always groans with a wide selection of meats, seafood, vegetables, and desserts. There's no Saturday lunch or Sunday dinner, but Trotter's is open for all other meals, every day. (See our West Ashley section of the Hotels and Motels chapter.)

Ye Ole Fashioned Ice Cream and Sandwich Café $
474 Savannah Hwy.
(843) 766-4854
10-A S. Windermere Blvd.
(843) 766-0921
1502 U.S. Hwy. 17 N., Mt. Pleasant
(843) 849-3698

This is a quick stop but a change from the usual fast food. There are several locations within our coverage area and a few more beyond. This café serves sandwiches, soups and, of course, lots of ice cream. There are scores of flavors. You'll find one next to Eckerd Drugs (that's one West Ashley location) and another in South Windermere. If you use the drive-through window, you may want to call ahead for soup and sandwich takeout orders. All the food is delicious, and local kids love this place. Hours are mid-morning through late night.

James, Johns, and Folly Islands, Kiawah, and Seabrook

People come from all over the Greater Charleston area to dine at some of the establishments on these islands. Whether you're looking for a quick deli sandwich or an elegant evening experience, you'll find it here. The following restaurants are on James Island unless otherwise noted.

Alano's Pizza $
The Shops at Bohicket,
1880 Andell Bluff Blvd., Seabrook Island
(843) 768-2424

If you are looking for pizza and want free delivery to the resorts, try this eatery between the entrances to Kiawah and Seabrook Islands in the Bohicket Marina Village. Alano's has good pizzas made fresh daily in three sizes, with a choice of 15 fresh toppings. It also has lasagna, wings, hoagies, and salads. Hours are late morning to late night every day.

AngelFish Restaurant $–$$
520 Folly Rd., Folly Beach
(843) 762-4722

In the Merchant Village Shopping Center, AngelFish has a bright, high-tech atmosphere with lots of chrome and glass. The menu is innovative and reflects the bounty of our local seafood and produce with a refreshingly light touch. Patrons enjoy shrimp Creole, vegetable stir-fry over rice, grouper, salmon cakes, grilled shrimp, and herb grilled salmon. There is an assortment of pasta dishes, other vegetarian entrees, quiche, omelets, and salads as well as a pita pizza with three cheeses and an artichoke egg roll. The daily menu features eight choices for dessert; and you can't go wrong with their pecan pie or chocolate cake. Cocktails are available. It's open for lunch and dinner Monday through Saturday.

Athens Greek Restaurant $$
325 Folly Rd., James Island
(843) 795-0957

The line moves quickly at Athens, in the Cross Creek Shopping Center, where there is usually a crowd eager to dine. Specialties at this popular Greek place include Greek chicken, spanakopita, lemon chicken soup, Greek salad with feta cheese, and baklava. A full range of spirits is available. Athens is open every day from lunch until late night except on Sunday, when only dinner is served.

Bear-E-Patch Café $–$$
801 Folly Rd., James Island
(843) 762-6555
1980-A Ashley River Rd., Charleston
(843) 766-6490
626 Coleman Blvd., Mt. Pleasant
(843) 971-8803

Every once in a while a simple, affordable, neighborhood restaurant strikes gold with the right combination of good food, generous portions, nice atmosphere, and friendly service. And that's what the Bear-E-Patch has going for it. This relatively small and unpretentious eatery on Folly Road (not far from the foot of the James Island Connector) is very popular with locals and beach dwellers—but it's now attracting Peninsula folk, too, who can zip over via S.C. 30 in almost no time at all.

Sister restaurants have opened along S.C. Highway 61 and in Mt. Pleasant. The breakfast menu is so hearty and creative with several specials offered daily that it's available until 3 PM and makes a dandy lunch. A deli-like lunch menu is offered also along with grilled burgers and such. But at least one down-home special is right out of grandma's Lowcountry cookbook. An on-site bakery turns out fresh bread (sourdough is a specialty) and pies which add to the allure. And now, dinner is served Monday through Thursday until 8 PM, and until 9 PM on Friday and Saturday.

Brett's $$–$$$
1970 Maybank Hwy., James Island
(843) 795-9964

A relative newcomer to the row of restaurants found these days along Maybank Highway on James Island is Brett's with its up-scale and sophisticated Italian-American cuisine. Once past the unpretentious exterior, you'll think you're in old Tuscany and the menu is old world, too. Choose from several Italian pastas, risottos, and gourmet pizzas, as well as beef, chicken, veal, and seafood dishes. Try their "Steak Napoleon" for a successful allied offering from Italy and France. A wine list from Italy and California has over 50 options. And Brett's desserts are seasonal and duly rewarding. Patio dining is available in warmer weather. Lunch is served from 11:30 AM until 2:30 PM, Monday through Friday. Dinner is served 5:30 PM until late, Monday through Saturday. Sunday brunch is from 10:30 AM until 2:30 PM. Please call ahead; reservations are recommended.

Café St. Tropez $$–$$$
1880 Andell's Bluff Blvd., Seabrook Island
(843) 883-3355

Those on the resort islands of Kiawah and Seabrook have a new option that's also a draw to people from downtown who know it's worth the drive. Formerly owned by the people who brought us Beaumont's (downtown), this is now under new ownership but with the same quality and standard of service. They call it "sophisticated contemporary with an international flair" with justification. For appetizers, try the duck liver mousse, foie gras, and black truffles with potato bread toast points; or the plum barbecued semi-boneless quail with honey-balsamic lentils. Special entrees have included a 14-oz. Argentine Delmonico steak with a four peppercorn whisky-cream sauce and French rack of Australian lamb with a blueberry five-spice demi-glace. Count 80 bottles of wine on their wine list, 17 of which are by the glass. As a finale, try the bourbon-pecan cheesecake with a chocolate graham-cracker crust and vanilla toffee sauce. Dinner is served daily starting at 5 PM.

Café Suzanne $$
4 Center St., Folly Beach
(843) 588-2101

Here's an unexpected oasis of genuinely good food and wine in a funky little building on the main drag at Folly Beach. The menu changes daily, but a number of tempting offerings are always ready to challenge the beachcombing gourmand in all of us. The secret to Suzanne's success is the tremendously talented staff who never seem to run out of new and delicious ideas. You'll like the pan-seared, crab-encrusted salmon with shrimp basmati rice or the grilled tenderloin of beef with rosemary Cabernet sauce. Officially, the fare is new American. Unofficially, it's just plain good eatin'. Café Suzanne is open only for dinner Monday through Saturday, and there is a Sunday brunch that's very popular.

Cappy's Seafood Restaurant $$
2408 Maybank Hwy., Johns Island
(843) 559-3552

It's good to have Cappy's back after their devastating fire, and it's fun to go by boat and tie up at the Buzzard's Roost Marina. The fresh seafood and view of the Stono River are splendid. Cappy's always has a number of daily specials with fresh shrimp, scallops, and fish. Look for their sweet potato-encrusted snapper or their grouper Romano. Dining is possible inside and out, and spirits are available. Lunch and dinner are served daily. (See our James and Johns Islands section of the Nightlife chapter.)

Charleston Crab House $$
145 Wappoo Creek Dr., James Island
(843) 795-1963
1101 Stockade Ln., (off Hwy. 17 N.),
Mt. Pleasant
(843) 884-1617

On the Intracoastal Waterway, the Charleston Crab House is open for lunch and dinner every day. The restaurant specializes in steamed garlic crabs (cooked until they are red, then placed before you for what locals call a "crab crack"). There is a raw bar, and outside tables for dining are close to the water. You can arrive by boat and moor at the restaurant dock. No reservations are necessary. There's a kid's menu and Mom and Dad may enjoy frozen tropical drinks. (See listing in the James and Johns Islands section of the Nightlife chapter.)

Dragon Gate Chinese Restaurant $
1739 Maybank Hwy., James Island
(843) 795-3398
Dragon Gate, in the James Island Shopping Center, serves authentic Chinese food. It has a full bar and a lunch buffet with all your favorite Chinese dishes such as sweet-and-sour pork, Szechwan beef and egg drop soup. The restaurant is open Monday through Sunday from lunch through late night.

General Store Deli $
1 Beachwalker Dr., Kiawah Island
(843) 768-9541
For a quick takeout breakfast or lunch, try this deli. The bakery items are fresh, but what kids like best are the fried chicken and enormous French fries. This is Kiawah's version of a convenience store (read, "upscale"), and sometimes that's just what's called for. Handy, quick, and close to everything on the resort island, the General Store is open daily from dawn to late night.

Gilligan's Steamer and Raw Bar $$
160 Main Rd., Johns Island
(843) 766-2244
1475 Long Grove Dr. (Seaside Farms),
Mt. Pleasant
(843) 849-2244
Gilligan's Steamer and Raw Bar has a great family atmosphere and delicious fresh steamed seafood. There are steaks and chicken as well, and the cooks will fry the seafood if you like. This is a place where you can order oysters by the bucket. Two veggies, a choice of salad or slaw, and hush puppies round out each meal.

Crayons are available so the kids can draw while they wait. Gilligan's is open for lunch and dinner every day.

The Jasmine Porch $$$
Kiawah Island Inn, Kiawah Island
(843) 768-2121
Views of the Atlantic Ocean surf framed by lovely live oaks are a big part of the experience at The Jasmine Porch. Although the restaurant is the signature dining experience on Kiawah, many Charlestonians have been great fans of the Sunday buffet and brunch for years. There's a vast array of delicious seafood displayed and always an impressive ice sculpture. Landlubbers can always find a good steak if seafood isn't your thing. Cocktails are served. Breakfast, lunch, and dinner at The Jasmine Porch are available seven days a week.

The Privateer Restaurant $$–$$$
1882 Andell Bluff Blvd., Seabrook Island
(843) 768-1290
With its "sophisticated casual" atmosphere, The Privateer serves delicious gourmet seafood and other entrees that appeal to landlubbers. Outstanding shrimp and scallop dishes, seafood pastas, broiled pink snapper, tempting veal, and steaks are all part of the menu. The views at the Bohicket Marina Village location are lovely. Try to arrive in time to watch the sunset. Dinner is served daily.

Rosebank Farms Café $$
1886 Andell Bluff Blvd., Seabrook Island
(843) 768-1807
Here's a delightful place to get typical Lowcountry cuisine (in other words, "Suh-thun' cookin'") done with a modern twist. Rosebank Farms Café is in the marina atmosphere of Bohicket Creek. This spot is especially popular during fishing tournaments at Seabrook. Along with choice steaks and fresh vegetables, try the honey and buttermilk fried chicken. Rosebank is open for lunch daily and reopens for dinner every night.

Starfish Grille $$
101 E. Arctic Ave., Folly Beach
(843) 588-2518

Here is the answer when the question is, "Where can we eat and look out over the ocean?" This attractive little bistro is perched right at the base of the 1,045-foot-long Folly Pier. (See our Fishing Piers and Bridges section of the Hunting and Fishing chapter.) Waves break under the dining room and seagulls ply the air around you. Atmosphere is the draw here, and the feeling inside is strictly casual. The Grille offers a full gamut of sandwiches, salads, and pasta dishes. Appetizers include coconut shrimp and spinach and fried oyster salad. Entrees range from Carolina crab cakes to fresh yellowfin tuna in a spiced red sauce. Of course, there's always a fresh catch of the day. The place is open for lunch and dinner every day of the week. It's a pleasant option for Sunday brunch, too. No reservations are required, but call ahead for parties of six or more. There's a full bar with 16 varieties of beer and a limited wine list by the glass. Don't forget their appealing array of frozen and dessert drinks. Note that the $5 parking fee at the pier is deducted from your bill if you show your receipt.

St. John's Island Café & David's Bakery
$–$$
3410 Maybank Hwy., Johns Island
(843) 559-9090

It's hard to know what to praise first at St. John's Island Café. The menu is typically American, with a definite Southern flair. The chalkboard lists the daily specials, which read a little bit like the dinners at Grandma's house when we were kids. Look for lasagna, pork chops, and meat loaf to die for. The added pleasure of fresh-baked breads, pies, and other desserts also draws a steady crowd of regulars from the offices in downtown Charleston and the resort islands of Kiawah and Seabrook. It's possible to order home-cooked food for take-out—the café even offers catering services these days. They're open for breakfast, lunch, and dinner Monday through Saturday. On Sunday, St. John's closes at 2 PM, following brunch.

Nightlife

When the sun goes down, all the people in Greater Charleston do not pack it in. In fact, locals and visitors who seek nighttime entertainment are met with an abundance of choices.

If you are interested in listening to live contemporary music, dancing, or just hitting the bar scene, start with the spots we've described below—you won't be bored. If you like beer and want to sample it straight from the folks who create it, try one of the brewpubs. Since many nightspots are actually lounges at restaurants where dining is the primary focus, we have added an indicator at the end of each club listing—(D)—for those places that are described in greater detail in our Restaurants chapter. We also have a category called Dinner Cruises for those who want to spend an evening on the waters of Charleston Harbor—cruising and dining, with live music and dancing as after-dinner options.

While Charleston is affectionately called the "Holy City" in reference to its many lovely churches, it also has a reputation for entertaining where socializing has a long and rich tradition. If you plan on enjoying a few beers or cocktails as part of the fun, be aware

As the sun sets in Charleston, residents and visitors have myriad options for evening entertainment.
PHOTO: COURTESY OF CHARLESTON AREA CONVENTION AND VISITORS BUREAU

of the legal restrictions in the Charleston area and know that area police departments actively enforce these laws. The minimum drinking age is 21 in South Carolina, and open containers are not allowed in moving vehicles. A charge of driving under the influence may be levied against anyone whose blood-alcohol content is measured at 0.10 or higher. In the city of Charleston, last call for liquor is usually 1:30 AM, and closing is mandatory at 2 AM.

The coffeehouse phenomenon has taken a firm hold in this area. We have several Starbucks these days, and there are at least a half-dozen non-chain houses to explore around the Peninsula. There are a number of conventional movie theaters showing first-run films here in the Lowcountry, and we have a downtown movie house called The Roxy that shows good foreign films and productions that might be called alternative (see subsequent listing). There's even a cabaret-style movie house on upper King Street, The American Theater, which shows some first-run and mainstream art films in a setting where you can snack and enjoy wine and beer while you watch the flick. We've listed theater names and phone numbers and suggest you call for titles after checking the local paper's movie listings.

For information about other entertainment options and cultural happenings, we suggest consulting The Arts and Annual Events chapters.

Bars and Nightclubs

Downtown Charleston

82 Queen
82 Queen St.
(843) 723-7591

A long-standing, favorite hangout for the local Broad Street business set and others, the bar at 82 Queen is narrow (but comfortable enough) and a good place to see friends. You'll find a fine mix of people there knowing and not knowing each other's names. Patrons especially like the back bar if the weather is nice. They enjoy hanging out in the courtyard while waiters zip by with tempting appetizers, and outdoor diners enjoy their fare beneath the stars. (D)

Bennett's at the Market
85 S. Market St.
(843) 534-1234

Like many of the venues in the Market area, this option is a restaurant as well as a night spot. That means this is a good choice for drinks and hors d'oeuvres—whether you stay on for dinner or not. In fact, you can choose from a number of plate "sizes" and define you experience there on your own terms. There's live dinner music and dancing Tuesday through Saturday and late night entertainment Thursday through Sunday. The daily Happy Hour starts things rolling along at 4 PM (through 7 PM).

Blind Tiger Pub
36 Broad St.
(843) 577-0088

If you are looking for British pub atmosphere, escape into this friendly environment with its dark English mahogany walls and cast-iron stools. Order Bass Ale or Guinness Stout, or try a Black and Tan—Bass on bottom, Guinness on top. Fear not: The beer is chilled appropriately for Charleston, not served lukewarm as in England. There is live music some nights, and a crowd that just keeps coming back. The back courtyard is a nice option when weather permits.

Carolina's
10 Exchange St.
(843) 724-3800

The bar at Carolina's restaurant is an upscale alternative and a very popular meeting spot for professionals. Seating is available at the bar proper and in the surrounding areas. Bar customers often feel comfortable staying on for dinner. Carolina's has an additional private dining room. Both areas are nice places to meet after work or after other events for a nightcap. (D)

Charlie's Little Bar
141 East Bay St.
(843) 723-6242

In Saracen Restaurant, you'll find this cozy bar upstairs overlooking the dining room below. It also has a thriving following of neighborhood patrons and after-work professionals who enjoy the atmosphere and premium spirits, cocktails, and hors d'oeuvres. Patrons who only want what the bar has to offer can enter through a small gate and rear back door off the bank's parking lot to the side. The service is friendly and the ambiance is a little like the speakeasy days of the 1920s. Great fun. (D)

Club Habana
177 Meeting St.
(843) 853-5900

Located in the swanky, upscale space directly above the Tinder Box (where all manner of tobacco products are sold), this is a late-night destination for a cigar and an after-dinner drink. The cozy spot has both male and female aficionados, so the company is always varied and interesting. Their plush couches and tasteful décor encourage patrons to puff away and sip a fine brandy in perfect comfort. Through a brilliant feat of air conditioning engineering, the atmosphere is actually breathable. They open daily for Happy Hour at 5 PM. On Sundays, they open at 8 PM.

Club Tango
39 Hutson St.
(843) 577-2822

Near the visitor center in the Camden Exchange complex, this dance club (styled after the New York nightclub scene of the late 70s) caters to a young crowd of latter day disco babies and swing aficionados doing their thing to a techno sound—making this a happening place on Thursday, Friday, and Saturday nights. You can shake your bootie there with the best of them or watch the action while imbibing your favorite cocktail. The nice thing about Club Tango is the dress code and cover charge, which bring in a nice mix of young professionals and upscale area visitors.

Cumberland's
26 Cumberland St.
(843) 577-9469

Happy hour here is a crowd-pleaser, particularly with the college crowd and 20-somethings, who rally to the cause most nights except Sunday. There is a full-service bar, and live music is a main drawing card—it features all kinds. Cumberland's even has its own ticket information line, so you can see who's on the docket for the night: Call (843) 577-4085 to see who's on the bill.

The Griffin
18 Vendue Range
(843) 723-1700

A popular hangout for young professionals is The Griffin, a cozy English pub with an easy, friendly atmosphere. Especially busy at lunchtime, workers from the financial and legal offices on East Bay and Broad streets stop here for simple, but hearty, sandwiches and maybe a cool brew. Others check in for happy hour and some stay for dinner. Every couple of weeks, they bring in live music in the evening that attracts a nice mix of locals and tourists out and about on East Bay.

Henry's
54 N. Market St.
(843) 723-4363

Henry's and its upstairs neighbor known as The Comedy Zone, used to be known for its Old Charleston meals and clubby side bar. Today, under different ownership, it has updated trappings and a new reputation for light food and live acoustic music. The ambiance is contemporary New Orleans, and the second floor is home to a popular comedy club. There is a happy hour from 4 to 7 PM on Monday through Thursday.

Horse & Cart Cafe
347 King St.
(843) 722-0797

Here's a pub that claims to have the largest selection of beers and ales in the city. Something for everyone seems to be the entertainment theme. Most weekends feature hot bands and solo artists from all over the South. Sundays feature imported beer sold by the pitcher. Tuesday's are DJ spinning nights. Other weeknights run the gamut from group drumming to Irish folk jams and open-mike poetry nights. Something fun is always scheduled. Food and music are available until 2 AM.

Mandalay
275 King St.
(843) 722-8507

This high-profile, high-style restaurant right on the corner of King and Wentworth Streets, with giant glass windows offering views all around, is hard to miss.

Mandalay tropical restaurant and brewery is located in a reworked 1897 building and offers a variety of house-made drafts and nightly drink specials. The second floor features a billiard room with mahogany pool tables and big screen TVs tuned to sports events. The third floor is called "Club Mandalay" where dancing to live acoustic music happens Tuesday through Saturday. The crowd here is young and hip.

McCrady's
2 Unity Alley
(843) 577-0025

Neatly tucked down Unity Alley off the hustle and bustle of East Bay Street is this small but attractive haven for a quiet drink. It lays claim to the fact that George Washington tipped a few here back in 1793. Today, this beautifully turned-out restaurant has an adjoining upscale bar that is a favorite with downtown business types and professionals because of its cozy fireside atmosphere. Its nice wine list and premium bar serve happy-hour specials to please the after-work crowd. And its popular dining room close by makes a natural progression from an after-work respite to an evening on the town. (D)

Mills House Hotel
115 Meeting St.
(843) 577-2400

Easily the best location in Charleston if you're looking to be at the center of things, the Mills House Hotel is home to two nightspots that deserve your consideration. The handsome bar just off the Barbados Room Restaurant is a classic Southern setting that oozes charm. There's a grand piano, and often someone is on hand to play your favorite Gershwin tune. The Best Friend Lounge is a separate, more intimate bar with quiet entertainment Tuesday through Saturday.

Mitchell's on the Market
102 N. Market St.
(843) 937-0300

This is Charleston's offering for those who want the hot Latin sound of Salsa and jazz. If you haven't got the steps quite down, they'll even teach you on the spot. Nightly lessons in the latest moves make everybody feel welcome—even if you're no match for Ricky Martin's pelvis. There's the Rhino Room Lounge for very late-night revelers upstairs where cigars, martinis, and desserts are served from 9 PM until 2 AM. They're usually open nightly, so rest up and come on out for the fun and spicy action.

Music Farm
32 Ann St.
(843) 722-8904

Now in its tenth year on the Peninsula, one of the most popular nightspots for contemporary music enthusiasts is the Music Farm—affectionately referred to by regulars as "The Farm." The beat goes on at weekly gigs when live bands—yes, favorite city sons Hootie and the Blowfish were once among them—perform here. The Farm's concert line, (843) 853-3276, has recorded information about upcoming entertainment. Sometimes there's a cover charge. The college crowd is thick, but also expect to see 30-somethings, 40-somethings, and older-somethings elbowing their way toward the bar. The Farm is across the street from the visitor center, and parking is available on the street as well as in the nearby garage.

O'Reilly's Irish Pub & Seafood Tavern
288 King St.
(843) 577-0123
There is live weekend entertainment at this pub, which has recently added a full compliment of seafood entrees and salads. The College of Charleston students love the fact that it is close to campus and tend to hand out here during their Happy Hour, from 4 to 7 PM Monday through Friday. The atmosphere is decidedly Irish, though, with plenty of tables and booths for gathering with friends. After Happy Hour, it appeals to past-college-days crowds or just anyone who appreciates a clean, not-too-well-lighted place that offers a wide assortment of draft and bottled beers and other bar beverages. (D)

Peninsula Grill
112 N. Market St.
(843) 723-0700
The Peninsula Grill at the Planters Inn offers a very beautiful, romantic, upscale bar tucked inside the restaurant. In warm weather, we recommend a drink here before and after dining outdoors in the gas-lit courtyard. This is always a well-dressed, attractive crowd and a classy oasis amidst the carnival atmosphere of The Market at night. (D)

Roof Top Bar & Restaurant
23 Vendue Range
(843) 723-0485
On the roof of The Library, one of the top restaurants in downtown Charleston, is this rare find on the Peninsula—a place (for cocktails) with a spectacular harbor view. (See The Library at Vendue in our Restaurants Chapter.) Newly renovated with two separate levels, the Roof Top Bar was much anticipated by locals. This

Insiders' Tip

Late-night revelers who need a rule of thumb to remember Charleston's bar-closing hours, try this: all bars in the Market area close at 2 AM. If you're getting a (very) late start or you feel the need to party even later than that, you'll have to go off the peninsula.

place is a lovely location for starting a summer evening in Charleston—catching the sunset and boats cruising in the harbor. The service is friendly and you can eat there, too, or move back downstairs for a quiet and slightly more formal dinner in The Library.

South End Brewery and Smokehouse
161 East Bay St.
(843) 853-4677
Here's a restaurant with its own microbrewery. Ice-cold hand-crafted brews made on the premises are served with baby-back ribs, oven-baked pizzas, and specials off the wood-burning grill. The glass elevator takes you up to a third-floor cigar lounge and billiard and game room with spectacular views over the city. South End has live entertainment nightly and serves both lunch and dinner seven days a week.

Tommy Condon's Irish Pub and Seafood Restaurant
160 Church St.
(843) 577-3818
Every day is St. Patty's Day at Charleston's only authentic Irish pub owned by an Irish family. In fact, families are indeed

welcome here. Tommy Condon's has traditional Irish sing-a-longs Wednesdays through Sundays and serves Irish spirits as well. The layout of the facility, with its big horseshoe bar, makes for a good party flow, and people mix and mingle all around. (D)

Vickery's Bar & Grill
15 Beaufain St.
(843) 577-5300
131 Shrimp Boat Ln., Mt. Pleasant
(843) 884-4440
Vickery's is a popular spot for a drink with friends. The restaurant does a booming daytime business with its Cuban-American cuisine, and there's a festive Latin flavor in the bar at night. There's a large outdoor seating area for imbibing or dining. Vickery's is just off King Street and offers limited (but possible) parking in the Market Corner Shopping Center's own lot. (D)

Wet Willie's
209 East Bay St.
(843) 853-5650
Across the street from the Custom House is this watering hole that's popular with the young professionals working up and down East Bay Street. Tourists are lured in as well because it's right on the street and very inviting by day or night with its big, wide open doors. On Sunday and Monday, there's karaoke; Friday and Saturday offer dancing with a DJ on site. You'll also find pool, pinball, and Foosball. Wet Willie's will ask you to support global cooling by drinking a famous frozen daiquiri.

East Cooper

Mt. Pleasant

Although Mt. Pleasant is still a family-oriented community, there are plenty of exciting destinations for grownups when the sun goes down. The tremendous growth of the Mt. Pleasant area and the subsequent boom in population has created a whole new market for after-hours entertainment. That's especially true now that all bars on Peninsular Charleston are mandated to close at 2 am. The days when this quiet East Cooper neighborhood was strictly a bedroom community for downtown Charleston are over. Some of Mt. Pleasant's night spots howl until 4 am! Mind you—this is no passport to drive irresponsibly or misbehave—and the Mt. Pleasant fuzz are out and about at all hours to prove it.

Bull & Finch Restaurant & Pub
1324 Theater Dr., Towne Centre
(843) 884-6455
For those vacationing on the barrier islands (Isle of Palms and Sullivan's Island), the convenience of Mt. Pleasant's giant Towne Centre is a pull with all their shopping opportunities. But when the shopping is done and it's time to kick back for a brew or a refreshing libation after a movie, there's this neat English pub to nicely fill the bill. They have a full menu of pub fare that runs the gamut from Lowcountry crab cakes to Beef Wellington, but the billiards, sports TVs, wide selection of domestic and imported brews, and friendly service are big draws as well. They open for business daily at 11:30 AM. (D)

Johnny Dollars Juke Joint
508 Mill St.
(843) 856-2123
One of Mt. Pleasant's newest clubs, this one is right on picturesque Shem Creek and it jumps with different activities nearly every night. Tuesdays, for instance, are dedicated to the country music fans with line dancing for those who can and do. On Wednesdays (ladies' night), they have karaoke so come prepared to wow the crowd. On Thursdays, the shag is the dance of choice. Friday night is disco and Rock & Roll night with all the favorites of that era. The joint closes its doors at 4 AM on Fridays.

Kaminsky's Most Excellent Café
1028 Johnnie Dodds Blvd.
(843) 971-7437
78 N. Market St.
(843) 853-8270

Kaminsky's Mt. Pleasant location is a wonderful café, (with a sibling establishment downtown in the Market area) that has broken new ground since the management declared Thursday to be jazz night. This has brought out an interesting crowd of music-loving revelers. The action starts at Happy Hour after work. The downtown Market Street location has live acoustic jazz on Monday and Tuesday nights. For more about the downtown location, see the Charleston section of our Restaurants chapter. (D)

Shem Creek Bar and Grill
508 Mill St.
(843) 884-8102

High on the list of casual nighttime destinations, Shem Creek is one of the most popular watering holes in the area. It certainly has some great things going for it—namely, the dockside bar overlooking the marsh, the raw bar inside, and the salty characters who make it their home away from home. The mood is usually upbeat, and the munchies are delicious. (D)

Sports
816 Johnnie Dodds Blvd.
(843) 881-6157

One of the hottest places in Mt. Pleasant on game night is this sports bar in the Lafayette Village Shopping Center off the US17 Bypass. Whether it's college game night, major league baseball, or NBA or NFL showtime, the big-screen TVs here show all the action while fans chow down on burgers and raise a few brews. Enthusiasm is the byword here—

the only taboo is not rooting for your team with all the gusto you've got.

Sullivan's Island and Isle of Palms

Although the islands east of the Cooper River are considered family beaches, there are several notable watering holes nestled behind the dunes. A word of warning: Don't let the casual setting lull you into ignoring the open container laws. In other words, don't stroll outside with an unsealed alcoholic beverage—police officers take it seriously.

Greater Charleston's after-hours entertainment is varied and well-suited to local tastes and to visitors' needs.

PHOTO: COURTESY OF SOUTH CAROLINA AQUARIUM

Banana Cabana
1130 Ocean Blvd., Isle of Palms
(843) 886-4361

The Banana Cabana is open seven nights a week and offers a volleyball net and putting green as well as lots of cool, refreshing libations and munchies. Locals and visitors seem to delight in visiting this place after a day at the beach. Sometimes the volleyball court is where you'll find macho men and their female challengers fresh from the beach boasting their sports prowess and their perfect tans. (D)

Bert's Bar
2209 Middle St., Sullivan's Island
(843) 883-3924

Many years ago, Bert's was Sullivan's Island's pharmacy and soda fountain. Gone are the ammonia Cokes and grilled-cheese sandwiches—blues and rock 'n' roll are what Bert's whips up these days. The kitchen serves burgers, soups, and salads. And Bert's even has an occasional Friday fish fry that draws a steady group of island characters. There is sometimes a cover charge for the live entertainment; it is generally a noisy, boisterous good time.

Dunleavy's
2213-B Middle St., Sullivan's Island
(843) 883-9646

A welcome watering hole for the island, Dunleavy's is an Irish pub with indoor and outdoor dining. The outdoor picnic tables are replete with dog bowls for patrons on a leash. The bar regularly attracts the beach crowd, and it's very family-oriented at the dinner hour. Fridays, Saturdays, and Sundays they feature a singer with acoustic guitar. Bill Dunleavy is usually on hand and makes one and all feel welcome.

Station 22
2205 Middle St., Sullivan's Island
(843) 883-3355

A handsome, comfortable bar with walls adorned with wonderful old pictures from the early days on the island, Station 22 has been a local favorite since it opened some years back. You can experience a quiet evening here as well as those occasional nights when the jukebox (said to be one of the best in town) is cranked loud. Revelers have been known to even cut a rug here. A charming train encircles the bar proper, and bartenders blow the whistle when the time is right. (D)

West Ashley

Nighttime activity west of the Ashley River is often on or near the water, in settings that are attractive but casual. Most nightspots are part of restaurants, and some with docks cater to the boating crowd.

California Dreaming Restaurant and Bar
1 Ashley Pointe Dr.
(843) 766-1644

This is the fort-like restaurant whose lights beckon from across the Ashley at night. After sundown, the scene is busy, lively, and fun. The bar is a great place to have a drink with a friend or a group of friends. You can see the lights of the Ashley and City Marinas, and it's adjacent to Ripley Light Marina—so the view is breathtaking. Because diners come here by droves, the bar is also a natural place to wait for a table. There's even a small floating dock for boat tie-ups. (D)

Gene's Haufbrau
817 Savannah Hwy.
(843) 225-4363

Recently reopened after a hiatus for remodeling, this West Ashley spot claims to be Charleston's oldest bar. Nothing luxurious, the new place is a comfortable neighborhood bar—friendly and spacious—with pool, shuffleboard, darts, good pub food, and more than 120 beers and 12 draft labels from which to choose. This is popular with the after-work crowd who toil across the Ashley River bridge. And it's still close enough to The Citadel to draw the thirsty (and legal) cadets who can smell a beer at forty paces.

Liberty Café and Pub
9 Magnolia Rd.
(843) 571-7255

The College of Charleston crowd and The Citadel cadets have found the Liberty café. The friendly, unpretentious scene has made this bar a popular off-campus gathering place where friends can meet and greet. There's a mix of students and locals, with after-work commuters adding to the enthusiastic assemblage. The café is known for its tasty steaks and burgers as well, so it's an affordable date destination. (D)

James and Johns Islands

Cappy's Seafood Restaurant
2408 Maybank Hwy., Johns Island
(843) 559-3552

Just across the Stono River Bridge at Buzzard's Roost Marina is this recently renovated seafood restaurant right on the water. The friendly little bar offers service inside and out, with libations that seem to taste better in the salty sea air. The lights on the boats moored at the nearby marinas add to the ambiance, and the restaurant always has a number of seafood specials sure to please. (D)

Charleston Crab House
145 Wappoo Creek Dr., James Island
(843) 795-1963
1101 Stockade Ln., Mt. Pleasant
(843) 884-1617

This popular spot on the Intracoastal Waterway near the Wappoo Cut Bridge has dockside tables and space for mooring boats. There is live entertainment on weekends after Memorial Day, and it always seems to be packed during the summer months. The deck is a lot of fun for drinks, appetizers, and watching those giant yachts go by. (D)

Coffeehouses

Gourmet Blend
354 Coleman Blvd., Mt. Pleasant
(843) 849-8949

Here's a trendy coffeehouse that's actually a cross between a place to grab some tasty hot java and a drive-thru dry-cleaner. Instead of freshly laundered shirts, they dispense coffee, gourmet sandwiches, and salads—to go. It's a favorite with morning commuters who can buy a newspaper while waiting in line for their coffee and/or lunch. It's open until 9 PM on weekends—so it's a good stop before an early movie and it makes a fun, but inexpensive date. The fare here is far more creative than fast food and almost as convenient.

O'Reilly's Irish Pub & Seafood Tavern
288 King St.
(843) 577-0123

There is live weekend entertainment at this pub, which has recently added a full compliment of seafood entrees and salads. The College of Charleston students love the fact that it is close to campus and tend to hand out here during their Happy Hour, from 4 to 7 PM Monday through Friday. The atmosphere is decidedly Irish, though, with plenty of tables and booths for gathering with friends. After Happy Hour, it appeals to past-college-days crowds or just anyone who appreciates a clean, not-too-well-lighted place that offers a wide assortment of draft and bottled beers and other bar beverages. (D)

Port City Java
159 Market St., Charleston
(843) 577-5282
261 Calhoun St., Cannon Park Place, Charleston
(843) 937-9352
1624 Palmetto Grande Dr., Towne Centre, Mt. Pleasant
(843) 216-2093

This trendy, chic coffee bar has four locations. The one at the corner of King and Calhoun Streets in the Francis Marion Hotel caters mostly to tourists and students. The draw there is all kinds of exotic coffees and some pretty fancy desserts. The Port City behind Saks appeals to tourists and King Street strollers offering a menu of small plates, salads, soups, and savories in addition to its selection of coffees and coolers. The location on Calhoun Street is supported by the MUSC crowd.

It does a sizable lunch business and has an even more elaborate menu. The newest location in Mt. Pleasant's Towne Centre is a haven for East Cooper shoppers. All Port City Javas (and the expanded Bistro versions) have hours that vary according to location. Most are open till 8 PM on weekdays and 10 PM on weekends.

Comedy Clubs

Theatre 99
30 Cumberland St.
(843) 853-6687

Called "Theatre 99" because the house seats exactly 99 souls, this is the home of a very popular improv comedy troupe known as The Have Nots! This three-member troupe has built a strong following in Charleston by finding the funny bone of local audiences and those out-of-towners who came for Piccolo Spoleto, alike. Some-

how, they always manage to take the ordinary and turn it into the absurd from point-blank audience suggestions. Having their own space gives them an option of using creative lighting as a prop, which seems to be a trick all their own. Audiences range from teens to tourists of the senior persuasion. Everybody seems to have a great time. They sometimes tour, so call ahead to be sure they're playing at their Cumberland street venue.

Dinner Cruises

Grayline Water Tours, Inc.
196 Concord St., Charleston
(843) 722-1112

The *Harbor Queen* is the dinner cruise boat—a larger vessel set up to provide passengers with a gourmet Southern buffet, cocktails, and live entertainment (usually a dance band). The music is relaxing—rhythm and blues, light jazz, and special requests. The menu reads like a downtown restaurant with plenty to choose from. You can have balsamic marinated pork loin, chili and garlic marinated shrimp, or roast chicken half with seasoned vegetables. Then, you finish the evening with flourless chocolate torte or strawberry shortcake. Of course, there's coffee and tea to drink.

Dinner Cruises are subject to weather and seasonal demand, so it's wise to call well in advance if you're visiting off-season or inclement weather. The *Harbor Queen* boards at the foot of Market Street

behind the ticket booth across the street from The U.S. Custom House. The evening's total fare is $36.72 for adults, $26.32 for ages 4 to 11, and $23.20 for children 3 and younger. There is a loading ramp to accommodate handicapped passengers. (See Cruise and Boat Tours in the Tours chapter.)

This cruise line has two boats that ply the waters of Charleston Harbor and offer entertainment to Lowcountry visitors. The *Charles Towne Princess* is primarily used for private charters. This vessel is equipped to offer amenities like cocktails and hors d'oeuvres and various forms of musical entertainment depending on your host's taste.

SpiritLine Dinner Cruise
40 Patriots Point Rd., Mt. Pleasant
(843) 722-2628

Dining and dancing aboard this 96-foot luxury tour boat while cruising historic

Sunset on the Lowcountry's tidal marsh is a time for reflection and rest. PHOTO: DAVID C. BERRY

Charleston Harbor make for one of those quintessential Charleston experiences. The *Spirit of Carolina* serves a three-course meal of she-crab soup, house salad, and a choice of five entrees such as prime rib, chicken, or seafood per prior request. All menu items are served with a nod toward the Lowcountry tradition of cooking. The boat makes its rounds up and down the waterways at sundown and is always a lot of fun. Live music and dancing are part of the weekday bill of fare. Entertainment is provided by a live band who can perform jazz, blues, shag, and coun-

try music as per your request. *Spirit of Carolina* is part of the Fort Sumter Tours group and conveniently departs from the docks at Patriots Point Naval and Maritime Museum, where there's free parking at the clearly marked boarding dock. The boarding begins at 6:30 PM and the cruise departs at 7 PM and returns at 10 PM. Rates and schedules change seasonally, but tickets are in the $39 range for adults (Sunday through Thursday) and $42 range on Friday and Saturdays. (See the Cruise and Boat Tours section of our Tours chapter.)

Movie Theaters

Downtown Charleston
The American Theater
446 King St.
(843) 722-FILM
In this restored Art Deco movie theater near the visitor center along up-and-coming upper King Street, is this cinema option. Here are two screening rooms that

now show first-feature films with this added treat: You can eat and drink during the show. Instead of regular theater seats, you sit at little tables and enjoy the movie while the film plays. Here's your chance to catch on the big screen current films and special televised events like Academy Awards Night and New Year's Eve in a

Insiders' Tip

Sometimes nothing will do after a long, hard day but to get up and over it all. About the highest place here in the Lowcountry that serves spirits for your attitude adjustment is the top floor of the Holiday Inn Riverview, known by locals as "The Round Holiday Inn." It's just across the Ashley River bridges from the Peninsula, and the restaurant and lounge is called High Spirits. The walls are practically all glass, and the view by night is fantastic.

party atmosphere. Upstairs in the "Stars" coffee and dessert bar, patrons can enjoy homemade desserts and taste the theater's own private label wine. Occasionally, a musician is on hand for live entertainment. Happy Hour is attracting a crowd of King Street workers on Monday through Friday. The venue can be rented for special events and children's birthday parties. (See our Kidstuff chapter.)

IMAX Theatre Charleston
360 Concord St.
(843) 725-4629

The IMAX movie format is technically a whole new world for those who've never experienced it. In a nutshell, the screen is five stories tall and the sound comes through the screen in quadraphonic fidelity at the audience who sits in Italian leather seats that feel like those in sports cars. The subject matter of the films is different, too. Every movie is shot exclusively for IMAX theatres throughout the world—and the level of creativity is nothing short of mind-bending. There's an IMAX film (usually about 40 minutes in length) for everyone in the family, and several titles are shown daily at various times throughout the day. Call ahead for what's playing and enjoy the IMAX experience for yourself. Here's a great idea and an entertaining option for those who opt for the S.C. Aquarium (next door) and the Fountain Walk Food Court on a rainy day.

The Roxy
245 East Bay St.
(843) 853-7699

Although there are traditional first-run movie theaters in West Ashley, East Cooper, nearby North Charleston, and even on James Island, the first-run theater downtown that might justifiably be called an "art house" is The Roxy. If you are interested in alternative films—some foreign, some avant-garde, some that will later be in the big commercial theaters—choose The Roxy. And if you enjoy taking your experience with a bite to eat and a glass of wine or bottle of beer—choose the Roxy. To find out what's currently showing (and what's playing at other area movie venues), see *The Post and Courier* entertainment section, "Preview." This section of the paper doubles as a free pick-up at shops, restaurants, and bars throughout the area.

James Island

Terrace Theatre
1956 Maybank Hwy.
(843) 762-9494

In the Terrace Oaks shopping center, this first-run, wide-screen movie house features current hits and classic films in an upscale and comfortable atmosphere. Its café, and lounge features gourmet snacks, coffee, and micro brews on tap. Desserts, wine, and champagne are also available to accommodate every taste. Call their Information Line (listed above) to hear what's on the current bill and to get matinee and nightly showtimes.

Concert Information and Venues

Greater Charleston's appetite for entertainment and artistic diversions is satisfied by a wide range of performance venues today. From the rafter-filling rock concerts attracting thousands to the most intimate recitals at the College of Charleston, we have a concert hall or a major facility that can handle the crowd.

TicketMaster is the high-tech way to get tickets to almost any concert or special event in the Lowcountry. This company, with nationwide ticket distribution, adds a surcharge for the convenience of buying tickets through them. You can get tickets by phone or at local kiosks in venues such as Publix and Piggly Wiggly grocery stores, which work like bank machines (handling charge cards). But the added cost is worth it for some. Others prefer to shop for their tickets to Spoleto and other hot concerts the old-fashioned way—by standing in line at the Gaillard Auditorium ticket window. You can access TicketMaster by calling (843) 554-6060. The Gaillard's box office is generally open from 10 AM to 6 PM year round. Before and during Spoleto, the hours are extended. (For more on Spoleto Festival USA and other performing arts events, see our chapters on The Arts and Annual Events.)

North Charleston Performing Arts Center
5001 Coliseum Dr., North Charleston
(843) 202-2787

With the advent of the 2,300-seat Performing Arts Center at the Charleston Area Convention Center complex, the Lowcountry won a place on the "road" itinerary for almost everyone who's anyone (or who's going to be) in the music industry. Finally, greater Charleston qualified as a viable destination for major shows and artists who only want to visit venues that seat audiences of 2,000 or so. When it opened in August of '99 with Harry Connick Jr. and his "Big Band" of sixteen hot New Orleans musicians, the $18-million facility was off to a roaring start. Since then, touring road companies of major Broadway shows, big name artists like George Winston and Melissa Manchester, and events that were inappropriate for the 14,000-seat North Charleston Coliseum have found a home. Their on-site ticket office is open from 10 am to 5 pm Monday through Saturday.

North Charleston Coliseum
5001 Coliseum Dr., North Charleston
(843) 529-5000

Opened in 1993, the North Charleston Coliseum is the largest and most diverse indoor entertainment facility in South Carolina. Various seating configurations are possible, but generally speaking, the coliseum's capacity is 14,000 seats. Because of this, Greater Charleston is now a viable audience for some of the biggest traveling shows and sports attractions in America. The coliseum has attracted the likes of Rod Stewart, James Taylor, the Ringling Brothers and Barnum and Bailey Circus, Reba McEntire, Metallica, World Cup figure skating, NHL hockey, and NCAA basketball, to name just a few. The coliseum is also the permanent home of the South Carolina Stingrays minor league hockey club, members of the East Coast Hockey League, and the fledgling Charleston Swamp Foxes—the Lowcountry's new arena 2 football team. (See our Spectator Sports chapter.) To get to the coliseum, take the Montague Avenue exit off Interstate 26 and follow the signs, or take the Montague Avenue exit off I-526 (Mark Clark Expressway). Ample parking is on-site, but be prepared to pay the price. Tickets for all Coliseum events may be purchased at their box office from 10 AM to 5 PM Monday through Saturday.

Gaillard Municipal Auditorium
77 Calhoun St., Charleston
(843) 577-7400

Built in 1968, Charleston's 2,734-seat Gaillard Auditorium is the premier venue in the city for major arts events. It was named in honor of longtime Charleston Mayor J. Palmer Gaillard Jr., and it always houses the major opera productions of Spoleto Festival USA (see our chapters on Annual Events and The Arts). The Charleston Symphony Orchestra performs here, and Gaillard hosts productions of the Charleston Concert Association and touring off-Broadway shows. At Christmastime, Charleston's children are awed by the Charleston Ballet Theatre's glittering presentation of *The Nutcracker.* The auditorium is easy to find—it occupies the half-block bounded

by Anson, George, Alexander, and Calhoun Streets. A city parking garage is next door. The Gaillard's box office hours are 10 AM to 6 PM Monday through Saturday.

Hotels and Motels

Downtown Charleston
East Cooper
Sullivan's Island, Isle
of Palms
West Ashley
Folly Beach
Kiawah and Seabrook
I-26 Corridor

If the Lowcountry knows a thing or two about putting up guests, it's because 4.2 million of them visited the Trident in 2000 and no one sees an end to this upward trend in sight. To accommodate these visitors, developers are poised to build new and better tourist accommodations both downtown and in the burgeoning North Charleston and Mt. Pleasant areas to reap the benefits of this incoming tide of dollars. Through the years, Southerners have established a reputation for hospitality, and they often compete to maintain the highest standards. Research and experience tell us that Charleston area visitors arrive with varying expectations, and a diverse accommodations industry has evolved to meet those needs.

We have included in this chapter and the one that follows what we consider to be good choices for people who may be looking for vastly different accommodations. We start with Trident area hotels and motels—some for the bargain-minded, some that are large and grand—then discuss the more intimate bed and breakfasts and atmospheric inns and vacation and beach rentals in the next chapters. Like friends in an eclectic

The grand double staircase at Charleston Place Orient Express extends a dramatic welcome to area visitors.
PHOTO: COURTESY OF CHARLESTON PLACE ORIENT EXPRESS

Hotels and Motels / 83

gathering, each accommodations category has something different to offer—prices vary greatly as well.

Downtown Charleston has the greatest number and the widest variety. We start our listings with downtown properties, then extend our coverage using the geographical order detailed in the How to Use This Book chapter. We end with information specifically helpful to the Lowcountry visitors who arrive by air and those among them seeking accommodations convenient to the airport. Unless we tell you otherwise, expect that these lodgings offer smoking and nonsmoking rooms and access for the handicapped and that they do not allow pets.

There are several viable lodging options in the East Cooper and West Ashley areas. The resort islands of Kiawah and Seabrook feature a vast array of cottages, villas, and condominiums. For the most part, rental companies for the resorts and other traditional vacation spots (Isle of Palms, Sullivan's Island, and Folly Beach) prefer to deal with stays of one week or longer. See our Vacation and Beach Rentals chapter for a list of companies that handle resort and vacation properties.

A friendly word of advice: Charleston attracts droves of visitors year round (there are major events scheduled nearly every month—see our Annual Events chapter), and we strongly recommend that you make reservations well in advance. For major events like Spoleto Festival USA and holiday weekends, it's advisable to plan up to six months in advance.

Price Code

Although rates are subject to change, we use the following pricing code to indicate the average rate for a one-night stay, in season, for two adults. Note that these rates do not include taxes, gratuities, or add-on services such as room service or premium TV channels. Off-season rates are, of course, lower. March through July and October through December are usually considered peak seasons.

$	Less than $65
$$	$66–95
$$$	$96–150
$$$$	$151–200
$$$$$	More than $201

Downtown Charleston

Best Western King Charles Inn $$$–$$$$
237 Meeting St.
(843) 723-7451, (800) 528-1234

The King Charles Inn, another in the Best Western chain, completed a major renovation of its facade and common areas a few years back. The location is ideal for those wanting to explore King Street shopping and the Market area on foot (see our Shopping chapter). Those of us who drive past on sweltering Charleston afternoons envy the guests we see frolicking in the second-level outdoor swimming pool. The nearby fountain makes a sparkling show for guests in the dining room. The decor is "traditional Charleston," with mahogany reproductions and Lowcountry art. Rooms feature 19th-century-like furniture, and some have adjoining guestrooms or balconies. The parking garage is underground and free for guests. The north area location is referred to as the Charleston International Best Western and is an atrium-styled hotel with many of these same amenities. (See our subsequent listings for other area Best Western locations.)

Charleston Place Orient Express $$$$$
130 Market St.
(843) 722-4900, (800) 611-5545

In terms of size, the former Omni is the granddaddy of Charleston hotels, with

490 luxury suites and superbly appointed rooms in the massive complex in the city's downtown shopping district. The hotel, with its impressive lobby and reception area, opens into the walkway of a mini-mall that includes such famous stores as Laura Ashley, Talbots, and Godiva (see our Shopping chapter).

The full-service European Spa with its on-staff masseur and masseuse has an indoor-outdoor swimming pool among the luxury amenities. Under the auspices of Orient Express, the rooms at Charleston Place have taken on the aura of Europe in the 1930s. Expect to find marble bathtubs and gold fixtures in the roomy baths. And notice the little touches in the rooms such as art deco lighting and the subdued use of color. They add just that much more romance to your lodging experience. Several superb dining options are available right under the Charleston Place roof. Foremost among them is the Charleston Grill on the main floor tucked away among the shops and boutiques. (See our Restaurants chapter for more on the Charleston Grill.)

Comfort Inn Riverview $$–$$$
144 Bee St.
(843) 577-2224, (800) 228-5150
As part of the Comfort Inn chain, the Riverview's 129-room version offers a string of discounts and other standard features plus its most desirable asset—views of the Ashley River. It is just outside the Historic District (but still on the Peninsula), and tours are available from the hotel. A fitness room appeals to many travelers, and the outdoor pool with its river view is a big hit with all ages. Continental breakfast is included in the price of the room, and there is no charge for parking.

Courtyard by Marriott/Riverview $$$$
35 Lockwood Dr.
(843) 722-7229, (800) 321-2211
$$$ 2415 Mall Dr., North Charleston
(843) 747-9122, (800) 321-2211
Overlooking the Ashley River at the base of the Peninsula is Charleston's newest hotel offering from Marriott. It opened in the fall of 1997. The 179 spacious guest-rooms all have two analog data-port phones, voice-mail messaging, and a work desk. In-room coffee makers and movies on demand via cable are some of the other amenities. A waterfront swimming pool, an indoor whirlpool spa, and fitness center are available as well as a daily breakfast buffet in the Courtyard Café. Golf packages are available for 19 Lowcountry courses. And there's ample on-site parking. This Courtyard by Marriott, which is near the Calhoun Street medical complex, cuts a high profile for those entering Charleston via S.C. 61, U.S. 17 and S.C. 30. A similar version is located along the I-26 corridor and convenient to the airport.

Days Inn Historic District $$$$
155 Meeting St.
(843) 722-8411, (800) 329-7466
The 124 units of this Days Inn are air conditioned and fairly typical of the rooms in this chain—clean and comfortable, with few frills. Enjoy a swimming pool and being only one block away from The Market, fine restaurants, plus shops and galleries. Limited free parking on-site is available. You can't beat this option for its ideal location and standard reliability. (See our East Cooper and I-26 Corridor sections below for other Days Inn locations.)

Doubletree Guest Suites/
Historic Charleston $$$–$$$$
181 Church St.
(843) 577-2644, (800) 222-8733
A relative newcomer to the Market area, and formerly known as the Hawthorn Suites, this comfortable courtyard hotel consists of oversized suites. Units have "the Charleston look" and include complete kitchens, separate bedrooms, and living rooms. Life is made easy with a complimentary breakfast buffet, and you can unwind with on-the-house refreshments at the afternoon reception. For those who enjoy burning the calories they consume, there's a fitness center and a heated whirlpool spa in the courtyard that seats at least 12 comfortably (great for

relaxing while gazing at the stars). When energy levels diminish, the hotel's VCR tape library is available to complement your cable television service. Five suites are completely wheelchair accessible. The hotel provides valet covered parking.

Embassy Suites $$$$–$$$$$
337 Meeting St.
(843) 723-6900, (800) 362-2779

This is one of Charleston's newest, all-suite luxury hotels. It's in the Historic District in what was originally The Citadel's first home (c. 1822). Unmistakably a military building, the echoes of young cadets marching off to the Civil War still seem to bounce off these old walls. Enjoy 153 handsomely furnished two-room suites with private bedrooms and living rooms. The decor recalls the grandeur of the colonial West Indies. All guest suites open onto a stone-floored atrium with giant palms and a three-tiered fountain. Amenities include in-room wet bars, telephones with voice mail and data ports, free, cooked-to-order breakfast, and complimentary beverages each evening. This is an ideal location—a stroll from the visitor center, The Charleston Museum, and special events in Marion Square Park. (See our I-26 Corridor section which follows for the north area location.)

Hampton Inn Historic District $$$–$$$$
345 Meeting St.
(843) 723-4000, (800) 426-7866
$$ 4701 Saul White Blvd.
(843) 554-7154, (800) 426-7866
$$$ 7424 Northside Dr., North Charleston
(843) 820-2030, (800) 426-7866

There are 171 rooms in the downtown Hampton Inn Historic District, conveniently located across from the visitor center, trolley transportation, and The Charleston Museum. One of downtown Charleston's newer inns, the Hampton offers the attractive features of an older, restored building mellowed with time but beautifully decked out in crisp, new furnishings. The courtyard is probably the

largest on the Peninsula, and the large pool is a welcome oasis for travelers. Double rooms have two queen beds, and an impressive continental breakfast is part of the deal—muffins, bagels, other breads, cereal, and coffee cake. Their Hampton Inn Airport/Coliseum—just off Ashley Phosphate on Northside Drive—is handy for airport travelers and convention visitors. This latest addition to the North Charleston convention complex serves the north area's sprawling industrial development.

Holiday Inn Historic District $$$$
125 Calhoun St.
(843) 805-7900, (877) 805-7900
$$ 6099 Fain St., North Charleston
(843) 744-1621, (800) 465-4329

For almost 40 years, the corner of Calhoun and Meeting was known by frequent Charleston visitors as the location of a convenient and affordable 1960s-style high-rise motel. It went by a number of names over the years, and is now open as a Holiday Inn with a recent $6 million facelift. Now there are 126 guest rooms and suites, a full-service restaurant and lounge, a fitness center, valet laundry, an outdoor pool, and courtyard. Best of all, it's still just steps away from King Street shopping, Marion Square, the visitor center, and Gailliard Auditorium. Business travelers have three phones with two lines, voice mail, and data ports in-room. The Holiday Inn Convention Center-Airport location offers 24-hour shuttle service from the airport and off-street parking.

Market Pavilion Hotel $$$$–$$$$$
225 East Bay St.
(843) 723-0500, (877) 440-2250

New to the landscape on peninsular Charleston and to the heart of the Market area you'll find this hotel at the corner of South Market and East Bay Streets. Called a "boutique" hotel with an emphasis on service and design, this option features guestrooms and suites for tourists and business travelers. For the latter, there are meeting rooms and banquet facilities, and an executive boardroom on tap. Guests have access to a rooftop pavilion with a pool and an open air bar providing spectacular views from this popular reception area. A full-service restaurant completes the picture for this newcomer to the local hospitality industry. Valet parking is available and the location couldn't be more convenient to the Market's shopping adventures and its after-hours nightlife.

Mills House Hotel $$$$$
115 Meeting St.
(843) 577-2400, (800) 874-9600
Of the city's grand hotels in the Historic District, the Mills probably enjoys the oldest, grandest reputation. Now managed by Bass Hotels and Resorts, it is on the corner of Meeting and Queen Streets, next door to the imposing white-columned Hibernian Hall (site of many a debutante ball and home of the Hibernian Society). Modern in its comforts and antebellum in its decor, the Mills House has always been a favorite with affluent travelers. The original (1853) Mills Hotel standing on that site was deemed unworthy of restoration in the early 1960s, so it was razed and replaced with a new, fire-safe structure (taller by a couple of floors) but with lobby areas and public rooms copied from the original hotel. So exacting are the reproduced details and antebellum appointments that frequently the Mills is used as a backdrop for movies and TV shows needing a "period" hotel setting. The beautiful courtyard, outdoor pool, and deck add a casual side to the Mills experience. The in-house restaurant and bar, called The Barbados Room, draws local patrons as well as the international set. You'll find live entertainment somewhere on the premises each night, and turndown service is part of the pampering. It's hard to beat the Mills for location, as it is only a stone's throw from the Four Corners of Law, the King Street antiques district, several museums and galleries, plus the bustling Market area.

Radisson Charleston Hotel $$$
170 Lockwood Dr.
(843) 723-3000, (800) 968-3569
$$ 5991 Rivers Ave., North Charleston
(843) 744-2501, (800) 333-3333
If you are crossing the Ashley River Bridge into Charleston, look to your left to see the towering Radisson Charleston Hotel behind riverside Brittlebank Park. There are 333 rooms and suites in this option, many with views of the river, and this venue is a popular one for conventions and meetings. A swimming pool is part of the facility, and the rooms have premium channels and movie rentals. Abundant parking is available at no charge. The Radisson Inn Charleston Airport location serves the north area.

Renaissance Charleston Hotel
$$$$–$$$$$
68 Wentworth St.
(843) 534-0300
Opened in early 2001 in the heart of the city's downtown business district, this is one of Charleston's newest major hotels from Marriott. It is steps away from King Street shopping and area restaurants, and the location is ideal for visitors to the College of Charleston campus just a short stroll away. Their 166 elegantly appointed rooms are decorated in a Charleston décor with bonnet beds and other charming details. Some rooms open onto the pool deck, others (32 of them, in fact) have balconies with city views. The on-site restaurant Brasserie des Amis serves a Southern-French-Mediterranean cuisine with a Charleston flair. There's a fitness center, a heated outdoor pool, and ample meeting space for business travelers and conventioneers. Hotel valet and self parking is just across Wentworth Street.

The Westin Francis Marion Hotel $$$$
387 King St.
(843) 722-0600, (800) 433-3733
Built in 1924 and beautifully renovated, the Francis Marion is now one of the city's most popular hotels. In all, there are 226 guest accommodations ranging from

rooms with two double beds to two-room king suites. All have been handsomely re-appointed with custom detailing. Twelve stories tall, the hotel affords visitors a bird's-eye view. It's near upper King Street's fast-developing shopping district, The Charleston Museum, the College of Charleston, and the visitor center. The hotel's signature restaurant is Elliot's on the Square (see our restaurant chapter), which offers a very pleasant atmosphere on the first-floor King Street side. Ample parking is just next door in a city-owned garage.

East Cooper

Comfort Inn $$$–$$$$
310 U.S. Hwy. 17 Bypass
(843) 884-5853, (800) 228-5150
$–$$ 5055 N. Arco Ln., North Charleston
(843) 554-6485, (800) 228-5150

This East Cooper motel has more extras than you might imagine and is a good value. Complimentary continental breakfast and a daily paper start the day off right. There is free cable TV with premium channels as well as laundry facilities for taking care of the beach sand in your shorts. Business guests will find phones with voice mail and data ports. You'll also find one of the two heated swimming pools available to tourists in Mt. Pleasant. The Comfort Inn Airport is just a mile from Charleston International Airport and the North Charleston Coliseum.

Days Inn Patriots Point $$
261 Johnnie Dodds Blvd.
(U.S. Hwy. 17 Bypass)
(843) 881-1800, (800) 329-7466

One of the most popular amenities at this Days Inn is the pool area—sheltered for privacy by mature shrubbery. All rooms are air conditioned, and the 24-hour on-site restaurant is a plus in our book for early risers who like to be close to that first cup of coffee. The rooms are in the standard Days Inn tradition: They're clean, comfortable, economical, and kid friendly.

Hampton Inn at Patriots Point $$$
255 Johnnie Dodds Blvd.
(843) 881-3300, (800) 426-7866
$$$ 1104 Isle of Palms Connector
(843) 856-3900, (800) 426-7866

This is a 121-room Mt. Pleasant hotel with inside hallways rather than the out-side breezeways that characterize many motels. There is no charge for local calls (often important to business travelers), and children younger than 18 stay free. The rooms here are a little grander than in most off-highway accommodations. The service says hotel, but the price says motel. A deluxe continental breakfast is on the house. Hampton Inn has added a new location on the Isle of Palms connector with deluxe suites, which are popular with traveling families.

Hilton Charleston Harbor Resort $$$$
20 Patriots Point Rd.
(843) 856-0028, (888) 856-0028

The 131-room Hilton Charleston Harbor Resort was a long time coming to this breathtaking waterfront spot at the very tip of Mt. Pleasant overlooking the Holy City. After 13 years, two different developers, and a major hurricane, this prime real estate resisted successful completion of a planned resort until Hilton arrived to save the day. Now the hotel and marina complex is one of Charleston's newest destinations for fun, sun, sea, and golf. The Hilton's decor is maritime—teak-trimmed and nautical. The state record blue marlin catch is triumphantly displayed in the main foyer.

Indoor facilities include meeting rooms, the Rockfish Grille restaurant, a cocktail lounge called the Reel Bar, and a ballroom. Suites and rooms are available with king-size beds or two double beds. Room phones have voice mail. Outdoors there's a swimming pool as well as a man-made, private sandy beach. The Yorktown and Patriots Point Maritime Museum is just next door. Golfers have discounted greens fees at the

Patriots Point course just outside the gate (see our Golf chapter), and the 450-slip marina opened in the summer of 1998. (See our Boating and Watersports chapter.) A water taxi service runs to downtown Charleston.

Holiday Inn/Mt. Pleasant $$$
250 Johnnie Dodds Blvd.,
(U.S. Hwy. 17 Bypass)
(843) 884-6000, (800) 465-4329

This elegant, full-service hotel has views of Charleston Harbor and the Cooper River and is only minutes away from the city as well as Patriots Point. Rooms are furnished with period reproductions, and a concierge level provides additional service and convenience. Visitors can enjoy a fitness center with a sauna, an outdoor pool, on-site restaurant, and bar.

Main Stay Suites $$$
400 McGrath Darby Blvd.
(843) 881-1722, (800) 660-6246
$$ 5045 N. Arco Ln., North Charleston
(843) 740-3440, (800) 660-6246

This 71-unit, three-floor, all-suite hotel opened in Mt. Pleasant in February of 1999 and offers unique accommodations to business travelers and vacationers who enjoy traveling as families. Half of the units at Main Stay have two bedrooms and two baths with doors that separate the kitchen, living area, and bathrooms from the sleeping rooms. The other half are roomy efficiencies with full kitchens equipped with all the necessities for preparing meals. All units have 25-inch TVs and VCRs. You'll also find a heated pool, an exercise room, and guest laundry services. There's even a barbecue area for

outdoor cooking. The check-in desk is manned only from 6 AM to 9 PM Monday through Friday. On weekends, it's open until 6. If you arrive outside of that envelope, follow the check-in instructions in the lobby. Another location in North Charleston serves visitors to the I-26 and I-526 area.

Masters Inn $$
300 Wingo Wy.
(843) 884-2814, (800) 633-3434
$ 6100 Rivers Ave., North Charleston
(843) 744-3530, (800) 633-3434

This 120-room option is a bargain and offers great proximity to the city (3 miles) and the Isle of Palms (7 miles). There are some extras as well, such as a pool, cable television, and free local phone calls. A lounge and restaurant are on-site, and free continental breakfast is served each morning. Efficiencies with kitchenettes are also available. Children younger than 18 stay free with parents. The North Charleston location is convenient to the airport and the Air Force Base.

Shem Creek Inn $$$$
1401 Shrimp Boat Ln.
(843) 881-1000, (800) 523-4951

With views of the shrimp boats moving in and out of their docks and the sun sparkling off miles of marsh, Shem Creek Inn is fun for both children and adults. Each of the 50 rooms has a private balcony, and king-size rooms have garden tubs. There is convenient parking under the building, and continental breakfast is served each morning. All the Shem Creek nightlife goes on close to the inn, and boat dockage is available.

Sullivan's Island, Isle of Palms

These two islands are popular vacation destinations and abound with rental property. With no hotel, motel, condominium, or resort development, Sullivan's Island has less to offer in terms of overnight rental but has an assortment of old and new island homes for rent in weekly increments. See our Vacation and Beach Rentals chapter for a list of companies that handle rentals on the islands.

On the Isle of Palms, in addition to weekly house rentals, Wild Dunes, a major resort, offers flexibility in length of stay (see subsequent listing). Please note: Summer reservations on both islands are often booked by late winter, so start making plans with a rental agency or other entity at least six months ahead. Most do not allow pets, but it is always worth asking.

The Boardwalk Inn at Wild Dunes $$$$
5757 Palm Blvd., Isle of Palms
(843) 886-6000, (800) 845-8880
Opened early in 1998, The Boardwalk Inn at Wild Dunes is a $12-million luxury hotel with 92 rooms or suites near Wild Dunes' two famous golf courses and 20-court tennis center. All this is situated along 2.5 miles of unspoiled white sand beach. The Boardwalk Inn has an on-site gourmet Lowcountry-style seafood restaurant and lounge plus a tropical pool complex. Even locals enjoy their attractive bed-and-breakfast packages for special occasions. Those start at about $198 per couple/per night in the summer months (high season).

Holiday Inn Express & Suites
1126 Ocean Blvd., Isle of Palms $$$–$$$$
(843) 886-3003, (800) 465-4329
1943 Savannah Hwy., Charleston $$$
(843) 402-8300, (800) 465-4329
7670 Northwoods Blvd. $$
North Charleston
(843) 553-1600, (800) 465-4329
New to the Isle of Palms, this beachfront hotel is a moderately priced option for traveling families. These rooms and suites are comfortable without the extras. There's still much to be desired with a pool, laundry facilities, sun deck, computer access ports, and free off-site parking. You're located near many of the island's most popular restaurants, too. The "Express" concept for this familiar chain seems to be growing—with locations in West Ashley and North Charleston.

Wild Dunes Resort $$$$–$$$$$
5757 Palm Blvd., Isle of Palms
(843) 886-6000, (800) 845-8880
Rental possibilities at Wild Dunes are widely varied. This 1,600-acre oceanfront golf resort is 30 minutes north of Charleston. Accommodations include one- to four-bedroom villas next to the ocean, golf courses, tennis courts, or lagoon. You can rent three- to six-bedroom homes with ocean, fairway, and Intracoastal Waterway views. Guests choose their location based on proximity to the beach, pool, tennis courts, marina, or fairways and, of course, price. The accommodations provide linens, dinnerware, televisions, and washers and dryers, plus a cleaning staff takes care of the messy parts of vacationing. You just focus on the fun. Golf is a big attraction, with two excellent courses: The Links, designed by Tom Fazio and ranked as a top course by Golf Magazine, and the Harbor Course, with holes along the Intracoastal Waterway (see our Golf chapter). There are Har-Tru tennis courts for day and night play, and tennis clinics and lessons are available. Of course, the sandy beach is beautiful, and there are many activities for families. Wild Dunes does not allow pets but will recommend local kennels.

West Ashley

The following West Ashley options provide good value with close proximity to the Peninsula. At most, you'll be about 20 minutes from the hustle and bustle of the Historic District. Note that most properties are on or near US 17, which is called Savannah Highway throughout this area.

Best Western Inn $$$
1540 Savannah Hwy.
(843) 571-6100, (800) 528-1234
This Best Western is only 3 miles from the Peninsula and is a very tasteful, affordable option. Continental breakfast is complimentary, and everyone loves the large outdoor pool. We think this is one of the area's real values, particularly since the spacious rooms have been recently refurbished. This

motel is convenient to the gardens and historic plantations along Highway 61.

Hampton Inn Riverview Hotel $$$
11 Ashley Pointe Dr.
(843) 556-5200, (800) 426-7866

Out of the mainstream, this Hampton Inn is on a road called Ashley Pointe Drive, off Albemarle Road west of the Ashley. Other nearby landmarks are Ripley Light Marina, and California Dreaming restaurant at the end of the street (see our Restaurants chapter). Ideal for visitors to the Lowcountry arriving by boat, this motel is a modern, multi-story facility with great views of the Ashley River and the adjoining marina. There are 175 rooms in all. Some have one double bed, others have two doubles, and there are VIP rooms with king beds and whirlpool baths. Continental breakfast is complimentary.

Holiday Inn Riverview $$$
301 Savannah Hwy.
(843) 556-7100, (800) 465-4329

For obvious reasons, locals refer to this circular hotel just across the Ashley River Bridge as "The Round Holiday Inn." Many of the 181 units and four suites have spectacular water views unmatched by any other accommodation in the city. Up top, a restaurant and bar offer panoramic vistas of peninsular Charleston and the meandering Ashley River. The pool area is an outside appendage to the hotel, unusual because of its elevated height and the view it provides. Guests enjoy the complimentary shuttle downtown and free on-site parking.

Lands Inn $$
2545 Savannah Hwy.
(843) 763-8885

This Lands Inn is about 6 miles from the city, which makes it more private and relaxing—not to mention more affordable. Guests can choose rooms with a king-size bed or with two doubles. It's basic lodging, a little farther from the madding crowd. A pool and private fishing dock for guests, cable TV, and a continental breakfast in the morning are available. Pets are welcome (with a $10 fee) and Citadel Mall is minutes away.

SpringHill Suites $$-$$$
98 Ripley Point Dr.
(843) 571-1711, (888) 287-9400

Across the Ashley just past the round Holiday Inn you'll find this all-suite Marriott hotel, which is popular with boaters tying up at Ripley Light Marina. Within close proximity to downtown and Hwy. 61 (out to the plantations), this hotel also offers many luxury amenities. Each suite has a mini-kitchen, a sitting area, cable TV, two-line telephones with data ports, voice-mail messaging, and a spacious work area. Guests also enjoy a free continental breakfast, outdoor pool and whirlpool spa, fitness center, and same-day valet service. Next door is the slightly more upscale Marriott Residence Inn offering one or two bedrooms, fully equipped kitchens, some suites with fireplaces, and other luxuries. Call (843) 571-7979 or (800) 331-3131 for reservations or more information.

Town and Country Inn $$$-$$$$
2008 Savannah Hwy.
(843) 571-1000, (800) 334-6660

What will strike you first about this West Ashley establishment is the electronic billboard out front that gives a running message about the services within. Next, you are likely to be amazed by the fact that this is as much a fitness center as it is a motel. Guests have access to facilities, and locals can buy memberships. With an indoor pool, racquetball courts, exercise equipment, sauna, and more, a stay here can qualify as a fitness vacation.

The regular rooms feature two queen beds or one king-size bed, and the bathrooms have marble tubs and built-in hair dryers. The phones offer voice-mail service, and the TVs all have 56 cable channels including HBO. Laundry service is an option and, if you are traveling light, efficiencies are available. The restaurant, Trotters, is popular as well (especially with the after-church crowd on Sundays) and runs unusual specials—just check the sign!

Folly Beach

Visitors interested in staying on Folly Beach will find a range of accommodations, including an oceanfront high-rise hotel (see listing) and old-style beach houses available for rent. Again, to rent a beach home, see the list of agents in our Vacation and Beach Rentals chapter.

Charleston on the Beach $$$$
1 Center St.
(843) 588-6464, (800) 465-4329
A Holiday Inn property, this is the only oceanfront hotel, restaurant, and bar in this part of the Lowcountry. Half the hotel's 135 rooms overlook the ocean at Folly Beach, and private balconies make wave-watching all the nicer. Standard rooms have either one king-size or two double beds. There is an oceanfront pool for those who do not dip in the salt water, and the Pierview Oceanfront Grill has terrific food and flowing spirits at its Riptides Beachfront dance bar. Another option for a cocktail is the Ocean Deck Lounge.

The Market Street fountain at Charleston Place is one of the city's loveliest nighttime views.
PHOTO: COURTESY OF CHARLESTON PLACE

Kiawah and Seabrook

These world-class resort destinations offer some extraordinary rental options that might be just what you are looking for—everything from a private villa to luxury homes to an upscale hotel. Look for our write-ups of Kiawah and Seabrook in the Neighborhoods, History, Area Overviews, and Parks and Recreation chapters.

Kiawah Island Resort $$$$–$$$$$
12 Kiawah Beach Dr., Kiawah Island
(843) 768-2121, (800) 654-2924

Called "South Carolina's joy of a resort isle" by Vogue magazine, Kiawah Island is a 10,000-acre, semitropical island with rental options galore. Choose from villas, cottages, and private homes, or stay at the 150-room Kiawah Island Inn. There are actually three resort areas, or villages, within walking or biking distance of island shopping and dining. Villas and cottages are fully equipped and have as many as four bedrooms, while luxury homes for rent in adjacent residential areas have as many as seven bedrooms and elaborate extras. The inn is an upscale hotel that features studio accommodations. Guests can choose from king-size or double beds with a kitchenette and dining room. Some units have porches with scenic views of the dunes or the ocean.

Other accommodations are basically clustered in the West Beach Village, the East Beach Village, and the Vanderhorst Plantation. In the West Beach Village, villas have views of the forest, ocean, lagoon, tennis courts, or golf courses. East Beach villas are parkside, linkside, courtside, or oceanside and offer some very appealing options. There are two pools for guest usage, one of which is an Olympic-size option in the 21-acre Night Heron Park, where guests will also find a covered pavilion, arcade, soccer field, and lake for fishing. The Vanderhorst Plantation is an exclusive gated community with very large homes and ample privacy.

Plan to swim, bike, shell hunt, boat, fish, and explore the many nature trails that encircle the island. Oh, and expect to break out the clubs too. According to Golf Magazine, Kiawah is one of the best golf resorts in America (see our Golf chapter). It was home of the 1991 Ryder Cup Matches and the 1997 World Cup of Golf. Kiawah's tennis program, with state-of-the art facilities at two centers, also ranks high nationally. Kiawah's kids' programs are a hit with young families.

Seabrook Resort $$$$–$$$$$
1002 Landfall Wy., Seabrook Island
(843) 768-1000, (800) 845-2475

This resort offers family vacations in a residential, island setting. Here you'll find one-, two-, and three-bedroom villas—some in the maritime forest, others overlooking the sea. There is no inn on Seabrook; the resort offers one-, two-, and three-bedroom privately owned villas for rent. These properties come equipped with spacious kitchens, sun decks or screened porches, cable hookups, and everything from linens to dinnerware. Some have maritime forest views, and others overlook the marsh or ocean. All are in

Insiders' Tip

The average daily rate for a room in Charleston peaks in April. In 2000, that average was $123.60 per night (according to the city's Convention and Visitor's Bureau). The occupancy rate for the city's hotel and motel accommodations is a very healthy 80.5%.

proximity to one of Seabrook's two golf courses, Ocean Winds and Crooked Oaks. Along with these championship courses (see our Golf chapter), Seabrook has a tennis complex and the area's only resort equestrian center. Swimmers choose between glistening pools and a beautiful stretch of beach along the Atlantic Ocean. Children can enjoy supervised, old-fashioned fun such as puppet shows, finger painting, and ice cream making while their parents relish precious private time.

I-26 Corridor (Charleston International Airport)

For business travelers, commuters to Charleston Area Convention Center meetings (in North Charleston), and vacationers who need accommodations convenient to the airport, a number of options await them along the I-26 corridor and the I-526 loop around the heart of the Lowcountry.

We've listed many of these options in the listings of well-known chain hotels and motels above. Here are a few more choices offering a variety of amenities and prices.

Charleston International Best Western
$$–$$$
7401 Northwoods Blvd., North Charleston
(843) 572-2200, (800) 528-1234
Conveniently located just off I-26 at Ashley Phosphate Road, this 197-room tropical atrium hotel has an indoor/outdoor swimming pool with separate whirlpool and sauna. There's a volleyball court as well as a game room for youngsters. A full buffet breakfast comes with the room, and there's free shuttle service to and from the airport. Rooms have premium channel cable TV, and guest laundry service is available.

Days Inn Airport-Coliseum $–$$
2998 W. Montague Ave., North Charleston
(843) 747-4101, (800) 329-7466
The familiar name in affordable comfort has 148 rooms with cable TV, pay-for-view movies, and refrigerators (on request). Like most others in the chain, this has an on-site family restaurant, an outdoor pool, and playground. This location is ideal for sports fans attending events at the Coliseum, only three blocks away. There's also free airport transportation for guests.

Embassy Suites
Charleston Convention Center $$$
5050 International Blvd.,
North Charleston
(843) 747-9882, (800) 362-2779
One of the first full-service hotels built to serve (and literally connected to via a climate-controlled skyway) the north area's new convention center complex, this 256-suite high-rise hotel is very impressive. Facilities include ample meeting space, a pool, and state-of-the-art business center for conventioneers. Services at the Embassy Suites include a complimentary breakfast as well as an evening reception and a free airport shuttle to make doing business here as pleasant and convenient as possible.

Ramada Inn Coliseum/
Convention Center $$
2934 W. Montague, North Charleston
(843) 744-8281, (800) 272-6232
A slightly more affordable alternative to the Convention Center hotel choices is this familiar name-brand hotel just off I-26. The 154-room facility has an outdoor courtyard pool, room service, in-room voice-mail, and video entertainment, plus some rooms have limited kitchen facilities and laundry service for long-term stays. The on-site restaurant is called The Porter House Grill and a sports bar always has a game on the big screen TV. The Ramada offers complimentary airport transportation.

Sheraton North Charleston $$$
4770 Goer Dr.
(843) 747-1900, (888) 747-1900
This recently renovated, 296-room hotel

Downtown Charleston has the greatest number and widest variety of accommodations.

PHOTO: COURTESY OF CHARLESTON AREA CONVENTION AND VISITORS BUREAU

is right off I-26 at Montague Avenue, five minutes from Charleston International Airport. Its refreshing indoor-outdoor pool and fitness center are a boon to the busy convention business. The Café is its on-site restaurant, and the nearby lounge is a favorite with guests and locals alike. Parking is free and so is the hotel's shuttle to downtown destinations as well as to the airport.

Bed and Breakfasts and Atmospheric Inns

For many visitors, the quintessential Charleston experience is staying in one of the city's many fine bed and breakfast inns. Indeed, some would say Charleston has raised bed and breakfast hospitality to an art form.

The real draw of our bed and breakfast inns is that they allow you to temporarily assume native status with a prime Charleston address. For a fixed price, you enjoy elegant lodging, breakfast, and a string of extras ranging from cocktails to turndown service, which usually means that your host folds back your bed linens and leaves delicious chocolates and a nightcap at your bedside.

There is some confusion over what constitutes a bed and breakfast in the strictest sense, and much of the discussion centers on the size of the operation and the amount of contact with the host family. It's even possible to find a small bed and breakfast establishment where personal contact with the owner never happens at all. Some operate as entities in houses that are not private homes, and some are rental arrangements in the primary residences of homeowners. The former operate as freestanding business establishments, while the latter are businesses operating in the midst of family routine. Each type appeals to certain travelers and not to others. We offer separate listings in this chapter for the larger properties that offer similar amenities (following the bed and breakfast inns listings). We call them atmospheric inns.

Both small bed and breakfast establishments and larger atmospheric inns are becoming more popular with business travelers. The requirements for doing business on the road are relatively simple; a private phone line for fax and computer e-mail, a little desk space, plus some peace and quiet usually fill the bill. If business entertaining is involved, you may want to clear that with your host to avoid any embarrassment.

Decide which type of accommodations you prefer, and call ahead for detailed information. While you have a contact person on the phone, ask a few questions to narrow your search. Make certain you understand what the host or hostess is offering. Ask if the guest quarters are in the owners' home and if there will be interaction with the family. Ask if the accommodation has a private entrance. Does it have kitchen facilities? What about a private telephone line, local calls, and long distance charges? What about parking; is it on-site and convenient or offered at a discount from a nearby garage? Is security for valuables provided? Ask what constitutes breakfast, and clear any special dietary needs. Find out about the inn's proximity to sightseeing and public transportation. Is concierge service part of the package? Be sure to ask if there are any curfews and if guests are issued keys.

If handling luggage is an issue, mention it to your potential host. Most bed and breakfast inns don't have staff available for handling your baggage unless special arrangements are made. Discuss wheelchair accessibility and whether children or pets are welcome, and find out what time you check in and check out. These details may seem picky, but they can color the experience and make a real difference to your stay. It's always best to know these things ahead of time to avoid unpleasant surprises.

If you would rather have someone else screen the possibilities, consider calling Historic Charleston Bed & Breakfast, (843) 722-6606 or (800) 743-3583, a local business that has been matching guests with in-home accommodations since 1981. The reservation service books more than fifty different private homes and carriage houses within the Historic District. With very few exceptions, these accommodations date from 1860 or earlier. Agents for Historic Charleston Bed & Breakfast know each property intimately: They know which ones are appropriate for children and which are not, they know which ones are accessible to the handicapped and elderly and which are not, and they can arrange for late arrivals and special transportation. Historic

These lacy wrought iron gates at Two Meeting Street welcome guests to a B&B experience on Charleston's famous battery. PHOTO: JAY TERVO

Charleston B&B also sends out excellent pre-arrival materials including maps and shopping and dining recommendations.

Accommodations booked through Historic Charleston Bed & Breakfast can range from $105 to $195 for two adults in a one-bedroom setting; an average of $350 for a two-bedroom accommodation; and as high as $500 to $600 for luxury three-bedroom offerings during high season. Rates can be slightly higher for special events and peak weekends like Cooper River Bridge Run, Spoleto Festival USA, and New Year's. Off-season rates are, of course, lower. March through July and October through December are usually considered peak season. Note that our pricing code does not reflect taxes, gratuities and add-on services such as room service.

Sometimes finding the right guesthouse or bed and breakfast inn to suit your needs and desires can be the start of a long-term relationship. Many proprietors and hosts entertain the same guests year after year, and properties are sometimes booked months in advance.

When choosing a bed and breakfast or an atmospheric inn, realize prices vary based on season, location, amenities, and various other factors. Properties in the Historic District obviously are the pricey option, but the payoff may be greater than you think. Being able to walk to major sites, stroll along The Battery, and sleep in an antique canopy bed make for a wonderfully traditional Charlestonian experience. It may warrant the price tag for many visitors.

Because bed and breakfasts and atmospheric inns are frequently in historic homes with architectural barriers, accessibility for the handicapped is rare. If that's a matter of concern, ask in advance. As for smoking, most of these properties are thumbs down, but there's usually a veranda, piazza, or nearby courtyard where you can light up.

When contacting these establishments, be sure to ask which forms of payment are accepted. Credit card policies vary, and some inns will take personal checks. We note in our listings those accommodations that do not accept credit cards, but if you want to rest more easily, it's worth a call to the property. When traveling with children, be sure to ask about roll-away beds and children's rates. Also, if there's a pet in your party, you will want to ask the inn personnel if pets are allowed.

Also note that an additional 4 percent accommodations tax is added to your bill for lodgings in smaller accommodations. At larger bed and breakfasts and guest houses (with six rooms or more), your total tax (including state sales tax) will be 12 percent.

Price Code

Although rates are subject to change, we use the following price code to indicate our listed properties' average rate per night, in season, for two adults.

$	Less than $65
$$	$66–95
$$$	$96–150
$$$$	$151–200
$$$$$	More than $200

Bed and Breakfast Inns

All properties listed, except for one Summerville and two Mt. Pleasant options, have Charleston addresses. They are arranged alphabetically.

Ann Harper's Bed & Breakfast
$$–$$$, no credit cards
56 Smith St.
(843) 723-3947

Ann Harper's charming suite is in an 1870 Charleston single house that is near King Street shopping, the College of Charleston, and the Medical University of South Carolina. This air-conditioned, two-bedroom suite is furnished with antiques, wicker, reproductions, and cherished family heirlooms. Couples may rent the guest suite with a double bed, a separate sitting area with television, and a private bath with one of the deepest tubs you've ever seen. A party of three persons might find this same suite to be just what they need, with its additional bedroom with a single. Full breakfast is served. The menu varies, but often you'll find Ann's famous shrimp and grits. Off-street parking is provided.

Ashley Inn Bed and Breakfast $$$
201 Ashley Ave.
(843) 723-1848, (800) 581-6658
A real taste of Charleston, this home was

built around 1832 and is a mansion even by today's standards—six bedrooms and a suite, with fireplaces throughout the house, and a lovely garden. All rooms have private baths and are tastefully furnished with antique, four-poster pencil-post or canopy rice beds. Breakfast is served on the piazza and features such gourmet delights as savory sausage soufflé or French toast with hazelnut-peach syrup. Afternoon tea and evening sherry are part of the hospitality. The inn has bicycles for guests to use and provides off-street parking. This may be the best option for guests wishing access to MUSC facilities—they are literally across the street.

Barksdale House Inn $$–$$$
27 George St.
(843) 577-4800
This bed and breakfast inn is in proximity to King Street shopping and the College of Charleston. In fact, the facility was once a fraternity house. No one would guess that fact today, as the Barksdale House Inn includes 14 beautifully appointed rooms, each one different from

the others. All have cable TV and private telephones. Five rooms are equipped with fireplaces and whirlpool baths (oh, what the frat brothers would have given . . .). Continental breakfast is served in your room or in the rear garden, and a nightly turndown service and sherry are included. Free parking is available.

Battery Carriage House Inn $$$$–$$$$$
20 S. Battery
(843) 727-3100, (800) 775-5575

The Battery Carriage House (c. 1843) is located right on The Battery, Charleston's very best address for a couple of hundred years. You couldn't be closer to the picturesque, historic park and beautiful views of Charleston Harbor. The eleven guest rooms to the rear and under the piazza are small, but completely charming—most with queen-size canopy beds and interesting furnishings. Three rooms are available with king-size beds. All rooms have cable TV with HBO, and you'll find individual controls for heating and AC. Some rooms have large steam showers; others have whirlpool tubs. Fluffy terrycloth robes and down pillows add to the pampering. Silver-service continental breakfast is served in the room or in the garden under the loggia, your choice. Happy hour wine is served in the lobby. The service here is very cordial, the ambiance very European—a bit like an Italian pension. And there's usually plenty of parking just across the street.

Bed, No Breakfast $–$$, no credit cards
16 Halsey St.
(843) 723-4450

Although this listing doesn't fit the bed and breakfast category in the strictest sense, it's a close relation. In fact, this is what *The New York Times* called "the no-frills option" in Charleston. You'll find two large, light-filled, air-conditioned rooms with a private entrance but, sorry, no eggs and grits. Actually, coffee, tea, and a refrigerator are available in each room, which means you can easily prepare your own continental breakfast. Both rooms

are non-smoking and there's a shared bath. Guests have their own TV and an in-room extension of the family phone line. There's a delightful courtyard, too, with a hammock that's ideal for an afternoon siesta. Guests appreciate the off-street parking and the fact that the College of Charleston and MUSC and the hospitals are within easy walking distance.

Belvedere Bed and Breakfast
$$$, no credit cards
40 Rutledge Ave.
(843) 722-0973, (800) 816-1664

The Belvedere gets its name from the handsome, Adam-style interior woodwork that was rescued from the 1785 Belvedere Plantation (torn down in the 1920s). Three rooms are offered in this handsome old mansion that faces Charleston's ornamental basin called Colonial Lake. Eclectically furnished with Oriental rugs, family heirlooms, and Charleston reproductions, you'll find a nice collection of antique Canton china along with several wonderful silver pieces throughout the public rooms. Guests all have keys to the front door and private keys to their rooms. Smoking is permitted on the balconies and porches. Local TV is available in each guest room, and a downstairs TV room offers premium cable channels and a VCR. Daily continental breakfast is provided, along with afternoon sherry and smashing views of the sunset over the lake.

Bennett-Hayne House $$$, no credit cards
113 Ashley Ave.
(843) 577-6056

The Wades have worked wonders in restoring their beautiful historic home (built in 1799) one block south of Calhoun Street on the Peninsula. From the spectacular Adam woodwork throughout the house (in particular on the second floor) to a lovely winding staircase, it's a tribute to 18th-century craftsmanship and 20th-century preservation efforts. One former drawing room is now used as a guest bedroom, and there are two more rooms on the third floor that offer interesting views of the city skyline and the Cooper and Ashley Rivers. Guest rooms are smoke-free, but smoking is allowed on the wide porch overlooking the garden, where guests enjoy an old-fashioned swing and tranquil surroundings. Breakfast at the Bennett-Hayne House is a major production-served in the formal dining room with all stops pulled out. Mrs. Wade does the cooking, and Mr. Wade serves as waiter and raconteur. Menus vary according to season and whim, but expect to find items like Belgian waffles with fresh strawberries or local creek shrimp with sausage and grits. Judging from guest evaluation cards, the Wades are serving up Charleston hospitality in tall order.

Cannonboro Inn Bed and Breakfast $$$$
184 Ashley Ave.
(843) 723-8572, (800) 235-8039
This historic 1853 home has eight beautifully decorated rooms for guests—all of which offer antique four-poster or canopy beds. The rooms are done in a handsome palette of mauves and pinks that complement the original hardwood floors. The house is furnished with an assortment of period antiques, and all rooms have air conditioning and private baths. Guests have TV and private telephones too. Complimentary tea and sherry are served each afternoon along with an assortment of home-baked goods. Awake to the aroma of sizzling sausage and freshly baked biscuits. A full gourmet breakfast is served each morning on the columned piazza overlooking a Lowcountry garden and fountain. Off-street parking is provided, and complimentary touring bicycles—an especially nice option in this part of town—are available for guests.

1837 Bed & Breakfast and Tea Room $$$
126 Wentworth St.
(843-723-7166, (877) 723-1837
Two artists have restored this historic (c. 1837) house near the College of Charleston and King Street shopping. All

nine rooms and the brick carriage house have air conditioning and are beautifully decorated. Guests are treated to a sumptuous gourmet breakfast and have access to off-street parking. The owners also take reservations from the public for afternoon tea in their parlor from 3 to 5 PM daily. Tea for registered guests is complimentary. Rooms have private entrances and baths, refrigerators, and televisions. To quote *The New York Times*, it is "a perfect place to unwind."

Fantasia Bed & Breakfast $$$–$$$$
11 George St.
(843) 853-0201, (800) 852-4466
Here in this 1813 classic Charleston Single House (See our chapter on Architectural Preservation), you'll find a charming bed and breakfast in Charleston's tradition of hospitality. The main house's two bedroom suites are upstairs over a pair of first floor drawing rooms that give visitors the feel and flavor of Charleston life before the Civil War. The piazza with its lazy hammock overlooks a handsomely landscaped garden accented with fountains and a cobblestone drive. A carriage and kitchen house with another bedroom actually sleeps four with a pull-out couch. A full breakfast is served in the main house and a continental breakfast is available for kitchen house guests. Wine and soft drinks await visitors after a busy day of shopping and touring the city's sites. Off-street parking is available and short term lease agreements are offered for the carriage and kitchen house facilities.

Guilds Inn Bed and Breakfast $$$
101 Pitt St., Mt. Pleasant
(843) 881-0510, (800) 331-0510
There are six bedrooms in the lovingly restored (c. 1888) Guilds Inn, each beautiful and typically "Old Village." Every room has a private bath, and continental breakfast is complimentary. Rooms vary in size; there's an executive suite, and honeymooners can request the special bridal suite with Jacuzzi. For upscale but intimate dining there's an intimate

If you arrive in Charleston without reservations, help is available at the Charleston Visitor Reception and Transportation Center at 375 Meeting Street. Open daily from 8:30 AM to 5:30 PM, the visitor center offers help finding rooms at inns, hotels, and motels in the greater Charleston area. This is, in effect, a clearing house of last-minute accommodations and a real life-saver for those impromptu visitors to the city. Later in the business day, these rooms are often offered at discounted rates. The desk personnel cannot secure reservations for you via phone; you must be there in person. They can, however, make a room reservation using your credit card once you're there.

restaurant downstairs called 101 Pitt Street. (See our Restaurants chapter). Guests enjoy the charm of this quaint neighborhood, where evening walks are a popular pastime.

The Hayne House $$$$
30 King St.
(843) 577-2633

Situated just one block off The Battery, The Hayne House was built in 1755 by Gen. Arthur Hayne, a hero of the Revolu-

tionary War. Innkeepers Brian and Jane McGreevy offer a total of six rooms and suites, each one with its own bath and interior theme. Furnished with heirloom antiques and artwork, the ambiance of family and tradition is all-prevailing at Hayne House. Guests enjoy the family's private garden and piazza and spending time in the drawing room and library. Expect to find plenty of good books and music, but no TV. A huge Southern breakfast is served in the formal dining room every morning at the family table. Well-behaved children of all ages are welcome.

King George IV Inn & Guests $$$–$$$$
32 George St.
(843) 723-9339, (888) 723-1667

At this four-story, Federal-style house with decorative fireplaces, wide-planked hardwood floors, and three porches, you're just off King Street with its many antiques shops and fashion boutiques. And Charleston's colorful City Market is only a five-minute walk away. This was originally the 1790s home of Charleston writer and early newspaper publisher Peter Freneau. Freneau was of Huguenot descent, and his brother, Philip, was called the "poet of the Revolution." All 10 rooms are furnished with antiques, TVs, and telephones, and have air conditioning. Eight of the rooms have private baths. Each morning, a continental breakfast is served with pastries, cereals, coffee, and juices. There is off-street parking for guests.

The Kitchen House $$$$
126 Tradd St.
(843) 577-6362

This block of Tradd Street, with its 18th-century homes and gardens, is in the Historic District. The Kitchen House (c. 1732), which was the former home of the surgeon general of the Continental Army, offers guests complimentary full breakfast, sherry, and wine. Guests can use the private patio to enjoy an herb garden and fish pond. There are two charmingly restored rooms in the original kitchen house and both have cable TV and air conditioning. *Colonial Homes* and *The New York Times* raved about this one. Ask about the honeymoon packages if you're in that market.

Lowndes Grove Plantation
Bed and Breakfast $$$
266 St. Margaret St.
(843) 723-8438

Now listed on the National Register of Historic Places, Lowndes Grove (c. 1786) is the only plantation on the Ashley River actually within today's city limits. The house and grounds, with spectacular views of the water, make a lush setting for wedding receptions and other festivities. There are six air-conditioned guest rooms with private baths and an air-conditioned guest cottage for families (babysitting is available). As elegant as the house is, the spacious grounds, pool, Jacuzzi, and river dock also make it a comfortable, almost rural setting. Continental-plus breakfast is served daily and includes at least one hot item—usually a Lowcountry favorite such as shrimp and grits. The house is especially convenient to The Citadel and Hampton Park, once the site of the 1901 West Indies Exhibition—a world's fair-like extravaganza that attracted dignitaries from all over the world. At the time, Lowndes Grove hosted former President Theodore Roosevelt.

Number Six Ambrose Alley $$$$$
6 Ambrose Alley
(843) 722-7551, (888) 722-7553

Here's an entire kitchen house with servant quarters and private garden (c. 1837) dedicated to hosting no more than four lucky Charleston visitors. Just a half-block north of Bull Street behind the Rutledge Victorian Guest House (see below), this charming 19th-century dependency is decorated as an English country cottage with an assortment of antiques. The living room, dining room, and two separate bedrooms make Ambrose Alley ideal for two couples visiting the city. This B&B option is not recommended for children

under 12. Afternoon sherry is offered along with a continental-plus breakfast each morning. Off-street parking is another definite asset.

The Long Point Inn Bed & Breakfast
$$$–$$$$
1199 Long Point Rd., Mt. Pleasant
(843) 849-1884

On an oak-draped, marshfront property next to historic Boone Hall Plantation in Mt. Pleasant, a large, rustic-looking log cabin has been lovingly renovated for Lowcountry visitors looking for a unique bed and breakfast experience. Each of the five guest bedrooms is individually decorated with an elegance that belies the informal exterior of the building. Inside, the rooms are furnished with a wide assortment of antiques and family heirlooms. Most guest rooms feature queen-sized beds along with private baths. All rooms have cable TV and VCRs. A cozy fireplace dominates the common great-room and a charming glassed-in porch is the setting for a full breakfast each morning. Vistas of the marsh can be enjoyed from the upstairs open-air porch and the view from the shrimping dock is a special joy at sunset. Nestled among 300-year-old Live Oaks, The Long Point Inn offers an unforgettable stay.

The Palmer Home $$$ and $$$$$
5 E. Battery
(843) 853-1574, (888) 723-1574

This bed and breakfast is in one of the most high-profile mansions on The Battery. This huge pink Italianate single house (sometimes called "The Pink Palace") offers spectacular views. From the piazza, guests can see across all of Charleston Harbor with Fort Sumter silhouetted on the horizon. There are four guest rooms on the third floor (there is an elevator) and a swimming pool in the garden for cool refreshment. There's also a more expensive carriage house (recently featured on a Travel Channel TV special) with two bedrooms that can accommodate up to eight adults. Continental breakfast is served in the rooms or on the piazza at your choosing. There's plenty of off-street parking, too.

Phoebe Pember House $$$–$$$$
26 Society St.
(843) 722-4186
This elegant, 200-year-old Federal-style home in Ansonborough was the birthplace of Civil War heroine Phoebe Pember. She was the wealthy daughter of a 19th-century Charleston businessman. As a nurse, she traveled to Confederate hospitals during the war and wrote about her experience in her memoirs, *A True Southern Lady's Story.* The interiors here are remarkably authentic yet very comfortable. The four guest rooms have fireplaces and canopy beds. Business travelers like the fact that rooms have desks, telephones, and fax machines. There's cable TV to enjoy once the work is done, and a popular day spa is just around the corner. The carriage house with its gardens is available for business meetings as well as short-term or long-term rental. You're only blocks from the City Market (see our Shopping chapter) and all the nightlife offered there. Special events at Gaillard Auditorium are virtually across the street. The College of Charleston is close by as well. There is off-street parking, and a silver tray continental-plus breakfast (this usually entails fruit, a selection of breads, and coffee, tea, or juice) plus evening wine and cheese is included.

Rutledge Victorian Guest House $$$$
114 Rutledge Ave.
(843) 722-7551, (888) 722-7553
This is the kind of guesthouse we can remember from the old days in Key West. The atmosphere is relaxed, the surroundings colorful and Bohemian. Take the exterior, for example—bright, painted Victorian, showcasing a large front porch filled with rocking chairs. Inside there are 11 rooms in all—some with hardwood floors, 12-foot ceilings, and fireplaces. Guests on business appreciate the private telephones and fax machine. There's

afternoon sherry for guests as well as nightly turndown service with chocolates and brandy. A continental-plus breakfast is served daily, and the dining room always features some kind of fresh-baked pastries, cookies, and teas—anytime. This guesthouse is not recommended for children under age 12.

Thirty-Six Meeting Street Bed & Breakfast $$$–$$$$
36 Meeting St.
(843) 722-1034
This handsome (c. 1740) home is only a little more than a block off The Battery and offers three guest rooms. Two are on the second floor and have queen beds and private baths. From there a spiral staircase leads to a third bedroom and bath. All rooms have queen-sized beds, kitchenettes, and there's an inviting walled-in garden with tables and chairs for relaxing after a busy day. A continental breakfast is provided in the kitchenette—ready whenever guests rise and wish to partake. Off-street parking is available.

The Thomas Lamboll House $$$
19 King St.
(843) 723-3212, (888) 874-0793
Named in honor of colonial era Judge Thomas Lamboll, this Charleston single house (c. 1739) is now a private home with two lovely third-floor guest rooms offered to bed and breakfast guests. Each is elegantly furnished with reproduction and antique furniture, has central air conditioning, a fireplace, cable TV, and a telephone. French doors lead onto the third floor piazza with distant views of Charleston Harbor over the peninsula's treetops. Continental breakfast is offered in the formal dining room every morning. Children are welcome and off-street parking is available.

Twenty-Seven State Street
Bed & Breakfast $$$$, no credit cards
27 State St.
(843) 722-4243
Owners Joye and Paul Craven operate this

bed and breakfast inn, built around 1800. Guests stay in one of the Cravens' two unique carriage house rooms. Each room includes a private entrance, bedroom, living room area, kitchenette, and private bath and is furnished with antiques, reproductions, and Oriental rugs. You'll find cable TV and private telephones. One room opens onto a lovely courtyard, the other onto a covered veranda. The Cravens ready the rooms with fresh flowers and fruit and provide an optional continental-plus breakfast and a newspaper each morning. Guests have access to bicycles for exploring the charming French Quarter and its lovely surroundings.

Two Meeting Street Inn
$$$$–$$$$$, no credit cards
2 Meeting St.
(843) 723-7322

This elegant 1890 Victorian mansion is at the intersection of Meeting Street and South Battery facing White Point Gardens. Guests stay in one of nine air-conditioned rooms, each of which has a private bath. All rooms are different, but each carries out the Victorian theme in every detail. Continental breakfast is served in the garden or the formal dining room, depending on the weather. The fare ranges from bakery-fresh lemon-blueberry muffins to fresh local strawberries to whatever is in season served with yogurt sauce. Afternoon tea is included in the rate. Much of Two Meeting Street's charm comes from the lacy Queen Anne-style veranda stretching across the front of the inn. Its lazy ceiling fans and rocking chairs make the scene an inviting option for afternoon tea.

Villa De La Fontaine Bed and Breakfast
$$$, no credit cards
138 Wentworth St.
(843) 577-7709

The owners of this columned mansion (c. 1838), with its spacious formal gardens, terrace, and fountain, offer four centrally air-conditioned rooms with canopy beds. Full breakfast served in the solarium is a special treat with homemade breads, jellies, and (depending on the day) Spanish omelets, eggs Benedict, and fresh waffles among the menu items. Two of Villa De La Fontaine's rooms have separate entrances. All rooms are furnished with exquisite museum-quality pieces, making the Villa quite a showplace. On-site parking is available.

Zero Water Street
$$$ and $$$$$, no credit cards
31 E. Battery
(843) 723-2841

Zero Water Street is actually a quiet, private entrance to 31 E. Battery, one of Charleston's classic mansion houses built on The Battery in 1836. Water Street is in the very heart of the old city's Historic District, and 31 E. Battery directly overlooks Charleston Harbor and Fort Sumter. Your room (with its private bath) and the adjoining piazza will offer spectacular views. Two guest suites with 12-foot ceilings are available plus an additional guest room. You'll have fresh-cut flowers arranged by the owner, a professional florist, and air conditioning, private telephone, TV, and off-street parking. A continental breakfast is provided either in your room or in the lovely Victorian garden with its antique play house.

Atmospheric Inns

Many inns in Charleston offer some of the same personalized touches that make the bed and breakfasts special, but on a larger scale. Most, but not all, operate in modernized facilities either renovated or built specifically for lodging. You can usually expect a great deal of charm along with complimentary continental breakfast, afternoon wine or sherry, and evening turndown service. What distinguishes one from another is location, authenticity of decor, trendy amenities, and management style. Prices per night vary with the seasons, and our price guides reflect the same coding ranges and caveats used for the bed and breakfasts. Again, all addresses are in Charleston.

Anchorage Inn $$$–$$$$
26 Vendue Range
(843) 723-8300, (800) 421-2952
Close to the Waterfront Park and some of Charleston's best restaurants, this fascinating luxury inn is one of the city's premier accommodations. While so much of Charleston revisits the 18th century, this inn replicates the ambiance of a 17th-century English coachman inn. Every detail is delightfully conceived—period antiques and handcrafted reproductions are one-of-a-kind, made specifically for the inn. Continental breakfast is served in the dining room. Afternoon wine and cheese is offered, and guests enjoy turndown service at night. There are two suites included in the inn's 19 rooms, and four rooms have Jacuzzi tubs. Ample parking is available in the city garage (at a rate of $10 for 24 hours) just to the rear of the inn.

Andrew Pinckney Inn $$$
199 Church St.
(843) 937-8800, (800) 505-8983
The Andrew Pinckney Inn is at the corner of Church and Pinckney Streets on the very edge of Charleston's historic Market. All of the Market's famous diversions—quaint shops, craft stalls, nightclubs, and fine restaurants—are nearby. Even the horse-drawn carriage tours are just a few steps away. The inn features a rooftop garden terrace for catching Lowcountry sunsets, and the attentive concierge service can arrange special golf and fitness packages on request. A continental breakfast is part of the package, and all rooms feature handsome antique-style furnishings. There's even a fully equipped conference room available for business or group travelers.

Ansonborough Inn $$$–$$$$
21 Hasell St.
(843) 723-1655, (800) 522-2073
The Award-winning Ansonborough Inn is at the end of Hasell Street off East Bay. Thirty-seven suites have been cleverly fashioned out of a turn-of-the-century warehouse. Heart-of-pine exposed beams (measuring 12 inches by 12 feet) and locally made red brick have been incorporated in the decor to give the inn—even with its magnificent 16- and 18-foot ceilings—a remarkably warm feeling. The facility's three floors are handicap-accessible and laid out around an open central atrium. The suites are equipped with full kitchens, and some have lofts. There's an on-site English-style pub and rooftop bar. Guests receive complimentary afternoon wine and a 24-hour monitored parking lot is available. One favorite amenity is the continental breakfast with fresh-baked breads. Choose from banana, apple-raisin, and blueberry muffins delivered each morning from Saffron's, a popular bakery just down the street. The business traveler is treated to multiple data ports and on-site conference facilities.

The Governor's House Inn
$$$$–$$$$$, no credit cards
117 Broad St.
(843) 720-2070, (800) 720-9812
Built in 1760 by John Laurens, this is the oldest house in Charleston currently being used as a bed and breakfast. Edward Rutledge, the youngest signer of the Declaration of Independence and once governor of South Carolina (1798–1800) lived here. Today, the house boasts 12 elegantly appointed guest rooms. The Grand rooms feature 12-foot ceilings with fireplaces and private verandas. The Roofscape room provides lovely views over the area's historic architecture. The Kitchen House suite has a separate living room, private porch, wet bar, and an original 1760 fireplace. A Southern continental breakfast is served, as is afternoon tea and evening sherry. The location is ideal from several standpoints: You're at the edge of the original Grand Modell city and today's prestigious Below Broad residential area, and you're within easy walking distance of King Street's shopping and antiques district.

Elliott House Inn $$$
78 Queen St.
(843) 723-1855, (800) 729-1855
Elliott House is next to the popular 82 Queen restaurant (see our Restaurants

Insiders' Tip

When negotiating your way through Charleston streets, you may encounter several street names that Charlestonians choose to pronounce in their own inimitable fashion. Here's a quick translation: If somebody mentions "Le-GREE" Street, it's Legare Street. And when directed to Hasell Street, note it is called "Hazel."

chapter) and across the street from the Mills House Hotel. This is life as it should be in the refined fast lane—breakfast served on silver service, afternoon champagne in the courtyard, and a heated Jacuzzi at night. Guests stay in one of 24 air-conditioned rooms, complete with Oriental rugs and period furniture. Since 82 Queen draws a big (but respectable) crowd to its bar, the action is just a few strides away for Elliott House guests. Complimentary bicycles are available for exploring the neighborhood, and parking is across the street in a city garage.

4 Unity Alley $$$$, no credit cards
4 Unity Alley
(843) 577-6660

Unity Alley is steeped in history; according to legend, George Washington quartered his horse here on his visit to Charleston back in 1791. Today this quiet alley in the bustling French Quarter boasts a renovated warehouse beautifully transformed into a grand home with charming guest accommodations.

Furnished with antique and reproduction furniture, the building surrounds a restful atrium garden—perfect for entertaining and dining. Opened in '98, 4 Unity

Alley offers three suites, each with a private bath. A full breakfast is served each morning and rarest of all—there's indoor parking available for guests.

French Quarter Inn $$$$
166 Church St.
(843) 722-1900, (866) 812-1900

Located in Charleston's original French Quarter district in the historic Market and Church Streets area, here is a new independent offering set for opening in the fall of 2001.

There are 50 rooms and suites elegantly appointed with an eclectic array of French pieces, Provencal beds, European-style bed dressings, and imported down comforters. Some of the rooms feature working fireplaces, whirlpool tubs, and balconies overlooking the festive Market area. Amenities include silver service breakfast in the room, afternoon wine and cheese, turndown service, and complementary 24-hour coffee, tea, and snacks. Valet parking is part of the upscale service.

Fulton Lane Inn $$$$–$$$$$
202 King St.
(843) 720-2600, (800) 720-2688

This cozy inn is a non-smoking facility nestled just off King Street in the heart of Charleston's fascinating antiques district. Built post-Civil War by Confederate blockade runner John Rugheimer, the inn is a fascinating taste of a time gone by. The 27 rooms are decorated in a Southern plantation style, and some feature fireplaces, king-size canopy beds, luxury baths, and whirlpool tubs. Nightly turndown service and a continental breakfast delivered on silver service are part of the hospitality here. Public parking is available just outside the door. This inn is part of the Charming Inns of Charleston group.

HarbourView Inn $$$$
2 Vendue Range
(843) 853-8439, (888) 853-8439

This is one of Charleston's newest luxury inns right in the heart of the downtown

Historic District. Its location, directly across from Waterfront Park, is one attraction. The 52 high-end, luxury rooms and suites close to the area's many fine restaurants, shops, galleries, and nightclubs are another. Opened in May of '98, the inn, with its handsome nautical appointments throughout, offers nightly turndown service, elegant in-room continental breakfast, and afternoon refreshments in the atrium. Top-floor rooms have spectacular views over Charleston Harbor—hard to find on the Peninsula. Ask about their special rate packages for honeymooners.

Indigo Inn $$$$
1 Maiden Ln.
(843) 577-5900, (800) 845-7639

The Indigo Inn fronts on Meeting Street and is across from a bustling shopping and restaurant district not far from Charleston Place. The three-story inn has 40 rooms around a private courtyard and fountain, and it prides itself on impeccable service. The traditionally decorated rooms feature massive four-poster beds and evoke a plantation atmosphere. A hunt (continental-plus) breakfast and the morning paper are complimentary, as is the on-site parking, a blessing in the heart of the city. Well-behaved pets are welcomed at an additional charge.

The Jasmine House $$$$$
64 Hasell St.
(843) 577-5900, (800) 845-7639

This classic Greek Revival (1843) mansion sits in the historic Ansonborough neighborhood, between the Market and Gaillard Auditorium. Six guest rooms are in the main house and feature 14-foot ceilings, Italian marble baths, and original architectural details. Four others in the carriage house open onto the private courtyard and Jacuzzi area and have charming brick floors and second-level piazzas. Guests enjoy a hot continental-plus breakfast and complimentary parking. Rooms in the main house are handsomely decorated in themes appropriate to the period of the house and Charleston's pre-Civil War heyday. Check-in is handled at the sister property, Indigo Inn, at the corner of Maiden Lane and Meeting Street.

John Rutledge House Inn $$$$$
116 Broad St.
(843) 723-7999, (800) 476-9741

Built in 1763 by John Rutledge, a signer of the U.S. Constitution, the house at 116 Broad Street has been completely renovated and transformed (as part of a three-building complex) into a swank inn with 19 rooms in all. The house is a designated National Historic Landmark, and the National Trust for Historic Preservation named it among the top 32 Historic Hotels of America for good reason. George Washington himself had breakfast here and was one of many patriots, statesmen, and presidents who came to call on Mr. Rutledge. The main residence contains elaborate parquet floors, Italian marble mantels, and molded plaster ceilings. Rooms have been modernized to include private baths, refrigerators, televisions, and individual climate controls. Afternoon tea is served in the ballroom, and evening turndown service includes chocolates at bedside. Continental breakfast and a newspaper are delivered to guests each morning. A full breakfast is available for a small additional charge. This inn is part of the Charming Inns of Charleston group.

Kings Courtyard Inn $$$$–$$$$$
198 King St.
(843) 723-7000, (800) 845-6119

The Kings Courtyard Inn has an interesting history in that the building has come full circle in its lifetime of nearly a century and a half. It began as an inn catering to 19th-century plantation owners and businessmen; then it was a private residence. After that, the downstairs housed some of Charleston's most fashionable shops, and now it once again serves guests with luxury accommodations. The Greek Revival-style inn is nestled among many fine antiques shops on King Street.

Rooms and suites are modernized with air conditioning and private baths, and no two are exactly alike. Some offer canopy beds; others feature fireplaces and many offer views of a lovely courtyard below. Wine or sherry is provided upon arrival. You may expect a continental breakfast and a newspaper delivered to you each morning, or you can have breakfast in the courtyards or the breakfast room. Guests may order from a menu if they like. One of our favorite details at the Kings Courtyard is the garden spa, used by guests year round. Cocktails are available in the courtyard bar, and brandy is provided each evening on the first floor. This inn is part of the Charming Inns of Charleston group.

Lodge Alley Inn $$$$$
195 East Bay St.
(843) 722-1611, (800) 845-1004

Set in a complex of 18th-century warehouses off East Bay Street in the French Quarter, Lodge Alley is a remarkable achievement in architectural balance. With 93 units of various sizes and configurations, it is large in capacity, but each room maintains the feel of an intimate Charleston dwelling. Many a celebrity has checked in at this address, because it offers luxury and discreet anonymity at the same time. Guests of the Lodge Alley enjoy special pamperings like fluffy robes, fireplaces, and stocked mini-bars. Some of the handsomely decorated rooms have complete kitchen facilities. Turndown service is complimentary, and off-street parking is offered for the minimal charge of $5.

Maison Du Pré $$$$
317 East Bay St.
(843) 723-8691, (800) 844-INNS

There are 12 elegant, air-conditioned guest rooms plus three suites at Maison Du Pré (c. 1804). Each has a private bath and is beautifully furnished with Oriental rugs and antiques appropriate for this charming compound of single houses in Charleston's fashionable Ansonborough section. In the spring and other temperate seasons, the garden patio—alive with flowers and the therapeutic splash of fountains—is a big draw.

In typical Charleston fashion, the piazza is a focal point for socializing with other guests and enjoying the garden views. The continental breakfast is complimentary as is the afternoon Lowcountry Tea—sometimes it's wine, cheese, fruits, and hors d'oeuvres with little tea in sight. Parking is free in a lot just across the street from the compound. This location is ideal for those attending Spoleto events at Gaillard Auditorium. Maison Du Pré has been featured in *Country Inns, Bed and Breakfast* magazine and cable TV's Travel Channel.

Meeting Street Inn $$$–$$$$
173 Meeting St.
(843) 723-1882, (800) 842-8022

In the heart of the city on bustling Meeting Street, this is a convenient option for a Charleston inn experience. The front portion of the inn is 140 years old, while the back section is a recent addition. Four-poster rice beds in every room add to the 19th-century ambiance of this elegant accommodation, convenient to many fine restaurants, antique shops, and the colorful City Market area. Continental breakfast may be taken in your room or out in the courtyard. The courtyard's heated Jacuzzi is popular with guests any time of the day. Afternoons at the Meeting Street Inn include complimentary seasonal refreshments and bar service in the lobby. Evening turndown service means a freshened-up room and bath plus a delicious chocolate on your bedtime pillow.

Middleton Inn $$$–$$$$
4290 Ashley River Rd.
(843) 556-0500, (800) 543-4774

In our estimation, Middleton Inn is the kind of place you really want to write home about. Situated on the grounds of one of the most beautiful and historic plantations in the South, Middleton Inn overlooks the Ashley River and the nation's oldest landscaped gardens and is just 14 miles from downtown Charleston. Guests have access to the nature trails, gardens, a swimming pool, and tennis courts. You'll also find croquet, canoeing, and an on-site café for continental breakfast. Middleton Place's famous restaurant is just a stroll through the woods away. The facility itself is of national award-winning design, contemporary, and starkly modern in its simplicity. It has 55 rooms with charming fireplaces and European baths. (See our Attractions chapter for more about Middleton Place.)

Planters Inn $$$$–$$$$$
112 N. Market St.
(843) 722-2345, (800) 845-7082
As charming and roomy as an antebellum Charleston home, this inn has a European flavor and an understated elegance that radiates quality. It came as no surprise to us some years back when Planters Inn captured *Lodging Hospitality* magazine's first-place award in the guest room category. From four-poster beds to mahogany armoires, authentic Charleston reproductions are showcased in spacious rooms with traditional high ceilings. The inn is in the colorful City Market area and is home to the popular Peninsula Grill (see our Restaurants chapter). Silver-service breakfast is delivered to your room, and an evening wine and hors d'oeuvres reception is a great way to meet other guests of the inn. Parking is available—a rarity for this busy location.

Vendue Inn $$$$
19 Vendue Range
(843) 577-7970, (800) 845-7900
Situated between East Bay Street and the famous "walk through" fountain of Waterfront Park is this upscale European-style inn with one of the best reputations going for fine service and attention to detail. There are 45 rooms and suites in all—each one carefully furnished with authentic antiques and 18-century reproductions. Junior and Deluxe suites offer gas fireplaces, marble baths, separate showers, and whirlpool tubs. Deluxe

Suites even go so far as to include separate living rooms, stocked wet bars, and fresh fruit baskets. A rooftop terrace and bar offer one of the best harbor views in the city and the Vendue's on-site restaurant, The Library, is one of Charleston's great dining adventures (see our Restaurants chapter). Guests start the day with a complimentary Southern breakfast buffet or enjoy a continental breakfast in their room. Business travelers will find 2-line phones in every room for making computer hook-ups easy. Wine and cheese in the Garden Room is available every afternoon.

Victoria House Inn $$$$–$$$$$
208 King St.
(843) 720-2944, (800) 933-5464
The Victoria House Inn is a 16-room luxury inn created within an 1889 Victorian building on King Street. Following the traditional inn format of serving light spirits in the lobby, providing evening turndown, and offering continental breakfast, the Victoria is another addition to the corporate family that includes Kings Courtyard Inn, Fulton Lane Inn, and the John Rutledge House Inn. Some rooms offer cozy gas fireplaces and relaxing whirlpool baths. Expect impeccable service and tasteful Victorian-style decor, but best of all is your handy access to the downtown antiques shops, restaurants, and watering holes.

Wentworth Mansion $$$$$
149 Wentworth St.
(843) 853-1886, (888) INN-1886
This elegantly refurbished inn was built from 1885 to 1887 as one of Charleston's few great Victorian town homes. Articulated in what is called the "Second Empire" style of architecture (after a French fashion popularized during the reign of Napoleon), it was originally the private estate of a Francis Silas Rodgers. Rodgers was a Charleston cotton merchant who made a fortune in phosphate after the Civil War. His mansion survives today as the city's most opulent ode to

"Creature" comforts await at Charleston's atmospheric inns. PHOTO: COURTESY OF PLANTERS INN

the long-lost Gilded Age of Innocence. Remarkably unchanged over the last century, the property has recently been converted into an inn of uncompromising luxury. It features 21 rooms and suites individually decorated and furnished with 19th-century antiques. All rooms have king-size beds and baths with oversize whirlpool tubs. Most have working gas fireplaces.

Guests enjoy the mansion's common rooms such as the Rodgers Library, the Harleston Lounge, and the atrium-like Sun Porch—where guests savor leisurely elegant breakfasts, afternoon teas, and evening wine and hors d'oeuvres hours. Private guides lead guests on tours of the city, and an on-site fine dining restaurant, circa 1886, opened in the fall of '99. (See our Restaurants chapter.) With its debut in the late spring of '98, Wentworth Mansion brought a whole new level of service to Charleston's already renowned tradition of unparalleled hospitality.

Woodlands Resort & Inn $$$$$
125 Parsons Rd., Summerville
(843) 875-2600, (800) 774-9999

Although this upscale option is beyond the geographic boundaries of this listing, it is so extraordinary that it should not be overlooked. Woodlands Resort & Inn is a unique venue in the best tradition of the "English country house hotel." Only this one has a decidedly Southern flair. The 42-acre estate, now called "Woodlands," was once the winter retreat (c. 1906) of a wealthy Northern industrialist. But today it is a 19-room luxury inn and conference center with tennis facilities, a croquet lawn, heated pool, and upscale spa facility. Each room is handsomely appointed and stocked with thoughtful personal amenities ranging from monogrammed robes of thick terry cloth to fresh-cut flowers and soothing glycerine soaps. The inn's on-site spa offers special pamperings such as fibro-therapy massage, herbal wraps, and body masques.

Perhaps best of all is the Woodlands dining experience. Chef Ken Vedrinski has consistently earned rave reviews from local and international food critics alike. He calls his cuisine "contemporary regional American," but we call it unforgettable.

Summerville is 30 minutes from downtown Charleston via I-26 (see our Daytrips chapter), and many Charlestonians plan mini-vacations to Woodlands just as their ancestors did a century ago when Summerville offered a pine-cooled retreat from Charleston's muggy humidity.

Vacation and Beach Rentals

Beach rentals, especially those on the barrier islands of Kiawah, Seabrook, Sullivan's Island, Isle of Palms (home of Wild Dunes), and Folly Beach are considered a real estate specialty here in the Lowcountry. Several companies deal exclusively in resort properties, while others target the less organized, more laid-back beach life on Sullivan's Island and Folly Beach.

Many of these beachfront accommodations are the second homes or would-be retirement homes for out-of-town owners. And it's fairly common to find the same real estate company that sold the property representing the owners in short-term lease arrangements to carefully screened area visitors.

Other companies, which deal in rental properties alone, offer vacation packages that make renting a beach house or oceanside condo a one-stop, one-call proposition.

Every company will have its own rules for renters, but keep these tips in mind when you're planning (and packing for) a Lowcountry beach rental. You can generally count on the rental company (or owner) to provide sheets, towels, blankets, pillows, paper products, kitchen cleaners (including dishwasher detergent), laundry products, bath soaps, and all your basic housewares.

You, on the other hand, will need to bring your own beach chairs and recreational equipment. You buy your own groceries—including staples like salt, pepper, and other spices plus condiments like ketchup and mayonnaise. You may want to throw in some plastic wrap or foil for leftovers. Also, ask ahead about bike or Moped, crib, and high chair rentals, when appropriate. Don't forget your camera and plenty of film.

Many families make longstanding reservations with the same company and make return visits for several years. They soon establish trusting relationships with agents and property owners that work to everyone's advantage. Here are some of the best options for beach rentals here in the Lowcountry.

Beachwalker Rentals
The Island Center, 3690 Bohicket Rd.,
Ste. 4-D, Johns Island
(843) 768-1777, (800) 334-6308
This independent resort-rental company specializes in Kiawah and Seabrook Island vacations. With almost two decades of experience, the company has built a solid reputation for value and friendly service. Many loyal families return to Beachwalker year after year, with these folks handling all the arrangements from bike rentals to golf. Call for the annual catalog of beachfront and nearby properties and ask about the off-season discounts.

Carroll Realty
103 Palm Blvd., Isle of Palms
(843) 886-9600
This firm which started in 1981 specializes in the sale and rental of resort homes on Isle of Palms and Sullivan's Island. Its offices are between the islands on Palm Boulevard.

Dunes Properties of Charleston
1400 Palm Blvd., Isle of Palms
(843) 886-5600
Specializing in coastal real estate and vacation rentals, Dunes Properties of Charleston has been doing business in the Lowcountry since 1989. Its staff of 15

agents handles rentals on Kiawah, Isle of Palms, Wild Dunes, Sullivan's Island, Dewees Island, Seabrook Island, and Folly Beach. About half this company's business comes from repeat customers who use its services year after year. Vacation planners can request Dunes Properties' annual catalog describing rental listings on the East Islands, West Islands, and Folly Beach. To ask about rental properties on Wild Dunes, call (888) 843-2322. For information about rental properties on Kiawah, call (800) 476-8444.

Great Beach Vacations
1517 Palm Blvd., Ste. C, Isle of Palms
(843) 886-9704, (800) 344-5105
Two Great Beach Center, Kiawah Island
(843) 768-2300, (800) 845-3911
This company offers rental homes, cottages, and villas on Wild Dunes, Isle of Palms, Sullivan's Island, Kiawah Island, and Seabrook Island. Accommodations range from 1 to 9 bedrooms (depending on the island). Golf packages and kids programs are available. They have a yearly catalogue of rental listings that's free upon request.

Fred Holland Realty
50 Center St., Folly Beach
(843) 588-2325
Experience is the key word for Fred Holland Realty when it comes to Folly Beach real estate and rentals. He's been finding vacation homes for Folly visitors for 25 years. The company handles about 150 beach rentals every year ranging from two- and three-bedroom condos to oceanside beach houses and even small apartments. The agents also arrange about 100 long-term (yearly) leases annually. About 65% of their business is repeat customers coming back for more. Their spring

brochure features the year's offerings for summer rentals. Call for more information.

Island Realty
1304 Palm Blvd., Isle of Palms
(843) 886-8144
Since 1977, this firm has been a major player in property sales and resort rentals on Isle of Palms (at Wild Dunes) and Sullivan's Island. Island Realty has 12 sales agents and 20 full-time employees in its resort-rental division. It also has a beachfront meeting and convention center with resort amenities available and golf packages at Wild Dunes.

Islands West
83 Center St., Folly Beach
(843) 588-6699, (800) 951-2470
This company handles real estate in the West Ashley area and exclusively handles Folly Beach rentals. Its office is in the first two-story building you'll see on Center Street as you come off the bridge to the island. It offers a variety of accommodations ranging from the most rustic of basics to oceanfront luxury condominiums. The 6-year-old company is "big enough to serve you and small enough to know you." Write or call for its yearly brochure of Folly Beach properties.

Pam Harrington Exclusives
The Island Center, 3690 Bohicket Rd., Ste. 2-C, Johns Island
(843) 768-0273, (800) 845-6966
This company, with headquarters near Kiawah in The Island Center, has a lion's share of business on Kiawah Island. It's been helping visitors secure luxury accommodations and premium real estate on Kiawah, Seabrook, and Johns Island since 1978. For sales information, call (843) 768-3635.

Shopping

Downtown Charleston
East Cooper
West Ashley
Shopping Centers
and Malls

For a city that's famous for all that's old and historic, shoppers today have easier-than-ever access to all things that are new and exciting. From fashions to home furnishings, from bestsellers to sporting goods, the Lowcountry has it all. The older shopping haunts have been updated and expanded plus whole new shopping destinations have sprung up in high-growth areas where the expanding population has called for them.

No matter how you look at it, the shopping opportunities here in the Lowcountry are almost unlimited. Communities that were geographically isolated only a dozen years ago are now within an easy commute to a diverse and interesting commercial/shopping adventure. The future looks bright and more shoppers are drawn to the area every day.

The variety ranges in size from specialty shop enclaves in downtown nooks and crannies to major shopping centers and the seemingly endless random strip malls. To provide a useful index for your shopping needs, we've categorized these shopping adventures by location and subject matter.

We'll start with the major shopping areas of downtown Charleston. Some of these famous old streets have been shopping meccas for two hundred years. Other streets have only recently become decidedly commercial. Much of downtown's Historic District houses a mix of shops and homes and every other aspect of daily life—with a certain deference made to keeping the historic fabric of the city intact.

Next, we'll survey the brightest and best shopping opportunities in the surrounding areas—like we've done with our chapters on accommodations, restaurants, and neighborhoods. Within each geographic designation, however, we've categorized stores by the type of merchandise that's dominant there. Included are the most exclusive boutiques and the just-as-welcome discount stores catering to the dollar-conscious consumer. In each case, we've tried to identify businesses with items of particular interest for our visitors and those frequented by a local clientele.

Finally, we'll offer newcomers a brief rundown of the major shopping malls here in the Lowcountry. We hope our guide is a tempting sample of the variety and quality of shopping options in this area. We do encourage you, however, to venture off the beaten track from time to time—new and hidden surprises are everywhere!

Downtown Charleston

King Street

Let's start with King Street, the mother of all Charleston shopping districts. This is the essence of downtown shopping, and it has been for a couple hundred years. While the street actually begins high on the Peninsula and ends as a narrow throughway past an extraordinary collection of pre-Revolutionary private homes, the real business and shopping district begins at about Mary Street and continues with greater intensity until it crosses Broad Street.

King Street is a busy two-way street until you reach Calhoun Street, where it becomes narrower and one-way heading south toward The Battery. Time was that King Street, like many of the other shopping thoroughfares in America's downtowns, was said to be dying. But the building of Charleston Place, a huge hotel and shopping complex, turned the tide. (Charleston Place was first an Omni hotel and later an Orient Express property; see our Hotels and Motels chapter.) It didn't hurt at all that Charleston Place contained a ground-floor shopping arcade featuring world-famous labels and merchandise. Today all of King Street is alive and well and enjoying a latter-day renaissance (particularly above Calhoun Street) that's amazing to watch. Old storefronts and facades are being restored and new construction seems always under way—from Calhoun to Mary Street and above. Apparently, there's no stopping in sight.

The area from Queen to Beaufain Streets is generally considered King Street's Antiques District (extensively covered in our Antiques chapter). Most other shopping adventures on King Street are found in the blocks between Beaufain and Calhoun. With the refurbishing of the Westin Francis Marion Hotel at Calhoun and King, plus the complete renovation of Marion Square (park), the shopping options don't necessarily cease at Calhoun anymore.

You'll find several chain stores along King Street. For fashions you can check out Abercrombie & Fitch, 260 King St., (843) 853-5888; Ann Taylor, 267 King St., (843) 722-8231; Laura Ashley, 146 Market St., The Shops at Charleston Place, (843) 723-3967; Banana Republic Men, 249 King St., (843) 722-6681; Banana Republic Women, 245 King St., (843) 958-8050; Gap, 269 King St., (843) 577-2498; Express, 230 King St., The Shops at Charleston Place, (843) 577-0379; Saks Fifth Avenue, 211 King St., Majestic Square, (843) 853-9888; Talbots, 238 King St., (843) 723-4802. You're also sure to recognize Victoria's Secret, 254 King St., (843) 723-0332 and The Body Shop, 216 King St., (843) 723-3300.

Listed below, by category of merchandise, are some of the more unique shops you'll find on King Street.

Bookstores

Boomer's Books & Collectibles
420 King St.
(843) 722-2666

This upper King Street bookshop buys, sells, and trades books. While popular reading material is the main thrust of the store, rare books, collectibles, Lowcountry memorabilia, and souvenirs are also for sale. Mind you, this store is a fooler. Its tiny storefront belies the seemingly endless series of rooms housing a vast selection of reading matter for every taste.

College of Charleston Bookstore
160 Calhoun St.
(843) 953-5518

The College of Charleston's bookstore, actually on Calhoun Street just off King, is typical of university bookstores. But it also carries a nice section representing local authors and local interest books as well as faculty publications. It's also fun to poke around in the college textbook sections just to see what's happening these days. Time flies.

The Preservation Society of Charleston
147 King St.
(843) 723-4381

The Preservation Society of Charleston Bookstore has what may be the most comprehensive area collection of books about Charleston, the Lowcountry, and all things Southern. Many Charleston and Lowcountry authors are represented here. You also can shop for art books, academic works, entertaining literature, and even some recorded material. (See our Attractions chapter for more on The Preservation Society of Charleston.)

University Books of Charleston
360 King St.
(843) 853-8700

This bookstore is not officially affiliated with the College of Charleston but is a popular source for college students and a place to browse for interesting academic titles. Along with textbooks and reference materials, University Books sells school logo items—everything from T-shirts to bumper stickers for your favorite college team.

Candy

Godiva Chocolatier, Inc.
The Shops at Charleston Place,
142 Market St.
(843) 722-6045

Tucked seductively inside Charleston Place's trendy shopping arcade, this is where you'll find those famous Godiva chocolates, loved the world over by serious chocoholics. Go all out and take home a whole box, or taste just the individual confections that catch your eye. Be prepared for the not-too-subtle aromatherapy when you walk in the door. It's very beguiling.

Children's Clothing

Sarah Anne's Ltd.
279 King St.
(843) 722-8675

In addition to wonderful toys and gifts, Sarah Anne's sells adorable children's clothes and accessories. You'll find Viva La Fete, Bailey Boys, Simi, Feltman Brothers among the lines in this upscale boutique. This is the exclusive outlet in downtown Charleston for Madame Alexander dolls and Steiff. Check out the hair accessories too. (Also see the Women's Clothing listings in the King Street section of this chapter.)

Straightlace
290 King St.
(843) 723-9571

If there is a little prince or princess in your life, ogle the display window at Straightlace. Handmade, special-order children's clothing such as smocked or embroidered linen suits, smocked coats, and christening gowns are all specialties. The off-the-rack clothing and gift selections are charming.

Worthwhile
268 King St.
(843) 723-4418

This boutique sells 100-percent cotton clothing for children and adults (see the Women's Clothing section under King

Street in this chapter). Shop here for earth-friendly, contemporary clothes that feel comfortable in the Charleston heat.

Gifts

Brittain's of Charleston
180 King St.
(843) 723-7309

When it's time to shop for a wedding or anniversary gift, this should be your first stop. Brittain's deserves a gold star for its complete selection of crystal and fine china. It carries Baccarat, Orrefors, Lalique, and Tiffany as well as a wonderful collection of accent pieces and decorating accessories. This is where many Charleston brides register their china and sterling patterns.

Con Garbo
165 King St.
(843) 853-0100

While Con Garbo holds its own among the antiques shops in King Street's famous antiques district, it is also a great resource of fine, imported Italian gift items. Sterling, leather, hand-painted dinnerware, and fine stationery supplies for the well-kept desk are samples of the merchandise on hand. To get to know the store better, Con Garbo hosts patrons to Café Expresso every Saturday from 2 to 4 PM. Come browse and learn about this relative newcomer to King Street with their wares and antique wonders from Italy. (See our Antiques chapter).

The Preservation Society Bookstore
147 King St.
(843) 722-4630

Along with all that's printed on Charleston and the Lowcountry, this terrific store offers local crafts, art prints, even recordings of Lowcountry lore told in the local Gullah dialect. Here, too, are the architectural drawings of Jim Polzois, whose studies of the city's architectural vernacular are beautifully done. They're simply the best available. (See previous listing under Bookstores.)

Riverrun
6 Beaufain St.
(843) 723-0200

This store is riding the crest of the new passion for all things Irish. Look here for fine imported Irish linens, crystal, Belleek china, jewelry, and women's apparel. The shop carries some home accents in pewter, brass, and stone, as well. Here's a great shopping venue for wedding gifts and anniversary presents or for starting family heirlooms of your own. Some brides have even shopped here for Celtic stationery for unique wedding invitations.

The Silver Puffin
278 King St.
(843) 723-7900

This King Street gift shop has a large selection of cards, mirrors, pottery, jewelry, and glassware. Some of the charming merchandise is domestic, some imported. The owners ship anywhere, so tourists can buy without having to carry things around during their Charleston adventures.

Uncork
333 King St.
(843) 577-9303

Sometimes, there's nothing like having a nice bottle of wine to enjoy in your hotel or B&B room at night after a day of shopping or sightseeing in Charleston. This shop, in the heart of the King Street shopping district, is the place to find just the right vintage. They carry a wide selection of wines and champagnes for all budgets as well as microbrews, cheese, and wine accessories. It's a good resource for finding a nice gift bottle for a friend or housesitter keeping the pets back home.

Home Accents and Decor

Claire Murray
295 King St.
(843) 722-0900

The artist Claire Murray has almost single-handedly revived the Old World art of rug hooking. She has created a worldwide market for her exquisite hooked rug designs, and this shop is her showcase.

Needleworkers love her kits for rugs, needlepoint, counted cross-stitch and knitting because they come with complete instructions and all the necessary materials. Many customers only know Claire Murray from her catalog; here's your chance to see her whole line in person.

Fred
237 King St.
(843) 723-5699

This smart, trendy resource for kitchen basics, high-tech housewares, and contemporary nifties is so chic you'll think you stepped into the culinary fantasy of a Danish designer. The emphasis here is on line and function, and almost everything you see is stark white. What a concept! What a neat store! But who the heck is Fred?

Historic Charleston Reproductions Shop
105 Broad St.
(843) 723-8292

The Reproductions Shop for the Historic Charleston Foundation is at the corner of King and Broad Streets. It's the showroom for home furnishings, accessories, and giftware authorized by the foundation. All items for sale have an accompanying product card explaining the item's historical significance to Charleston's history and the Charlestonian lifestyle. The shop features Baker Furniture's Historic Charleston collection of 18th- and 19th-century reproductions of furniture from famous Charleston homes. It also carries dinnerware patterns and brass accessories, fabrics, and wallpaper as well as rugs and jewelry. (For more, see our chapter on Architectural Preservation.)

Holiday Traditions Inc.
356 King St.
(843) 723-1020

No matter what the calendar says, it's always Christmastime here. Whether you're looking for holiday gifts or decorations for the home, this is a cornucopia of Yuletide celebratory glee. Look for the European glass ornaments featuring Christopher Radko, Old World Christmas, and the Polonaise Collection. Tourists love to take home a Charleston ornament for the Christmas tree, and locals know they can find decorative items for other holidays as well. Thanksgiving, Easter, and Halloween get the full treatment here, and it's all fun and attractive.

Le Creuset
241 King St.
(843) 723-4191

Most folks don't know that the famous French enameled cast-iron cookware known as Le Creuset has a manufacturing plant right here in the Lowcountry. It's in Yemassee, South Carolina, about an hour's drive from Charleston, and the good news is the factory outlet on King Street. The ordinarily pricey cookware is considerably discounted here—a boon to gourmets who happen across this downtown store. You're likely to pick up some wine and champagne accessories, too, along with some nifty cooking gadgets.

Palais Royal
The Shops at Charleston Place,
246 King St.
(843) 853-4331

This is the store for fine French linens—everything for the bed, bath, and table. All the merchandise is natural fiber—either linen or Egyptian cotton. Palais Royal also carries goose-down duvets and pillows that veritably evoke pastel mornings on the Left Bank. To complete the scene, the shop carries a variety of hand-painted porcelain and other table graces. If you love Paris, there's a little bit of it here.

Raymond Clark
429 King St.
(843) 723-7555

Only a block from the visitor center, Raymond Clark offers affordable but original American crafts. From interesting, one-of-a-kind gifts to handmade jewelry and very arty home accessories, the look is contemporary and distinctive. Half store, half gallery, this is really fun to see.

Studio
314 King St.
(843) 722-2762

For those in the market for upscale contemporary look, Studio is a cornucopia of merchandise and ideas. The key word, here, is contemporary. They carry lighting and interesting accent pieces plus furnishing by famous names like Nambè, Knoll, American Leather, Artemide, and the Museum of Modern Art (MOMA). They can work with your interior designer or outsource decorating services for the special "look" you're seeking.

Jewelry

Charles Kerrison and Company
285 King St.
(843) 577-6104

This impressive and trusted store has a reputation for carrying superior merchandise including Baume & Mercier and Maurice LaCroix watches. Look here for Waterford crystal, Mikimoto pearls, and Fabergé. Many a bride has found her dream ring at Kerrison, and scores of graduates have been remembered with fine jewelry from here. It is also a wonderful source for wedding gifts, and the window displays are always elegant.

Croghan's Jewel Box
308 King St.
(843) 723-3594

This is a shop that some will remember as a tiny space unobtrusively tucked away behind a small awning on King Street but filled with quality merchandise. It's tiny no more. After 80 years as a Charleston shopping institution, this family-owned jewelry store finally has the space to show its worth. Now, expanded into the space next door, Croghan's carries exquisite jewelry and wonderful gifts for all the important occasions. The rings are to die for, and there seems to be no end to the trays of earrings, shelves of silver and crystal, and other delights. A Croghan's package delivered to your door or under the tree—sometimes the smaller the better—is cause for real excitement. (See our Antiques chapter.)

Joint Venture Estate Jewelers
185 King St.
(843) 722-6730

Joint Venture is unusual in that it focuses on jewelry on consignment. The inventory at any time can include heirloom and contemporary jewelry as well as watches, and the staff is happy to appraise, restore, or repair your possessions. (See our Antiques chapter.)

Norma May International
315 King St.
(843) 577-8884

This high-end resource for truly distinctive fashion art and accessories offers an international collection of one-of-a-kind and limited edition jewelry. Also, check out their selection of beautiful silk shawls, scarves, and wraps. This is clearly one for the bold and the beautiful and those who dare to wear the different.

Perry's of Charleston
233 King St.
(843) 958-8866

Perry's of Charleston has a fascinating shop on Charleston's legendary King Street dealing in antique, estate, and fine jewelry and one-of-a-kind pieces. There are literally hundreds of choices. Owner and president Ernest Perry has more than 30 years' experience in this highly specialized industry. He and his associates offer a full range of appraisal services including retail replacement and fair market value for estate, donation, gift, damage, customs evaluation, or divorce settlement purposes. (See our Antiques chapter.)

Men's Clothing

319 Men
319 King St.
(843) 577-8807

Part of the King Street men's clothing scene for 16 years now, this shop is a favorite among discriminating shoppers whose tastes edge toward Italian designs. The owners of 319 Men claim to carry the most recognizable designer labels in town, and they probably do. You can always count on personalized service and a pleasant shopping experience.

A.J. Davis & Company
296 King St.
(843) 577-3088

This store joined the King Street cadre of men's clothiers several years ago and has been a pacesetter ever since. The accent here is on quality and service—the store even delivers to downtown hotels. Look for designer names such as Barry Bricken, Zegna, Ike Behar, Zanella, Kenneth Cole, Joseph Abboud, and Corneliai. You'll find everything from formal wear to sportswear and accessories to boot. A recent addition, a ladies boutique, A.J. Davis for Her, carries such designers as Bernard Zins, Margaret O'Leary, and Barry Bricken.

Ben Silver Collection
149 King St.
(843) 231-7458, (800) 221-4671,
(800) 577-4556

Here is a must-see, whether you're shopping for men's or women's clothing. Ben Silver only maintains shops in Charleston and London, so here's your one chance on this side of the Atlantic. Along with ultra-fine British and American clothes and furnishings, you'll also discover exclusive blazer buttons for virtually every college or university in the United States and abroad. In fact, Ben Silver carries button sets for more than 600 fraternal organizations and military schools as well. It's a classy place for a nifty gift idea.

Berlin's Clothiers
114 King St.
(843) 722-1665

Since 1883, Berlin's has been a Charleston institution. Four generations of young Charleston gentlemen have purchased their first good suit from Berlin's. You can find all the classics here, from wing-tip shoes to navy blazers, knit shirts to madras shorts. Look for European designer names, too, among the classics such as Brioni, Canali, Hickey-Freeman, Hart Schaffner &

Marx, and more. Berlin's offers custom sizing, a complete formal wear department, and a big-and-tall section. Patrons love the convenient parking across the street for their own shopping or shopping for something nice for the lady in their life from Berlin's for Women next door. (See listing under Women's Clothing.)

Grady Errin & Co.
313 King St.
(843) 722-1776

The sign says, "Classic Clothiers to Gentlemen," and that pretty much sums it up for this shop. This smart store is among King Street's collection of fine men's shops, and it's a real contender. You'll find a complete selection of traditional blazers, yachting wear, sports clothes, and accessories. Expect quality, style, and gracious Old World service.

M. Dumas & Sons
294 King St.
(843) 723-8603

Charleston men and boys have been buy-

ing their outdoor sports clothes at M. Dumas since 1919. This store is all about practicality mixed with style and boasts one of the most complete inventories—hunting jackets, camouflage hats, flannel shirts, corduroy pants, shoes, and even snakeskin boots—in town. Dumas was doing the "hunting look" before doing the hunting look was cool.

Margaritaville
282 King St.
(843) 577-4145

"Parrot Heads" will recognize the name instantly. This new store is Jimmy Buffett's own 2,000-square-foot retail outlet on Charleston's King Street selling men's and women's super casual clothing, Buffett's compact discs, and assorted Jimmy Buffett memorabilia. JB loves Charleston and this is his second retail store—the other being in Key West, of course. Here is a haven for chilled-out college kids and good fun for the laid-back crowd.

Max's
328 King St.
(843) 722-4024

This attractive men's shop always has a handsome collection in its display windows, offering a virtual visual index of what the well-dressed (and inherently conservative, of course) Charleston man wears at work and play. It's been serving patrons since 1933 with trusted brand names such as Corbin, Burberry, Southwick, Robert Talbott, Hilton, Bass, Hickey-Freeman, Gitman Brothers, and many others.

Natural Beauty

Spa Adagio
387 King St.
(843) 577-2444

This is one of those places you can go for those special pamperings that bring back harmony to your life. The Spa Adagio therapists know just the song your sore muscles need to hear (through massage). Their soft aromas sing to your senses and their relaxing sounds soothe your soul.

You'll find Spa Adagio in the lower level of the Francis Marion Hotel.

Stella Nova
292 King St.
(843) 722-9797
78 Society St.
(843) 723-0909
1320 Theatre Dr. (Towne Centre),
Mt. Pleasant
(843) 884-3838

Stella Nova sells Aveda pure plant products and services for the hair, skin, and body. Check out the natural solutions to stress, ranging from aromatherapy to basic, old-fashioned pampering. Ask about the Micro Nova Botanical Salon on-site with Stella Nova's natural hair-color process and skin-care programs. Call (843) 723-0909 for day spa appointments.

Shoes

Bob Ellis
332 King St.
(843) 722-2515, (843) 722-2605,
(843) 723-5204, (800) 253-8628

Experience the shoe-store phenomenon that is Bob Ellis. People from all over the country make the pilgrimage to Charleston to do just that. Suffice it to say that the downtown tradition's three telephone lines into the women's section say something about the store's popularity. High fashion, a huge selection, and friendly, highly qualified sales folk create the magic. They carry women's sizes 4 to 12 AAAA, AAA, AA, and B. In men's, they carry sizes 6 to 16 and widths from A to EEE. If you love shoes (and fine matching bags), don't miss Bob Ellis.

Ellison's Shoes
307 King St.
(843) 577-2297, (800) 611-2353

Ellison's is another well-respected, top-of-the-line store that specializes in women's shoes for walking, comfort, and leisure. The shop's Arche line is high fashion and comfortable at the same time. It also carries Mephisto. Generations of Charlestonians have shopped here with complete satisfaction.

Pete Banis Shoes
297 King St.
(843) 577-0950
Northcutt Plaza, Mt. Pleasant
(843) 881-4414

This is a great shoe shop for the young and trendy at heart. It carries women's shoes by names such as Van Eli, Unisa, and American Eagle. Expect to find style, selection, service, and smart shoes with a little sass.

Rangoni of Florence Shoes
270 King St.
(843) 577-9554

Many think the level of personal service here is simply the best in town. Rangoni's fine collection of Italian-designed shoes for men and women is superb in both quality and style. For women, the store carries (even in hard-to-find sizes) the elegant Rangoni shoes, along with the more fashion-forward Anne Klein, Claudia Ciuti, and Clark. Also, look for Donald J. Pliner, Andre Assous, and others. For just the right accessory to complement those stylish new shoes, choose from one of the largest selections of handbags in town. Men's lines of footwear include Cole-Haan, Bally, Moreschi, Donald J. Pliner, Clark, and Johnston & Murphy among others.

Sports

The Extra Mile
336 King St.
(843) 853-9987

This is a service-oriented, specialty sports shop with products preferred by competitive runners and swimmers. It sells Nike, New Balance, Asics, Saucony, Zoot Sugoi, and other name brands. It also has a shop in the Mt. Pleasant area.

Half Moon Outfitters
320 King St.
(843) 853-0990
425 Coleman, Blvd., Mt. Pleasant
(843) 881-9472

When friends were gearing up to travel through South America one Christmas season, where did they head first? That's right—Half Moon. They were after brands such as Patagonia, Simple Shoe, and Birkenstock. Half Moon carries other lines in its wide assortment of supplies for outdoor activity.

Sportsman Shop
359 King St.
(843) 722-0072
Shop here for sporting equipment of all types, plus clothing and accessories. For years the simply named Sportsman Shop has served the needs of area school teams as well as the serious and weekend athletes of Charleston.

Women's Clothing

Anne's
312 King St.
(843) 577-3262
Anne's has developed a loyal following among petites in the community because of the wonderful selection, all the way down to size 3. There are happy customers in all the other sizes as well (up to 24½), because Anne's carries name-brand merchandise and gives personalized service. Many a bride has dressed herself and her wedding party in beautiful gowns from Anne's. Shop here for contemporary clothing appropriate for business and casual occasions as well as evening attire.

Berlin's for Women
114 King St.
(843) 723-5591
At the corner of King and Broad is family-owned Berlin's—one of Charleston's oldest and nicest clothing stores. Established in 1883, Berlin's built a reputation as a fashion landmark specializing in sportswear, lifestyle, and special occasion dressing. It carries one of the largest selections of evening and special occasion dresses in the Southeast and attracts customers from all over. Some of its designer lines include Nicole Miller, Tahari, Wolford, and Zelda. A beautifully renovated store, excellent service, and free parking across the street make it a pleasure to shop here.

Bits of Lace
212 King St.
(843) 577-0999
For sexy, pretty lingerie, visit Bits of Lace. Please note: These are undergarments that should be treated with care. In fact, many are silk and should be washed only by hand. Most items are simple, top-of-the-line articles of clothing that definitely give the impression that someone cares.

Christian Michi
220 King St.
(843) 723-0575
At the corner of King and Market Streets, across from Saks Fifth Avenue, Christian Michi offers collections for women by fashion designers such as Etro, Piazza Sempione, Strennesse, and Alberta Ferretti. The shop also sells Kiehl cosmetics and toiletries plus assorted home furnishings like imported crystal, and Diptyque candles. Check out their handmade 22-karat gold jewelry.

Ellington
193 King St.
(843) 722-7999
Classic style with a new arrangement is Ellington's claim to fame. The retailers say they are to clothing and furniture what jazz is to music. Some of the chic lines of women's clothing they offer include Barry Bricken, Margaret O'Leary, and Zanella. Accents and accessories include Joan & David belts and purses. Things for the home include lamps (new and old), bedding, and some American and European antiques (from couches to accent tables). Look for names like Pacifica and (Italian) Dialogica. Ellington ships anywhere.

Granny's Goodies Vintage Clothing
301 King St.
(843) 577-6200
This is a decidedly acquired taste, but for those who love the avant-garde, Granny's Goodies is a gold mine. Everything from old designer labels to castoffs from estate sales—the goods are there for the getting.

It's not unheard of to choose an ensemble from Granny's, hit the club or the art gallery openings, and make a fashion splash. Movie makers and costumers love this place. And the prices are right.

Luna
334 King St.
(843) 853-LUNA

Like its sister store in Columbia, South Carolina, this new King Street shop (where Elza's was formerly located) features clothing, jewelry, accessories, shoes, candles, Mexican pottery, and home furnishings. Eclectic style, lots of color, and sheer exuberance are the keynotes here.

Urban Cotton
287 King St.
(843) 937-8500

Southerners wish they could dress like this every day—hooray for coolness, comfort, and class! Urban Cotton clothes are casual but more than a little sexy in that they are so soft and subtle. This is where you'll find that essential little black dress and all sorts of other surprises.

Nancy's
342 King St.
(843) 722-1272

Nancy's is another interesting, upscale boutique on King Street that's a must-see for ladies with a strong sense of style. Look here for such designer labels as Parameter, View Collection, and Essendi. Of special note are the one-of-a-kind metal bracelets imported from Europe exclusively for Nancy's. Belts of leather, chain, and even rhinestones are among the accents found here. The look is chic but timeless—appropriate for the young and the merely young at heart.

Putumayo
445 King St.
(843) 958-0900

Formerly of New York City, this company moved lock, stock, and barrel to Charleston in 1997 and opened its retail outlet on Charleston's King Street. The shop sells fashions collected from exotic markets all over the world. Its contemporary, well-priced women's apparel consists of exclusive prints, embroideries, and tapestries that are comfortable and casual yet unusual and bold. This shop appeals to women from age 18 to 60.

RTW
186 King St.
(843) 577-9748

For interesting clothes that are always on the cutting edge of fashion, visit RTW. Look for designers such as Sylvia Heisel, Maria V. Pinto, Peter Coen, and Loree Rodkin Jewelry, and others who present trunk shows here with some frequency. RTW is diagonally across King Street from George C. Birlant & Company (see our Antiques chapter).

Sarah Anne's Ltd.
279 King St.
(843) 722-8675

Sarah Anne's sells novelty sweaters, tops, and jackets for women by designers such as Michael Simon, Marisa Christina, Christine Rotelli, Robert Scott, David Brooks, Susan Bristol, and Geiger of Austria. In addition to good-looking, fun clothes, Sarah Anne's offers entertainment for impatient youngsters with toys and live animals on the prowl or in the pen, depending on the need for confinement. (See our previous listing under Children's Clothing.)

Worthwhile
268 King St.
(843) 723-4418

Selling unique casual and contemporary clothing made from only natural fibers, Worthwhile is, well, a worthwhile boutique on Charleston's trendy King Street. Look for brand names such as FLAX, Kishori, Jeanine Payer, and Giraudon. (See the previous Children's Clothing listings in the King Street section of this chapter.)

Meeting Street and the City Market

The cross street that, along with Broad Street, defines the "Four Corners of Law" is Meeting Street, another wide avenue of history, prosperity, and faith. Here, after all, is the location of the original church that gave the street its name (see the Historic Churches section of our Attractions chapter). It runs virtually the length of the Peninsula and ends at White Point Gardens.

Meeting Street boasts many of Charleston's most famous and historic homes, but above Broad Street, the scenery changes from residential to commercial. Here, again, the options run the gamut from banks to museums to office buildings, hotels, and churches. But you should get to know a gem or two along the way that offer valuable information along with quality merchandise.

Meeting Street takes you smack-dab into the historic Market, one of the most colorful and popular tourist destinations in the city. The Market's shopping area is flanked by busy, one-way streets (called N. and S. Market Streets) and East Bay Street.

The Market may be one of the oldest "shopping malls" in the United States. It was built on land that Charles Cotesworth Pinckney, who was a signer of the U.S. Constitution, ceded to the city in the 18th century for use as a public market. Made up of low brick buildings that have survived hurricanes, earthquakes, tornadoes, fires, and even Civil War bombardment, these sheds also were used by vendors selling fish, meat, and vegetables in bygone days.

The figurehead building that gives a dignified front to all the Market's craziness is the 1841 Market Hall, designed by Charleston's famous 19th-century architect, E.B. White.

This faithful copy of a Roman Temple sitting where Market Street intersects Meeting is now owned by the city and has recently undergone extensive renovation. But the building is better known to locals as The Confederate Museum, run by the Daughters of the

A Lowcountry lacemaker displays her handiwork in Charleston's historic market. PHOTO: DAVID C. BERRY

Confederacy. To visitors it's a prelude to the cornucopia of color and noise, food and fun the legendary Market has in store.

Originally built as a municipal shelter for merchants and farmers bringing their wares and produce into the city for sale, the spirit of the Market survives today. Everything from odd pieces of sterling silver flatware for the table to handmade children's toys and even tie-dyed clothes is offered on tables and from booths set up daily by a cadre of merchants. The traditional Charleston basket ladies are here in force with their signature sweetgrass baskets galore (see the Close-up on sweetgrass baskets in this chapter). Artists ply matted and framed prints of famous Charleston scenes, and you can even buy packages of mixed rice and beans—all ready to cook up as "Hoppin' John" or black-eyed pea soup.

The Center Market, stretching from Meeting to Church streets, is a string of specialty shops, boutiques, and eateries. Here, vendors of all types rent spaces and booths to hawk their wares.

Then at N. Market Street, Rainbow Market is an unusual cluster of small shops. Each has a separate facade but is situated within the parameters of two 19th-century buildings. From Birkenstock shoes to needlepoint patterns, the merchandise and services in Rainbow Market appeal to a varied clientele.

Continuing along the open air section, between Church and East Bay Streets, local artisans and international importers sell their wares. Here you can watch the local "basket ladies" actually weaving their regional treasures—sweetgrass baskets of all sizes and shapes.

Sooner or later, everybody ends up at the Market—Charleston's traditional melting pot. For shoppers looking for the unusual in jewelry, art, or crafts, for tourists in search of the quintessential souvenir, for college kids on spring break too sunburned for the beach, and even for the occasional out-of-work musician who will play for loose change, all Charleston roads lead to the Market.

Galleries and restaurants flank the Market on both sides—some of which come alive at night as jazz clubs and gourmet restaurants. All the chefs have their own slant on Charleston's "she-crab soup," and the seafood is always fresh and succulent.

The Market has become something of a second stop for any and all other events going on in the city. So it's a popular nighttime destination for the young and restless.

The Market is a must-see for every Charleston visitor—and its magic seems to lie in its eternal spontaneity. It's an ever-changing kaleidoscope of things and smells and sounds and people who all seem to be in a carnival mood. It's different every day; and it's always the same. The Market is a Charleston enigma. Don't miss it.

Bookstores

Chapter Two Book Store/
Chapter Two Book Store for Kids
249 Meeting St.
(843) 722-4238

Chapter Two for adults and its expanded section devoted to children are wonderful sources for books of all kinds. The staff is knowledgeable about the inventory, and what they don't have they'll order for you. Chapter Two is a most gracious supporter of local novelists, and book signings are fairly regular happenings. Don't forget to look upstairs where their extensive collection of travel books is found, and they display a comprehensive selection of local interest titles and Lowcountry authors. There's also a limited amount of free parking to the rear of the store—just off Wentworth St.

Historic Charleston Foundation
Museum Shop and Bookstore
108 Meeting St.
(843) 724-8484

This store is in the Frances R. Edmunds Center for Historic Preservation and, as you might expect, stocks books regarding preservation and restoration. From beautiful coffee table books to fascinating reference material, choose from works about everything from gardening to selecting

Victorian house colors. The store's selection of gift items also is keyed to the Charleston taste with brasses and china accents and linen tableware. (For more, see our Attractions chapter and the Gifts listings in the Meeting Street section of this chapter.)

Waldenbooks
120 Market St.,
The Shops at Charleston Place
(843) 723-6186
2070 Sam Rittenberg Blvd., Citadel Mall
(843) 766-5879
Waldenbooks, a national chain bookstore featuring a wide selection of reading material, opened in 1997 in Charleston Place. The shop's windows face the busy traffic at the corner of Market and Meeting in the upscale downtown shopping area and frequently display interesting titles. Park in the Charleston Place garage if you can, and expect to be seduced along your way to the bookstore by the sights and smells of the other merchants' wares and goodies inside the complex. All the latest bestsellers, a wide range of specialty titles, and a complete selection of local interest topics can be found here and in the chain's other Charleston locations.

Candy

Lucas Belgian Chocolate Inc.
73 State St.
(843) 722-0461
You can't miss the cheerful pink awning just a half-block south of S. Market Street next to Häagen-Dazs Ice Cream Shoppe. This was one of the first truly fine chocolatiers to open in the Market area, and its longevity is fair testimony to the quality of its chocolate and presentation skills. Not only is just about every chocolate confection offered, but your purchases are also beautifully wrapped and the service is charming.

Market Street Sweets
100 N. Market St.
(843) 722-1397
As if the distractions of the Market aren't

enough, here's a candy store that hands out free samples. Woe be to the poor dieter who happens to pass by here. Market Street Sweets opened in this location in 1984 selling gourmet Southern candies. The devil has had his way with sweet-tooth sufferers here ever since. The shop is most famous for its pralines but also turns out beautiful bear claws, chocolates, and other homemade specialties. This is a first stop for many Charleston visitors who have passed this way before. Market Street Sweets ships anywhere, so no one is really immune.

The Peanut Shop of Charleston
76 N. Market St.
(843) 723-6052
Down in the Market where the tourists swarm, the Peanut Shop offers a Low-country tradition by the tinful: peanuts. We're talkin' only the top-grade, Southern peanuts that are hand-cooked in pure peanut oil and vacuum-packed in resealable tins. The irresistible marketing ploy here is the free samples the shop offers—sure to close a sale. Once you're sold, you can look over the other fine foods and gifts, including the delicious Smithfield hams.

Flowers and Garden Accents

Blumengarten
62 Queen St.
(843) 722-4266
What do you get when you cross a German-trained architect with a floral shop in Charleston? The answers are: Blumengarten and the best designs in flowers and floral decor for special occasions this side of the Rhine. No two arrangements come out of Blumengarten alike. The shop's bulletin board filled with "thank yous" from grateful customers testifies to that. The folks here do everything with equal flair—from giant Charleston weddings to the simplest gesture of hospitality. The shop is like a breath of Europe just off Meeting Street on Queen. Look for the simple sign and a doorway bursting with blooms.

Charleston Gardens
61 Queen St.
(843) 723-0252
Across Meeting Street from the Mills House and half a block or so down Queen is this popular shop offering beautiful home and garden furnishings. Here, you'll find English garden furniture, statuary, fountains, hand-thrown pottery, handcrafted ironwork, garden books and tools, topiary, paintings, and prints. Charleston Gardens always has a great gift idea for that hard-to-shop-for friend with a green thumb.

Charleston Hammock Co.
75 S. Market St.
(843) 723-3011
There's nothing quite so Southern as a hammock in the summertime. That's why real, hand-tied Southern hammocks are so popular—here in the Lowcountry and even in the North. Here's a resource for genuine, front (or back) porch, sip-your-lemonade hammocks in a variety of sizes and configurations. The Hammock Co. will ship your purchase anywhere, so what's holding you back? A little rope?

Gifts
Alpha Dog Omega Cat
40 Archdale St.
(843) 723-1579
In Majestic Square on the corner of Market and Archdale Streets, this shop is strictly for the dogs (and cats). Gifts range from gourmet pet biscuits, designer collars, and leashes to jewelry, toys, and clothes. We're talking indulgence here! And this shop is serious about it all. Only a pet lover would really understand.

Carolina Wine & Cheese
54½ Wentworth St.
(843) 577-6144
A half-block off Meeting Street on Wentworth is this tiny shop specializing in wine-and-cheese gift baskets and picnic setups. Call ahead for special occasions, or drop in for the selection of fine wines, beers, and champagne (domestic and imported). Those into home brewing can find supplies and equipment to make their own labels. Look for special, imported meats and cheeses to make your picnic complete and unforgettable.

Cat's in the Doghouse
40 N. Market St., Rainbow Market
(843) 853-1915
As the name implies, this is a shop for pet lovers who go all out when shopping for their four-legged friends. There are gifts galore for the humans, too, who love (and spoil) their pets. Collars, toys, treats, and other goodies await, plus name-brand art objects and humorous gifts dedicated to pet-lovers. Located in the Rainbow Market where so many other gift items are found, this shop is an impromptu reminder that our furry friends are worthy of our devotion, as well.

The Charleston Museum Gift Shop
360 Meeting St.
(843) 722-2996
Here in America's oldest municipal museum, there's a gift area that's both comprehensive and tasteful. The emphasis is on items (such as books, jewelry, models, textiles, and educational toys) that have some connection to Charleston and the Lowcountry. It's an ideal place to pick up a souvenir from your vacation while visiting the must-see museum (see the Other Sites and Museums section of our Attractions chapter as well as Kidstuff).

Gibbes Museum of Art Shop
135 Meeting St.
(843) 722-2706
The shop at the Gibbes is just inside the front doors of the museum and is open to the public with no admission charge. This is one of the Lowcountry's best stops for art books, jewelry, stationery, small reproductions, and art prints of all kinds. Many locals go in early November for the best selection of fine Christmas cards in the city. (For more on the Gibbes Museum of Art, see our Attractions, The Arts, and Kidstuff chapters.)

When searching for gifts, don't forget the Gibbes Museum of Art. Many of the locals go here early in November for one of the Lowcountry's best selections of Christmas cards. PHOTO: COURTESY OF GIBBES MUSEUM OF ART

**Historic Charleston Foundation
Museum Shop and Bookstore
108 Meeting St.
(843) 724-8484**

A stop at the Frances R. Edmunds Center for Historic Preservation is usually for visitor orientation and resource offerings on preservation and restoration, but this also is easily one of the best gift boutiques in town. Miniatures, reproductions in brass and china, books, textiles, and even some crafts abound here. Quality reigns, even in gifts for the children. (See our Attractions chapter and the Bookstores listing for Meeting Street earlier in this chapter.)

**House of Versailles
129-A Market St.
(843) 722-4242, (800) 264-2506**

This is more than a resource for famous men's and women's fragrances, it's a place where you can have your compatibility tested for various scents. Located just across the street from Charleston Place, you can research hard-to-find fragrances here, as well. Expect to find such designer names as Annick Goutal, Comptoir Sud Pacifique, Lady Primrose, Jean Patou, Caron, and Givenchy. Attractive bottles for holding your distinctive selections are available for gift presentation.

**Kites Fly'n Hi
40 N. Market St., Rainbow Market
(843) 577-3529**

Something about flying a kite brings out the best in people. That's the philosophy behind this colorful little shop in Rainbow Market that is all about kites—of every kind and size. Look here for diamonds, deltas, boxes, and dragons plus wind socks and flags of fantastic design. The shop even has stunt kites for advanced fliers. Put the products to use here on the Lowcountry beaches or take them home to your own sky.

**Market Leather of Charleston
40 N. Market St., Rainbow Market
(843) 722-1156**

Here's a shop in the Rainbow Market that's all about leather accessories for men and women. They import several lines of ladies' handbags, belts, and worktotes for the home or office. For men, they have a wide selection of billfolds, duffles, and utility kits. Look for leather backpacks, passport covers, attachés, briefcases, garment bags, wallets, computer briefs, plus handsome cases for phones and palm pilots. This is a gold mine of gift ideas when holidays and birthdays come around.

The Mole Hole of Charleston
94 N. Market St.
(843) 723-0881

Here's the Market's version of the staple shop for arty collectibles and accents for the home and garden. Folks into Bovano and Wee Forest Folk will find a nice selection here. The shop features cut glass and birdhouses, Wolford oil lamps and Hummel figurines—a myriad of beautiful keepsakes from which to choose.

Noah's Nook
City Market, Shed A
(843) 722-8002

For those travelers who like to find a year-round Christmas shop and buy that special ornament for the tree that's sure to recall their Charleston vacation, here's one that nicely fills the bill. This shop, tucked away in the Market between Meeting and Church Streets, is a division of Light Be and features exclusive lines of hand-painted, locally made ornaments with a Charleston theme. Their collectible lines include Buyers' Choice, Annalee, Seraphim Angels, Little Street People, Fontanini, and many others. Even on the hottest days of summer, there's a little bit of the North Pole here.

Home Accents and Decor

Metropolitan Deluxe
164 Market St.
(843) 722-0436

Ever since it opened, the Metropolitan Deluxe has been the home furnishings store that marches to a different drummer. This seductive and eclectic mix of European-style furniture, bedding, and linens is across Market Street from Majestic Square and straight out of the latest magazines. Look here for tableware that's chic beyond the pale and special accents and accessories that delight decorators and casual browsers alike. The collection of candles and dried flowers alone is worth the trip. A corner devoted to cards and stationery is one of the major pulls as is the bit of free parking in front of the store.

Jewelry

Nice Ice Fine Jewelers
145 Market St.
(843) 577-7029

Cross Market Street from Charleston Place to find Nice Ice. Check out the many cases of costume designs along with displays of the real stuff. Expect to be a bit surprised by the good prices. Some of the most unusual pieces seen around town have been created by Nice Ice. Look here for Steven Dweck, Doris Panos, Hidalgo, Barry Kronen, and Judith Ripka.

Shogry's Gold Showcase
90 N. Market St.
(843) 722-7211

Tucked away amid the noise and confusion of the Market area, Shogry's is a nice jewelry store specializing in gold pieces. Check the window display for examples of bracelets and other items—they're as well-priced as they are lovely.

Women's Clothing

Everything But Water
130 Market St.,
The Shops at Charleston Place
(843) 722-5884

If you are looking for a bathing suit, try Everything But Water in Charleston Place. The store carries contemporary swimwear and accessories by such designers as Anne Cole, Gottex, La Blanca, and Oscar de la Renta, in sizes 4 through 26.

Oroton
120 Market St.,
The Shops at Charleston Place
(843) 722-2800, (800) 676-8661

As one of only two outlets in the U.S. to date (the other in Los Angeles), this high-style boutique in Charleston Place is a rare find for those who love all things Oroton. That's the Australian Oroton line of products with the distinctive "O." Best known for their fine leather handbags, Oroton also carries women's shoes, belts, wallets, small leather goods, jewelry, eyewear, and executive accessories—all interpreted with classic lines and timeless style.

Church Street

This is a street with romantic charm to spare. It's the heart of Charleston's French Quarter, where the Huguenots first set up their houses and shops in the 18th century. It was once the very center of the old city, and much of its early ambiance and heritage remains in evidence today.

Although Church Street runs from the Market area to White Point Gardens, past houses where presidents slept and folk operas were inspired, the shopping section is largely limited to the area between Market and Tradd Streets. Here you'll find everything from charming little fashion boutiques to bookstores and antiques shops.

Bookstores

The Charleston Rare Book Co.
66 Church St.
(843) 723-3330
Tucked away on one of Charleston's most charming streets, The Charleston Rare Book Co. deals in just that—rare books—particularly those concerning Charleston, the Lowcountry, and books by classic authors of the South. The Civil War, antebellum Americana, Winston Churchill, Victorian literature, and naval and maritime history are all special interests of the buyers.

The Southern Literary Tradition
83 Cumberland St.
(843) 722-8430
Here's a bookstore that's an adventure in architectural history and the city's rich literary tradition. It's located in the Nicholas Trott House (1709), next door to the Powder Magazine, in what is said to be Charleston's first brick residence. The store offers formal tea and a house tour as well as rare first editions, and books about the South and the Lowcountry. You can see a wonderful private collection of rare books, but many volumes are for sale, as well. A $5 admission charge includes a house tour (given at 10 AM and 2 PM) plus tea. After 3:30 PM, only the garden is open for tea. If you're looking for a hard-to-find book, the proprietors will search for lost titles for you and watch the marketplace for your favorite author's work.

Children's Clothing

82 Church Street
108 Church St.
(843) 723-7511
Moms have been shopping at 82 Church for generations. That's why (when the shop moved up the street) they kept the well-known name. Here you'll find conservative, traditional clothing for children and a shopping adventure that is charming in its own right. The "Charleston Bonnet" for baby girls (puffed with a front-top bow and chin tie) and hand-smocked dresses are sold here. A full range of imported and American-made merchandise is available, and the shop's precious display windows are always an escape into fashion innocence.

Gifts

The Boutique
102 Church St.
(843) 722-1441
Without a doubt the Lowcountry's most gorgeous nightgowns, bathrobes, slips, and the like come from The Boutique. This store, located at the corner of Church and Broad, is where the "hat man" is painted on a wall. The shop also sells fine costume jewelry, linens, and other quality gift items, including the Lilly Pulitzer collection.

Charleston Memories
170 Church St.
(843) 577-0323
Here's another gift shop in the Market area (formerly known as Linning House Galleries) locals choose for occasions when the gift must be special. There's an extensive inventory of quality items, from crystal figurines to accents and other decorative accessories for the home. The selection of children's gifts is pretty special too.

East Bay Street

This was once a street of bustling cotton warehouses in the mid-19th century, where silks and satins from exotic lands were bought and sold among the rice and indigo merchants who labored here. The old warehouses that survived the rigors of war and economic stagnation were "rediscovered" in the late 1970s, when a new epoch for the street began. Although below Broad Street, East Bay can claim the famous Rainbow Row of town houses and the High Battery along Charleston Harbor. Today you'll find a concentration of galleries, nightclubs, restaurants, and bookstores along East Bay between Market and Broad Streets. Beyond this area, other clusters of shops have emerged worth noticing. Here are some of the shopping venues you won't want to miss.

Bookstores

Atlantic Books
191 East Bay St.
(843) 723-7654
310 King St.
(843) 723-4751

These shops sell used, rare, and collectible books. Specialties are books on South Carolina, Americana, the Civil War, and things nautical. If you are interested in buying or have something special to sell, the owners are eager to talk to you.

Candy

Charleston Chocolates
190 East Bay St.
(843) 577-4491, (800) 633-8305

We'll warn you about this place again in our East Bay Street Gifts section, but there's no better way to lose the battle of the bulge than with Charleston Chocolates. Go ahead and surrender. Succumb to the morsels called Black Forest and Vanilla Butter Rum, then sample the scores of other ways to go. That's why they say this is "a taste of heaven from the Holy City."

Gifts

Amelia West & Company
30 Pinckney St.
(843) 853-9922

Near the Market at the corner of Anson and Pinckney Streets is this unique gift and decorative accessories shop. You'll find contemporary picture frames, hand-crafted trays, fine linens, hand-painted ceramic dinnerware, very special pillows, and more unusual stuff.

Enjoy the charm of Charleston shopping. PHOTO: FLETCHER NEWBERN

Charleston Chocolates
190 East Bay St.
(843) 577-4491, (800) 633-8305

One thing we neglected to say in our previous mention of this chocolo-rama is that all the hand-dipped chocolates here—including the other-worldly Charleston Chocolate Truffle—have no additives or preservatives. It's chocolate as it's supposed to be: beautifully made, joyously presented, handsomely wrapped, and, alas, too quickly gone. These little morsels make the perfect gift for almost any occasion.

Clowns' Bazaar
56 Broad St.
(843) 723-9769

This is Charleston's only tax-exempt showcase for folk art, collectibles, and gifts handmade by challenged artisans. By "challenged," the shopkeepers mean crafted by people in Third World countries and faraway lands too-seldom accessible by international traders. You'll find crafts from India, Pakistan, Kenya, Cameroon, Chile, Peru, Jerusalem, Bangladesh, and Indonesia. Along with tableware, hand-loomed cloth, ceramics, pottery, carvings, and baskets, there's even some clothing from Tibet. (See our listing in the Arts chapter under Galleries.)

Indigo
4 Vendue Range
(843) 723-2983

If you gravitate toward the eclectic, you'll love Indigo. The inventory ranges from antique luggage to Mexican folk art to Brazilian textiles. In this shop, you'll find village baskets nestled near Shaker boxes next to Edwardian bamboo and old Italian marble. You'll never fail to find something wonderful here.

Luden's
78 Alexander St.
(843) 723-7829

Since 1867 Luden's has been selling Charlestonians top-quality, brand-name clothing, equipment and gear for hunt-ing, fishing, and boating. Anyone who goes for this outdoor gear will love Luden's for the myriad of gift items available here. Shop here for tide clocks, ship's logs, nautical cookbooks, and all kinds of rigging and boat accessories. Luden's is a block off East Bay Street, just below Charlotte Street on Alexander. There's free parking on-site. (Also see Luden's in the Hunting and Fishing chapter.)

O'Hara & Flynn, Ltd.
32 Laurens St.
(843) 534-1916
1640 Palmetto Grande Dr., Towne Centre,
Mt. Pleasant
(843) 216-1916

Here's a direct importer of fine wines and gourmet cheeses plus fresh pates, smoked salmon, and saucissons for the discerning connoisseur. With a shop downtown, near Harris Teeter, and another in Mt. Pleasant's Towne Centre, they're handy for locals who know their tastes and want the best. They even have in-shop tastings every Friday evening from 5 to 7 PM. Ask about their Thursday wine classes at Vintage Restaurant (on S. Market Street). Call (843) 577-0090 for more information.

The Smoking Lamp
197-B East Bay St.
(843) 577-7339

Forget the no smoking signs. Between High Cotton Restaurant and Atlantic Books, this always-fragrant tobacco shop features a complete selection of fine pipes, cigars, tobacco, cigarettes, and smoking accessories.

Home Accents and Decor

Wilton House Ltd.
211 East Bay St.
(843) 723-6929

Wilton House is a great resource for traditional and English-style home furnishings priced right, plus great gift items and decorative accessories. Fine pillows, ceramics, mirrors, and collectibles make this a delightful stop along busy East Bay, just around the corner from the Market.

Jewelry

Dazzles
155 East Bay St.
(843) 722-5997
86 Queen St.
(843) 722-5950
The Shops at Charleston Place,
226 King St.
(843) 722-5951

This family of jewelry stores is best known for its 14-karat-gold slide bracelets that have the look, style, and feel of an heirloom. Dazzles has a large selection to choose from, or you may design one of your very own. Gold slide bracelets can be set with diamonds and precious stones in various shapes and motifs. Dazzles also has a large selection of gold enhancers for Omega necklaces too.

Geiss and Sons Jewelers
116 East Bay St.
(843) 577-4497

Geiss is on the first floor of a charming little 18th-century brick building on East Bay, just south of Broad. While the shop sells custom-designed diamond and colored-stone rings, it is also known for its inventory of watches by Rolex, Tissot, and Breitling.

Natural Beauty

Earthling Day Spa
334 East Bay St.
(843) 722-4737

Here in Ansonborough Square is a great source for skin and body products and books and tapes on health and well-being. Earthling also offers the unique Palates method of conditioning. With Palates, clients work out with trained professionals who guide them through a therapeutic body-conditioning regimen of stretching, strengthening, alignment, and toning exercises. There are other gifts for the mind and spirit such as aromatherapy candles, spa treatments, therapeutic massage, and a nice selection of natural cosmetics.

East Cooper

Bookstores

Barnes & Noble Booksellers
1716 Towne Centre Way, Towne Centre,
Mt. Pleasant
(843) 216-9756
1812 Sam Rittenberg Blvd.,
Westwood Plaza, Charleston
(843) 556-6561
7620 Rivers Ave., Northwoods Mall,
North Charleston
(843) 572-2322

The nation's biggest bookseller has opened three locations in the area. All stores are huge (25,000 square feet), and each carries approximately 175,000 different titles for adults and children. In addition, all stores have coffee bars and music departments.

Children's Clothing

Gwynn's of Mt. Pleasant
916 Houston Northcutt Blvd.,
Village Pointe Shopping Center,
Mt. Pleasant
(843) 884-9518

The department for children at Gwynn's is special indeed. For infants through teenagers, Gwynn's offers top-line brands, attractive accessories, and shoes. It's another of those Charleston traditions: outfitting the little one at Gwynn's.

Radical Rags
210 Coleman Blvd., The Common,
Mt. Pleasant
(843) 884-8763

Radical Rags in The Common sells cute, traditional clothing for girls size 7 to 14, along with some preteen outfits. Boys' sizes range from 8 to 20. The staff is friendly and helpful, and the selection is terrific.

Ragamuffin Shop
210 Coleman Blvd., The Common,
Mt. Pleasant
(843) 884-4814

Also in The Common, Ragamuffin Shop shares staff and floor space with Radical Rags. Its specialty is clothing for infants up to size 6X in girls and 7 in boys.

Southern Belles
280 W. Coleman Blvd., Mt. Pleasant
(843) 881-4070
This shop is near Wonder Works in Northcutt Plaza and carries traditional clothing for preemies through preteens. Expect lots of smocked outfits, coordinated sibling attire, and crib shoes. It also has toys, picture frames, signature gift items, and scrapbook supplies.

Gardening
Abide-A-While Nursery & Garden Center
1460 U.S. Hwy. 17 N. Bypass, Mt. Pleasant
(843) 884-9738
Here in Charleston, where gardens are so beloved, there has to be a nursery where people go to get perennials, seeds and shrubbery, trees, and ornamentals. One of the best is Abide-A-While. Its selection is enormous, the quality is good, and you can always count on getting knowledgeable gardening advice.

Gifts
Rana
320 W. Coleman Blvd., Ste. K,
The Shops of Mount Pleasant,
Mt. Pleasant
(843) 884-1983
This exclusive gift boutique tucked away in The Shops of Mt. Pleasant is a veritable cache of fine china, crystal, linens, and gifts you'd be proud to give or receive. Locals find Rana inspiring when wedding gifts are called for and Santa needs a little help for someone very special. Parking is free.

Wonder Works
280 W. Coleman Blvd., Mt. Pleasant
(843) 849-6757
975 Savannah Hwy.
(843) 573-9300
This is a toy store with an educational theme for kids and adults. Departments include geography, nature, arts and crafts, and a special section with developmental toys for infants and toddlers. There are many of the most famous names in educational toys, such as Brio and Playmobil, and Wonder Works is the largest seller of telescopes in the southeastern United States.

Home Accents and Decor
The Brick House
1465 Stuart Engals Blvd., Mt. Pleasant
(843) 881-8911
These folks have created a unique and fun marketplace for very fine, "gently used" home furnishings. They say good taste doesn't have to be expensive, and this store proves the point. Designer and owner Mary Chason will also visit your home for consultation on items you wish to consign. You'll find The Brick House on the bypass frontage road near Wal-Mart and Wando Crossing Shopping Center.

By The Yard
695 Coleman Blvd., Mt. Pleasant
(843) 849-0711
975 Savannah Hwy.,
St. Andrews Shopping Center, Charleston
(843) 571-5142
Don't let the name fool you. This is much more than a yard goods outlet. It's a one-stop option for the home, carrying rugs, gifts, lamps, mirrors, furniture, framed art, accessories, and fabrics. The store offers complimentary design assistance from a well-trained staff of friendly sales folk.

East Bay Gallery
280 W. Coleman Blvd., Northcutt Plaza,
Mt. Pleasant
(843) 216-8010
The latest incarnation of this well-known gallery of home accents and objets d'art is located in the Specialty Shops of Northcutt Plaza. Here's a treasure chest of contemporary decorative accessories that range from hand-crafted, one-of-a-kind art pieces to the eclectic object that makes a home truly distinctive. Look for blown glass, wrought iron, jewelry, mirrors, accent chairs, clocks, wind chimes, children's toys, and interesting collectibles. More than 100 artists and craftspeople are represented here—carefully juried by the owners. (See the listing in Arts, under Galleries.)

Kitchens By Design
234 Mathis Ferry Rd., Mt. Pleasant
(843) 849-6890
Since 1980, this unique shop has offered

Close-up

Lowcountry Tradition: Sweetgrass Baskets

Tne art form practiced here in the Lowcountry has been recognized and celebrated virtually all over the world. Examples of this rare craft are found in the art museums of New York and Rome and among the Smithsonian collections in Washington, D.C., and yet the work is evident all along the sidewalks of Charleston's Four Corners of Law at Meeting and Broad streets. You'll easily find it downtown in the Market and here and there in makeshift stalls along Lowcountry highways—especially along U.S. Hwy 17 N.

We're talking about the weaving of sweetgrass baskets, a traditional African-American art practiced here in the Lowcountry since the early 18th century.

These baskets are handmade of long bunches of sweetgrass, pine needles, and bulrush that are bound together with fiber strips from native palmetto trees. The bunches are coiled and formed to create a wide variety of baskets—all shapes and sizes, each one unique. The baskets are both functional and beautiful.

Creating these baskets requires skilled craftsmanship and long hours of hard work. A simple, average basket may require 12 hours or more to make, while larger, more complicated versions may take up to two or three months.

The craft of weaving sweetgrass baskets has been a part of the Lowcountry since the earliest days of slavery. The skills are largely passed on from generation to generation. Traditionally, the men harvest the fiber and other plant material from the local marshes and swamps, then the women weave the baskets.

While the bulrush, pine needles, and palmetto strips are indigenous to and traditionally obtainable throughout the Lowcountry, coastal land development has begun to threaten the artisans' supply. Today, some weavers have to travel as far as Florida and along the Savannah River in Georgia to find natural stands of sweetgrass growing in roadside marshes. Because of this threat to one of the Lowcountry's most endearing traditions, Historic Charleston Foundation sponsored a test project on James Island to cultivate the growing of sweetgrass as a crop. Over the past few years the experiment has been a resounding success. It looks as if the sweetgrass basket tradition—in terms of raw material, at least—is more secure now than it has been for many years.

A Lowcountry local works on a sweetgrass basket.
PHOTO: DAVID C. BERRY

The result of all this labor and talent is spectacular. Each sweetgrass basket is utilitarian and beautiful, rich in the natural tones of the varied grasses and elegant in its ethnic simplicity. The baskets are true objects of art, and so they're not cheap. We feel the investment (usually $50 or $60 for a standard basket) is very worthwhile. Be sure to discover the wonderful sweetgrass baskets of the Lowcountry for yourself.

creative design services for new and renovated kitchens and baths. The showroom displays and sells fine kitchen furnishings, gourmet cookware, and tools.

Celadon Home Furnishing & Accessories
621 Johnnie Dodds Blvd., Mt. Pleasant
(843) 884-7005

Celadon Home Furnishing & Accessories is one of those stores where you could almost outfit a home from cellar to dome. Its large inventory of sofas, chairs, tables, and accessories is only outdone by the number of options available "by order." Choose from more than 700 fabrics and your upholstered sofa or chair can be delivered in about two to four weeks.

Jewelry

Skatell's Manufacturing Jewelers
1036 Johnnie Dodds Blvd., Mt. Pleasant
(843) 884-8488
1798 Ashley River Rd., Charleston
(843) 763-8925

The outstanding thing about Skatell's is that customers come here to have jewelry made to their own specifications. Skatell's is a direct importer of diamonds, and it tries to pass the savings on to the buyer.

Music

Millennium Music
1732 Towne Centre Way, Ste. L,
Towne Centre, Mt. Pleasant
(843) 971-2005
372 King St., Charleston
(843) 763-2000

There are two locally owned Millennium Music stores (East Cooper and downtown), and we recommend both for your listening and music purchasing pleasure.

The Towne Centre location is handy for Mt. Pleasant residents who love to spend time and money there. Purchasing a membership gives you a break on costs for CDs and tapes (be sure to ask about the initial membership charge to determine if it's worth your while), but listening—at a long wall of sampling stations where you can pick a CD and don the headphones—is free.

Both Millennium Music stores have an area dedicated to children and their music, and behind a lovely set of doors downtown is a glassed-in classical music listening room. Millennium carries all major categories of music and then some.

Natural Beauty

Gallery for Hair & Skin Care
320 W. Coleman Blvd.,
The Shops of Mt. Pleasant, Mt. Pleasant
(843) 881-4546

This full-service hair- and skin-care shop offers massage by a certified therapist and specialists in hair color, skin care, and makeup. For women who know their skin- and hair-care products by name, this option carries, Montage, Fudge, Kenra, Nioxu\in, Joico, Biolage, Matrix, Goldwell, KMS, Sebastian, and Tigi, among others.

Stella Nova
1320 Theatre Dr., Towne Centre,
Mt. Pleasant
(843) 884-3838
292 King St.
(843) 722-9797
78 Society St.
(843) 723-0909

Stella Nova's location in Towne Centre

makes a pleasant stop before or after a movie. They carry Ahava, Kusco Murphy, Terax, and Le Clerc make-up, among many other lines. They have Aveda pure plant products and services for the hair, skin, and body. Services include haircuts, styling, pedicures, facials, and scalp treatments. Ask about their day spa programs.

Women's Clothing

Copper Penny
280 W. Coleman Blvd., Northcutt Plaza, Mt. Pleasant
(843) 881-3497
311 King St., Charleston
(843) 723-2999
This boutique sells comfortable, stylish clothes for contemporary women. In Northcutt Plaza near Wonder Works, this shop is a good source for unique, casual yet sophisticated clothing that works from day into evening. Gifts and distinctive accessories fill out the inventory, and its shoe department is gaining notice. Their newest location is in downtown Charleston on King Street.

Gwynn's of Mt. Pleasant
916 Houston Northcutt Blvd., Village Pointe Shopping Center, Mt. Pleasant
(843) 884-9518
Locals have shopped at Gwynn's in several locations through the years, and they have always been pleased. A nice thing about this store is the wide range of departments under one roof. Women's clothing is a specialty, and the shoe and accessory departments carry top-of-the-line merchandise. Sales consultants are most helpful and will coordinate outfits to your specifications.

West Ashley

Bookstores

Book Exchange
1219 Savannah Hwy.
(843) 556-5051
The Book Exchange sells new and used paperback and hardback books as well as collectible comics. Reader-friendly, this is where the serious mystery novel addicts go for a fix and where the neighborhood kids swap comic books.

Books-A-Million
832 Orleans Rd.
(843) 556-9232
2150 Northwoods Blvd., North Charleston
(843) 764-2377
Books-A-Million is one of Charleston's largest chain bookstores. With its small coffee shop section and expansive inventory, Books-A-Million has a lot to offer. For instance, it stocks nature-related gift items, calendars, and toys. The magazine section covers a big back wall, and the children's section has a video area to entertain the young ones while parents shop. Books-A-Million offers several discounts, and you can buy a one-year club membership for $5 to maximize your savings.

Books, Herbs and Spices
1409-D Folly Rd., Berle Shopping Ctr., James Island
(843) 762-3025
This is primarily a health-food store, but there's a large section of books about foods, herbal remedies, and other health-oriented matters. While you're shopping, treat yourself to something tasty from the kitchen or the blender. There's also a refrigerator case that's always filled with fresh vegetarian sandwiches and exotic juices promising health benefits.

Indigo Books
3714 Betsy Kerrison Pkwy., Johns Island
(843) 768-2255
A great hit with the Kiawah and Seabrook crowd, this small but well-stocked bookstore in the Island Center Plaza is the

place to pick up a great summer vacation read. The shopkeepers do a great job of keeping a wide variety of books on hand, and they special order anything you cannot find post haste. Their section of Southern authors is especially interesting, and the inventory of Lowcountry titles is as good as the major chains. Even wintertime islanders find Indigo a good place to shop for holiday gifts to send grandkids up North.

Ravenous Reader
520 Folly Rd., James Island
(843) 795-2700
This is a favorite bookstore on James Island, and thanks to the James Island Connector, it's now very convenient to those coming from town as well as those traveling Folly Road. The Ravenous Reader is expanding and has great books and a friendly staff who'll answer your questions and order just about anything you want.

Children's Clothing
Kiawah Kids
Straw Market, West Beach Village,
Kiawah Island
(843) 768-2341
Visitors and residents on Kiawah Island find cute things for children at Kiawah Kids. From dressy dresses (even some smocked) to T-shirts and shorts, this store in the festive Straw Market shops offers a wide selection for girls. Boys aren't left out; look here for T-shirts, shorts, and swimwear, too.

Gardening
Cross Seed Co., Inc.
840 St. Andrews Blvd.
(843) 766-1687
You can always tell when spring is coming to the Lowcountry when Cross Seed starts displaying the new early-blooming plants along the front of their West Ashley store. Charleston gardeners for generations have shopped at Cross Seed for gardening

supplies, pet products, and all things natural for the well-dressed outdoors. Along with seeds and bulbs, here's a great source for information on when to plant and how to nurture the quintessential Charleston garden.

Hyams Landscaping and Garden Center
870 Folly Rd.
(843) 795-4570
Here's another favorite of Charleston gardeners. The selection of room-filling house plants is spectacular, but you'll also find bedding plants, seeds and bulbs, fountains, birdbaths, hanging planters, and more. And there's always someone nearby with helpful answers to your gardening questions.

Gifts
Charleston Collections
625 Skylark Dr.
(843) 556-8911
Straw Market, East Beach Village,
Kiawah Island
(843) 768-7487
This shop sells an incredible assortment of things Charlestonian. Look for Charleston wind chimes, Charleston art prints and originals, Charleston seashell lamp kits, Charleston cookbooks, Charleston note cards, and even Charleston jewelry. Get the drift? The clerks are prepared to ship goods anywhere, so this is a great stop for souvenirs to send home.

Elegant Options
1899 Andell Bluff Blvd., Bohicket Marina,
Seabrook Island
(843) 768-5542
Here's a safe bet: Whatever the occasion, Elegant Options has a great gift waiting for you (or the one you're trying to please). Weddings, anniversaries, birthdays, Christmas, christenings, even graduations and housewarmings—Elegant Options has it all. The emphasis here is on elegance for the home with art, furniture accents,

ceramics, brass, collectibles, and even some jewelry—all of which has been carefully chosen to represent the best in taste and style.

Home Accents and Decor

Charleston Lighting and Interiors
1640 Sam Rittenberg Blvd.
(843) 766-3055

Locals and newcomers looking to brighten their homes with distinctive chandeliers, lamps, ceiling fans, and interesting accents in occasional furniture are discovering this new option west of the Ashley. Their collections include both period and high-tech pieces that work well in traditional as well as contemporary settings—but still have that Charleston touch of class. Look for names like Quoizel (Tiffany), Iris, Wilshire, Minka, and Tech Lighting—to name a few.

In Good Taste
1901 Ashley River Rd.
(843) 763-5597

This is a store for the serious gourmet, with all kinds of kitchen items, live herbs, wines, cheeses, coffees, teas, and gift baskets. It often sponsors wine tastings and fun cooking classes that have proven very popular with a devoted clientele. Look for In Good Taste near the Port City Grille restaurant. (See our Restaurants chapter.)

Jewelry

Polly's
1890 Sam Rittenberg Blvd., Citadel Plaza
(843) 763-0017
270 King St.
(843) 722-9228
976 Houston Northcutt Blvd., Mt. Pleasant
(843) 884-2447

Look for the Citadel Plaza on Sam Rittenberg Boulevard, and you will find Polly's, a large, locally owned jewelry store. Polly's specializes in diamonds, gold jewelry, and watches. There is ample free parking, and the staff is most helpful. The downtown and Mt. Pleasant stores are a similar source for diamonds, gold, and watches. Customers can have jewelry designed or repaired on the premises.

Traditions by Garfield
8 Windermere Blvd.,
South Windermere Shopping Center
(843) 571-3099
345 King St.
(843) 722-7936

Traditions by Garfield is South Windermere Shopping Center's unique jewelry store. Traditions is not only a full-service shop with cases of pretty jewelry and nice watches, but also a good source for estate jewelry (be sure to check out the little case of lovelies in the back) and gorgeous children's gifts. The shelves around the front part of the store are filled with handsome gifts.

Men's Clothing

Stein Mart
St. Andrews Shopping Center,
975 Savannah Hwy.
(843) 763-2444

The men's (and boys') section of this high-end discount store is quite extensive. You can find a good selection of suits and sport coats in short, regular, and long sizes. Expect to see designer labels as well as fine Italian cuts among the lot. Shirts, ties, sport clothes of all kinds, and underwear complete the selection.

Barton & Burwell
47 Windermere Blvd.,
South Windermere Shopping Center
(843) 766-3220

Serious anglers know Barton & Burwell like they know the back creeks of the Lowcountry. Any and everything associated with the sport of fishing is here to be found: clothes, shoes, boots, reels, lures, and any other kind of tackle. Any 10-year-old kid worth his or her spinning rod would be thrilled with a gift certificate from here. (See our Hunting and Fishing chapter for information on where to put your new equipment to use.)

Toys

Hammett's Learning World
2245-D Ashley Crossing Dr.
(843) 766-3315

Parents like shopping at Hammett's, and

children are inspired here as well. This store carries top-of-the-line educational toys, publications, and supplies—from the perfect multi-cultural lesson planner to read-by-phonics tapes—along with school necessities.

The Learning Center
67 S. Windermere Ctr.
(843) 556-1200
The Learning Center offers educational books and toys. Located behind the South Windermere Shopping Center, the shop is staffed by knowledgeable employees who are prepared to help parents, teachers, and interested friends and relatives find appropriate learning tools

for kids with an appetite to learn as well as play.

Women's Clothing
Stein Mart
975 Savannah Hwy.,
St. Andrews Shopping Center
(843) 763-2444
It claims to be the only "upscale, off-price specialty store in America," and it may be true. Stein Mart has frontline women's fashion apparel in its Boutique section and accessories that are considerably discounted. There are hats, shoes, purses, jewelry, hair accessories, and hosiery too. The store also carries a large selection of gifts, linens, and special things for the home.

Shopping Centers and Malls

Charles Towne Square
2401 Mall Dr., North Charleston
(843) 529-1946
This was Greater Charleston's first major mall. Just off Interstate 26 in North Charleston, it was originally built 20 years ago to serve the military community and the north area of the Trident, which was experiencing mushrooming growth at the time. Since then, the scene has dramatically changed. Today, Charles Towne Square has undergone a major remodeling and rebuilding program that completely redefined the mall as old-timers knew it.

The patrons of Piccadilly Cafeteria were glad to see them survive the evolution. Movie fans love the 18-screen multiplex movie theater, Regal Cinemas, which has stadium seating. The brightly colored movie house is in a separate building on the ultra-landscaped, campus-like location.

Citadel Mall
2070 Sam Rittenberg Blvd.
(U.S. Hwy. 17 and S.C. Hwy. 7 at I-526)
(843) 766-8511
When Citadel Mall opened in the early 1980s, it was the merchandising hit of the decade. Major anchors are Dillard's, Sears, Parisian, and a Belk store that

opened in the spring of 2000. The whole mall has undergone a complete refurbishing with updated and re-landscaped bench areas for foot sore shoppers, a new children's play area, and a multi national food court for catching a quick bite before launching into further shopping expeditions. There are more than 100 shops to satisfy every shopper's needs. The location, at the intersection of I-526 and U.S. Hwy. 17, makes Citadel Mall convenient for almost anyone in the Lowcountry. Call the Customer Service Center for information as to business hours and special events.

South Windermere Shopping Center
22 Windermere Blvd. (at Folly Road)
(843) 766-0261
With shops that front on Folly Road and others on a second row behind, South Windermere is a popular shopping center in the West Ashley area. There is also a shopping strip that borders the center itself, and those stores have addresses on Windermere Boulevard as well. The major anchor is Belk, but there are other worthwhile stops in the complex. There's Robinson's Bicycle Shop, founded in 1888 and still very popular with bike enthusiasts. The Open House is a gift shop with

elegant paper goods ranging from Crane stationery to whimsical gift wrap. Traditions by Garfield is a jewelry store and gift shop that always has enticing window displays (see previous listing). A more recent tenant called Earth Fare is a popular outlet (set up like a chain grocery store) for all-natural, organically grown food. Shoppers at Earth Fare can also order from a counter and dine in a convenient on-site café. Other shopping options are Phillips Shoes and Barton & Burwell, a favorite of local anglers (see previous listing).

Towne Centre
U.S. Hwy. 17 N., Mt. Pleasant
(843) 216-9900

This is the Lowcountry's first major offering to shoppers of the newest trend in retailing—the replication of a traditional downtown shopping district in a suburban setting. The fantastic growth of Mt. Pleasant and the whole East Cooper area provoked Towne Centre, a whole "new town" that has the best of the old and all the convenience of the new. The look of Towne Centre is based on Charleston's famous King Street—with traditional-looking storefronts (60 of them so far) and attractive sidewalk settings. The difference is—ample free parking with lush landscaping added to avoid the "vast sea of asphalt" look offered by the shopping malls of yore.

Towne Centre was a $40-million, 47-tenant project when it opened in the summer of 1999. Since then, new stores and entertainment options have been climbing aboard at a steady rate. Among the pioneers in this venture were the major anchors of Belk, Old Navy, Barnes & Noble, Morgan Stewart Furniture Galleries, plus Bed, Bath & Beyond. Soon, a 16-screen, 3,100-seat movie theater called Palmetto Grande joined the crowd. Newcomers include Banana Republic, Bull & Finch Pub, Game Pro, Casual Corner, Chico's, Chili's Bar & Grille, Hallmark Creations, Learning Express, Gap, Victoria's Secret, and Pier One. Even Millennium Music moved to Towne Centre to be part of the action.

Towne Centre is located on U.S. Highway 17 in Mt. Pleasant. The location is convenient to nearly everyone because of the nearby Isle of Palms Connector (S.C. Hwy 517) and the proximity to I-526, which almost completely encircles the Lowcountry.

St. Andrews Shopping Center
975 Savannah Hwy.
(843) 556-9442

Generations of Charleston kids have identified St. Andrews Shopping Center by the Coburg Cow revolving on a sign at the edge of its parking lot on Savannah Highway. The life-size plastic bovine lights up at night and signals to travel-weary kids that they are almost home (or at the shopping center). The major anchor here is Stein Mart, the upscale, off-price department store that features items for the home and clothes for men, women, and children (see previous listing). Other stores include an old-fashioned barber shop called Mooney's and By The Yard, a large fabric store that also carries lamps, rugs, furniture, and accessories (see previous listing). One of the newer tenants is Norwalk, the Furniture Idea, with its nice selection of items for the home. St. Andrews is the handy location of a Weight Watchers and Ladies Choice Fitness Center, as well.

Antiques

For the Insider who wants to buy, sell, study, or just window shop for antiques, Charleston is a mother lode. Because it was first an English city, the Charlestonian sense of taste in antiques is decidedly British. And fittingly, Charleston's many antiques shops and galleries—many of which are clustered along King Street—tend to reflect that English bias.

The affluent, British-educated, 18th-century Charlestonians proudly decorated their homes with the latest in English good taste as an obvious symbol of their cultural status and social position. If they couldn't import their heart's desire for finery and furniture, they imported tradesmen who could re-create it for them on this side of the Atlantic. Eventually, Charleston produced a new generation of silversmiths and cabinetmakers who earned their own reputations for fine craftsmanship. Indeed, early furniture from Charleston is among the best of the pre-1830 furniture crafted in this country. But it's safe to say that long after Britain ceased being a political factor in the colonies, Americans still looked to Mother England for direction in taste. In fact, this artistic and cultural co-dependency has lingered in Charleston for more than 200 years.

During the late 18th and mid-19th centuries, drastic events greatly altered the city's economic health. There were earthquakes, wars, fires, and storms, all of which took their toll on Charleston's grandeur (including the city's remarkable resource of period antiques). The collapse of the indigo and rice trades, the hardships of Reconstruction, and the opening of America's vast Western frontier left poor Charleston with few viable resources to rebuild its economy.

Many of the elegant old homes fell into neglect as Southern families struggled to cope with all the social and economic changes swirling around them. In many cases, their only recourse was to sell some of the old family furniture, silver, crystal, and china remaining from the former days of glory. Charlestonians did what they had to do to survive.

By the early 1900s, a few savvy antiques dealers from New York had discovered Charleston's cache of fine English furnishings. They soon learned the quality of the furniture was outmatched only by the city's economic distress. By the 1920s, what amounted to an antiques industry was going strong in Charleston. Unfortunately, it was mostly out-going. Along with fine furnishings, dealers were carting off architectural details like wrought iron balconies, shutters, and even whole paneled rooms.

Today, Charleston no longer relies on furnishings from her local homes and the misfortunes of her old families to fill today's antiques shops and galleries. Local dealers and buyers attend auctions and estate sales up and down the Eastern seaboard, and some make regular buying trips to Europe. Ships carrying 40-foot containers filled with early-to mid-19th-century English antiques arrive regularly in Charleston Harbor. Much of the merchandise is sold in local shops, while some of it goes to discerning dealers all over America. Still, Charleston enjoys the lion's share of the top-quality merchandise, largely because of the demand. Many of Charleston's old homes were built to showcase such furnishings, and each new owner cherishes the opportunity to refurbish his or her home appropriately.

From St. Michael's Alley and King Street to the shops in Mt. Pleasant and along Savannah Highway, there are dozens of opportunities to shop for some of the best antiques sold in America.

One particular section along King Street, between Beaufain and Queen Streets, is sometimes referred to as the Antiques District, where you'll find a high concentration of quality shops and fascinating merchandise. But the shopper who really wants to "do" the antiques market in Charleston will have to expand their search well beyond King Street these days. Quality shops are found tucked away in nearly all the commercial areas and seeing them all is getting to be something of a crusade. Lookers are almost always welcome, but if you're a serious collector or a dealer, be sure to talk to the proprietor and make your wishes known. Often, there are back rooms or upstairs galleries available only to those interested enough to ask.

At the corner of King and Queen Streets is a good place to start. Walking north from there, you'll find some of the best antiques stores the city has to offer. Most shops are open Monday through Saturday, but hours of operation can be as eclectic as the selections at many of these shops, so if in doubt, call ahead. We've alphabetized the following store and merchandise descriptions for easy reference.

Acquisitions
273 East Bay St.
(843) 577-8004, (843) 722-0238
This shop offers full interior design services and specializes in English pine originals and beautifully made reproductions of English mahogany and antique painted furniture. It is a great resource for accent pieces as well. These designers are very popular with the Kiawah and Seabrook Island crowd, and one look at their handsome displays tells you why.

Alexandra
179½ King St.
(843) 722-4897
Climb the stairs just through the King St. doorway to find this exclusive shop of antique French furniture, decorative wares, fine linens, pillows, china, and oil paintings—all reflecting the French Provencal ambiance now gaining popularity in Charleston.

Ali's Alley Antiques & Interiors
28 Hasell St.
(843) 577-5770
This shop in trendy Ansonborough is full of fine English and Continental furnishings such as armoires, farm tables, mirrors, and paintings. Roberta Ketchin is the owner and decorator who is known for her colorful and contemporary treatments of period rooms. She offers reproductions, new and vintage upholstered

pieces, plus a large selection of decorating accessories. Shipping can be arranged to anywhere.

Antiques Market
634 Coleman Blvd., Mt. Pleasant
(843) 849-8850
Only ten minutes from downtown Charleston, you'll find this mall with antiques and collectibles that are fun and decorative. This market hosts more than 100 booths under one roof with furnishings, sterling silver, antique button jewelry, and other interesting treasures for the finding. Less serious, perhaps, than some of the King Street antiques stores, this is a great place for browsing through the keepsakes and surprises. Parking is free and convenient—just off Coleman Boulevard.

Architrave
153 King St.
(843) 577-2860
Open since 1991, Architrave carries an assortment of fine American 18th- and early-19th-century furniture. But its strongest suit may be the wide assortment of antique chandeliers and other vintage lighting fixtures. In fact, its chandelier restoration and rewiring is getting to be a popular specialty. The owners buy from estates and dealers all over the Southeast and can ship virtually anywhere in the world.

charming of all, there are two (otherwise very friendly) West Highland terriers on site who are trained to (and do) growl at the mention of the word "Yankees."

D. Bigda Antiques
178 King St.
(843) 722-0248

This King Street dealer specializes in sterling silver with pattern-matching of new, old, and obsolete patterns. You'll also find a large selection of hollowware of all styles and periods, fine estate jewelry, art, and some furniture. The owners generously offer a referral service to those having difficulty finding rare and obsolete patterns.

A'riga IV
204 King St.
(843) 577-3075

Open since 1976, this shop carries a wide assortment of interesting early ceramics, decorative arts, and period accessories. There are no reproductions here at all. Look for an eclectic assortment of 17th- through 19th-century furniture. A'riga IV is best known, however, for its fascinating assortment of antique medical and scientific instruments. This is a special treat for the many docs and nurses who come to Charleston for medical conventions. A'riga has been the subject of a nice write-up in *The New York Times*.

Merrill Benfield Interior Design &
Decorative Accessories
285 E. Bay St.
(843) 853-9559

Formerly known as Poppe House, this charming shop is now open in a new location with their collection of 18th- and 19th-century antiques, decorative accessories, and fine reproductions. This is Merrill Benfield's shop, and it also houses his highly successful interior design business. They do a lot of custom buying for clients and special manufacturing to order. The shop is also especially known for its unusual lamp conversions. Most

George C. Birlant & Company
191 King St.
(843) 722-3842

This is one of Charleston's oldest and largest antiques stores, having been around since 1929. The owners are direct importers of l8th- and 19th-century English furniture and faithful English-made reproductions. They also specialize in antique silver, china, crystal, and brass. Birlant is the exclusive source for replicas of a Charleston Battery Bench like those found in White Point Gardens. It actually owns the original cast-iron molds.

Carolina Prints
188 King St.
(843) 723-2266, (800) 328-6256

This shop deals in pre-1945 American art, antique prints, sporting and Southern genre art, and museum-quality framing. It has an extensive assortment of art from Charleston's "Renaissance Period" of the 1920s and '30s, including works by Alfred Hutty, Elizabeth O'Neill Verner, and Alice Ravenel Huger Smith. Purchases can be framed and shipped anywhere.

Carolopolis
2000 Wappoo Dr.
(843) 795-7724

Away from the King Street crowd on

James Island, this is a treasure hunter's delight. Carolopolis is John Brown's constantly varying selection of antique and vintage furniture, along with offbeat lighting, mirrors, paintings, architectural items, and other assorted finds. Some items are rustic while others are finished and ready to use. All are fun to browse through on a rainy day.

Carpenter's Antiques and Restorations
976 Houston Northcut Blvd., Mt. Pleasant
(843) 884-3411
Since 1980, Carpenter's has been a resource for restoring antique furniture. It carries affordable restored furniture from the late 1800s and early 1900s. The owners have recently expanded their merchandise to include a variety of designer accessories and lamps. Also, look for original oil paintings from local artists.

Century House Antiques
56½ Queen St.
(843) 722-6248
Century House is a charming shop on lovely Queen Street specializing in English and Chinese Export porcelain of the 18th and 19th centuries, plus rare early prints, antique maps, and out-of-print books on Charleston.

Charleston Rare Book Co.
66 Church St.
(843) 723-3330
Book lovers will enjoy this one, specializing in rare and out-of-print books on Charleston, the Lowcountry, and South Carolina. There's plenty on the Civil War, of course, and on antebellum America. Look for maritime history, Winston Churchill, and Victorian literature too. Its book search service will find the most obscure titles for you. It's great browsing here. (See our Shopping chapter.)

Chicora Antiques
102 Church St.
(843) 723-1711
This is C. Lyman McCallum Jr.'s collec-

tion of finer pre-1840 American furniture and decorative arts with an emphasis on Federal and Classical period pieces. An especially nice aspect of this shop is the detailed documentation of every piece for sale. He proudly guarantees the authenticity in writing of every item offered and maintains a client request file to notify customers when objects of special interest become available. Mr. McCallum also offers an inspection and authentication service, by commission, for any piece offered at an estate sale or auction anywhere in the country. This is a must-see for the serious connoisseur of fine American furniture.

Church Street Galleries
100 Church St.
(843) 937-0808
Here you'll find fine English and American furnishings from the 18th and early 19th centuries, along with exceptional Oriental screens and accessories. These dealers proudly say they've been in the trade for more than 25 years and have been collecting for more than 45.

Classics of Charleston, Ltd.
154 King St.
(843) 853-0333
Here is a resource for extremely high quality and well-documented English period antiques. Owner Lynn Anne Christensen also does appraisals and consultations for clients here and all over the country. The shop shows only a fraction of her entire inventory and some out-of-town customers shop here "electronically." Accent pieces include American sterling, Staffordshire dogs, gilt mirrors, oriental porcelains, and cranberry glass.

Con Garbo
165 King St.
(843) 853-0100
This is a new comer to King Street and shoppers who have traveled to Italy will adore this direct importer of all things Italian. Everything in the store comes

from Florence. In addition to beautifully restored Italian antique furniture, you'll find accent and gift items such as sterling, leather, hand-painted dinnerware, and even a wide variety of imported stationery and desktop items—all with that distinctive Italian flair for design.

Croghan's Jewel Box
308 King St.
(843) 723-3594
Croghan's is another Charleston institution. Many a sterling wedding gift or baby cup has come from here. Croghan's specializes in antique jewels and elegant jewelry, children's jewelry, rings, estate silver, hollowware, and unusual gifts. Here is where you can find those wonderful Charleston (or plantation) rice spoons—traditionally found on every well-set Charleston table (see our Shopping chapter).

D&D Lines
190 King St.
(843) 853-5266
This is a boat lover's delight tucked away inside one of the doorways down the Historic Alley at 190 King Street. Inside, you'll find wonderful old pond boats of every shape and size, vintage fishing gear, toy motorboats, ship's wheels, and other decorative accessories with a nautical theme. We even saw a Navy uniform and a maître d' jacket from an old ocean liner. And this is real pay dirt for a browser, with a recently expanded collection of rare books on boats, fishing, Charleston, and the sea. The proprietor, Tony DeRista, is fun to talk to and a wealth of information on all things nautical.

Decorators Alley
177½ King St.
(843) 722-2707
This upstairs adventure is always a trip into the unusual: antiques, mirrors, lamps, rugs, decorative accessories, linens, garden ornaments, and quirky architectural embellishments. The lion's share of the merchandise is gleaned, they say, from

the "Gilded Age." Naturally, professional decorators are frequent callers, but the public is welcome and always entertained by the interesting finds.

Devonshire, the English Garden Shop
152 King St.
(843) 579-0022
Here is a heady mix of antique and carefully selected new items for the garden or the garden-like interior. The "look" is decidedly English and Devonshire has several popular shops in exclusive locations on both coasts that cater to devotees of this popular decorating trend. You'll find exclusive lines of hand-forged iron, old and new stone ornaments, iron gates, and attractive architectural elements along with a vast assortment of prints and books on garden decor.

English Patina Inc.
179 King St.
(843) 853-0308
Here is a direct importer of quality English and European 18th- and 19th-century furniture and accessories. The major specialty here is the large collection of handsome English chests, but we saw some fine Country French pieces as well. Be sure to see the large selection of antique brass spyglasses à la Capt. Ahab and Moby Dick.

Estate Antiques
155 King St.
(843) 723-2362
At Estate, you'll find a wide assortment of fine early American 18th- and 19th-century (pre-1830) furniture, plus Oriental rugs, prints, paintings, and other decorative accessories. The focus is on Charlestonian and Southern furniture, and the owners keep a keen eye out for interesting local estate sales. They carry no reproductions. Estate makes every effort to authenticate (and document) every piece on display. Past customers have the right to exchange previously purchased items for current merchandise or

Antiques / 147

The Antiques District of King Street is a favorite of window shoppers. PHOTO: FLETCHER NEWBERN

store credit. The owners are exclusive distributors of the video series "Authenticating Antique Furniture," by noted expert John Bivins, an excellent reference for beginners and professional collectors alike.

Gates of Charleston
73 Broad St.
(843) 958-0040

Facing the main thoroughfare of Broad Street is this fascinating shop dealing with garden decor. These folks can make your garden or patio into a showplace. Look for antique architectural products, wrought iron, planters, wall hangings, and other unique decorative items (old and new).

Gateway Antiques & Consignments
161½ King St.
(843) 722-3381

This is Mary Moore Jacoby's shop of estate consignments. This is as close as

you'll get to the old days of King Street antique shopping with a changing inventory of mostly English furniture (many pieces have a Charleston background). There's an interesting collection of smaller pieces, too, such as silver, porcelain, clocks, lamps, Majolica, and out-of-print books on Charleston.

John Gibson Antiques
171, 183 King St., 151 S. Market St.
(843) 722-0909

This firm has been dealing in antiques on King Street for about 20 years. Because genuine 18th-century pieces are getting increasingly difficult to find (not to mention more costly), this shop can make up remarkably convincing pieces by combining different old but incomplete antiques. Many handsome pieces of furniture have resulted from this practice, but be advised that their value (like the price) has been compromised. This crowded, fascinating shop features mostly 19th-century furniture along with some fine old reproductions. Estate appraisal, interior design, restoration, and gold-leafing services are offered.

Ginkgo Leaf
159 King St.
(843) 722-0640

This charming little shop has been around since 1990. It is a festive and eclectic mix of antique furniture and decorative accessories. There's a smattering of 18th-, 19th-, and 20th-century pieces, with an emphasis on the English and Country French look. Ginkgo Leaf also carries textiles, majolica, bamboo, and unique topiaries and makes custom dried-flower arrangements to order.

The Goat Cart
18 E. Elliot St.
(843) 722-1128

This little nook is one of Charleston's original consignment shops and offers an assortment of antiques, trifles, Oriental furniture, porcelains, decorative items, rugs, and 18th- and 19th-century American and English furniture. Locals as well as visitors shop here for unusual pieces (many of local origin) and a changing assortment of creative accessories.

Golden & Associate
206 King St.
(843) 723-8886, (843) 853-4706

Clearly, this is one of King Street's largest displays of imported and locally acquired pieces. The vast array of merchandise includes—but is not limited to—furniture, mirrors, chandeliers, sconces, fireplace accessories, and garden items from the 18th and 19th centuries.

Hoover Watches & Jewels
202 King St.
(843) 958-8002

This bright shop specializes in antique, vintage, and contemporary fine jewelry and personal timepieces. They carry names like Patek, Philippe, Rolex, plus many rare American wristwatches. Their selection of antique and designer engagement rings and wedding bands is another strong suit. Hoover has another store in New Orleans with additional inventory.

Hungryneck Antique Mall
401 Johnnie Dodds Blvd., Hwy. 17 Bypass, Mt. Pleasant
(843) 849-1744

Here is one of the largest antique malls in Mt. Pleasant with more than 60 dealers sharing 15,000 sq. ft. under one roof. They buy and sell antiques and collectibles of all kinds. Look for sterling silver, mahogany and oak furniture, Victorian pieces in wicker and ornamental iron. We've seen wicker, dolls, architectural pieces, and even linens here. It's always a changing scene and there's plenty of parking right out in front of the mall.

Helen S. Martin Antiques
169 King St.
(843) 577-6533

The specialties here are antique weapons with names like Remington and Williamson. There are 19th-century English, French, and even Confederate firearms to see, plus fine bronzes and rare antique books. Look for Oriental rugs, European ivory, and a large collection of sterling silver. We especially admire the shop's collection of fine European beer steins.

Mary Frances Miller Antiques and Interior Design
190-C King St.
(843) 958-0400

Tucked away down the alley beside D&D Antiques (with the toy boats and nautical antiques) is this shop of fine furniture and accessories of the 18th and 19th centuries. They also carry a selection of mid-sized oriental rugs. The furniture selection is both English and French—with some Chinese and Japanese accent pieces. Also look for brass and porcelain. The owner has shops in Charlotte and Atlanta, as well.

Antiques / 149

Jack Patla Co.
181 King St.
(843) 723-2314
Established back in 1951, this name has long been associated with fine 18th- and 19th-century antiques and English garden ornaments in the classic Charleston tradition. The ownership changed in 1997, but the tradition goes on, and the reputation for reliability still applies. Even the same management is on hand. Look for the extensive collection of antique brass fireplace fenders, English-made, lead garden ornaments, and wooden boxes of all kinds. Shipping is never a problem.

James Island Antiques
2028 Maybank Hwy., James Island
(843) 762-1415
Here, lucky shoppers will find 17th-, 18th-, and 19th-century furniture and accessories, including Jacobean oak. Look here for delft, pottery, Staffordshire, pearl ware, decorated stoneware, pewter, iron, tinware, and woodenware. This shop is open by chance or by appointment, so call ahead.

Joint Venture Estate Jewelers, Ltd.
185 King St.
(843) 722-6730
This is the area's largest estate and pre-owned fine jewelry consignment shop. The inventory ranges from the most elaborate Victorian ornaments to a very modern, contemporary look. Variety is the strong suit here—with more than 1,200 consignors offering jewelry, flatware, and hollowware for every taste and pocketbook. Specialties found here are platinum, diamonds, sapphires, emeralds, rubies, pearls, and a large assortment of vintage watches. Repairs, restorations, and appraisals are done on site.

King Street Antique Mall
495 King St.
(843) 723-2211
Here is the only antiques mall, per se, on the Charleston Peninsula—which means you see a whole lot of merchandise under one roof. There are about 75 dealers currently participating in this 9,000-sq.-ft. showroom of affordable antiques, collectibles, and fine art. You'll find everything from costume and estate jewelry to furniture and rugs to garden statuary and Civil War memorabilia. The location—only a block from the Visitors Center—puts you near convenient parking and (DASH Trolley) transportation elsewhere downtown.

Livingston & Sons Antiques Inc.
163 King St.
(843) 723-9697, (843) 556-6162
Livingston is a direct importer of fine English and European antiques whose displays can be seen at either its King Street shop or in its 39,000-square-foot warehouse at 2137 Savannah Highway. Look in these locations for an eclectic mix of merchandise from larger pieces such as chests and cabinets to handsome old wood boxes and clocks plus collectible majolica, Wedgewood, and Staffordshire.

Moore House Antiques
150 King St.
(843) 722-8065
Here is a delight for fanciers of Chinese Export porcelain. There's always a fine assortment of Canton, Rose Medallion, Fitzhugh, and others from the early 19th century. Look for the shop's 18th- and 19th-century furniture and Persian rugs too. This merchandise is beautifully documented, and safe shipping to anywhere is never a problem.

Peacock Alley
9 Princess St.
(843) 722-6056
Here's a charming assortment of fine antiques, reproductions, and decorative accessories in a restored warehouse just off King Street. The merchandise includes some interesting consignments from old Charleston homes and fine pieces from

Insiders' Tip

Every spring, as a scholarship fund-raising project
for the College of
Charleston's School of Arts,
there's a fabulous Antiques
Symposium appealing to
antiques lovers everywhere.
This three-day event is
held on campus and fea-
tures scholarly presenta-
tions, focused-study
sessions, private viewings
of merchandise from Charleston's best dealers and, of
course, tours of breathtaking historic homes. Speakers are all nationally
recognized leaders in their
particular fields. The cost
varies according to the
year's specific program and
the number of events you
want to attend. This is a
must-do for serious academics and novices to the field
alike. For more informa-
tion, call (843) 953-6339.

and decorative accessories. Owner Chet Kellogg is a veteran of the antiques trade and really knows his stuff. Quality and value are the bywords here. Framed prints and wall hangings are a special forte.

Perry's of Charleston
233 King St.
(843) 958-8866

A relative newcomer to Charleston's leg-endary King Street, Perry's of Charleston is a welcome one—with an unusual and fascinating shop. They deal in antique, estate, and fine jewelry and one-of-a-kind pieces that are truly the stuff of dreams. Owner and president Ernest Perry has more than 30 years' experience in buying, selling, and consigning fine jewelry and sterling tableware. He and his associates offer a full range of appraisal services including retail replacement and fair mar-ket value for estate, donation, gift, dam-age, customs evaluation, or divorce settlement purposes. Every piece at Perry's has a story, and the staff relishes each and every one. (See more in our Shopping chapter.)

Petterson Antiques and Appraisal Service
201 King St.
(843) 723-5714

Petterson bills itself as "the last curiosity shop in America." In addition to furni-ture, the merchandise includes classical eclectic curios, objets d'art, old books, porcelain, Depression glass, old art, mag-azines, movie and sports posters, and other decorative accessories. Look through its wonderful collections of antique Charleston postcards for a peek at Charleston B.C. (before crowds). Appraisals are offered, and Petterson has full auction service.

abroad. Peacock Alley is a half-block off King Street beside Saks Fifth Avenue. Out-of-town buyers can relax; the shop can ship anywhere.

Period Antiques
194 King St.
(843) 723-2724

Period Antiques is a small shop with an interesting, unusual, and ever-changing selection of choice 18th- and 19th-cen-tury American and European antiques including furniture, paintings, mirrors,

Queen Charlotte Antiques, Ltd.
173 King St.
(843) 722-9121

A newcomer to the King Street antiques scene is this shop, a sister to the original store open for a number of years in Charlotte, NC.

Their specialty is 17th- and 18th-century English and French fine antiques and decorative accessories. They also carry garden ornaments that are either old or reproductions of old garden decorations (recreated in new, more durable materials). The philosophy here is to provide merchandise for the Charleston market that has the formal elegance of 18th century England combined with the livability and casual charm of the French countryside. A nice collection of coffee table books illustrating that delightful mix makes this shop a pleasure to visit.

Ridler Page Rare Maps
205 King St.
(843) 723-1734

In the large, white building across the alley from Saks Fifth Avenue, this rare shop sells authentic antique maps covering all parts of the globe. It handles maps from the 16th through the 19th century, old coastal charts, and local map renderings. This place is as interesting to historians as it is to the antiques buffs and decorator types.

Roumillat's Antiques
2241 Savannah Hwy.
(843) 766-8899

This is something of a departure from the veddy, veddy serious antiques tradition of King Street in Charleston, but it's an

awful lot of fun. Roumillat's has a vast array of used furniture and antiques that can surprise you. Some people find real gems in the rough. Roumillat's says the selection includes American and English antiques, Victorian, Edwardian and plain old-fashioned stuff. Call ahead for directions to its West Ashley warehouse and the twice-monthly auction dates, then go and enjoy.

Shalimar Antiques
2418 Savannah Hwy.
(843) 766-1529

Five miles south of the Ashley River Bridge on US17, Shalimar has a large stock of quality antiques, clocks, and furniture. It offers expert clock restoration and carries the area's largest stock of American primitives, which are somewhat hard to find here in the Lowcountry.

The Silver Vault of Charleston
195 King St.
(843) 722-0631, (843) 571-4342

This is a hard-to-find resource for silver-plating, repairs, and full restorations of all metals, including brass and pewter. This is the companion shop of The Brass & Silver Workshop at 758 St. Andrews Boulevard. The owner, Alfred Crabtree, has more than 30 years' experience in silver repair and restorations.

Terrace Oaks Antique Mall
2037 Maybank Hwy., James Island
(843) 795-9689

Terrace Oaks is a fun place to browse for those unexpected finds. It has two floors and 11,000 square feet of American, European, and primitive furniture along with a wide variety of other related goodies including porcelain, collectibles, estate jewelry, and sterling. And, there's ample free parking.

287 East Bay
287 East Bay St.
(854) 723-0964

In what was once old warehouse space across from the Harris Teeter grocery store in Ansonborough is now a charming shop featuring English, French, and American antiques. Its collection includes a large and creative assortment of accessories, artwork (original oils and old prints), lamps, and objets d'art. They do competent restorations, too. Worldwide shipping is available.

Wine & Pine
208 King St.
(843) 723-0447

In the heart of the antiques district you'll find this slight anomaly that—when you stop to think of it—is actually a great idea. The shop is an off shoot of the East Bay Street store, Acquisitions, which is described earlier in this chapter. Here you'll find English and European wine cabinets and armoires (both antique pine and reproductions) as well as other inter-esting furniture associated with fine dining. But the surprise here is their vast collection of European and California wines plus the best accessories to go with them. The staff is well versed in domestic and imported wine as well as antique pine furniture, so stopping here is educational as well as fun. Picking up a nice bottle of wine to enjoy after a day's antique shopping on King Street is nothing short of inspired.

Zinn Rug Galleries
269 East Bay St.
(843) 577-0300

Zinn is a direct importer of exquisite antique and semi-antique Oriental, Caucasian, and Turkish rugs, kilims, and kilim accessories. It features a large selection of Aubussons and needlepoint as well. Also look for Suzanis and Ottoman furniture.

Experience the grandeur of Drayton Hall, built along the Ashley River's west bank.
PHOTO: COURTESY OF CHARLESTON AREA CONVENTION AND VISITORS BUREAU

Attractions

Visitor Information

House Museums

Plantations and
Gardens

Forts

Historic Churches

Museums and
Other Sites

However varied the attractions of the Lowcountry and Greater Charleston may be, this is a place where people are drawn to, captured by, and never completely escape from the clutches of history. In fact, it's fair to say we focus more on history—a deeper, richer, more romantic history (and more of it)—than any other Colonial city in America. At least, that's the traditional and prevailing Charlestonian attitude.

Whether you're a newcomer to the Lowcountry (and soon to be an Insider yourself) or just a visitor to this gentle land, it's easy to be overwhelmed by the amount of history offered here and the seriousness with which Charlestonians deal with it in their daily lives.

Charlestonians very much want to share their history with newcomers and guests. They'll proudly do so as long as you pay close attention, clearly make an effort to learn and seek factual information from reliable sources. People here aren't very interested in the tired Southern cliches put out by Hollywood and the peddlers of all that moonlight and magnolia nonsense. The true story of Charleston's past is far more interesting than any of the fiction you might have read or heard. Good listeners are richly rewarded for their investment of time and attention.

For obvious economic reasons and other reasons equally valid in this community (such as pride and passion), the subject of tourism in historic Charleston is seriously studied. There are many points of view, of course, but tourism has for many years been a rather sensitive and often volatile topic of discussion.

A good example of this debate can be found in a Charleston Chamber of Commerce brochure published for (attracting) the tourist market in 1904, a time when the city's fortunes were at a rather low economic ebb. Charleston is described as a lady—one of unquestionable breeding and dignity—who has been forced onto the wicked stage of tourism by unseemly circumstances far beyond her control:

"The conservatism which has always characterized Charleston has hitherto prevented her merits from becoming so widely known as they should be," the pamphlet reads. "But conservatism in matters connected with the welfare of the community is no longer in accord with the spirit of our times. Charleston has always been justly famed for her hospitality, and still delights to honor all those who are deserving of (her) respect and admiration."

Then, with further Victorian modesty, the brochure goes on to laud the city's apparently unlimited historical attractions:

"The lover of history finds deep interest in her (Charleston's) connection with every important historical event from the planting of the early colonies down to the present day and the sentimentally inclined can discover in the city and vicinity the scenes of many a legend and story."

Obviously, tourism and Charleston have a long working (if sometimes strained) relationship. Charleston and tourist management, on the other hand, are relatively recent and wary acquaintances. In other words, the sheer volume of visitors (especially during the past decade) has begun to seriously impact the fragile charm Charlestonians have stubbornly held onto for the past 200 years.

The quaint, genteel, quiet residential flavor of the 18th-century peninsular city (even with its 19th- and 20th-century scars) is by definition with the economic, cultural, and environmental consequences of 4.2 million tourists visiting annually. This collision of mores and economics has resulted in a very carefully planned and closely monitored tourism experience for today's Charleston visitor. We, as the city's guests (whether for a week or a lifetime), are very much the fortunate winners in this tug-of-war between then and now.

Because we truly care and because it helps to preserve our city's unique cultural identity, Charleston's historic attractions are, for the greatest part, well organized, highly accessible, and intelligently interpreted. In short, there are delightful experiences in Charleston for visitors of all ages and all areas of interest.

In this chapter, we will begin by steering you to visitors centers and information outposts. Then we'll take you on a written tour of the Lowcountry's brightest and best attractions, beginning with the house museums, followed by plantations and gardens, forts, historic churches, and other museums. There is a lot to see and do here, and we hope this guide will help you plan well and miss nothing of interest to you. Unless otherwise noted, all addresses are in Charleston.

Visitor Information

Charleston Visitor Reception and Transportation Center
375 Meeting St.
(843) 853-8000, (800) 868-8118

Because parking in the old Historic District is nearly always a problem, visitors are encouraged to make their first destination the Charleston Visitor Reception and Transportation Center. Its location on upper (meaning the northern end of) Meeting Street offers visitors a welcome opportunity to leave their cars behind and see Charleston's large Historic District (mostly on the southern end of the Peninsula) by any of several alternative transportation options. This is the major, general information resource site in Charleston proper, and when we make a general reference to "the Visitor Center" in our guide, the Visitor Reception and Transportation Center is the place to which we refer.

The Visitor Center building, erected in 1856 by the South Carolina Railroad and originally used as a freight depot, makes a perfect place to get your bearings and plan your adventure in historic Charleston. Inside, you'll find a three-dimensional diorama model of the peninsular city, while a multi-screen video display introduces you to the sights and sounds you're likely to encounter here.

You'll find a comprehensive collection of free brochures, maps, fliers, and other publications detailing the special tours, dining adventures, and lodging options in the city, along with information on various recreational offerings and transportation venues. There is also a central ticket office for most of the area's attractions, special events, and performances.

If you're arriving without reservations for lodging, there's even a desk here that can offer visitors a rescue for last-minute accommodations. The Lowcountry Reservations desk, near the ticket and information counter, keeps track of the city's hotel, bed and breakfast, and motel rooms that are still available as of that day and their sometimes discounted prices. Bear in mind, this is risky business during spring and fall or on weekends when it is entirely possible that the city's visitor accommodations are fully booked. But on the other hand, if you're looking for a last-minute room, this is the place to go first. And sometimes you can get a great deal.

Once you've taken in the city's overview of itself, it's time to go out and see the real thing. It's always best to start with a professional tour of some kind. If you're new to Charleston, this will be your only "first impression," so why not make it an informed one with a guided tour?

Guided walking tours usually begin in the morning and last from one to two hours. They start from various central locations in the Historic District—at most of the large hotels and bed and breakfast inns. The cost is about $15 a person. You may also choose to ride in a comfortable, air-conditioned minibus. These guided, motorized tours take about an hour, and prices range from $15 to $20. Or you might want to take one of Charleston's famous carriage tours and see the city at a clip-clop pace. (See our chapter on Guided Tours for complete information on tour options and prices.)

Inexpensive and convenient motorized shuttle buses called DASH (Downtown Area Shuttle System) cost 75 cents per ride and leave the old depot behind the center at 15- or 20-minute intervals and carry passengers to the old City Market in the heart of downtown. So, it's very possible to "do" the city and leave your car at the visitor center lot or garage.

Also at the Visitor Reception and Transportation Center, you'll find the 20-minute slide presentation called "Forever Charleston." This audiovisual introduction to the cornucopia of Charleston history and culture is a good one, well worth seeing. The work includes some remarkable photography by three of Charleston's nationally known photographers: Tom Blagden Jr., Ron Anton Rocz, and Bill Struhs. In air-conditioned comfort, you'll see breathtaking vistas over and beyond the city and check out (up close) some of the architectural detail that has been the signature of historic Charleston for at least 200 years. You'll hear tidbits from some of the city's local philosophers, and you'll get to peek behind usually closed gates into a few Charlestonian gardens and lifestyles.

"Forever Charleston" is shown every 30 minutes from 9 AM to 5 PM daily. The admission charge is $2.50 for adults and teens, $2 for seniors, and $1 for kids ages 6 to 12. It's free for children younger than 6. The visitor center is open daily from 8:30 AM to 5:00 PM.

Frances R. Edmunds
Center for Historic Preservation
108 Meeting St.
(843) 724-8484

Those who find themselves downtown in the vicinity of 108 Meeting Street (across from the Mills House) have another option for starting their historic Charleston odyssey. The Frances R. Edmunds Center for Historic Preservation is its official name, but it's the Historic Charleston Foundation's version of visitor orientation. You'll find a well-planned cultural and architectural overview and free and friendly tourist advice.

The center's museum shop carries a fine array of merchandise, including many items from the foundation's Reproduction Collections. You'll find a comprehensive selection of books and reference materials relating to preservation, restoration, and Charleston's 18th- and 19th-century cultural life. You can also buy tickets for the foundation's signature house museum, the Nathaniel Russell House, and Middleton Place Foundation's Edmondston-Alston House (see the House Museums section of this chapter). The Frances R. Edmunds Center is open Monday through Saturday from 10 AM to 5 PM. Sunday hours are from 2 to 5 PM. Admission is free.

The Preservation Society of Charleston
147 King St.
(843) 722-4630

Another friendly informational oasis for the sore-footed traveler (especially handy for those touring the many antiques venues scattered along King Street) is The Preservation Society of Charleston.

Its bookstore offers a fine collection of books, reference materials, and gift items pertaining to Charleston and the Lowcountry. The accommodating staff of volunteers offers free tourist information as well.

Every fall, starting at the end of September and running through October, The Preservation Society's evening candlelight tours of private homes and gardens are very popular. This is a lovely time of year to see the city. Tickets are priced at $40 a tour and often sell out early, but you might check here at the bookstore at the last minute and still be able to join one of these self-guided, neighborhood walking tours. (See our Annual Events chapter for more on the tours.)

The 147 King Street location serves as headquarters and resource center for the organization (founded in 1920) originally known as "The Society for the Preservation of Old Dwelling Houses," one of America's premiere preservation organizations. (See our Architectural Preservation chapter for more information.) The Preservation Society bookstore is open from 10 AM to 5 PM, Monday through Saturday. (See our Shopping chapter.)

House Museums

According to a recently completed study, peninsular Charleston contains more than 2,800 historic buildings rated as "architecturally significant." Overwhelming as that may seem, it's even more amazing to realize the vast majority of those buildings are private homes. And of these homes, literally hundreds could legitimately qualify as house museums—not only for their exterior architectural sophistication but also for their sumptuous interiors. In fact, preserving these homes and their remarkable collections of art, china, fine furniture, and fabrics has become an integral part of today's Charleston lifestyle.

It's staggering to think that even after Charleston's devastating earthquakes, wars, fires, and hurricanes—not to mention the ever-changing tides of the city's economy—these houses still stand. More than a few of them contain many of their original furnishings and treasured family heirlooms, some having been in place since before the American Revolution.

While most of these historic homes remain in private hands and are rarely opened to public tours, seven Charleston house museums offer visitors unique adventures behind normally closed doors.

Most of the following house museums are open year round and operated by various nonprofit preservation organizations in the city (see our Architectural Preservation chapter for more information). Others are privately owned and run as businesses. In either case, Charleston's house museums afford a fascinating glimpse into the style and sophistication of the city's interiors during a number of heydays in the development of American decorative arts.

From 18th-century Georgian to late-19th-century Victorian, Charleston's house museums are presented here in the chronological order of their construction dates. As a quick reference for those who don't happen to keep the eight basic architectural styles of historic Charleston constantly top-of-mind, the following definitions (courtesy of the Historic Charleston Foundation and the National Trust for Historic Preservation) are offered:

• *Colonial* refers to the period from 1690 to 1740. Look for a very low foundation, beaded clapboard siding, a high-pitched gable roof (sometimes with flared eaves), hipped dormers, and raised panel shutters. A good Charlestonian example is the John Lining House, 106 Broad Street at King Street.

• *Georgian* refers to the architectural style popular in England during the reign of Anne and the four Georges. Here in America, the style is generally assigned to the years 1700 to 1790. Look for a hipped roof, box chimneys, triangular pediments (often with oval lights), columns, a raised basement, and a belt course between floors. An excellent Charleston example is the Miles Brewton House, 27 King Street.

• *Federal* is the American architectural style seen chiefly between the years 1790 and 1820.

In England, the style is called "Adam," in reference to the English-Irish architect Robert Adam. Look for geometric rooms, ironwork balconies, a low-pitched roof, decorative bands around interior rooms, exterior trim, spiral stairs, and elliptical fan lights. The Nathaniel Russell House, 51 Meeting Street, is a fine Charleston example.

• *Classical Revival* is the architectural return to the lines and look of ancient Greece (and later, Rome). It was popular in America from about 1820 to 1875. Look for large, heavy columns and capitals, temple pediments, triglyph and guttae, and all the other details in classic Greek architectural order. In Charleston, a great example is Beth Elohim Synagogue, 90 Hasell Street.

• *Gothic Revival* refers to the period between 1850 and 1885, when many American building designs borrowed from the upreaching lines of western European architecture between the 12th and 16th centuries. Look for pointed arches, buttresses, stone tracery, and finials. At 136 Church Street, the French Huguenot Church exemplifies this style.

• *Italianate* is shown in the popular building style seen here between 1830 and 1900. Look for paired brackets and round head arches, balustrades, a low-pitched roof, and the loggia (or veranda). A classic Charleston example is the Col. John Algernon Sydney Ashe House, 26 South Battery.

• *Victorian* refers, of course, to England's Queen Victoria, who reigned from 1836 to 1901. In American architecture, however, it was a popular style between the years 1860 and 1915. Look for a multi-gabled roof, elaborate wood bracket work (sometimes called gingerbread), turrets, and roof decorations. A rare Charleston example is the Sottile House, on the College of Charleston campus at Green Street.

• *Art Deco* is exemplified in the highly stylized look that many American buildings took during the years between the world wars, roughly 1920 to 1940. Look for decorative panels, narrow windows, flat roofs, and multicolored bands. Charleston's most outstanding example is the beautifully restored Riviera Theater, 225–227 King Street.

Thomas Elfe House (1760)
54 Queen St.
(843) 722-9161

This delightfully miniature single house is one of Charleston's wonderful little treasures that, for the past several years, has been open to the public on a limited basis. (For more information on single houses, see the Close-up on this architectural idiom in our Architectural Preservation chapter.) Built well before the American Revolution, it was a modest craftsman's home like many others throughout the city. The particular craftsman who owned this one, however, was most extraordinary.

Thomas Elfe arrived in Charleston from England in about 1747, bringing along a unique skill for woodworking. Here in Charleston, he became one of the most prolific and acclaimed cabinetmakers of the Colonial era. His work appears in many other house museums and private homes throughout the city, as well as in other fine museums all over the country.

During the period of 1768 to 1775, his own records show that Elfe created more than 1,500 pieces of cabinetwork. He worked primarily in mahogany, with distinctive fretwork, unique leg design, and inner-drawer construction being telltale signs of Elfe's craftsmanship.

Restored in 1970, the house interiors show many finishing touches that are attributed to its first, now-famous owner. All four rooms display exquisitely proportioned fireplace walls of cypress paneling. There are china cabinets and deftly scaled closets artfully worked into each chimney alcove. The slightly lowered dados give the effect of higher ceilings and greater space.

The fact that its first owner was a major contributor to the art and lifestyle of Colonial Charleston makes it interesting today. Any serious student of fine, Charleston-made, 18th-century furniture or an antiques buff with a nose for history

The deftly-scaled dining room of the Thomas Elfe House (1760) is presented much as Elfe would have left it in the mid-18th century. PHOTO: COURTESY OF THOMAS ELFE HOUSE

will want to see this house. It is a show-place for 18th- and early-19th-century furnishings. The tour schedule is Monday through Friday from 10 AM until noon. Occasionally, the house is open afternoons and weekends, so call ahead to check. Admission is $5.

Heyward-Washington House (1772)
87 Church St.
(843) 722-0354

This handsome, early Charleston "dwelling house" is now known by two names because of two prominent Americans associated with it—one an owner, the other a distinguished guest.

It was built in 1772 by Daniel Heyward, a wealthy rice planter and the father of Thomas Heyward Jr., a South Carolina signer of the Declaration of Independence. It is documented that the younger Heyward lived in the house until 1794.

In 1791, President George Washington made a grand tour of the new nation and included Charleston on his itinerary. In anticipation of this distinguished visitor, the city rented Heyward's house for Washington's accommodations, and Heyward was thus displaced to his country house for the duration. In Washington's diary, he

recorded his visit to the property, saying, "The lodgings provided for me in this place were very good, being the furnished house of a gentleman at present residing in the country; but occupied by a person placed there on purpose to accommodate me."

Today the house is furnished with a magnificent collection of period antiques, especially some fine, Charleston-made furniture of the 18th century. Look for the famous Holmes bookcase that still bears the scars of an incoming British mortar from the days of the American Revolution. This is the only 18th-century house museum in the city with original outbuildings (kitchen, carriage house, and necessary) still a part of the courtyard. You'll also find a small formal garden, in keeping with the period of the house.

Heyward-Washington House was saved from destruction in the early 1920s by The Preservation Society of Charleston. It is now a National Historic Landmark owned and operated by The Charleston Museum. It's open daily, Monday through Saturday from 10 AM to 5 PM and Sunday from 1 to 5 PM. No entry is allowed after 4:30 PM. Admission is $8 for adults and teens and $4 for children 3 to 12. Note that The Charleston Museum offers discounted combination ticket prices for this house, the Aiken-Rhett House, and the Joseph Manigault House—$12 for two museum sites, $18 for three.

Joseph Manigault House (1803)
350 Meeting St.
(843) 723-2926

At the beginning of the 19th century, Charleston architecture was still very much dominated by what was fashionable in Mother England. This house, designed and built in 1803 by Charleston gentleman-architect Gabriel Manigault for his brother Joseph, was certainly no exception. Today it remains one of America's most beautiful examples of the graceful Adam style.

Both Manigault brothers were wealthy rice planters with sophisticated tastes. Gabriel had studied in Geneva and London, where the Adam influence was at its height, and he maintained an extensive architectural library of his own.

The house is distinguished by one of the most graceful staircases in the city and displays an outstanding collection of Charleston, American, English, and French furniture of the period. Don't miss the charming gate temple in the rear garden. During the 1920s, when the Manigault House was very nearly torn down in the name of progress, Gabriel Manigault's classical gate temple was used as the restroom for an oil company's service station, then on the garden site. Later, during World War II, the house served as a USO canteen for servicemen passing through Charleston's busy Navy Yard en route to battle stations overseas.

Today it is a National Historic Landmark owned and operated by The Charleston Museum. Hours are 10 AM to 5 PM Monday through Saturday and 1 to 5 PM on Sunday. The last tour begins at 4:30 PM. Admission is $8 for adults and teens and $4 for children 3 to 12.

Nathaniel Russell House (1808)
51 Meeting St.
(843) 724-8481

Prominent shipping merchant Nathaniel Russell decided to build his great "mansion-house" on Meeting Street, practically within sight of the busy wharves that produced his wealth. When his house was completed in 1808, Russell was 71 and he had reportedly spent $80,000 on the project—an enormous sum at that time.

Like the Manigault house, Russell's new home was inspired by the work of English architect Robert Adam, whose delicate style was influenced by the airy classical designs only recently uncovered (literally) in the Italian excavations of Pompeii and Herculaneum.

Today's visitor is immediately dazzled by the dramatic, free-flying, elliptical stairway floating up through three floors without any visible means of support. Finely proportioned, geometric rooms are furnished with another outstanding collection of Charleston, English, and French pieces, including rare china, silver, and paintings.

Unlike most other Charleston house museums, the Russell House has never been through a sad period of decline and disrepair. First as a fine town house, then as the home of a South Carolina governor, and later as a school for girls and even a convent, 51 Meeting Street has always been a respected and cared-for landmark. Today it is owned and operated by Historic Charleston Foundation, an organization that has done much to preserve and illuminate the city's architectural heritage (see our Architectural Preservation chapter).

The house is open for tours Monday through Saturday from 10 AM to 5 PM and Sunday from 2 to 5 PM. The last tour begins at 4:30 PM. The house is closed on Christmas Day. Admission is $7 a person; for children younger than 6, admission is free. Call (843) 724-8482 for tickets and group tour information.

Edmondston-Alston House (1825–1838)
21 E. Battery
(843) 722-7171

In 1825 Charles Edmondston, another wealthy merchant and wharf owner, built this handsome dwelling where he could enjoy an uninterrupted view over the expanse of Charleston Harbor. In 1828,

The second floor Drawing Room of the Edmondston-Alston House is a fine example of why Charleston's famous house museums are a must-see. PHOTO: COURTESY OF CHARLESTON AREA CONVENTION AND VISITORS BUREAU

the house was bought by Col. William Alston, a rice planter. His son, Charles, redecorated the house in the 1830s, favoring the fashionable Greek Revival style.

Incredibly, today's visitor can still find many family documents, portraits, silver pieces, and fine furnishings—including Charles Alston's almost-intact library—in place. Much of it dates back to the 1830s. The house is notable for its unusual Regency woodwork, as well as its uncompromising views of the harbor. The intimacy and authentic details of the house may leave guests feeling as if the Alstons only recently left the property, perhaps on a visit to the country.

The Edmondston-Alston House is owned by Middleton Place Foundation. Tours are offered from 10 am to 4:30 pm Tuesday through Saturday and 1:30 to 4:30 pm Sunday and Monday. Admission is $8 a person and free for children younger than 6.

Aiken-Rhett House (1817, 1833, 1857)
48 Elizabeth St.
(843) 723-1159

Unlike any other house museum in Charleston, the Aiken-Rhett house is a time capsule of Charleston's history and taste. It was the home of Gov. William Aiken from 1833 through 1887, and it owes most of its eerie charm to him.

The structure was built in 1817 by John Robinson as a typical Charleston single house, much like many others built in the city at the time. However, under the later ownership of South Carolina railroad magnate Aiken (who was governor at the time of the Civil War), the house was drastically altered and enlarged. In 1833 it was remodeled to conform to the bold Greek Revival style popular then. Again in 1857 alterations were made, this time in the heavily ornamented Rococo Revival style that was gaining popularity in antebellum Charleston. Rococo Revival, which was popular in 18th-century France, is noted for curvilinear lines, as in shells, foliage, and scrolls.

Here again, an uncanny amount of furnishings and other objects belonging to Governor and Mrs. Aiken can still be found, including portraits, statuary, library volumes, and elaborate chandeliers the couple brought back from Paris in the 1830s. The difference here is that much of the house is unrestored. It is instead preserved, largely as it was presented to The Charleston Museum in 1975 by descendants of the Aiken family.

As a result, the visitor can almost feel the presence of Jefferson Davis, president of the Confederacy, who was a guest in the house in 1863. You can easily picture Confederate Gen. P.G.T. Beauregard using the house as his headquarters during the almost relentless Federal bombardment of Charleston in 1864. And the haunting, life-size portrait of Mrs. Aiken dressed in her finery belies the emotional and economic hardship she suffered after the war when the governor was arrested and briefly imprisoned for treason.

Another miracle of the Aiken-Rhett house is the remarkably well-preserved (but unrestored) slave quarters and outbuildings (including stables and a privy) to the rear of the house. A high masonry wall surrounding the stable yard and slave quarters somehow managed to keep out the forces of time and change. They're shown as they are, unrestored and unromanticized, making an eloquent statement about slavery and the sociology of the 19th-century South. If woodworking detail is any measure of worth and respect, the horses at the Aiken-Rhett house were more important than the slaves who worked as house servants. The horse stalls have Gothic arches and turned pillars; no such adornment graces the utilitarian slave quarters.

The fragile textures of time and the changing fortunes of war very much show in this remarkable house museum. Surely this is its most romantic and tragic charm. The Aiken-Rhett House is a must-see. One-hour house tours are given from 10 AM until 4:30 PM, Monday through Saturday. Last tour starts at 4:15 PM. On Sundays, tours are from 2 to 5 PM, with the last tour starting at 4:45 PM. Admission is $7 a person; for children younger than 6, it is free.

A combined ticket that includes admission to the Nathaniel Russell house is $12, and a ticket for the two house museums plus the Powder Magazine is $1

Calhoun Mansion (1876)
16 Meeting St.
(843) 722-8205

Here is one of Charleston's few Victorian palaces. A possible reason Victoriana is under represented in Charleston's decorative arts is a fiscal one—the city's economy was devastated by the Civil War. Clearly, during most of the Victorian era (1860–1915), no great amount of mansion building was being done here. But the 25-room, 24,000-square-foot, elaborately decorated house now known as the Calhoun Mansion is one spectacular exception.

It was built by George Walton Williams, a merchant and banker who, unlike most wealthy Southerners, was financially undaunted by the war (his fortune was largely invested north of the Mason-Dixon line). At the time of construction, the house was immodestly described in New York, Atlanta, and Charleston newspapers as "the handsomest and most complete home in the South, if not the country."

The Calhoun Mansion has 14-foot ceilings, ornate plaster moldings, and all the elaborate woodwork, lighting fixtures, and window treatments you would expect from the period. A grand staircase climbs to a 75-foot domed ceiling, and there's a ballroom with a glass skylight 45 feet high. A remarkable collection of fine furnishings of the Victorian era makes a grandiose statement in this fascinating anomaly of Charleston's decorative arts.

The house is open for tours from 10 AM to 4 PM Wednesday through Sunday. Admission is $15 for adults and $7 for children ages 6 to 11. Special tours may be arranged upon request.

Plantations and Gardens

Without a doubt, no visit to Charleston is complete without a journey to the plantations. And nowhere is Charleston's late, great plantation culture more evident than along the old route to Summerville via the Ashley River Road (S.C. Highway 61).

This is the state's oldest highway, and it once provided secondary, back-road access to some of the most beautiful Colonial plantations in the Lowcountry. Primary access to the early plantations was by river—a much faster, more convenient route.

It might be helpful to remember much of the wealth and sophistication of Charleston in the 18th and 19th centuries was derived from the plantation system. And the plantation system was, after all, an agricultural economy based on the practice of slavery. As beguiling as it may appear to be, the opulence and wealth so evident in the downtown Charleston houses and outlying plantations built during these years may be viewed with a newfound perspective when remembering this grim reality.

This is where the Charleston visitor may fall prey to a trite old Southern cliche: namely, that there was a time when the bucolic romanticism of the Old South largely swirled around the moonlit, magnolia-scented lives of Southern aristocracy. While some of that romantic imagery may be true, it by no means tells the whole story.

Today, much more than in the past, greater emphasis is being placed on showing visitors a realistic picture of the society as a whole. That includes the lives of slaves, trades people, merchants, women, and children. Look for that emerging slant as you go about your adventures on the old plantations.

It might also be helpful to know that America's version of the plantation system did not originate here at all. Like almost everything else in the early colonies, it was imported. It came to Charleston from England through the West Indies. In fact, many of Charleston's early planter families emigrated from older plantations in Barbados.

While a number of influences brought its concept to America, slavery clearly flourished here in the Lowcountry. Today's visitor has a rare opportunity to see the plantation system in its various forms and eras. Indeed, today's more enlightened stance offers the chance to see where slavery took root in South Carolina—and where it ended.

Here's a suggested route you may want to take:

Starting on the Peninsula, take U.S. Highway 17 S. Once across the Ashley River bridge, you'll drive through some of Charleston's post-World War II urban sprawl. You may choose to start your plantation tour at the very beginning—at Charles Towne Landing State Historic Site, South Carolina's unique state park at the site of the colony's original settlement. There, you'll explore a reconstruction of an early settler's cabin and see the "experimental garden" where test crops of various kinds held the settler's best hope for survival in this brave new world.

Next, you may want to take the same architectural quantum leap Charlestonians did— from that early, crude settler's cabin to the classical grandeur of Drayton Hall (begun in 1738), which was built along the Ashley River's west bank only a generation later.

At Middleton Place (developed c. 1740) and Magnolia Plantation (started in the 1680s, then expanded about 1840), you can explore the vast gardens so important to these early planter families. Magnolia's informal design (typical of 19th-century gardens) makes an interesting contrast to Middleton's strict geometric patterns (so popular in 18th-century France).

In fact, the geometrically designed formal gardens at Middleton Place show the incredible strength of Europe's artistic influence here in Charles Towne, just 40 years before the American Revolution. At Middleton Place House (1755) you can trace the story of the distinguished Middleton family, which included Arthur (1742–1787), a signer of the Declaration of Independence. At the Middleton Place stable yards, you can interact with some of the daily activities of a working plantation.

In the spring, you'll want to include Cypress Gardens, originally part of Dean Hall plantation on the Cooper River. Follow S.C. Highway 61 from Middleton Place to S.C. Highway 165, join U.S. Highway 17-A through Summerville to Moncks Corner and follow the signs. There, in a 163-acre, black-water cypress swamp, is an incredible azalea garden started in the 1920s and now owned and operated by the City of Charleston Department of Parks. You'll find charming little bateaux (flat-bottomed boats) to use, and there are 3 miles of walking paths through the vibrant spring colors reflected in the mirrorlike waters.

Back through Charleston and 6 miles north along US 17 is Boone Hall, the picturesque, 738-acre plantation used extensively in the ABC TV miniseries "North and South," filmed in and around Charleston several years ago. Boone Hall's best features include the famous avenue of live oaks and the original "slave street" of nine brick slave cabins (c. 1743).

You won't be able to visit all these plantations in a single day. If you must select only a sampling of Greater Charleston's plantation culture, the following in-depth review of these sites should help you choose.

You won't regret the investment of time and travel it takes to digest these plantations and gardens. They're so much a part of the city—so vital to its development—to see just one side of Charleston life and not the other might seriously handicap your understanding of the area as a whole.

Charles Towne Landing State Historic Site
1500 Old Towne Rd., between I-26 and S.C. Hwy. 171
(843) 852-4200

Surely this is one of the most unusual state parks in South Carolina, if not America. Charles Towne Landing State Historic Site was created as part of South Carolina's 300th anniversary celebration in 1970 on the plantation belonging to Dr. and Mrs. Joseph I. Waring. Today the property isn't presented to the public as a plantation per se. Rather, the vast acreage is devoted to re-creating and interpreting the first English settlement in the Carolinas, which existed on this plantation site back in 1670.

Once inside the gate, visitors travel down a long alley bordered by ancient live oaks and swamp. Eventually you come to a parking lot and a large complex of modern buildings that serve as a starting point for your adventure.

Here are some highlights:

If at all possible, begin your visit with the wonderful 30-minute film "Carolina," shown free in the nearby theater pavilion at scheduled intervals. This film, directed by Carlos Romers in 1969, features wonderful music by the London Philharmonic Orchestra and is still the best introduction to Charleston around. Filmed entirely without actors, this motion picture sensitively traces the settlers' long, arduous voyage across the Atlantic and shows the strange new world that awaited them. The camera celebrates the settlers' eventual success with a feast of the city's art, flowers, and rich architectural detail. The film gives newcomers a clear sense of the first settlers' struggles, and what must have been their surprise and wonder at the wild new land that would hold their future.

The giant Interpretive Center at the main pavilion once included an unusual underground museum that interpreted the first 100 years of the colony with artifacts, exhibits, recordings, and art. This area was closed because of damage sustained in Hurricane Hugo and has not reopened. Many of the exhibits, however, have been moved to the lobby of the theater pavilion and can be seen there.

Along the river, you may board a full-scale replica of a typical 17th-century trading vessel called the *Adventure*. Picture it as a common work vehicle of the early plantation system, plying the waters loaded with fur pelts, indigo shipments, and rice to sell on the wharves in Charleston. These boats also carried people and supplies to the widely scattered plantations upriver.

The post-Hugo redesign of the Animal Forest boasts a 20-acre natural habitat zoo with wolves, pumas, bears, bison, snakes, and alligators—all part of the Lowcountry landscape when settlers first arrived in the 1670s.

The Settlers' Life Area, with its replica Colonial buildings, is a handsome example of what early colonists saw every day. You'll see candle-making, open-fire cooking, woodworking, and, depending on the season and the weather, even the colony's first printing press in action. Special exhibits and demonstrations can be found here on holidays.

Charles Towne Landing is open all year. The hours are 8:30 AM to 5 PM, extended from June through August to 6 PM. Picnic tables, a snack bar, and a gift shop are all on site. The park is largely accessible to handicapped visitors. Admission is $5 for adults and teens older than 14, $2.50 for children 6 to 14, $2.50 for seniors (in-state seniors are free) and free for handicapped visitors and children younger than 6. Bicycle rentals are $2 an hour with a $2 deposit. Tram tours are $1 a person. (See our Kidstuff chapter.)

Drayton Hall
3380 Ashley River Rd.
(843) 766-0188

Not a tour of a reconstructed working plantation or the collected decorative arts from a bygone era, Drayton Hall offers an adventure in architecture. Yes, architecture and a great deal more.

If for no other reason, Drayton Hall should be seen and experienced as the sole survivor of the ugly 1865 rampage by Union troops, who looted and burned nearly every other plantation house along the Ashley River. But there is more to Drayton Hall, as it also stands as a survivor of many other changes, influences, forces, and times.

It was built between 1738 and 1742 as the country seat (primary home) of John Drayton (1716–1779), whose family had emigrated to Charles Towne from Barbados and settled nearby at Magnolia Plantation a generation earlier. The house is considered one of the oldest and finest examples of Georgian-Palladian architecture in America. Its recessed, two-story portico may have been inspired by Italy's Villa Pisani, designed in 1552 by Andrea Palladio. The portico is one of the architectural signatures of Palladianism, and Drayton Hall's portico may be one of the earliest built in America.

The story of how this very sophisticated English Palladian villa came to be built along the west bank of the Ashley, and how it survived the ravages of time, wars, earthquakes, and hurricanes, is a fascinating saga.

Maybe the greatest curiosity of all is how the old Drayton house survived the enormous forces of changing architectural taste. Oddly, the house was never modernized for 20th-century use. Drayton Hall has never seen plumbing or central heat; it never had gas installed for lighting or heating purposes. Its only link with modern electricity is the one meager line that brings life to its sadly necessary modern security system.

Quite simply, Drayton Hall is an architectural time capsule. The structure remains almost untouched as an eloquent statement about 18th-century thinking, craftsmanship, technology, and design. It's one of the few sites left in Colonial America so pure, unaltered, and uncompromising.

Visitors will find the Drayton Hall story—how it all came to pass—interpreted by a small group of professional guides. These storytellers lead you through 250 years of time, family genealogy, architectural history, and a smattering of the economic and social realities of the plantation system.

A word or two about "interpretation" might be helpful here. Because each guide at Drayton Hall develops his or her own perspective of the house, every tour will be slightly different. That is, each guide bears the responsibility of interpreting and synthesizing the tremendous amount of research data collected about the property. You hear the guide's words, not a written script. Thus, return visits will only deepen your understanding of the house, its people, and its times. The bare fact that you're touring virtually unfurnished rooms is hardly noticeable, since each room is chock-full of interesting information and rich architectural detail.

Drayton Hall comes to life because imagination is a wonderful artist. Imagination can paint in the faded colors of Drayton Hall's early days, when the settlement of Charles Towne was barely 70 years old. It can flesh out the heady, pre-Revolutionary days when the Ashley River plantation system was at its zenith. Now, through imagination, the visitor can even see Drayton Hall in the grim, dark days following the Civil War, when vagrants and vandals used it at will. Imagination can find the returning prosperity and almost hear the laughter of the Drayton parties and other family occasions held here as recently as the 1960s. All it takes is an informed interpreter and your attentive ear.

Research is an ongoing process at Drayton Hall. The staff has recorded oral histories of the Drayton family as well as the African Americans so closely associated with the house and its survival. Preserved but unrestored, Drayton Hall and its faded hues and subtle shading, its frayed places and telling stains are all pure Charleston. The house serves to illuminate the whole Ashley River plantation system in a rare and strangely haunting light.

In the spring of 1997, Drayton Hall added another dimension to its interpretation of the site. A map is now provided to visitors for a self-guided nature walk through the Drayton property. You can walk through various natural environments including marsh, riverfront, and forest areas. Minimal signage along the trail offers interpretation of each environment. Archaeological as well as historic sites can be seen and understood as to their relevance to the 18th- and 19th-century Drayton Hall lifestyle. Major portions of the nature trails are handicapped-accessible.

An ongoing project at Drayton Hall is an education program for students in kindergarten through grade 12. Several curriculum-coordinated programs feature student tours, plantation games, archaeology studies, and preservation workshops for both teachers and students.

This historic site is now jointly owned by the National Trust for Historic Preservation and the South Carolina Department of Parks, Recreation, and Tourism. Admission prices include a guided tour of the historic house. Admission to the grounds only is $3 per person. Tours are offered on the hour from 10 AM to 3 PM November through February and 10 AM to 4 PM March through October. A written tour in English, French, or German can be purchased. Group rates, AAA and military discounts, handicapped access, and pre-arranged student programs are available. During peak season (March and April, September and October), admission is $10 for adults, $8 for ages 12 to 18, $6 for children ages 6 through 11. Admission is $2 less off season and always free to members of the National Trust and Friends of Drayton Hall who show their membership cards. (See our Annual Events chapter for information on the Annual Spirituals Concert at Drayton Hall.)

Magnolia Plantation and Gardens
S.C. Hwy. 61
(843) 571-1266

This is where Thomas Drayton Jr., father of Drayton Hall's John Drayton, settled when he came to Charles Towne in 1676. Early on, the home that Drayton, a successful

English planter from the island of Barbados, built for himself and his family was destroyed by fire. The house built to replace it was subsequently burned by Union troops in 1865. The present structure is said to have been a Drayton family hunting lodge that was moved down the Ashley River in 1873 and placed atop the foundations of the old plantation house.

Magnolia Plantation is the original (and continuing) home of the Drayton family, now owned and managed by a ninth-generation descendant. It is famous for its expansive, informal, English-style gardens, which are the legacy of the Rev. John Grimke-Drayton, the plantation's owner during the Civil War, whose parish was nearby at St. Andrews. In 1843 the Rev. Grimke-Drayton imported numerous specimens of *Camellia japonica*, and in 1848, *Azalea indica*. Due to a bout with tuberculosis in the late 1840s, he left his parish for a time and devoted himself entirely to his garden.

By 1870, despite the tragedy of the war and the burning of the main house, the gardens at Magnolia Plantation had grown in size and reputation. That year, the property was first opened to the public. Paddle-wheeled steamboats from Charleston made regularly scheduled excursions to Magnolia, where tourists relaxed, took picnics, and strolled along the blossom-laden paths. But for all its lacy bridges arching gracefully over mirrorlike cypress ponds, one little-known, smaller area is well worth finding.

Look for the garden called Flowerdale. This is where it all began. Here is Magnolia's earliest garden area (planted in the late 1680s), and it was possibly the inspiration for the Rev. Grimke-Drayton's larger, more ambitious plan a century and a half later. Surely the reverend sat here in the 1850s, pondering the moral issues facing his plantation world as the political storm clouds gathered over the South. Perhaps it was amid the beauty of Flowerdale that Grimke-Drayton first thought of expanding the garden plan to create an

The world-famous gardens at Magnolia Plantation are colorful year-round.
PHOTO: COURTESY OF MAGNOLIA PLACE

oasis of beauty so large and lasting it might someday sustain his family home.

Today the gardens boast 250 varieties of azaleas and 900 varieties of camellias. These, plus many other flowers added through the years, keep Magnolia Gardens in colorful bloom all year long. Its most spectacular season, however, is spring, when the dazzling, vibrant azalea colors seem to vibrate on the landscape as far as the eye can see.

Visitors can get an overview of the property in a 12-minute video on the plantation's history shown at regular intervals in the orientation theater. Magnolia Plantation offers additional activities for nature lovers. Canoes can be rented to glide through the eerie beauty of its 125-acre waterfowl refuge. There are walking and bicycle trails, plus a wildlife observation tower that's very popular with birdwatchers. There's an herb garden, a horticultural maze, an antebellum slave cabin, a typical Ashley River rice barge, and even a petting zoo for children (as well as adults). You'll find picnic areas, a snack shop, and a gift shop there too. (See our Kidstuff chapter.)

The property is open daily from 8 AM to 5 PM. Group rates are available. Regular admission is $11 for adults, $8 for teenagers, $5 for children ages 6 through 12, and free for those younger than 6 (an additional $5 provides admission to the Audubon Swamp Garden as well). The house tour is an additional $6; but children under 6 cannot tour the house. However, the 30-minute Nature Train tram ride is $5 for adults, $4 for teenagers, $3 for children 6 through 12, and $1 for children under 6.

Audubon Swamp Garden at Magnolia Gardens
S.C. Hwy. 61
(843) 571-1266
In the 1980s, Magnolia Plantation and Gardens added a new element—the Audubon Swamp Garden. This separate attraction encompasses a 60-acre, black-water cypress and tupelo swamp. The visitor has the opportunity to see an otherwise inaccessible natural area via boardwalks, dikes, and bridges, which provide an intimate view of the horticultural beauty and wildlife, including a few alligators.

The swamp garden gets its name from the great 19th-century American naturalist and wildlife artist, John James Audubon, who visited Magnolia in search of water bird specimens during his many lengthy stays in Charleston.

This attraction, a 45-minute self-guided walking tour, is operated apart from the rest of Magnolia Plantation and may be seen at half the price of Magnolia's general admission. That means $5 for adults, $4 for teens, $3 for kids ages 6 through 12, and free for those younger than 6.

Middleton Place
S.C. Hwy. 61
(843) 556-6020
Middleton is one of the Lowcountry's most famous plantations and another National Historic Landmark along the rich and fascinating Ashley River. This was the home of Henry Middleton, president of the First Continental Congress, and his son, Arthur, a signer of the Declaration of Independence.

The sheer size and scope of Middleton's gardens tell a great deal about the man and his grand vision. When he began his garden plan in 1741 (the framework for it remains unchanged today), the French influence for adopting a formal, geometric design was still very much in vogue. This was the Age of Reason, where philosophy held that the essence of true beauty lay in humankind's conquest over nature. Thus, all great gardens of the time imposed order and geometric form over the otherwise natural, unruly landscape.

Legend says it took 100 slaves almost a decade to complete the sweeping terraces, walks, and artificial lakes—vistas that are still pleasing to the eye today. But the gardens at Middleton Place are only part of

The surviving flanker building at Middleton Place is a house museum in its own right boasting rare art and fine furnishings. PHOTO: COURTESY OF CHARLESTON AREA CONVENTION AND VISITORS BUREAU

the plantation story interpreted here. Unlike some of the plantations closer and more convenient to Charleston, Middleton Place was a world unto itself. The 12-acre greensward, with its grazing sheep and strutting peacocks, creates an unforgettable image for the first-time visitor. This bucolic, pastoral scene belies the frenzy of activity and the vast labor force needed to maintain this busy world.

Now open on the Middleton Place grounds is Eliza's House, an actual freedman's dwelling. It is furnished as it might have been found in the 1870s, when African Americans who stayed on the plantation after emancipation lived there. Middleton Place Foundation conducts ongoing research into the lives of the slaves, freedmen, and tradespeople who were so important to the Middleton Place scene. The lively plantation stableyards, with active displays of day-to-day life, provide another glimpse into that busy world. Chances are you'll find a blacksmith, a potter, weavers, and carpenters all busy at

work and eager to explain and demonstrate their skills.

The main house, built sometime before 1741, was—like Magnolia's—burned in 1865 by Union troops. It is said the soldiers drank wine and dined in splendor at Middleton Place house, then set fire to it as they left.

The south flanker building (added about 1755) was least damaged by the fire, and it was essentially rebuilt in the early years of this century in its present form. Inside, you'll find Middleton family memorabilia displayed, along with a remarkable collection of important family portraits that include works by Benjamin West and Thomas Sully.

Not to be missed is the view of the Ashley River from the high terraces of the gardens. The green grass ripples down the hillside to the graceful butterfly lakes below. Off to one side, the old rice mill counterbalances the picture-perfect composition of the landscape.

The Restaurant at Middleton Place

serves authentic Lowcountry cuisine and a daily lunch is available to visitors. At night, from 6 to 10 PM, the restaurant serves a delightful candlelight dinner and there's no admission charge for entry to the property. (See our Restaurants chapter for details on dining at Middleton Place.)

In addition to the sensitive and skillful interpretation of the plantation's glorious past, there's an unexpected contemporary side to its present-day life. Just past the rice mill, a path leads into the forest and up a hill to The Inn at Middleton Place, a 55-room riverside oasis for discerning overnight travelers. The Inn was designed by Charleston architect W.G. Clark, and it seems to have been born "of" the forest rather than "in" it. With vine-covered stucco and unblinking modern glass walls, each suite looks out over a green, woodland setting or the quiet waters of the Ashley River. A visit to The Inn is well worth the short stroll from yesterday into the present (see our Bed and Breakfast & Atmospheric Inns chapter for more). The Inn has won numerous architectural awards, plus a place in *Time* magazine's "10 Best of '86" list and a spread in *Architectural Digest Travels*.

Middleton Place is open daily. Hours are 9 AM to 5 PM for the gardens and stable yards. House tours begin at 10 AM, except on Mondays, when they begin at 1:30 PM. House tour admission adds $8 a person to Middleton Place rates: $15 for adults and teens and $7 for children ages 6 to 12. Group rates are available, special events with food service may be arranged on the property. (See our Annual Events chapter for special events at Middleton.)

Cypress Gardens
Off S.C. Hwy. 52,
8 miles south of Moncks Comer
(843) 553-0515

For those with time and the inclination to go even farther afield, there's yet another treat in store. Discover the beauty and wonder of Cypress Gardens—a true Southern cypress swamp and a 162-acre water forest of uncommon natural beauty.

This park, once part of Dean Hall Plantation, is now owned and operated by Berkeley County. You'll find meandering footpaths for hikers, but the traditional way to see Cypress Gardens is by bateau—a flat-bottomed boat poled or paddled by expert young boaters who are always on hand to do the work for a small price. You have the option of rowing yourself if you like, but the serenity of the black waters mirroring springtime azaleas, dogwoods, daffodils, and wisteria deserves your undivided attention.

In a separate building, Cypress Gardens' new 24,000-gallon aquarium features fish and turtles native to the Lowcountry and has a display of venomous and non-venomous snakes.

Cypress Gardens is closed the entire month of January. Call ahead for seasonal hours and special admission prices. Hours are usually 9 AM to 5 PM. In-season admission is $7 for adults and teens, $6 for seniors, and $2 for students ages 6 to 12. Admission is free for children younger than 6.

Forts

Among the most visited attractions in the Lowcountry are the area's famous forts—standing today in mute testimony to the great strategic role Charleston Harbor played during the conflicts of the past 300 years.

Of course, the most famous of these fortresses is legendary Fort Sumter, where the Civil War began. But Greater Charleston has a number of other forts and former military fortifications that offer fascinating stories, both for the serious historian and for us regular Insiders too. There's Fort Moultrie on Sullivan's Island, Fort Johnson on James Island (now site of the South Carolina Wildlife and Marine Resources Center), and Battery Wagner on Morris Island.

We'll sketch brief histories of these sites—just enough to send you off to see the real thing with a taste of the very real drama and sacrifice associated with these places.

Fort Sumter National Monument
Charleston Harbor
(843) 883-3123

Almost every Charlestonian knows the story by heart: The year was 1861. South Carolina had seceded from the Union. And yet just a few miles east, there at the mouth of Charleston Harbor, Union forces were still stationed at Fort Sumter. The Confederacy officially demanded that Fort Sumter be vacated, but the North adamantly refused. At 4:30 AM on the morning of April 12, a mortar shell burst over the fort, fired from nearby Fort Johnson. The Civil War had begun.

At first—largely as a matter of honor—the Union forces defended Fort Sumter. But after 34 hours, they surrendered. It was practically a bloodless battle—no one was killed, and only a few men were wounded.

Amazingly, the Confederates held the fort for the next 27 months, against what was the heaviest bombardment the world had ever seen. Over the course of almost two years, no fewer than 46,000 shells (about 3,500 tons of metal) were fired at the island fort. In the end, the Confederate troops abandoned Fort Sumter, but they never surrendered. It was February 17, 1865. By April, the war and the cause would be lost.

Today Fort Sumter is a national monument administered by the National Park Service of the U.S. Department of the Interior. It is still accessible only by boat, and the only public tour of this tiny man-made island and world-famous fort is offered through Fort Sumter Tours.

You can board the Fort Sumter tour boat at the National Park Service's new facility at the foot of Calhoun Street on the Cooper River. The impressive $15-million interpretive center took three years to build and adds a dramatic new dimension to the Fort Sumter experience. Here, visitors are immersed in the Fort Sumter story with interactive displays and graph-ics while Park Service rangers are on hand to answer questions. Among the sights found here, you'll find the actual 33-star Garrison Flag that flew over the fort that historic first night of the Civil War. The trip out to Fort Sumter takes about two hours and 15 minutes. The boat ride affords delightful views of Charleston's waterfront and a narrated history of Charleston Harbor given en route. The specially built sightseeing boats are clean, safe, and have on-board restrooms.

Insiders' Tip

Parking can be a hassle in Charleston. See our Getting Here, Getting Around chapter for a list of the city's parking garages. For the lucky few who happen upon a parking meter, here's the story: Most of the older meters have a two-hour maximum time limit and take nickels, dimes, and quarters. If the meter is painted red, you're limited to only 15 minutes. Here and there, we're starting to see new digital meters that take only quarters. But here's the worst news of all: The meter maids (and misters) in Charleston tend to be quick on the draw when issuing tickets. If you want to be a good citizen, you can report a broken meter by calling (843) 724-7368.

Once you're at Fort Sumter itself, you can walk freely about the ruins. There's another interpretive museum area on site with National Park Service rangers there to answer any questions you may have.

You'll need to check in for your tour at least 15 minutes early for ticketing and boarding. Departure times vary according to the season and the weather, so call the number listed for departure information. During the busy summer season, there are usually three tours a day. Prices are $11 for adults and teens and $6 for children younger than 12. Children younger than 6 are admitted free, but a boarding pass is required for them. Handicapped access is available. Group rates are available, but advance reservations for groups are encouraged. (See the Cruise and Boat Tours section of our Guided Tours chapter or our Kidstuff chapter for additional information.)

Fort Moultrie
1214 W. Middle St., Sullivan's Island
(843) 883-3123

From the earliest days of European settlement along the Eastern seaboard, coastal fortifications were set up to guard the newly found, potentially vulnerable harbors. In this unique restoration, operated today by the National Park Service, visitors to Fort Moultrie can see two centuries of coastal defenses as they evolved.

In its 171-year history (1776 to 1947), Fort Moultrie defended Charleston Harbor twice. The first time was during the Revolutionary War, when 30 cannons from the original fort drove off a British fleet mounting 200 guns in a ferocious, nine-hour battle. This time, Charleston was saved from British occupation, and the fort was justifiably named in honor of its commander, William Moultrie.

The second time the fort defended the city was during the Civil War. For nearly two years, the Charleston forts (and the city itself) were bombarded from both land and sea. The walls of Forts Sumter and Moultrie crumbled under the relentless shelling, but somehow the forts were able to hold back the Union attacks.

Today the fort has been restored to portray the major periods of its history. Five different sections of the fort and two outlying areas each feature typical weapons representing a different historical period. Visitors move steadily back in time from the World War II Harbor Entrance Control Post to the original, palmetto log fort of 1776.

Fort Moultrie is open from 9 AM to 5 PM year round. It is closed on Christmas Day. Groups should make reservations for guided tours. Pets are not allowed. Admission is free.

From Charleston, take US 17 N. (Business) through Mt. Pleasant to Sullivan's Island and turn right on Middle Street. The fort is about 1.5 miles from the intersection.

Fort Johnson
Wildlife and Marine Resources Center
217 Fort Johnson Rd., James Island
(843) 762-5000

Fort Johnson is another Charleston area fortress steeped in history and adaptively reused for modern needs. Since the early 1970s, the waterfront James Island site has been the home of the South Carolina Wildlife and Marine Resources Department, which researches and promotes the state's marine industries.

But savvy military buffs know Fort Johnson in another role. Like Fort Moultrie, this site has military significance that dates back several hundred years.

No trace now exists of the original Fort Johnson that was constructed on the site in about 1708. It was named for Sir Nathaniel Johnson, proprietary governor of the Carolinas at the time. A second fort was constructed in 1759, and small portions of that structure remain as tabby ruins there today. (Tabby is an early building material made from crushed lime and oyster shell.)

Records show the fort was occupied in 1775 by three companies of South Carolina militia under the leadership of Lt. Col. Motte. During the American Revolution,

Close-up

The "Best Friend of Charleston" Comes Home

The very first steam locomotive to offer regular passenger and freight service in the United States chugged out of Charleston in 1830. A near-exact replica of that train, known as "The Best Friend," finally came back home in 1993 to rest and be displayed in a building next to the visitor center on Ann Street. And you can see it there—absolutely free. This city-owned facility has a charming little gift shop, too, with lots of interesting railroad memorabilia. Groups are welcome and with advance notice they can meet a railroad-uniformed storyteller who will dramatize the "Best Friend" story for kids of all ages. To schedule group visits, call (843) 973-7269.

The replica (built in 1928 and refurbished in 1969) was originally commissioned by Norfolk Southern Railroad Co. to celebrate the 100th anniversary of its parent company, the South Carolina Canal and Railroad Co.

The now-famous train (consisting of an engine, a tender, and two open passenger coaches) made its first run on Christmas Day of 1830. About 140 brave Charlestonians climbed aboard this curious-looking contraption at Line Street and chugged a dazzling 6 miles out to Dorchester Road—which was as far as tracks had been laid to date.

Newspaper accounts at the time said, "We flew on the wings of the wind at the varied speed of 15 to 25 miles per hour." Soon, the tracks were extended 136 miles up to Hamburg, South Carolina, creating the first viable train transportation system in the country. Eventually,

The Best Friend, America's first passenger and freight train, would have been a wondrous sight to behold as it traveled the length of its run from Charleston to Hamburg, South Carolina, in the 1830s.

PHOTO: COURTESY OF CITY OF CHARLESTON

those first railroad tracks would find their way over the Smoky Mountains to Knoxville, Tennessee, where they would carry the first U.S. mail over the mountains and carry the first military troops into the Civil War.

As for the original "Best Friend," it sadly came to an early demise. Just six months into the operation (in June 1831), the train was idle at one of its stops en route when the engineer became annoyed by the constant hissing of the noisy escape valve. He instructed a slave fireman to tie off the valve with his handkerchief and fix the nagging problem. In due course, the engine exploded, killing the poor fireman, scalding the engineer, and destroying the original locomotive.

the fort remained in Colonial hands until 1780, when the British forces advancing on Charleston reported finding it abandoned. A third fort was built in 1793, but a hurricane destroyed it in 1800. Some work on Fort Johnson was done during the War of 1812, but the following year another storm destroyed that progress. Shortly afterward, Fort Johnson was dropped from official reports of U.S. fortifications.

During early 1861, South Carolina state troops erected mortar batteries and an earthwork of three guns on the old fortress site. Unbeknownst to most Americans, the actual signal shot that opened the bombardment of Fort Sumter and marked the beginning of the Civil War was fired from the east mortar battery of Fort Johnson on April 12, 1861. Fort Sumter was fired upon, not vice versa.

During the Civil War, building activity increased until Fort Johnson became an entrenched camp mounting 26 guns and mortars. However, apart from routine artillery firing from the site, the only major action at the fort occurred on July 3, 1864, when its Confederate defenders repulsed two Union regiments totaling about 1,000 men. The Union forces sustained 26 casualties and lost 140 men as captives. The Confederate loss was one killed and three wounded. On the night of February 17, 1865, Fort Johnson was evacuated during the general Confederate withdrawal from Charleston Harbor.

After the Civil War, Fort Johnson became a quarantine station operated by the state and the city of Charleston. It continued to be used in that capacity until the 1950s. Today's inhabitants at the site (the Marine Resources folks) do not prohibit exploration, so you might find this history-drenched spot worth a visit.

Battery Wagner, Morris Island

Of all the forts and battlegrounds that dot the Lowcountry landscape and pay quiet tribute to the area's military history, perhaps the most muted one is Battery Wagner on Morris Island. The story is a brief one in the long struggle of the Civil War, but it is a significant one that is especially poignant today. In 1989, the story of Battery Wagner was portrayed in the acclaimed film *Glory*, which starred Matthew Broderick, Denzel Washington, and Morgan Freeman.

Time and tides have long since removed all traces of Battery Wagner. Today, Morris Island is vacant and uninhabited. It was recently annexed by the city of Charleston and is expected to one day be developed to become a vital part of the ever-growing metropolitan area surrounding the city. Although a monument at Battery Wagner is planned, the site remains remarkably overlooked by the public at large. But whatever its future may hold, the story of Morris Island will always include the story of Battery Wagner and the 54th Massachusetts Regiment.

Because Charleston was the "cradle of Secession," it was a primary target for the Union's high command. On June 16, 1862, the Union forces' first attempt to capture the city failed at the Battle of Secessionville on James Island. Union commanders decided to mount a two-pronged attack using both land and naval forces. There were two possible lines of approach to the city: through Sullivan's Island, which was heavily defended, or through Morris Island, which was more lightly guarded. On Morris Island, the main defense was Battery Wagner, a quickly built fortification with thick sand walls and more than a dozen cannons.

Choosing the Morris Island approach, Union forces landed on July 10, 1863, and opened fire the following day with little success. A week later, they tried again. Even after a 10-hour artillery bombardment, Battery Wagner stood firm.

At dusk on July 18, the Union infantry advanced up the beach toward heavily defended Battery Wagner. Spearheading the attack was the 54th Massachusetts Regiment under the leadership of Col. Robert G. Shaw, the 25-year-old son of a wealthy Boston abolitionist. The regiment under Shaw's command was made up entirely of free blacks from the North. It was one of the 167 black units that fought against the Confederacy in the Civil War.

The bloody, hand-to-hand struggle at Battery Wagner saw 272 men from the 54th (more than 40 percent of the unit) fall dead and 1,500 Union forces lost, including Col. Shaw. The valor and courage displayed in the battle proved once and for all to Northern and Southern leaders that black soldiers could and would fight. The story of the 54th was widely publicized at the time and, as a result, the Union Army began to enlist blacks in growing numbers. By 1865, a total of 178,895 black soldiers had enlisted, which constituted 12 percent of the North's fighting forces.

The fight for Battery Wagner continued for 10 more weeks until the Confederates finally abandoned the work on September 6. The 54th continued to serve along the southeast coast for the remainder of the war. It was mustered out of service in Mt. Pleasant on August 20, 1865.

Historic Churches

In a city that was a major contributor to the American ethic of religious freedom, there's a deep reverence for church architecture. The "Holy City," as it likes to be called, has dozens of beautiful 18th- and 19th-century churches that bear witness to this history and the 21st-century pride that goes with it.

Several churches are notable because of their early date of construction, while others impress with their architectural grandeur. Some are survivors of cataclysmic events; a few speak volumes about their ethnic and sociological origins. Here are some churches whose history enriches Charleston and her citizenry, but remember, they are only a few of many. Unless otherwise noted, all are in the downtown vicinity and are still active houses of worship. They are listed in alphabetical order.

Cathedral of St. John the Baptist (1890–1907)
Broad and Legare Sts.

The first Cathedral of St. John the Baptist was completed in 1854. It was an outstanding example of Gothic architecture, built of Connecticut sandstone with a 200-foot spire. The building was completely lost in the great fire of 1861. By 1890, work had begun on what is almost an exact duplicate of the 1854 building. It was designed by P.C. Kelly of Brooklyn, New York, and followed closely the plans for the original structure. The exception is the square tower that, for monetary reasons, replaced the tall spire. The newer building is made of Connecticut brownstone. The nave is tiled, measures 150 by 80 feet, and seats 700 people.

Cathedral of St. Luke and St. Paul (1815)
126 Coming St.

The church that is now the Cathedral Church for the Episcopal Diocese of South Carolina was originally known as St. Paul's, Radcliffeborough. It was organized as a mission in 1806.

This building, designed by the architects James and John Gordon, was completed in 1815. At the time of its building, the load of the tower proved too heavy for the supporting walls, and the tower was dismantled. A lighter, Gothic Revival-style parapet was added, which is in contrast to the Classical Revival building below. Inside, the original color schemes have been reproduced as part of the intensive restoration of the building following severe damage in Hurricane Hugo.

Circular Congregational Church
(1891–1892)
150 Meeting St.

This church was originally called the Independent Church of Charles Towne and was established in 1681 by some of the first settlers of Charleston. It was one of the first two congregations created in the settlement (the other being St. Philip's Church; see subsequent listing).

The first building was of white brick and was known by locals as the White Meeting House. It is from this early euphemism that Meeting Street takes its name. That building was outgrown and replaced in 1806 by the first "Circular Church," an impressive structure designed in the Pantheon style by Charleston's famous architect Robert Mills. It is said to have seated 2,000 people, both black and white. The great fire of 1861 swept across the city and took this building with it. The ruins stood mutely until the earthquake of 1886 turned them to rubble.

A third (and the present) building on this site was completed in 1892 and is circular in form, but Romanesque in style. The church's graveyard is the city's oldest, with monuments dating from 1696. This is the burial ground of Nathaniel Russell.

(See the Nathaniel Russell House listing under House Museums in this chapter.)

Emanuel A.M.E. Church (1891)
110 Calhoun St.

The African Methodist Episcopal Church had its beginnings in 1787 in Philadelphia with the founding of the Free African Society, based on the doctrines of Methodism and the teachings of John Wesley. A similar organization was founded in Charleston in 1791 by the Rev. Morris Brown, a free black preacher affiliated with another Methodist church in the city. This show of independence from the blacks led to a secession from the Methodists and the founding of three black churches in Charleston, known as the Bethel Circuit.

The Emanuel A.M.E. congregation is one of those churches. The original building was in the Hampstead neighborhood in the east side of the city. By 1818, it had 1,000 members. In 1822, Denmark Vesey, a carpenter who bought himself out of slavery, laid plans in the church for an insurrection. Word of the rebellion leaked out, and Vesey and some of his followers were executed. The Hampstead church was burned to the ground. By 1834, all black churches in South Carolina were closed by the state legislature.

During the years following the Denmark Vesey incident, some of the congregation returned to white churches, but others continued the traditions of their African church and met underground. The congregation resurfaced in 1865—3,000 strong—and today's building was completed in 1891. The original gas lamps that line the sanctuary have been preserved. With seating for 2,500, the church has the largest seating capacity of Charleston's African-American congregations.

First Baptist Church (1822)
61 Church St.

Here is the oldest Baptist church in the South. The congregation originally emigrated from Maine to the Carolinas in 1783. The building was designed by the first American-born architect, Robert Mills, in the popular Greek Revival style. Mills didn't mince words, saying of his creation, "[it is] the best specimen of correct taste in architecture in the city. It is purely Greek in style, simply grand in its proportions, and beautiful in its detail." Wood for the solid mahogany pulpit was brought from the West Indies for the staggering sum (in 1822) of $1,000. First Baptist's fabulous organ dates from 1845 and was made by Erben.

First (Scots) Presbyterian Church (1814)
53 Meeting St.

The Scots Kirk (or Scots Meeting House) was organized in 1731 by 12 Scottish families who believed in a strict subscription to the Westminster Standards (church laws) and the Presbyterian form of church government. Their first simple structure on this site was built in 1734. It was replaced in 1814 by the present structure, which is the fifth-oldest church building in Charleston. By unanimous vote of the congregation, the church bell was donated to the Confederacy in 1862 and has never been replaced.

Although the church was badly damaged by a fire in 1945, it was lovingly repaired. In the window over the main door appears the seal of the Church of Scotland, the Burning Bush, with a Latin motto that reads, "*Nec Tamen Consumbatur*" ("Nevertheless it was not consumed").

French Huguenot Church (1845)
136 Church St.

French Huguenots were followers of the 16th-century French reformer John Calvin. After Louis XIV revoked the Edict of Nantes (1685), there was an enormous flight away from France by Protestants, many of whom came to the Carolinas.

The Huguenot Church in Charleston was organized in 1681, and groups of believers arrived in this area between 1680 and 1763. In 1706, the Church Act established the Anglican Church as the official religion in South Carolina, and slowly,

> ## Insiders' Tip
> Some downtown churches are open to visitors who respectfully wish to see these historic interiors during weekday daytime hours. The schedules may be erratic because these are active, working religious organizations with busy calendars of church events scheduled for the congregations. However, if the doors are open, the sanctuary is deserted (usually there's a sign posted for visitors), and you know you're disturbing no one, feel welcome to quietly enter and briefly look around.

most Huguenot churches were absorbed into what became Episcopal congregations. The Huguenot Church in Charleston is the outstanding exception—it is the only remaining independent Huguenot congregation in America.

This church was the city's first to be built (1845) in the Gothic Revival style. It was designed by Edward Brickell White, a noted Charleston architect who is credited with popularizing the Gothic style in America. The church was damaged by shelling during the Civil War and nearly demolished by the 1886 earthquake. Each time, it was painstakingly restored. The building just underwent a major refurbishing in 1997.

The church's famous Tracker organ, restored in 1967 by The Preservation Society of Charleston and the Charleston chapter of the American Organists Guild, is one of the city's true musical treasures. It is one of the last of its kind anywhere in the country.

Grace Episcopal Church (1848)
98 Wentworth St.

Another magnificent example of Gothic-style church architecture in Charleston is Grace Episcopal Church, designed by Edward Brickell White. This building was completed in 1848.

The memorial windows in Grace Church are teaching windows, each containing scenes from the life of Christ as well as lay persons and clergy associated with the church. The largest window, over the rear doorway, took more than a year to complete and contains more than 10,000 pieces of glass. A small window on the Epistle side of the narthex contains an angel with the face of a small girl who drowned on Sullivan's Island.

Grace Church was closed for a year in 1864 because of the terrible bombardment from Morris Island, but it reopened soon after the evacuation of Charleston, during Federal occupation.

Kahal Kadosh Beth Elohim (1840)
90 Hasell St.

This is the oldest synagogue in continuous use in the United States. The present congregation was organized in 1749. It is also the longest surviving Reform synagogue in the world. Beth Elohim is acknowledged as the birthplace of Reform Judaism in the United States, tracing its origins back to 1844. It's a branch of Judaism that places more emphasis on traditional religious and moral values, instead of rigid ceremonial and ritualistic detail. The present 1840 Greek Revival structure was designed by Cyrus L. Warner. The graceful but massive wrought-iron fence that faces onto Hasell Street dates back to the original 1749 synagogue.

St. John's Lutheran Church (1817)
10 Archdale St.

This is Charleston's mother church of Lutheranism, with a history spanning more than 250 years. The congregation was organized in 1742 and worshiped in various places until the present structure was completed in 1817. Frederick Wesner was the architect. The steeple is said to have been designed earlier by famous Charleston miniaturist Charles Fraser and constructed in 1859. The original bell was given to the Confederate cause (bells were often melted down for use in ammo, cannons, ships, firearms, and the like) and was not replaced until 1992.

St. Mary's Catholic Church (1837–1839)
89 Hasell St.

Called "the Mother Church of the Carolinas and Georgia," St. Mary's was the first Catholic church established in the English colony. Its first pastor came from Ireland in 1788. Originally known as "The Roman Catholic Church of Charleston," St. Mary's officially took its present name in 1837. The Greek Revival building on the site today was consecrated in 1839, replacing an earlier edifice lost in the city's great fire of 1838. Early communicants were mostly Irish immigrants and French refugees from the West Indies. In fact, church records were kept in French until 1822. Today, the crowded churchyard contains gravestones written in Latin, French, and English representing a congregation that spanned 17 nationalities, three continents, and two centuries. Inside, over the main altar, hangs a painting of the Crucifixion, painted in 1814 by John S. Gogdell, a noted Charleston artist. The current organ is a Jardine (built in 1874 and restored in 1980) that is often featured in Piccolo Spoleto concerts held in May.

St. Matthew's Lutheran Church (1872)
405 King St.

The huge influx of German immigrants to Charleston during the first half of the 19th century caused the city's second-oldest congregation of Lutherans to greatly expand their house of worship. The magnificently Gothic church, with its tall, German-made stained-glass windows, was finished in 1872 with a 297-foot spire that stands taller than any other in the state. It was designed by John H. Devereaux.

In a spectacular 1965 church fire, the spire collapsed into the street below—the very point, in fact, piercing the sidewalk just to the left of the church's front door. That steeple point is still there (encased in concrete) and commemorated by a plaque honoring the congregation's courage and determination to restore the architectural treasure.

St. Michael's Episcopal Church (1752–1761)
80 Meeting St.

While St. Philip's can claim to be the oldest congregation in Charleston, St. Michael's lays claim to having the oldest church structure. There is some mystery as to whom the actual architect of St. Michael's might have been. But there's no question this magnificent edifice is one of the great treasures of the city.

The church has remained essentially unchanged over the centuries, with the exception of a sacristy added in 1883. However, the structure has undergone major repairs several times because of natural and man-made disasters. In the earthquake of 1886, the steeple tower sank eight inches, and the church cracked in several places. St. Michael's was damaged by a tornado in 1935 and again in 1989 by Hurricane Hugo. During both the American Revolution and the Civil War, the spire was painted black to make it less visible as a target for enemy gunners.

During his visit to Charleston in 1791, President George Washington worshiped at St. Michael's, where he sat in the Governor's Pew—so marked by a small plaque. In later years, the Marquis de Lafayette and Gen. Robert E. Lee sat in that same pew. Buried in St. Michael's churchyard are several distinguished members of the congregation, including Gen. Charles Cotesworth Pinckney, Revolutionary hero, signer of the Constitution, and Federalist presidential candidate; and John Rutledge, signer of the Constitution and member of the U.S. Supreme Court.

St. Philip's Episcopal Church (1835–1838)
146 Church St.

St. Philip's is the mother church of the Episcopal Diocese of South Carolina. And for more than 300 years, this church has been a vital force in the life of Charleston. Today, there are more than 1,500 communicants. It is believed the name is derived from the Anglican parish in Barbados, the island from which many early Charleston planters came after emigration from England.

The first St. Philip's was built in 1680–81 on the site of what is now St. Michael's Episcopal Church at Meeting and Broad Streets. A new edifice was authorized for what was considered to be the "new" gates of the city (the present site on Church Street) in 1710. This building was destroyed by fire in 1835. The present building was designed by Joseph Nyde, who was influenced by the neoclassical arches inside London's St. Martin's-in-the-Fields Church (1721) designed by James Gibbs.

The history of Charleston is traceable just by reading the names of the memorial plaques around the walls of the sanctuary and in the churchyard outside. Buried here are Col. William Rhett, officer of the Crown; Edward Rutledge, signer of the Declaration of Independence; Charles Pinckney, signer of the U.S. Constitution; and the Hon. John C. Calhoun, statesman and vice president of the United States. Here, too, is the grave of DuBose Heyward, author of *Porgy* and collaborator with George Gershwin on the libretto for the folk opera *Porgy and Bess*.

Unitarian Church in Charleston (1780, 1854)
8 Archdale St.

The first building on this site was under construction when the American Revolution began. During the British occupation of the city, the church was used as quarters for the British militia, and its newly installed pews were destroyed. The church, of Georgian design, was finally repaired and in use by 1787. For the next 30 years it formed one corporate body with the Meeting Street Independent Church (now Circular Church; see previous listing), but in 1839, this congregation was re-chartered as the Unitarian Church.

Charleston was experiencing a period of great prosperity in the 1850s, and the Unitarians hired the young architect (and church member) Francis D. Lee to remodel the building in the popular Gothic Revival style. He was commissioned to incorporate the old walls and tower into his new design. Lee was inspired by the Henry VII chapel at Westminster Abbey—especially the delicate and lacy fan tracery ceiling there. He duplicated that amazing ceiling in this church, and it is considered to be some of the finest Gothic Revival work extant in America.

Museums and Other Sites

American Military Museum
44 John St.
(843) 723-9620

Directly behind the visitor center on Johns Street is the American Military Museum, which will be of interest to dedicated re-enactment buffs. Here you'll find hundreds of uniforms, patches, and insignia plus legions of military miniatures and toy soldiers. The museum's collection includes items from Desert Storm, the Vietnam and Korean wars, World Wars I and II, the Spanish American War, Indian wars, the Civil War, and the American Revolution. Admission is $5 for adults, $1 for children 12 and younger, and free to military personnel in uniform. Hours are 9:30 AM to 5:30 PM, Monday through Saturday. Sunday hours are from 1 to 5 PM.

The Battery

One can argue that Charleston's White Point Gardens, which most people know as The Battery, shouldn't officially be called an "attraction," like a museum or a fort. On the other hand, it's a darn good bet that no first-time visitor to the city ever left here without making it a point to walk there or at least drive by.

In a city where almost every other building or street holds some historical significance, few sites have afforded a better view of Charleston's 300-year-long parade of history than The Battery.

That seaside corner of land at the end of East Bay Street, where it turns and becomes Murray Boulevard, is now a pleasant park with statues and monuments, long-silent cannons, and spreading live oak trees. There's even a Victorian bandstand that looks like it could sport a uniformed Sousa band any Sunday afternoon. But the atmosphere on The Battery hasn't always been so serene.

The Battery has been a prominent feature in Charleston since the earliest days of the English settlement. Then, it was known as Oyster Point because it was little more than a marshy beach covered in oyster shells—bleached white in the Carolina sun.

At first, it was mostly a navigational aid for the sailing vessels going into and out of the harbor. The peninsula was still unsettled, and the first Colonial effort was farther upstream on the banks of the Ashley River at what is now called Charles Towne Landing. Later, when the settlement was moved to the much more defensible peninsula site, the point was a popular fishing area—too low and too easily flooded to be much of anything else. Charts used during the years 1708 to 1711 show only a "watch tower" on the site and just a few residences built nearby.

Remember, Charles Towne was still a walled city at that time, the southernmost wall being several blocks north, near what is now the Carolina Yacht Club on East Bay Street. The point was definitely a "suburban" location. The area took a decidedly higher public profile about a decade later, when the pirate Stede Bonnet (pronounced bo-NAY) and some 40 or 50 scalawags like

Close-up

Ashley River Road: Backroad to the Plantation Life

Before Hurricane Hugo struck the Lowcountry in September of 1989—destroying an estimated 7 million board feet of prime, standing lumber—the Ashley River Road (S.C. Hwy. 61 from Church Creek to Bacons Bridge Road) was oak-lined, moss-laden, sun-dappled, and almost unbearably beautiful. Certainly, that's how many Lowcountry old-timers remember it.

Most of the huge oak trees were hundreds of years old and stood so close to the road they became a hazard to speeding cars. So, for several years, every serious accident (and there were many) became a new excuse to remove more trees and more of the road's ambiance. Then came the slow but relentless encroachment of commercial businesses and the addition of more and bigger real estate developments, each taking an even higher toll on the once scenic highway.

In the late 1990s, however, preservationists woke up to the fact that old S.C. Hwy 61 was a unique natural resource—of Lowcountry history and beauty—and it was quickly vanishing in the name of progress and development. Turning back these forces, once under way, turned out to be nearly impossible. But through years of planning and negotiation, a new plan has emerged which hopes to preserve as much of the old road's ambiance as possible. The group seeks to qualify the road for National Scenic Byway status after wining State Scenic Byway status in 1998.

The stretch between Drayton Hall and Middleton Place still has the densest tree canopy.

The canopy of Live Oaks over the Ashley River Road is quintessentially Southern. This Lowcountry vista is becoming increasingly rare as development encroaches along the scenic old highway.
PHOTO: FLETCHER NEWBERN

That is, the live oaks reach up and over the road, creating a sun-filtered canopy through which you'll feel you're driving into the past.

Remember, the Ashley River itself is always on your right—sometimes just through the trees. Bear in mind, too, that the old road (originally a trail for Native Americans) was only a back road to the Ashley's colonial plantations. It was slow, rutted, and practically impossible to navigate in wet weather. Most social and business traffic to and from the far-flung plantations went by water. Thus, the great houses were actually built facing the river, the avenue to all agricultural wealth. Still, European settlers are recorded using the back road as early as 1707.

If you look carefully, you'll notice some unexplained low ridges along the roadside. Chances are, these are old rice dikes indicating where the land was flooded and the fields cultivated for rice.

In other places through the forest (now drastically thinned by Hugo), you'll see larger, unnatural-looking mounds—especially noticeable in the wintertime. These are the outcroppings from old, abandoned phosphate mines. After the Civil War, during the late 1870s, phosphate (an early fertilizer product) was discovered in the ground along the west bank of the Ashley. For a brief but reckless period, this entire landscape was crudely strip-mined. As ecologically careless and harmful as these practices were, the phosphate era provided desperately needed income for a few of the old planter families that had somehow managed to hold onto their properties through the war and Reconstruction.

If the phosphate mining years were not the Ashley River's finest hour, at least they helped rescue what little was left of the plantations after the cataclysmic year of 1865. In February of that year, as the war was winding down, Union troops advanced toward Charleston on the Ashley River Road, looting and burning as they came. Of all the great houses once standing along the high, west bank of the river, only Drayton Hall survived.

Once, there were scores of plantations along the Ashley. They had wonderful, lyrical names: MacBeth and Runnymede, Millbrook and Schievelin. Today, three of the old properties are open to the public. These are Drayton Hall, Magnolia, and Middleton Place (see our Plantations section in this chapter). Each is unique and remarkable in a different way and offers special insight into the Ashley River's fascinating plantation story.

him were hanged there from makeshift gallows. These executions were apparently quite effective in bringing an end to the pirate activity that had plagued the Carolina coast.

The first of several real forts built on the site came along as early as 1737. This and subsequent fortifications were crudely built, however, and none lasted long against the tyranny of the sea. By the time of the American Revolution, White Point was virtually at the city's door and no longer considered a strategic site for defense.

Hurricanes in 1800 and again in 1804 reduced whatever fortification remained there to rubble. Another fort, this version constructed for the War of 1812, apparently gave White Point a popular new name—The Battery. At least, the new name appears on maps beginning about 1833.

The seawall constructed along East Battery (the "high" one) was built after a storm in 1885. Storms and repairs have traded blows at the seawall for many years—in 1893, 1911, 1959, and, of course, with Hugo in 1989.

The area's use as a park dates back to 1837, when the city rearranged certain streets to establish White Point Gardens. It

A sunrise as seen from the heroic Confederate Memorial at White Point Gardens.

PHOTO: COURTESY OF CHARLESTON AREA CONVENTION AND VISITORS BUREAU

was from this vantage point that Charlestonians watched the battle between Confederate fortifications across the river and the small band of Union troops holed up in Fort Sumter on April 12, 1861. This, of course, was the beginning of the Civil War. Once the war had started, this peaceful little garden was torn up and convulsed into two massive earthwork batteries—part of Charleston's inner line of defense. And while one of these battery sites housed a huge Blakely rifle (one of the two largest weapons in the Confederacy), neither battery ever fired a shot in anger. (Some incoming artillery rounds probably landed here during the extended bombardment of the city from late 1863 until Charleston fell in February 1865.)

The end of the Civil War was the end of The Battery's role in Charleston's military defense, although several subsequent wars have left poignant souvenirs behind for remembrance. Today no fewer than 26 cannons and monuments dot The Battery's landscape, each of which is described on a nearby plaque or informational marker.

Over the years, The Battery has become something of a balm for the Charlestonian soul. In 1977, Warren Ripley wrote a detailed booklet called *The Battery*, which is still available through *The Post and Courier* offices. In it, Ripley sums up the reasons The Battery is so special:

"It has watched the elaborate drill of colonial militia and the 'goose step' of Hitler's sailors on parade before WWII. It has suffered through 're-enactments' of historic events it witnessed in the first place, seen parades, air shows, and fireworks displays without number.

"It has observed three centuries of ocean traffic, watched the evolution from sailing ship to steam and nuclear propulsion as warships and cargo slipped in and out of port.

"It has echoed Sunday afternoon band concerts and heard the weekday cries of street vendors hawking wares to the neighborhood homes. It has harked to the whispers of countless lovers and warmed to the daylight shouts of happy, playing children."

For Charlestonians, clearly The Battery is more than a pleasant little park. Far more, indeed.

The Bells of St. Michael's
Meeting and Broad Sts.

If your timing is lucky, a visit to the very heart of Charleston and its "Four Corners of Law" at the intersection of Broad and Meeting Streets will be delightfully punctuated by the resonant chime of mighty church bells ringing overhead.

Indeed, the bells of St. Michael's Episcopal Church make more than just a pleasant sound. Their ringing is very much a part of Charleston—one of its oldest and most endearing attractions. In fact, their ringing is another of Charleston's object lessons in faithful perseverance, stubborn Southern survival, and the fleeting passage of time.

St. Michael's Episcopal Church, built in 1761, is the oldest church edifice on the Peninsula and the second-oldest congregation in the city (see previous listing in the Historic Churches section of this chapter). This is the church where George Washington worshiped on his famous 1791 presidential tour that included a stay in Charleston (see Heyward-Washington House listing in the House Museums section of this chapter).

The eight bronze bells hanging in St. Michael's spire were originally cast at the Whitechapel Foundry of London in 1764. Church records say the bells first sounded here in Charleston on September 21 of that same year, having safely made their first journey across the Atlantic Ocean. Amazingly, the bells have made that long journey back to England three times since.

Their first journey "home" was in 1782 during the War of Independence. The bells had rung in defiance of the Crown during Charleston's protest of the Stamp Act in 1765, and British soldiers confiscated them as a punishing prize of war. Once back on English soil, however, the bells were purchased by a private speculator and promptly returned to Charleston and again placed in St. Michael's steeple.

In 1862, during the Civil War, seven of the bells were removed from the steeple and taken to Columbia for what was hoped to be safekeeping. Charleston was such a likely target that many of the city's treasures were sent to Columbia at that time to escape the Union's wrath. Only the large tenor bell was left behind, to ring the alarm for Charlestonians still in the city. In 1865, the year Charleston fell, the bell rang dutifully until it cracked. Meanwhile, Gen. William T. Sherman's Union army selected upstate Columbia as an artillery target, and South Carolina's entire capital burned in what was one of the most dramatic episodes of the war.

In 1866, St. Michael's vestry arranged to have the seven charred bells from Columbia and the one cracked bell remaining in the church returned to England to be recast once more in their original molds at the Whitechapel Foundry. When they were returned in 1867, church records show that the melodies of "Home Again" and "Auld Lang Syne" rang from St. Michael's steeple.

The last journey of the bells back to England and the Whitechapel Foundry—still in business after all these years—was in 1993. Their recasting, once more in the original molds, was part of St. Michael's $3.8-million restoration and repair project undertaken as a result of damages suffered in Hurricane Hugo.

The bells of St. Michael's rang anew on July 4, 1993, in a special, daylong hand-ringing ceremony done in the English style. Nostalgic Charlestonians from all denominations made special trips past St. Michael's all day to hear the bells celebrate Independence Day and acknowledge another homecoming for the bells of St. Michael's at the Four Corners of Law.

Postal History Museum
Meeting and Broad Sts.

Unknown to most of the tourists who pass through the intersection of Meeting and Broad Streets (the Four Corners of Law), there's a fine and fascinating little gem right there, deftly tucked into one of the corners.

The Postal History Museum is a special room inside the Charleston post office showing visitors some of the interesting tidbits of postal history associated with this coastal Colonial town.

For instance, Charleston's first postmaster (on the job before 1694) was actually known as the city's "powder receiver." Not only was he responsible for the mail, he also collected a percentage of gunpowder from every ship that arrived (see subsequent listing for Powder Magazine). He was required to post incoming letters in a public room in his house for 30 days and collected his commission only when the letters were picked up by the recipient. Imagine being in London in 1700, addressing a letter to "John Doe, Charles Towne, Carolina," and it actually getting here.

This little museum is a must for philatelists or anyone else who ever wondered how 18th- and 19th-century mail was handled. It is open during regular U.S. post office hours, and admission is free. It's a great excuse to see Charleston's elaborately detailed 1896 post office building, the oldest continuously operating post office in the Carolinas.

Powder Magazine
79 Cumberland St.
(843) 805-6730

Only a couple of blocks from the bustling market area is, quite simply, the oldest public building in the Carolinas. And yet, as Charleston attractions go, the Powder Magazine is relatively unknown to tourists and to some locals as well.

Perhaps the site is overlooked because it's dramatically upstaged by Charleston's sumptuous house museums and romantic streetscapes. And in truth, the utilitarian Powder Magazine actually predates Charleston's legendary aesthetics. It was built for a time when the still-new English settlement was predominantly interested in self-defense and basic survival.

In the early years of the 18th century, Charles Towne was still threatened by Spanish forces, hostile Indians, rowdy packs of buccaneers, and an occasional French attack. It was still a walled city, fortified against surprise attack.

In August 1702, a survey of the armament in Charles Towne reported "2,306 lbs. of gunpowder, 496 shot of all kind, 28 great guns, 47 Grenada guns, 360 cartridges, and 500 lbs. of pewter shot." In his formal request for additional cannons, the royal governor requested "a suitable store of shot and powder ... (to) make Carolina impregnable." And so in 1703, the crown approved and funded such a building, which was completed in 1713 on what is now Cumberland Street.

The Powder Magazine was the domain of the powder receiver, a newly appointed city official entitled to accept a gunpowder tax levied on all merchant ships entering Charleston Harbor during this period.

The building served its originally intended purpose for many decades. But eventually, in an early Colonial version of today's base closings, it was deemed unnecessary (or too small) and sold into private hands.

This multi-gabled, tile-roofed, architectural oddity was almost forgotten by historians until the early 1900s. In 1902, it was purchased by The National Society of Colonial Dames of America in the State of South Carolina. It was maintained and operated as a small museum until 1991, when water damage, roof deterioration, and time had finally taken too high a toll. What the Powder Magazine needed to survive at all was a major stabilization and restoration—something beyond the resources of the owners.

In an agreement whereby the Historic Charleston Foundation did the needed work under a 99-year lease, the Powder Magazine has undergone a $400,000 preservation effort, its first ever. This included a temporary roof over the entire structure, allowing the massive walls to dry out before necessary repairs could even begin. Much-needed archaeological and archival research was also done on the site.

The Powder Magazine was opened to the public in the summer of 1997. Inside, a new, interactive exhibit interprets

Only four majestic columns remain at the former site of the old Charleston Museum. A turn-of-the-19th-century building once housed the museum's priceless collection, which was moved to a new (Meeting Street) facility in the late 1970s. PHOTO: COURTESY OF CHARLESTON AREA CONVENTION AND VISITORS BUREAU

Charleston's first 50 years—a time when it was still a relatively crude Colonial outpost of the British Empire. Admission is $2 for everyone 6 and older.

The Charleston Museum
360 Meeting St.
(843) 722-2996

Directly across Meeting Street from the Visitor Reception and Transportation Center is one of Charleston's finest jewels: The Charleston Museum. Because it is the first and oldest museum in America, having been founded in 1773, the museum's collection predates all modern thinking about what should be kept or discarded in preserving the artifacts of a culture.

Instead, The Charleston Museum is heir to the collected memorabilia of real American patriots, early Charlestonian families, and early Colonial thinkers, explorers, scientists, and planters. It is their opinion of what mattered then and what they thought should matter to us today. Although the collection is housed in modern buildings and has the benefit

of modern conservation methods and enlightened interpretation, the collection is uniquely eloquent. It speaks of a city that already knew it was great and sought early on to record itself for posterity. That difference alone makes The Charleston Museum a must-see.

The museum's scope is the social and natural history of Charleston and the South Carolina coastal region. Objects from natural science, cultural history, historical archaeology, ornithology, and ethnology are presented to illustrate the importance each had in the history of this area. The Charleston Silver Exhibit contains internationally recognized work by local silversmiths in a beautifully mounted display. Pieces date from Colonial times through the late 19th century.

Visitors will see what the museum's many archaeological excavations have revealed about some of the city's best and worst times. Some artifacts date from the early Colonial period, while others are from the Civil War years. Some exhibits focus on early Native Americans who lived in this region. Others trace changes in trade and commerce, the expansive rice and cotton plantation systems, and the important contributions made by African Americans.

Children will be intrigued by the Discover Me room with amazing things to touch, see, and do. They'll see toys from the past, games children played, the clothes they wore, furniture they used, and more. The photographs, ceramics, pewter, and tools reveal a very personal portrait of Charlestonians from the past.

Because the Charlestonian lifestyle is so much a part of the city and its history, the two house museums owned and operated by The Charleston Museum are an important part of its offering. (See previous listings for Heyward-Washington House and Joseph Manigault House in the House Museums section of this chapter.) In these appropriate settings, you'll see some of the museum's remarkable collection of antique furniture and other decorative arts.

The Charleston Museum is open Monday through Saturday from 9 AM to 5 PM and 1 to 5 PM on Sunday. Admission is $8 for adults and teens and $4 for children ages 3 to 12. (See our Kidstuff chapter for more on children's programs.) Combination tickets, which include admission for the two house museums, sell for $12 for two sites and $18 for all three.

Old Exchange & Provost Dungeon
122 East Bay St.
(843) 727-2165
A public building has stood on this site at East Bay and Broad Streets since Charles Towne was moved from its original settlement to its present location in 1680. The early settlers built their court of guard here. They imprisoned pirates and Native Americans in the building's lower level and held their town meetings upstairs in the hall.

The British built the present building to create an impressive presence in the bustling Colonial port. With its striking Palladian architecture, the Exchange surely did just that. It was completed in 1771, and

quickly became the social, political, and economic hub of the growing city.

From its steps, the independent colony of South Carolina was publicly declared in March 1776. During the Revolution, the building was converted to a British prison, where signers of the Declaration of Independence were to be held. In 1788, the convention to ratify the U.S. Constitution met in the building, and President George Washington was lavishly entertained here several times during his Southern tour. From 1818 to 1896, the building served both the Federal and Confederate governments as the Charleston post office. In 1917, Congress deeded the building to the Daughters of the American Revolution of South Carolina.

During an excavation of the dungeon in 1965, part of the original seawall of Charles Towne was discovered. Today, the Old Exchange & Provost Dungeon is leased to the state of South Carolina and open to the public as a museum. The building has two halls that are available to rent for private events. Hours are 9 AM to 5 PM daily. Admission is $6 for adults and teens, $3.50 for children 7 to 12, and free for kids younger than 6. Senior discounts and group rates are available.

Gibbes Museum of Art
135 Meeting St.
(843) 722-2706
Established in 1905 by the Carolina Art Association, the Gibbes Museum of Art stands a block and a half north of the Four Corners of Law. As locations go, that's fairly close to what Charlestonians traditionally believe to be heaven. And clearly, the Gibbes represents Charleston's most uplifting experiences in art.

Museum members, residents of the city, and visitors all have access to a distinguished and growing collection along with year-round exhibitions, educational programs, and special events. The building itself stands as a memorial to James Shoolbred Gibbes, a wealthy Charlestonian who bequeathed funds to the city of Charleston and the Carolina Art Association to create a permanent home for the association's collection.

Today that rich and fascinating collection includes American paintings, prints, and drawings from the 18th century to the present. There are landscapes, genre scenes, views of Charleston, and portraits of notable South Carolinians. Faces associated with history (and architectural landmarks all over the Lowcountry) seem to come to life here. You'll find Thomas Middleton painted by Benjamin West and Charles Izard Manigault by Thomas Sully. There's John C. Calhoun painted by Rembrandt Peale, plus an outstanding collection of more than 400 exquisite, hand-painted miniature portraits of 18th- and 19th-century Charlestonians.

The Elizabeth Wallace Miniature Rooms offer 10 miniature interiors representing different traditions in American and French architecture, decorative arts, and design. The Gibbes also has an outstanding collection of early Japanese woodblock prints in a special Oriental gallery.

In addition to the regular schedule of exhibitions on loan from international, national, and regional collections, the Gibbes presents major exhibitions in the visual arts during Spoleto Festival USA every May through June. Members and the public are invited to join museum tours, gallery talks, lectures, seminars, and meet-the-artist events and to see films and videos made for schools and community groups.

One of the most popular aspects of the Gibbes is the museum shop, which offers an excellent selection of art books, posters, note cards, jewelry, and other gift items. Shop early for the best Christmas cards. Museum members receive a 10 percent discount on all purchases. Admission to the shop, which is open during regular museum hours, is free.

The Gibbes also has a working studio at 76 Queen Street that provides professional instruction in everything from painting and photography to textile silk-screening and jewelry-making. Classes and workshops are designed for all ages and levels of experience. Contact the Gibbes

Museum Studio at (843) 577-7275 for additional information.

Memberships to the Gibbes Museum of Art are renewable on an annual basis. Dues are tax-deductible. You'll find applications for membership at the information desk, or you can call the Gibbes at (843) 722-2706. Guided tours are available by appointment. Ask for the education department to make arrangements. Admission is $7 for adults, $5 for children ages 6 to 18. It's $1 less for seniors, military, and college students with school IDs. Members are admitted free. Museum hours are Tuesday through Saturday from 10 AM to 5 PM and 1 to 5 PM Sunday. The museum is closed on Mondays. The Gibbes is fully handicapped accessible. (For more on the Gibbes, see our chapters on Kidstuff and The Arts.)

IMAX Theatre Charleston
Fountain Walk
(next to the S.C. Aquarium)
(843) 725-IMAX

Just next door to the South Carolina Aquarium you'll find another attraction making a hit with children and adults alike. In the summer of 2000, Charleston got its own IMAX theatre, which brings the moving picture experience into a new dimension. Incredible photography notwithstanding, the screen is five stories tall and the theatre seats are ergonomic delights for the weary spine—upolstered in light blue Italian leather. The ultra-dynamic sound comes literally "through" the screen at the viewer and many of the newer IMAX movies are now photographed in 3-D. Some of the titles that locals and tourists have recently enjoyed include *Dolphins*, *Everest*, and *T-Rex*. Shows run on the hour from 10 AM to 9 PM with different titles shown throughout the day. Call for the day's movie schedule and catch the incredible IMAX experience if you haven't already done so.

Magnolia Cemetery
70 Cunnington St.
(843) 722-8638

One of the most telling places in all of

Magnolia Cemetery is a resting place for Confederate dead and many Charleston luminaries.
PHOTO: DAVID C. BERRY

Charleston has to be the remarkably distinctive 19th-century cemetery at the north end of the Peninsula, not far off East Bay Street (which becomes Morrison Drive).

Not on any contemporary beaten path and clearly not a tourist destination, Magnolia Cemetery is the quiet, final resting place of many important Charlestonians and other players in the city's long-running and colorful drama. It is also an intriguing collection of Southern funerary art in an almost unbearably romantic setting.

The site was originally on the grounds of Magnolia Umbria Plantation, which dates back to 1790 and where rice was the principal crop in the first half of the 19th century. By 1850, however, a 181-acre section of that land had been surveyed for a peaceful cemetery, dedicated on November 19, 1850, on the edge of the marsh. From that time on (even to the present), many of Charleston's most prominent families chose Magnolia as the place to bury and commemorate their loved ones.

Many of the city's leaders, politicians, judges, and other pioneers in many fields of endeavor are interred beneath the ancient, spreading live oaks of Magnolia. Among them are five Confederate brigadier generals. There is a vast Confederate section, with more than 1,700 graves of the known and unknown—84 South Carolinians who fell at the Battle of Gettysburg are included.

There are literally hundreds of ornate private family plots, many of which bear famous names. You will find the monument of Robert Barnwell Rhett—"Father of Secession," U.S. senator, attorney general of South Carolina, and author. There's also the grave of George Alfred Trenholm, a wealthy cotton broker who served as treasurer of the Confederacy and organized many a blockade run for the cause. Trenholm is thought by many to be the man on whom Margaret Mitchell's Rhett Butler was based. Among the famous artists and writers buried in Magnolia are Charleston's Alice Ravenel Huger Smith, and John Bennett.

To find Magnolia, drive north on East Bay (Morrison Drive) and turn right at the traffic light onto Meeting Street (S.C. Highway 52). Turn right at the first opportunity onto Cunnington Street, and Magnolia's gates (open daily from 2 to 6 PM) are at the end of the street.

Patriots Point
Naval and Maritime Museum
40 Patriots Point Rd., Mt. Pleasant
(843) 884-2727

Patriots Point is the name given to a huge maritime museum complex that consists mainly of four in situ ships (permanently situated): a submarine, a destroyer, a Coast Guard cutter, and an aircraft carrier with 25 vintage aircraft. For this, one of Charleston's major attractions, you'll need comfortable shoes and plenty of time.

Considering all there is to see, Patriots Point Naval and Maritime Museum is a real bargain. Admission is $11 for adults and teens, $5 for children ages 6 to 11, and free for children younger than 6. There's a $1 discount for senior citizens and anyone with a military ID. Plan on spending the better part of your day at Patriots Point; it's open from 9 AM to 6:30 PM. Gift shop hours are from 9 AM to 5:30 PM. Here's a detailed rundown of the ships on display.

Yorktown **(Aircraft Carrier)**

No one comes or goes through Charleston via U.S. 17 across the Cooper River bridges without noticing the giant aircraft carrier moored off Mt. Pleasant. It dominates— no, commands—a vast stretch of the Cooper's Mt. Pleasant shore at the very gates into Charleston Harbor.

She is none other than the *Yorktown* (CV-10), the famous "Fighting Lady" of World War II and the proud flagship of Patriots Point, the world's largest naval and maritime museum.

Of the four vessels permanently anchored and open to the public, the *Yorktown* is the most impressive. Commissioned April 15, 1943, in the darkest days

of the war, the ship fought valiantly in some of the worst engagements ever witnessed at sea, inflicting heavy losses against the Japanese at the Truk and Mariana Islands, and supporting the American ground troops in the Philippines, at bloody Iwo Jima, and Okinawa.

Shortly after the ship was commissioned and sent into battle, 20th Century Fox put a film crew on board to record— on still-rare Technicolor film—the continuing war story of a typical Navy carrier in action. The spectacular footage shot at unnamed, secret locations during then-unnamed battles became the Academy Award-winning documentary film feature of 1944. The film was called *The Fighting Lady*, and it is shown daily at the *Yorktown*'s on-board theater at regularly scheduled intervals. Don't miss it. Nothing brings the World War II drama of the *Yorktown* to life like this amazing celluloid time capsule. The terrible explosions and blistering fires, the fierce fighting, and all the brave young faces who served on the *Yorktown* are there to be seen and appreciated by generations then unborn.

But the *Yorktown* story doesn't end there. Not at all. The ship went on to patrol the western Pacific during the Cold War and even fought in Vietnam. In fact, the *Yorktown* received the crew of Apollo 8, the first manned space flight around the moon, in 1968.

The flight deck, hangar deck, and many of the *Yorktown* crew's living and working quarters are open to visitors today. You'll find actual carrier aircraft and Vietnam-era anti-sub planes on display—25 aircraft in all. And there are other fascinating exhibits on everything from mines to shipbuilding.

One of the newer exhibits is the true-to-scale Vietnam Naval Support Base, showing the living conditions and work areas of a typical support base during the Vietnam War. You'll also find the Congressional Medal of Honor Museum, featuring displays representing the eight different eras of our military history in which the Medal of Honor was awarded. You'll see actual Medals of Honor and some of the artifacts related to their original recipients.

Mercifully, you'll find a snack bar on board the *Yorktown* and another in the riverside gift shop, so excited youngsters and foot-weary veterans can stop for lunch and a rest.

Laffey (Destroyer)

The heroic destroyer *Laffey* (DD-724) was commissioned on February 8, 1944, and participated in the giant D-Day landings of Allied troops at Normandy four months later. Transferred to the Pacific, she was struck by five Japanese kamikaze suicide planes and hit by three bombs off Okinawa during one hour on April 16, 1945. The *Laffey*'s gallant crew not only kept the ship afloat but also managed to shoot down 11 planes during the attack. After World War II, the *Laffey* served during the Korean War and then in the Atlantic Fleet until she was decommissioned in 1975.

A tour route on the *Laffey* lets you see the bridge, battle stations, living quarters, and various displays of destroyer activities.

Clamagore (Submarine)

The World War II submarine *Clamagore* (SS-343) was commissioned on June 28, 1945, and operated in the Atlantic and Mediterranean throughout its entire career, patrolling tense Cuban waters during 1962. Twice modified, the *Clamagore* survived as one of the U.S. Navy's last diesel-powered subs until it was decommissioned in 1975.

The *Clamagore* tour route covers the control room, berth and mess areas, engine rooms, maneuvering room, and displays of submarine warfare. Note: Spaces are very cramped on-board. Visitors with health problems or claustrophobia are strongly cautioned.

Ingham (Coast Guard Cutter)

The *Ingham* was the most decorated vessel in the U.S. service, with a total of 18 ribbons earned during its career of more than 50 years. Commissioned in 1936, the *Ingham* took part in 31 World War II convoys, six Pacific patrols, and three Vietnam tours. In 1942, it sank the German U-boat 626 with one depth charge, called "*Ingham*'s Hole-in-One."

In recent years, the cutter tracked illegal immigrants and drug runners. The *Ingham* was decommissioned in 1988 and is now open for tours.

South Carolina Aquarium
100 Aquarium Wharf,
Calhoun at Concord Sts.
(843) 720-1990

In May of 2000, after years of planning, controversy, and nervous anticipation, Charleston's new $69-million South Carolina Aquarium opened to rave reviews as a major new attraction in the Lowcountry. This non profit, self-supporting institution is dedicated to educating the public about and helping to conserve South Carolina's unique aquatic habitats. Their mission is to display and interpret the state's diverse range of habitats—from rushing mountain streams to the oceanic depths of the Atlantic. It was the first aquarium in the country to open with a complete Education Master Plan in place. Admission is free for South Carolina school children enrolled in the Aquarium's academic programs. Extensive field studies and outreach programs are also in place.

Among the 60 exhibits in the 93,000-sq.-ft. building are more than 10,000 living organisms, representing more than 500 species. The Aquarium is home to otters, birds, turtles, fish, venomous snakes, other reptiles and amphibians, aquatic invertebrates, and insects. The exhibit path leads visitors through five major regions of the Southeast Appalachian Watershed as found in South Carolina, the Blue Ridge Mountains, the Piedmont, the Coastal Plain, the Coast, and the Ocean. They use a wide variety of media to enhance the visitor experience—some are interactive, some are for very young children, some are education "sta-

Alligators thrive in the Lowcountry salt marshes and up-river swamps. Occasionally they make unwelcome appearances on area golf courses and in the backyards of creek-side, suburban homes!

tions" for discovery labs and classrooms. Admission to the South Carolina Aquarium is $14 for adults, $12 for teens and seniors over 62, and $7 for children 4–12. Hours vary according to time of year: (from August 16 to June 14) it's open 9 AM to 5 PM; (from June 15 to August 15) it's 9 AM to 6 PM. The Aquarium is closed on Christmas Day. Parking is available across Concord Street from the Museum's entrance.

The Citadel Museum
171 Moultrie St.
(843) 792-6846

This museum showcases The Citadel, the Military College of South Carolina. The museum covers the history of the school from 1842 to the present. Various displays represent the military, academic, social, and athletic aspects of cadet life.

The museum is on campus, on the third floor of the Daniel Library—the first building on the right inside The Citadel's main gates. Hours are Sunday through Friday from 2 to 5 PM and Saturday from noon to 5 PM. The museum is closed for college, national, and religious holidays. There is no charge for admission. (See more on The Citadel in our Education chapter.)

Karpeles Manuscript Museum
68 Spring St.
(843) 853-4651

This is one of seven museums in the United States funded by California businessman David Karpeles. They are all nonprofit endeavors to "preserve the original writings of the great authors, scientists, statesmen, sovereigns, philosophers, and leaders from all periods of world history," according to the museum's mission statement.

Scholars, educators, students, and lovers of books and manuscripts are invited to enjoy these collections free of charge. This unusual but fascinating collection is housed in the former St. James United Methodist Church, one of

Charleston's best 19th-century replicas of a classical Roman temple. Special exhibits change from time to time, but the permanent collection includes some of the rare, original writings that helped build our country's unique form of government. Among the Karpeles manuscripts is one of the four original drafts of the Bill of Rights and the Emancipation Proclamation amendment to the Constitution.

The museum is open Tuesday through Saturday from 11 AM to 4 PM. For more information on exhibits or special programs, contact Caroline Dame at the museum. Admission and parking are free.

John Rivers Communications Museum
College of Charleston, 58 George St.
(843) 953-5810, (843) 792-8016
The College of Charleston's John Rivers

Communications Museum offers a unique opportunity to explore the world of broadcasting and communications. John M. Rivers was a Charleston-born banker, businessman, and broadcasting executive who introduced television to the Lowcountry in 1953.

Visitors to the museum can hear early sound recordings, learn about the lives of famous inventors such as Marconi and Edison, and trace the advancements in science from the box camera to television, from the phonograph to radio.

The museum is open Monday through Friday from noon to 4 PM, except during College of Charleston holidays. Summer hours may vary and group tours are conducted by appointment only, so call the museum for scheduling. Admission is free, but donations are appreciated.

Architectural Preservation

If anything is more remarkable than Charleston's softly pastel streets, graceful church spires, and elegant old homes with their exquisite interiors, it has to be the fact that any of it still exists at all.

No other Colonial city has suffered so many calamities as often as Charleston. Time after time, fire has left vast areas of the city in ashes. The city was bombarded during war twice—once by the British during the Revolution and again by Northern cannon in the War Between the States.

Mother Nature has repeatedly hurled fierce hurricanes and tornadoes at the city, and it has been cracked and shaken periodically by terrible earthquakes.

And yet, as you walk through the large and little streets south of Calhoun, you find them lined with fascinating architectural relics of the past. It's hard to imagine that much of what looks so timeless and permanent today could so easily have been swept away by any number of man-made disasters or devastating natural happenstances.

Indeed, Charleston's ethic of architectural preservation and restoration comes by no accident. It's the result of hard work and sacrifice by a few early visionaries and the regularly tested courage of today's preservation organizations.

Insiders need to know about these organizations. Being savvy of the preservation laws can actually have financial benefits here. Qualified Charleston property owners (newcomers and old Charleston families alike) can donate Conservation Easements to either of the city's two major preservation organizations and receive certain tax benefits in exchange. This is one of the ways our federal government rewards and encourages historic preservation in the community. An easement is "partial interest in a property, set out as protective covenants or restrictions and conveyed by recorded deed." In other words, the easement runs with the land in perpetuity and affects each succeeding owner, but the grantors and successor owners retain full use and enjoyment of the property, subject to the terms of the easement. In exchange, the Internal Revenue Service recognizes a tax deduction for the gift of a perpetual conservation restriction on the use of real property.

Charleston buildings within the registered Historic District that are of some architectural integrity and more than 50 years old usually can receive this certification. Properties eligible for easement donation (mostly below Calhoun Street) include agricultural, commercial or residential structures, or historically important acreage.

This award-winning preservation and tax strategy has been growing in popularity during the last few years. The Historic Charleston Foundation, for instance, holds protective covenants on more than 279 structures and easements donated by commercial and residential owners in the greater Charleston area. This is a viable means through which concerned property owners can actively participate in the long-term preservation of Charleston.

It is important to recognize the dues that already have been paid to properly stand guard against the pitfalls and challenges that lie ahead. Historic preservation in Charleston remains an active and vital force. The organizations responsible for keeping Charleston beautiful continue to need public support and enlightened participation.

What follows is a brief description of Charleston's principal preservation organizations along with membership and other support information.

Close-up

Charleston's Architectural Idiom: The Single House

You'll see a thousand examples—from grand, brick, or stucco structures three or four stories tall to more modest clapboard houses with one or two floors. As different as they may seem, they all share a common denominator. They all are exponents of a unique architectural invention: the Charleston single house.

In its simplest definition, the single house is one room wide (butted against the street) and two or more rooms deep. Frequently a side porch is featured—in Charleston, it's called a "piazza"—giving welcome shade and adding extra room for outdoor living. Piazzas, in turn, may also be one or multiple stories in height. All single-house piazzas, however, will have one formal opening onto the street that serves (more or less) as the property's front door.

Experts love to debate the origins of this architectural phenomenon. There are several theories. Some say the architectural roots lie in the Bahamas; others say it evolved here in Charleston as the English custom of primogeniture (whereby the eldest son inherits an entire property) began to break down. This in turn led to inherited properties being subdivided again and again into narrow, strip-like lots—the houses built on them ultimately had to conform. Another possibility is tied to residential properties in 18th-century Charleston being taxed according to their frontage on the street.

You can choose a theory and join in the fray if you like, but genuine 18th- and 19th-century single houses are quintessentially Charlestonian. And they're a point of much-deserved pride and satisfaction for those who own or live in them.

The other side of that coin, of course, is the maintenance factor. Charleston single houses are all very old. Some of them are turn-of-the-century Victorian versions; others are Revolutionary-era houses with rare paneling and priceless interior detailing. In any case, we're talking high maintenance here. Really big bucks.

Oh, and those charming side piazzas? Be advised that every three years or so—they need painting. Depending on the style of balustrade (railing) and the number of levels to the piazza, the paint and labor bill can run several thousands of dollars. Don't forget to plan for that in your budget along with the cost of taxes and other routine maintenance.

Charleston single houses are obviously treasured. This distinctive architectural style, indigenous to this city, is very much a part of living here. And every beautifully maintained Charleston single house you'll see is tangible evidence that the city's architectural traditions remain sacrosanct.

This is a typical Charleston single house, the city's distinctive contribution to urban American architecture.

PHOTO: THOMAS P. FORD

The Preservation Society of Charleston
147 King St., Charleston
(843) 722-4630

In the early 1920s, Charleston was fortunate to have a remarkable group of people who sensed the value of their historic town and its wealth of architecturally significant buildings. These people jealously guarded that heritage and saved a great portion of it from its two worst enemies—the many decades of past neglect and the future's natural gravitation toward urban "renewal."

The city's first preservation organization, The Society for Preservation of Old Dwelling Houses, was founded in 1920 and incorporated in 1928. It evolved into what is now The Preservation Society of Charleston.

The organization is dedicated to preserving the heritage of the city. Its varied activities include advocacy on behalf of protective acquisition and restoration of historic properties, active participation in meetings of Charleston's Board of Architectural Review, and representation at a variety of city meetings and boards dealing with preservation issues. One of the Society's most innovative ideas is its Neighbors Labors program, where volunteers help repair homes owned by elderly or disabled residents unable to afford needed maintenance.

The Society works to keep both its membership and the general public informed about current preservation philosophies, techniques, and issues. To that end, the group publishes a quarterly newsletter, *Preservation Progress*, and schedules regular meetings with informative speakers.

In 1931 the Society played an important role in promoting the first Historic Zoning Ordinance in the United States. Other successes have included the initial saving of the Joseph Manigault House, the Heyward-Washington House (see the section on House Museums in our Attractions chapter), and the East Bay Street area now known as Rainbow Row.

In its early years, the society depended on the generosity of its founding members for financial support. Today it continues to depend in large part on its membership (about 2,000 people scattered all over the country) for monetary and moral support. To augment this base, the Society engages in limited publishing efforts and maintains the beautiful, well-stocked Preservation Society Bookstore, which carries associated gift items from the Lowcountry (see our Shopping chapter). The store is open daily at the Society's 147 King Street headquarters. Additionally, the Society sponsors the annual Fall Candlelight Tours of Homes and Gardens (see our Annual Events chapter), which are very popular with tourists. Funds earned from these activities are used to further preservation objectives.

Dues for annual membership are as follows: student and institutional membership, $20; individual, $30; family, $40; contributor, $100; business membership, $100; sustaining, $250; patron, $500; and benefactor, $1000.

The Preservation Society is a nonprofit, tax-exempt institution. Membership dues and contributions may be deducted for income and estate tax purposes. Memorial gifts are invited. Write The Preservation Society of Charleston for more information at P.O. Box 521, Charleston, SC 29402.

Historic Charleston Foundation
40 East Bay St., Charleston
(843) 723-1623

Historic Charleston Foundation is a nonprofit, educational organization dedicated to the preservation and conservation of the nation's architectural and cultural heritage as represented in Charleston and the Lowcountry.

Organized and incorporated in 1947, the Foundation has undertaken programs that concentrate on property conservation, plus neighborhood and business zone revitalization. The Foundation seeks the stabilization of Charleston's architecturally significant urban environment, which traces its origin to the 1670s.

The Foundation's primary efforts have centered in Charleston's Old and Historic District—the oldest in the United States—which encompasses more than 3,600 structures and represents approximately 25 percent of the Peninsula's buildings. Additional preservation efforts and survey work extend into the outlying tri-county area—the original settlement area of the Carolinas.

Foundation programs serve as realistic alternatives to urban decay; provide protection for vulnerable buildings, housing and neighborhoods; and promote heritage education and citizen participation in urban planning. In fact, the Foundation's efforts in these areas serve as models for many other communities throughout the nation.

Seen here on the Palmer Home (c. 1848), the shade-giving piazza is a Charleston architectural signature—and a cool pleasure on a hot summer day. PHOTO: COURTESY OF THE PALMER HOME

The work of the Foundation is divided into five basic areas: preservation programs, house museum and curatorial efforts, heritage tours and education, Historic Charleston Foundation Reproductions, and public relations and development. Staff offices and the organization's new Preservation Resource Center are at 40 East Bay Street in the historic waterfront building known as the Missroon House (1808).

The Foundation owns and operates three of Charleston's famous museums—the Nathaniel Russell House at 51 Meeting Street, the Aiken-Rhett House at 48 Elizabeth Street, and the Powder Magazine at 79 Cumberland Street. (See our Attractions chapter for in-depth descriptions of these museums.)

The Foundation's Frances R. Edmunds Preservation Center at 108 Meeting Street provides additional offices and serves as an orientation center with free exhibits about the city's architectural history. Here, too, you can buy tickets to the Foundation's house museums (and the annual house and garden tours). Call (843) 724-8484. Also housed in the Edmunds Center, across from the Mills House, is the Foundation's museum shop, where you'll find a comprehensive selection of books, gifts, Lowcountry crafts, and heritage-related items for adults and children (see our Attractions chapter for more on the Foundation's museum shop).

The Historic Charleston Foundation Reproduction Shop, at 105 Broad Street (at the corner of Broad and King), is a retail showroom displaying exclusive, Charleston-inspired furniture as commissioned by the Foundation for reproduction. The offerings have been assembled from the Foundation's own collections as well as from The Charleston Museum, Middleton Place Foundation, and various private collections in the city. This shop is open Monday through Saturday, 10 AM to 5 PM. Call (843) 723-8292.

For more information about any Historic Charleston Foundation merchandise, see our Shopping chapter or write P.O. Box 622, Charleston, SC 29402.

A recent restoration project of the Foundation was the Powder Magazine at 79 Cumberland Street (see our Attractions chapter). This utilitarian structure, once used for storing gunpowder, is the only public building remaining in the Carolinas from the period of the English Lords Proprietors. Today it is restored to its mid-19th century appearance and serves as an interactive interpretive center for Charleston's first 50 years. Call (843) 805-6730 for more details.

Historic Charleston Foundation has no membership, but its work is augmented by the active support of about 600 volunteers who annually donate thousands of hours to the Foundation's programs and special events. The largest concentration of volunteer support is provided by the board of trustees, homeowners, and docents for the enormously popular Festival of Houses and Gardens each spring (see our Tours chapter for more information). Volunteer opportunities include duties as house museum docents and service on standing and special interest committees.

Financial support for Foundation programs comes from a variety of sources including earned and endowment income, public and private grant money, and tax-deductible gifts of cash securities or objects. The Foundation welcomes gifts from those who wish to participate in the study, conservation, and protection of Charleston's heritage. All contributions and bequests are tax-deductible.

South Carolina Historical Society
100 Meeting St., Charleston
(843) 723-3225

In 1855, as the last of America's Revolutionary generation was dying off, their recorded thoughts, accomplishments, and aspirations were dying with them. The founders of the South Carolina Historical Society recognized this fact and

saw the need to preserve existing records of that era for the future of South Carolina and generations to come.

That year, they invited "contributions of every sort . . . [to] illustrate . . . social, political or ecclesiastical [life], our industry, [and] our resources . . . " This 19th-century call for the vanishing evidence of South Carolina's past became the foundation for the Society's collection.

Simply restated for today, the Society's mandate is to collect information respecting every portion of our state, to preserve it and, when deemed advisable, to publish it.

The Society's holdings now constitute South Carolina's most important private repository of history. Members and researchers find and study the papers of governors, members of Congress, generals, architects, poets, artists, soldiers, and planters, along with young girls' diaries and love letters, the records of churches, banks, grocery stores, plantations, and shipping companies. Together, they all record the rhythms of daily life in South Carolina—then and now.

In addition, the Society holds more than 40,000 maps, photographs, and architectural drawings and 55,000 books, pamphlets, and serials that trace the lives of South Carolinians. Their collection includes over 1,300 linear feet of manuscripts, papers of individuals and institutions. Their Tower Collection of Civil War material is especially strong. The Society maintains an Internet website with 65,000 records pertaining to 18,000 South Carolina surnames—a boon to genealogists checking in from all over the world.

Partly as a result of the increasing awareness of heritage and the growing popularity of genealogy during the past five years, researchers—historians, genealogists, authors, lawyers, scholars, and film makers—have flocked to the Society in record numbers for the wealth of information available.

The South Carolina Historical Society seeks membership among all who share an interest in the state's past, whether they be students, adults, natives, or newcomers. Members enjoy a rich variety of programs and benefits including the quarterly *South Carolina Historical Magazine*; a newsletter, *Caralogue*; and invitations to Society-sponsored lectures, tours, and social functions.

The Society maintains its offices and collection in the Fireproof Building, built on Charleston's Meeting Street in 1826 and designed by South Carolina's premier antebellum architect, Robert Mills.

Membership dues encourage easy participation by all those interested in South Carolina history. They are as follows: undergraduate student membership, $25; regular, $50; libraries and institutions, $50; contributor, $60; and sustainer, $100. Various levels for corporate and major donor memberships are also available.

For a membership application or more information, call the number above or write South Carolina Historical Society, 100 Meeting Street, Charleston, SC 29401.

Tours

Charleston's African-
American History

Ethnic Tours

Other Guided Tours

Upon first impression, visitors to Charleston are usually taken with the city's architectural charm. Part of that fascination comes from the unspoken questions that leap to mind about Charleston's early good times. People want to know more about how a city of such wealth and architectural sophistication did, in fact, evolve.

The next impulse many visitors have is to seek out some kind of tour to find answers to some of those questions. Understandably, people want a visual, geographic, or ethnic overview, a point of reference, some kind of perspective. But most of all, they want to hear the stories about Charleston—when everything old was shiny and new, political independence was still a dream, and the name of Charles Towne was world-famous as the brightest jewel in the British Colonial crown.

That's why the telling of Charleston's story has literally become an industry. In fact, it's so important that to become an officially licensed tour guide here, one must take a city-sponsored course (and pass very tough written and oral exams) just to get the job. Charlestonians, you see, care enormously that their story be told well. That's simply because the real truth is interesting enough to make mere half-truths, downright lies (told by unscrupulous tour guides), and corny amateurism wholly unnecessary. It's deceitful and not at all Charlestonian.

Tours of the city are available in several forms. Most of the walking or riding (be that in a carriage, car, or van) tours depart from the Charleston Visitor Reception and Transportation Center on Meeting Street (simply referred to as the "visitor center" hereafter) or from the City Market area. You may also choose to meet a private guide at your inn or hotel and depart from there. Ask your hotel clerks or concierges to book your tour reservations—they have plenty of experience doing so.

Whichever tour mode you choose, you'll have a wonderful adventure. Included in this chapter are some of the tours currently available that we consider especially good and interesting. We've listed categories of tours alphabetically, and we start with a little background information to help you explore Charleston's rich African-American heritage.

Charleston's African-American History

As we've mentioned in several places in this book, no visit to Charleston would be complete without gaining a better understanding of and appreciation for the strong African influences on this society, past and present. The folkways, lifeways, culture, and achievements of these people have been infused into every fiber of the Charleston experience since the very beginning of the 1670 English settlement.

Among the first settlers in Charles Towne were black and white indentured servants and enslaved Africans. Within a decade, the English settlers had implemented the plantation system (already flourishing in Barbados) to sustain themselves here and create a product for economic exchange. Their labor force came from Africa—particularly the West Coast of Africa—from areas now known as Sierra Leone, Ghana, and Benin.

European and American traders plied the Atlantic waters off these areas, capturing Africans, imprisoning them until they could be boarded onto slave ships. Typically, each African was afforded a mere four square feet of living space while chained down in the

Close-up

Gullah: A Language, an Ethic, a Lowcountry Folklore

Part of our country's growing trend toward ethnic self-awareness has been a renewed interest in Gullah, the colorful language and accompanying lifestyle that once flourished on the South Carolina sea islands—from Georgetown to Daufuskie.

Researchers reported that as late as 1979, 100,000 South Carolinians spoke Gullah. But in the census of 1990, only 180 families still listed it as the language they spoke at home. Without intervention, the Gullah language will soon live only in scholarly textbooks and on fragile academic recordings.

The origins of Gullah date back to a sad chapter in America's past. When slave traders sailed to West Africa and stuffed their ships full of men, women, and children to be sold as slaves to Southern planters, Gullah was conceived. As that black culture meshed with the white, Gullah was born. A thick, lilting mix of African and English dialects, it started as a makeshift second language used among the sea island slaves, and it slowly evolved into the unwritten native tongue of their descendants.

Oddly, slavery and the antebellum South fed energy to the language. Gullah served a very practical transitional purpose and its use and culture actually developed during those years. After the Civil War, however, the separation between the black and white cultures became highly exaggerated for nearly a century and a half. Cut off from the cultural homogenization that occurred everywhere else in America, life along the sea islands changed very little. Sea

Obo Addy performs Gullah rhythms and song at the MOJA Arts Festival, a celebration of the city's African and Caribbean heritage. PHOTO: COURTESY OF CITY OF CHARLESTON OFFICE OF CULTURAL AFFAIRS

islanders still fished the coastline, shrimped the marsh, hunted for game in the woods, and spoke their native tongue unashamedly.

Gullah stubbornly survived in this splendid isolation—until the outside world rediscovered the islands and invested millions of dollars to develop them as resorts. Suddenly, bridges were built that introduced paved roads, indoor plumbing, better education and access to higher-paying mainland jobs. Gullah became thought of as "bad English." Soon it was something to be ashamed of or denied. Then television, the greatest homogenizing influence of all, came along and nearly snuffed the language out altogether.

Finding true Gullah today is like finding gold. It's rare and it's kept hidden from "outsiders." Still, there are a few islanders determined to keep it alive. There still are those who knit their own fishing nets—rather than buy the ones made in Japan. There are those who still cook the Gullah receipts (recipes) and serve their families whole meals fresh from the sea. Thankfully, there are still those who take what's left of the sweetgrass from the riverbanks and fashion baskets of great skill and beauty—just like their ancestors did back in Sierra Leone.

hold. Under these grim and inhumane conditions, untold numbers of Africans died en route to the New World. From coastal Africa, the ships would sail to the West Indies where some of the human "cargo" would be sold into slavery. The rest was brought to the South Carolina coast.

Awaiting the slave ships on Sullivan's Island off the coast from Charles Towne were crude structures called "pest houses." Here, the unwilling passengers would be held for a period of at least 40 days—to be checked for diseases and infections—during which they would be also groomed for sale. If maladies were suspected or discovered, the captives would be quarantined onboard their ships.

In just the five years between 1803 and 1808, an estimated 40,000 Africans were imported to America. The sheer volume of incoming slaves became a cause for concern among the relatively few white slave holders who feared an uprising. In 1808 the importing of additional slaves was banned. However, this ban did little to stem the flow, and slave trade continued as late as 1858.

Once sold, most of the Africans would toil in the fields. Their labor made the early plantation life of coastal South Carolina not only possible but highly profitable. Africans also brought with them vital knowledge of rice and indigo production, cattle tending, boat building, and ironworking. Eventually, their food, language, religion, and music all mingled with the European traditions to create the Lowcountry culture called "Gullah" we celebrate today.

Not all Africans living in America were enslaved. From 1690 on, a few free people of color were living in the Carolina. They were mostly multiracial and usually lived in the urban areas where they could find work in various trades. There were cobblers, carpenters, wheelwrights, brick masons, and smithies. Some became wealthy and owned slaves themselves.

With the end of the Civil War and the Emancipation Proclamation, all African Americans were technically free. However, the opportunistic post-war Reconstruction period and the advent of Jim Crow laws led to Constitutional struggles over the 13th, 14th, and

15th amendments. The much-longed-for freedom of African Americans in Charleston was shallow, indeed.

Many people of color left their rural homes and sought a better life in urban settings—sometimes moving to large northern cities—where opportunities for work and education were better. Those who remained behind tended to live in small, rural, self-sustaining villages that were clustered around their beloved churches—mostly free of white control. Visitors to the Lowcountry today can see evidence of this social pattern in communities such as Snowden, in Mt. Pleasant, and Maryville, west of the Ashley. During the Civil Rights Movement of the 1960s, Charleston blacks gathered at sites like the old tobacco factory at 701 East Bay Street and Moving Star Hall on Johns Island to organize and peacefully gain rights granted to all Americans by the U.S. Constitution.

Because more than one-fourth of the African slaves shipped to the 13 original American colonies before the Revolution came through Charleston, this city's role in African-American history can hardly be overstated. In the years between 1700 and 1775, an estimated 200,000 slaves were put ashore on Sullivan's Island. One expert on slave history has even dubbed Sullivan's Island the "Ellis Island of black Americans" (in the literal, if not the symbolic, sense). And yet, until very recently this fact was little known by most contemporary Americans—even South Carolinians. Realistically, this was not a popular subject for Charleston tour guides in the pre-Civil Rights era. History buffs felt awkward describing the tragedy of 18th- and 19th-century slave trade along with the city's upbeat tourist attractions. As a result, Charleston has been criticized in the national media for taking a shortsighted view of its own black history. Thankfully, a more enlightened attitude is starting to emerge. More and more of our nation's 34 million African-Americans are discovering Charleston in their efforts to explore their cultural heritage.

Today, the annual MOJA Arts Festival in October is Charleston's official celebration of its African and Caribbean culture. (See more about MOJA in our chapters on The Arts and Annual Events.) But many of our popular tourist destinations feature special exhibits and events pertaining to Charleston's African-American history. We'll start with the best resource for related information and then describe some of the places and events you'll want to see on your own. After that, we offer the names of companies that can provide guided tours geared toward showcasing the city's African-American heritage.

African American National Heritage Museum
College of Charleston
Avery Research Center, 125 Bull St.
(843) 953-7609

As Charleston proceeds into the new millennium, a more enlightened approach to presenting the city's rich African American heritage is starting to bloom. The African American National Heritage Museum is a multi-site, cooperative educational effort undertaken by the Avery Research Center for African American History and Culture, the City of Charleston, Historic Charleston Foundation, and the South Carolina African American Heritage Council.

At four primary historic sites, these entities are working together to provide insight into the greater Charleston African American experience. At these sites, visitors can start to explore the origins of the culture and the role African Americans played in shaping Charleston, the South Carolina Lowcountry and, in fact, the nation. Historical exhibits, living history demonstrations, site interpretation, and cultural events are offered at the following venues.

Slave Mart Museum
6 Chalmers St.

The one longtime local outlet for black cultural information in Charleston was the Old Slave Mart at 6 Chalmers Street. At this site, reproduction slave-made wares and crafts were sold and actual slave-era artifacts were displayed. Unfortunately, the museum failed as a privately owned tourist attraction and it closed in 1988. The building was bought by the City of Charleston that same year, and it reopened in 1999 as the focal point of a multi-site black history museum and tour dedicated to illustrating the drama of the city's African-American saga.

The building encloses part of the rear yard of a now-gone tenement building known to have been used for slave auctions as early as 1856. First called "Ryan's Mart" and later, the "Mart in Chalmer's Street," this was one of several sites in this neighborhood where African Americans were sold into slavery. The last auctions in this location were in 1863.

Visitors to the Slave Mart Museum experience presentations and exhibits which include sources of the African cultures, the middle passage, Caribbean influences, emancipation, reconstruction, arts, ethnic cuisine, and Charleston's quiet role in the Civil Rights Movement.

From here, visitors are encouraged to move on and explore the other three facets of this unique museum. The Slave Mart Museum is open from 10 AM to 5 PM Monday through Saturday and from 2 to 5 PM Sunday. It is closed on Thanksgiving, Christmas, and New Year's Day. Admission is $6 per person.

McLeod Plantation
325 Country Club Dr., James Island
McLeod Plantation dates back to the late 17th century when it was one of the first profitable farms to be established along the Ashley River system. This property was acquired in 1993 by Historic Charleston Foundation and its fine collection of antebellum buildings is considered to be among the best preserved in the American South.

In addition to the main house (c.1854), there are barns, stables, a gin house, kitchen, and a dairy plus a street of several slave cabins. According to a census taken in 1860, there were 74 slaves living in 26 dwellings on the plantation whose work was the cultivation of sea island cotton.

McLeod was occupied by both Confederate and Union forces during the Civil War. The main house served as a field hospital and it housed officers from the famous 54th and 55th Massachusetts Volunteers. It also became the main office for the Freedman's Bureau serving the James Island area during Reconstruction years. McLeod Plantation is only open by special advance arrangement through Historic Charleston Foundation and the Avery Research Center. Call (843) 953-7609 for more information. Admission is $6 per person.

Aiken-Rhett House
48 Elizabeth St.
(843) 723-1159
It is rare, indeed, that a property of such prominence and historic importance as this would survive to this day in so authentic a state. But here is a house museum that affords the uncanny opportunity to view an "urban" household of great privilege as it was on the eve of the Civil War.

The central section of the Aiken-Rhett House (see House Museums in our Attractions chapter) was built in 1818 in the Federal Style popular at that time. However, when William Aiken, Jr. and his wife bought the property in 1831, they did an extensive remodeling of the first floor in the robust Greek Revival style, which was all the rage at that time. When Mr. Aiken was elected Governor of South Carolina, wings were added with a dining room and ballroom for formal entertaining and even an art gallery eventually came along. But in effect, the decor of the house was arrested in 1857, shortly before the Civil War began. And because of the war's drastic impact on Gov. Aiken and his family, the house and the outbuildings that supported it (including the on-site slave quarters) remained remarkably unchanged from that point on. In fact, the house came into the hands of The Charleston Museum in 1975 almost as a sealed time capsule of pre-Civil War taste and technology.

Most notable are the servants' quarters to the rear of the house which are in sharp contrast to the rest of the property—far more plain and utilitarian than the horse stables and even the privies.

A portable pre-recorded tape with appropriate sound effects is available for self-guided tours of the property and docents are on hand to answer any questions you may have.

The museum house is open from 10 AM to 4:30 PM Monday through Saturday. Sunday hours are from 2 to 4:30 PM. Admission is $7 per person; for children younger than 6, it is free.

Avery Research Center for African American History and Culture
125 Bull St., College of Charleston
(843) 953-7609

In Charleston, the rich culture of South Carolina's African Americans is recognized for its unique national significance. However, the materials that document this culture have been widely scattered over time, and much has already been lost. The College of Charleston's Avery Research Center for African American History and Culture was established to document, preserve, and make public the unique historical and cultural heritage of this significant group for this and future generations.

In October 1990, the center was established at 125 Bull Street in Charleston's Historic District. Here, at long last, a growing archival collection and on-site museum could share the purpose of gathering together these valuable materials and encouraging scholarship on the subject.

The research center is on the site of the former Avery Normal Institute, the local normal school (for teachers-to-be), and college preparatory school that served Charleston's black community for nearly 100 years. Avery Normal Institute was organized in October 1865 by black minister F.L. Cardozo of the American Missionary Association for (in his words) "the

education of colored children." In 1868, the school moved into the Bull Street building just five blocks west of the College of Charleston. There, for nearly a century, the school produced teachers for the community and gifted leaders for South Carolina and the nation.

Today, the center is actively soliciting manuscript collections: the personal and professional papers of individuals and organizations, oral and video histories, photographic records, and other related documents. Donors may be assured their gifts will receive the care needed to store and preserve them properly.

The archival collections are regularly used for exhibits and educational programs for the public. These activities are planned in conjunction with local and national African-American celebrations and holidays.

The Avery Research Center reading room is open to the public Monday through Saturday from noon to 5 PM. Morning hours are available by appointment. Walk-in visitors can enjoy tours of the building and the museum galleries 2 and 4 PM on weekdays and Saturday from noon to 5 PM. Group tours are available by appointment.

For more information, call Annette Teasdell at the number listed above. Written inquiries should be addressed to Avery Research Center for African American History and Culture, 125 Bull Street, College of Charleston, SC 29424.

Battery Wagner, Morris Island

The first Union regiment of free black soldiers, the now-famous 54th Massachusetts Volunteer Infantry Regiment, fought on Morris Island during the Civil War. The bloody battle was an undeniable confirmation of the bravery, courage, and valor of the black soldiers and their willingness to fight for the North. Although the site is not (yet) memorialized formally, the island can be viewed briefly during Fort Sumter harbor tours, which leave from Patriots Point in Mt. Pleasant or from Charleston's City Marina on Lockwood

Drive. What you'll see are just small hills that were originally built as artillery fortifications, a few shanties, and truck-farm areas. Call (843) 884-2727 for departure times. Ft. Sumter Tours are from 9 AM to 6:30 PM Monday through Friday. The fare is $11 for adults and teens and $5 for children ages 6 through 11. No tours go out to the fort on Christmas Day. (See more on Battery Wagner in the Forts section of our Attractions chapter.)

Boone Hall Plantation
U.S. Hwy. 17 N., Mt. Pleasant
(843) 884-4371
Once one of the largest cotton plantations in the South, Boone Hall dates back to the 1680s. At one time Boone Hall was home to more than 1,000 slaves. Nine of the original slave houses still stand on the plantation's "Slave Street." These structures, now frequently used by film makers for their stark authenticity, are open to the public on this still-working farm. Boone Hall is open Monday through Saturday from 8:30 AM to 6:30 PM and Sunday from 1 to 5 PM, April 1 through Labor Day. After Labor Day until April 1, hours are 9 AM to 5 PM Monday through Saturday, Sunday 9 AM to 4 PM. Admission is $12.50 for adults and teens and $6 for children ages 6 to 12. Seniors 60 and over pay $10. The Plantation Kitchen Restaurant is open 9 AM to 3:30 PM Monday through Saturday. (See our Lowcountry Daytrips chapter for more on Boone Hall Plantation.)

Cabbage Row
89–91 Church St.
This downtown area was claimed as the inspirational setting for DuBose Heyward's 1925 book, *Porgy*, and for George and Ira Gershwin's beloved folk opera, *Porgy and Bess*, which premiered in 1935. Cabbage Row, the scene of the story, took its name from the vegetables regularly sold from carts and windowsills by the area's black residents. Today, this section houses quaint little shops, but anyone familiar with the opera and its distinctive

stage settings will readily see that this place and the alleys around and behind it could easily have been the story's original scene.

Was the story based on truth? Was there ever a crippled vendor named Porgy who won, then lost, the love of a troubled woman named Bess? Many older Charlestonians recall a poor, crippled man who lived here in the early 1920s and used a small goat cart to get around. His name was Samuel Smalls. The other details of the story are hard to pin down. But Charleston certainly had enclaves of black families who struggled against very difficult circumstances. And their sagas of survival and social interdependence were not unlike Porgy's. Charleston obviously experiences the wrath of hurricanes, and in those days terrible storms struck with little warning. And surely then, as now, the ugly specter of drugs and violence dramatically influenced the lives and loves of these people. We may never actually know if Heyward ever heard of Samuel Smalls, but the connections are intriguing and the story is timeless.

More avid music lovers and Porgy fans may want to visit Smalls' grave, which is well-marked in the churchyard of James Island Presbyterian Church, about a 6-mile drive from the Charleston Peninsula on Folly Road. The grave was unmarked for many years until an anonymous but concerned Charlestonian took the responsibility of funding a suitable marker for this legendary Charleston icon. To get to the church, take the James Island Connector (S.C. Highway 30) over the Ashley River and turn left on Folly Road. The church is at 1632 Fort Johnson Road, the intersection of Folly and Fort Johnson Roads. Look for the marker to Porgy just outside the fenced churchyard.

The Charleston Museum
360 Meeting St.
(843) 722-2996
America's first museum, founded in 1773, has exhibits and art depicting African-American life in the South Carolina Lowcountry.

Additional photographs and treasured information on African-American history and culture are housed in the museum's archives. Archival research is welcome—call the museum for an appointment. The Charleston Museum is open Monday through Saturday from 9 AM to 5 PM. Sunday hours are from 1 to 5 PM. Admission is $8 for adults and teens and $4 for children ages 3 through 12. The doors are closed on Thanksgiving, Christmas, and New Years Eve. (See The Charleston Museum entry in our Attractions chapter for more information.)

Drayton Hall
3380 Ashley River Rd.
(843) 766-0188
This Colonial-era plantation house is shown to the public today as an architectural museum. It is considered to be the finest and earliest example of Palladian architecture in America. Built between 1738 and 1742, the structure serves as a monument to 18th-century European and African-American artisans, who displayed highly sophisticated building skills at a remarkably early time.

Now a property of the National Trust for Historic Preservation, Drayton Hall's research and education departments are in the vanguard of the nation's effort to document and acknowledge the contribution of African Americans to the Colonial South. Special events and educational programs at Drayton Hall offer insight into this culture and its modern legacy. For more information, ask for Dr. George W. McDaniel, director, or Karen Nickless, director of research and education.

Drayton Hall is open daily, except Christmas and Thanksgiving. Admission is $10 for adults, $8 for students ages 12 through 18, and $6 for children ages 6 through 11. Admission to the grounds only is $3. Admission is free to card-holding members of the National Trust for Historic Preservation. (See the Drayton Hall entry in our Attractions chapter.)

One of our most treasured exponents of African-American heritage is the Low-country gospel spiritual. For a little slice of heaven, attend one of the special holiday candlelight concerts performed by local African-American choirs at Drayton Hall during the Christmas season. These concerts, originally sponsored by the Friends of Drayton Hall, are now open to the public and offer a rare opportunity to hear authentic Lowcountry spirituals (with their distinctive double hand-clapping) in an original setting. See our Annual Events chapter or call the number listed for more information.

Eliza's House at Middleton Place
S.C. Hwy. 61
(843) 556-6020
After the Civil War, a number of freed slaves chose to remain living and working on the huge rice plantation that was Middleton Place. They were most likely responsible for constructing in the 1870s the building that was later named "Eliza's House." It was named in memory of Eliza Leach, a South Carolina African American born in 1891 and the last person to live in the building. For 40 years or so, she worked at Middleton Place, performing a variety of duties from working in the gardens to greeting visitors. She died in 1986 at age 94, and almost to the end of her life she lived in the house in much the same way her predecessors did.

The building has been restored and is now shown along with the other former plantation outbuildings that house demonstrations of weaving, spinning, blacksmithing, candle-making, carpentry, and pottery-making—all tasks of the plantation slaves. Eliza's House was originally built to house two families: One half of the building now depicts typical living quarters; plans are in the works to set up the other half for exhibits of artifacts from Middleton Place slaves.

Eliza's House is open daily from 9 AM to 5 PM. Middleton Place house tours are Tuesday through Sunday from 10 AM to 4:30 PM. Admission is $15 for adults and teens to see the plantation gardens and stable yards (including Eliza's House) and

$7 for children ages 6 through 12. There is an additional $7 charge (for adults and children alike) for a guided tour of the plantation house. (See more about Middleton Place in our Attractions chapter.)

Snee Farm Charles Pinckney National Historic Site
1254 Longpoint Rd., Mt. Pleasant
(843) 881-5516, (843) 883-3123
The interpretation of African-American history at Snee Farm centers on the influence of enslaved people of West African origin on the development of Charles Pinckney's Colonial farm. This offering has struck a cord with a large population of Charleston tourists and in the peak year of 1997, more than 40,000 people (individuals, families, and school groups)

visited the site. Snee Farm was established in 1988 to highlight the contributions of Pinckney, a famous statesman, politician, and signer of the U.S. Constitution. The contribution of people of African descent is shown through exhibits, park handouts, archaeology displays, and a video program. These contributions were in the form of language, food, agricultural skills, and craftsmanship.

The site has a small gift shop where various publications are sold that help illuminate the African-American story. Sometimes even a maker of sweetgrass baskets is on hand to demonstrate that distinctive local art form. Park hours are from 9 AM to 5 PM most of the year, with an extended hour offered in the summer months. There is no admission charge for this site.

Ethnic Tours

Gullah Tours Inc.
(843) 763-7551
This group offers Charleston folk tales told in Gullah, the distinctive language spoken by Lowcountry blacks that's a separate and unique cross between English and various African dialects. Your guide is Alphonso Brown, licensed guide, lecturer, and author of *A Guide to Gullah Charleston*. You will tour many of the important local African-American sites. All tours leave from Gallery Chuma on 43 John Street, across from the visitors center. Weekday tours are at 11 AM and 3 PM. Saturday tours are at 11 AM and 1 and 3 PM. No tours are given on Sunday. These all-adult tours are $15 a person.

Sites and Insights Tours
(843) 762-0051
Visit little-known black history sites and gain a knowledge of Charleston's past from an African-American perspective. Hear stories of slavery, free blacks, the Denmark Vesey Slave Uprising, the Stono Rebellion, Catfish Row, and Charleston's colorful sea islands. These are one- and two-hour motor tours that depart from the visitor center. Rates are $10 a person

of any age for the shorter tour and $15 for the two-hour program. Call for schedules.

Tourific Tours African American History
(843) 853-2500
This company, owned by a native Charlestonian and civic leader, offers two tours of African-American history departing from the visitors center. Tour #1 lasts two hours and takes visitors on a stroll through the streets of Charleston to the boundaries of the original walled city. You'll see typical Charleston "single houses" and antebellum mansions, historic churches, the Dock Street Theater, cobblestone streets, and the famous Four Corners of Law. Tour #2 takes visitors through the picturesque College of Charleston campus where free people of color lived prior to the Civil War. Hear about the early contributions of African Americans to the city's history and see on-site examples of work by Charleston's famous wrought-iron worker Philip Simmons. Learn about slave uprising leader Denmark Vesey and visits African-American churches. Reservations are required for these tours, and all require a minimum of two people to begin. Each tour is $15 per person.

Other Guided Tours

Bus and Van Tours

Bus and van tours are very comfortable—if for no other reason than the fact that these tour vehicles are air conditioned. In the summer months, that certainly counts for a lot. Most of these vehicles have small PA systems so hearing the driver and tour guide is no problem. Be advised, however, that only certain streets are approved for larger tour vehicles, so you'll miss some of the tiny side streets and alleys that give Charleston so much of its charm. Here are some of the best of the motor tours offered:

Adventure Sightseeing
1090 Ft. Sumter Dr.
(843) 762-0088, (800) 722-5394

This company offers a variety of tours of the Historic District. You may choose one of the bus or van tours with special features such as The Citadel Dress Parade (Fridays only), a tour through the Old Exchange or one of Charleston's house museums. Adventure Sightseeing offers free pickup service from downtown hotels, the visitor center, the City Market, and the City Marina. Reservations are accepted from 8 to 10 AM daily.

Fares for two-hour tours are $23 for adults and teens, $14 for children 5 to 11, and free for children 4 and younger. For Adventure's 1½-hour tour, adult fares are $15, and $11 for children 5 to 11. The shorter, 1¼-hour tour is $13 for adults and $9 for children.

Adventure also offers narrated walking tours ($12.50 a person) that leave from the visitors center and require reservations. These tour groups must consist of ten or more persons. All Adventure tours include a complete history of the city; two-hour tours include one house museum.

Charleston's Finest Historic Tours
P.O. Box 263, Ridgeville, SC
(843) 724-6263

This company offers three daily sched-uled tours—all in a luxury touring coach. Tour A begins at 10 AM and is a city-centered adventure including seeing and hearing about noteworthy mansions and churches, Civil War forts, The Battery, and Slave Mart (allow 90 minutes). Adult fare is $15; youths 10 through 17, $10; children age 9 and under free. Tour B begins in the afternoon at 2 PM and lasts 3 hours. It includes a visit to Boone Hall Plantation (including the mansion house and slave cabins tour) plus the nearby Charles Pinckney Plantation. Adult rates are $30; ages 10 to 17 years, $25; children 9 and under, free.

Charleston Tours Inc.
545 Savannah Hwy.
(843) 571-0049

These guides say they're "the Southern specialists for city or plantation tours." Tour A is a 90-minute city tour that includes the French Quarter and the Slave Market plus a stop at The Battery. The fare for adults and teens is $15; children ages 6 through 12, half-price. Tour B goes out to the plantations and lasts four hours. It includes a visit to Magnolia Plantation and Gardens, Middleton Place, or Drayton Hall. Adult and teen fare is $45, and children ages 6 through 12, $22.50. Tour C includes Boone Hall Plantation, which has been featured in many movies. Adults and teens go for $35, children ages 6 through 12 go for $17.50. Tour D is billed as an "all-day adventure" that includes the city tour (you do lunch on your own) in the Market area, then continues on to Boone Hall Plantation. Adults and teen admissions are $45; children 6 through 12 go for $22.50. All tours depart from the visitor center with free pickup service from most downtown locations.

"Doin' the Charleston" Tours
P.O. Box 31338, Charleston, SC 29417
(843) 763-1233, (800) 647-4487

Here's something of a high-tech motor tour—a new twist on historic interpretation. You travel around Charleston in a minibus with large windows while historic views of many of the same places you're seeing are displayed via laser disc on a screen inside your motor coach. There's even a musical soundtrack to your guide's live narration. Allow 90 minutes for this tour, which includes a stop at The Battery. Rates for adults and teens are $15, and the price is $9 for children 6 through 11. Daily tours leave promptly from the visitor center at 9:30 AM, noon, and 2:30 and 4:30 PM* (*during daylight savings time only). Free pickups from downtown lodgings are offered. Call for reservations.

Gray Line Bus Tours
P.O. Box 219, Charleston, SC 29402
(843) 722-4444, (800) 423-0444

Gray Line offers four tours of Charleston in various configurations—all in air-conditioned minivans with large windows.

The Historic Charleston Tour #1 (allow 75 minutes) includes a stop at The Battery and points out dozens of historic sites. Adult rates are $14, children younger than 12, $9. Tour #1-A is an expanded version of Tour #1 (allow 90 minutes for this one). For this, adult rates are $16, children $10.

Tour #2 is called Historic Charleston-Patriots Trail (allow two hours). This tour includes a stop at The Battery and one of Charleston's house museums (which one will vary according to season and availability). Adults and teens are charged $22, children younger than 12, $15.

Tour #3 is a combination Bus and Boat Tour with an optional all-day shuttle pass. This is a special pricing of Tour #1 along with a boat tour of Charleston Harbor. Also included is an all-day pass on the downtown area shuttle that travels to and from the boat tour as well as the City Market, the King Street shopping district, and most downtown hotels and motels. Adult and teen rates are $22, and children younger than 12 pay $15. Tours depart the visitor center every 30 minutes (on the hour and half-hour) and the tour bus stops at 102 N. Market Street 20 minutes before then.

Talk of the Towne
2166 St. James Dr.
(843) 795-8199

Enjoy panoramic views of The Battery, Rainbow Row, and all the major downtown landmarks from a minibus designed especially for touring Charleston. The two-hour tours leaving from the visitor center include a 35-minute guided tour of the Nathaniel Russell House or the Edmondston-Alston House. Pickup from all major downtown hotels is available. The rate for adults and teens is $22; children 12 and younger go for $13. The 75-

Insiders' Tip

With all the horse-drawn carriage tours on city streets, you will be pleased to learn that Charleston horses wear "diapers." Should a horse's diaper need changing and the street in any way become sullied (they say it can happen to even the best of horses), there's a very civilized Charleston solution. A special truck patrols the carriage routes during tour hours carrying a huge, black tank of perfumed disinfectant. In the event of an "accident," carriage drivers are carefully instructed to throw out weighted flags to mark the spot and drive on with dignity unruffled. The truck then scurries to the scene for a welcome squirt, a quick wash, and a gracious apology. What can we say? It happens.

Close-up

Gateway Walk

Looking for a way to see Charleston that's a little off the beaten path? Gateway Walk is a free walking tour many find unique, and it's right through the heart of the Historic District.

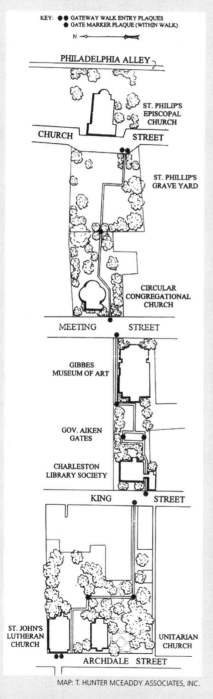

KEY: ●● GATEWAY WALK ENTRY PLAQUES
      ● GATE MARKER PLAQUE (WITHIN WALK)
N

PHILADELPHIA ALLEY

ST. PHILIP'S
EPISCOPAL
CHURCH

CHURCH   STREET

ST. PHILLIP'S
GRAVE YARD

CIRCULAR
CONGREGATIONAL
CHURCH

MEETING   STREET

GIBBES
MUSEUM OF ART

GOV. AIKEN
GATES

CHARLESTON
LIBRARY SOCIETY

KING   STREET

ST. JOHN'S
LUTHERAN
CHURCH   UNITARIAN
                          CHURCH

ARCHDALE STREET

MAP: T. HUNTER MCEADDY ASSOCIATES, INC.

In 1930 Mrs. Clelia Peronneau McGowan, president of the Garden Club of Charleston, came up with the idea for a walkway that would connect the city's churchyards, garden areas, and tucked-away courtyards. She was inspired by a trip to Paris where she embraced the idea of meandering through serene gardens in the midst of a bustling cityscape. The plan was designed by noted Charleston landscape architect Loutrel Briggs and opened on April 10, 1930, to celebrate the 250th anniversary of the founding of Charleston on its peninsula site.

The Walk is designated by unobtrusive plaques and foot stone markers that lead through historic sites but depart from the sidewalk viewpoint and beckon you into the hidden core of the city blocks between Archdale Street and Philadelphia Alley. This self-guided stroll covers four blocks where you may amble through four churchyards full of fascinating old tombstones with a variety of blooming flora. It continues through the gardens of the Charleston Library Society and Gibbes Museum of Art, with its rose garden that features the Governor Aiken gates, fountain, and sculpture. Winding your way through several centuries of Charleston history, you'll discover how Gateway Walk was named for the beautiful wrought-iron gates along the way.

An inscription on one of the plaques attributed to Mrs. McGowan reads:

"Through hand wrought gates, alluring paths
Lead on to pleasant places,
Where ghosts of long forgotten things
Have left elusive traces."

The Walk underwent its first restoration in 1953 with the continued support of Mr. Briggs. In 1992 the garden club initiated a three-year restoration designed by T. Hunter McEaddy Associates and spearheads its ongoing maintenance through an endowment established at the Community Foundation. The Gateway Walk is free and open 8:30 AM to 5 PM Monday through Friday.

minute version is a nonstop, 7-mile ride through Charleston that includes The Battery, Rainbow Row, and the Four Corners of Law. Adult and teen fare is $13; children ages 12 and younger go for $8.

Taylored Tours of Charleston
1300 Lenevar Dr.
(843) 763-5747

This group offers four historic tours of Charleston. Tour #1 is a general history tour (allow 75 minutes) covering more than 90 points of interest including a stop at The Battery overlooking Fort Sumter. Adults and teen admissions are $12; children younger than 12, $7. Tour #2 is a 90-minute trip specializing in specific subjects: the Colonial period and the Revolution, the Civil War, black history, and architectural points of interest. Reservations for these tours are required a day in advance, and the cost is $17 a person. Tour #3 offers 90 minutes of general history (same as Tour #1) followed by a guided tour of one of Charleston's house museums (the Nathaniel Russell House, Heyward-Washington House, or the Aiken-Rhett House). Rates for adults and children are $21; children younger than 12 are charged $11. Tour #4 is a plantation tour lasting about three and a half hours. It includes a trip up the historic Ashley River Road and visits one of two historic Lowcountry plantations (your choice), either Middleton Place or Magnolia Plantation. This tour costs $21 per person. Free pickups from downtown hotels are available. All tours depart from the visitor center. Interested parties may ask about their day-long tours of Savannah, Georgia, as well.

Walking Tours

Walking tours are great if you're up to the exercise. The pace is slow, the interpretation is personal, and the detail you'll see and hear is incredible. These tours—by definition—have the excitement and feel of a treasure hunt, and treasure is always found. Every one of these tours bears the

stamp of your particular tour guide, and this seems to make the experience more intimate and fun. On the other hand, you cover a relatively small part of the historic Peninsula and see only a microcosm of all there is to see. Here are some of our favorites:

Anna's House & Garden and
Walking Tours
122 Queen St.
(843) 577-5931

Anna Taylor Blythe is a 2nd generation tour guide in Charleston and has been collecting stories for Charleston visitors for many years. Her tour includes refreshments in the Palmer home on East Battery with its spectacular views over Charleston Harbor, a stroll through "Mrs. Whaley's garden" as described in the popular gardening book, and ends in a charming shop at 61 Queen Street. Tours begin under the green awning at 61 Queen Street at 9:45 AM and 2 PM Monday through Saturday, rain or shine. The rate is $22 per person; reservations are required.

Her 1½ hour Ghost Walk tour is also a visit through 18th- and 19th- century neighborhoods—this one with tales of ghosts, plateye, voodoo, graveyards, and "Hags & Haints." These tours begin at 5 PM in front of the Mills House at 115 Meeting Street, as well as 7 and 9 PM leaving from TG's, 170 Church Street in The Market. Adult fare is $13, children age 7 to 12, $7; with reservations required.

Architectural Walking Tours
(843) 893-2327, (800) 931-7761

These are two-hour tours of Charleston's remarkable architectural heritage. Your guide through seven local public buildings is Fern Williams Tuten, a local art historian and licensed city guide. The tour of 18th-century buildings begins at 10 AM; the tour of 19th-century buildings is at 2 PM. Both tours depart from the Meeting Street Inn, 173 Meeting Street (tours depart 10 minutes earlier from Hawthorne Suites). No tours are offered on Tuesday or Sunday. The charge is $15 a person. Special theme tours and group tours are available with advance notice. These include a house museum along with public buildings.

Charleston Strolls
Walk with History
(843) 766-2080, (843) 884-9505
This is the walking tour recommended by *The New York Times* and *Southern Living*. It operates Monday through Saturday all year long, leaving from Charleston Place at 9:30 AM, from Days Inn at 9:40 AM and from the Mills House at 10 AM. A personal guide brings to life Charleston's history from Colonial days through the Civil War to the present. You'll stroll cobblestone streets, find hidden gardens, walk in famous footsteps, and much more. Rates are $16 for adults and teens, and children 12 and younger are admitted free. Reservations are accepted, but not required.

From March 15 through November 15, this company offers "The Ghost Walk," an eerie journey into Charleston's haunted past. This tour departs at 5 PM from the Mills House courtyard at 115 Meeting Street. Regular rates apply.

Charleston Tea Party Walking Tour
(843) 577-5896, (843) 722-1779
These two-hour tours end with a tea served in the private garden of your guide after a walk through the oldest section of the Historic District. The tours include Colonial and 18th-century architecture, Civil War history with quotations from diaries, church history, Charleston gardens and interiors, plus insight into Charleston's preservation story. Tours begin at the King's Courtyard Inn, 198 King Street, and cost $15 for adults and children 12 and older and $6 for children younger than 12. For the 9:30 AM tour, call 577-5896; for the 2 PM tour, call (843) 722-1779. Reservations are required.

Civil War Walking Tour
(843) 722-7033
This walking tour departs from the Mills

House courtyard, 115 Meeting Street, at 9 AM daily. You'll hear the personal accounts and colorful anecdotes of the late Charlestonians who lived through it all. The tour includes comparisons of photos of Charleston from the 1860s with those of today. Reservations are appreciated. The adult rate is $15. Children younger than 12 can tour free. Group rates are available, and the route is wheelchair accessible.

Charleston's Original
Ghost Hunt Walking Tour
(843) 813-5055
Here's another offering for those interested in chasing down Charleston's famous ghost stories with Nicholas Herron as your guide. The tour departs from the sidewalk area in front of the United States Custom House on the corner of S. Market Street and East Bay at 7 and 9 PM

(weather permitting). The adult fare is $10; children, $5. Reservations are required.

The Original Charleston Walks
(843) 577-3800, (800) 729-3420
This group specializes in educational and group tours. Choose from the following seven options: The Charleston Walk, Wicked Charleston, The Civil War Walk, The Maritime Walk, Lowcountry Ghost Walk, Historic Homes Walk, and In Slavery & Freedom. One of these options is bound to please the most finicky traveler. Tours depart Washington Park (the Broad Street gates) at the corner of Meeting and Broad Streets. Call for times and reservations. Tours are $14 for adults and $8 for children 7 to 14. The Historic Homes tour is $22 for adults and $18 for children (age 7 to 14).

On The Market, Get Set, Tour!
(853) 853-8687
Tommy Drew is your host (and licensed guide) for this ghost tour with grizzly tales of murder and death, unrequited love, tragedy, and other old Charleston lore. Daily tours begin at the steps of Market Hall on Meeting Street, between South Market and North Market Streets, at 6 and 8 PM. Ghost Tour adult fare is $14; children (12 and under), $8.

General history tours from Tommy Drew start from the same location and begin at 11 AM and 1 and 3 PM. Reservations are required. Adult fare is $13; children (12 and under) pay $5.

The Story of Charleston
(843) 723-1670, (800) 854-1670
Reservations are required for this walking tour that claims to show visitors the Holy City "from a Charlestonian's point of view." In addition to architecture and history, this intimate, 90-minute-plus tour profiles some of the city's legendary personalities and recounts the impact of wars and disasters. Tours leave from in front of the circular fountain at Water-

It's best to see Charleston (first) at a clip-clop pace—letting the city's rich architectural detail and graceful gardens soak into your consciousness. PHOTO: COURTESY OF CHARLESTON AREA CONVENTION AND VISITORS BUREAU

Close-up

The Pest Houses on Sullivan's Island

Today there's just a bronze plaque. And even that plaque is a very recent addition to the history being interpreted for the public at Ft. Moultrie on Sullivan's Island. But it is, at least, a beginning. The plaque commemorates a grim chapter in Charleston's history—the advent of the "pest houses" on Sullivan's Island during the city's booming slave trade in the 18th and 19th centuries.

In 1707, the local government was in fear of the diseases carried by slave ships arriving at the colony from West Africa. As a remedy for this, a law was passed requiring all slave ships to dock at Sullivan's Island and unload their human cargo for a period of quarantine—usually 10 days or so. The place for holding these unfortunate people was called a "pest house," in reference to the pestilence hopefully kept inside its primitive walls. After a period of time during which the "cargo" was inspected for disease, the captives were moved across the harbor and sold at public auction into slavery. An estimated 40 percent of black Americans have ancestors who came through the pest houses of Sullivan's Island.

There are no surviving eyewitness accounts of what actually went on in these long-vanished structures, but in 1759 a Charleston physician, Dr. Alexander Garden (for whom the gardenia blossom was named), left this description of the slave ships:

"I have often gone to visit those Vessels on their first Arrival," he writes. "But I have never yet been on board one that did not smell most offensive and noisome, what for Filth, putrid Air, putrid Dysenteries...it is a wonder any (people) escape with Life."

The plaque on Sullivan's Island is a step in the right direction, but a far too small (and too late) gesture of acknowledgment for what is clearly an important chapter in American history.

front Park (at the foot of Vendue Range) at 10:30 AM and 5 PM. Rates are $14 for adults and $8 for children 12 and younger.

The same company, called Tour Charleston, offers The Ghosts of Charleston tour, which is based on the new book *Charleston Ghosts and other Macabre Aberrations* by Edward Macy and James Buxton. This 70- to 90-minute adventure is a big hit with those interested in the paranormal and departs from the fountain at Waterfront Park at 5 and 7:30 PM. The same pricing applies.

The company's newest offering is The Pirates of Charleston, where you'll walk in the footsteps of Blackbeard, Stede Bonnet, Richard Worley, Anne Bonny, and other famous rogues of the sea. This tour begins at 10 AM and 4 PM—leaving from Waterfront Park. The same pricing applies.

Carriage Tours

Carriage tours are an enduring Charleston tradition. There's nothing like seeing an 18th- and 19th-century city at an appropriately slow, leisurely, clip-clop pace. You'll ride through neighborhoods above and below Broad Street (ones that are approved for horse-drawn vehicle traffic) while your driver tells the Charleston story. The ambiance is wonderful, but again, you're restricted to certain areas of the city for traffic management purposes and you receive a somewhat limited view of the city's many charms. Here are the carriage tour options now available:

Carolina Polo & Carriage Company
(843) 577-6767

All tour guides on these carriages are city licensed and trained by a company tour director who has been doing carriage tours since 1978. These tours depart from 16 Hayne Street and 181 Church Street (from the lobby of the Doubletree Hotel on the corner of North Market and Church Streets). Adult and teen rates are $17; children 12 and younger pay $8. Private carriage tours are available upon request.

Classic Carriage Tours Inc.
(843) 853-3747

One of the South's best-known carriage works, Classic Carriage, specializes in the construction and restoration of 19th- and 20th-century carriages, wagons, and surreys. With Percheron draft horses and experienced, licensed tour guides as drivers, these one-hour tours are popular with visitors and those planning special events in the Charleston area. These carriages are especially popular for traditional Charleston weddings. Reservations are strongly encouraged for the daily tours, which leave from the corner of Church and Market Streets in the City Market area from 9 AM to 5:30 PM daily. Adult and teen rates are $17; children 12 and younger are $8.

Old South Carriage Co.
(843) 577-0042

These are the carriage tours narrated by licensed guides wearing red sashes (Confederate uniforms, of sorts). The 50- to 60-minute tours depart from 14 Anson Street, at the corner of N. Market and Anson Streets, every 20 minutes beginning at 9 AM daily. Adult fares are $17, and fares for children ages 6 through 11 are $8.

Old Towne Carriage Co.
(843) 722-1315

These carriage tours by licensed guides leave the company barn at 20 Anson Street near the City Market starting at 9 AM. Tours are given until dusk and run from 45 minutes to an hour. Fares for those older than 11 are $17, and fares for ages 4 to 12 are $5.

Palmetto Carriage Tours
(843) 723-8145

Experienced guides narrate this one-hour

carriage tour that meanders through 25 blocks (2 miles) of antebellum neighborhoods at a clip-clop pace. Tours begin and end at the red barn behind the Rainbow Market, 40 N. Market Street. Hours are 9 AM to dusk daily. Adult rates are $17, and children ages 4 to 11 are $6.

Cruise and Boat Tours

These tours offer the absolute joy of being on the breezy waters of Charleston Harbor and the wide Cooper River, both of which offer an entirely new perspective on Charleston. It's a perspective that was, after all, the one first seen by pirate scalawags and some of our country's founding fathers. This was the first view for those aboard heavy-laden packet boats and cotton barges as well as those on the first ironclad warships and the crowded slave vessels out of Africa and the Caribbean. Maritime history is clearly one of Charleston's long suits, but we suggest you supplement a boat tour with another type of tour so you don't miss the urban story. Here are some of our favorite water tours:

Coastal Expeditions
(843) 884-7684

Scheduled and spontaneous kayak tours are an unusual way to see the coastal waterways. Don't be shy just because you've never snuggled into one of these sleek boats before—even half-day tours include an instruction clinic. Rates vary, but two tours are the half-day Shem Creek Tour, $55 a person, and the full-day Adventure Tour, $85 a person.

Charleston Gray Line Water Tours
(843) 722-1112, (800) 344-4483

The Gray Line folks say they've been giving water tours of Charleston Harbor since 1908. Their current tour boat, *The Charleston Princess*, is the only paddle wheeler on the Harbor, and she is the only tour boat that departs from the Historic District (at the end of Market Street one block from the Market). The Gray Line

Harbor of History tour includes 75 points of interest including a ride past Fort Sumter. Tour hours are 11:30 AM, 1:30 and 3:30 PM. Adult fare is $11, and children 5 to 15 go for $5. The Harbor Lights Dinner Cruise features gourmet dining and live entertainment. After dinner enjoy the romantic nighttime views from the 3rd-level "sky deck." Reservations are required for the dinner cruise only. The dinner cruise departs at 7 PM; adult fare is $36.72, and children's fare is $26.32. A combo ticket with a carriage ride is discounted to $22 for adults, $11 for children.

Schooner Pride
(843) 559-9686, (888) 571-2486

Ah, here's a fantasy that is delightfully achievable. See Charleston from the water—as countless settlers and 19th-century immigrants saw it—from the decks of a tall ship, the *Schooner Pride*. She's 84 feet long and U.S. Coast Guard-certified to carry 49 day passengers or 20 overnight guests. The two-hour cruise of Charleston Harbor costs $17 for adults and kids 12 and older, and $11 for children younger than 12.

Experienced sailors and quick learners may help with the ship, or you can simply sit back and enjoy the wind, sea, and unexpected pleasure of almost soundless propulsion. Call for afternoon or evening schedules and reservations. Schooner Pride is moored at the City Marina, and all tours depart from there. No tours are offered after November 26 and begin again on May 1.

SpiritLine Fort Sumter Tour, Harbor Tour, and Dinner Cruise
(843) 722-2628

This is the only boat tour from Charleston that actually stops at the Ft. Sumter National Monument where the Civil War began. Tours leave daily from two locations: the City Marina on Lockwood Boulevard, and from Patriots Point in Mt. Pleasant. Tour hours vary seasonally, so call for details. Adult rates are $11,

> ## Insiders' Tip
>
> For a more extensive look at the hidden historical treasures of the Charleston area, look into one of the day-long excursions planned annually by the South Carolina Historical Society. Every year, the membership is invited to participate in a caravan tour deep into the Lowcountry hinterlands, touring private plantations and fascinating little-known sites. For membership details, you can write the Society at 100 Meeting Street, Charleston, SC 29401.

children age 6 to 11, $6. A new point of departure for the Ft. Sumter Tour Boat is planned for the Charleston Maritime Center on Concord Street sometime after the summer.

SpiritLine also has a non-stop Harbor Tour that departs from the City Marina and from Patriots Point (only on weekends in January and February). The tour lasts approximately 1½ hours and cruises past The Battery, Patriots Point Maritime Museum, Castle Pinckney, Fort Sumter, and Fort Johnson. Adult rates are $10.50; children (age 6 to 11) $5.50.

Their Dinner Cruise is aboard the new *Spirit of Carolina* and departs from Patriots Point in Mt. Pleasant at 7 PM and returns at 10 PM (boarding begins at 6:30 PM). A sumptuous three-course meal is served—prepared to order—with table-side service, spirits, live entertainment, and dancing. Reservations are required. The weekday fare is $37.85 per person, the weekend rate is $40.85.

Air Tours

Flying High Over Charleston
(843) 569-6148

If getting the "overview" is something you want—literally—there are even a couple of airplane tours available to Charleston area visitors. Jim Ellison is an FAA licensed commercial pilot with 14 years of flying experience in the Charleston area. His Package A: Historic Charleston & Sea Island Tour includes historic plantations, harbor and aircraft carrier *Yorktown* views, beautiful beaches and sea islands, The Citadel, Ft. Sumter, Morris Island lighthouse, and miles of ocean coastline vistas—in addition to Historic Charleston from the air. This is an hour-plus tour in a photo-friendly airplane. His Package B: Taste of Charleston Sightseeing Tour is about 40-minutes in length and slightly more limited in subject matter, but just as exciting. Tours are available seven days a week (weather permitting) and take off from Johns Island, 15 minutes from downtown Charleston. The rate for Tour A is $149. Tour B is $119.

The Arts

Festivals
Organizations
and Venues
Theater
Dance
Music
Galleries

Some people would tell you the verdict on Charleston and the arts is still out—that after an early, spectacular (even historic) start, the city fell asleep artistically and has stayed that way since...well, the Civil War. Others would have you believe this city is a virtual Mecca for experimental and traditional artists of all kinds, if only during Spoleto Festival USA. The truth probably lies somewhere in between. While there have been dormant stretches, there have also been times, such as the 1920s and early '30s, when Charleston experienced artistic stirrings that resulted in truly exciting art.

In literature, there was Charleston's own DuBose Heyward (1885–1940), whose legendary 1925 novel, *Porgy*, inspired a renaissance of artistic effort in and about the city and its people. The story, for those who may not be familiar with it, is based on the life of a poor, crippled black street vendor and his tragic love for an abused, drug-addicted woman. The novelist's playwright wife, Dorothy, co-wrote the successful stage play that opened on Broadway in 1927.

In 1926, none other than George Gershwin—already famous for "Rhapsody in Blue" and bound for immortality as the composer of dozens of American musical standards—was fascinated by the story. He felt Porgy was just the vehicle he was looking for to create a new art form: the American folk opera.

One of the city's favorite legends is about the long, hot summer George Gershwin spent in Charleston (actually, in a house on Folly Beach) working on the opera. Yes, he did come here. And no, the house isn't still standing. It washed out to sea years ago in a storm long since forgotten, although you might hear otherwise from alleged Insiders. During that summer, with the help of the Heywards and Gershwin's lyricist brother, Ira, the project eventually made the transformation from the literary page to a legitimate, hauntingly beautiful opera.

Although it took several years to finally put it on the boards, the world-famous work known as *Porgy and Bess* was at last produced by New York's Theatre Guild in 1935. While it was never a staggering financial success (not many things were in 1935), the work was universally and artistically acclaimed. Since then, the opera has played all over the world, including in Milan's prestigious La Scala. But no audience could love it more than an audience in Charleston, where it was performed most recently in 1990 in a marvelous production at Gaillard Municipal Auditorium. In 1989, immediately following the devastation of Hurricane Hugo, a bruised and battered Charleston was given a special gift when a New York City production of *Porgy and Bess* was flown in to give an impromptu performance for the people of Charleston. Over the roar of portable generators and the sound of distant buzz saws clearing streets still filled with debris, the New York cast sang a concert version of the opera on the steps of the Customs House. The cathartic effect of that emotion-filled performance is difficult to describe. Suffice to say—it created an indelible memory for those Charlestonians who were there to witness it.

Neither DuBose Heyward nor George Gershwin would live to see *Porgy and Bess* reach the zenith of its fame. Gershwin died of a brain tumor in 1937, and Heyward succumbed to a heart attack in 1940. The Heywards, along with their daughter, are buried in the graveyard of St. Philip's Episcopal Church, not far from the real Catfish Row on Church Street, a couple of blocks below Broad.

Another highlight of the Charleston renaissance period would be the work of Alice Ravenel Huger Smith (1887–1958), watercolorist and "preservationist" of the Lowcountry's rice plantation landscapes. In the late 1930s, when she began to realize the old plantation lifestyle—especially the rice plantation lifestyle of the 1850s—was dying out and might soon be forgotten, she recorded it in a series of paintings that are now integral to the permanent collection of the Gibbes Museum of Art (see the section on Other Museums in our Attractions chapter).

Yet another important artist of the city's renaissance years would be Elizabeth O'Neill Verner (1883–1979). Her fascination with the architecture and streetscapes of Charleston can be traced back as early as 1903. One passion was etching, and her works (including many illustrations of Charleston) are highly acclaimed. The work of Verner, from about 1923 until the late 1960s, has almost come to define Charleston's renaissance school of art.

But what about today? And what is all this Spoleto hoopla about? Following is an introduction to the big event, along with a couple of other popular festivals. After that, we offer listings and information under self-explanatory headings: Festivals, Organizations and Venues, Theater, Dance, Music, and Galleries. Unless otherwise noted, all addresses are in Charleston.

During Spoleto Festival USA, you'll find street concerts and impromptu performances almost anywhere in Charleston. PHOTO: WILLIAM STRUHS

Festivals

Spoleto Festival USA
**Various locations, P.O. Box 704,
Charleston, SC 29402
(843) 722-2764**

Not every newcomer to the Lowcountry is familiar with the city's spectacular May showcase for the arts called Spoleto Festival USA. By the same token, no one stays in Charleston very long before hearing "Spoleto this..." and "Spoleto that..."

For openers, know that Spoleto (pronounced spo-LAY-toe, like tomato) is the New World counterpart to the summertime arts extravaganza in Spoleto, Italy, called the "Festival of Two Worlds." The latter was founded back in 1958 by Pulitzer Prize-winning composer-librettist-director Gian Carlo Menotti.

Menotti saw the quaint, medieval town of Spoleto's rich architectural heritage, suitable performing facilities, and central European location (about 60 miles north of Rome) as the perfect backdrop for an interdisciplinary arts celebration. There, he created a world-famous showcase and exchange for international talent both young and old, rich and poor.

By 1977, Menotti was looking for an American home for his festival, and for many of the same reasons he chose Spoleto, Italy, he thought Charleston could neatly fill the bill here in America. With support and encouragement from Charleston Mayor Joseph P. Riley Jr., other important members of the local community, and the then-well-funded National Endowment for the Arts, Spoleto Festival USA premiered as a two-week explosion of opera, jazz, theater, visual arts, and dance, including classical ballet. It explored new ways to look at traditional works as well as the cutting-edge and the avant garde. Tickets to Spoleto events are sold in packages as well as for individual events. They aren't inexpensive, but much of Spoleto's infectious enthusiasm is palpable on the city streets—that is, free, and available to everyone.

Almost anyone would agree that Charleston takes on a special glow during the festival. Maybe the illumination comes from the corps of international critics who review performances daily in a special section of *The Post and Courier* or the crowded restaurants and traffic-clogged streets. Perhaps it's the joyful noises that seem to be floating on the air all over town, the street performers, the sudden profusion of sidewalk art galleries and the excitement of a population swollen with young, animated, talented people. But for whatever reasons, Spoleto is a time of great fun and good art. Don't miss it.

When the festival is over and, alas, they pack up the sets and costumes and truck them off to distant parts, take heart. The arts in Charleston—and by that we mean a number of quality offerings—don't completely cease. They just slow down a bit after those hectic weeks of intense saturation. We try to think of it this way: The spirit of Spoleto fosters the development of greater and more appreciative audiences for arts activities in and around Charleston throughout the year. (See our Annual Events chapter for more on Spoleto.)

Piccolo Spoleto
**133 Church St.
(843) 724-7305**

Piccolo Spoleto (translated from the Italian "Little Spoleto") is the city of Charleston's way of saying, "Encore! Encore!" It is Charleston's official companion festival (a series of festivals, really) running concurrently with the internationally acclaimed Spoleto Festival USA.

Piccolo's focus, however, is on local and regional talent of every artistic discipline. There are literally hundreds of events offered every year through Piccolo, most of which are relatively low-cost or free. Expect to see performances ranging from chamber music and provocative theater to experimental dance and visual arts.

The city's Office of Cultural Affairs handles the project and sees to it, through its Artreach program, that the festival's high spirits and fine performances are exported to artistically neglected sections of the community. This way, the arts can be experienced by everyone, regardless of economic status or educational background. (For more on Piccolo Spoleto, see our Annual Events chapter.)

MOJA Arts Festival
133 Church St.
(843) 724-7305
The MOJA Arts Festival in September is the city of Charleston's celebration of the Lowcountry's rich and wonderful her-itage from the African and Caribbean cultures. This 16-day performance schedule offers exciting theater, visual arts, dance, music, films, and lectures.

"MOJA" is a Swahili word meaning "one" and "unity" or "the source" and "the beginning." Hence, the city's celebration of black arts is indeed appropriately named, as Charleston was the port of entry for thousands of slaves during the 18th and 19th centuries. Their contribution to American culture is clearly enormous. The festival is sponsored by the city's Office of Cultural Affairs and is funded in part by the South Carolina Arts Commission. (See our Annual Events chapter for more on MOJA.)

Organizations and Venues

City of Charleston
Office of Cultural Affairs
133 Church St.
(843) 724-7305
The city of Charleston devotes this office in the Dock Street Theatre to advocating, providing services for, and helping fund the various arts organizations that contribute to promoting the city. In the summer, for example, these folks sponsor the Storefront School for the Arts, a program for inner-city children co-administered by the Parks and Recreation Department. The Office of Cultural Affairs also maintains the revolving exhibits of the City Gallery in the Dock Street Theatre and produces the MOJA Arts Festival each fall and Piccolo Spoleto in the spring. Call Ellen Dressler Moryl, executive director, for more details.

North Charleston Cultural Arts Program
Sterett Hall
(former Charleston Navy Base)
PO Box 190016, North Charleston
(843) 745-1087
The Cultural Arts Program for North Charleston was created in 1979 to plan for and support artistic and cultural activities throughout the community. It provides programs and services intended to enhance the quality of life for citizens and assists in the cultural and economic development of the area. The Cultural Arts Program is located in Sterett Hall on the former Navy Base and many of its performances are held in the recently renovated Park Circle Auditorium.

The program's other offerings include the North Charleston City Gallery at 3107 Firestone Road. Gallery hours are Monday through Saturday from 9 AM to 5 PM. The Dinner Theatre series in Park Circle Auditorium is another popular feature. By far the largest project undertaken through the program is the annual North Charleston Arts Festival, held every spring. Admission and parking are free for this two-day extravaganza mounted in the giant North Charleston Coliseum. The festival is a kaleidoscope of color and images with original artwork, photography, arts, and crafts plus live entertainment and food concessions. For more information, call Marty Besancon at the NCCAP office or write the group at P.O. Box 190016, North Charleston, SC 29419.

The North Charleston Performing Arts Center has added a new dimension to the Lowcountry's year-round entertainment. ARTIST'S RENDERING: COURTESY OF N. CHARLESTON PERFORMING ARTS CENTER

North Charleston Coliseum
5001 Coliseum Dr., North Charleston
(843) 529-5050

This beautiful venue has already helped put the Lowcountry on the map for many nationally known performing arts groups. Opened in 1993, the much-anticipated North Charleston Coliseum is the largest and most diverse indoor entertainment facility in South Carolina. Various seating configurations are possible, but, generally speaking, the coliseum's capacity is 14,000 seats. Because of this, Greater Charleston is now a viable audience for some of the biggest traveling shows and sports attractions in America. The coliseum has attracted the likes of Rod Stewart, Neil Diamond, the Ringling Brothers and Barnum and Bailey Circus, James Taylor, Metallica, World Cup figure skating, NHL hockey, and NCAA basketball, to name just a few. The coliseum is also the permanent home of the South Carolina Stingrays hockey club, which began play in the East Coast Hockey League in the fall of 1993 (see our Spectator Sports chapter). Tickets for all coliseum events may be purchased at the Coliseum box office or by phone (888) 386-8497. To get to the coliseum, take the Montague Avenue exit off Interstate 26 and follow the signs, or take the Montague Avenue exit off I-526 (Mark Clark Expressway).

Theater

In the 18th century, when Charles Towne was the capital of the Colonial province and a thriving port of entry, there were reports in England that it was "the gayest, politest, and richest place in America." So naturally, it follows that Charles Towne was one of the first American towns to patronize the cultural arts—including the world of drama.

According to Eola Willis and her copious 1933 study of the city's early theatrical life, *The Charleston Stage in the 18th Century*, drama was alive and well here as early as the 1730s. The city's first newspaper, *The Charleston Gazette*, described at some length the theatrical season of 1734. That year on January 18, the *Gazette* carried the following notice:

"On Friday the 24th instant, in the Court-Room will be attempted a Tragedy called

'The Orphan, or the Unhappy Marriage.' Tickets will be delivered out on Tuesday next at Mr. Shepheard's at 40s each."

Apparently, the season's opening performance was a hit because on February 8, the *Gazette* published its first review, in which the prologue to *The Orphan* was reprinted in its entirety. Quickly following on February 18, *The Opera of Flora* or *Hob in the Well* opened with the dance of the two Pierrots and the pantomime of Harlequin and Scaramouch. This was another first for Charleston theater—the first time a musical play had been performed on American shores. Apparently, the theatrical life of Charleston was off and running by 1734 and shines just as brilliantly today.

Dock Street Theatre
135 Church St.
(843) 720-3968, Box Office: (843) 965-4032

Much ado is made about Charleston's many firsts, not the least of which is the story about the Dock Street Theatre being the first and oldest theater in America.

Let's split hairs here just for accuracy's sake. It has been academically determined that the first theater in America was erected in Williamsburg, Virginia, in the second decade of the 18th century. The second was built in New York in 1732. The third was in Charles Towne in 1736, while poor old Philadelphia didn't have a playhouse until 1749.

In the early 18th century, certain buildings were called theaters though they were no more than "long rooms"—rooms big enough to hold an audience. These places lacked a traditional stage and other theatrical facilities. The 1734 production of *The Orphan*, for instance, was actually performed in a courtroom—just such a place.

Charleston's first (technical) theater was on the site of the old Planters Hotel on Church Street, which was then the only major route running the entire length of the city. It ended at White Point, which is now known as The Battery (see more on The Battery in our Attractions chapter). Thus, Church Street was the thoroughfare for all the traffic to and from the bustling and noisy docks. It made good sense to build a theater near this main traffic route, so in 1736 the first building was constructed on the south side of Queen (then called Dock) Street, just a little west of heavily traveled Church Street. Records show it was less than 100 yards from the Huguenot church and St. Philip's Episcopal Church. It was said to have had a stage, pit boxes, and a gallery. Some ill fate likely soon befell this building, because no mention of it is found after 1737.

Eventually, a second theater was constructed nearby, and an early hotel was built on the rear portion of the old theater lot. The year was 1800. It was called the Planters Hotel because it was popular lodging for Lowcountry planters and their families, who would traditionally leave their plantations at certain times of the year. It was customary to be in town for the winter social season and for Race Week, an exponent of Charleston's torrid 19th-century love affair with horse racing. In 1835, the Planters Hotel was remodeled and expanded.

The old Planters Hotel is the structure that was still standing, but in ruins, when in the 1930s the New Deal's Work Projects Administration—giving work to unemployed architects and craftsmen during the Depression—rebuilt it as the theater we know today. Technically, it is the oldest building still standing that was part of a Colonial theatrical enterprise. But the charming stage proscenium and the handsome paneled boxes we encounter today in the Dock Street were not around for the prologue to *The Orphan*. Not in 1734, anyway. It would be more than 200 years later, on November 26, 1937, that Charleston's own DuBose Heyward, already famous for *Porgy*, would write a special dedication to reopen a new facility. The reconstructed theater was called the Dock Street in honor of those early Charleston productions on the site.

None of the above, of course, takes

anything away from Dock Street Theatre's enormous popularity and charm or the tremendously important role it plays in the theatrical life of the city today.

The reconstruction of the Dock Street auditorium recaptures the spirit of early Georgian theaters. It seats 463 people, with a pit and a parquet of 13 boxes. The walls are paneled with natural local black cypress, rubbed soft and mellow. The wood was treated with an old formula of iron filings dissolved in vinegar and then waxed to bring out the grain. The lighting fixtures carry out the feeling of candle brackets, and the cove ceiling has exceptional acoustic properties, as did many theaters of the time. Over the stage hangs a carved wood bas-relief of the Royal Arms of England (obligatory in all Georgian theaters), duplicated from an original that still hangs above the altar in Goose Creek's chapel of ease, built in 1711. (See the Close-up, "Lowcountry Chapels of Ease," in our Worship chapter.)

The Dock Street's stage has a proscenium opening of 34 feet (somewhat larger than the original would have had) and features an apron forestage with "proscenium doors" on either side. This is typical of Georgian theaters. Today's Dock Street stage floor is flat, whereas the original was most likely tilted. The rebuilt Dock Street was never intended to be a museum piece or an exact reconstruction. It is, however, a modern theatre capable of handling a wide variety of productions and an integral part of Charleston's rich cultural life.

Acting Companies

Whether you're a confirmed theater patron, an experienced actor, or just a Thespian wannabe, there's a Lowcountry theater company that will interest you. Some of these companies are longstanding members of the Greater Charleston arts community; others are embryonic or just getting off the ground.

The College of Charleston's Theater Department is flourishing, with four groups currently taking bows. The work is first-rate, and these quality productions stand out as some of the best bargains in town. All college productions are mounted in various venues in the Simons Center for the Arts at 54 St. Philip Street on campus. Thumbnail sketches of some of our local theater groups follow.

Art Form and Theater Concepts
133 Church St.
(843) 723-5399, (843) 722-2220

This exciting young African-American theater group recently presented its high-energy comedy *It's Showdown Time*, and the members are busy preparing for their next MOJA production. Auditions are traditionally in June, and the director is Art Gilliard. Call (843) 813-0750 for more details.

Center Stage
Simons Center for the Arts,
54 St. Philip St.
(843) 953-8228

Center Stage is the College of Charleston student organization that, together with the school's Theatre Department, produces a varied season from October through April in the Emmett Robinson Theater. Productions are staged and directed by faculty and guest directors. Admission is free. Separate from these productions are the experimental one-act plays (also free) staged by students in the Simons Center's flexible and highly creative "black box" Theatre 220. For more information, contact Mark C. Tiedje at the number listed above.

Charleston Guerrilla Theatre
217 Lucas St., Mt. Pleasant
(843) 762-6685

Here's a community theater group that does everything from lively classics to innovative modern works—Shakespeare to Broadway. Its venues have found the group everywhere from Dock Street Theatre to public parks and the odd warehouse for community outreach programs. Open auditions are publicly announced before major productions. Call Bill Stewart for more information.

Charleston Stage Company
133 Church St., Ste. 7
(843) 577-5967, (800) 454-7093
This group presents a full season of family-oriented plays and children's theater from September through April in the Dock Street Theatre. It also offers various educational programs that explore stage management, scene study, projection, and creative dramatics for beginners and advanced students. Volunteers are encouraged to contact Julian Wiles at the theater to become involved.

Flowertown Players
133 S. Main St., Summerville
(843) 875-9251
This is a community theater in Summerville whose educational and literary objectives are to stimulate interest in the arts, music, literature, and drama in people of all ages. It has a regular season of productions and its own home facility in downtown Summerville. General manager is Naomi Nimmo; volunteers are welcome. Call the theater for more information.

The Footlight Players
20 Queen St.
(843) 722-4487
This group recently celebrated its 69th season of producing quality community theater in Charleston. It enjoys strong support from Charleston's theater community for its long-standing record of exposing local audiences to interesting, instructive, and cultural plays that are in keeping with Charleston's traditional mores. Since the early 1940s, The Footlight Players have performed in their converted cotton warehouse (c. 1840) on Queen Street, easily one of the city's most charming theatrical venues. Office manager is Karin B. Stewart; volunteers are welcome. Call for additional information.

Robert Ivey Ballet Productions
1910 Savannah Hwy.
(843) 556-1343
Although Robert Ivey Ballet is primarily a dance company with a full-time studio, this production operation offers popular musicals on a fairly regular basis. Recently, the RIB mounted a production of *West Side Story* at the College of Charleston as ballet company in residence. For theater productions, open auditions are held, usually in the fall. Call Robert Ivey for more information on ballet, modern, and jazz dance instruction at the Charleston Dance Studio.

Main Stage
Simons Center for the Arts,
54 St. Philip St.
(843) 953-6306
Main Stage produces several plays each semester that are exclusively directed and designed by faculty from the college's department of theater. Productions—often of classical or traditional works such as Shakespeare's *Macbeth* and Ibsen's *Ghosts*—are at the College of Charleston's Emmett Robinson Theater. For production information, call (843) 953-6306, or the box office at (843) 943-5604.

Premiere Theater at the College of Charleston
Simons Center for the Arts,
54 St. Philip St.
(843) 953-6306
These productions are contemporary plays featuring the work of local professionals as well as faculty and graduate students from the College of Charleston theater department. Sometimes, professional directors are brought in as guests for special works. For additional information, contact Evan Parry's office at (843) 953-5439, or the box office at (843) 943-5604.

Shakespeare Project at the College of Charleston
College of Charleston,
Simons Center for the Arts,
54 St. Philip St.
(843) 953-7735
Now four years old and still growing is the college-sponsored Shakespeare group who recently mounted a wonderful production

of *Romeo and Juliet*. These performances by student and community-based actors are presented in August under a wing of the Theatre Department and are done in the Emmett Robinson Theater. There's general seating with adult tickets costing $10, student seating, $6. For more specific information, call Todd McNerney at the number above.

Theatre on the Side
30 Cumberland St.
(843) 853-4894
This is Charleston's newest grass-roots thespian group and one dedicated to performing short plays by contemporary playwrights. Spearheading this effort is Jenny Devine, a veteran of the Footlight Players group. Performances have been mounted at Theatre 99 at 30 Cumberland Street in the past, but the group may find other venues. For more information, call the number above.

Workshop Summer Theatre
20 Queen St.
(843) 722-4487
This all-volunteer organization has a unique focus on community theater at the grassroots level. It is dedicated to providing talented newcomers and first-time directors with a forum for the dramatic arts. Almost 20 years old, the Workshop Summer Theatre usually (but not always) performs in The Footlight Players Workshop at 20 Queen Street and usually (but not always) during the summer months. For more information, contact the current director by mail or the switchboard at The Footlight Players.

Dance

Dance Companies

Anonymity Dance Company
26 27th Ave., Isle of Palms
(843) 886-6104
This professional modern dance company has been Charleston-based since 1985. It performs throughout the state with a wide repertoire of styles and works. The company is available for master classes in technique, improvisation, choreography, and classroom creativity for children. Contact Jennifer D. Strelkauskas, artistic director, at the number above for more information.

Charleston Ballet Theatre
477 King St.
(843) 723-7334
This energetic group presents professional dance concerts in Charleston and throughout the Southeast. Its wide range of performances includes such classics as *The Nutcracker*, *Sleeping Beauty*, and *Swan Lake* as well as contemporary works. Call Don or Patricia Cantwell, artistic directors, for more information. The group's resident facility, near the visitor center, includes a 300-seat theater space, public parking, and spacious studios. Charleston Ballet offers an annual series. For box office information, call the number above.

Robert Ivey Ballet
1910 Savannah Hwy.
(843) 556-1343
Robert Ivey Ballet is an international touring company performing mostly classical productions and Broadway musicals. The senior company consists of about 30 dancers who have represented the United States on tours to the former Soviet Union and South America. Robert Ivey's youth company performs with about 25 dancers. Open auditions are held on a regular basis. Call Robert Ivey at the number listed for more information.

Dance Schools

In a town that gave its name to a famous dance step that put flappers of the '20s on the world map, it should be no surprise that Charleston is still the scene for a variety of dancing and dance instruction. Below we have listed some good schools but we encourage new residents to also check with your local area's recreation department and/or continuing education programs.

Ballet Academy of Charleston
1662 Savannah Hwy.
(843) 769-6932
Ballet Academy of Charleston is under the direction of Mara Meir, former ballerina with Ballet de Paris and prima ballerina of the Israeli Opera. This is a fee-based school offering scheduled semesters of classical ballet training for children ages 4 through 17, with separate adult classes. Trial classes for children are offered. No recital performances are held. Instead, parents view their children's progress through regularly scheduled, end-of-year open classes and periodic conferences with the director.

Charleston Ballet Studio
477 King St.
(843) 723-7334
This school is affiliated with the professional dance company Charleston Ballet Theatre. Classes and workshops are offered for ages 3 through adult, and performances—a serious goal for serious students—are held at the Gaillard Municipal Auditorium and Sottile Theater.

Charleston Dance Studio,
Robert Ivey Ballet
1910 Savannah Hwy.
(843) 556-1343
Robert Ivey, himself a professional dancer, directs this dance company and school. His professional instructors teach classes in ballet, jazz, and dance exercise. The school has a nurturing attitude toward children, and their families and friends appreciate the seasonal performances that let the students show off their talents.

Robert Ivey Ballet is shown here using the Lowcountry as a backdrop for interpretive dance.
PHOTO: COURTESY OF ROBERT IVEY BALLET

Music

Charleston Community Band
14 George St.
(843) 763-4528

Started in 1977, this all-volunteer concert band performs 20 free concerts a year throughout the area. The group provides a wonderful opportunity for talented local adults to continue their musical pursuits. Call current band president Susan DuPuis at the number listed above or at (843) 747-8340 for more information.

Charleston Concert Association
Gaillard Municipal Auditorium,
77 Calhoun St.
(843) 722-7667

The Charleston Concert Association (CCA) is Charleston's oldest nonprofit presenting arts organization. Founded in 1936 as a sister organization with the Charleston Symphony Orchestra (CSO), CCA's original mission was to bring internationally acclaimed musicians to Charleston as a complement to CSO. Back in 1931, the symphony's aim was to create an avenue for local musicians to develop their skills.

Insiders' Tip

Another small concert series presented by the Charleston Symphony Orchestra is the "Sunday Family Series" at Gaillard Auditorium. These four concerts scattered throughout the year offer families a fun but low-cost outing in the arts and some wonderful exposure to semi-classical music.

Today, the CCA's mission is to provide local access to classical artists of international caliber throughout the year (whereas Spoleto Festival USA is a more concentrated exposure of only two weeks). In recent years, the CCA has expanded its vision to include all of the performing arts, including theater and film as well as dance. Among the CCA's recent presentations were the highly acclaimed Moscow Virtuosi from Russia, I Musici de Montreal from Canada, and New York's modern dance sensation, the David Parsons Dance Company. Tickets are sold by subscription to the series, and individual prices range from $15 to $35. The executive director is Jason A. Nichols. Call for subscription rates and concert season details.

Charleston Symphony Orchestra
14 George St.
(843) 723-7528

Charleston has a long, rich, and varied musical history. Records indicate several different orchestras were organized in the city during the years from 1819 to 1919. Today's organization, known as the Charleston Symphony Orchestra, has been in existence for more than 50 years.

In December 1936, Miss Maud Winthrup Gibbon and Mrs. Martha Laurens Patterson founded what is known today as the Charleston Symphony Orchestra, and they presented a concert in Hibernian Hall on Meeting Street. The orchestra provided music for the official grand opening of the newly restored Dock Street Theatre in 1936. And the Dock Street in turn became the orchestra's official home for its first three years. Through the 1940s and '50s, Memminger Auditorium was home for the group, as it brought in such famous artists as Robert Merrill, Jan Pierce, Blanche Theirbom, and Eleanor Steber. The orchestra played under the batons of conductors J. Albert Frecht, Tony Hadgi, Don Mills, and, from 1962 to 1982, Lucien DeGroote.

In the late 1970s, the orchestra emerged as a fully professional organization with the employment of a core of full-time, conservatory-trained, first-chair players. The orchestra achieved "metropolitan" status in the American Symphony Orchestra League and adopted Gaillard Auditorium as its official home. In 1984, David Stahl became music director and conductor. Under his leadership, the CSO has become one of the leading arts organizations in the Southeast. The orchestra's budget under Stahl increased from $250,000 in 1984 to about $2.4 million in 1999. Stahl new assistant conductor Lara Webber and a resident orchestra of about 40 professional, full-time musicians now perform a demanding concert schedule on stage and throughout the community, including special events and school programs throughout the state.

The orchestra has four major concert series—Masterworks, Chamber Orchestra, Light & Lively, and Pops. In addition, the CSO performs other special concerts that cover a broad range of musical tastes. Individual ticket sales are handled through the Gailliard Auditorium box office or by phone at (888) 386-8497. Ticket prices vary according to the series, but they range from $10 to $35 for individual concerts.

Charleston Symphony Orchestra League
14 George St.
(843) 766-2161

Although it's mostly known in the community as sponsor of the annual Symphony Gala and the Symphony Designer Showhouse, the 300-member Charleston Symphony Orchestra League serves its namesake group in many ways.

Through fund-raising events, the league provides major financial support to the orchestra. It annually awards scholarships to orchestra musicians for advanced study and to school-age musicians who are members of the Charleston County Youth Orchestra. Members volunteer many hours of service in the CSO office promoting the orchestra and aiding in the sale of season tickets, and they also serve as con-

cert ushers. The league welcomes anyone wishing to join and support the CSO.

CSO Chorus
14 George St.
(843) 723-7528

First organized as the CSO Singers Guild in 1978 to be the choral complement of the Charleston Symphony Orchestra, this group is now called the CSO Chorus. The group performs with the CSO in major works several times a year. In addition to the large concert group of nearly 125 singers, there are two smaller performance groups that appear throughout the season. The Chamber Singers, under the direction of CSO assistant conductor Lara Webber, perform 20th-century music. The second group, Songs of the South, is under the direction of Hank Martin and performs Civil War-era music for conventions and local organizations. Participation in CSO Chorus groups is by regularly scheduled audition. Call CSO president Kristine Turner at (843) 577-5884 for more details.

International Piano Series,
College of Charleston
44 George St. (Sottile Theatre)
(843) 953-6575

Since 1989, the School of the Arts at the

Insiders' Tip

Watch for the "Small Fry Concerts" given by the Charleston Symphony Orchestra at the Gibbes Museum of Art. There are four of them every year— specially created for kids from ages 2 to 10. It's a fun outing and a great way to introduce young ears to fine music and good art.

College of Charleston has had an annual spring International Piano Series that's also open to the general public. The series was designed to introduce students and the Charleston community to an array of fine, established performers from around the world. This is a major inspiration to music students on campus who have come from as far away as Spain, Korea, China, and Costa Rica to study in the college's piano performance program. All concerts are at 8 PM in the Sottile Theatre on George Street just off King and admission is $15 at the door. Call the number above for a performance schedule and a calendar of School of the Arts events.

Monday Night Concert Series,
College of Charleston
Simons Center for the Arts,
54 St. Philip St. (Recital Hall)
(843) 953-8228

This is one of those little gems that few people know about and yet it's one of the best arts events going on in the city. These regularly scheduled Monday night concerts, free of charge, are usually presented in the Simons Center Recital Hall and feature faculty and adjunct faculty talent from the Music Department. The programs vary from jazz to Renaissance music, from organ concerts (at the Cathedral of St. Luke and St. Paul, 126 Coming Street) to choral works from the College's Gospel Choir (at the nearby Sottile Theater, 44 George Street). The overall quality of the concerts is always quite wonderful, and the admission price can't be beat. Call Mark Tiedje at the School of the Arts for more information and specific concert schedules.

Vox eterna
P.O. Box 13268, Charleston, SC 29422
(venues vary)
(843) 556-5826

The name means "voice eternal," but the group is only four years old. This is a choral group of about 20 singers who get together to perform serious 20th-century music in four planned concerts a year. Performances are held in various

> ## Insiders' Tip
> The Spoleto finale concert at Middleton Place is a great site for an all-day picnic. Go early and spread out a blanket to reserve your spot on the tiered lawn facing the butterfly lakes. Eat, drink, and toss the Frisbee all afternoon. Stroll the magnificent gardens. Then settle down for a great evening of festival music under the stars.

churches and concert halls throughout the city to explore the many acoustical possibilities and find the appropriate space to match the music. Many of the singers hold advanced degrees in music or related fields and the quality of their concerts is earning praise from local critics. The group is professionally conducted by Scott Atwood, who auditions new singers by appointment. Admission to the concerts is free (for now), but that may change soon. Call the number above for concert dates and audition information.

East Cooper Concert Series
1516 Pine Island, Mt. Pleasant
(843) 884-9090

This annual four-concert series, held on spring Saturday nights at 8 PM at Christ Our King Church, benefits East Cooper Community Outreach. Admission to all concert events is a monetary donation or a food or paper product. Performers include various ensembles from the Charleston Symphony Orchestra, visiting concert choirs and individual artists. The church is at 1122 Russell Drive in Mt. Pleasant. Contact Loma Tedesco for scheduling and more details at the number above.

Galleries

With so much history and architecture to brag about, Charleston may not be terribly famous for its art. But the fact is the city has produced a number of fine artists over the years. The charming illustrations Elizabeth O'Neill Verner created from the 1920s to '40s were certainly not the first artistic views of the city to catch the public's eye, but they were (and still are) among the most popular. Other great talents include Charles Fraser and Samuel Morse (the inventor of the telegraph), who were portraitists working here. Some of the works of those artists are on display at the Gibbes Museum of Art (see the Other Museums section of our Attractions chapter).

Today, downtown Charleston hosts an amazing array of fine art galleries that expand the view and viewpoint far beyond the city Elizabeth O'Neill Verner loved to draw. Generally, when you're browsing in any of the downtown galleries, you're within easy walking distance of another...and another...and another. All are free to enter.

The serious shopper with an appetite to see more than just a few galleries may want to park the car and use Charleston's DASH shuttle system between stops. If you decide to give it a try, take the Meeting-King Street route. (For more on DASH, see our Getting Here, Getting Around chapter.)

African American Art Gallery
43 John St.
(843) 722-7568

There is always a colorful and changing collection at this showcase for African and African-American art. Just across from the Charleston Visitor Reception and Transportation Center, the exhibition room features original works from local, national, and international artists. New exhibits are mounted every two months. The gallery's prints and custom framing department has more than 1,500 limited-edition prints and posters.

The African American Gallery also offers a number of educational programs for schools, local community groups, and visitors. These include gallery tours, lectures, poetry readings, meet-the-artist events, classes, workshops, multimedia presentations, and more. African-American heritage tours to areas of historic importance in and around Charleston are offered in conjunction with licensed tour guides (see our Guided Tours chapter). Hours are 10 AM to 6 PM, Monday through Saturday.

Downstairs, Gallery Chuma features the large format, stunning imagery of Jonathan Green, famous Gullah artist now of Naples, Florida.

American Originals
153 East Bay St.
(843) 853-5034

This unique gallery, between Broad and Queen Streets, occupies more than 2,500 square feet in an old, historic sugar and cotton warehouse. Bright and colorful, the shop carries decorative fine crafts and wearable art. They feature original works by Rogers Oglesby, Zernie Smith, and Chaz Walter. Look for oils, watercolors, mixed media works, and contemporary handcrafts made by more than 350 local and regional artists. American Originals has silks and batik, tile art, metal sculpture, pottery, jewelry, and mobiles. Hours are 10 AM to 6 PM, Monday through Thursday; 10 AM to 7 PM on Friday; 10 AM to 10 PM on Saturday, and Sunday 11 AM to 4 PM.

Audubon Wildlife Gallery
177 King St.
(843) 853-1100

This is the official gallery of the annual Southeastern Wildlife Exposition with exhibits of SEWE artists all year long. The gallery and store are very popular with tourists, nature lovers, and wildlife fans. You'll find old and new limited-edition nature prints, traditional Audubon prints, 19th-century city views, engravings, and antique plates. It carries original wildlife art and a wide assortment of merchandise related to birding, stargazing, and nature study. Hours are 10 AM to 5:30 PM Monday through Saturday.

Beyond the Image
148 East Bay St.
(843) 722-4121

The name of this gallery says just what it is—fine art and beyond. Specifically, the gallery goes beyond carrying original works by local and nationally known artists to offer expert custom-framing services. Hours are Monday through Friday, 10 AM to 5 PM; Saturday, 11 AM to 5 PM.

Birds I View Gallery
119-A Church St.
(843) 723-1276, (843) 795-9661

Anne Worsham Richardson is a South Carolina artist and naturalist who is recognized across America for her wildlife paintings—especially her birds. She maintains a private wildlife sanctuary outside her studio, where she often takes in sick or injured birds. They frequently recover under her care and are returned to the wild, but while they are healing, many birds have been models for her paintings. Richardson has received many honors during the past few years, her latest being induction into

the South Carolina Hall of Fame at Myrtle Beach. Gallery hours are Monday through Saturday from 10 AM to 5 PM.

Blink!
62-B Queen St.
(843) 577-5688

Appropriately named, this is a gallery you might miss if you blink—literally. Located in a tiny slice of a building on Queen Street, it features some of the most interesting ceramics, jewelry, glass, and textiles found in the French Quarter. Hours are Monday through Saturday, 10 AM to 5 PM.

Carolina Fine Paintings & Prints
188 King St.
(843) 723-2266

This gallery specializes in pre-1945 American art (including a fine selection from Charleston's own Renaissance Period) and what's called sporting art. Carolina Prints has been around for almost 30 years, putting artists and collectors together. You'll find a wonderful selection of works by Alfred Hutty, Alice Smith, Anna Heyward Taylor, and Elizabeth O'Neill Verner plus antique prints, original paintings, and botanicals by Besler, Schwert, and others. The gallery carries Audubon prints and architectural drawings too. The staff is qualified to act as framing consultants. Hours are Monday through Friday, 10 AM to 5 PM; Saturday, 9 AM to 5 PM; or by appointment.

Eva Carter Gallery
132 East Bay St.
(843) 722-0506

In what used to be called the New Gallery, next to the Old Exchange Building on East Bay, is now Eva Carter's own—displaying her bold abstract paintings. Her sophistication in the arrangement of line, color, space, and texture creates emotional intensity to even drivers passing by her windows. One of Charleston's better-known artists, Eva Carter's work is a must-see for contemporary art lovers. The gallery also features abstract works of the late William Halsey and sculptural works in steel by Gretchen Lothrop. Hours are Monday through Saturday, 10 AM to 5 PM.

Charleston Renaissance Gallery
103 Church St.
(843) 577-6039
This charming gallery is at the intersection of St. Michael's Alley and Church Street. Recently restructured to present a mix of old and new works, it appeals to visitors from all over the world as well as local Charlestonians. It features 19th-century Southern masterworks and the art of the Charleston Renaissance period (1920s and '30s). Also, the gallery has exclusive representation of contemporary plein air painter West Fraser. Gallery hours are Monday through Saturday, 10 AM to 5 PM.

Charleston Crafts Inc.
87 Hasell St.
(843) 723-2938
This gallery, just next to the Charleston Place parking garage, showcases the works of South Carolina's finest craft artists. Exhibits include works in clay, fiber, wood, jewelry, metals, glass, photography, paper, traditional crafts, basketry, leather, toys, and even soap-making, with exhibitors chosen by a jury of other artists and gallery owners. Charleston Crafts offers a wide variety of gifts—from traditional to contemporary, from utilitarian to decorative, from affordable to exclusive. Demonstrations and featured craft artists change every week. Hours are from Monday through Saturday from 10 AM to 5:30 PM. Sunday hours are seasonal and posted accordingly.

Charleston Frame Works and Gallery
816 St. Andrews Blvd.
(843) 556-9373
Across the Ashley River about a mile down St. Andrews Boulevard, this gallery, formerly known as the Blue Knight Gallery, is making a name for itself as a source for affordable artwork. Pre-matted and framed prints and posters are featured here. There is a custom framing department that's well-stocked and creative. Hours are Monday through Friday from 10 AM to 6 PM and Saturday from 11 AM to 3 PM.

City Gallery
133 Church St.
(843) 724-7305
This city-owned art gallery is actually next door to (and connected with) the city's historic Dock Street Theatre. That means there's a lot of heavy traffic, and to be shown here is a real coup for an artist. Local talent is shown exclusively and all exhibitions are juried. Hours are Monday through Friday 9 AM to 5 PM and during all performances at the Dock Street.

Clowns' Bazaar
56 Broad St.
(843) 723-9769
Here is Charleston's only tax-exempt folk art showcase, a gallery exclusively set up to provide employment for disadvantaged artisans. It features the work of several groups of talented artists who, for one reason or another, fall under the auspices of this special category. The showcase represents artists from SERRV (which includes many Third World countries), Ten Thousand Villages (mostly African art), and Charleston Sunday Artists (local artists who are retired from the mainstream gallery scene). Hours are 11 AM to 5 PM daily.

Cobblestone Studios
40 N. Market St.
(843) 853-5829
426 Broadway, Mt. Pleasant
(843) 971-9227
Look for Cobblestone Studios in the Rainbow Market in the old City Market area. It carries fantastic watercolors and oils, flowers, and exciting Charleston reproductions, plus handmade gifts and jewelry. Hours are Monday through Saturday from 10 AM to 5:30 PM and Sunday from 11 AM to 4 PM.

Coleman Fine Art
45 Hasell St.
(843) 853-7000
This is the needle in the haystack for anyone

looking for an art restoration specialist. Services include cleaning and revarnishing damaged or dirty oil paintings, plus museum and custom framing for art of all kinds. It carries children's books illustrated by Mary Whyte plus other original works and some limited-edition prints as well. Commissions are accepted for portraits. Hours are Tuesday through Saturday 10 AM to 6 PM or by appointment.

John Carroll Doyle Art Gallery
54 Broad St.
(843) 577-7344

Visitors to the Market area who stop in at A.W. Shucks for lunch or for oysters and beer are totally surrounded by the unique work of popular Charleston artist John Doyle. His bold colors and striking figures are filled with life, drama, and his very special treatment of light. Doyle is nationally known for his energetic paintings of blues musicians, blue marlins, and blue hydrangeas. His studio is right on Broad Street, and special showings of his work or private commissions can be arranged. Gallery hours are Monday through Saturday, 10 AM to 5 PM.

East Bay Gallery
280 West Coleman Blvd., Mt. Pleasant
(843) 216-8010

Here is a gallery of eclectic, functional art that houses the work of more than 400 American artists. You'll find art glass, jewelry, pottery, contemporary wood and metal art, textile art, and much more. Although the name implies the location is on East Bay Street in Charleston, this gallery is actually in Mt. Pleasant—in the specialty shops of Northcutt Plaza where there's plenty of free parking.

Gayle Sanders Fisher Gallery
124 Church St.
(843) 958-0010

This is the showcase for Gayle Sanders Fisher's imaginative originals in oil and watercolor. The Carolina Lowcountry, its unique architecture, nature, and color have been Fisher's subjects for the past 30 years. Her work is included in many private and corporate collections throughout the country. Gallery hours are Monday through Saturday, 10 AM to 5 PM; Sunday 1 to 4 PM.

Gallery Two Queen
2 Queen St.
(843) 853-8512

Here is the combined gallery of well-known Charleston artist Marty Whaley Adams and newcomer Paige Hathaway Thorn. Adams' impressionistic paintings, reminiscent of Matisse and Cassatt, are light-filled and delightfully personal. She works in oils and watercolors and creates monotypes as well. Thorn is a graduate of the Savannah School of the Arts and her work is in hand-dyed textiles. Her inspiration is frequently from nature with botanical themes wrought in silk-screened fabrics for pillows, scarves, and other wearable art. Hours are 10 AM to 5 PM Monday through Saturday and 1 to 5 PM on Sunday.

Halsey Gallery at the
College of Charleston
54 St. Philip St.
(843) 953-5680

The Halsey Gallery in the Simons Center on St. Philip Street between Calhoun and George Streets is administered by the School of the Arts at the College of Charleston. It exists to advocate, exhibit, and interpret visual art with an emphasis on contemporary art. In addition to housing seven major exhibitions each year, the gallery serves as an extension of the undergraduate art curricula and sponsors interpretive programs such as accompanying lectures and seminars. While the primary audiences served include the college's students, faculty, and staff, the gallery is open to the public and participation in its programs is encouraged. Gallery hours vary according to the building's use for performances and school-related functions. Call for more specific details.

Bernie Horton Originals Gallery
111 Church St.
(843) 858-0014

Here you'll find fascinating marshscapes and Lowcountry images of shrimpers, crabbers, clammers, and oyster harvesters done in oils and acrylics. The works of Mark Horton are also featured. Gallery hours are Monday through Saturday, 10 AM to 5:30 PM and Sunday 12:30 to 5 PM.

Gallery Joporo
340 King St.
(843) 577-4777

On fast-changing King Street, this contemporary gallery of unique artwork, includes originals, Giclees, and bronze "frog" sculptures. Regularly featured artists include Dean Vella, Mat Lively, Leonard Wren, and Tim "Frogman" Cotterill. Hours are Monday through Friday, 12:30 to 6 PM; Saturday 10 AM to 6 PM.

Steven Jordan Gallery
463 W Coleman Blvd., Mt. Pleasant
(843) 881-1644

Steven Jordan's enormously popular work has always been well worth the trip over to Mt. Pleasant. He works primarily in transparent watercolor and occasionally in acrylics and pastel. Jordan's subjects range from Lowcountry to international scenes. For 10 years, Jordan was on the faculty at the Gibbes Museum of Art, and he is a member of the American Watercolor Society. More than 40 of his works are available in print. His gallery includes handcrafted jewelry, pottery, and some sculpture. Hours are Monday through Saturday 10 AM to 6 PM.

Terry Katz Gallery
65 Broad St.
(843) 534-2020

Terry Katz' work has been shown in galleries as far away as Zurich and in New York, Atlanta, and Palm Beach closer to home. Her impressionistic brushstrokes, layering of paint, and treatment of light and water have been compared to Monet with flashes of the spirit of Van Gogh. She brings her talent to bear on traditional Lowcountry scenes with delightful results. Her gallery hours are Monday through Saturday, 10 AM to 6 PM.

Charlynn Knight Gallery
829 Savannah Hwy.
(843) 556-7070

This gallery out on Savannah Highway carries a variety of originals and prints by Charlyn J.M. Knight and Trish McKinney. Also, you'll find stained glass by Valerie J, Oldham. Art lessons and classes in stained glass are offered for adults those 18 and older. Hours are Tuesday through Saturday, 10 AM to 5 PM.

E.S. Lawrence Gallery
229 Meeting St.
(843) 853-4280

This gallery is a branch of the upscale gallery of the same name in Aspen, Colorado, and features works by Chi Tak

Hak, Steve Hanks, Graciela Rodo Boulanger, Zvonimir Mihanovic, A.J. Finley McRee, Tomasz Rut, Jack Dowd, Richard Haman, Dalva Duarte, Leon Bronstein, Tom Sierak, and Dr. Suess. Hours are Monday through Wednesday, 10 AM to 8 PM; Thursday through Saturday, 10 AM to 10 PM; and Sunday 1 to 6 PM.

Nina Liu and Friends
24 State St.
(843) 722-2724
Nina calls this "a gallery of contemporary art objects." We call it fun. This quaint gallery is quite possibly the heartbeat of Charleston's French Quarter art scene. Her gallery makes bold and changing statements with very distinctive collections of glass, porcelain, jewelry, decorative ceramics, and fiber art. Solo shows by nationally known artists are featured periodically, and you'll find paintings, photography, and sculpture as well. Her gallery/salon is in a 19th-century town house on State Street, which attracts an international clientele of shoppers and art patrons. Hours are Monday through Saturday from 10 AM to 5 PM, or by appointment.

Lowcountry Artists Ltd.
148 East Bay St.
(843) 577-9295
Nine local artists operate this gallery on East Bay Street's busy gallery row. The quaint shop has a fine selection of original watercolors, woodcuts, pottery, oils, and prints. The specialty here is Charleston and Lowcountry scenes. You'll also find collages, hand-painted tiles, colored-pencil drawings, linocuts, monoprints, etchings, and other graphics. Portrait, fine art, and commercial art commissions are welcomed. Every month, one of the participating artists has a show of new works. Hours are Monday through Saturday from 10 AM to 5 PM, or by appointment.

Elizabeth Lyle Gallery
161 King St.
(843) 723-2600, (888) 847-0937
One of the city's upscale, international galleries gaining more attention these days, the Elizabeth Lyle Gallery specializes in the works of contemporary American, European, and Peruvian artists, featuring Yvonne Mora (Peru), David Fernandez (Peru), Martin Jewell (USA), David Borenstein (USA), and Paolo Turri (Italy). Gallery hours are 10 AM to 5:30 PM every day but Sunday.

Martin Gallery
57 Queen St.
(843) 723-7388
Here's a showcase for contemporary works by nationally acclaimed artists working in oils and acrylics—including those of Italian master painter Imero Gobbato; bronzes by wildlife sculptor Leo Osborne, marble, bronze, and terra cotta sculpture by Claire McCardle and photography by Michael Kahn. Hours are Monday through Saturday, 10 AM to 6 PM; Sunday 1 to 5 PM and by appointment.

McCallum-Halsey Studios
20 Fulton St.
(843) 723-5977
Longtime Charleston favorite Corrie McCallum's and her late husband William Halsey's work is shown at their Fulton Street studio (second right turn off King Street past Charleston Place). The works are primarily in oils but often incorporate interesting textiles (sometimes even objects). Graphics and sculptures are included. William Halsey, by the way, is the artist for whom the College of Charleston named its exhibition gallery in the Simons Center for the Arts. Hours are by appointment only.

Margaret Petterson Gallery
125 Church St.
(843) 722-8094
Seeing the Lowcountry through Margaret Petterson's artistic eye is to see it in a new light. Her work blends old and new, traditional and contemporary. And you're invited to visit with the artist as she paints in her Church Street studio. You'll also find original pottery by Jo Jeffers Wing-

field. Gallery hours are Monday through Saturday from 11 AM to 5 PM and by appointment.

Pink House Gallery
17 Chalmers St.
(843) 723-3608
In one of the city's most picturesque buildings (first used in 1694 as a tavern) is this quaint gallery featuring architecturals, wildlife, and florals. Look here for original works by Alice Stewart Grimsley, Bruce W. Kruckle, and Alexandria H. Bennington. Ravenel Gaillard's remarkable Lowcountry scenes are featured here, as well. Works are shown on all three floors and special exhibits are held in the courtyard just off the cobblestone street. Hours are Monday through Saturday, 10 AM to 5 PM.

Reflections South
125 Meeting St.
(843) 577-9351
This gallery features the popular work of one of the city's best-loved painters, Virginia Fouché (pronounced foo-SHAY). Her original paintings and lithographs illuminate Charleston, the Lowcountry, and its people. Through the years, Fouché has received many awards and honors, the latest being a Grumbacher Silver Medallion for her watercolors. Her works hang in public and private collections across the country. The gallery also carries block prints and lithographs by Walter Ingilis Anderson, one of the South's foremost painters of barrier island and wildlife scenes. Gallery hours are Monday through Saturday, 10 AM to 5 PM, and Sunday 1 to 5 PM.

Amelia Rose Smith Garden Gallery
113 Church St.
(843) 958-0666
Along with the popular watercolors and pastels of Amelia Rose Smith, this gallery carries the original works of Jean Sinclair Beck, Frances London DuBose, J. Michael Kennedy, Joan A. Davis, and Carroll Morrell. Hours are Monday through Saturday, 10 AM to 5 PM.

Tippy Stern Fine Art
154 Market St.
(843) 534-0028
This contemporary gallery is attracting notice for its interesting shows of works by established and emerging artists. The shows are group, solo, and themed exhibitions that are handsomely mounted in their distinctive space located across the street from Saks Fifth Avenue's side entrance (behind the Riviera Theatre). The gallery has shown works by Charles Ailstock, Richard Hagerty, and Juan Logan, and is open Tuesday through Saturday, 11 AM to 5 PM, and Sundays by appointment.

Tidwell Art Gallery
323 King St.
(843) 723-3167
This gallery features prints and oils from local, state, and nationally known artists including Martin Ahrens, Irene Charles Batt, Miles Batt, Deborah Cavanaugh, Carolyn M. Epperly, Joyce Hall, Matt Constantine, Vernon Washington, Christopher Zhang, and Patsy Tidwell. Look for color graphics and original watercolors too. Hours are 9:30 AM to 5:30 PM Monday through Saturday, and Sunday, 1 to 5 PM.

Utopia
27 Broad St.
(843) 853-9510
This small fashion boutique/art gallery on Charleston's very traditional Broad Street seems like a non sequitur, but it's a welcome and refreshing break. It also displays alternative and avant-garde fashions and art which is attracting a dedicated following. Hours are Monday through Saturday from 11 AM to 7 PM; on Sunday, it's noon to 5 PM.

The Verner Gallery
79 Church St.
(843) 722-4246
Located at the corner of Church and Tradd, this gallery has changing exhibits of visual artists working with Lowcountry themes and other subjects. The gallery

regularly features the popular work of Elizabeth O'Neill Verner and contemporary artists such as Daphne von Baur, Mary Walker, Lonnie Stewart, Gene Speer, Paul Bertholet, Robert Stark, Manning Williams, Lese Corrigan, and others. Hours are 10 AM to 5 PM, Monday through Saturday or by appointment.

Karen Vournakis Studio-Gallery
125 King St.
(843) 723-3921

Some Charleston arts fans may know Karen Vournakis for her Piccolo Spoleto award-winning posters for 1996, 1998, and 2000. Her style is hand-painted photo and mixed media. She combines her interest in architecture and archaeology with her artistic talent. She reinterprets her own photographic images in her studio by adding wax crayons, pencils, and oil directly on the archivally processed original gelatin silver prints, resulting in a post-Modernist blend of photography and painting. She is frequently working "in the field" so you may want to call ahead. But regular gallery hours are Monday through Saturday, 11 AM to 5:30 PM. The gallery is closed Wednesdays and Sundays.

Waterfront Gallery
215 East Bay St.
(843) 722-1155

This is Charleston's largest art gallery and they have recently moved to this location. A cooperative gallery, the Waterfront features 19 South Carolina artists working in oils, watercolors, pastels, monotypes, and hand-colored photography. Every participating artist has works in residences and businesses around the world. Commissions are accepted, several of the artists do portraits, and others do calligraphy and sculpture. Gallery hours are 11 AM to 6 PM, Monday through Thursday; weekends 11 AM to 10 PM.

Wells Gallery
103 Broad St.
(843) 853-3233

The Wells Gallery presents a diverse palette of original work from artists who enjoy regional, national, and international success. Works range from contemporary realism to abstract expressionism, from landscape to figure, from full color to somber neutrals. Regular gallery artists include Betty Anglin-Smith, Rhett Thurman, Susan Mayfield West, Mickey Williams, Betty H. Robinson, Joseph Cave, Shannon Smith, Jennifer Lynn Smith, William Jameson, John Hulsey, Randall McKissick, Karen Larson Turner, David Goldhagen, and Harvey Walford. Gallery hours are 10 am to 6 pm, Monday through Saturday.

Gordon Wheeler Gallery
180 East Bay St.
(843) 722-2546

The gallery of local artist Gordon Wheeler offers original acrylic paintings of Charleston and other Lowcountry scenes. He's mostly known for his commission work, but the shop has limited edition prints and some very popular golf art. Gallery hours are 10 AM to 6 PM, Monday through Saturday; 11 AM to 5 PM Sunday.

Annual Events

Tradition is of utmost importance to Lowcountry residents, and successful annual events always fall into that category. Events in the Trident area run the gamut from the Lowcountry Oyster Festival—where salty oyster juice stains and face-painting masterpieces serve as souvenirs—to the sophisticated and comprehensive arts festival that is Spoleto Festival USA. Charlestonians and visitors alike turn out in big numbers for all the events listed in this chapter, so we strongly suggest you make your reservations early.

For information about any of the activities, we recommend contacting the Visitor Information Center of the Charleston Metro Chamber of Commerce (part of the area's convention and visitors bureau) at (843) 853-8000 or (800) 868-8118. Offices are in the Charleston Visitor Reception and Transportation Center at 375 Meeting Street. The City of Charleston Office of Cultural Affairs, 133 Church Street, (843) 724-7305, and the automated ticketing service, Ticketmaster at (843) 554-6060, are other good sources for information. The following listings will serve as good starting points in your efforts to dive into the traditions of the Trident. Unless otherwise noted, all events take place in Charleston proper.

January

Lowcountry Oyster Festival
Boone Hall Plantation,
1235 Long Point Rd., Mt. Pleasant
(843) 577-4030

The very first Lowcountry Oyster Festival gathered a small but hardy crowd back in 1982. That was then. And now? Well, now we would marvel if snow scared off the thousands who loyally appear. This festival, organized by the Greater Charleston Restaurant Association, is built around the mighty oyster but is geared to the whole family's appetite for fun. The gates of beautiful Boone Hall Plantation in Mt. Pleasant open at 11 AM, and ticket holders are welcomed until the gates close at 5 PM. An oyster-eating contest as well as other competitions and games are held, all in the name of fun and support of local children's charities. Barbecue and chili fill the void for non-oyster eaters, and if the winter temps aren't enough, there are plenty of chilled beverages—beer being the most popular—to keep things cool. Usually scheduled the week before Super Bowl

Sunday, admission to the festival is $8 in advance and $10 at the gate.

Citadel Dress Parade
The Citadel, 171 Moultrie St.
(843) 953-5000

Almost every Friday during the school year, the nearly 2,000-member Corps of Cadets at the Citadel marches in retreat parade or review on Summerall Field to close out each week. In addition to the family and friends turnout, the Dress Parades are a long-standing local and visitor favorite due to the impressive precision of the Corps. Spectators are welcomed (for free)—just be sure to take your seat before 3:45 PM when the action commences. Call for a schedule.

Make Your Own History
Charleston Area
Convention and Visitors Bureau,
P.O. Box 975, Charleston, SC 29402
(843) 853-8000

If you are a local and haven't quite gotten

around to seeing all the wonderful attractions in your own town, this is your big chance. Purchase this pass with local I.D. and play tourist during the month of January. For $15 per person, this pass entitles Charleston-area residents to free admission to more than 10 of the area's best attractions. Some of the most popular house museums such as the Aiken-Rhett House and the Edmonston-Alston House are on the list. Plantations include Boone Hall, Charles Pinckney National Historic Site, Middleton Place, and Drayton Hall. Patriots Point Maritime and Naval Museum, Charles Towne Landing State Historic Site, Fort Moultrie, several county parks, and the Gibbes Museum of Art are a few more on the diverse menu of attractions that may be just a little less crowded in January and well worth checking out. (See our Attractions chapter for more on these special sites.) Passes may be picked up at the visitor center at 375 Meeting Street.

February

Budweiser Lowcountry Blues Bash
Various locations, P.O. Box 13525,
Charleston, SC 29422
(843) 762-9125

In the past, as many as 35 acts have participated in the Lowcountry Blues Bash. Musicians such as Dave Peabody and Rob Mason, The Love Dogs, Big Boy Henry, Lil' Brian & the Zydeco Travelers, Carl Weathersby, and Shrimp City Slim have played to enthusiastic crowds at more than 10 venues throughout the area. The event proudly showcases some of the area's older blues musicians along with ones up-and-coming on the scene. Tickets range from free to $12 per performance. The 10-day event is held in early February. Festival promoter, musician, and radio personality Gary Erwin runs the show, and you can call him for more information about the Bash and other blues happenings around town at (843) 762-9125 from 10 AM to 6 PM, Monday through Saturday. A Budweiser Lowcountry Blues Bash brochure is available by sending a self-addressed, stamped envelope to the above address.

Annual Benefit Tour of
Historic Bed & Breakfasts
Various downtown locations
(843) 722-7551, (888) 722-7553

This afternoon tour lets you walk or use a free shuttle to check out ten or more area bed and breakfast inns for future stays. Guides are quick with stories about ghosts, goblins, and even movie stars who have found a haven at certain inns. While we can't promise flowers in early February, inn owners typically care for their gardens or front-door presentations so that, whatever the season, it's a lovely and interesting tour. Expect prices to run in the $25 range. The shuttle makes it easy to get from one inn to the next. Proceeds benefit MUSC Children's Hospital and other local charities. For information on the tour, call the numbers listed above.

The Junior League of Charleston
"Whale of a Sale"
Charleston Area Convention Center,
5001 Coliseum Dr., North Charleston
(843) 763-5284

This is the rummage sale to end all rummage sales. And if you don't believe it, ask the dozens who camp out the night before in the parking lot to be the first ones through the door. Everything from large appliances, furniture, and computers to toys, sports equipment, clothing, and "you name it" is donated by the Junior League's membership, and there is new merchandise from area merchants. Of course, it's all available at rock-bottom prices. This event is a treasure hunter's paradise, so come prepared to search for loads of bargains. The doors open at 8 AM and close at 4 PM, usually on the first Saturday in February.

Southeastern Wildlife Exposition
Various downtown locations
(843) 723-1748

This exposition is said to be the largest celebration of wildlife art anywhere. Incredible displays of paintings, prints, sculpture, carvings, photography, collectibles, and crafts are all inspired by the boundless wonders of nature. More than 40,000 ticket-holding guests crisscross between the dozen or so exhibition sites on the Peninsula during the three-day event. Most are also interested in the expo's conservation motif. Hence, the booths, student contests, and the like are devoted to the green theme. Tickets for the 2001 event, held on Presidents' Day weekend, were $12.50 a day or $30.00 for a three-day pass (children 12 and under are free with a paying adult). VIP packages start at $100 and include an Insiders' look at the Expo. VIPs get opportunities to preview and purchase original artwork, attend special receptions and parties, and enter exhibits through separate entrances and move to the front of lengthy lines. For more information on the next annual exposition or advance ticket purchases, write the SWE at 211 Meeting Street, Charleston, SC 29401.

March

Historic Charleston Foundation's
Festival of Houses and Gardens
Various downtown locations
(843) 723-1623, (843) 722-3405 (festival info)

Those who want to move beyond a passive, coffee table book enjoyment of Charleston's private homes and gardens wait for this event each year. It's a mouthful, but what the foundation undertakes and offers is also expansive. For a month's time in March and April, more than 600 volunteers make it possible to tour more than 150 private houses and gardens. Every day the itinerary changes, with the

Roasted oysters are a Lowcountry delicacy—steamed over an open fire and served piping hot by the shovelfuls. PHOTO: FLETCHER NEWBERN

focus on historically and architecturally distinct dwellings and gardens. To further broaden the experience, the foundation also hosts oyster roasts at Drayton Hall Plantation, and there is a series of garden-only tours. Tickets are $40 and are available from the Frances R. Edmunds Center for Historic Preservation at 108 Meeting Street or by calling the number above. Proceeds support Historic Charleston Foundation's many preservation programs. (See our chapter on Architectural Preservation for more on Historic Charleston Foundation.)

Kids Fair
Gaillard Municipal Auditorium,
77 Calhoun St.
(843) 571-6565

Since 1988, the Jewish Community Center has sponsored this indoor fair for children at the Gaillard Auditorium. We like the safety precaution of not allowing any adult to enter if not accompanied by a child and appreciate the wide range of age-appropriate entertainment—from face-painting to health-issue booths, all free of charge. The hours are 10 AM to 5 PM on a Saturday in mid-March. In a nice change of pace, parents are admitted free

with children, whose tickets are $2. Parking is free, too.

Charleston Symphony Orchestra League
ASID Designer Showhouse
Location varies, 14 George St.
(843) 723-7528

Each year a private historic dwelling is placed in the capable hands of volunteers from the Charleston Symphony Orchestra League to be presented in all its dazzling glory to the public in a one-house tour. The annual showhouse event, which opens in late March and continues for a month, is sponsored by the orchestra league, and each room is decorated by an ASID designer. It provides a great opportunity to tour an attractive home, shop the in-house boutique and have lunch at the same residence in the tea room. Sometimes the boutique might be in a garage or carriage house; the tea room might be set up in the garden. It all depends on the layout of the chosen home. Tickets are $12 in advance or $15 at the door, and proceeds benefit our outstanding orchestra. Hence, it's a win-win situation and another opportunity to experience the inside of Charleston.

Christian Family Y Tea Room
21 George St.
(843) 723-6473

Just don't miss it—the she-crab soup, shrimp-paste sandwiches, and incredible Huguenot torte at the Y Tea Room. While the Y volunteers have been serving this late-March lunch for nearly 30 years, it is still a wonderful surprise when, lo and behold, it's time for the Tea Room again. Conveniently located on George Street at the Y, just off King Street, the lunch is perfect for a midday break. Why not get take-out food for your own picnic? The food is delicious and is the real McCoy in terms of Lowcountry cooking. Expect to order a complete lunch with dessert for around $10. The Tea Room is open only one week each spring, Monday through Friday from 11:30 AM to 2 PM. Proceeds benefit the Christian Family Y's programs.

Charleston Antiques Symposium
School of the Arts, College of Charleston,
Charleston, SC 29424
(843) 953-6527

Looking for a way to immerse yourself in the decorative arts? The School of the Arts at the College of Charleston has the answer each spring when it coordinates the Charleston Antiques Symposium during the first weekend in March. Noted scholars and collectors of the fine and decorative arts present lectures, study sessions, and programs for both the novice and the connoisseur. The venues add to the experience—some sessions take place in historic homes, some in studios of artists and craftsmen, and others on the College of Charleston campus. Past speakers have included Ron Hurst, Curator of Collections at Colonial Williamsburg; Bradford Rauschenberg, Director of Research at the Museum of Early Southern Decorative Arts; and Theodore Landsmark, President of the Boston Architectural Center. Ticket prices range from $35 to $75 for single events and package prices are available too. Call the number listed for details.

April

Cooper River Bridge Run
P.O. Box 22089, Charleston, SC 29413
(843) 792-0345, (843) 792-6611

The Bridge Run, as the natives call it, is a social event as much as it is a run. Men, women, and children begin training for the run months before the race date, and some even attend clinics scattered around the area as part of their preparation. Bumper stickers dare us with words like "Gone Runnin'," and banners fly around the city for weeks ahead of time—we can't say we just forgot. Still, a 10-kilometer (6.2-mile) run or 4.4-mile walk is a bit much for some of us, if not too great a challenge for the 30,000 or so participants who pound the pavement each year (usually in early April). The race begins in Mt. Pleasant, continues across the bridge it's named for, and finishes downtown. The early entry fee for the shorter walk is $15, and the run is $20. All entrants receive a T-shirt and other goodies. For more information and an application, write to the Cooper River Bridge Run, P.O. Box 22089, Charleston, SC 29413. (For more information, see our Spectator Sports chapter.)

Flowertown Festival
900 Crosscreek Rd., Summerville
(843) 871-9622

Summerville, a 20-mile drive from Charleston, is the setting for this wonderful small-town festival each spring (see more on Summerville in our Lowcountry Daytrips chapter). If the winter has been kind, the city—affectionately called Flowertown—will be ablaze with color on the first weekend in April, and the events are nonstop. Sponsored by the Summerville Family YMCA, the festival is a three-day affair that includes arts and crafts displays with more than 400 vendors, a youth festival, sports tournaments, the Taste of Summerville food festival, and much more. There is no admission fee, but there are charges from individual vendors for food and activities. (For more on Summerville, see our Lowcountry Daytrips chapter.)

Lowcountry Cajun Festival
James Island County Park,
871 Riverland Dr.
(843) 762-2172

Crawfish-crazed connoisseurs take heart: There's a chance for you to get your fill this side of New Orleans at the annual Lowcountry Cajun Festival. Set in mid-April, it's a stompin' good time at the James Island County Park, where more than 5 tons of crawfish, eating contests, crawfish races, and a genuine Louisiana Cajun band make up the mix for family fun. Sponsored by the Charleston County Park and Recreation Commission, tickets

The Spoleto Festival's magic begins in late May and continues into the month of June. PHOTO: DAVID COOPER

for the festival are $6 for adults and free for kids under 12 with a paying adult.

The Garden Club of Charleston's Walking Tour of Private Houses and Gardens
Various downtown locations
(843) 406-7626

Some of Charleston's finest Historic District homes and gardens are showcased on The Garden Club of Charleston's tours on two Saturday afternoons in early April. The members have organized this tour for more than 65 years and continue to delight tourists and locals alike with the selection of private homes, breathtaking gardens, and their own flower arrangements that enhance the homes' interiors. Tickets are in the $25 range and can be purchased by calling the number listed or by writing to P.O. Box 20652, Charleston, SC 29403.

Family Circle Cup
Daniel Island Tennis Centre,
161 Seven Farms Dr.,
Daniel Island, Charleston
(843) 534-2400, (800) 677-2293

Take in some tennis at the $9 million Daniel Island Tennis Centre, the new home of the Family Circle Cup. This tournament relocated in 2001 to Charleston after a long-time run in Hilton Head, South Carolina. The nine-day, Women's Tennis Association Tier I event attracts many of the top seeds in women's tennis. Some of the past competitors were Conchita Martinez, Monica Seles, Arantxa Sanchez-Vicario, Jennifer Capriati, and Mary Pierce. Held in mid-April, the Family Circle Cup is another highlight in Charleston's spring events line-up. Ticket prices range from $20 for qualifying matches up to $50 for the finals. Call the number above or write to Family Circle Cup, 416 King Street, Charleston, SC 29403 for more information. (See our Spectator Sports chapter for more on the Family Circle Cup.)

Ashley Hall House Tour
Various downtown locations
(843) 720-2855

Organized by the Alumnae Association of Ashley Hall school, this self-paced tour runs from 2 to 5 PM one Saturday in April.

Each year the tour features a different downtown neighborhood of historic homes and gardens, many of which will not be found on any other tours in the city. For this reason, alums, locals, and visitors jump at the chance to see inside some of Charleston's most beautiful private homes. Tickets are $30 with advance purchase encouraged; some tickets are available the day of the tour at the visitor center. For more information contact the Alumnae Association of Ashley Hall at 172 Rutledge Avenue, Charleston, SC 29403.

Charleston Farmers Market
Hutson St. (between King and Meeting)
(843) 724-7305
Held every Saturday from mid-April through October just above Marion Square (King, Meeting, and Calhoun Streets), the Charleston Farmers Market gives you a chance to pick out fresh fruit and veggies from our best local growers. Each week brings a variety of special activities, and the food and family fun are offered from 8 AM until 1 PM. Music, arts and crafts, and "Ask a Master Gardener" are just a few of the attractions. A holiday market is held an early Saturday in December, too, so you can gather loads of fresh greenery and goodies to "deck the halls." We know lots of folks who are regulars at the Farmers Market—hooked on that fresh-harvested produce and free fun.

Blessing of the Fleet
Alhambra Hall, 131 Middle St.,
Mt. Pleasant
(843) 849-2061
The town of Mt. Pleasant and the shrimping industry pull out their finest when they invite the public to celebrate the Blessing of the Fleet. Along with prayers for a successful shrimping season and a parade of shrimp boats, organizers offer a wide range of entertainment and culinary delights. From shrimp-eating contests to educational displays and face painting, the formula is for fun, and the setting—beautiful. With its gorgeous view of Charleston, Alhambra Hall can't be beat. The festival is held the last weekend in April. Drawing more than 10,000 people each year, the Blessing of the Fleet is Mt. Pleasant's largest tourism event. The festival is sponsored by the town of Mt. Pleasant and the Blessing of the Fleet Committee. Admission is free, but food from a variety of East Cooper restaurants ranges from about $2 to $5.

May

Lowcountry Senior Sports Classic
P.O. Box 21912, Charleston, SC 29413
(843) 762-2172
Attention all 50- and older athletes: These senior games feature competitions in more than 40 recreational events, so display your competitive nature. No matter what your interests, there is something for you in this five-day event in early May. The events include bowling, golf, croquet, swimming, basketball, tennis, track and field, and softball, held at various locations such as The Citadel and the Naval Weapons Station. In addition to the competitive events, other opportunities for friendship and fun include the opening social with live Big Band music, a Senior Expo, and a sunset cruise. And who knows—qualifying here may lead to the chance to compete at the state and national senior sports classics. Registration, which includes events and the banquet, is $15, with additional fees for golf and bowling. The softball tournament fee is $40, and the sunset cruise costs $10. Registration forms are available at area recreation departments or by using the address or phone number listed.

Dining With Friends
Lowcountry AIDS Services,
1501 Manley Ave., North Charleston
(843) 747-2273
Hundreds of volunteers host private dinner

parties for friends in their homes in a joint fund-raising effort supporting Lowcountry AIDS Services one Saturday in May. (For more information on the services provided by LAS, see our Healthcare chapter.) The kinds of parties run the spectrum from barbecue to black tie. Guests make a tax-deductible donation and enjoy a pleasant evening with old and new friends topped off with a Champagne and Dessert Grand Finale at 9 PM at the Charleston Maritime Center.

North Charleston Arts Festival
Performing Arts Center of the Charleston
Area Convention Center Complex,
5001 Coliseum Dr., North Charleston
(843) 745-1087
Bring the family and spend some time at the North Charleston Arts Festival. The indoor/outdoor entertainment at this nine-day festival encompasses everything from juried adult and youth art exhibits, a photography competition and a local arts and crafts show and sale, to puppet and magic shows, live theater, and dance performances. Just listening to the variety of musical entertainment (including African drumming, school choral groups, classical music, and a finale by the Charleston Symphony Orchestra) is reason enough to check it out. Event hours are 10 AM to 4 PM daily. Also a fun run, a walk, and a wheelchair race are held for the more active set. Some events are free, and others are ticketed events in the $10 range. The festival wraps up with a gala priced at $40 per person. Ample parking is available for free.

Spoleto Festival USA
Various locations
(843) 722-2764, (843) 723-0402
Since 1977, Spoleto Festival USA has continued as a bright star on Charleston's arts calendar. One resident put it well when she said that anticipating Spoleto each year is "like looking forward to another Christmas, without having to dread the discarded gift paper mess." Already accustomed to an unusually strong year-round arts agenda, the city becomes blissfully hyperactive during Spoleto with world-class theater, music, dance, opera, and visual and literary presentations. It begins on Memorial Day weekend and lasts 16 days or so.

The 2001 Spoleto was highlighted by the Puccini opera, *Manon Lescaut*, Compania Nacional de Danza from Spain, The Royal Shakespeare Company in *A Servent with Two Masters* and an ever-popular chamber music series directed by Charles Wadsworth. Tickets for individual Spoleto events range from about $15 to $75. For an up-to-date schedule, contact the event box office at P.O. Box 157, Charleston, SC 29402, or call Ticketmaster at (843) 554-6060. (See The Arts chapter for more on Spoleto.)

Piccolo Spoleto Festival
Various locations
(843) 724-7305
We are particularly proud of Piccolo Spoleto, the city of Charleston's creative companion to Spoleto Festival USA. Piccolo events—including jazz cruises, a children's festival, a juried art exhibit, cabaret, and "brown bag and ballet"—are held in unusual places (anywhere from boats to parks to churches) and showcase local as well as national talent. The calendar is booked, and the ticket prices are very reasonable, ranging from free events to others that are almost always less than $15. For a more comprehensive schedule of events, write the City of Charleston Office of Cultural Affairs, 133 Church Street, Charleston, SC 29401. (For more on Piccolo Spoleto, see our chapter on The Arts.)

Grace Episcopal Church Tea Room
98 Wentworth St.
(843) 723-4576
Another of Charleston's special spring tea rooms is the one put on by the volunteers of Grace Episcopal Church, near the College of Charleston. Lowcountry specialties are the fare here, and who can pass up an opportunity to sample a few of these: crab and okra soup, ham bis-

cuits, and shrimp remoulade with an assortment of freshly baked desserts. Prices run from $2 to $5 an item, and you may find yourself returning several times during the two weeks the tea room is open. The dates correspond with the Spoleto Festival, the last week of May and first week of June. Lunch is served Monday through Friday from 11:30 AM to 2 PM, and takeout is available for your own Spoleto picnic. Proceeds benefit church outreach programs.

Charleston Air Expo
Charleston Air Force Base, North Charleston
(843) 963-5608

Gates open at 9 AM for the crowds of up to 175,000 folks who turn out each year for this free air show. Launched from the Charleston Air Force Base, the aerial demonstrations of the Charleston Air Expo may feature the U.S. Air Force Academy Parachute Team and the Wings of Blue, as well as the U.S. Air Force's Thunderbirds, whose daring maneuvers will leave you in awe. Other flying events include B-2 Stealth Bombers, F-117 Stealth Fighters, vintage World War II bombers, and other military and civilian aircraft. Static displays allow access to look in cockpits and cargo areas-a real hit with the kids. Crowd control and parking are well organized, and food and souvenir concessions are on site. A special preview of the annual show is held the day before for people with disabilities and special needs. For more details on the Charleston Air Expo, write to Air Expo, 437 AW/PA, 102 East Hill Boulevard, Charleston Air Force Base, SC 29404-5154. (For more on Charleston's military facilities, see our Military chapter.)

June

Carolina Day
1214 Middle St., Sullivan's Island
(843) 883-3123

Sullivan's Island in the summer is cause for celebration in itself. Add to the natural charm of the venue an event like Carolina Day, and you're in for some serious fun. No admission is charged for this annual re-enactment program at Fort Moultrie, and it is a wonderful opportunity to learn about the history of the patriots' Revolutionary War victory over the British Navy on June 28, 1776. Other Carolina Day events include a special church service and the ringing of church bells in Charleston, Mt. Pleasant, Sullivan's Island, Isle of Palms, and North Charleston. An open house at the South Carolina Historical Society (see our Architectural Preservation chapter for more information) and a South Carolina Art Tour at the Gibbes Museum of Art (see the section on Other Museums in our Attractions chapter) are both free of charge. A procession takes place in the afternoon. It is composed of historical and lineal groups that make up The Palmetto Society of Charleston, the group that sponsors Carolina Day. The parade moves from Washington Park downtown to White Point Gardens at The Battery, where a wreath-laying ceremony and band concert wrap up the procession. The program runs from 9 AM to 8 PM. (See our Kidstuff and Attractions chapters for more information on Fort Moultrie.)

July

Festival on the Fourth
Brittlebank Park
(843) 577-6947

If you are looking for a large time—as in large crowds of 40,000 or more people and the large amounts of music, food, and beverages needed to satisfy them— plan to spend the Fourth at Brittlebank

Park. We particularly like the fireworks display exploding at the end of the festival and suggest watching it from the park or, if you get there in time to be a patron, one of the nearby restaurants or bars. Admission is free, and local bands and restaurants provide the music and food for purchase.

August

**Evinrude Outboards/
Hydra-Sports Boats Fishing for Miracles
King Mackerel Tournament
Charleston Harbor Marina Resort,
24 Patriots Point Rd., Mt. Pleasant
(843) 766-0011**
This king mackerel fishing tournament, held the third weekend in August, is one of the largest saltwater fishing tournaments in South Carolina. Based out of Charleston Harbor Marina Resort, cash prizes (and we're talking more than $160,000 in total prize money) are awarded for the biggest catch as well as other categories. The tournament proceeds benefit the Medical University of South Carolina Children's Hospital (see our Healthcare chapter) and the Coastal Conservation Association of South Carolina. The entry fee is $265 before August 1 and $315 thereafter. (For more on this and other fishing tourneys in the area, see our Hunting and Fishing chapter.)

September

**Folly River Float Frenzy and Fish Fry
121 Center St., Folly Beach
(843) 588-3059**
This crazy, fun time on the river is a must for the not-so-fussy who aren't afraid of a little water. Participants—some in costumes, some in not much at all—float down the river during an early-September weekend in an array of vessels. Live music, endless refreshments, and the ambiance of laid-back Folly Beach set the tone for raft competition and fun. The rewards are many, not the least of which is the fish-fry supper for one and all at the Folly Marina on W. Ninth Street. Admission to the event is free to watch, $10 if you want to enter a raft. The city of Folly Beach and the Folly Association of Businesses sponsor the fun, and proceeds go to beautification projects.

**Scottish Games and Highland Gathering
Boone Hall Plantation,
1235 Long Point Rd., Mt. Pleasant
(843) 529-1020, (843) 884-4371**
The tartan-clad clans gather and traditions abound when the Scottish Games and Highland Gathering, sponsored by The Scottish Society of Charleston, is held at Boone Hall Plantation. All ages are incorporated into the festivities, which range from highland and country dancing and bagpipe music to tossing the caber. Those interested in finding out more about their Scottish roots enjoy talking to clan members at various booths, and everyone has a chance to sample Scottish culinary delights such as meat pies, scones, and shortbread. Boone Hall Plantation is a lovely setting for all of this, and September is usually a very temperate month in the Lowcountry. Advance tickets for the 9 AM to 5 PM gathering are $10 for adults and teens and $4 for children 6 to 12. Gate prices will be $12 and $5, respectively. Parking is $3 per car, which includes a program. For more information, contact The Scottish Society at P.O. Box 31951, Charleston, SC, 29417-1951.

**The Preservation Society of Charleston's
Fall Candlelight Tours of
Homes & Gardens
Various downtown locations
(843) 722-4630, (800) 968-8175**
Beginning in September and running through October, the candlelight tours, sponsored by The Preservation Society of Charleston, are a splendid opportunity to

experience the interiors of homes and churches in Charleston at night. Tourists and locals alike enjoy the romantic walk along several city blocks between dwellings and the commentary on the architecture, history, and folklore of each property by the volunteer guides. Tours run from 7 to 10 PM on Thursday, Friday, and Saturday nights. The Sunday afternoon garden tea tours are enchanting, too. Tickets are $35 per tour or $90 for the weekend package of three, which feature different locations in the Historic District each week. You can find out more about the tours by writing The Preservation Society at P.O. Box 521, Charleston, SC 29402. (Please see our chapters on Architectural Preservation and Attractions for more information about the society.)

MOJA Arts Festival
133 Church St.
(843) 724-7305, (843) 577-7400

Running for ten days in September and October, MOJA—a Swahili word for "source" or "beginning"—celebrates the long and fascinating African-American and Caribbean traditions and contributions to western cultures. Charleston becomes a stage for lectures, theater, and dance performances, art exhibits, concerts, and general festivities. Activities for the young and old provide the opportunity for sharing good times and harmony amongst people. Expect broad strokes of color, graceful movement, and beauty and revelry in abundance. Check *The Post and Courier* for special features and a listing of specific events with admission prices (many events are free), or call the above numbers for more information. (See our Tours and The Arts chapters for more about MOJA and Charleston's African-American tradition.)

Friends of the Library Used-Book Sale
Gaillard Municipal Auditorium,
77 Calhoun St.
(843) 805-6977

Organized by the Friends of the Library's volunteers to raise money for Charleston County libraries, this used-book sale just gets bigger and better. Since 1983, the event held at the Gaillard Auditorium has included categories such as fiction, nonfiction, history, cooking and travel, just to name a few. The books all are donated by the public—paperbacks sell for $1; hardbacks are $2. A "better book" section has individually priced books. Peruse the selection of more than 50,000 books, tapes, and CDs during the three-day event, which has a $2 admission fee (on Friday only) for adults and teens. Children younger than 12 are admitted free. Event hours are Friday from noon to 8 PM, Saturday from 9 AM to 4 PM, and Sunday from noon to 4 PM.

Festival Hispano
Wannamaker County Park,
8888 University Blvd., North Charleston
(843) 762-2172

Celebrate the sights, sounds, and tastes of the Latino world at Festival Hispano on a Saturday in early September. In between nachos, salsa, and chicken tamales, delight in the red-hot beat of hot Latin music. The Parade of Nations and folk dances add to the colorful display of the beautiful ethnic costumes. Over 4,000 attended the 2000 festival, making it the second largest event sponsored by the Charleston County Park and Recreation Commission—second only to the Lowcountry Cajun Festival (see April's events). Admission is $6 for adults, and children under 12 are free with a paying adult.

October

Charleston Garden Show
Gaillard Municipal Auditorium,
77 Calhoun St.
(843) 577-7400

Charleston's botanical treasures are many, and the garden show celebrates the long history of them all. From lectures to tours to hands-on activities for children and adults, the show is a comprehensive and informative early October weekend for the experienced and the newly interested. Vendors are on hand at Gaillard Municipal Auditorium with plant materials and garden accouterments, all ready to be incorporated into your landscape scheme. It's all for sale, and widely acclaimed landscape designers are scheduled for informative sessions with participants. Tickets can be purchased in packages or for individual events and range from $25 for a garden tour to $40 for a symposium and $60 for the popular plantation tours. General admission to just take a look at the exhibits and marketplace vendors is $6, and mini-lectures at Gaillard Auditorium are free.

Taste of Charleston
Boone Hall Plantation,
1235 Long Point Rd., Mt. Pleasant
(843) 577-4030
If you have ever dreamed of sampling just a bite here and a bite there from the great restaurants all around town, this event is your dream come true. The Taste of Charleston is an all-day affair at Boone Hall Plantation, where more than 50 restaurants, all members of the Greater Charleston Restaurant Association, sell their specialties in sample proportions at bite-size prices. The fare may include shrimp and grits, beef kabobs, Greek chicken, seafood dishes, and a variety of desserts. Plan to nibble your way around the plantation grounds, then watch the Waiters Wine Race (make a bet on who'll spill) and ice-carving competition. Adults love the beer and winetasting booths, and children delight in the pony rides and face-painting. The event is usually scheduled for a Sunday in October, and admission is $6 in advance or $8 at the gate. Children 10 and under are admitted free with an adult.

Komen Charleston Race for the Cure
P.O. Box 20637, Charleston, SC 29413
(843) 792-9186
A relatively new entry into the road-race circuit in the Charleston area, the Race for the Cure has quickly grown in popularity among runners of all ages to become the largest 5K race in South Carolina. The event is held by the Susan G. Komen Breast Cancer Foundation, which spon-

The opening ceremonies for Spoleto Festival USA brings together all aspects of the arts in an exciting and colorful spectacle. PHOTO: WILLIAM STRUHS

sors the 5K Race for the Cure around the country. It is a breast cancer awareness race in which participants are invited to wear the name of loved ones who have battled cancer. The race takes place in downtown Charleston, and early registration fees (before October 1) are $15 for the 5K run/walk and the 1-mile fun run/walk. Children under 5 are free but must be registered. After October 1, the cost goes to $20. Proceeds benefit both local and national grants awarded for breast cancer prevention and research.

Mt. Pleasant Children's Day Festival
Patriots Point Sports Complex,
Mt. Pleasant
(843) 849-2061

On an October Sunday afternoon, the town of Mt. Pleasant holds the Children's Day Festival to honor the children of the community and provide them with live entertainment, games, food, and fun. The event is organized by the Mt. Pleasant Recreation Department and East Cooper schools that all set up game and food booths. Games are free, with prizes awarded, and food sales benefit the school PTAs and PTSOs. Last year's entertainment lineup delighted more than 10,000 children and families. The Rhine-

stone Roper, Mandrake the Magician, Becky Becker's Box of Puppets, The Gravity Brothers Comedy Juggling Duo, The Citadel Cheerleading Squad and the Wando Show Choir have all performed here. If that's not enough to make the little ones' eyes light up, there's laser tag, jump castles, a climbing wall, a giant slide, plus mechanical animal rides. A Halloween costume contest also puts the children in the spotlight. Parking and admission are free.

Greek Festival
Greek Orthodox Church of
The Holy Trinity, 30 Race St.
(843) 577-2063

Another in Charleston's delectable, ethnic festivals is the Greek Fest held in mid-October every year at the Greek Orthodox Church. Greek food, dancing, jewelry, crafts, and cooking demonstrations are some of the highlights of the weekend-long family fun. Dine in or take out the gyros, Greek chicken dinners, spanakopita, and pastries. Check out the bazaar and take in a tour of the beautiful church. You're bound to be speaking a little Greek by the time you leave. Hours are 11 AM to 8 PM Friday and Saturday; 12 to 7 PM on Sunday. Admission is free.

November

Plantation Days at Middleton Place
4300 Ashley River Rd.
(843) 556-6020, (800) 782-3608

No wonder so many brides ache to marry close by the spectacular butterfly lakes of Middleton Place: The grounds are the essence of romanticism and classic beauty (for more on Middleton Place, see our Attractions chapter). Perhaps it's a fantasy about living in a magnificent setting like Middleton, with the mythical prince, until death do you part. Back here in reality, consider getting a feel for plantation life at Middleton Place's Plantation Days. On every Saturday in November, visitors can observe craft workers in action as

they showcase the tasks necessary for existence on an 18th- or 19th-century plantation. It's not hard to imagine the harvest season in full swing as you watch demonstrations of actual quilting, dyeing, candle-making, leather tanning, and cider-making. Sweetgrass baskets, like those sold downtown at the City Market (see the Close-up in our Shopping chapter), are fashioned before your eyes as you immerse yourself in a different era. Regular gate admission to see the stable yards and gardens during Plantation Days is $15 for adults and teens and $8 for children 6 through 12. An additional $8 is charged to see the house.

Charleston Cup Steeplechase
5365 Forest Oaks Dr., Hollywood
(843) 723-1748, (843) 766-6208
Every November the horsey set (and those who like to horse around once a year) don chapeau and equestrian attire to picnic and watch the steeplechase events at Stono Ferry, south of Charleston in Hollywood, South Carolina. The Charleston Cup Golf Classic on Friday and a black-tie gala the next evening kick off the fun. The Sunday track races the next day provide good excuses for some friendly mingling and informal betting on your favorite name horse. All proceeds go to benefit a local charity. The gates open at 9 AM for the infield setup of some pretty fancy spreads complete with candelabra and flowers, and the races commence at 1 PM. The reserved infield parking is $100 or $200 for the front row. Advance tickets for general admission are $12 or $15 at the gate. Parking is $5 per car and a shuttle provides transportation to the track. (See our Spectator Sports chapter for more on this event.)

The Battle of Secessionville
Boone Hall Plantation,
1235 Long Point Rd., Mt. Pleasant
(843) 884-4371
Sponsored by the Palmetto Brigade of Charleston, the Battle of Secessionville is re-enacted right before your eyes with all the splendor and tragedy of the Civil War. Some of the activities to witness on this mid-November weekend include cavalry and artillery performances, battle aftermath re-enactments, uniform demonstrations, and tours of the Boone Hall Plantation house and slave village. (For more on Boone Hall, see our Lowcountry Daytrips and Tours chapters.) Camps open at 9 AM and the battle commences at 2 PM. Admission prices are $12.50 for adults and $6 for children 6 to 12. (To learn more about the Battle of Secessionville, see "Battery Wagner" in the Forts section of our Attractions chapter.)

Holiday Festival of Lights
James Island County Park,
871 Riverland Dr.
(843) 762-2172
Young and old delight in the more than 125 magical lighting displays set up in the James Island County Park from mid-November through New Year's. Set your own pace as you take the three-mile driving tour, winding through the park and enjoying the spectacle. The lights burn from 5 to 10 PM Sunday through Thursday and until 11 PM on Friday and Saturday. Admission is $10 a car and $25 for 15-passenger vans. A Holiday Festival of Lights Fun Run and Walk the day before opening gives participants a preview of the 600,000 glittering lights. The 5K Fun or the 2-mile walk is a $5 entry fee in advance or $20 per family. Start a new family tradition of viewing the dazzling display every year.

December

Gibbes Museum of Art
Holiday Tour of Homes
Various downtown locations
(843) 722-2706
When it's time to get in that Christmas spirit, this is the tour to inspire you. Organized by the Women's Council of the Carolina Art Association of the Gibbes Museum, the Holiday Tour of Homes regularly sells out early. Many of Charleston's finest private homes, decorated by the homeowners and volunteers for the holidays, are on display. Held in early December from 1 to 4 PM, locals and tourists enjoy the opportunity to experience the holidays Charleston-style and gather some new decorating ideas for the season. Tickets are $30 and can be reserved by calling the number above. (For more on the Gibbes Museum of Art, see our

Attractions, Kidstuff, and Shopping chapters.)

Annual Spirituals Concert
Drayton Hall, 3380 Ashley River Rd.
(843) 766-0188

African-American spirituals, rooted in the work songs of West Africa and developed during the days of slavery, are incredibly moving. A cappella voices and rhythmic double-clapping are characteristic of the songs. The opportunity to hear them performed is rare. This early-December event begins with an informal candlelight house tour and refreshments each night at 6 PM followed by the hour-long concert around 7 PM. To order tickets at $35 a person ($30 for Friends of Drayton Hall), contact Drayton Hall at 3380 Ashley River Road, Charleston, SC 29414. Seating is limited in the Great Hall of Drayton Hall, so advance reservations are required. (For more on Drayton Hall, see our Attractions chapter.)

Christmas Parade of Boats
Charleston Harbor
(843) 762-2172

For over 20 years, privately owned boats have been turning out for this event, which is sponsored by the Charleston County Park and Recreation Commission, on the first Saturday evening in December. The boats are decorated in holiday themes with a nautical twist, and they parade and compete for cash prizes. The fleet of 50 or so vessels cruises from Patriots Point and the Wando River past the Peninsula, finishing at the Ashley Marina on the Ashley River. Spectators can enjoy the maritime spectacle, including a fireworks display, for free and pick their favorites while watching from points along the waterfront such as The Battery, the USS *Yorktown* at Patriots Point, and Waterfront Park.

Family Yuletide
Middleton Place, 4300 Ashley River Rd.
(843) 556-6020, (800) 782-3608

There's a fire for chestnut-roasting, Jack Frost could very well be nipping at your nose, and you can bet that yuletide carols are going to be sung by a choir. It's all part of Family Yuletide at Middleton Place, which is usually held on the third Thursday in December. There will be holiday storytelling by the bonfire, and crafters will be working by torch light in their shops to get the venerable plantation ready for Christmas. The children can make angels out of corn husks, and a live nativity scene is planned. Reservations are recommended for this family event. Admission is $10 per adult and $5 for children 3 to 12.

Kwanzaa
Various downtown locations
(843) 724-7305

Like the traditions of Mardi Gras, the Chinese New Year, and Cinco de Mayo, Kwanzaa is a celebration of culture and heritage. Based on the ancient African harvest, the focus is on the African-American family and is meant to be observed at home, where participants reflect on principles such as unity, self-determination, purpose, and creativity. A variety of events

Insiders' Tip

If you're here during the Christmas season, be sure to visit Candyland on King Street. The local merchants association closes a couple of blocks to traffic and decorates the temporary park in a festive holiday theme with a giant Christmas tree, a miniature train, snowmen, the works. Shops along the street offer free parking vouchers to holiday shoppers, adding to the spirit of the season.

takes place around the Lowcountry, allowing opportunities to learn more about Kwanzaa. During the last week of December through New Year's Day, singing, dancing, poetry readings, and speakers are a part of the observance. A naming ceremony is held to receive indigenous African names. A children's ceremony and final celebration with the lighting of candles share the holiday with the community. All events are free and open to the public.

First Night Charleston
Various downtown locations
(843) 852-6423, (843) 554-6060 (Ticketmaster)
The inaugural First Night Charleston was held on New Year's Eve 1997 and met with great success. First Night Charleston, a local interpretation of the event started in Boston in 1976, marks the passage of one year into the next with a broad selection of arts and cultural performances in the downtown Historic District. The slant is a family-oriented, affordable, nonalcoholic, entertaining

way to ring in the New Year. The 30- to 45-minute offerings include ballet, theater, improvisational comedy, puppetry, and an array of music from choral, chamber and ethnic, to folk and Big Band. Much of King Street is blocked off for pedestrian-only traffic, allowing a festive atmosphere at every turn with roving musicians and actors, jugglers, facepainters, and dancing. All the events are within walking distance, and performances take place several times over the course of the evening so that participants may attend as many shows as they like. Children's programming begins at 2 PM; the major events begin at 7 and last until 11 PM, when a grand finale and fireworks conclude at midnight at the U.S. Custom House. An $8 button ($12 after 12/20), $5 for children 6 to 12, gains access to more than 60 indoor and outdoor events. Buttons are available in advance through Ticketmaster at the number listed or onsite at booths the night of the event. Free parking at City of Charleston garages comes with the presentation of a button.

Kidstuff

For starters, know that Greater Charleston is a fabulous vacation destination. Over three million people come to the Lowcountry every year, and a majority of those visitors arrive in the form of families.

A quick glance through our Attractions chapter might give you the impression that Charleston primarily serves up nothing but history—forts, house museums, plantations and historic sites. While this wouldn't seem to be very kid-friendly, we've found that, almost without exception, Charleston's major annual events and attractions have been designed (at least partially) with children in mind.

And don't forget that kids love to learn. Greater Charleston is a living, breathing, three-dimensional, full-color, interactive classroom for learning about America (which is really learning about ourselves). And here's the best part: It's a classroom with a beautiful ocean nearby, and that means beaches! Are we talkin' fun, or what?

So, let's take stock. What have we got here? Interesting (new and old) places to go with really neat stuff to see; places where people used to live and work (and play) hundreds of years ago; ships of all types and all sizes that you can actually climb around on; and beaches close by with plenty of sand and sunburn to go around. We've got ball parks, game parks, and parks where you can swim. There are places to camp, rivers to explore, even new foods to taste. Ever eat a crawfish? We've got farms where you can pick your own strawberries and blueberries when the season is right. We've got something for every kid out there.

So this chapter is dedicated to fun activities that children and parents can do together. Let's get started.

Outdoor Explorations

As you will note in our Parks and Recreation chapter, there are many public parks in the area. We have found that some are particularly appealing to children, and we describe those in more detail below. Whatever outdoor plans you make, be sure to bring plenty of sunscreen during the warm months and bug repellent for those pesky no-see-ums (gnats) present most of the year.

Charles Towne Landing State Historic Site
1500 Old Towne Rd., between I-26 and S.C. Hwy. 171, Charleston
(843) 852-4200

This state park is many things to many people, and it really is a terrific introduction to a hands-on history lesson. Founded in 1970, Charles Towne Landing State Historic Site is 663 acres of walking, bicycling, and in-line skating paths, an animal forest, an area dedicated to the depiction of the lives of settlers, and more. Kids can expect to see native animals such as wolves, alligators, pumas, otters, bison, and maybe even a bear or two in a natural habitat setting. Children enjoy the craft-making demonstrations and appreciate the period clothing worn by the park staff. Recent archaeological digs are centered on uncovering information about the original settlement of Charles Towne prior to its relocation on the peninsular site. These excavations are bound to stir some excitement among visitors of all ages.

We recommend the $1 per person tram ride, a 30-minute narrated tour through the park that goes past the original house and down to Old Towne Creek, where a reproduction of a 17th-century trading vessel named *Adventure* is often docked. Bike rentals are available for a $2 deposit plus $2 an hour. Wonderful special events throughout the year as well as summer and holiday day camps attract a steady flow of young people. The park is open daily (except Christmas Eve and Christmas) all year. Hours are 8:30 am to 5 pm from September through May and extend to 6 pm from June through August. Adult admission is $5, and admission for children 6 to 14 is $2.50. Children younger than 6, handicapped, and senior citizens get in free. (See our History, Attractions, and Parks and Recreation chapters for more information.)

Fort Sumter National Monument
Charleston Harbor
(843) 883-3123 (National Park Service)
What could be a more awe-inspiring setting and thrilling experience for a young person than arrival by tour boat at Fort Sumter, the fort where the Civil War began? In the middle of Charleston Harbor, Fort Sumter looks much like it did a century ago and affords an incredible view of the city and surrounding islands. We recommend careful supervision of children, as the fort is surrounded by water and there are many precarious climbs. The gift shop has an array of interesting items (a kit of historically accurate paper dolls or replica buttons, for example) and Civil War books, and it is air conditioned—a major plus after a hot day scouring the fort. National Park Service rangers are on-site to answer questions, and there is a museum.

Admission for adults and teens to Fort Sumter is $11; children 6 through 12, $6 accompanied by a ticketed adult; and

those younger than 6, free. Tour boats depart from the new tour boat facility at the foot of Calhoun Street at the Cooper River. Call for schedules; the fort is open year round. (For more on Fort Sumter, see the Forts section of our Attractions chapter and our Tours chapter.)

Hampton Park
55 Cleveland St., Charleston
(843) 724-7326
As children, we came to Hampton Park to play around the 60 inner-city acres, so it's a particular treat to experience the park these days with the next generation. Kids delight at the same simple pleasures we remember: feeding ducks and geese in the pond, smelling the gorgeous roses, and just frolicking in the wide-open spaces. The police department's horse stables are a real draw for the little ones, who can stand outside the ring and admire the animals, and the parcourse exercise trail is a favorite of older children and adults. The Piccolo Spoleto finale, a city-sponsored Easter Egg hunt, and in-line skating night during warm weather are great reasons to plan a Hampton Park visit. The park is free, but keep in mind the midtown location and possible safety concerns if you're venturing to Hampton Park at night. (See our Parks and Recreation chapter for more information.)

James Island County Park
871 Riverland Dr., Charleston
(843) 795-7275
This beautiful, 643-acre park offers biking, keowees (junior-size kayaks), skating, fishing or crabbing, a climbing wall, a super playground, and much more. Splash Zone, however, is the James Island park's great water attraction. With two 200-foot tube slides, a 500-foot lazy river is enlivened by a spray-filled, waterfall-peppered "adventure channel." There's a leisure pool perfect for kiddies and a Caribbean play structure with interactive elements. Splash Zone is simply awesome. Showers, concessions, lockers, and rest-

rooms are available. Splash Zone hours are 10 AM to 6 PM on May weekends and daily from Memorial Day through Labor Day. The annual Holiday Festival of Lights will dazzle young and old alike with more than 100 lighting displays on view mid-November through New Year's. (See Annual Events for more on this festival.) Park daily hours are 8 AM to 6 PM in March, April, September, and October; 8 AM to 8 PM from May through August; and 8 AM to 5 PM November through February. Gate admission is $1 per person (2 years and under are free), but Splash Zone will run you an additional $7.95 for Charleston County residents ($6.95 for children under 42 inches tall) and $9.95 for non-residents. The Holiday Festival of Lights admission is $10 per car. (For more, see our Parks and Recreation chapter.)

Leland Farms
S.C. Hwy. 700, Wadmalaw Island
(843) 559-1296
During the spring and summer months, area farms offer you-pick-it produce, and one of our favorite spots is Leland Farms on Wadmalaw Island south of Charleston. Children carry buckets out into the fields and delight in gathering and eating seasonal berries right off the vine. Strawberries, blackberries, and blueberries are carried home by the pound and can stimulate some creative pie and ice cream making later. This can be a pleasant morning or afternoon that teaches kids that food doesn't just come from the grocery store or drive-through. The Leland Farms fields are open 8 AM to 5 PM Monday through Saturday in season; call the Berry Hotline number listed for directions and produce selections.

Magnolia Plantation and Gardens
S.C. Hwy. 61, Charleston
(843) 571-1266, (800) 367-1266
While the horticultural maze and antebellum cabin (an original, dating back to around 1840) are first stops for the little ones, the petting zoo with African pygmy goats, deer, and other friendly animals is the real calling card for toddlers and elementary school kids visiting Magnolia. They can buy handfuls of grain to feed the gentle creatures but should expect an occasional nibble on the posterior from a pushy goat or two. The topiary gardens, trimmed to resemble animals, and Barbados Tropical Garden (with plants native to Barbados—homeland of the original settling family—and points south) are also fun to see. Older children can rent canoes or bikes (or you can bring your own), and everyone enjoys the 45-minute, 4-mile tram ride through the property. Leashed pets are welcome too.

Magnolia is open 365 days a year from 8 AM to 5 PM. Admission for adults is $11, and the price for children varies according to age: $8 for teens; $5 for ages 6 through 12; $1 for under 6. For the house tour (where children younger than 6 are not allowed), nature train, and swamp gardens, there are additional charges of $5 to $6 per activity for adults, $4 for teens, and $3 for kids 6 to 12. (See our Attractions chapter for more on Magnolia Plantation and Gardens.)

Middleton Place
4300 Ashley River Rd., Charleston
(843) 556-6020
In addition to being lots of fun for the kids, the incredible beauty of the gardens and forest trails of Middleton Place tends to leave parents lingering, trying to drag out the good times a little bit longer. A shady picnic area near the Greensward is a delightful place to enjoy the vistas. And here's the chance for everyone to milk a cow, card wool, or grind corn. Middleton is a working plantation: Free-range farm animals mill about, and craftspeople are hard at work so that visitors can observe or even take part in the re-enactment of history.

Plantation Days are a fun, educational series of Saturdays in November when demonstrations of plantation harvesting, candle dipping, syrup making, shepherding and more take place (see our Annual Events chapter). Gates are open daily from 9 AM until 5 PM. Middleton Place is open year round. Garden and stable yard admission is $15 for adults and teens and $7 for children 6 to 12. Kids younger than 6 are admitted free. An additional $8 fee is charged for the house tour. (For more on Middleton Place, please see the Plantations and Gardens section of our Attractions chapter.)

Palmetto Islands County Park
444 Needlerush Pkwy., Mt. Pleasant
(843) 884-0832

This nature-oriented park is on more than 900 acres of typical Lowcountry terrain and features a mile-long wilderness trail along a boardwalk through the marsh. Little children enjoy playing at The Big Toy, a play area with lots of wooden equipment such as towers, slides, and swings, and their older siblings enjoy the tunnel, slide, and view associated with the observation tower. Pedal boats and canoes are for rent, and many visitors enjoy exploring on bicycles—rent one or bring your own.

Splash Island is the hot new attraction here for warm-weather patrons. A 200-foot slide, a 16-foot otter slide (no otters, just a fun name), sprays, waterfalls, geysers, and a delightful sand play area await. In addition to the park admission of $1 per person, Splash Island admission is $5.99 for Charleston County residents, $6.99 for non-Charleston County residents, $4.99 for children under 42 inches tall, and free for children younger than 3. A flat $3.99 is charged after 3 PM Monday through Friday. Splash Island is open from 10 AM to 6 PM on weekends in May and daily from Memorial Day through mid-August. Park daily hours vary by season as follows: May through August, 9 AM to 7 PM; March, April, September, and October 9 AM to 6 PM; and November through February, 10 AM to 5 PM. (See our Parks and Recreation and Boating and Watersports chapters for more information on this park.)

Sullivan's Island Park
1610 Middle St.
(Station 21 and Middle St.),
Sullivan's Island
(843) 883-3198

Involved parents and other residents of Sullivan's Island have worked hard to make this park the little gem that it is. With two sections of play equipment, lots of wooden things to crawl in and on, and sliding-friendly apparatuses, children are fairly contained and easily occupied. There is even a fence around one area for additional safety for younger children. The man-made mound, left over from World War II, was built as a mortar battery to store ammunition. It is referred to by locals as "The Hill" and is the place to go if your kids are into sliding. Wear tennis shoes and play clothes, bring a big piece of cardboard and your steady nerves, then climb to the top and slide down...over and over and over again. At least that's the way it works with kids. While this is the same good, clean fun we had here as children, be forewarned that there is danger in the shape of a huge pit in the mound's center that is not particularly well-marked. Keep children away from the edges and also avoid letting the kids make solo treks into the bamboo groves or other isolated areas. Although Sullivan's is an island of good neighborhoods, there is safety in numbers where children are concerned. There is no admission charge. (See our Parks and Recreation chapter for more on Sullivan's Island Park.)

Waterfront Park
Cumberland St. to N. Adgers Wharf,
Charleston
(843) 724-7326

Just off East Bay Street in downtown Charleston, the lovely Waterfront Park is another nice picnic and cool-your-heels spot. Sea breezes keep the tables under the covered pier area perfect for just these pursuits. Children have fun splashing around in the pineapple-shaped fountain or getting soaked in the circular spray fountain. We've seen pictures of half a kindergarten class in one of the large swings that line the pier, a 400-foot extension into Charleston Harbor. No admission is charged. (See our Parks and Recreation chapter.)

White Point Gardens at The Battery
South tip of East Bay and King Sts.,
Charleston
(843) 724-7326

Frisbee-throwers and cannon-climbers love White Point Gardens. Children can run free beneath the canopy of trees and pretend to lift the immensely heavy and immovable cannonballs. Lots of photo ops here! There is usually a pleasant breeze off the water (the harbor circles around the point), and this open space is a much-loved haven of respite in the city. We used to search through the oyster-shell fill along the walks to find ancient shark teeth or other treasures. Don't expect any more luck than we had decades ago, but do plan to enjoy the leisurely pace of an old-fashioned park. Of course, no admission is charged. (For more info, see our Parks and Recreation, History, and Attractions chapters.)

Kid-Friendly Beaches

Though there are many great beach destinations in a coastal area like this one, one of our favorite swimming areas for children is on Folly Beach at the Folly Beach County Park, (843) 588-2426. Unlike some other area beaches, this one has its own parking, lifeguards, and facilities. Take a right off Folly Road onto Center Street and follow it to its end. Young surfers will want to head for the midsection of the island, where waves are best. Admission is $5 a car.

Kiawah, most of which is a private resort community, does offer public access at Beachwalker Park, (843) 768-2395, on the west end. Lifeguards, parking, restrooms, and equipment rentals are available from April through October. Turn just before the gates to Kiawah to find the park. The ocean frontage is somewhat off-the-beaten-path, thus allowing for eleven miles of unspoiled sand and surf. A $5 fee is required per car.

We can cautiously recommend the beaches on Sullivan's Island and the Isle of Palms, but urge parents to keep several general cautions in mind before you send the

Sun and sand keep little hands busy for hours. PHOTO: THOMAS P. FORD

kids skipping to the surf. Note that strong, tricky currents are prevalent at each end of Sullivan's Island as well as the south end of the Isle of Palms. Convenient parking can be tough to find on both islands, but the Isle of Palms County Park, (843) 886-3863, located mid-island, offers lots of parking and lifeguards on duty during the summer months for a $5-per-car entrance fee. Walk-ins and bicycles are admitted at the three beach parks at no charge. (Our Parks and Recreation chapter offers more information on all of these parks.)

Cultural Fun

Charleston Ballet School
477 King St., Charleston
(843) 723-7334

If your youngsters fancy standing on their tippy-toes, put that talent to good use by enrolling them in the Charleston Ballet Theatre's official school. Classes in creative movement, ballet, and jazz dance for ages 3 and older are offered. While the school's graduates dance with major companies throughout the country, students without professional ambition are welcome. The school and its parent theater company are located in a new King Street facility downtown, just a block from the Charleston Visitor Reception and Transportation Center. Call the number above for class offerings and fees. Regular ballet performances and Spoleto tickets are $15 for adults and $10 for children. Season tickets for five performances are $125 with discounts for children younger than 18 and seniors. The annual *Nutcracker* ballet, performed by many of the ballet school students during the Christmas season, is a longstanding favorite. (See The Arts chapter for more on the Charleston Ballet Theatre.)

The Charleston Museum
360 Meeting St., Charleston
(843) 722-2996

In addition to being the oldest history, art, and science museum in the country (founded in 1773), The Charleston Museum is one of the best resources for children in the city. We love to try to keep pace with the kids as they scamper through the modern complex (the facility is well designed and very kid-older-than-4 friendly). There are interesting classes

throughout the year—with such titles as "Babies, Bunnies, and Beasties," "Treasure's Ahoy," and "Mummies, Monsters, and Make-Believe"—that usually last one afternoon session and cost about $8. We've found that starting off on a rainy day in the Discover Me room, with its "touch-me" exhibits, is the best way for little ones to unwind and connect with the museum. The museum is across the street from the visitor center. It is open 9 AM to 5 PM Monday through Saturday and 1 to 5 PM on Sunday. Admission is $8 for adults and teens and $4 for children ages 3 to 12. Free parking is available in a small lot behind the museum. (For more information, see our Attractions chapter.)

Gibbes Museum of Art
135 Meeting St., Charleston
(843) 722-2706
Gibbes Museum of Art Studio
76 Queen St., Charleston
(843) 577-7275

The Gibbes is a source of pride for many Charlestonians. Not only are the collections impressive, but the facility itself and enthusiasm of the membership also spark creativity in the young and old alike. Studio art classes at the Gibbes are very popular with Charleston children. From drawing to working with clay to watercolor art or photography, the offerings appeal to many levels of artistic interest and skill. Classes cost between $65 and $95, and semesters run about eight weeks.

"Sensational Saturdays!" are family-oriented programs for ages 3 and older held one Saturday a month from September through March (except December). Gallery visits, games, and hands-on art

"Tom Sawyer" courts "Becky Thatcher" in a recent youth production of the Mark Twain classic at the Dock Street Theatre. PHOTO: COURTESY OF CHARLESTON STAGE COMPANY

activities for children and parents are presented between 10 AM and noon. Admission is $1 for children who are Gibbes members, $4 for nonmember children, and parents are free.

One Sunday during October, November, February, and March the Gibbes, in conjunction with the Charleston Symphony Orchestra, hosts Small Fry Concerts especially for children ages 2 to 10, parents, and grandparents. The Conductor presents programs at 2 and 3:30 PM to the delight of the children gathered around on floor cushions. An instrument petting zoo allows children to try out the musical instruments. Tickets are $8 available at the Gibbes the day of the concert or $25 for the season. And with exhibits ranging from the contemporary to the abstract, a simple visit to the museum any time can be a visual thrill. Hours are 10 AM to 5 PM Tuesday through Saturday and 1 to 5 PM on Sunday. The museum is closed on Mondays. Adult admission is $7 (with a $1 break for seniors, military personnel, and college students); for children 6 to 18, $5. Annual family memberships are $60, and they include a 10 percent discount on museum shop purchases and classes. (For more on the Gibbes, see our chapters on The Arts and Attractions.)

Charleston Stage Company
Theatre School
Dock Street Theatre, 133 Church Street,
Charleston
(843) 577-5967

"All the world's a stage"...and maybe your youngster would like a chance to learn more about it. Charleston Stage is a prime creative outlet for that dramatist in the family. The Theatre School offers a variety of acting and theatre education opportunities for children in grades K–12. The program introduces theatrical skills in classes designed to enhance acting skills, bolster self-confidence, and encourage self-expression. Advanced students may participate in KidsRep, the performing troupe for middle school students and TheatreWings, the apprentice program for high school students. The Theatre School students are encouraged also to audition for roles in the Charleston Stage's Main-Stage and KidStage productions each season. Classes are offered year round in two-week summer sessions to weekly afternoon classes throughout the school year at the Dock Street Theatre downtown and in their rehearsal studios in Northcutt Plaza in Mt. Pleasant.

Indoor Fun and Games

American Theater
446 King St., Charleston
(843) 853-0246

Make your child a "star" for the day and line up his or her next birthday at the American Theater "Stars" room. What birthday child wouldn't be delighted to see their name in lights on the marquee? Saturday and Sunday afternoons the party starts 30 minutes prior to the film screening so that children can gather to sing happy birthday, blow out the candles (you provide the cake), and open presents. During the movie food, beverages, and cake are served. Three birthday packages are available depending on the menu selected and range from $6.50 to $11 per person with a 10-person minimum. The Saturday and Sunday matinees all year long are shown for kids and make for a fun afternoon's entertainment.

Carolina Ice Palace
7665 Northwoods Blvd., North Charleston
(843) 572-2717

Charleston's coolest place for family fun is the Carolina Ice Palace with two NHL-size ice rinks for recreational skating, instruction, hockey teams and leagues, and birthday parties. Open seven days a week for you to perfect that double axle, the Ice Palace's general-public hours are 11 AM to 3 PM Monday through Friday with after-school skating from 3 to 5:30 PM Monday, Wednesday, and Friday. The palace is also open from 7 to 9 PM Monday through Wednesday, and Thursday night is family night with a $25 package of skate rentals, pizza, and soda for a family of four. Friday and Saturday hours extend to 11:30 PM, and Sunday hours are 1:30 to 6 PM. Other on-site attractions are the video arcade, virtual reality center, and giant pro shop for skate rental and sharpening. Burgers and pizza can take care of the hungries and an alcohol-free lounge with satellite TV provides a little relaxation while watching your future Olympic star. Admission prices are $5 for children 4 to 12 and seniors, $2 for children 3 and younger, $6 for adults with a $2 charge for skate rental. After-school skating is $4 including skate rental. Discount coupon books offer savings for 12 admissions. Skating and hockey classes conducted by professional instructors are available on a group or individual basis.

Charleston County Library Storytimes
68 Calhoun St., Charleston
(843) 805-6893

"Tell me a story, please." Charleston County Libraries have the answer. They offer a series of storytimes for young children ages 12 months to 8 years old. "Wee Reads" is a 20-minute weekly morning program for ages 12 to 23 months. "Time for Twos" is another weekly morning program lasting 30 minutes for ages 24 to 36 months. All toddlers must be accompanied by a parent or caregiver. There is a pre-school storytime for ages 3 to 6 which includes 30 minutes of interactive storytelling, sometimes with videos and crafts. Children 6 and under may come in their pajamas for the evening "Sleepytime Storytime" to hear stories and sing songs. Call the number above or your branch library to register. (See our Education chapter for a list of branch libraries.)

Christian Family Y
21 George St., Charleston
(843) 723-6473, (843) 853-5453

The Christian Family Y has been a part of the Charleston community since 1903, offering dozens of programs and services for children and adults. With the completion of the Lindstedt-Hawk Aquatics and Fitness Center, the Y has one of the best pool facilities in town, complete with a lap and therapy pool. The children's swim programs at the Family Y include parent-tot swim sessions for ages 6 months to 3 years, children's swim lessons, and birthday swim parties. (The Y supplies the pool and lifeguards; you bring the cake and ice cream.) Other children's classes at the Y include karate, dance, cheerleading, and ceramics. Red Cross Babysitting Certification and Proper Manners for Children also fill a need for training youngsters. Call the Family Y for a schedule of current programs. Memberships are $25 for adults and $15 for seniors 55 and older and children 16 and younger. Pool membership costs an additional fee starting at $95 for individuals or $90 for senior citizens. Family memberships are available too and vary according to family size. Swimming parties are $75 for up to 15 children, with additional children admitted for $3 each. The two-hour parties are offered from 11 AM to 3 PM on Saturdays.

Frankie's Fun Park
5000 Ashley Phosphate Rd.,
North Charleston
(843) 767-1376

This is Charleston's answer to the kiddies' cry for an amusement park. Kids can spend money on a variety of activities—from bumper boats and a batting cage to go-carts and the "trampoline thing." A rock-climbing wall offers another challenge. Two miniature golf courses and a lighted, 90-position driving range offer a slower-paced, less gravity-defying experience. There is no general admission, but park activities cost between $1 and $4.50 each. A family with two kids can expect to spend $20 to $30 at Frankie's if Mom and

Dad don't participate; it'll likely be $40 or more if everyone joins in. There are picnic tables, a snack bar, and clean restrooms. Hours are nine to midnight Monday through Sunday during the summer. Otherwise, its noon to 9 PM Monday through Friday, 10 AM to 11 PM Saturday, and noon to 9 PM on Sunday. Frankie's is closed on Thanksgiving, Christmas Eve, and Christmas.

South Carolina Aquarium
100 Aquarium Wharf, (near Calhoun and Concord Sts.), Charleston
(843) 720-1990

The newest major attraction in Charleston is the South Carolina Aquarium, opened in May 2000. Located at the edge of historic Charleston harbor, two-thirds of the building projects over the water and multiple decks complete the views of the Cooper River, both the bustling activity of the shipping industry and the serene natural landscape. The Aquarium interprets South Carolina's diverse variety of habi-tats from mountain streams to the depths of the Atlantic Ocean. The 93,000-square-foot facility displays more than 60 exhibits representing over 500 species with 10,000 living organisms. Otters, birds, turtles, fish, reptiles, aquatic invertebrates, and insects are all a part of the habitats here. Visitors will experience five major regions of the Southeast Watershed of South Carolina: the Blue Ridge Mountains, the Piedmont, the Coastal Plain, the Coast, and the Ocean. The Education Master Plan, developed with local teachers, naturalists, and community leaders, encompasses interactive displays, special Toddler Exhibits, an Education Center, a Discovery Lab, and several Education Stations. August 16 through June 14, the hours are 9 AM to 5 PM; June 15 through August 15 hours are 9 AM to 6 PM. Adult admission is $14, teens 13 to 17 are $12, and children 4 to 12 are $7. (See our Attractions chapter for more on the South Carolina Aquarium.)

Teaching youngsters about the Lowcountry's maritime habitat is part of the South Carolina Aquarium's primary mission. PHOTO: COURTESY OF SOUTH CAROLINA AQUARIUM

Day Camps

Many community centers, schools, and churches operate day camps around the Trident. Extended-day programs are available for many working parents and run from the end of the school day until 6 or 6:30 PM at most schools and centers. Like camps, some offer enrichment courses such as karate, piano, foreign language study, drama, and arts and crafts.

Charleston County After School
Charleston County Community Education,
75 Calhoun St., Charleston
(843) 937-6421, (843) 762-2172
Working parents of school-age children will be glad to take advantage of the extended-day programs available in many of the local public elementary and middle schools. These programs provide a safe, supervised, and educational environment at your child's own school. This affordable after-school alternative offers organized activities, snacks, and time to complete homework assignments, and many have a selection of enrichment courses. The average cost is $30 a week, but it varies by school and activity. The following community school directors' offices can provide additional information:

Downtown, (843) 724-7276 or (843) 529-3926; Mt. Pleasant, (843) 849-2829; North Charleston, (843) 566-1839 or (843) 764-2236; James Island, (843) 762-2793; Johns Island, (843) 559-6460; West Ashley, (843) 763-1552 or (843) 763-1599; McClellanville, 887-3244; Yonges Island, (843) 889-6852.

Davis Community Center,
4800 Park Cir., North Charleston
(843) 745-1028
The recreation department offers after-school programs at all 20 community center locations throughout North Charleston. Supervisors direct help with homework, games, sports, and arts and crafts. No fee is charged. Contact the number listed for more information.

Summer Camps

It has an all-too-familiar ring: "Mom, Dad, I'm bored."

Once school is out, you better have a plan to keep the kids occupied and happy on those never-ending, lazy summer days. Fortunately, several of the recreation departments, county parks, private schools, arts organizations, churches, and scout groups around the Trident area offer summer day-camp adventures. Lots of fun stuff is organized to pique your child's interest in something new or improve skills in a favorite pastime. Some of the day camps with a mix of activities are listed below, plus a few sports- and arts-oriented camps. Prices may vary slightly.

Brickhouse Plantation
Summer Riding Camps
Brickhouse Plantation Equestrian Center,
2669 Hamilton Rd., Johns Island
(843) 559-2867
Giddy-up and go! Brickhouse Plantation's equestrian center provides professional instruction, marvelous facilities, and an ongoing commitment to safety. Beginner, intermediate, advanced, and adult camps are offered with hunt seat, dressage, cross-country, hunter jumper events and vaulting riding styles. The one-week sessions run during June and July and are sure to

make a horse lover out of anyone. The camps last from 8 AM to 2 PM Monday through Friday. What fun! Fees are in the $250 per week range. (See the Horseback Riding section of our Parks and Recreation chapter for more information.)

The Citadel Basketball Camp
McAlister Field House, The Citadel,
Charleston
(843) 953-5286, (843) 723-2005
Citadel head basketball coach Patrick Dennis serves as camp director of this popular, 20+-year-old basketball program

for boys and girls ages 6 to 16. The staff includes Citadel basketball coaches, area high school coaches, and collegiate players. The younger Bulldog campers (ages 6 to 8) play on scaled-down facilities, and all instruction takes place in McAlister Field House, where the big Bulldogs play their college games. The one-week sessions run from 9 AM to 4 PM on Monday through Thursday and from 9 AM to noon on Friday. Fees are $175 for the week ($165 before May 1), or send two or more children for $155 each. The Citadel also offers baseball, soccer, tennis, and wrestling camps. Contact the school's athletic department for more information. (For more on The Citadel's academic offerings, see our Education chapter.)

City of Charleston
Junior Summer Tennis Camp
Charleston Tennis Center,
19 Farmfield Ave., Charleston
(843) 724-7401

The city's Junior Summer Tennis Camp has an excellent program for your budding tennis enthusiast. The camp is for beginners to advanced intermediate students and meets from 9 AM to noon Monday through Friday. Daily instruction includes working on fundamental strokes, video analysis, and personal attention. Games and prizes add to the positive, fun environment. Fees are $65 for one week and $120 for two consecutive weeks. (See the Tennis section of our Parks and Recreation chapter for more information.)

Co-ed Summerfest
Ashley Hall, 172 Rutledge Ave.,
Charleston
(843) 965-8485, (843) 722-4088

Ashley Hall's campus provides a perfect in-town setting for summer programs designed to entertain, educate, and challenge your children. (See our Education chapter for more on Ashley Hall.) Day camps, athletics, enrichment adventures, academic skills, and computer workshops

> ## Insiders' Tip
> Plan to bring swimsuits but leave the coolers at home for your day at Splash Island or Splash Zone at Palmetto Islands or James Island County Park. Proper swimming attire is required, and no outside food or beverages are allowed.

let you sign 'em up for a variety of sessions throughout those long summer months. The day camps keep campers on the go with tennis, swimming, gymnastics, group games, and arts and crafts. Athletic challenges sap up some of that boundless energy with basketball, volleyball, dance, soccer, scuba, swimming, and tae kwon do.

The enrichment adventures allow students to explore and develop new interests in areas such as basic photography, marine biology, fiction writing, and French. Computer skills and a study and reading skills workshop are some of the academic offerings Contact the school for a complete brochure outlining sessions. Day-camp sessions cost $125 per one-week session with an additional $10 a day for extended days. Athletic challenges start at $35 a week and go up to $90. The enrichment adventures begin at $25 and climb to $60. The Study and Reading Skills Workshop is $225.

Creative Spark
757 Long Point Rd., Mt. Pleasant
(843) 881-3780

Let your child's creativity and imagination be sparked. Creative Spark Center for the Arts presents a wonderful variety of summer camps in the performing and visual arts to do just that. Art, an improvisational drama workshop, and musical theater camps, along with creative writing, dance, and private music instruction, are among the choices for ages 3 and older. Call the above number for a complete brochure with details on sessions. The art camps cost $170 for one two-week session with a 20% sibling or multi-camp discount. The creative camp combines acting, singing, playing instruments, and making artistic creations for $130 for two weeks. Creative writing is $55. Dance classes range from $15 to $60, and music classes are $60 up to $150 for every eight lessons. Birthday parties with an art, music, or dance theme are fun options here. A cake, favors, activities, supervision, and cleanup are provided for up to 12 for $150 on Saturdays.

East Cooper Gymnastics
497 La Mesa St., Mt. Pleasant
(843) 849-6668
Preschool- and kindergarten-level camps

are offered in June and July for $75 to $125 a week. The goal of each camp is to provide a fun and relaxed atmosphere where each child can build strength, flexibility, and coordination. Instruction covers vault, bars, beam, tumbling, and Tumbl-Trak. Campers also have play time in the tumble jungle—an indoor, soft playground.

Junior Kids Art Camp
Colorful Kids Art Camp
Gibbes Museum of Art Studio,
76 Queen St., Charleston
(843) 577-7275
Hands-on art and imaginary travels await your 4½- to 6½-year-old at the Junior Kids Art Camp at the Gibbes studio. Each of the three one-week sessions encourages creativity, helps develop fine motor skills, and builds confidence. Classes like "Jurassic Art" (drawing and painting Earth's prehistoric creatures) and "Magical Masks" (making tribal and masquerade

Shining faces, beautiful faces: That's life for kids in the Lowcountry. PHOTO: THOMAS P. FORD

masks) are sure to get those little hands busy. Camps meet Monday through Thursday from 1 to 3:30 PM. Tuition is $85 a week for Gibbes members, $95 per week for non-members, or $205 for members and $250 for non-members for all three weeks.

The Colorful Kids Art Camp is for ages 7 to 12 and focuses on learning about different artists (and their styles) each week. Offerings have included "Picasso's Faces," where students learn to draw faces by painting portraits of classmates as well as a self-portrait. "O'Keeffe's Flowers," "Caulder's Mobiles," and "Van Gogh's Landscapes" carry on the famous-artist projects, stimulating your child's own artistic expression. The Colorful Kids camps meet Monday through Thursday from 1 to 4 PM. Tuition is $85 per week for Gibbes members, $100 a week for non-members, or $335 for members, $410 for non-members for all five weeks. (See our Attractions chapter for more about the Gibbes Museum of Art and the Gibbes Studio.)

Summer Fun on the Island Day Camp
James Island Recreation Complex,
1088 Quail Dr., Charleston
(843) 720-3808

Sponsored by the City of Charleston Department of Recreation, Summer Fun on the Island is a camp for youth between the ages of 6 and 12 years old. Monday through Friday from 9 AM to 3 PM, campers are engaged in arts and crafts, swimming, storytelling, movies, music, aerobics, and gymnastics divided by age groups. Once a week, campers venture out on field trips to great spots such as James Island and Folly Beach County Parks, Middleton Place, Riverbanks Zoo, and Splash Zone. Five sessions are offered from June to mid-August, with fees for city residents set at $125 per session. Non-residents of the city pay $150 per session.

Lowcountry Daytrips

It Was (Once) All about Rice . . .

Summerville, Flower-town in the Pines

A Walk on the Wildside

The Story of Santee

Cancel

Here are some daytrip adventures into the very heart of the Lowcountry—great excuses to go afield in search of unusual fun and a deeper understanding of what makes this area unique.

The first is a day-long journey into a land of winding rivers offering a fascinating look at some of South Carolina's early rice plantation history. The second will allow you to spend an afternoon discovering a real Lowcountry gem, Summerville, and all the strange twists of fate that have led to its various incarnations: railroad boomtown, international health resort haven, and azalea paradise (a title the community still proudly boasts). The third is a morning walk on the Lowcountry's wild side—along Marrington Watchable Wildlife Trail near the town of Goose Creek in Berkeley County. A fourth daytrip is a must for families with school-age children—Old Santee Canal State Park up in Moncks Corner. Kids and parents alike enjoy the interactive adventures at the park, where the Lowcountry's days of canal-building and horse-drawn barges are revisited.

It Was (Once) All about Rice . . .

In the 18th and early 19th centuries, this Lowcountry land and its waters spawned a rich, romantic, fragile culture largely based on a single cash crop—rice. Any real understanding of the Lowcountry and its ethic includes an appreciation for rice and the major role it played in the development of the area.

To that end, on our first daytrip we will visit the sleepy fishing village of McClellanville—once a cool summer home for old rice plantation families, more recently the brave survivor of 1989's devastating Hurricane Hugo.

We'll pay a call on two important 18th-century rice plantations presented to the public in totally different, but equally valid, ways. And we'll explore old Georgetown, formerly the "Rice Capital of the Carolinas." On the way, we'll encounter charming little chapels of ease that served the faithful plantation dwellers so far flung and isolated in South Carolina's earlier days.

And finally, we'll wander the quiet paths of Brookgreen Gardens, a unique and unexpected museum of 19th- and 20th-century American sculpture, built on rice plantation lands once granted to Lowcountry colonists by King George II of England.

Start at the foot of Charleston's Cooper River Bridge on U.S. Highway 17 N. Follow the signs on the bridge for Georgetown and Hwy. 17-701. Do not take the right lane at the end of the bridge leading to the village of Mt. Pleasant.

The Cooper River Bridges

Once described as "a new traffic epoch" by its Jazz Age builders, the old Cooper River Bridge on your left is now the overcrowded, often-cursed foil for rush-hour commuters to and from peninsular Charleston. Officially named the John P. Grace Memorial Bridge, in honor of a former Charleston mayor, the span was the fifth-longest suspension bridge in the world when it opened in 1929. It took 14 months to complete, at a cost of 14 bridge workers' lives and more than $5.7 million. Its narrow, roller-coaster 2.7-mile ride provides a spectacular view of the Cooper River for some travelers, sweaty palms and a pounding heart for many others. In 1946, the freighter Nicaragua Victory, adrift in gale-force winds, crashed into the eastern approach of the bridge, tearing away a 100-yard section of the roadway and sending one car carrying a family of five to a watery grave below. So vital was this single Charleston-to-Mt. Pleasant traffic link that an old iron bridge was barged in to serve as a temporary patch. Huge cranes hoisted it up to the span so cars could gingerly cross while permanent repairs were planned.

By 1966, increasing traffic and an impatient public demanded better access to and from the Peninsula, so a second, wider span was added. The new bridge was named the Silas N. Pearman Bridge, in honor of a South Carolina commissioner of public works. Both bridges, now obsolete, are scheduled to be replaced with a new, state-of-the-art span sometime in the first few years of the new millennium. The new bridge is to be named for long-time local politician and South Carolina State Senator Arthur Ravenel. The bridge is currently in its final design phase.

Continue along the U.S. 17 Bypass for about 8 miles through commercial development. Then look to your right for a small, tin-roofed chapel with an octagonal cupola. Pull into the churchyard through the open gate.

Christ Episcopal Church
2304 U.S. Hwy. 17 N., Charleston
(843) 884-9090

Here's your first chance to encounter one of the Lowcountry's most charming undiscovered treasures, one of the little-known but much-loved chapels of ease (see the Close-up on chapels of ease in our Worship chapter). Millions of tourists visit the area and never even know these little testimonies to the Lowcountry's bygone plantation era still exist. Amazingly they do exist, in various forms and in varied states of repair and use. First, however, a little background information is required.

The colony of Carolina was founded with the Anglican Church as its established religious force. Early on, Anglican congregations received financial assistance from the British government to construct houses of worship. These first Anglican churches also tended to benefit from the generosity of wealthy planters in their congregations. As a result, these churches were built with greater architectural sophistication than the early buildings of other religious organizations. And it's mostly these better-built, early Anglican structures that survive today as mute witness to the strength of religion in the early colonies and the isolation of plantation life.

Christ Church Parish was one of 10 parishes established by the Church Act of 1706. The following year, a wooden building was in place on this site, serving a slowly growing number of communicants. After fire destroyed the wooden building in 1725, a brick structure was completed in 1726.

In 1782, British soldiers burned the church to the walls during the Revolution, and it wasn't restored until about 1800. In 1865, during the Civil War, fire all but destroyed the church again, and although it was once more rebuilt, regular services were discontinued by 1874. Finally, in 1925, both the structure and the congregation were restored by caring descendants of early Christ Church parish families. Despite its long, hard struggle for survival, Christ Church is a viable, active congregation today. Sunday services offer Holy Eucharist at 8, 9, and 11:15 AM.

Chances are, your initial excursions into the Lowcountry's plantation past (including many of the sites documented in our Attractions chapter) led you along the Ashley River, not the Cooper. If so, you missed the opportu-

nity to visit some of the vast plantations that once flourished along the Cooper. First, we'll stop at Snee Farm, country home of one of America's founding fathers, Charles Pinckney (1757–1824), then we'll visit one of America's most photographed plantations, Boone Hall.

To find Snee Farm and Boone Hall Plantation, cross the four-lane highway opposite Christ Church to Long Point Road and look for the sign. Less than a mile up Longpoint Road on your left is the entrance to Snee Farm.

Snee Farm
1254 Long Point Rd., Mt. Pleasant
(843) 881-5516, (843) 883-3123

Only 28 acres remain of what was once the expansive Snee Farm, Colonial plantation home of Charles Pinckney, a major molder of the U.S. Constitution. But those relatively few acres are fast becoming a home-base for thousands of African Americans who come to the Lowcountry seeking more information about their heritage and the important role Charleston plays in that story.

Let's begin with Charles Pinckney, the man. He began his public career at age 22, when he was admitted to the South Carolina Bar and the South Carolina General Assembly. Pinckney served as one of four South Carolina delegates at the Constitutional Convention in Philadelphia. He served as governor of South Carolina, was ambassador to Spain from 1801 to 1805, and held seats in both the state and national legislature. He retired from public life in 1821 and died three years later.

Originally, Snee Farm was part of a 500-acre royal grant awarded in 1698 to Richard Butler. By 1754, the farm comprised 715 acres and was purchased that year by Pinckney's father. The property was the family's "country seat" and an integral part of Charles Pinckney's life. Like many other Charleston aristocrats, Pinckney relied on slave labor (mostly imported from West Africa) to raise the "Carolina gold" (rice) that grew on Snee Farm.

Today, the contributions of those people of African descent are being unearthed by National Park Service archaeologists.

Historians working behind the scenes are following the threads of African contributions to the Lowcountry culture in the fields of language, diet, agriculture, mechanics, and craftsmanship. And the Pinckney site is a rich resource for this information.

The present house on the site, built in the 1820s, is an excellent and charming example of the type of coastal cottage once common here in the Lowcountry. Guests will find interesting interpretive exhibits in and around the house. There's an informative 18-minute video telling of Charles Pinckney, Snee Farm, George Washington's Colonial-era visit to the property and the United States as a young, emerging nation. Park hours are from 9 AM to 5 PM. Admission is absolutely free, a real bargain.

Turn left back onto Long Point Road, and less than a mile down the way is Boone Hall's entrance.

Boone Hall Plantation
1235 Long Point Rd., Mt. Pleasant
(843) 884-4371

Today's Boone Hall Plantation is a 738-acre estate dating back to the 1680s, when the Lords Proprietor made this sizable land grant to an early English settler, Maj. John Boone.

During the 18th and 19th centuries, Boone Hall was a thriving cotton plantation covering more than 17,000 acres. Brick was also a plantation product and was used in the construction of the original mansion, cotton gin house, slave cabins, and circular smokehouse. Later, Boone Hall was famous for its large groves of pecan trees, many of which are still productive today.

Boone Hall is a favorite of photographers and filmmakers because of its magnificent avenue of live oaks and the nine original, unrestored slave cabins (c. 1743) that once housed the plantation's skilled craftspeople and house servants. The original Boone Hall mansion was lost in a tragic fire. The present structure dates

Close-up

Angel Oak: A Lowcountry Treasure

Don't laugh, but we're about to suggest taking a drive to the countryside of Johns Island for the sole purpose of seeing . . . a tree.

That's right, a tree. It's an oak tree, but it's a very special one, a very old one, and a very famous one.

The tree is called Angel Oak, and everything about it is pure Lowcountry. No visitor has really seen the Charleston area without making the trip out to the island—to be summarily awed and embraced by the Angel Oak's mighty outstretched arms.

Let's start with some background information.

Live oak trees (*Quercus virginiana*) are native to the Lowcountry and found throughout the area, but they are especially common on the sea islands. During the 18th and 19th centuries, lumber from the live oak forests was highly valued for shipbuilding. In fact, most of the area's ancient live oaks were harvested during those two centuries.

This live oak, however, survived. Angel Oak has been reported to be in excess of 1,400 years old, although the exact age is difficult to calculate. Very old live oaks are prone to heart rot (they become hollow at the center), which makes core sample ring-counting unreliable. This much is documented: Angel Oak is only 65 feet tall, yet its circumference is 25½ feet. The area of shade under this huge canopy is an incredible 17,000 square feet, and the longest outstretched limb reaches out 89 feet and has a circumference of more than 11 feet.

Clearly, the Angel Oak is ancient. It knew the Lowcountry long before the English settlers arrived. It was already an old tree when the Kiawah tribe lived on this land and no doubt enjoyed its shade. It knows more than any of us ever will about hurricanes, wars, fires, earthquakes, and time. To see it is to gain worthwhile perspective on the entire Lowcountry environment.

The property where the Angel Oak stands was originally part of a land grant to Abraham

The Angel Oak may be the oldest living thing east of the Mississippi River. PHOTO: FLETCHER NEWBERN

Waight in 1717. Waight became a prosperous planter with several plantations in the Low-country, including one known as The Point, where the Angel Oak stands. The property passed through generations of the Waight family, acquiring the Angel name when Martha Waight married a Justis Angel in 1810.

The Angel family plantation was sold in 1959 to the Mutual Land and Development Corp., but a small parcel of land and the old tree itself were held back and leased to the South Carolina Agricultural Society for $1 a year. The society cared for the tree until 1964, when it became the property of an S.E. Felkel, who eventually fenced in the tree and charged visitors a small fee to view it.

The City of Charleston acquired the Angel Oak property in 1991, and it was opened to the public with no admission fee on September 23, 1991. Generations of Charlestonians have journeyed to the property for picnics, family reunions, weddings and private parties. Permits are required for large events and the consumption of alcoholic beverages at the site.

You won't regret making the effort to visit the old Angel Oak. It's part and parcel of the Lowcountry experience. To get there, take U.S. 17 to Main Road, looking for the signs to Kiawah and Seabrook. After Main Road crosses Maybank Highway to become Bohicket Road, look for Angel Oak Road on your right. Signs mark your route to this magnificent tree of life. For more information, call (843) 559-3496.

from the mid-1930s. Extensive location filming was done here for the ABC-TV miniseries "North and South."

Admission is $12.50 for adults and teens and $6 for children 6 through 12. The property is open every day except Thanksgiving and Christmas. Hours are Monday through Saturday from 9 AM to 5 PM and Sunday from 1 to 4 PM. From April 1 through Labor Day, hours extend to 8:30 AM to 6:30 PM on weekdays and 1 to 5 PM on Sundays. (For more on Boone Hall, see our Attractions chapter.)

Return to U.S. 17, and turn left. (Note that this is a four-lane highway, and use extreme caution while crossing the two oncoming lanes before turning left.) Follow U.S. 17 and note the signs designating the Francis Marion National Forest on both sides of the highway.

Francis Marion National Forest
U.S. Hwy. 17 N.
(843) 336-3248, (843) 887-3257

This quarter-million-acre tract includes sections of both Charleston and Berkeley Counties. Once the battleground where the legendary Gen. Francis Marion—the Swamp Fox—engaged Col. Banastre Tar-

leton's British troops during the American Revolution, this vast park is now a wildlife reserve and a microcosm of the Lowcountry's natural habitat.

Here, as in no other place, the power and destructive range of 1989's Hurricane Hugo is dramatically apparent. The tall, mature forest was completely devastated by the storm, yet nature's recovery process is equally fascinating. Today, what is most obvious to passing visitors is not the storm's aftermath but the lush thicket of natural regrowth that has appeared over the past several years.

The Francis Marion National Forest offers a wide variety of recreational activities, including picnicking and camping sites, boat ramps, fishing ponds, rifle ranges, and hiking, horse, and motorcycle trails. For more information, contact the Witherbee District Ranger in Moncks Corner or the Wambaw District Ranger in McClellanville at the numbers listed. (For more on camping options in Francis Marion National Forest, see our Parks and Recreation chapter.)

Continue on U.S. 17. At about mile marker 33, look for the sign on the right marking the intersection of S.C. Highway 45. Turn right to discover McClellanville.

McClellanville

This sleepy old fishing village, nestled among the live oaks along Jeremy Creek, was once the summer haven for rice planters living along the Santee River. More recently, however, McClellanville is best known as one of the small towns where residents bravely and miraculously survived Hurricane Hugo in 1989.

Eons before the town was known as McClellanville, it was one of the small villages occupied by the Sewee Indians. Archaeology shows it's one of the few sites in South Carolina that have been continuously occupied by humans for thousands of years.

The beginnings of the existing village date back to the mid-1800s, when riceplanters on the Santee River built retreats here, away from the disease-ridden backwater plantations. A devastating hurricane in 1822 had completely wiped out a village of planter homes on nearby Cedar Island, and the new site was thought to be safer from storms. After the Civil War, economics forced some of the area planters to completely abandon their large plantations and move into the little summer village on a permanent basis.

McClellanville wasn't actually "McClellan-ville" for many years, until it became necessary to christen it something for postal and other municipal purposes. Several names were discussed, including "Jeremy" or "Jerryville," after the creek of the same name. Even "Romain" was considered, after Cape Romain. But the village was finally named McClellanville for one of its early citizens, A.J. McClellan.

In the 1920s, it became one of the first places in the state where shrimpers from the west coast of Florida would come to trawl the rich coastal waters. Eventually, the town developed into one of the major shrimp ports in the state. The old buildings in McClellanville reflect the architectural development of the town from a summer retreat for plantation families to a thriving, incorporated municipality. You'll find residential, commercial, religious, and educational properties dating from the 1860s to the 1930s.

Of the hundreds of thousands of stories spawned by the forces of Hurricane Hugo on September 21, 1989, the story of McClellanville is among the most memorable.

A small plaque has been placed on a wall near the cafeteria door in McClellanville's Lincoln High School. It's a little more than 6 feet above the floor, and it shows how high the water rose that night. But no 8-by-10-inch plaque can measure the level of fear experienced by the 400 or so people who had gathered at the school for shelter against the storm.

In the pitch-black night, as the storm center pushed violently over peninsular Charleston some 35 miles to the south, the accompanying tidal surge rushed in on McClellanville with horrendous force and speed. The school was a designated storm shelter, and what was almost the entire population of the town had just settled in for what they hoped would be only a moderately uncomfortable night. There was excitement, to be sure. And dread. And worry. But the primary concern was getting the children and older people settled in as comfortably as possible. To that end, people were scattered throughout the building in various hallways and classrooms. Suddenly, they heard a strange, rushing noise above the already fierce storm. The cold, black water of Hugo's tidal surge rushed in from everywhere, pinning the exit doors shut and turning the school into a nightmarish death trap.

Some people scrambled onto the bleachers in the gymnasium as the waters quickly climbed after them. Others crowded up onto the school's stage and literally held their children over their heads as the water surged in up to their chests. They sang and prayed, cried and comforted each other throughout the seemingly endless night. Finally, the water began to recede. What the stunned survivors found outside by dawn's earliest light was unrecognizable.

Amazingly, no one drowned in the McClellanville calamity at Lincoln High School. One life was lost, later (a heart attack victim). But it could easily have been a disaster costing hundreds of lives. Today, McClellanville is remarkably recovered. If you drive into the village via Pinckney Street, note the "new" Wappetaw Presbyterian Church (c. 1830) on the right. Turn right on Oak Street and drive about two blocks to St. James Santee Episcopal Church. There, the congregation dates back to 1706. This charmingly pure, shingled Gothic structure was built in 1890. Don't leave town before you drive up to the docks for a view of the McClellanville shrimp fleet harbored along the Intracoastal Waterway.

Return to U.S. 17 via Pinckney Street and turn right. About 100 yards up the road, a sign marks the intersection of S. Santee Road (marked S.C. 857). Turn left and follow it about 2 miles to the entrance of Hampton Plantation.

Hampton Plantation
1950 Rutledge Rd., McClellanville
(843) 546-9361

The origins of Hampton Plantation (c. 1750) can be traced back to the earliest European settlement of the Santee delta. The Horry family, who built and developed the property, were descendants of French Huguenots who had immigrated to Carolina in search of religious freedom and economic advancement.

The Horrys are thought to have acquired the land on which Hampton now stands during the period between 1700 and 1730. The actual date of construction for Hampton's main house is not known, but according to early records, Col. Daniel Horry built it around 1750.

The Horry land holdings on Wambaw Creek comprised some 5,000 acres, and they all were worked by slaves like most other Lowcountry plantations at the time. Rice was grown on the swamplands along the water, and these fields were connected by a complicated system of canals and ditches. The fields were flooded and drained as the demands of the rice-growing season required.

Indigo—used in the dyeing of wool— was another Hampton cash crop. For a time, there was a profitable demand for indigo because England used it in vast quantities for the dyeing of British naval uniforms. In fact, the Daniel Horry who supposedly built Hampton Plantation married the daughter of the famous South Carolina woman Eliza Lucas Pinckney, who is credited with growing the first successful indigo crop in the Lowcountry.

During the American Revolution, while most of the prominent men were off engaging the British enemy at various locations, a colony of wives and children sought refuge at Hampton—relatively isolated from the military action. The dozen or so ladies sheltered there represented something of a Who's Who of South Carolina Colonial history. Women with names such as Drayton, Middleton, Rutledge, Izard, and Huger were in attendance at various times.

Hampton's famous portico played an interesting role in the plantation's long story. It may have been built specifically to impress one of Hampton's distinguished early visitors. In 1791, President George Washington made a grand tour through the still very young United States of America. On May 5, according to Washington's own diary, he "breakfasted and dined at Mrs. Horry's about 16 miles from Georgetown." The traditional story is that as the president was brought up the steps of the glorious new portico at Hampton, Mrs. Horry and her mother, along with the youngest Horry daughter, greeted Washington wearing "sashes and bandeaux" hand-painted with likenesses of the president.

Another story is that Washington was asked whether a young oak tree growing directly in front of the house should be removed to improve the view. The president is supposed to have suggested the tree be spared, and so it was. At any rate, what remains of a giant old live oak can still be seen today directly in front of the house.

Circumstances found the actual welfare of Hampton Plantation left largely up to the Horry women during the busy years between the Revolution and the beginning of the Civil War. As ownership passed down (and the married name became Rutledge), Hampton faded as a viable agricultural operation.

In 1865, when he was just 22, the young master of Hampton, Henry Middleton Rutledge, joined the 25th Regiment of North Carolina. Eventually, he was elected to lead his unit through the war. Before the war was over, his regiment had suffered 200 killed in action, 280 dead from disease, and 470 wounded, with 140 of those wounded more than once.

Of course, life at Hampton was drastically altered following the war. The family struggled to cope with the financial requirements of maintaining the house, but the altered economic climate made life very difficult. Rice was no longer profitable, and Hampton was too far from the struggling markets to try to raise cotton, corn, or tobacco in any volume. Hampton, during those years, must have presented quite a strange juxtaposition: the proud, classical portico once surrounded by a formal lawn now planted in string beans and crowded with chickens.

By 1923, both Col. Henry Rutledge and his wife, Margaret Hamilton Seabrook, were dead. Hampton sat empty and neglected for a number of years until 1937, when the colonel's youngest son, Archibald Rutledge, retired to his family's ancestral home.

Archibald Rutledge, was a man of letters—he'd published his first book of poetry in 1907. His prowess with poetry and prose always reflected his love and nostalgia for life on the Santee. By 1934, in recognition of his burgeoning literary reputation, Archibald Rutledge was named poet laureate of South Carolina. In 1941, he published his most popular work, *Home by the River*, in which he described his efforts to restore Hampton Plantation

to its former glory. Over the course of more than 30 years, hundreds of visitors were eventually received at Hampton, drawn to the plantation and its owner by the popular works of Archibald Rutledge. By 1971, in failing health, Rutledge sold the house and 75 acres to the state of South Carolina. He died in 1973 and was buried in the family cemetery on Hampton's grounds.

When Hampton Plantation became a state park in 1971, the house had been unoccupied for several years. Initial inspections quickly indicated that an extensive renovation would be absolutely necessary. While documentary research about the house and its owners went on, another story began to unfold—the evolution of the house itself.

The exposed fabric of the house revealed that most of the interior walls had been covered with modern materials at various times over the course of the previous century. As the newer surfaces were removed, the ancient framework of Hampton became exposed. This afforded researchers an excellent opportunity to display sections of the original house as well as the different patterns of modernization and change that evolved in a Lowcountry plantation house on the Santee delta.

Like Drayton Hall on the Ashley River, Hampton Plantation offers visitors an architectural look at the sophisticated lifestyles pursued by some of the Lowcountry's earliest families.

Admission to Hampton Plantation—the state park—with its picnic grounds and screened cabanas is free, and the grounds are open daily from 9 AM to 6 PM. The house is open Thursday through Monday (from Memorial Day through Labor Day) from 11 AM to 4 PM. Admission to the house is an amazingly low $2 for adults, $1 for youths 6 to 16, and free for children younger than 6.

As you leave Hampton and return to S.C.

857, turn right and go about a half-mile. This will bring you to a sandy road leading off to the left. This remote, almost abandoned stretch of wilderness eventually brings you to another early chapel of ease—this one built for the spiritual needs of the planters along the Santee delta.

Bear in mind, you're well off the beaten track here. Real Insiders shouldn't be daunted by a lonely, sandy road apparently leading into the pages of history and the beguiling mists of time . . . But we'd better add that if the road is wet and muddy, proceed at your own risk. If you see recent tire tracks, you can be safely encouraged to try it. When you get there, you won't be disappointed.

St. James Santee Church
Off S.C. Hwy. 857

Finding this incredibly sophisticated, early architectural treasure sitting here alone in the apparent wilderness is your first surprise. Your second jolt may be learning it was built (in about 1768) not as the first, but as the fourth church to serve St. James Santee Parish. Let this simple fact dramatically emphasize just how important religion was to these early Carolina settlers.

St. James Parish was a thriving neighborhood of planters who petitioned the church for a "new" chapel that would be more conveniently located near Wambaw Creek. The building eventually provided for them was finished shortly after the completion of St. Michael's in Charleston at Meeting and Broad streets. In fact, the impressive design of St. Michael's may have influenced this structure in that both designs employ the use of two bold, classical porticos. Here the porticos are supported by four gently fluted brick columns complete with brick bases and brick Doric capitals.

If you're lucky, the church will be open, and you can see the high-backed, boxed pews separated by a cross axis of clay tile flooring. If the church isn't open,

discreet window peeking is definitely called for.

Amazingly, these beautiful, hand-hewn box pews have never been painted, never in the church's history, although sometime in the 18th-century they were rearranged so the chancel might face the east wall. What is now the rear portico has been enclosed as a vestry room, and the simple pulpit on the north wall is a modern replacement. But the general ambiance of this little chapel in the wilderness is overwhelmingly authentic.

Sitting here so proudly in this quiet, woodland setting, St. James Santee Church seems to generate its own will to survive. This relic of the Lowcountry's plantation past is so powerful that although the church's communion silver was stolen during the Civil War, it was quietly returned at a later date.

In the churchyard, barely legible tombstones (best translated by paper rubbings) relate stories of fierce Revolutionary battles and the closely held relationships between the strong early families of the Santee delta.

Turn around, go back to U.S. 17 and turn right, heading northeast toward Georgetown. At about mile 56, there's a sweeping curve in the road that preludes the delta of the South Santee River and its plantation system. Your vista both to the right and the left is not natural marsh but what remains of vast rice fields, once worked by 19th-century slaves when Georgetown was the "Rice Capital of the Carolinas." Just across the high bridge over the North Santee—another branch of the Santee's widespread watershed to the Atlantic—you'll encounter the painted white gates of Hopsewee Plantation on your left.

Hopsewee Plantation
U.S. Hwy. 17,
12 miles south of Georgetown
(843) 546-7891

Hopsewee Plantation was built in 1740 and was the birthplace of Thomas Lynch

Jr., a signer of the Declaration of Independence. This is the only early rice plantation in Georgetown County that is currently open to the public.

Amazingly, only five families have ever owned Hopsewee. Today, it is owned by Mr. and Mrs. Franklin D. Beattie, who graciously open their home and its grounds to the public. Theirs is a remarkably refreshing attitude toward historic preservation in that the Beattie's actually live in Hopsewee, but with a respect for its place in history.

Although the main house at Hopsewee has been modernized for today, it is handsomely furnished with fine antiques and family-owned period furniture that make it very easy to picture life here as it was in Thomas Lynch's day. Be sure to visit the two cook houses, as so few of them survive today. These are furnished with tools, crockery, and cooking utensils appropriate to their original purpose. It's important to realize that the work in these "dependency" structures—like the backbreaking work done in the rice fields— made the more formal life of the main house possible. Guests are invited to walk along a marked trail past quiet rice fields and the foundations of 18th- and 19th-

century slave cabins—mute testimony to the countless African Americans who worked the plantation in another era.

Hopsewee is on the North Santee River overlooking the river's broad, flat delta. Imagine the beautiful views Lynch was able to see every day as he pondered the dangers and daring consequences of national independence.

Hopsewee is open "by chance or by appointment," as their literature puts it. But the Beattie's have a refreshingly generous attitude about sharing their historic property. Chances are you'll find Hopsewee open and well worth the investment of your time. Tours of the house are hourly, and there's a nice gift shop to browse through if you need to wait a few minutes until the next tour. Hopsewee is usually open 10 AM to 4 PM. Admission is $8 for adults and $5 for children ages 5 to 17. For carloads entering the grounds but not touring the house, the fee is $2.

Continuing north on U.S. 17 for about 12 more miles past Hopsewee Plantation, you'll cross a high bridge over the Sampit River and pass a large industrial complex (Georgetown Steel Corp.) on your right. Then, once in Georgetown proper, turn right off U.S. 17, and you'll quickly find yourself downtown.

Georgetown

More than any other South Carolina community of its size, age, and historical importance, Georgetown is respectful of its past. What the visitor sees here today—streets and streets lined by charming 18th- and 19th-century homes—reflects this consciousness quite beautifully.

Several preservation organizations in the community can share credit for this effort. They include the Georgetown County Historical Society, the Georgetown County Historical Commission and the Historic Georgetown County Foundation. These groups were instrumental in collecting data pertaining to the community, marking and preserving historic homes and sites, and educating new generations about the former rice capital of the Carolinas.

Downtown Georgetown was recently revitalized and now has interesting shops and restaurants backed up against the once-bustling riverfront docks. At the intersection of Front and Scriven Streets, you'll see an interesting old brick building with a clock tower. This is Georgetown's famous Rice Museum—a great first stop in your search to understand the giant rice industry that made Georgetown the thriving agricultural focus of the Lowcountry.

Rice Museum
Front and Scriven Sts., Georgetown
(843) 546-7423

The real story of the rice culture of Georgetown County is one of the most exciting and colorful chapters in the history of South Carolina—maybe even in the whole history of American agriculture. It's all been captured here in the Rice Museum through fascinating maps, pictures, artifacts, exhibits, and intricate dioramas that portray a rice crop from planting through processing and eventual shipment to markets all over the world.

The Rice Museum is in the Old Market Building, which locals call "the town clock." This clock tower has become the architectural symbol of Georgetown, and this is an appropriate place to browse through booklets and tourist information pertaining to Georgetown County.

Look for the exhibit called "The Brown's Ferry Vessel." This is what remains of an early commercial river vessel that plied the waters of the Carolina coast during the first half of the 18th century. Heretofore, very little has been learned about South Carolina river vessels of this early period. This one, which was carrying a load of bricks when it sank near Brown's Ferry in about 1740, has been excavated from its longtime resting place in a river bank and laboriously preserved for this display. The remaining sections of its hull and keel shed invaluable light on a dimly lit facet of the Lowcountry's transportation history. There you'll also find a 15-minute video presentation called "Garden of Gold," which beautifully illustrates the area's rice culture. The gallery is open from 10 AM to 4 PM Monday through Saturday.

Museum hours are 10 AM to 4:30 PM, Monday through Saturday. Admission is $5 for adults, $4 for seniors, but students, children, and members of the museum get in free. Admission to the next-door gallery, which features changing exhibits of paintings, crafts, and sculpture relating to Georgetown, is free.

Eighteen miles north of Georgetown, still on U.S. 17, is the entrance to another adventure, Brookgreen Gardens. Rest assured it's well worth the long drive.

Brookgreen Gardens
U.S. Hwy. 17, Georgetown
(843) 235-6000, (800) 849-1931

Brookgreen Gardens plugs nicely into the plantation theme of this daytrip in that the property encompasses four 18th- and 19th-century plantations: The Oaks, Springfield, Laurel Hill, and (old) Brookgreen. But since the late 1920s, agriculture has hardly been the primary harvest here. Instead, Brookgreen now has 350 acres of beautifully landscaped gardens specifically designed to display more than 500 pieces of outdoor sculpture—all created by leading American artists of the 19th and 20th centuries.

Brookgreen Gardens was the brainchild of noted American sculptor Anna Hyatt Huntington, who, with her late husband, philanthropist Archer M. Huntington, planned and endowed a museum back in the 1930s. Today the property is managed by a private organization—Brookgreen Gardens, a Society for the Southeastern Flora and Fauna. You may choose to get an initial orientation at the visitors pavilion for an overview of the property, or you may want to wander the seemingly endless paths and encounter the breathtaking sculpture by surprise. Brookgreen has a tour boat that takes guests four times daily on a brief trip out into the swamp waters and estuaries. There's also a nature area where wild animals native to these plantations are housed and viewable in natural settings.

Brookgreen's hours are 9:30 AM to 8 PM, every day except Christmas. Admission is $8.50 for adults and teens, $4 for children ages 6 to 12 and free for members of The Brookgreen Society and children 6 and younger.

To return to Charleston, follow U.S. Highway 17 S. back to Mt. Pleasant and cross the Cooper River Bridge into the city.

Summerville, Flowertown in the Pines

Our second daytrip suggestion is perfect for either a crisp spring afternoon or one of those Lowcountry summer scorchers that's so hot you will gain a true appreciation for the natural wonder that is your destination. We're headed to Summerville, the Flowertown in the Pines.

If you're coming from Charleston along S.C. Highway 61 (the old Ashley River Road), veer to the right on Bacons Bridge Road, which is S.C. Highway 165. This will lead you into Summerville at S. Main Street (U.S. 17-A). If you're arriving via Interstate 26 from Charleston, take the second Summerville exit onto U.S. 17-A, then follow the signs.

In Summerville, you're 25 miles inland from the Atlantic Ocean on a ridge that's just 75 feet above sea level. The longleaf pine forest all around you helps keep temperatures moderate, with air freshly scented with refreshing pine vapors borne on soft sea breezes.

These are the basic elements that first attracted a few planter families to build summer camps in this pineland spot—away from the mosquitoes and deadly swamp fevers that plagued the lower areas. The first few families to establish summer homes in Summerville settled between the end of the Revolutionary War and 1790. By 1828, there were 23 houses in the village. Two years later, a chapel of ease to St. Paul's Episcopal Church was built, indicating a growing desire of some families to maintain full-time residences there. The summer homes were often built high on pilings with large, wraparound porches to catch the breezes. Today, you still find many of them scattered in the half-mile Old Town area around St. Paul's Episcopal Church.

By 1832, the South Carolina Railroad had come to Summerville, and the new areas of growth (unlike Old Town) had the benefit of better planning. There were regularly spaced streets running parallel to and at right angles with the train tracks. A large, open space was reserved for a town square, and today's town hall overlooks that site. Victorian commercial buildings soon sprang up around the square, and many of them are still standing. With its umbilical railroad connection to Charleston at last in place, the once sleepy village started to grow rapidly, and in 1847, Summerville was incorporated.

A series of fever epidemics struck Charleston during the late 1850s, sending even more new residents to this relatively disease-free locale. As a Charleston newspaper lamented during those difficult years, "The eyes of Charleston sadly turned toward Summerville . . ." By 1860, the population had grown to 1,088 residents—548 white, 540 black.

The Civil War brought an abrupt end to Summerville's growth and prosperity. Not until the end of the century would the town see another boom. When it did come, however, it would bring the pineland village international fame.

In 1889, a world congress of specialists in respiratory diseases met in Paris and named Summerville, South Carolina, of all places, one of the two best resort areas in the world for the cure of lung and throat disorders. This widely publicized "Tuberculosis Congress" introduced a whole new era for Summerville. Special excursion trains came in from New York and St. Louis, and numerous establishments were built to accommodate the flood of health-minded visitors. The grandest of these lodges was the Pine Forest Inn (unfortunately, no longer standing), where President Theodore Roosevelt, among other luminaries, stayed.

But alas, the fame of Summerville as a health resort waned with the coming of the Depression. But post-World War II prosperity in the Lowcountry gave the town new reason to succeed.

Summerville has traditionally been known as a center for azalea culture. The lushly landscaped gardens and homes all seem to be extensions of the city's own Azalea Park, which is a focal point on the town's Main Street. Come spring of every year, Summerville still earns the title "Flowertown in the Pines." What follows are listings that give information on places and events you will want to see on your visit to Summerville, including an auto tour of more than a dozen architecturally significant homes.

Greater Summerville
Chamber of Commerce, 402 N. Main St.
(843) 873-2931

Daytrippers to Summerville may first want to check in at the city's chamber of commerce, located right on Main Street near Town Square. This green-roofed building serves as a mini welcome center with newcomer information, maps, brochures, and friendly advice. It is open Monday through Friday from 9 AM until 5 PM, Saturday from 10 AM to 3 PM, and Sunday, 1 to 4 PM.

Dorchester Museum
00 E. Doty Ave.
(843) 875-9666

The Dorchester Museum is an easy walk from the chamber offices, and it is another must-see on your visit to Summerville. Officially opened in 1993 for the Flowertown Festival (see the following listing), this museum gives visitors a fascinating look at the city's and the county's past. The inspiration was simple enough—it was intended to be a place where the area's children could learn about their own hometown, and visitors could see some of the area's rich and romantic past. You'll find local fossils, natural history, memorabilia from an earlier Summerville, and photographic displays tracking the city and Dorchester County from the days following the Great Earthquake of 1886 to the present. There is a special emphasis on the area's historic architecture and Summerville's many memorable characters.

The building was formerly a police station and is in the same block as the chamber of commerce, less than a block from Town Square. Admission is $2 for adults, and $1 for children. Under age 5, it's free. Museum hours are Tuesday through Saturday 10 AM to 2 PM.

Flowertown Festival
Various sites
(843) 873-2931

If you're lucky enough to be stopping in town sometime around Easter, chances are you'll see vestiges of Summerville's biggest annual bash, the Flowertown Festival. The entire town participates in this gala, planned for when the town is ablaze with color and the area's spectacular azaleas, camellias, and dogwoods are all in bloom.

The fun has been going on each spring since 1973 and includes concerts, dancing, a food fair, a health fair, kiddie rides, historic house tours, and craft exhibits of all kinds. In fact, the Flowertown Festival (originally sponsored as a fund-raiser for the Summerville Family YMCA) is highly regarded in craft circles up and down the Eastern Seaboard—the quality of crafts traditionally displayed here is exceptional.

Each year, tens of thousands of visitors celebrate spring in the Lowcountry by attending the three-day event. The atmosphere is like an old-fashioned country fair. For more details, call or write the chamber at P.O. Drawer 670, Summerville, SC 29484. (Also, see our Annual Events chapter for more on the festival.)

If, however, the calendar finds you in Summerville when the flowers are not quite so showy, don't fret. There's more to see in this special little town. The following driving tour will take you through the Old Town section of Summerville, with its winding streets, architecturally significant homes, and gleaming aura of uniqueness.

Summerville's Old Town

The cool, shady streets of this part of Summerville recall the days when this was a hot-weather retreat for wealthy planters. The charming homes and well-kept gardens seem little changed from those days in the mid-1800s.

For a nice driving tour, turn from U.S. 17-A—Main Street—onto W. Carolina Avenue and begin at St. Paul's Episcopal Church. The church parking lot is a good place to pause and get your bearings.

St. Paul's Episcopal Church
111 Waring St.
(843) 873-1991

The history of St. Paul's Episcopal Church dates back to 1828, when the Rev.

Philip Gadsden, rector of another Lowcountry chapel of ease, followed the growing number of communicants moving to the thriving village of Summerville.

Services were first held in the leaky old village hall or a parishioner's residence. But in 1829 a decision was made to build a proper house of worship. The first church building, dedicated in 1832, stood just a few feet south of the present structure, but Summerville's rapid growth soon made this simple wooden building inadequate for the growing number of believers. By 1857 a new church (the present structure) was built at a cost of $5,000.

The terrible earthquake that rocked the Lowcountry on the night of August 31, 1886, badly damaged the building, but somehow the sturdy church survived. Inside, you can still note the metal earthquake rods running through the structure for reinforcement.

There was a move in the early 20th century to replace the building with a more modern structure. Fortunately,

The Cooper River bridges never fail to evoke awe or fear (or both) in newcomers. PHOTO: DAVID C. BERRY

those plans were never realized. Today St. Paul's rector, vestry, and congregation work to preserve the old church, an architectural focal point for Old Town and Summerville.

Exit the church parking lot left onto Gadsden Street, which will take you back to W. Carolina Avenue. Take a right, then an immediate left onto Sumter Avenue, where in a few short blocks you will encounter at least 13 architecturally significant homes or "cottages" dating from the mid- to late 19th century. What follows are brief descriptions of the homes, arranged in geographical order for a brief but pleasant driving tour past some of the most charming houses of Summerville's Old Town.

Gelzer Brothers House (c. 1819)
413 Sumter Ave.

This home, like several others on this end of Sumter Avenue, was actually built facing a street that's no longer in existence. You're viewing what was originally the rear of this very early Summerville dwelling.

Brailsford-Browning House (c. 1830)
408 Sumter Ave.

Here is an example of early Summerville architecture in which the house is lifted high off the ground to catch cool breezes. The lower area was once open; the present enclosure was added after 1915. Early records show this house was occupied in 1838 by a Dr. W.M. Brailsford, when it was listed among 29 houses in the growing village of Summerville.

Brownfield House (c. 1875)
320 Sumter Ave.

This residence belonged to the Brownfield family, who built on the site of a defunct boarding school for girls known as The Brownfield Academy. In 1893, the school was advertised as "particularly desirable for Northern young ladies with impaired health who would probably be successful in following their studies in this health-giving climate."

Buckheit House (c. 1884)
317 Sumter Ave.

Existing documentation indicates that in 1862 a baker from Charleston named Philip Buckheit bought this land. Perhaps because of the war, he didn't actually build his house until more than two decades later.

Disher House (c. 1862)
303 Sumter Ave.

Deeds for this property go back to 1862, when Robert W. Disher bought 2 acres of land from A.W. Taylor. Disher's house (and presence) on this site must have been noteworthy, as the adjoining road now called Charleston Street was formerly known as Disher Street.

William Prioleau House (1896)
302 Sumter Ave.

Built by Charleston druggist William H. Prioleau, this is one of the many Victorian homes built during the big health resort boom around the turn of the century. The lacy architectural style is called Queen Anne.

Kinloch House (c. 1861)
233 Sumter Ave.

This house was built in 1861, shortly after the shelling of Fort Sumter in Charleston Harbor, on land formerly owned by the Rev. Philip Gadsden, first rector of St. Paul's Episcopal Church.

Purcell House (c. 1820)
224 Sumter Ave.

Records date this home to between 1811 and 1828. The architecture is typical of the very early hunting lodges or summer homes built by nearby planters.

Preference (c. 1885)
223 Sumter Ave.

Note the West Indian character of this home. The broad porches and high elevation would have offered friendly shade and cool breezes to residents and guests.

Although the exact date of construction

They call it "crabbing." Tie a chicken neck to a string and drag it along a creek bottom. The result: makings for delicious she-crab soup! PHOTO: THOMAS P. FORD

is unknown, this handsome Victorian house is thought to have been built for one Mary Webb around 1885. As for the unusual name, it seems that after the Civil War many summer homes took on the names of the owner's former plantations, most of which were lost or sold after the conflict.

Charles Boyle House (c. 1888)
220 Sumter Ave.

This house was built by Summerville attorney Charles Boyle around 1888 on land that at one time straddled the Colleton-Berkeley county line.

Samuel Prioleau House (1887)
217 Sumter Ave.

This was the home of Dr. Samuel Prioleau, in whose honor the first Summerville infirmary was named. The land was given to the doctor's wife by her mother, Mrs. Benjamin Rhett, who lived next door.

Rhett House (1882)
205 Sumter Ave.

Dr. Benjamin Rhett served as a surgeon for the Confederacy and later practiced medicine in Summerville. His Victorian house was built on land that was once owned by the South Carolina Canal and Railroad Co. during Summerville's first boom days in the 1830s.

Samuel Lord-Elizabeth Arden House (1891)
208 Sumter Ave.

This handsome Victorian house was built for Samuel Lord in 1891 by the same contractor who built the town's celebrated Pine Forest Inn. With its three stories and impressive double piazzas, the ornate house was purchased in 1938 by Elizabeth Arden, the famous cosmetics magnate, who used it as her winter retreat. It remained in her possession until 1954.

To return to Charleston, stay to the right on Sumter Avenue until it intersects with W. Fifth Street at the First Baptist Church. Turn right and follow W. Fifth back to Main Street, take a left and follow U.S. 17-A through town until you see signs for I-26 S. That will be your quickest route back to Charleston.

A Walk on the Wild Side

In a city famous for its bittersweet history and sophisticated architecture, it's easy to follow that same suit when you go afield in search of some Lowcountry daytrip adventures. The previous sojourns (to the fishing village of McClellanville and the quaint metropolis of Georgetown) basically offer more of the same with a country flavor. So, for the sake of variety and an adventure into another world, here's a daytrip expressly for nature lovers, serious birders, wildlife photographers, and anyone who wants an up-close and personal look at the Lowcountry's true environment—the Carolina wetlands.

Marrington Plantation is on land now owned by the Charleston Naval Weapons Station outside the town of Goose Creek. It was a typical working plantation during Colonial times. In the late 1600s, when rice was introduced to this area and became a major cash crop, this was only one of hundreds of rice operations flourishing here. By the 1850s, more than 150,000 Lowcountry acres were under rice cultivation.

Rice fields were man-made. They were comprised of an elaborate system of dikes and canals used to control different water levels needed for planting, growing, and harvesting the rice. Today, many of those agricultural fields—long since gone feral—have become natural wetlands, teeming with wildlife.

Under the Navy's Natural Resources Program and its local initiative dubbed "Watchable Wildlife," some of Marrington Plantation's former rice fields (not used for any military purposes) were developed in 1995 as a self-guided nature trail for the public. The mile-long trail opened in 1997 and includes more than 1,200 feet of boardwalk that winds its way around several ponds.

Today, these ponds offer a natural habitat for wading birds, migratory waterfowl, alligators, eagles, hawks, wood ducks, snakes, turtles, frogs, and insects. White-tailed deer, river otters, gray squirrels, and other wildlife can sometimes be seen there too.

Even winter visitors are treated to many of the Lowcountry's natural delights. Look for egrets, herons, and ring-necked ducks. But lower temperatures usually drive the alligators and snakes out of view for the Lowcountry's short cold season. (This may or may not come as welcome news to hard-core nature lovers.)

Two observation towers offer a panoramic view of the 1,000-acre plantation, and 27 numbered stations serve as markers along the way—each with a corresponding paragraph in an accompanying brochure that explains the cultural and natural history of each feature.

To find this nifty natural diversion, take I-26 to the Goose Creek/Moncks Corner exit (at Northwoods Mall) and follow

Insiders' Tip

Drop those windows (or the convertible top) and breathe in the Lowcountry. If you're looking for a picture-perfect afternoon drive, head out in the early evening down the twisting ribbon of Bohicket Road and enjoy the summer sun filtering through the spreading canopy of live oaks as you approach Kiawah.

S.C. 52 about 2 miles, past a number of auto dealerships and commercial buildings. Turn right on Snake Road (which crosses the Goose Creek Reservoir), and turn right, again, onto Redbank Road (County Road 29). You'll pass several signs announcing the Naval Weapons Station, and after 2 miles or so you'll see a large green sign for Marrington Plantation. Follow the dirt road to the parking lot, where you'll see the trail's starting point and some accompanying brochures for interpretation. A tip to the wise: Pack plenty of insect repellent for this outing.

The Story of Santee Canal

Old Santee Canal State Park
900 Stony Landing Rd., Moncks Corner
(843) 899-5200

Another fun daytrip adventure is to Old Santee Canal State Park, a wonderful addition to the South Carolina park system just 45 minutes from Charleston. Opened about a decade ago, Old Santee Canal State Park interprets the building and operation of America's first man-made inland waterway.

To find this colorful and kid-friendly park, take I-26 north from Charleston to Exit 208 (S.C. Highway 52), then follow S.C. 52 about 18 miles past Goose Creek and into Moncks Corner. Two miles down the main road of the town (S.C. 52), look for an Old Santee State Park sign on the right. Plan to bring a picnic basket (rain or shine—there's a large, covered picnic area with tables) and spend your day absorbing the tranquil inland beauty.

Santee Canal was America's first summit canal, a type of canal that uses a multi-lock system to raise and lower cargo-laden barges. It was praised as a great engineering and economic development in the 1800s. The canal provided a cost-efficient, dependable way to ship crops between the uplands and the coast. While ideas for such a solution had been tossed about as early as the 1700s, the Revolutionary War intervened, and it was not until 1793 that construction actually began. Seven years and $650,000 later, with the labor of 700 men who worked with shovels and picks, a canal 22 miles long, 30 feet wide, and 5fi feet deep was a reality.

At first, mules and horses walked alongside the canal and pulled the heavy barges or boats with their cargo. Later, crewmen with poles replaced the beasts. In all, there were 16 years of profitable operation before severe droughts in 1817 and 1819 dried up the canal and ended operations for the time being. The rains returned, and 1830 was the canal's busiest year, with 700 cotton-heavy barges passing through the waterway.

Progress in transportation technology within the state spelled disaster for the canal, however, when a railway between Columbia and Charleston was completed in 1840 and took a substantial portion of the canal's business. The final blow came in 1846, when the railroad tracks were laid to Camden. In 1850 the shareholders threw in the towel.

Today, most of the canal is covered by the waters of Lake Moultrie. But where the still waters of Biggin Creek and the nearby swamps intersect with the southernmost section of the canal, the South Carolina Department of Parks, Recreation, and Tourism has created the Old Santee Canal State Park. Included in the park is the plantation house at Stony Landing bluff, built after 1840 by John Dawson. The house—restored and open to the public free of charge—faces Tail Race Canal (flowing from the Santee Cooper lakes, created during the 1940s). Throughout the 19th century, cement and building blocks were made here, and during the Civil War, gunpowder was manufactured.

After a house tour, a good place to get oriented is the park's interpretive center. There are nifty exhibits showing the canal in different phases, a 30-foot simulated oak tree with man-made wildlife inhabitants (we bet you can't tell the difference!), and a cave. Short films about canals and the environment are also up-to-date and well-done. If it's a pretty day, we suggest a hike on a nature trail—either the swamp walk, the creek walk, or the canal walk—or renting a canoe.

In the winter, the park is open from 9 AM to 5 PM, but those hours are extended until 6 PM during summer. For more information, call or write Old Santee Canal State Park, 900 Stony Landing Road, Moncks Corner, SC 29461. Admission is $3 for adults; seniors pay $2; children age 6 and younger get in free.

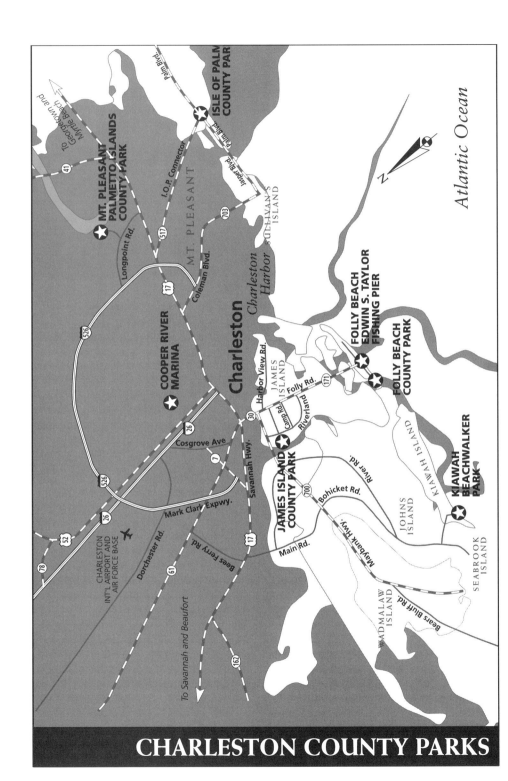

CHARLESTON COUNTY PARKS

Parks and Recreation

The warm climate and natural resources of the Lowcountry make recreation and physical fitness top priorities with locals. This chapter deals specifically with some of the things we do for fitness and fun and offers a sampling of the public places designated for them. Spectator sports, boating and watersports, fishing, hunting, and golf are detailed in separate chapters due to the immense popularity and numerous outlets for these recreational activities.

As you will see reflected in many of the listings in this chapter, the Charleston County Park and Recreation Commission and Charleston County Community Education Program provide wonderful opportunities for recreation. The school programs are set up at public schools after regular hours to serve adults and sometimes children who are interested in non-credit self-enhancement courses. For detailed information, write to Adult and Community Education Programs, Charleston County School District, 75 Calhoun Street, Charleston, SC 29403 (the phone is (843) 937-6421), or call Charleston County Park and Recreation Commission at (843) 762-2172. Free brochures on recreational opportunities are often available at one of the public libraries.

Another wonderful resource for young and old is the Christian Family Y at 21 George Street, (843) 723-6473. The Family Y offers self-enrichment and exercise classes and a full schedule of aquatic programs. Membership is open to all at $25 for adults, $15 for seniors 55 and older, and $15 for children 16 and younger. There is an additional fee of $95 per quarter to use the pool, weight room, and exercise facilities. A day pass for visitors is $10 a day.

The following is an overview of specific places, organizations and businesses that keep the fun flowing through the Lowcountry. The listings will let you know how to go about participating in some of the Trident's most popular recreational activities. We start off with descriptions (arranged geographically) of the public parks and recreation centers where you and your family can fashion your own fun. Then we get more specific, breaking down information on individual recreational pursuits by type of activity (arranged alphabetically).

Parks and Recreation Centers

The parks we like best are sizable tracts of land that give young and old alike a chance to enjoy the great outdoors. We make a distinction here between "park" and "playground" because, although the former may include the latter, "park" implies more space and characteristics that appeal to both children and adults. We list several playgrounds under a separate heading later in the chapter. For more information on the public parks, call the City of Charleston Department of Parks and Recreation, (843) 724-7326. Call (843) 724-7327 if you would like to schedule a special event at one of the parks.

Also included here are several community center complexes scattered throughout the Lowcountry. These offer various indoor activities, usually at a bargain price. All listings are arranged geographically, starting with parks and centers in Charleston and East Cooper (including Mt. Pleasant, Sullivan's Island, and Isle of Palms). Then we go to West Ashley and James, Folly, and Kiawah Islands. Welcome to a few of our favorite places.

Downtown Charleston

Officially this subject comes under the auspices of the Charleston Department of Parks and Recreation. It offers an extensive program of activities, sports, special events, and multi-generational recreation for residents and visitors. Here are the best-known spots.

Hampton Park
55 Cleveland St., Charleston
(843) 724-7326

Near The Citadel, Hampton Park is a 60-acre downtown park with a lake (complete with lots of resident ducks for feeding), one of the largest rose gardens in the state, grassy areas, a trail for workouts, a bandstand (the site of many an afternoon concert) and even the police department's horse stables (sorry, no touching). A giant Easter egg hunt and the Piccolo Spoleto finale are held here. Sometimes the park is closed off (usually Tuesday and Thursday evenings from April to September and Saturday mornings year round) for walkers, runners, joggers, skaters, and bikers—a great traffic-free treat for city kids and their parents. (For more, see our Kidstuff chapter.)

Waterfront Park
Cumberland St. to N. Adgers Wharf, Charleston
(843) 724-7326

Just off East Bay Street, from Cumberland Street to N. Adgers Wharf, this is one of the city's most popular and most delightful parks. On site are a 400-foot pier for viewing harbor activity and two inviting fountains in which the young and young-at-heart are allowed to play. You'll also enjoy grassy areas and swings (see our Kidstuff chapter).

White Point Gardens
South tip of East Bay and King Sts., Charleston
(843) 724-7326

At the tip of the Peninsula, boxed in by East Bay Street, Murray Boulevard, King Street, and South Battery, White Point Gardens has a beautiful view of the harbor and some of the homes of The Battery. Kids love to climb on the old cannons (and stacked cannonballs) or picnic in the grassy areas. You may even catch a glimpse of a bride and groom exchanging vows here in the old bandstand. It is often crowded on Sunday when the weather is nice but less so during the week. (For more on the history of White Point Gardens, see our History chapter; see Kidstuff for more on fun activities.)

Mt. Pleasant

Alhambra Park
131 Middle St., Mt. Pleasant
(843) 884-2528

This simple, lovely park across from Alhambra Hall is wide open, with free public admission from sunup to sundown. It offers a nice lawn and scenic view of Charleston Harbor. The selection of playground equipment (swings, slides, climbing toys, and a merry-go-round) keeps the children busy. For picnics, there are several tables under the shade of big oaks.

Richard L. Jones Recreation Complex
391 Egypt Rd., Mt. Pleasant
(843) 884-2528, (843) 884-2278, ext. 6773

Opened in March 1991, this large, modern building provides a facility for scheduled recreation programs, a gymnasium, a six-lane pool, and an activity room. There is a one-year membership fee of $2 each for everyone 5 and older. The pool usage fee is $2 a day, but it's free for kids younger than 5 and $1 for seniors 50 and older. Non-Mt. Pleasant residents pay $100 for an annual family membership. There are separate fees for T-ball, softball, basketball, baseball, and soccer. Crafts, painting, dance and theater classes, swimming lessons, and gymnastics camps (half-day and full-day) are some of the activities offered. The Mt. Pleasant Recreation Department also sponsors a track team for children ages 8 to 18. The season runs January through mid-March. Monthly fees are $25 for Mt. Pleasant residents and $50 for nonresidents. The buddy baseball, basketball, flag football, and soccer leagues provide the opportunity for children with disabilities to play with children their own age. The hotline number, the second one listed previously, gives more information on programs, athletics, and current events.

Palmetto Islands County Park
444 Needlerush Pkwy.
(843) 884-0832
This family-oriented, 943-acre nature facility is in a heavily wooded area, with a 2-acre pond and 1-mile canoe trail. You'll enjoy a well-designed playground, picnic sites, and boat docks. It is a perfect place to jog, walk, or rent a pedal boat or a bike. Rates are $3.50 per half-hour for boats (plus a $2 deposit) and $3.25 an hour or $10 for a full day on a bike (again, add in a $2 deposit). Splash Island, with its 200-foot water slide, is quite popular in the warm months. Park admission is $1 per person (no charge for children younger than 3) with an annual individual pass available for $10 for Charleston County residents, $20 for nonresidents. Additional fees ($5.99 for Charleston County residents and $4.99 for children under 42" tall; $6.99 for nonresidents) are charged for entry to Splash Island. Annual family and senior passes are available also. (For more on this park, see our Kidstuff and Boating and Watersports chapters.)

Sullivan's Island, Isle of Palms

Isle of Palms County Park
1-14th Ave., Isle of Palms
(843) 886-3863
Everyone can hit the beach straight off the Isle of Palms Connector at one of the newer county parks. Enjoy one of the area's nicest beaches, open daily year round, with the convenience of paved parking, outdoor showers, restrooms, a sand volleyball court, and children's play area. Just in case you forget your beach gear, you'll find chairs, umbrellas, bicycles, and boogie boards available for rent. The summer season hours are 9 AM to 7 PM with lifeguards on duty. The park is open daily from 10 AM to 6 PM in April, September, and October, and the November through March hours are 10 AM to 5 PM. Admission is $5 per car, $10 per camper, and $20 per bus. (See the Kid-Friendly Beaches section of our Kidstuff chapter for more information.)

Isle of Palms Recreation Department
24-28th Ave., Isle of Palms
(843) 886-8294
This comprehensive facility includes a big playground (complete with separate equipment and areas for different ages), a volleyball court, athletic fields (for soccer, football, and kickball), baseball fields, tennis courts, and basketball courts. An indoor center houses night basketball courts, tumbling equipment, Ping-Pong tables, and more. There are also sheltered tables and grills for picnics.

The department sponsors special programs such as a summer day camp, youth dances, and a senior citizens group and organizes events such as kite-flying and sand-sculpting contests. The park is open from sunup to sundown; the recreation building is open from 8:30 AM until 6 PM (with the kids' programs in the morning), Monday through Friday, and from 12:30 until 5 PM on Saturday.

Sullivan's Island Park
1610 Middle St., Sullivan's Island
(843) 883-3198
Sullivan's Island has a nice park at The Mound (constructed by the military during World War II) on Middle Street between stations 20½ and 22 (street names on Sullivan's are based on the old streetcar station stops). There is a bandstand, plus basketball courts, two tennis courts, and children's wooden play equipment in a fenced-in tot lot (see our Kidstuff chapter). Although there is no official recreation department on Sullivan's Island,

Towne Landing, see our Attractions, History, and Kidstuff chapters.)

Insiders' Tip

For children (and adults) with physical, social, and behavioral disabilities, Anchors Away! is a special program for recreational opportunities designed by the Department of Physical Medicine and Rehabilitation of the Medical University of South Carolina. Options include JetSkiing, fishing, water-skiing, canoeing, harbor tours, sailing, swimming, kayaking, and more. For additional information call (843) 792-0721 or (800) 734-4785.

Caw Caw Interpretive Center
5200 Savannah Hwy., Ravenel
(843) 889-8898

A bit further out but worth the trip (about 15 miles south of Charleston on Highway 17S) is the Caw Caw Interpretive Center in Ravenel, South Carolina. Part of the Charleston County Park system, this 654-acre park is managed specifically for birds and wildlife. There are seven miles of interpretive trails, a 1200-foot swamp boardwalk, and a bird and butterfly garden. Loads of educational programs, daily walks, workshops, and demonstrations complete the natural, cultural, and historical experience. Admission is $4 for adults, $2 for seniors and youths ages 3 to 12, and free for children 2 and under. Hours are 9 AM to 5 PM, November through February; 9 AM to 6 PM, March, April, September, and October; and 8 AM to 7 PM, May through August. The park is closed on Mondays.

one member of the town council serves as head of recreation.

West Ashley

Charles Towne Landing 1670
U.S. Hwy. 171, Charleston
(843) 852-4200

In West Ashley, this is a wonderful, low-key park for all ages on the site of the original settlement called Charles Towne. There is an animal forest, playground, replica of the ship *Adventure*, early settlement village, gift shop, restaurant, and even a movie, *Carolina*, about the history of the Lowcountry. It shows every half-hour. You can take the tram around the property and learn about the park's history or rent bikes. Ask about the annual bike passes for $10 and vehicle passes for $40 (good at any state park)—they are good deals if you are going to be spending lots of time here. (For more on Charles

James Island

James Island County Park
871 Riverland Dr., Charleston
(843) 795-7275

This incredible, 643-acre park offers biking, nature trails, a climbing wall, an elaborate playground, pedal boats, kayaks, hydrobikes, 16 acres of lagoons, a Spray-Play fountain area, a fishing and crabbing dock, and picnic areas. There are 10 vacation cottages, camping sites (see "Camping" later in this chapter), and three picnic shelters that can accommodate 200 or more people each. Admission is $1 per person (no charge for children younger than 3). Individual passes are $10 for Charleston County residents; $20 for nonresidents. The ever-popular Splash Zone costs an additional $7.99 (residents) and $6.99 for children under 42 inches tall or $9.99 (nonresidents), but most agree it is well worth the price to escape to the land of the tropics via slides, waterfalls, and spray effects (see our Kidstuff chapter). Annual family and senior passes are also available.

Folly Beach

Folly Beach County Park
1010 West Ashley Ave., Folly Beach
(843) 588-2426
At the tip of Folly Beach, this county park is an easy-to-reach, family-oriented beach destination. Enjoy the sand and waves, or bring along binoculars for viewing feathered friends in the marsh or nearby Bird Key. In addition to beach chair, boogie board, and umbrella rentals, you'll find a snack bar and gift shop. The Pelican Watch Shelter provides natural gas, an oyster-roasting pit, and barbecue cookers.

Due to recurring winter high tides, erosion is a problem at this beach park. Each year a renourishment program replenishes the sand, but the parking has been cut to 220 spaces. This may make parking here more difficult in the summer months so it's best to get there early in the day. Admission is $5 per car, $10 per camper, or $20 per bus. Walk-ins and bicy-

cles are free. Hours are 9 AM to 7 PM from May through August, 10 AM to 6 PM in April, September, and October, and 10 AM to 5 PM November through March. (See the Kid-Friendly Beaches section of our Kidstuff chapter for more details.)

Kiawah Island

Beachwalker Park
1 Beachwalker Dr., Kiawah Island
(843) 768-2395
This park, just outside the gates into Kiawah (take a right on Beachwalker Drive), is open April through October. Summer hours, May through August, are 9 AM to 7 PM; in September, October, and April the hours are 10 AM to 6 PM (weekends only in October and April). This is 10 miles of pristine beach with white sand. Admission is $5 per car, $10 per camper, or $20 per bus, and all 150 parking spots often fill early. Walk-ins and bicycles are free. There are lifeguards, outdoor showers, and restrooms, and beach chair, boogie board, and umbrella rentals are available. (Also see the Kid-Friendly Beaches section of our Kidstuff chapter.)

Kiawah Island's 36 miles of bike paths offer easy exploration. PHOTO: FLETCHER NEWBERN

Recreation

What follows is a good representation of the recreational opportunities scattered throughout the Lowcountry. Categories are in alphabetical order and so are the businesses that are listed with each type of activity.

The following departments are also good clearinghouses for information on specific sports and recreational opportunities throughout the Lowcountry. In Charleston, call the City of Charleston Department of Recreation, (843) 724-7326, or the James Island Recreation Complex, (843) 720-3808. In Mt. Pleasant, call the Richard L. Jones Recreation Complex, (843) 884-2528. For Isle of Palms information, call the town's Recreation Department, (843) 886-8294. Sullivan's Island Town Hall, (843) 883-3198, can provide information on options on that island, and the North Charleston Recreation Department, (843) 745-1028, can answer recreation questions in that area.

Aerobics

Individual recreation departments often offer aerobics classes. The parks and recreation departments and facilities listed in the Recreation introduction are good places to look for further information. The Christian Family Y has a choice of aerobics classes including kickboxing and step and water aerobics for $40 a month for adults and $35 a month for students. Also, most full-service fitness centers offer a plethora of aerobics classes (see our Fitness Centers section in this chapter).

Charleston County
Community Education Program
Charleston County School District,
75 Calhoun St., Charleston
(843) 937-6421

This program offers moderately priced aerobic classes at locations all over the county. For a schedule and more information, write to the above address or pick up a free brochure at one of the public libraries.

Archery

Carolina Rod & Gun Inc.
1319 Savannah Hwy., Charleston
(843) 571-7972

Bow-and-arrow enthusiasts will find a fine source of archery equipment and information here. Carolina Rod and Gun employs full-time technicians and offers custom services such as bow-tuning and arrow-building. It is by far the most popular archery services vendor in the Lowcountry. See our Hunting and Fishing chapter for more on Carolina Rod & Gun.

Aviation

Two companies in Charleston County offer flying lessons. Two are based at the Charleston Executive Airport on Johns Island, and one is East Cooper at the East Cooper Airport. Call any of the three to get advice on what's required by law.

Palmetto Air Service
700 Airport Rd., Mt. Pleasant
(843) 884-8914

For primary flight instruction east of the Cooper River, talk to the instructors at Palmetto Air. Their lessons are $81 an hour for dual instruction and $56 an hour to learn solo in a Cessna 152. They also offer sightseeing flights over Charleston for those of us who are not yet ready to earn our wings.

Pro Flight
2700 Ft. Trenholm Rd., Johns Island
(843) 559-3331

Open seven days a week, Pro Flight teaches all levels from primary flight training to instrument and commercial flight instruction. For instruction in a Cessna 150, the rental is $45 an hour plus $25 for the instruction. The cost is $59 an hour to rent a Cessna 172 and $87 an hour for an Arrow, with the same $25 instructor's fee. Aircraft rental and scenic tours are also available.

Baseball

The area's recreation departments organize baseball leagues (T-ball for toddlers through baseball for teens), and there's a batting range for those who want to go it alone. Call the department in your area for information about spring registration, and plan to have on hand your child's birth certificate, social security card, and insurance as well as a registration fee of about $10 for city residents, $25 for non-residents.

Frankie's Fun Park
5000 Ashley Phosphate Rd.,
North Charleston
(843) 767-1376
You're never too old to swing it! Frankie's has a nine-position baseball batting cage with a variety of pitch-speed options. It costs $1 for 12 pitches, or 72 swings for $5. (See our Kidstuff chapter for more about Frankie's.)

Basketball

Public basketball courts are adjacent to most local playgrounds. Here are a few spots for shooting the rock convenient to various parts of the Greater Charleston area. More playgrounds are listed later in this chapter.

Moultrie Playground, across from Colonial Lake at 41 Ashley Avenue, and Hazel Parker Playground, next to the Carolina Yacht Club at 70 East Bay Street, both have outdoor courts that are very convenient if you are downtown.

In Mt. Pleasant, the Richard L. Jones Recreation Complex on Egypt Road (see previous listing in Parks and Recreation Centers) has an indoor gymnasium and active basketball programs for youth ages 5 to 15, adults, and seniors age 50 and older.

If you are on one of the East Cooper beaches, consider playing at the Isle of Palms Park, 24-28th Avenue, which has one outdoor lighted court and one indoor court. There are youth and adult basketball leagues organized by the recreation department there as well. Another island option is the lighted court at Sullivan's Island Park, conveniently located on Middle Street in the center of the business district and usually swarming with players eager to shoot some hoops.

If you are in West Ashley, try playing outdoors at St. Andrews Park on Playground Road or the St. Andrews Family Fitness Center on Sam Rittenberg Boulevard for indoor courts. The James Island Recreation Complex has an indoor court that is open for recreational play daily and organizes adult and youth leagues January through March. For more information, contact the area recreation departments.

St. John's Community School offers coed adult (18 and older) pickup basketball and a men's league for those 20 and older. The school is at 1518 Main Road on Johns Island.

Bicycling

Coastal Cyclists
P.O. Box 32095, Charleston SC 29417
(843) 442-1589
Coastal Cyclists is an organization of bike riders and racers that meets once a month (usually on the first Monday) at an area restaurant. Members enjoy supper together and have a meeting with a guest speaker. Coastal Cyclists organizes club rides for Class 1 to Class 4 riders covering 20 to 40 miles on average. The group has a racing team that travels to compete around the state. Annual family membership costs $25, single membership is $15 and includes a newsletter on upcoming events. This group is open to riders of all levels.

Bowling

Bowling is popular in the Lowcountry, with active leagues playing every night on area lanes right next to the occasional group or office outing. For information about leagues, talk to the management at the following lanes, and beware of those gutter balls!

AMF Triangle Lanes
1963 Savannah Hwy., Charleston
(843) 766-0241

Just off the Mark Clark Expressway, west of the Ashley, Triangle has automatic scoring, a pro shop, and a lounge. There are 24 lanes and leagues every evening. You can bowl here for $3 a game, with shoe rental for $2.50. This is a choice venue for birthday parties.

Ashley Lanes
1568 Sam Rittenberg Blvd.,
Charleston
(843) 766-9061

Ashley Lanes has numerous leagues and a total of 24 lanes. The per-game cost to bowl before 6 PM is $1.70 for adults, $1.45 for children, $1.24 for seniors, and $2.45 after 6. It's $2.10 for shoe rental. In addition to bowling, you'll find an amusement center with a snack bar and several video games, plus a restaurant, lounge, and nursery.

Twin River Lanes
613 Johnnie Dodds Blvd.,
Mt. Pleasant
(843) 884-7735

Twin River Lanes is the East Cooper venue for bowling and offers 16 lanes for play. Before 6 PM prices are $2.75 per game and $2.75 for shoe rentals. After 6 it goes up to $3.75 per game. You can rent lanes by the hour for $19.99. Other fun activities are the arcade with the laser tag room, the sports bar and grill, and the pizza counter.

Camping

There are government-owned, public places for camping in the Charleston area as well as private options, and the best clearinghouse for information on them is the Charleston County Park and Recreation Commission, (843) 762-2172. We've

At Middletown Place, "The Seated Wood Nymph" was buried to s[ ] it the wrath of Union soldiers in 1865. Long ago, she was returne[ ] her rightful place—gracing the gardens in thoughtful repose.
PHOTO: COURTESY OF CHARLESTON AREA CONVENTION AND VISITORS BUREAU

included our favorites here.

If you've got a youngster who wants to get outdoors, the Boy Scouts are on top of things at their two campsites, Camp Hona-wah on Wadmalaw Island and Camp Moultrie on Lake Moultrie. For more information on joining the Boy Scouts of America or if you would like to volunteer to help out, call the Coastal Carolina Council of the BSA, 1025 Sam Rittenberg Boulevard, Charleston, (843) 763-0305.

The Girl Scout Outdoor Program Facility is a wonderful site in Cordesville (about 38 miles from Charleston) that's listed on the National Register of Historic Places. The summer resident camp is called Camp Low Country and runs June through August. The site includes a Junior Olympic-size pool, 20-stall stable, lighted riding ring, screened dining hall, three units of platform tents, and one cabin unit. For more information about the Outdoor Program Facility or other Girl Scout programs, call (800) 868-9911.

Capers Island
c/o 5CDNR, P.O. Box 12559,
Charleston, SC, 29412
(843) 762-5075

This 2,000-acre barrier island can only be reached by boat but is well worth the effort of securing a ride. You may travel in your own boat or contact Coastal Expeditions, (843) 884-7684, to arrange water transport. South Carolina's only primitive beachfront camping area, Capers has no facilities, and camping here is absolutely in the rough—exactly the way plenty of people want it. It is protected under the Heritage Trust Program and managed by the South Carolina Department of Natural Resources Marine Resources Division. Contact the Marine Resources Division at Fort Johnson on James Island at the number listed above for a permit.

Francis Marion National Forest
Pinckney St., near intersection of U.S.
Hwy. 17 and S.C. Hwy. 45, McClellanville
(843) 887-3257

There are four sites in the Francis Marion National Forest, a little more than 2 miles past Awendaw. It's hard to beat this place for seclusion and an opportunity to get back to nature. The forest still bears scars from Hurricane Hugo, but it stands testimony to nature's resilience. To get there, take US 17 N. toward Georgetown. Just after the intersection of US 17 and S.C. Highway 45 about 33 miles from Charleston, turn right onto Pinckney

Street and look for the ranger station. All the sites are free except at Buck Hall Campground, which costs $15 a day on a first-come, first-served basis. Call for information about availability, or write the Wambaw Ranger District, P.O. Box 788, McClellanville, SC 29458.

James Island County Park
871 Riverland Dr., Charleston
(843) 795-9884, (800) 743-7275

One lovely spot is the James Island County Park, with 125 camping sites. Campers can spend the night in tents or in recreational vehicles. Most sites are equipped with full water, sewer, and electricity hookups. Prices for tent sites range as follows: $16.15 for Charleston County residents; $17.10 for nonresident seniors; and $19 for nonresidents. For full hookups, these are the rates: $21.25 for Charleston County residents; $22.50 for nonresident seniors; and $25 for nonresidents. (Please note that these fees do not include the 12% accommodations tax levied here.) Round-trip shuttle service is available to downtown Charleston, Folly Beach County Park, and Folly Beach Fishing Pier for $5, $4 ages 3 to 12.

KOA Kampground
3157 Hwy. 17 North, Mt. Pleasant
(843) 849-5177, (800) KOA-5796

This Mt. Pleasant KOA campground offers large pull-through sites with 20-, 30-, and 50-amp hookups. Amenities include restrooms, showers, heated swimming pool, convenience store, laundry, firewood, and propane. There is a 30-acre lake fully stocked for fishing and water recreation. The 2.5-mile hiking trail and bike rentals offer other opportunities for enjoying the great outdoors. Deluxe and wilderness tent sites are available for those who really want to get away from it all. Located on Highway 17 North, this location has many nearby attractions like Boone Hall Plantation, SeeWee Wildlife and Nature Center, Patriots Point Maritime Museum, and historic Charleston. (See our Attractions,

Kidstuff, and Daytrips chapters for more on these and other area points of interest.) Weekly and monthly rates range from about $199.80 per week and $305 per month plus water and electricity. Nightly rates are around $30.

Oak Plantation Campground
3540 Savannah Hwy., Johns Island
(843) 766-5936
This is an RV campground with modern facilities. Campers park on concrete pads with 30- and 50-amp hookups available. The campground is landscaped with privacy in mind, and campers enjoy fishing for bream and bass in the freshwater lake. There is a playground with swings, a swimming pool, a small grocery with propane, and a shuttle bus for those who wish to leave the RV behind and catch a ride into the city. The office is open from 7:30 AM to 7 PM, and nightly rates range from $13.20 to $22.

Fitness Centers

Lifequest
610 Coleman Blvd., Mt. Pleasant
(843) 849-1414
35 Folly Rd., Charleston
(843) 571-2828
Lifequest centers are locally owned, state-of-the-art fitness centers. The two facilities are sparkling clean and attractive with an antibacterial aerobics floor, free weights, a dumbbell section, circuit-training machines (of Lifequest's own design), cardiovascular equipment (including steps, bikes, and treadmills), a ladies-only section, and a self-defense studio. Childcare for children 3 months and older is an option. Lifequest memberships for 12 months are about $44 a month for a single with each additional family member at $27 a month. Call for more information and special package rates.

St. Andrews Family Recreation Center
1642 Sam Rittenberg Blvd., Charleston
(843) 763-3850
Affiliated with the St. Andrews Park and

Playground Department, this is a full-service health fitness facility. The whole family (even the little ones, who play in the nursery) can enjoy aerobics classes, eight racquetball courts, a squash court, a basketball court, a Junior Olympic pool, Nautilus equipment, free weights, an indoor track, stair machines, treadmills, personal trainers, and more. Annual, three-month, student, and daily passes are available, and prices vary according to factors such as residence and age. St. Andrews Public Service District residents pay about $36 a month for a single membership or $60 a month for a family membership with a $64 or $103 one-time enrollment fee. Full-time students pay on a month-to-month basis, usually about $50 a month. Daily passes are available for $8. Hours are 5:30 AM to 9 PM, Monday through Thursday, Friday closing at 8 PM; 8 AM to 5 PM on Saturday and 2 to 5 PM Sunday.

Town and Country Inn Fitness Center
2008 Savannah Hwy., Charleston
(843) 571-1000
Although it's in a motel complex, this $1-million fitness center is open to the public for memberships. For an initiation fee and monthly payment, members can use the Cal Gym exercise equipment, stair machines, stationary bikes, dumbbells, two racquetball courts, a lap pool, showers, and sauna. Memberships run $120 per quarter for singles or $179 for family memberships, including a one-time initiation fee of $25.

Football

There are many leagues for youth football. For more information about children's teams, contact Youth Sports at (843) 724-7330. Registration is held throughout the month of August. Children must be 8 through 14 to play, and be sure to bring your child's birth certificate when you sign up. Play starts in mid-September and runs through the fall. Also, the Mt. Pleasant Recreation Department offers flag football for kids ages 7 and 8 during the fall.

Frisbee Golf

Charleston is on top of the Frisbee fun. On a pretty day, White Point Gardens (down by The Battery) is usually covered with young people throwing Frisbees. Call the City of Charleston Department of Recreation, (843) 724-7326, for more information.

Gymnastics

It seems most extracurricular community programs and recreational department programs offer gymnastic courses. Another option we can recommend is Charleston Gymnastics Training Center.

Charleston Gymnastics Training Center
1088 Quail Dr., Charleston
(843) 720-3808
This is a very serious, well-respected program that is safety-certified. Competitive teams go to the state, regional, and national level. Preschool to advanced classes are offered throughout the school year. There is a $15 registration fee, and once-a-week one-hour classes cost $88 for an 18-week session. One-and-a-half hour classes are $135 for a week session.

Horseback Riding

The equestrian set is quite active in the Greater Charleston area. We've included one stable each in Mt. Pleasant, West Ashley, Hollywood (south of Charleston on the way to Edisto Island), and Seabrook, and two on Johns Island.

Brick Church Farm
1131 Wando Rd., Mt. Pleasant
(843) 881-1310
This is a popular riding school, away from city congestion with caring, competent personnel. Call for directions and information. This is primarily a private show barn that prepares riders for hunter jumper competitions on the local and southeastern levels. No horse rentals are available here, but boarding for hunters and jumpers is $400 a month. Lessons are offered on a limited basis (on your own horse) in the $35 to $65 range for a half-hour private lesson or an hour-long group lesson.

Brickhouse Plantation Equestrian Center
2669 Hamilton Rd., Johns Island
(843) 559-2867
Ponies are the specialty at Brickhouse. Lessons in hunt seat, dressage, and combined training cost $30 for a once-a-week group lesson or $100 for a month of group lessons. Private lessons cost up to $40 per lesson or $140 for a month of lessons. Boarding is offered in three locations. Stall boarding in the main barn is $415 a month, and it's $380 in the pony barn. Pasture boarding is $230 a month. Brickhouse also has a summer camp (see our Kidstuff chapter for summer camp information).

Middleton Riding and Hunt Stables
4280 Ashley River Rd., Charleston
(843) 556-8137
A premier boarding and lesson facility, Middleton has a dressage arena, cross-country course, and lighted ring for evening riding. Stall boarding is $450 a month, and lessons are offered for $25 a half-hour (private or group lessons) or $20 for a half-hour lesson on a monthly basis. Trail rides are offered through the nearby Middleton Inn (see our Bed and Breakfast and Atmospheric Inns chapter) for ages 10 and older for $40. Contact Coastal Equestrians, (843) 556-5272, for these walking trail rides through the Middleton woods and wetlands.

Mullet Hall Equestrian Center
2662 Mullet Hall Rd., Johns Island
(843) 795-4FUN (4386)
Opened in April 2001 by the Charleston County Park and Recreation Commission, this 60-acre equestrian center features fenced warm-up and open-lunge areas, three permanent show rings, and jump sets. For riders who trailer their horses in, there are seven miles of riding trails through the 738-acre park site.

Passes are required for trail riding. Ample parking is available for all kinds of vehicles. This facility serves as the host site for a variety of competitive horse shows. Call for more information about upcoming events.

Seabrook Island Equestrian Center
Seabrook Island
(843) 768-7541

This center is at Seabrook but is open to the public. Reservations should be made for private lessons, trail rides into the undeveloped portions of the island's woods and marshes, rides on the beach in the summer, and boarding. The walking trail rides for ages 8 and older are $50 a person. The advanced rider may go on a trotting/cantering trail ride for $60 a person; beach rides are $70 a person for advanced riders. Parent-led pony rides are $25 per half hour. Lessons cost $25 per hour for semi-private sessions, and $40 per half-hour for private training. Boarding fees here are $400 a month. Advanced riders may also call for more information on the monthly adopt-a-horse program.

Stono Ferry Stables
5304 Stono Ferry Course, Hollywood
(843) 763-0566

Stono Stables offers lessons, dressage, hunter jumper training, boarding, and sales. Staff members are involved in polo, and this is a good source for information about that sport as well. Stall boarding runs $375 a month, and lessons for children are $78 a month for one lesson a week. These can either be one-hour group lessons (with a maximum of five riders) or half-hour private sessions.

Stono River Stable
2962 Hut Rd., Johns Island
(843) 559-0773

This established riding school offers weekly and private lessons with a children's summer camp. The escorted daily trail rides cover miles through the heart of a sea island maritime forest area and

> ## Insiders' Tip
> It's a Charleston tradition to enjoy an oyster roast at sunset along some Lowcountry creek when there's a nip in the air. Locals like their oysters with crackers, drawn butter, and a pinch of horseradish.

cost $20. There is dressage, show jumping, and a cross-country course at this 200-acre facility. The owners welcome visitors, and children regularly drop by to feed a favorite pony a carrot. Lessons are $30 an hour for a private lesson and $25 for a half-hour private lesson or a one-hour group lesson. Stall boarding is available for $300 a month. A new 10-stall barn is offered for show and transit horses, so bring your horse on vacation with you!

Martial Arts

There are numerous martial arts studios in the Charleston area. In addition, some courses are also offered at many of the recreation centers mentioned in the Parks and Recreation Centers section in this chapter.

International Taekwon-Do Center
1750 Savannah Hwy., Charleston
(843) 556-4391

International offers classes for men, women, and children ages 5 and older who are interested in tae kwon do and self-defense. Classes are taught at the Savannah Highway studio and at Sunshine House on Long Point Road in Mt. Pleasant. There is a $50 registration fee, with a monthly lesson fee of $70, a four-month fee of $62 a month, and a yearly fee of $50 a month. Call for special packages, and check it out with a free trial class.

Masters Studio of Self Defense
1021 Rifle Range Rd., Mt. Pleasant
(843) 881-4866
1888 Wallenberg Blvd., Charleston
(843) 766-4376
7671 Northwoods Blvd., North Charleston
(843) 797-1031
848 Folly Rd., James Island
(843) 762-1640

With four locations convenient to a good portion of the Greater Charleston area, Masters Studio offers classes for all ages in a variety of self-defense disciplines—shaolin kempo, karate, jujitsu, and t'ai chi. Group as well as private lessons are available. The twice-weekly, one-hour classes are $67 a month for adults and $62 a month for kids ages 5 to 12. If already enrolled in a class, private lessons are $17.50.

Minigolf

Classic Golf
1528 Ben Sawyer Blvd., Mt. Pleasant
(843) 881-3131

Classic Golf has two 18-hole courses and is a great place for a birthday party. Charges vary with age: Adults pay $6 a round; and kids, $4. Special group and off season rates are available. Hours are 11 AM to 10 PM or later in the summer. Chow down at the Island Clubhouse restaurant next door for Caribbean and island-style food after your round.

> ## Insiders' Tip
> After finishing lunch at one of the fine restaurants scattered along East Bay Street, take a stroll through Charleston's Waterfront Park. It's safe, nearby, and perfect for "taking the air," as the old-timers in this area might put it.

Sand Dollar Minigolf
1405 Ben Sawyer Blvd., Mt. Pleasant
(843) 884-0320

With enormous, friendly looking, plastic animal obstacles, this course is especially fun for children. Gazebo rentals for birthday parties are encouraged, and there are special group rates. Sand Dollar stays open year round with extended hours April through Labor Day. After a round of golf, head into the gift shop to look at the huge collection of shells and souvenirs for sale. A round here is $1.50 for children 12 and younger and $3 for adults. Group rates are available also.

Playgrounds

There are 17 playgrounds in the city, some of which are downtown and in West Ashley. The playground and special events coordinator for the Charleston Department of Recreation can be reached at (843) 724-7336. We've described some of our favorites.

Moultrie Playground
41 Ashley Ave., Charleston
(843) 724-7398

Completion of an extensive renovation relocated four new tennis courts beside the existing two along Broad Street. The new baseball field moved to the old tennis court site and opened in spring 2001. New concrete walkways and bleachers were installed also. The playground has nice equipment for kids including climbing sets, swings, and a sand pit, plus basketball courts. Moultrie is across from Colonial Lake and is a popular destination for families.

Hazel Parker Playground
70 East Bay St., Charleston
(843) 724-7397

Open sunup to sundown, this park has playground equipment as well as athletic fields, a tennis court, and basketball hoops. You can see Charleston Harbor from the grounds, and you are in skipping distance of The Battery.

St. Andrews Park and Playground
1095 Playground Rd., Charleston
(843) 763-4360
This recently revamped playground features the basic fun stuff—monkey bars, slides, and swings. This is the headquarters for the St. Andrews Park and Playground Commission, and up-to-date information on sporting events and activities is available here. There are lighted tennis courts, athletic fields for baseball, softball, football, and soccer, basketball courts, and a gymnasium. A picnic shelter is available.

Mary Utsey Playground
1350 Orange Grove Rd., Charleston
(843) 724-7337
West of the Ashley, this playground's shady areas are much appreciated during the hot months in Charleston. It has swings and other standard playground equipment.

Racquetball

Racquetball enthusiasts can find camaraderie and court time at the fitness centers listed above and at some recreation centers and playground complexes. (See both categories in this chapter for phone numbers.)

Running

Running is a very popular Lowcountry activity, and most every weekend offers a charity benefit run/walk for the serious and not-so-serious runners here. By far the largest race is the Cooper River Bridge Run drawing an international field of competition of over 30,000 participants.

Along with the Cooper River Bridge Run, other annual races include a 5K and 10K that happen in conjunction with the Flowertown Festival in Summerville. Other 5K runs are the North Charleston Arts Festival run, the Holiday Festival of Lights run, and the South Carolina Race for the Cure. See our Annual Events chapter for more on these happenings. Also, the James Island County Park sponsors a triathlon series during June, July, and August. (See the Parks and Recreation Centers section of this chapter for more on this county park.)

Charleston Running Club
P.O. Box 31216, Charleston, SC 29417
(843) 971-2889
The Charleston Running Club holds meetings the last Tuesday of every month at the MUSC Wellness Center and has about 600 members. The organization publishes a substantial newsletter monthly in booklet form (with results from races, stories, book reviews, and a calendar). The club sponsors about a dozen races and a summer track series. They also organize a schedule of Charleston area group runs at Colonial Lake, MUSC Harper Student Center, and the James Island Post Office. Members enjoy a party after the Cooper River Bridge Run and discounts at local athletic stores. Write for more information and a membership application.

Skating

People in this area skate indoors and outdoors and even have a club—the Charleston Roll Patrol—to promote their interests. Hampton Park and James Island County Park, where you can also rent inline skates, are great outdoor skating sites (see our Parks and Recreation Centers section in this chapter).

With the advent of the Professional Ice Hockey team, The South Carolina Stingrays, ice skating has seen a surge of interest in the Lowcountry. For more about the Stingrays see our Spectator Sports chapter. The North Charleston Coliseum and the Carolina Ice Palace (see below) are the venues for this type of skating fun.

Here are some popular indoor rinks for roller skating followed by one for ice skating.

Hot Wheels Skating Center Inc.
1523 Folly Rd., Charleston
(843) 795-7982

Even the little ones can skate here in clamp-on skates. The management at Hot Wheels is enthusiastic, and this is a very popular place for birthday parties, which are often booked weeks in advance. A snack bar stocks light refreshments. Skating prices range from $1 (plus $1 skate rental) on Wednesday evenings, 7 to 9 PM, and up to $5 on Friday and Saturday nights, 7 to 11 PM.

Stardust Skate Center
2035 Spaulding Dr., North Charleston
(843) 747-0111

A popular skate center, Stardust is large and can accommodate several parties and many individual patrons at the same time. Supervision and safety are emphasized at this family-oriented center. The snack bar is extensive, and there are many video games to play. Skating prices vary, ranging from about $3.50 per person on school nights (and for children under 12 on Saturday mornings) up to $7 per person on Fridays and Saturdays between 7:30 and 11:30 PM. Skating lessons for children 12 and younger are $3.50.

Carolina Ice Palace
7665 Northwoods Blvd., North Charleston
(843) 572-2717

The Carolina Ice Palace has two NHL-sized ice rinks for public skating year round. This is a fun atmosphere for family entertainment with youth and adult hockey and figure skating. The facility encompasses an arcade, virtual reality center, full service pro shop, party rooms, and a jumbo TV lounge. Hours are 11 AM to 3 PM Monday through Friday. After-school skating is scheduled from 3 to 5:30 PM Monday, Wednesday, and Friday. The palace is also open from 7 to 9 PM Wednesday and Thursday night. Friday and Saturday hours extend to 11:30 PM, and Sunday hours are 1:30 to 6 PM. Skating fees are in the $4 to $6 range with $2

for skate rental. (See our Kidstuff chapter for more on the Ice Palace.)

Soccer

The popularity of soccer in this area has led to new venues for the sport. The recently dedicated Ansonborough Fields, downtown near the Charleston Maritime Center, are providing fields for soccer and football. In the fall of 2001, a new soccer complex opened on James Island off Ft. Johnson Road.

Again, the area recreation departments are the clearinghouses for information on soccer. They can steer adults and children alike to a soccer team in their area. Sign-up includes a modest fee of $10 to around $25 and commitment to weekday practices and weekday and Saturday games or both. Birth certificates are required. Call the recreation departments previously listed for more information on youth and adult leagues.

Softball

In the spring, it seems softball games pop up everywhere in the Lowcountry. To learn more about teams and competition for youth and adults, call the city and town recreation departments listed at the beginning of the Recreation section of this chapter. Also check with churches, as many sponsor their own teams.

Tennis

An empty tennis court on a pretty day is hard to come by in this area. The city of Charleston maintains 56 hard courts, 41 of which are lighted and available on a first-come, first-served basis for free (except for a nominal fee at the Charleston and Maybank Tennis Centers). With headquarters at the Charleston Tennis Center, the city organizes leagues, round-robins, socials, and tournaments for tennis enthusiasts of all ages. Lessons can be arranged by calling (843) 762-7706. A new

$9-million tennis complex was constructed on Daniel Island instigated by the announcement that the Family Circle Cup would move to Charleston from its long-standing run in Hilton Head. This is fostering the further growth of tennis here.

The very popular local United States Tennis Association league has 45 men's and ladies' teams competing at nearly every National Tennis Rating Program level of play on public and private club courts around the area. There are nine ladies' city league teams as well. Call the city tennis coordinator at (843) 724-7401, or one of the tennis centers listed below, for more information about specific locations, court reservations, and joining tennis leagues. The following list will give you some ideas about the options.

Charleston Tennis Center
19 Farmfield Ave., Charleston
(843) 724-7402

These city of Charleston courts are conveniently located in West Ashley and are popular with the tennis crowd. Hours are based on demand, but are generally Monday through Thursday, 8:30 AM to 10 PM; Friday from 8:30 AM until 7 PM; Saturday from 9 AM until 6 PM; and Sunday, 10 AM until 6 PM. Junior Summer Tennis Camps are held in July and August (see the Summer Camps section of our Kidstuff chapter). Court fees vary, so please call for information.

Creekside Tennis and Swim
790 Creekside Dr., Mt. Pleasant
(843) 884-6111

Creekside Tennis and Swim has 12 lighted courts. Members enjoy use of lockers, a lounge, and a six-lane swimming pool. The club hosts active adult and junior programs. There are no court fees, but monthly dues and an initiation fee are charged. Nonmembers can take lessons. (See our Neighborhoods chapter for more on the Creekside community.)

Kiawah Island Resort
12 Kiawah Beach Dr., Kiawah Island
(843) 768-2121, Ext. 4012

In November 1996, Kiawah was rated the third-best tennis resort in America by

The city's youth soccer leagues encourage competition, sportsmanship, team play, and just plain fun.
PHOTO: THOMAS P. FORD

Tennis magazine, which bases its top-50 selections on quality of instruction, off-court amenities, and facilities. The resort has two separate tennis complexes. The West Beach Tennis Club, open year round, has 14 Har-Tru clay courts, two lighted hard courts, and a backboard for practice. The East Beach Tennis Club, open mid-March through November 1, boasts nine Har-Tru courts, three hard courts, two lighted courts, and a fully automated practice alley. Nonmember play is available for a $20 per hour fee ($15 in the off-season). (For more on Kiawah, see our Neighborhoods chapter.)

Maybank Tennis Center
1880 Houghton Dr., Charleston
(843) 406-8814

Another city-owned tennis facility is the Maybank Tennis Center with a full-time staff on site. You'll find a total of 11 courts here, eight lighted hard courts and three Har-Tru. A fee of $2.50 to $3 per person per hour is charged for the hard courts and $7 to $7.50 per hour for the clay courts. The hours are 8 AM to 8 PM Monday through Friday, 8 AM to 6 PM on Saturday, and 12 PM to 8 PM on Sunday, or until you wind up that heated match.

Wild Dunes Resort, Isle of Palms
5757 Palm Blvd., Isle of Palms
(843) 886-2113

Wild Dunes features 17 Har-Tru tennis courts, one hard court, a ball wall, and a stadium court for tournaments. Five of the courts are lighted. Resort guests and members have priority, but nonmembers can take part in clinics, lessons, and round-robins. (See our Neighborhoods chapter.)

Volleyball

Some bars on the beach provide a volley-ball net and encourage random competition, which we hear can get pretty fierce among beer buddies. If you are interested in something more predictable and organized, there are teams put together by the Mt. Pleasant and Isle of Palms recreation departments. The Isle of Palms Recreation Department, (843) 886-8294, organizes coed adult teams in January and February. The Mt. Pleasant folks can be reached at (843) 884-2528. There is a charge of about $25 for participation. Teams are also often sponsored by local restaurants and merchants. Inquire at one of the area recreation departments about signing up.

Golf

Better by Design
Signature Holes
Scenery
Charleston Area
Golf Courses
Courses at
Lowcountry Resorts

Greater Charleston can take justifiable pride in the variety of golf challenges available to the area's visitors and residents.

If you're a serious tournament player with world-class experience, or if you're just one of those relatively harmless twice-a-year duffers, Charleston has you well covered when it comes to golf. After all, this is the site of America's very first golf course—among the city's many claims to fame. The actual site of the first course, laid out in 1786, known as "Harleston Green," has long ago been overtaken by subsequent urbanization, but golf is always proudly mentioned when the list of Charleston's "famous firsts" comes up.

Today, Lowcountry golf is a wealth of opportunity. From the world-ranked resort courses to the ever-popular public tracks, from the private courses to the semi-private offerings, it's possible to golf every day for nearly a month and play a different 18-hole course each day.

Clearly, the great drawing card for Lowcountry golf is the weather. Here the winter chill hardly ever discourages the stouthearted player, and the summer's sweltering heat only adds another challenge to the dedicated would-be pro. Indeed, for the vast majority of the year Charleston area golf courses sing the siren's call to golfers from (literally) all over the world.

We'll start with some of the famous designer names that are associated with Lowcountry golf courses. Then, we'll take you on a brief tour of some of our infamous signature holes, where even the best players are tested to make birdie.

We'll give you a tour of the area's public courses and then go out to the island resorts where an array of designer courses await the serious golfer determined to be tested by the very best.

Better by Design

Every area course is different in some way. Each has its own charm and individual characteristics, not to mention frustrations. That, in part, may be because most of the world's best golf architects have designed courses here in the Lowcountry. You'll find the work of Pete Dye, Tom Fazio, Arthur Hills, Jack Nicklaus, Gary Player, Robert Trent Jones Sr., and Rees Jones, among them.

Pete Dye's name is one of the biggest in the industry. His most famous courses include Harbour Town on Hilton Head Island and the Stadium Course at PGA West in La Quinta, California. A more recent Dye offering is The Ocean Course at Kiawah Island, which hosted the 1991 Ryder Cup matches and the prestigious World Cup of Golf in November 1997. The latter was the world's most-watched golf competition when the event was transmitted via satellite to more than 80 countries. Won by the Irish for the first time since 1958, the team's four-day total of 31-under-par led the field by five strokes. Each team player pocketed $200,000 for his effort.

The Ocean Course rivals Tom Fazio's Lowcountry masterpiece, The Links Course at

Wild Dunes Resort, which is ranked among the world's best by *Golf* magazine. Fazio's golf courses are possibly the best known here in the Lowcountry because he designed both courses on Wild Dunes (The Links and Harbor Course), and he also laid out Kiawah's popular Osprey Point.

Whereas Pete Dye frequently uses railroad ties (a signature of his work), Arthur Hills prefers to use more of a site's natural elements in his designs. Hills did the newest course at Dunes West, which opened in 1991 and showcased the 1992 Amoco Centel Championship. Hills' other famous golf course designs include Eagle Trace, a TPC course in Coral Springs, Florida, cited in *Golf Digest*'s "100 Best Courses in America."

Another name to note among the Charleston area's most popular golf designers is Torri Jackson, who gave us Patriots Point in Mt. Pleasant back in 1981. He's also responsible for the course on Edisto Island at Fairfield Ocean Ridge (1978) and the one at Crowfield Plantation (1990) in Goose Creek.

Newest of the "name" designers to provide Charleston-area golfers with a challenge to their skills is Dr. Michael Hurdzan. His contribution is the new 27-hole Golf Club at Wescott Plantation in North Charleston. Named "Architect of the Year" in 1997, Dr. Hurdzan's design allows players to enjoy the natural elements on the course and "play in various directions and lengths" around them.

Signature Holes

Here's a sampling of the flavor of Lowcountry golf—a few of the area signature holes you'll want to be prepared for.

Patriots Point has its famous No. 17, a par 3, 112-yard island green that catches the uninitiated off-guard. This hole requires the player to take into careful consideration the ever-changing winds off Charleston Harbor.

The No. 6 hole at Fairfield Ocean Ridge is another island hole that can be a spoiler. It's a tough 380-yard, par 4 challenge.

Crowfield Plantation offers its par 5, 500-yard No. 7 hole that features treacherous mounds that make players feel as if they've found a bit of old Scotland.

Rees Jones' Charleston National design, which opened in 1990, features the demanding No. 15 hole, a par 3, 183-yarder from the white tees. It plays 210 yards from the blue tees and has an innocent-looking pond on the right that attracts errant balls like a magnet.

On The Links Course at Wild Dunes, No. 9 is said to be the most difficult. It is a long, straight 451-yard par 4 that often plays even longer because it is usually played into the wind. The green is closely guarded on the left by a hidden pond. This green is also the most unforgiving on the course—it slopes severely from back to front. All things considered, a par on No. 9 is an excellent score.

The signature hole at Wild Dunes' Turtle Point is No. 11. There's water along the entire right side from the tee past the green. According to Jack Nicklaus, its designer, "You can drive the ball as far as you want, but the farther you drive it, the greater the chance of slicing it into the water. There is a secondary landing area, or an out where those who won't want to chance it can play the shot. Then putt it or chip it or, as the Scots say, 'play a bumble' back into the green."

Scenery

Pete Dye's Ocean Course and Tom Fazio's Links Course both make spectacular use of the Atlantic Ocean in their designs. Fazio's Harbor Course on Wild Dunes uses the Intracoastal Waterway as a backdrop. The Links at Stono Ferry, designed by Ron Garl in 1989, is another opportunity to play along the colorful and busy Intracoastal.

But most of the Lowcountry's golf courses take full advantage of the beautiful salt marshes, signature of the area itself, in their layout designs. Gary Player's Marsh Point on Kiawah is probably the best example. A curious alligator has even been known to occasionally wander onto the course.

In fact, the area's multiple charms make the Lowcountry a favorite destination for golf widows and widowers and the assorted family members who often get swept up in a spouse's or parent's pursuit of the sport. The rationalization usually goes something like this: While golfers are challenged to play the many private, semi-private, and public courses throughout the area, the unenlightened can always explore the beautiful Lowcountry plantations, the splendid museums, the beaches, and the interesting shops, thus staying contented and amused.

And that brings up another benefit of Charleston area golf: Because there are so many other things to do here, the area courses are relatively uncrowded. That means excellent starting times and an unhurried atmosphere.

Here we provide brief profiles of the area courses, so tee up when it suits you, and play at least 18 relaxing and scenic Lowcountry holes. You'll find descriptions of who designed the courses and when, plus who can play them, how much it costs (during high season) and where to call for more details. Greens fees quoted are in-season rates (unless otherwise noted) and exclude tax.

Many golfers have met their Waterloo on No. 4 at Wild Dunes' Links course. PHOTO: THOMAS P. FORD

Charleston Municipal Golf Course
2110 Maybank Hwy., Charleston
(843) 795-6517

This public course, only five minutes from downtown Charleston, has been around since 1927. Although it lost some 350 mature trees in Hugo's wrath, the course was beautifully replanted and is now in very good shape. The par 72 course is 6500 yards long from the middle tees; it's 5200 and par 72 from the forward tees. You'll find small greens, well-tended fairways, and an on-site pro shop with a snack bar. PGA- and LPGA-trained instructors are on hand for lessons, and this is the only public course in South Carolina with a Slazenger club-fitting system available for beginners and experts alike. Individual greens fees are $12 (for walkers) or $22 (with cart). The rate goes up to $25 on weekends. Charleston residents get a $3 discount. Call about a week in advance for tee times.

Coosaw Creek Country Club
4210 Dorchester Rd., North Charleston
(843) 767-9000

Coosaw Creek, a 645-acre residential community in North Charleston, offers an Arthur Hills course designed in 1993. The par 71 course is 6593 yards long from the middle tees. The bonus here is on accuracy instead of length; good tee shots as well as a deft short game are the keys to low scoring. Hills had more natural topography to work with at Coosaw Creek than most Lowcountry layouts offer—you'll find rolling fairways, subtle mounding, and gradual elevation changes. The best opportunity to score low is on the front nine, as the back side brings more of the water and wetlands into play. Eric Landfried is the pro on hand. In-seasonal weekday greens fees are $57; Saturday and Sunday fees are $63, taxes and cart included. After Labor Day, the greens fees go down to $39 for weekdays and $44 on weekends.

Charleston National Country Club
1360 National Dr., Mt. Pleasant
(843) 884-7799

The idea for Charleston National Country Club was conceived more than 20 years ago, but the once-private golf community was just coming into focus when Hugo struck in 1989. Redesigned and refurbished with input from original designer Rees Jones, the par 72, 18-hole course (now semiprivate) is 6928 yards long. Charleston National has a beautiful 8,000-square-foot clubhouse with luxury amenities, including a pool and tennis center. This is the home course for the College of Charleston and The Citadel golf teams. Charleston National's pro is Bart Wolfe. Weekday greens fees are $60; and $40 after 1:30 PM. Twilight greens fees are $27.95. Friday through Sunday fees are $75; and $49.95 after 1:30 PM. Weekend twilight fees are $29.95. Carts are included in the price.

Crowfield Golf and Country Club
300 Hamlet Circle, Goose Creek
(843) 764-4618

Crowfield Golf and Country Club offers championship golfing on a semiprivate course designed in 1990 by Tom Jackson and Bob Spence. Their par 72, 18-hole layout is 7003 yards long. The course is slightly Scottish in that it has a rolling terrain accompanied by acres of fairway and green-side bunkers. Shooting ability is of prime importance here. Undulating greens and imaginative pin placements test the nerves of the most skilled players. Crowfield's pro shop is well-stocked, and there's a restaurant and cocktail lounge on-site. Breakfast, lunch, or dinner may be ordered from the menu. Call pro Bert Yelverton for lesson details. Tee times are accepted up to one week in advance. Weekday greens fees are $49; Saturday and Sunday fees are $59, and that includes a cart. Locals pay $32 on weekdays and $42 on weekends.

Dunes West
3535 Wando Plantation Wy., Mt. Pleasant
(843) 856-9000, (888) 955-1234

Ten miles northeast of Charleston in the fast-growing East Cooper area, Dunes West is part of a 4,700-acre residential community that's been in development since the late 1980s. The highly rated course—set on a high, marshy peninsula bounded by three tidal creeks—was designed by Arthur Hills on the site of the historic Lexington Plantation house.

Like its sister course on Isle of Palms, Dunes West takes full advantage of its natural setting. The par 72 championship course is 6871 yards long. The opening holes, cut from tall pines, have fairway corridors leading to elevated and bunkered greens. The back nine has a typical Lowcountry flavor with moss-draped oaks lining the fairways and expansive views of the marsh from several of the tees and greens. There's a handsome clubhouse with every modern luxury amenity. The pro is Kevin Zmickas. The Hills course at Dunes West was the site of the 1992 Amoco Centel Championship, and it is now a public course. Greens fees Monday through Thursday are $69; Friday through Sunday, they are $85.

Eagle Landing
1500 Eagle Landing Blvd., Hanahan
(843) 797-1667

This semiprivate golf course was constructed in 1987 and is slightly different in that it was built at "executive length." You play with a regulation ball, but the course itself is slightly shortened to use less land. The concept is very popular in Japan (where they know a thing or two about space limitations and miniaturization), but it's still fairly rare here. The par 65 course is 4164 yards long from the middle (traditionally the men's) tees, but only par 62 and 2910 yards from the forward (or ladies') tees. This foreshortened course takes some getting used to, but many of the residents of the associated Eagle Landing retirement community find the difference refreshing.

The Eagle Landing clubhouse features a fully stocked pro shop and snack bar. Pro instruction is available from Dwight Thomas. You'll also find a driving range and putting greens at this well-maintained facility. This unusual golf challenge is next to the Eagle Landing residential community. The course is public, but club memberships are available. Weekday fees are $12 before 1 PM, $13 after. Saturday and Sunday play will run you $18 before 1 PM, $15 after. Carts are included.

Edisto Beach Golf Club
1 King Cotton Rd., Edisto Beach
(843) 869-1111

The course closely associated with Fairfield Ocean Ridge resort on Edisto Island is a semi-private, 18-hole championship layout designed by Tom Jackson in 1976 and has been considerably updated since then. The 6400-yard course features water holes, dense subtropical vegetation, and (for early risers) frequent visits by native wildlife. Fairfield has its share of old bull gators, but local wisdom says they prefer sunning and running to fighting.

The course has dune ridges throughout. Where the Nos. 2 and 3 tees are now situated was once a Confederate stronghold. The overall feel of the course is natural, as it was primarily carved from tidal marsh and jungle-thick Lowcountry vegetation. The No. 1 green provides a spectacular view of the Atlantic.

Fairfield's other amenities add to the mix, and you'll find a fully stocked pro shop with club and cart rentals available. Clinics and private instruction are offered by PGA-trained pros. Tee-time reservations are required. Weekday rates are $48 for 18 holes before 2 PM and $41 after 2, but call direct for more information—rates change seasonally.

The Links at Stono Ferry
5365 Forest Oaks Dr., Hollywood
(843) 763-1817

This 18-hole, par 72 course, owned and managed by Jim Colbert Golf Inc., is on

S.C. Highway 162, off U.S. 17 S. near the little town of Hollywood, about 15 miles or a half-hour from Charleston. The Links opened in 1989 and was designed by Ron Garl to accompany the exclusive Stono Ferry Plantation development. The course is 6606 yards long and open to the public seven days a week. It has three scenic holes on the Intracoastal Waterway, and it is a fair test from the back tees. You'll find a complete pro shop and a driving range, plus a full-service restaurant. PGA-trained teaching pro Kevin Zemnickas is on hand for tips and lessons. Rental clubs are available. Advance registration is required. Weekday greens fees are $41 before 1 PM, $35 after. Saturday and Sunday, they are $45 before 1 PM, $35 after. Locals get a $10 discount before 1 PM, a $5 break after. There's a twilight fee after 4 PM and seniors pay $20 on Mondays only. Cart fees are included.

Patriots Point Golf Links
100 Clubhouse Rd.,
(off U.S. Hwy. 17 Bus.), Mt. Pleasant
(843) 881-0042

Operated by Kemper Sports Management, this 18-hole public course is across the Cooper River bridges in Mt. Pleasant, just off U.S. 17 N., near the towering USS Yorktown, anchored in Charleston Harbor. (See our Attractions chapter.) The par 72 layout, open since 1980, has just had a $2.1-million upgrade with a new state-of-the-art irrigation system installed. Patriots Point affords spectacular views of the harbor, with oceangoing cargo ships frequently passing by.

The course is 6838 yards in length, with well-contoured fairways and well-bunkered greens. Pro Chad Leonard is on hand for lessons and more information. Amenities include a complete pro shop, a driving range, rental clubs and carts. A grill and snack bar are available too. Call ahead for tee times. Weekday greens fees are $62; Saturday and Sunday fees are $79. Twilight fees begin at 3 PM and are $30 on weekdays, $35 on weekends. Locals pay $38 for weekday play and $43 on weekends; their twilight rates are $24 and $27. Cart rental is included.

Pine Forest Country Club
1001 Congressional Blvd., Summerville
(843) 851-1193

The 18 holes at Pine Forest Country Club

It's a given: Golf is great in the Lowcountry. PHOTO: THOMAS P. FORD

Insiders' Tip

When you're playing on one of the Lowcountry's many marsh-front golf courses like Cougar Point on Kiawah or the Harbor Course at Wild Dunes, don't be surprised if you find yourself sharing the green with a curious alligator. The unofficial rule is: Let the gator keep the ball; no penalty stroke incurred.

in Dorchester County wind through the tall Summerville pines with some live oaks, dogwoods, and a lake system thrown in for good measure. Designed by architect Bob Spence in 1992. Pine Forest is maintained and run by Kemper Management noted for their ambitious and well-kept golf challenges. It is one of the most talked about USGA courses in the Lowcountry. The course is 6905 yards long from the middle tees, with an equal representation of straightaways, doglegs, and elevation changes. It is nicely balanced, with fun in store for golfers of all abilities. Rental clubs and carts are available. The local pro is Bert Yelverton. Call for reservations. Weekday greens fees are $30. Saturday and Sunday fees are $38, dropping to $32 after 1 PM. Carts are included in the prices.

**Shadowmoss Plantation
Golf and Country Club
20 Dunvagan Dr. (off S.C. Hwy. 61),
Charleston
(843) 556-8251, (800) 338-4971**

Public play is welcome at this scenic course, designed by Russell Breeden and opened in 1973 along S.C. Highway 61, the old Ashley River Road. In 1986 the 18-hole, par 72 course was extensively

renovated, and several water hazards were added to increase the challenge. Other modifications were made after Hurricane Hugo. The course is 6701 yards long and cuts through pines, oaks, and hickories. A mosaic of ponds and streams comes into play in an area once dotted with early 18th-century and 19th-century plantations.

You'll find a well-stocked pro shop, a snack bar, a grill with a lounge, and locker rooms. There's also a putting green as well as a chipping green and driving range. The golf pro at Shadowmoss is Bob Wolfe. Tee times can be arranged through a number of local hotels and inns or by calling Shadowmoss. Monday through Thursday greens fees (with cart rental included) are $35, Friday fees are $41, and Saturday and Sunday fees are $45. After 1 PM, weekday rates are $30; weekend rates are $39.

**The Golf Club at Wescott Plantation
5000 Wescott Club Dr., North Charleston
(843) 871-2135, (866) 211-GOLF**

Opened in the fall of 2000 with the full 27 holes up and ready for play early the following year, The Club at Wescott Plantation is North Charleston's worthy answer to the trendy designer courses on the resort islands closer to the coast. Designed by Dr. Michael Hurdzan who took full advantage of the natural elements on the course, all 27 holes are treelined with plenty of definition to each hole. Each hole has five tees so golfers can choose tees from 5,120 yards up to 7,100 yards—depending on their ability. The course winds through streams, ponds, wetlands, and key sentinel trees, with holes playing in various directions and lengths from these features. The club also features a full driving range, a completely outfitted pro shop, a full-service restaurant, and meeting/conference spaces. Thomas Robertson is currently head pro. Monday through Friday (except holidays), fees are $36.50; weekend play (and holidays) costs $46.50. Prices are less for juniors and during twilight hours.

Courses at Lowcountry Resorts

Wild Dunes

Only 15 miles from Charleston is Wild Dunes, which offers a total of 36 holes of Tom Fazio golf among its many upscale amenities.

Wild Dunes Links
10000 Backbay Dr., Isle of Palms
(843) 886-2164, (888) WDR-GOLF

The Links opened in 1980, with a 6722-yard, par 72 layout from the middle tees. Because two of the finishing holes (a par 4 and a par 5) are right on the Atlantic, you'll want to pray for a non-windy day. Indeed, wind can make the course different every day, but the scenery compensates for its fickle nature. The course is in great condition from tee to green, with rolling fairways and oak and palm trees in abundance. The Links (and Wild Dunes' other offering, Harbor Course), have a new high-tech yardage system for golf guests. Using a golf cart-mounted display screen linked to a Global Positioning Satellite System, players can determine the distance to a target with pinpoint accuracy. The pro shop is first rate, with Marty Mikesell riding herd on the whole golf program. Head pro at the Links is David Jeffcoat. *Golf Magazine* currently includes Wild Dunes Links among its Top 100 courses in the country. From Monday through Thursday (March 23 through May 31), the daily greens fees are $119 from 7 AM until noon; $109 until 2 PM, and $95 after—cart included. Weekend rates are $185 until noon and $165 after.

The Harbor Course
5881 Palmetto Dr., Isle of Palms
(843) 886-2164, (888) WDR-GOLF

The Harbor Course, which opened in 1985, has four holes set directly along the Intracoastal Waterway. The course is a par 70, with a 6446-yard layout that really challenges players. Two holes play from one island to another across the

Yacht Harbor, where the wind can be a major factor. Frequent players say to beware the challenging 17th hole. The pro is Kenny Gargiulo, and instruction is available through the fully stocked pro shop. From Monday through Sunday (March 23 through May 31), the greens fees are $119 from 7 AM until noon; $99 until 2 PM, and $79 after—cart included.

Kiawah Island Resort

Internationally famous Kiawah Island offers no fewer than six separate, distinct golf layouts for the adventurous Lowcountry golfer. Popular Lowcountry golf personality Tommy Cuthbert heads Kiawah's golf program. The River Course is exclusively reserved for property owners on the island. But Kiawah golf is so famous and popular there's still great opportunity for the tour elite, low handicappers, and the average player too. The Oaks on Johns Island is the newest acquisition. And four Kiawah courses—Cougar Point, Turtle Point, Osprey Point, and The Ocean Course, made famous by the internationally televised 1991 Ryder Cup Matches—are semi-private and open to homeowners, guests visiting the island, and Lowcountry vacationers who call specifically for reservations at least 24 hours in advance. Call Kiawah's main switchboard and check with each course individually for tee times.

Oak Point
4255 Bohicket Rd., Johns Island
(843) 768-7030

Recently acquired by Kiawah Island Golf, and now another part of its comprehensive golf package, is Oak Point. Tucked away within Hope Plantation adjacent to Kiawah and Seabrook islands, it was designed by Clyde Johnson and built in 1989. The par 72, 6759-yard-long course is challenging to both the novice golfer and the experienced professional.

Wide areas of windswept fairways stretch along salt marshes and heavily foliaged woodlands. There are numerous vistas of freshwater ponds and winding creeks. Word is that some area golfers prefer this course to Kiawah's Turtle Point, and it's a great choice for 36-hole-a-day players seeking a variety of challenges in the Kiawah-Seabrook area. The pro shop was recently renovated, and PGA pro Mike Arthur provides instruction for golfers at all levels of play. Hours can vary seasonally; call for tee times and more information. Daily greens fees in season are $90, cart included. Summer rates (June 8 through September 6) are $69.

Cougar Point
West Beach Village, Kiawah Island
(843) 768-2121, (800) 654-2924

Cougar Point, formerly called Marsh Point, reopened in 1996 after a complete, year-long makeover by original (1981) course designer Gary Player. Now, this par 72 course has a 6925-yard layout from the championship tees. Ric Ferguson is the resident pro with a top-flight shop to boot. There's even a halfway house on the 10th hole. Sometimes, four-footed furry creatures, along with alligators, ospreys, hawks, and a few snakes, have been known to be in the gallery here. Daily greens fees in season are $149, cart included. Summer rates (June 8 through September 6) are $119.

Turtle Point
East Beach Village, Kiawah Island
(843) 768-2121, (800) 654-2924

Turtle Point, designed by Jack Nicklaus, is an 18-hole, par 72 course that's 6914 yards long from the middle tees. It opened in 1981. Turtle Point is a low-profile design with fairway and green settings blended into the existing landscape. Nowhere is this more evident than along the spectacular three-hole stretch woven through rolling sand dunes directly along the Atlantic Ocean. Head pro at Turtle Point is Ronnie Miller. Turtle Point has been the site of the Carolina Amateur and the 1990 PGA Cup Matches. Daily greens fees in season are $149 cart included. Summer rates (June 8 through September 6) are $119.

Insiders' Tip

The list of designers whose courses carve beautiful curves through the Lowcountry reads like a who's who in the industry. Pete Dye put his signature railroad ties to use at The Ocean Course on Kiawah Island, home of the 1991 Ryder Cup and 1997 World Cup of Golf. Arthur Hills designed the new course at Dunes West, which showcased the 1992 Amoco Centel Championship. Tom Fazio crafted both The Links and Harbor Course at Wild Dunes, and Torri Jackson is responsible for Patriots Point, Fairfield Ocean Ridge, and Crowfield Plantation, all of which are more than a decade old and maturing gracefully. Throw in Rees Jones (Charleston National), Gary Player (Cougar Point at Kiawah) and the Golden Bear himself, Jack Nicklaus (Turtle Point), and you see that Lowcountry courses have come off the drawing boards of the very best.

Osprey Point
Vanderhorst Plantation, Kiawah Island
(843) 768-2121, (800) 654-2924
Tom Fazio designed Osprey Point in 1988. The par 72 course is 6678 yards from the middle tees and has four large, natural lakes. At Osprey Point, Fazio used this superb natural canvas to create a golf challenge of amazing playability and variety. In addition to the natural lakes, there are fingers of saltwater marsh and dense forests of live oaks, pines, palmettos, and magnolias. Jim Kelechi is pro here, and the club has a restaurant, bar, lounge, and locker rooms. Daily greens fees in season are $179, cart included. Summer rates (June 8 through September 6) are $129.

The Ocean Course
1000 Ocean Course Dr., Kiawah Island
(843) 768-2121, (800) 654-2924
The Ocean Course was designed by Pete Dye and completed just in time for the Ryder Cup matches in 1991. That year, *Golf Digest* named The Ocean Course "best new resort course of the year." Now the magazine calls it America's Toughest Resort Course. The cliffhanger finish of the 1991 Ryder Cup put the course on the must-play list of pros and amateurs everywhere. Dye's beautiful design gives you a par 72, 6824-yard challenge from the championship tees.

All 18 holes of the Ocean Course offer panoramic views of the Atlantic Ocean, and 10 holes play directly along the pristine, windswept beach. The clubhouse includes a restaurant, bar, pro shop, and locker rooms. The head pro at The Ocean Course is Brian Gerard. Daily greens fees in season are $245, cart included. Summer rates (June 8 through September 6) are $175.

Seabrook Island

Golf on Seabrook Island is limited to island residents, friends of club members, and visiting resort guests. There are two distinctly different golf challenges on the island: Crooked Oaks, designed by Robert Trent Jones Sr., and Ocean Winds, designed by Willard Byrd. Both courses have been executed in beautiful, undisturbed surroundings for challenging championship play. Seabrook's golf courses are the only ones in all of South Carolina that have earned full certification in the Audubon Cooperative Sanctuary Program.

Crooked Oaks
1002 Landfall Way, Seabrook Island
(843) 768-1000, (800) 824-2475
Crooked Oaks is an 18-hole, 6832-yard, par 72 course that meanders through the lush maritime forest and around several black water lagoons. When Jones designed it back in 1979, he described it as his "hard par-easy bogey" course. Most of the greens are elevated or well-bunkered—there are no lucky shots to the greens. It has rolling fairways weaving through stately live oaks, Spanish moss, sea marsh, and thick forest. Private and group instruction is offered by PGA pro Alan Walker. The fully stocked pro shop has sports fashions as well as equipment. Peak season greens fees are $125, cart included. The nine-hole rate is $65.

Ocean Winds
1002 Landfall Way, Seabrook Island
(843) 768-1000, (800) 824-2475
Ocean Winds, designed by Willard Byrd, is slightly older (1973) and is a 6805-yard, par 72 course from the middle tees. It plays a bit closer to the ocean. As a result, the Atlantic breezes can be a real test for even the best golfer. Ocean Winds golfers enjoy the benefits of a full-service clubhouse facility and a large pro shop, plus clinics and private instruction offered by an excellent teaching staff. Tournament coordination is available from PGA pro Alan Walker. Daily greens fees are $125 and include golf cart. The nine-hole rate is $65.

Boating and Watersports

Boating is an integral part of the Lowcountry lifestyle. State figures reveal that Charleston County is home to the most boats in South Carolina—28,483 registered watercraft in 2000. That's an amazing statistic—about one boat for every four households on a per capita basis. The Trident area logged 50,629 registrations in 2000, which represents around 13 percent of the South Carolina total.

There seems to be no end in sight for the boating frenzy, as newcomers and old salts alike discover and rediscover the pleasures of spending time on the water. From moonlight sails and family picnics on barrier islands to morning hunts in the back creeks and deep-sea fishing adventures, many are the occasions when "by boat" is the only way to go.

You can bring your own, or you can buy, rent, or charter a boat while you are here. Whatever the case, make certain to acquire, in navigational terms, "local knowledge" before you leave shore. We recommend contacting the U.S. Coast Guard about its Auxiliary Public Education Courses. These cover information about navigational rules, aids to navigation, legal requirements, safety equipment, trailering, and coping with emergencies. State law requires that any person younger than 16 operating a boat or personal watercraft with an engine of 15 horsepower or greater without adult supervision must complete the boating safety training. The courses are held several times a year. For a schedule, call (843) 559-5221 or (800) 277-4301.

Note that laws governing boating under the influence are strictly enforced on South Carolina waters. Boat operators will be tested for blood-alcohol content in the event of accidents. For more information, call the Boating Safety Division of the South Carolina Department of Natural Resources at (843) 762-5041. The local Marine Resources Division is at 217 Fort Johnson Road and can be reached at (843) 762-5000. We suggest you request the department's pamphlet on equipment requirements, rules, and regulations. To find out specifically about licensing, boat titles and registration, call (843) 762-5064.

Those who want to launch their boat in the Lowcountry will be happy to know that there are a number of landings for public use. On weekends they are generally crowded, and early risers will find it easier to park a car and trailer. The parks department is nearing completion of a major renovation project to improve the public access to 19 area boat ramps. For more information about the status of area landings, contact the Charleston County Park and Recreation Commission at (843) 762-2172.

Marinas

If you are interested in docking your boat at a Lowcountry marina, consider the following options. We offer several choices, scattered throughout the Trident area and listed alphabetically.

Ashley Marina
33 Lockwood Dr., Charleston
(843) 722-1996

This 180-slip marina, at intracoastal marker 470 on the Ashley River, is on the Peninsula and convenient to all areas of the city. Diesel and gasoline are available at the fuel dock, and there is room for 860 feet of boat docking. In addition to a captain's lounge, ship's store, showers, and a laundry, there is a fax machine, and a notary public is on the premises. The marina also deals in new and brokered sailboats, trawlers, sportfish, and motor yachts. Marina managers can supply names and phone numbers of charter boats that leave from their marina. Some sample prices of charter opportunities are as follows: A captained fishing charter on either a 28- or 42-foot boat is around $900 for a full day offshore and $700 for a half-day. A three-hour rental for cruising inland waters is $300 plus $75 for each additional hour. (See our Hunting and Fishing chapter for more on charters.)

Bohicket Marina
1880 Andell Bluff Blvd., Seabrook Island
(843) 768-1280

Next to Kiawah and Seabrook resorts, Bohicket is 20 miles south of Charleston but just 6 miles from the Intracoastal Waterway. Within minutes, boaters are in the open sea. Bohicket's 200 wet slips and floating docks are on deep water, and dry storage is available. Shower and bathroom facilities, a laundry, shops, and restaurants make this marina a first-class destination. Boat charters, parasailing, and water tours are offered, and fuel is available at the ship's store. Bohicket Marina is a Boat U.S. facility with member discounts for transient dockage.

Buzzard's Roost Marina
2408 Maybank Hwy., Charleston
(843) 559-5516

Near Intracoastal marker 11, Buzzard's Roost is a deepwater marina that's just minutes from the city's municipal golf

course. There are 190 wet slips along with dockage for transients. A laundry, shower, and gas and diesel fuel are available but no launch facilities. You will find a restaurant and small ship's store here.

Charleston Harbor Marina Resort at Patriots Point
24 Patriots Point Rd., Mt. Pleasant
(843) 856-9996, (888) 856-9996

Opened in June 1998, the Charleston Harbor Marina created a lot of excitement among area boaters. This full-service marina offers convenient ocean access with its location at the southwestern tip of Patriots Point in Mt. Pleasant. (See more about Patriots Point Naval and Maritime Museum under the Other Sites and Museums section in our Attractions chapter.) This deepwater marina with 460 permanent and transient slips features state-of-the-art design with wide floating docks and protective breakwaters.

Amenities include gasoline and diesel fuel, a laundry, restrooms, and showers, electric and manual courtesy carts, a ship's store, and potable dockside water. Other special services are a water taxi and shuttle service to downtown Charleston and the Charleston International Airport; rentals of power boats, sailboats, and windsurfers; and inshore and offshore fishing and sailing charters. Adjacent to the Charleston Harbor Hilton Resort (see our Hotels and Motels chapter) and the Patriots Point Links (see our Golf chapter), this resort complex provides endless opportunities for entertainment and recreation.

Charleston Maritime Center
10 Wharfside St., Charleston
(843) 853-DOCK (3625)

The Charleston Maritime Center has an all season, deep-water marina with floating docks for 30 wet slips. Located on the Peninsula's Cooper River side, this facility is near the city market with loads of shops and restaurants for exploring and a major grocery store, Harris Teeter. The Maritime Center is part of Charleston's waterfront area development that includes the South Carolina Aquarium and IMAX Theatre complex nearby. (For more on these sites see our Attractions and Kidstuff chapters.) On-site there are showers, a dock shop, pump-out stations, gas and diesel fuel, ice, and 30- and 50-amp power. Transient boaters are a specialty here. Boat U.S. members receive a discount on fees.

City Marina
17 Lockwood Dr., Charleston
(843) 723-5098

This marina is close to all the action around the Peninsula. There are 300 slips and transient dockage, and there is a convenient downtown shuttle service. This marina can accommodate vessels as large as 300 feet. Electric 30-, 50-, and 100-amp power as well as gas and diesel fuel are available. The Marina Variety Store restaurant and Salty Mike's Deck Bar are adjacent for a little land-side dining and recreation. In season, parasailing and jet ski rentals are available through Tidal Wave Watersports (see listing under Personal Watercraft and Other Wet Toys below). The marina is nearing completion of a five-year expansion and improvement project, adding more slips and facilities such as the ship's store, the reception center, and state-of-the-art control room.

Cooper River Marina
2430 Thompson Ave., Charleston
(843) 554-0790

Your fastest tack to Charleston Harbor may be the Cooper River Marina, located 2 miles north of the Cooper River bridges at the former Charleston Naval Base. This deepwater marina is operated by the Charleston County Park and Recreation Commission and has floating, concrete docks with electric hookups and plenty of free parking. Boat yard storage, security, laundry, fax and e-mail service, restroom facilities with a shower, and ice are available. Charleston County residents receive a discount on slip fees.

Daniel Island Marina
669 Marina Dr., Charleston
(843) 884-1000

This 20-year-old marina has 220 slips with more under construction. Forty-four wet storage slips and 300 in dry stack stor-

Shrimp and other fishing boats supply the area with fresh seafood. PHOTO: SHEM CREEK

along with complete on-site engine, hull, and accessory service. Short-term dockage is available, and the facility is equipped with showers, a laundry, a lounge, and a restaurant.

Duncan's Boat Harbour
4354 Bridge View Dr., North Charleston
(843) 744-2628, (800) 287-2252

Duncan's, on the Ashley River in North Charleston, is both a wet and dry storage marina. It has 60 wet slips, 30 outside dry slips, 225 inside dry stack spaces, and a ship's store plus restrooms and showers. Duncan's offers repair service for Mercruiser and Mercury and sells new boats, including the Bayliner, Trophy, Maxum, and Robalo lines.

Isle of Palms Marina
50 41st Ave., Isle of Palms
(843) 886-0209

This marina, on the Intracoastal Waterway at Wild Dunes Resort, is a full-service facility with 30 wet slips, floating docks, a restaurant, bathrooms, showers, a laundry, and a ship's store with supplies for boating. Isle of Palms Marina also offers inshore- and offshore-chartered trips, eco-tours, and jet ski rentals. (See our Hunting and Fishing chapter.)

Mariner's Cay Marina
3-A Mariner's Cay Dr., Folly Beach
(843) 588-2091, (800) 446-6194

Mariner's Cay is part of Mariner's Cay Resort and is on the Folly River across from the Folly boat ramp. Just 2 miles from the ocean and 9 miles from the Intracoastal Waterway, this 77-slip marina is one of Charleston's closest facilities to the Atlantic and has gas and diesel fuel, ice, and 24-hour security. A laundromat, restrooms with showers, cable TV hookups, and a ship's store complete the amenities.

Ripley Light Marina
56 Ashley Pointe Dr., Charleston
(843) 766-2100

Just west of the Ashley, in the shadow of

age offer boaters more options. With the development of Daniel Island (see our Neighborhoods chapter), the marina is seeing more traffic and has a ship's store, a shower, and restrooms. Fuel, ice, and live bait are available. No ramp is here, but work racks and a boat washing area are offered.

Dolphin Cove Marina
2079 Austin Ave., North Charleston
(843) 744-2562

Dolphin Cove is on very deep water on the Ashley, between the Ashley River Bridge and the North Bridge. The marina offers 125 wet slips with an additional 250 in dry stack storage. Gas is available here

California Dreaming (see our Restaurants chapter), you'll find Ripley Light. The 79-wet slip marina has showers, a laundry facility, a courtesy vehicle for transport to the Peninsula area, floating concrete docks, and boating supplies. Fuel, bait, and dry storage are available as well.

Shem Creek Marina
526 Mill St., Mt. Pleasant
(843) 884-3211
Shem Creek offers 124 dry stacks for boat storage. Convenient for East Cooper residents, Shem Creek is often filled to capacity, but don't expect amenities other than fuel and ice. Adjacent to the Shem Creek boat ramp, this marina bills itself as "Mt. Pleasant's neighborhood marina."

Stono Marina
2409 Maybank Hwy., Johns Island
(843) 559-2307
Just 4 miles from the Charleston Peninsula, Stono Marina is next to Buzzard's Roost Marina (see previous listing). Boat repair and service are available, and the ship's store carries boat supplies and ice. There are bathrooms and showers, but no fuel facilities.

Toler's Cove Marina
1610 Ben Sawyer Blvd., S.C. Hwy. 703 at
Intracoastal Waterway, Mt. Pleasant
(843) 881-0325
East of the Cooper, Toler's Cove—surrounded by the Marsh Harbor development—is across the harbor from Charleston and across the Intracoastal Waterway from Sullivan's Island and the Isle of Palms. Toler's Cove can accommodate vessels up to 100 feet in length. The marina has showers and a laundry as well as gas, bait, ice, and other necessities.

Wild Dunes Yacht Harbor
40-41st Ave., Isle of Palms
(843) 886-5100
Wild Dunes offers docking for 40- to 50-foot boats with access to the resort's amenities, which include golf, tennis, swimming, and a beach. Metered electric 30/50-amp power hook-ups, gas and diesel fuel, and cable TV are some of the options available here. Wild Dunes also provides access to laundry, showers, and restroom facilities is provided. Wild Dunes Yacht Harbor is in the process of converting to dockominiums, so talk with the management about leasing or purchasing your dock space.

Boat Sales and Repairs

If you are in the market for a new boat, shop the retail stores in the Trident area for reliable sales and service. Beware of fly-by-night operations selling boats out of cow pastures, however, as they are sometimes fronts for liquidation operations and may not be there to help mediate with the manufacturer when your new boat springs a leak.

From the city out to North Charleston, here's a sampling of some of the older establishments. These are also good places to start if you find yourself in need of a boat mechanic while visiting the Lowcountry. If you require a boatyard for more extensive repairs and maintenance contact one of the following: Delta Marine Technologies at (843) 747-2628, Halsey Cannon Boatyard at (843) 884-3000, or Ross Marine at (843) 559-0379.

Charleston Yacht Sales
3 Lockwood Dr., Ste. 201, Charleston
(843) 577-5050
These knowledgeable yacht brokers handle both sail and powerboats with a large selection to choose from. They also offer service, repairs, appraisals, delivery, and surveys. They're next to the municipal marina and are a longtime fixture on the Peninsula.

Longshore Marine
2650 Clements Ferry Rd., Wando
(843) 849-0569
Recently relocated to Daniel Island at the entrance to Daniel Island Marina Village,

Longshore Marine is a Mercury and Yamaha Outboards dealer. They continue to work on all models with parts, service, and accessories available. Some of its popular lines of new boats are Edgewater, Angler, and Glacier Bay.

Renken Boat Center, Inc.
5840 Dorchester Rd., North Charleston
(843) 767-0515
Renken sells a variety of boats including Hurricane, Sea Fox, Crownline and Johnson, Evinrude, Mercruiser, and Yamaha outboards. It also offers parts, service, and accessories. The Renkens have been doing business for many years in the Lowcountry, and theirs is a trusted name.

Sea Ray of Charleston
4415 Sea Ray Drive (off Leeds Ave.),
North Charleston
(843) 747-1889
This store is the area's exclusive Sea Ray dealer, selling sport boats, cruisers, and yachts as long as 68 feet. Mercruiser and Mercury are other brand names here, and service and accessories are also offered.

Seel's Outboard
1937 U.S. Hwy. 17 S., Charleston
(843) 556-2742
2910 Hwy. 17 N., Mt. Pleasant
(843) 849-8788
Seel's carries Evinrude, Johnson, Volvo Penta, and Yamaha motors and Grady White boats as well as Chaparral, Stinger, Alumacraft, and Sea Hunt. With two locations, on Savannah Highway in West Ashley and the bypass in Mt. Pleasant, Seel's is an established boat dealership that has been in operation since the 1960s.

St. Barts Yachts
3 Lockwood Dr., Ste. 302-A, Charleston
(843) 577-7377
In recent years Beneteau USA moved its North American corporate headquarters to Charleston, and St. Barts is the local dealer for Beneteau Yachts. Beneteau's factory in Marion, South Carolina, builds sailboats from 31 to 46 feet long as well as custom lengths. St. Barts also represents the Waquiez line and Rampage sportfishing yachts and handles brokerage of all types of sailboats.

Sailing Instruction

Sailors or aspiring sailors will find plenty of company in the Lowcountry. If you are interested in learning more about the sport or the local regatta schedule, talk to the enthusiasts at the College of Charleston Sailing Association. They are based at the Charleston Harbor Marina and can be reached at (843) 953-5549. (See listing.)

The following listings will steer your ship in the right direction when it comes to sailing instruction and service.

College of Charleston Sailing Association
Charleston Harbor Marina, 24 Patriots
Point Rd., Mt. Pleasant
(843) 216-8450, (843) 953-5549
The College of Charleston offers adult noncredit sailing classes that meet at the Charleston Harbor Marina. Equipment is furnished, and no advanced skills are required. Basic and intermediate classes are offered April through September. The cost is $275 for 15 hours of sailing instruction on J-22 boats and 4 hours of classroom instruction. Call the association for details.

Ocean Sailing Academy
Charleston Harbor Marina,
24 Patriots Point Rd., Mt. Pleasant
Bohicket Marina Village,
1880 Andell Bluff Blvd., Seabrook Island
(843) 971-0700, (800) 971-4888
The Ocean Sailing Academy offers US Sailing Certification courses from the Learn to Sail level on up through Open Ocean Passage Making. They even guarantee skippering ability at the conclusion of any of their courses. Completion of just one course will give you the freedom and

certification to rent a boat and head out for a day of sailing. Instruction is given on a range of boats including J/24s, J105s, Waquiez Pretorian 35s, and Beneteau 411s. Classes may be customized to fit your needs, or you may participate in one of their regularly scheduled courses. They operate Charleston's only public charter sailing club. For more information about classes, the sailing club, team-building programs, and prices, call the number above.

Charters

If you are dreaming of gliding across Charleston Harbor at sunset or entertaining your friends on a weekend outing, several area power and sailboat charter companies have all types and sizes of yachts to match your fantasy.

Bohicket Boat Adventure and Tour Co.
1800 Andell Bluff Blvd., Johns Island
(843) 768-7294

Bohicket Boat provides all kinds of boating fun for visitors and locals alike. They offer powerboat rentals, sailing charters, river and kayaking tours, and sunset cruises. Bohicket Boat even customizes tours geared to your special interest, be it dolphin-watching, crabbing, shrimping, shelling, or fishing around the barrier islands in the Lowcountry. Prices range from $30 an hour for a 16-foot skiff to $185 a day for a 22-foot Catalina sailboat. The custom tours cost $190 to $325 for two to four hours with up to six passengers. Call for a monthly calendar of activities and reservations. (For more information on sportfishing trips, see our Hunting and Fishing chapter.)

Charleston Air Sea Charters
P.O. Box 309, Isle of Palms, SC 29451
(843) 886-8663, (800) 524-3444

Charleston Air Sea Charters is a watersport facility at Wild Dunes Yacht Harbor (see previous listing). Bareboat rentals of kayaks and 16- to 21-foot skiffs are available by the hour or half-day and full-day. Prices range from $30 an hour up to $455 for the full day. Other adventures here are private sailing charters, including day sails, harbor cruises, sunset sails, or island beach excursions. Their fleet of inshore and offshore fishing boats consists of all types—flats boats, sportfishing yachts, island hoppers, and headboats. Charters are arranged for 1 to 100 people by the hour, or half or full day. Group charters are offered for parties and special events, and catering with customized menus is available. Charleston Air Sea Charters is a part of AquaSafaris, Inc., which handles charters worldwide. Call the number listed for reservations and more details on pricing.

Schooner Pride
17 Lockwood Dr., Charleston
(843) 559-9686

Sit back, relax, and take a two-hour harbor cruise on a three-masted, gaff topsail schooner (class C tall ship). What better way to enjoy the vistas of Charleston's historic waterfront? Reservations are recommended, and the fee is $18 for adults and kids 12 and older and $12 for children ages 3 to 12. The *Schooner Pride* is also available for private parties of up to 49 people. The two-hour group rate is $750 Friday or Saturday after 6 PM and $650 all other times. The *Pride* departs from the City Marina (see earlier listing). (Also, see the Cruise and Boat Tours section of our Tours chapter for more on the *Pride*.)

Canoeing

With the amazing system of waterways in the Lowcountry, there are many great opportunities for canoeing. The Charleston County Park and Recreation Commission, (843) 795-4386, can help with a list of community school courses in paddling. Also, each spring it co-sponsors the East Coast Canoe & Kayak Symposium with the Trade Association of Paddlesports (TAPS). The event is held at James Island County Park. The symposium regularly attracts more than 1,000 paddling enthusiasts of all skill levels for a weekend of lectures, on-water demos, and classes. Reflecting the growing national interest in paddling, local support has made this one of the top events of its kind in the country.

Lowcountry Paddlers
C/O Charleston County PRC,
861 Riverland Dr., Charleston
(843) 762-2172

Regular meetings are open to anyone interested. Guest speakers talk about their experiences as well as conservation issues and upcoming trips. Meetings are held the third Monday of each month at North Charleston High School. An all-day trip is planned for the third Saturday of the month. This family-oriented group publishes a monthly newsletter and has about 100 members. The annual membership (which includes membership in the American Canoe Association) is $27 for an individual or $35 for a family. Call the Charleston County Park and Recreation Commission for contact information about this group.

Palmetto Islands County Park
444 Needlerush Pkwy., Mt. Pleasant
(843) 884-0832

This 943-acre nature facility is in a heavily wooded area, with a 2-acre pond and 1-mile canoe trail. It is a perfect place to canoe (rentals are no longer available, but you can bring your own), and a nominal admission fee of $1 a person is charged. (See our Parks and Recreation and Kidstuff chapters for more on this exciting park.)

Charleston Harbor, once the haven of war vessels, is now home to a peaceful fleet of recreational boats and luxury yachts. PHOTO: DAVID C. BERRY

Kayaking

Not too many years back, Charlestonians didn't know a whole lot about kayaks. But this is the here-and-now, and kayaking has definitely become a cool and popular sport. The waterways around Charleston make an ideal venue for both the beginning and expert kayaker to take in the scenery and tranquility. To find out more, check into the following groups and venues.

Charleston Watersport Outfitters
1547 Johnnie Dodds Blvd., Mt. Pleasant
(843) 884-9098
Charleston Watersport carries a complete line of quality watersport equipment and accessories. They handle sales and rentals of the Ocean Kayak line of kayaks. The store is conveniently located on the U.S. Highway 17 By-Pass in the K-Mart shopping center to serve vacationers on nearby Sullivan's Island and the Isle of Palms. A full-day kayak rental costs $35, plus $20 for each additional day, and $50 for an entire weekend. In addition to kayaks, Charleston Watersport has a large selection of surfboards (Gordon and Smith, Maya, Stewart, Hobie, and Hansen), water skis (Ho Sport Extreme Ski Co.), and wakeboards (Hyperwhite). The friendly staff can help you choose your on-the-water fun.

Coastal Expeditions Tours
514-B Mill St., Mt. Pleasant
(843) 884-7684
Coastal Expeditions rents kayaks and offers kayak tours all over the Lowcountry from marsh creeks to secluded beaches. Naturalists and instructors certified by the American Canoe Association and British Canoe Union run this operation and take groups of 2 to 40 on nature tours. A quality operation, Coastal Expeditions welcomes beginners and experienced kayakers and also sells new and used equipment. It offers private and group lessons as well. The half-day tours are $55 a person and $85 a person for a

full day. Single kayaks rent for $35 for a half-day and $45 for a full day; double kayaks are $45 for a half-day and $55 for a full day. Overnight expeditions for four or more people are a fun option too.

James Island County Park
871 Riverland Dr., Charleston
(843) 795-7275
James Island County Park offers lots of classes, clinics, and day, after-work, and overnight tours are offered in sea kayaking and canoeing. Canoe lessons range from $15 to $25 for Charleston County residents and $22.50 to $37.50 for nonresidents.

Kayak classes and tours range from $15 for county residents and $22.50 for nonresidents for a basic course, up to $60 for residents and $90 for nonresidents for more advanced offerings. Contact the Park for their quarterly program guide to check out the variety of paddler offerings.

Middleton Outdoor Program
4290 Ashley River Rd., Charleston
(843) 556-0500
Middleton offers nature-based kayaking on the Ashley River year round and in the black-water cypress swamp seasonally from December through April. Learn to roll and rescue while perfecting your paddle techniques, then follow your guide on a Lowcountry adventure. The basic kayak instruction with guided two-hour tour costs $35 a person. A three-hour tour of shipwrecks is $45 per person. Kayak rentals are also available for $20 per hour.

Watersports

Other water recreation opportunities abound in our area and don't necessarily involve owning or chartering a boat. Local waters offer lots of spots that are waiting to be explored on personal watercraft or investigated by scuba diving. Surfing, windsurfing, and water-skiing provide ways to catch a wave or a breeze or jump a wake while demonstrating your finesse. Or maybe just plunging into a pool for a refreshing swim is your answer to the oft-daunting Lowcountry heat. A list of the folks who can help you get started follows.

Personal Watercraft and Other Wet Toys

To jump on your own Jet Ski and zip around the endless waterways, inlets, and creeks in the Lowcountry for the day, contact one of the following for rental or purchase of personal watercraft.

Champion Honda Yamaha BMW
4155 Dorchester Rd., Charleston
(843) 554-4600
Champion Yamaha sells the full line of Yamaha watercraft and accessories at competitive prices. It is a full-service center open Monday through Friday from 9 AM to 6 PM and Saturday from 10 AM to 3 PM.

Tidal Wave Watersports
60 41st Ave., Isle of Palms
(843) 886-8456
17 Lockwood Dr., Charleston
(843) 853-4386
Tidal Wave Watersports' two locations have personal watercraft rentals, parasailing, and a water-ski school. The Jet Ski

rental rates are $55 a half-hour and $75 an hour, with a $15 passenger fee.

A special safari tour from Wild Dunes (that's the Isle of Palms address) is a very popular, 90-minute guided excursion by WaveRunner. You venture out into the ocean, up to Capers or Bulls Island (with a stop for beachcombing) and return on the Intracoastal Waterway. The 30-mile round trip starts at $95.

Parasailing choices are offered at both locations, with flights costing $50 (at Isle of Palms beach or at Charleston Harbor) for the 600-foot pull and $70 for the 1200-foot thrill (it's a 1.5-hour trip). What a way to check out the beach from a bird's-eye view. Believe it or not, takeoff and landing

Set sail. PHOTO: COURTESY OF CHARLESTON AREA CONVENTION AND VISITORS BUREAU

tions are open seasonally in the warmer months. Call ahead for more information.

Trophy Lakes
3050 Marlin Rd., Johns Island
(843) 559-2520

Trophy Lakes is the place for water-skiing, kneeboard, and wakeboard lessons taught by instructors who are nationally-ranked on the pro tours. The lessons are taught on two private lakes on Johns Island and are scheduled by appointment. The rates are $53 a half-hour for novice lessons and $37 for 20-minute intermediate lessons. Water-ski and wakeboard pulls are $21 for 15 minutes. Weekly rates also are available. Water-skiing competitions are held here as well, so call Trophy Lakes for a schedule of events.

are dry, and anyone age 2 and older may try it. (The minimum weight requirement is 80 pounds, or you fly with someone else.)

Tidal Wave Watersports also holds a water-skiing school at the Wild Dunes location, with U.S. Coast Guard-licensed and insured instructors. Ninety minutes of instruction is $165 for up to four people and includes a boat, captain, and equipment. Tidal Wave Watersports loca-

Yamaha Suzuki Sea-Doo of Charleston
5870 Dorchester Rd., Charleston
(843) 552-7900

Representing the Sea-Doo line, Yamaha Suzuki Sea-Doo has the largest selection in the area of personal watercraft and jet-powered boats for sale. They run from 85 to 310 horsepower, with lengths up to 20 feet. These boats are good for touring, skiing, and all-around family fun.

Scuba Diving

There are many scuba enthusiasts in this area. Diving the numerous wrecks under Charleston's waters is a real kick. For information about dive trips and activities, our listings give you some good places to start. The College of Charleston also offers a scuba class from time to time. Contact Coach Bruce Zimmerman at (843) 953-5960 to find out information about the next scheduled class.

Aqua Ventures
426 Coleman Blvd., Mt. Pleasant
(843) 884-1500

Aqua Ventures offers beginning dive classes and certification. The evening classes are held twice a week for three weeks and cost $195. Open-water certification is a $60 weekend fee (transportation not included) for training at Clear Water Springs in north-central Florida.

Aqua Ventures also organizes trips to many locations including the Caribbean, the Bahamas, and Florida. To dive our local waters, call to schedule offshore dive charters.

Charleston Scuba
335 Savannah Hwy., Charleston
(843) 763-DIVE

This conveniently located store is a center

for diving enthusiasts. It provides retail sales, gear rentals, on-site repairs, scuba charter trips, and classes—open-water certification through dive master. Basic classroom and pool sessions are $249 for the twice weekly, three-week classes. An additional $145 covers four open-water dive sessions that are necessary for certification. Charleston Scuba is adjacent to the Holiday Inn Riverview West of the Ashley.

Wet Shop
5121 Rivers Ave., North Charleston
(843) 744-5641

The Wet Shop is a PADI and NAUI, five-star facility offering open-water classes beginning every three weeks. The Wet Shop conducts offshore and river charters every weekend and sometimes during the week. A fee of $225 includes classroom instruction, open-water dives in Florida, rental gear, and books.

Surfing

The surfing craze has been reborn among the young crowd, much to the delight of all those baby-boomer surfer dudes. The Lowcountry's most popular spots for wave action are on Folly Beach and the Isle of Palms. The Washout at East Ashley Avenue, a designated surfing area on Folly Beach, attracts all ages in search of the perfect wave. Other good surf can be found near the Folly Pier at East Atlantic Avenue, 10th Street on Folly Beach, and near the pier and the county park on the Isle of Palms. (Keep in mind that it is illegal to surf closer than 200 feet to a pier.) Bert's Break, at Station 22 on Sullivan's Island, is probably the best low tide break in the area. Local surf shops are equipped with surfing and beach-going needs. A couple of options follow.

McKevlin's Surf Shop
1101-B Ocean Blvd., Isle of Palms
(843) 886-8912, (843) 886-9283 (Surf Line)
8 Center St., Folly Beach
(843) 588-2247, (843) 588-2261 (Surf Line)

Opened back in the '60s, McKevlin's carries a full line of surfboards, clothing, and accessories. Some of its better-known board brands are Natural Art, Hawaiian Island Creations, Lost, T. Patterson, Harbour, and Seasoned. Its two locations offer rental of surf and body boards and videos. Call the Surf Line for the latest on wind and wave conditions, tides, and water temperatures.

Local Motion Surf Shop
1909 Hwy. 17. N.,
Sweetgrass Shopping Center, Mt. Pleasant
(843) 881-2898

Local Motion Surf Shop rents and sells new and used surfboards (Surf Prescriptions and Matt Kecheley), men's and women's clothing and accessories (O'Neill, Hurley, Surf the Earth, and MCD). It can take care of your surfboard repairs too. The shop is open 10 AM to 6 PM, Tuesday through Saturday, and 12 to 4 PM on Sunday. Winter hours are 1 PM to 5 PM, Tuesday through Friday, and 10 AM to 6 PM on Saturday.

Swimming

Christian Family Y
21 George St., Charleston
(843) 723-6473

There are two pools at this Y—one is a therapy pool that stays at about 93 degrees with jets for massage; the other is the 25-yard, four-lane "cool pool" for laps. Swimmers can use the full showers and locker rooms, and the Y is available for lessons and parties. Lessons and parent-tot swim classes run about $55 per session. (For a complete rundown of prices, see our Kidstuff chapter.)

James Island Recreational Complex
1088 Quail Dr., Charleston
(843) 720-3806

Operated by the city's Department of Recreation Aquatics Division, this 25-yard, outdoor pool with lifeguards is open June through August. Water fitness classes and swimming lessons are planned for the mornings, and open swimming is the norm in the afternoon. Adult city residents can swim for $1.50, nonresidents for $3; residents 17 and younger pay $1; nonresidents, $2. City residents pay $20 for youth swimming lessons and $25 for adult lessons; parent and tot swims are $15. Nonresidents pay $30 for youth lessons, $35 for adults, and $20 for parent and tot swimming.

Palmetto Islands County Park
444 Needlerush Pkwy., Mt. Pleasant
(843) 884-0832

The outdoor water playground at Palmetto Islands County Park is open 10 AM to 6 PM on weekends in May and every day from Memorial Day until Labor Day. Charges for county residents are $5.99 for an adult and $4.99 for a child under 42 inches tall; nonresidents pay $6.99 for an adult and $5.99 for a child. Children younger than 3 can swim for free. Swimming fees are in addition to a $1 per person park admission. (For more on this and other Charleston County parks, see our Kidstuff and Parks and Recreation chapters.)

Richard L. Jones Recreation Center Pool
391 Egypt Rd., Mt. Pleasant
(843) 884-2528

There is a six-lane, indoor swimming pool at the Richard L. Jones complex. Swimming lessons, aquatic exercise classes, lap and recreational swimming are some of the many options. Membership is open to anyone. Mt. Pleasant residents pay only $2 for a one-year membership plus $2 each time they swim. Children 4 and younger swim free. Nonresidents pay $100 for yearly memberships. Swimming lessons range from

Insiders' Tip

Old salts (and new ones too) will want to pick up a copy of *The Boating News* for the latest scoop on all the area's waterfront info. The monthly tabloid, published in Charleston, is distributed along the coast from Virginia to Florida. Along with news about legislation, boat shows, boatyards, marinas, and other maritime matters, commentary and letters make this a lively read. The free paper can be found at marinas, boating supply stores, and nautical shops, or call (800) 723-2703 to subscribe.

$20 to $35 for residents and from $22 to $39 for nonresidents.

W. L. Stephens Aquatic Center
780 W. Oak Forest Dr., Charleston
(843) 724-7342

This is a good place to start your exploration of swimming pools in the Greater Charleston area, as the City of Charleston Aquatics Division has an office here. Open year round, this indoor pool has six lanes and is 25 yards long. It is a popular winter birthday-party venue—nothing like a warm swim when there's frost on the windows—and draws its share of regular lap swimmers. There are full showers. The price to use the pool is $2 for adults and $1.50 for children younger than 17. Swimming lessons for residents are $20 for children and $25 for adults; nonresidents, $25 for children and $35 for adults.

Hunting and Fishing

Hunting and fishing are major recreational traditions in the Trident area. When the Hon. William Elliott published *Carolina Sports by Land and Water* in 1846, it was called a "description and defense" of these sports in the Lowcountry. Today, the best defense of these outdoor activities is that many who participate in them are also conservation-minded people who help implement and adhere to laws protecting wildlife. Limits, seasons, and a licensing program are part of an overall system that fosters responsible sportsmanship and helps maintain diversity and numbers in fields and streams.

Hunting

Hunting is one of the most important industries in the state. Deer hunters alone contribute more than $180 million to South Carolina's economy. Overall, there are more than 200,000 licensed hunters here. To ensure the future of the industry, the South Carolina Department of Natural Resources sponsors a number of events to expose youth to hunting. Parent-child and adult-youth hunts for doves, ducks, and turkeys are among the outings they organize. The DNR also works closely with the many active conservation groups to promote youth and adult hunting.

From raccoons to deer, turkeys to ducks, there are both variety and quantity in Lowcountry habitats. Deer hunting has overtaken dove hunting as the most popular type of hunting in South Carolina. The high deer population and the relative ease of accessibility, combined with the long Lowcountry season (usually August 15 to January 1), are factors in its popularity. There are a lot of public and private lands set up specifically for deer hunting in this area.

The mourning dove continues to be popular quarry for hunters. It's ranked as the No. 1 game bird in South Carolina. Dove shoots are quite common in September, late November, and late December/early January and provide social events for many Lowcountry hunters. The sport is strong, but a slight decline in the dove population during the last few years has led to some restrictions, including the elimination of morning hunts during the first three days of the season and a bag limit of 12 doves per hunter per day. Turkey hunting has grown in popularity because of a very successful restoration project that moved turkeys from the Francis Marion National Forest in the 1950s and from the Piedmont and Savannah River Plant areas in the 1970s to other habitats across South Carolina. The season lasts four to six weeks in the spring and is an option in every county in the state.

Small game hunting for squirrel, rabbits, fox, raccoon, opossum, and quail provides more springtime hunting opportunities. Most quail hunting takes place from late fall to early spring on public shooting reserves. On private lands in the Trident area, the season usually runs from late November to early March with a limit of 15 birds per hunter per day because of the limited numbers of coveys of quail.

Waterfowl hunting has experienced a big rebound after more than a decade of drought in the Canadian breeding grounds. More abundant moisture on the grounds and more acreage of nesting cover provided by the Conservation Reserve Program have increased the continent's waterfowl population. The past couple of years have seen the Lowcountry's numbers increasing as well. Blue-winged teals and northern shovelers are at all-time population highs, according to the Office of Migratory Bird Management for the U.S. Fish and Wildlife Service. Other species on the rise include greenwings, golden-eye, and buffleheads, in addition to the diving ducks such as canvasbacks and redheads.

Before Taking to the Field

So how does the would-be hunter in the Lowcountry get set for those early-morning outings in a duck blind or late afternoons in a deer stand?

The South Carolina Department of Natural Resources publishes a booklet, *South Carolina Rules and Regulations for Hunting, Fishing, and Wildlife Management Areas in South Carolina*, that details hunting areas, regulations, education, limits, and check stations. For your free copy, write to the department at P.O. Box 167, Columbia, SC 29202, or call locally at (843) 762-5065. The booklets can also be found at local sporting goods stores and the sporting goods departments at large retailers (such as Wal-Mart and Kmart), where you also can purchase hunting and fishing licenses. (Licenses are also available by phone 24 hours a day at (888) 434-7472 with an additional $3.95 processing fee.) Turkey, migratory bird, and waterfowl hunting regulations and seasons are outlined in even more detail in separate brochures available just before the various seasons. Initiated in 1998, a migratory game bird permit is required in South Carolina. To get the free permit, hunters must obtain a migratory bird Harvest Information Program (HIP) permit by answering a few questions on forms available at all license vendors.

The South Carolina DNR Wildlife and Marine Resources Division designates private land in the Trident area as Game Zone 6. In addition to laws restricting hunting by personal invitation on private property, state game wardens also actively enforce regulations on other lands—marked as either Wildlife Management Areas (WMAs) or U.S. Forest Service property—where public hunting is allowed.

Obviously, residents or visitors must be licensed to hunt in the Trident area. Remember that seasons, prices, gender restrictions, and limits change virtually every year. Deer season generally lasts from mid-August to January 1. Migratory game bird season always comes in the fall. Other hunting season dates are available by calling (843) 762-5065. As we go to press, the annual price for a state resident to hunt in a management area is $30.50, with an additional $6 needed to hunt big game. For nonresidents, it costs $100 for an annual license to hunt small game. A 10-consecutive-day, non-resident, small-game-only license costs $50, and a three-consecutive-day one costs $25. Non-resident fees for hunting big game are $89 plus $76 for a management area permit.

For annual waterfowl season, hunters may buy a management area permit (in addition to their state hunting license and all necessary stamps) to hunt in designated areas (prices are the same as listed in the previous paragraph). Always make sure you know that you are within the scope of state and federal game laws before you head out to hunt.

For information about the South Carolina Department of Natural Resources' free, 10-hour hunter education course, contact the department at the address given and mark the letter: "Attention: Hunter Education." You can call the department at (843) 734-3888 or (800) 277-4301 or locally at (843) 762-5041. The course combines classroom instruction (covering hunting ethics, hunter-landowner relations, and basic conservation and wildlife management principles) and hands-on experience in hunter safety and hunting techniques. It is required that all residents and nonresidents born after June 30, 1979 successfully complete the course before a hunting license can be obtained. This course is accepted by other states that require safety certification for licenses, and South Carolina recognizes certification from other states.

Fishing

The Trident area offers some of the best fishing on the East Coast. Charleston County, blessed with some 60 miles of protected coastline, is a fishing enthusiast's paradise. The fresh waters of the Ashley and Cooper Rivers, with their adjacent rice field breaks and salt creeks, bays, and (of course) the ocean are all open to the public. Fish for largemouth bass, bream, trout, flounder, or spottail bass in these rivers and bluefish in the harbor, or head out to the deep water to match wits with dolphin, wahoo, marlin, sailfish, or tuna.

Berkeley County's Marion and Moultrie Lakes cover 170,000 acres with striped bass, largemouth bass, sunfish, white bass, crappie, and catfish aplenty. Dorchester County includes part of the Edisto River, home to striped bass and American shad—the roe of which, often prepared and served with grits, is a Lowcountry delicacy. Largemouth bass, redbreast, and bluegill bream and catfish also swim the Edisto.

Before You Drop a Line

Residents and out-of-state visitors pay fees to fish or shrimp, with rates varying according to the fishing venue and angler's age. (No license is necessary for dock or pier fishing.) For residents and nonresidents, saltwater fishing licenses (Marine Recreational Fisheries Stamps) are $5.50. Freshwater licenses are $10 on an annual basis for South Carolina residents. For out-of-state anglers, annual licenses to fish only fresh waters cost $35, and one-week freshwater licenses are $11. Ask the South Carolina Marine Resources Division about combination discounts if you plan to be both hunting and fishing.

In an effort to protect the fish population, South Carolina has also established regulations regarding limits on the sizes and number of fish that may be taken, the use of seines and gill nets, and guidelines concerning crabbing, shrimping, and other fishing activities. Saltwater fishing conservation and ethical angling practices are not only encouraged but enforced. Undersized fish and fish over the quantity limits should be released, helping to ensure future fish populations. Fortunately, the number of saltwater finfish tagged and released in South Carolina waters is increasing each year as more and more anglers take up this practice. Already, it is conserving resources and providing valuable information on the growth and movement of fish for further study and management. Again, for more specific information about seasons, rules, and licenses, refer to the South Carolina Department of Natural Resources' annually issued rules and regulations booklet (see Hunting for details on how to pick up a copy) or contact the Marine Resources Division at (843) 795-6350.

Deep-sea Fishing

Deep-sea fishing is a popular sport, and charter boats allow visitors and locals alike to enjoy the experience. Locals say that the best offshore fishing is during the months from May through September, when water temperatures are warmer, although, weather permitting, you can venture out at other times of the year. Charter trips are on luxury boats—air conditioned and large enough to ride out the ocean swells, yet small enough to put you on a first-name basis with the captain. The average cost for ocean reef charter trips—although prices can vary at the captain's discretion—is $700 for a half-day (that's for up to six passengers) and $900 for a full day (again, for six passengers).

Gulf-stream charters are only offered on a full-day basis and run about $1,000 for 10 hours, $1,150 for 12 hours, and $1,300 for 14 hours for six passengers. A gratuity is not

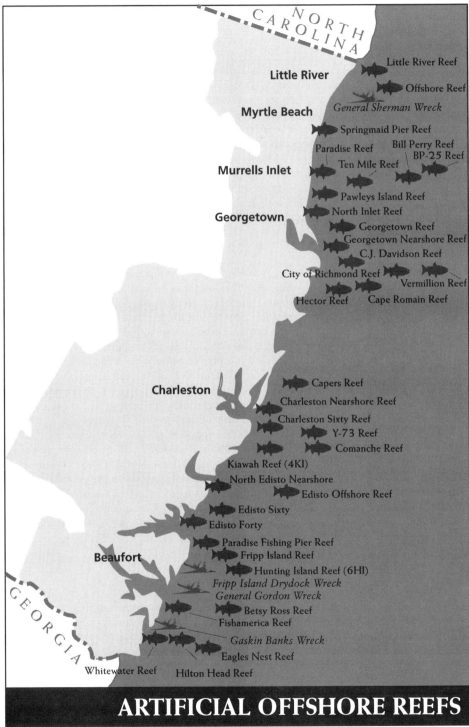

NORTH CAROLINA

Little River

Myrtle Beach

Murrells Inlet

Georgetown

Little River Reef

Offshore Reef

General Sherman Wreck

Springmaid Pier Reef

Paradise Reef   Bill Perry Reef
                 BP-25 Reef
Ten Mile Reef

Pawleys Island Reef

North Inlet Reef

Georgetown Reef

Georgetown Nearshore Reef

C.J. Davidson Reef

City of Richmond Reef

Vermillion Reef

Hector Reef   Cape Romain Reef

Charleston

Capers Reef

Charleston Nearshore Reef

Charleston Sixty Reef

Y-73 Reef

Comanche Reef

Kiawah Reef (4KI)

North Edisto Nearshore

Edisto Offshore Reef

Edisto Sixty

Edisto Forty

Paradise Fishing Pier Reef

Fripp Island Reef

Beaufort

Hunting Island Reef (6HI)

Fripp Island Drydock Wreck
General Gordon Wreck

Betsy Ross Reef

Fishamerica Reef

Gaskin Banks Wreck

Eagles Nest Reef

Whitewater Reef   Hilton Head Reef

GEORGIA

ARTIFICIAL OFFSHORE REEFS

included, and you'll want to tip the captain and mates whether the fish were biting or not. These guys earn their keep by charting the course, baiting the lines, and doing their best to find the fish. On both charter and "head" boats, which accommodate dozens more people on a "per head" basis at a fraction of a charter's cost, all rods, reels, bait, and tackle will be provided. Visiting anglers may be amazed to see that a little bit of everything is used to catch fish here—from ballyhoo with skirts to live bait to lures without bait. On charter boats, anglers usually bring along food and a drink cooler. On head boats, you can almost always count on a snack bar.

Call at least a month before you visit to book a charter. It is not normally necessary to contact a head boat more than a couple of days before you want to go out. Most captains are going to lead you to the reefs (see the artificial reef chart in this chapter for the locations of some of these) or the Gulf Stream and want you to plan on a long, physically challenging but exhilarating day. Be prepared: If you tend to get seasick, ask your doctor to recommend good over-the-counter preventive medicine. General common sense suggests you get a good night's sleep before your day on the boat, which will usually begin before dawn.

While on the sea, drink lots of nonalcoholic fluids, and don't forget your sunglasses and sunscreen, a long-sleeved shirt, a hat that shades your face, deck shoes with good traction, a couple of towels for drying off periodically, and a camera to prove the size of that mighty one that got away.

Expect to land fish such as king and Spanish mackerel, cobia, sea bass, and even barracuda if you are on the reefs. In the Gulf Stream, you'll likely pull blue or white marlin, wahoo, tuna, dolphin, or sailfish, so break out the recipes. Bottom fishing in the Gulf Stream could lead to good hauls of snapper, grouper, porgy, or amberjack—all good eating.

Inshore Fishing

Perhaps inshore fishing is more to your liking. The ubiquitous winding rivers, creeks, and inlets in the Trident area offer lots of action without the lengthy trip out to the Gulf Stream. The quiet beauty of the setting and the salt marsh smells can afford a memorable experience and, we hope, some good eating afterward. Go after flounder, king mackerel, trout, jack crevalle, spottail bass, or redfish.

The cooler months of the year, usually from September through April, are the best times to wet a line inshore. The clarity of the water is good then, and in shallow water you may even see the fish and cast directly to them. (The summer months may be slightly less inviting for fishermen because of the heat and prevalence of gnats and mosquitoes.) Anglers use light-tackle rods and reels and saltwater fly rods for snagging most inshore catches.

Charter Boats

The main charter operators in the area are based around five marinas: Charleston Harbor Marina Resort, (843) 856-9164 or (888) 856-9996, Isle of Palms Marina, (843) 886-0209, and Toler's Cove, (843) 881-0325, in East Cooper; Ripley Light Marina, (843) 766-2100, west of the Ashley; and Bohicket Marina, (843) 768-1280, on Johns Island. Contacting them should provide the latest information on available charters for all kinds of fishing.

The following listings should give you a good head start on some of the head or charter boats available for offshore or inshore fishing. Take note that these salty seagoing veterans don't always like to be tied down to specific price ranges. Be ready to bargain. (For more information, see our Boating and Watersports chapter.)

Bohicket Charters
Bohicket Marina
1880 Andell Bluff Blvd., Johns Island
(843) 768-7294

Bohicket offers inshore, flats, offshore, and Gulf Stream fishing trips out of Bohicket Marina, near Kiawah and Seabrook Islands. Charters include full-, three-quarter-, and half-day trips on 25- to 55-foot passenger boats. Rates start at $250 for two people for four hours of flats fishing for redfish and trout. Inshore family fishing for four to six passengers begins at $275 for three hours. Offshore rates are $400 to $1,000 for half-days, $700 to $1,450 for three-quarter days, and $900 to $1,650 for full-day trips. Boat rentals from 15-foot skiffs to 23-foot Deck Boats are also available, along with tackle, trips to find shells, sunset cruises, and other customized journeys. Rates begin at $125 to $225 for half-days and $150 to $390 for full day. (For more on Bohicket Marina, see our Boating and Watersports chapter.)

Carolina Clipper
Shem Creek, 825 Creekside Dr.,
Mt. Pleasant, SC 29465
(843) 884-2992

This large, comfortable boat, complete with snack bar and electric reels, is air conditioned and takes off each day, year round at 7 AM. Early bird and overnight trips are available as well. Home base is on the north side of Shem Creek Bridge in Mount Pleasant, behind The Trawler Restaurant. Capt. Billy Knight is owner and operator.

Capt. Peter H. Brown
522 Old Bridge Ct., Mt. Pleasant
(843) 830-0448

Full-time guide Capt. Peter Brown spends 280 days a year targeting gamefish along South Carolina's coast. And what does he do on his days off? Goes fishing, of course! His full-, three-quarter-, and half-day private charters are aboard an 18-foot flats skiff, ideal for stalking big fish in very shallow water. Rods and tackle are

provided for year round inshore light tackle and fly fishing. U.S.C.G. licensed and insured, Peter specializes in sight casting, and (depending on the season) he'll put you on the red drum, black drum, trout, flounder, Spanish mackerel, and Jack Crevalle.

Capt. Richard Stuhr
Inshore, Light-Tackle and Fly Fishing
547 Sanders Farm Ln., Charleston
(843) 881-3179

Capt. Richard Stuhr—a native Charlestonian with lifelong experience on the water—offers custom trips into the inland waters of the Lowcountry on his 18-foot Action Craft. His specialties are inshore light-tackle and fly fishing. This Orvis-endorsed guide offers full- and half-day trips for one to three people year-round. Prices range from $300 for half-days to $375 for full days.

Captain Ivan's Island Charters
805 Duck Hawk Retreat, Charleston
(843) 762-2020

Specializing in live bait and light tackle fishing, Captain Ivan's two 30-foot, wide-beam boats have custom rods, reels, and tackle and are Coast Guard certified. Half-day trips for up to four passengers are $550 with each additional passenger adding $100. Full-day trips for up to four are $900, adding $100 for each additional person. Gulf Stream trolling or bottom fishing runs $1,300 for up to four with additional passengers adding $100 each. Specialty trips for shark fishing and tournaments are available for booking, too.

Fin Stalker Charters
1287 Hampshire Rd., Charleston
(843) 795-4707

Lowcountry native Captain Chris Chavis really knows his way around the area's inshore estuaries, tidal creeks, and barrier island waters. He offers full- and half-day charters for light-tackle and fly fishing year round. All equipment is provided, and trophy photos are available. His Action Craft "flats boat" is ideal for stalking redfish, trout, Jack Crevalle, tarpon, Spanish mackerel, sharks, and cobia, among other sportfish challenges. No license is required. Call for more information and reservations.

Harbor Fishing Charters
1196 Russell Dr., Mt. Pleasant
(843) 670-6767

To fish the backwaters of the Lowcountry, including Charleston Harbor and the barrier islands, charter with Reid Simmons, an experienced inshore guide. Using light tackle and live bait, you will pursue spottail bass, trout, and flounder on his 17-foot flats boat. Half-day rates start about $300, and a full day is about $425.

Isle of Palms Marina Charters
41st Ave. at Intracoastal Waterway, Isle of Palms
(843) 886-0209

Isle of Palms Marina offers inshore and offshore fishing trips with three-quarter- and full-day options. Inshore flats fishing for four hours is $300. For inshore fishing around the jetties, the cost is $450 for six hours. Offshore fishing on a 10-hour trip is $1,200. Crabbing trips, shelling, beach-combing, motorboat rentals, as well as sunset and moonlight cruises are also available. (See our Boating and Watersports chapter for more on Isle of Palms Marina.)

Palmetto Charters, LLC
Charleston Harbor Marina Resort
24 Patriots Point Rd., Mt. Pleasant
(843) 849-6004, (843) 854-5538

Palmetto Charters operates an offshore/inshore fishing charter fleet located at the beautiful Charleston Harbor Marina at Patriots Point. The fleet encompasses a dozen boats ranging in size from 30 to 61 feet. Palmetto Charters offers some of the best guides and offshore fishers with the better known sportfishing yachts in the area. The offshore trips for up to six passengers range from $475 for a half-day up to $1,300 for a full day depending on the size of the boat. Inshore rates for two peo-

> ## Insiders' Tip
>
> Some Lowcountry hunters are fortunate to participate in the South Carolina Department of Natural Resources' computerized-draw hunts, offered each year in Wildlife Management Areas. Special hunts for deer, turkey, waterfowl, and quail are organized by DNR, which offers an excellent value (the cost is always well below market value). These hunts are comparable to ones on a private preserve. Contact SCDNR offices for applications, and test your luck of the draw.

ple range from $300 to $500 depending on the length of time booked.

Sea Dawg Charters, Inc.
506 Ann St., Mt. Pleasant
(843) 556-3526, (843) 442-9230

Full- and half-day trips for six people are available by chartering the Sea Dawg out of the Charleston Maritime Center. Chase the sportfish, including marlin, sailfish, dolphin, wahoo, and tuna offshore on this classic 28-foot Bertram. Fully equipped with the latest electronics and fish-finding equipment, rods, reels, bait, and tackle are provided for your convenience. Rates range from around $550 for a half day to $750 for a full day in the Gulf Stream. (For more on Charleston Maritime Center, see our Boating and Watersports chapter.)

Sea Fix Offshore Charters
633 Royal Ave., Mt. Pleasant
(843) 577-0800, (843) 881-0180

Sea Fix Charters offers a 54-foot Craig Blackwell sportfishing yacht designed for a comfortable ride with twin 800-horsepower diesel engines to get you to the Gulf Stream fast. An air-conditioned salon, top-of-the-line electronics, and tournament-grade tackle set you up for a great day of fishing. Book this boat for Gulf Stream, full-, three-quarter, half-day, and tournament charters. Up to six passengers may go, and the charters depart from Toler's Cove Marina in Mt. Pleasant. Rates range from $600 for a half day to $1,100 for a full day. This charter service also offers a 28-foot Bertram.

Fishing Piers and Bridges

Maybe you just want to escape for a couple of hours to see what you can find by dropping a line in the neighborhood waters. After all, scheduling a charter or putting the boat in the water often takes advance planning and a major commitment of time. Or perhaps you have the kids in tow—those attention spans may only be good for an hour or so. The Charleston area provides ample opportunity for this leisurely walk-up pastime. A number of piers and bridges for saltwater fishing are maintained and operated by the Charleston County Park and Recreation Commission and the city of Charleston.

Folly Beach Edwin S. Taylor Fishing Pier
101 E. Arctic Ave., Folly Beach
(843) 588-FISH

Extending more than 1,045 feet into the Atlantic Ocean, this 25-foot-wide pier is noted for the distinctive design of a diamond-shaped platform at its end. The platform itself covers a 7,500-square-foot area, with part of it under a covered shelter. The pier is 23 feet above sea level and affords great fishing, walking, birding, and viewing of Folly Beach and the ocean. Landward, a large facility provides restrooms (unisex restrooms are available,

too, for the handicapped and parents with small children), a tackle shop and the Starfish Grille (see our Restaurants chapter). The pier is open daily from 6 AM to 11 PM April through October, 7 AM to 7 PM March and November, and from 8 AM to 5 PM December through February. Parking is $4, and the fishing fees are $5 for an adult Charleston County resident ($8 for king mackerel fishing), $3 for children 12 and younger, and $8 for a nonresident adult ($10 for king mackerel fishing). You can also rent rods and get annual passes here.

Palmetto Islands
County Park Fishing Dock
444 Needlerush Pkwy., Mt. Pleasant
(843) 884-0832

Wind down a paved walking trail to this large, floating dock at the Peninsula Center on Horlbeck Creek and Boone Hall Creek. There are also several smaller docks for peaceful fishing and crabbing within the Palmetto Islands County Park, which offers full facilities. Hours are 9 AM to 7 PM from May through August; 9 AM to 6 PM in March, April, September, and October; and 10 AM to 5 PM from November through February. Park gate admission is $1 a person, with children younger than 3 free. (For more on the Palmetto Islands County Park, see our Kidstuff and Parks and Recreation chapters.)

James Island County Park Dock
871 Riverland Dr., Charleston
(843) 795-7275

On a tidal creek on the Stono River, this floating dock offers tranquil fishing and crabbing with complete facilities and handicapped access. Crabbing classes, which give pointers on catching and cooking crab, are offered here from time to time. Part of the dock is covered and picnic tables are nearby. The park has plenty of parking and is open daily, May through August, from 8 AM to 8 PM; September, October, March, and April from 8 AM to 6 PM; and November through February, 8 AM to 5 PM. The individual admission

Lowcountry Lunkers

Several state-record-size gamefish have been landed in Lowcountry waters. Here's a listing of several, with the type of fish, weight (in pounds and ounces), port, year, angler, and angler's hometown noted.

Bluefish—21-0; Charleston, 1975; by J.A. Curtis, Charleston.

Croaker—4-9; Charleston, 1979; by C.I. Frasier, Charleston.

Dolphin—74-6; Mt. Pleasant, 1994; by W.C. Etheredge, Columbia, S.C.

Southern Flounder—17-6; South Santee, 1974; by L.C. Floyd, Florence, S.C.

Gag Grouper—48-8; Charleston, 1997; by R.L. Price, Summerville.

Red Grouper—30-2; Charleston, 1976; by G. Frost, Belvedere, S.C.

Scamp Grouper—23-10; Charleston, 1972; by R.E. Tobin, Mt. Pleasant.

Crevalle Jack—40-1; Charleston, 1993; by J. Benich, Mt. Pleasant.

Ladyfish—5-14; Charleston, 1994; by B. Raver, Charleston.

King Mackerel—62-0; Charleston, 1976; by J. Brownlee III, Charleston.

Blue Marlin—752-6; Johns Island, 1993; by D.F. Pearce II, Mt. Pleasant.

White Marlin—108-0; Charleston, 1981; by D.C. Critz Jr., Savannah, Ga.

African Pompano—35-8; Mt. Pleasant, 1997; by M.L. Wireman, Charleston.

Florida Pompano—8-12; Charleston, 1975; by C. Mullinax Sr., Charleston.

Jolthead Porgy—18-4; Charleston, 1984; by J. Currie, North Charleston.

Bigeye Thresher Shark—406-0; Edisto Island, 1978; by J.H. Mixson, Johns Island.

Bull Shark—477-12; Stono Inlet, 1985; by C.R. Faust, Folly Beach.

Dusky Shark—466-12; Charleston, 1981; by M. Almond, Charleston.

Lemon Shark—332-0; Charleston, 1983; by J. Weirman, Charleston Heights.

Hammerhead Shark—588-3; Charleston, 1989; by B. Bass, Charleston.

Sandbar Shark—199-4; Charleston, 1984; by T. McGuiness, Charleston.

Sand Tiger Shark—350-2; Charleston, 1993; by M. Thawley, Summerville, S.C.

Silky Shark—248-0; Charleston, 1981; by R. Keenan, Charleston.

Spinner Shark—159-0; Mt. Pleasant, 1998; by J. Short, Ellenboro, N.C..

Sheepshead—15-4; Charleston, 1969; by J. Percival, Hanahan, S.C.

Vermillion Snapper—6-10; Charleston, 1975; by D.H. Long, Charleston.

Atlantic Spadefish (tie)—11-16; Edisto Island, 2000; by R.F. Cothran Jr., Manning, S.C.

Longbill Spearfish—53-0; Mt. Pleasant, 1986; by H.L. Johnson Jr., Mt. Pleasant.

Spot (tie)—1-1; Charleston, 1967; by J. Stehmeyer, Charleston.

Tripletail—25-8; Mt. Pleasant, 1971; by R. Hanckel Jr., Charleston.

Albacore Tuna—37-4; Charleston, 1976; by W. Crump, Johns Island.

Skipjack Tuna—25-14; Charleston, 1986; by D.L. Stubbs, Charleston.

Yellowfin Tuna—241-12; Charleston, 1979; by T.C. Lewis, Mt. Pleasant.

Little Tunny—29-7; Charleston, 1975; by C. Edwards Jr., Columbia, S.C.

This information is provided courtesy of the South Carolina Department of Natural Resources Marine Resources Division.

price is $1, with no charge for children younger than 3. (See our Kidstuff and Parks and Recreation chapters for more about the recreational opportunities at James Island County Park.)

Brittlebank Park Pier
Lockwood Dr., Charleston
(843) 724-7321
Operated by the city of Charleston, this pier with a floating dock extends 200 feet out onto the Ashley River on the west side of the Peninsula. At Lockwood Drive and Fishburne Street next to the Joseph P. Riley Ballpark, the 10-acre park is a venue for many large outdoor concerts and events. Parking is available, but there are no restrooms or other facilities. No fee is charged. It is open sunrise to 11 PM daily.

Waterfront Park Pier
Cumberland St. to N. Adgers Wharf,
Charleston
(843) 724-7321
Waterfront Park is quite a popular spot for tourists and locals because of its setting overlooking Charleston Harbor toward Mt. Pleasant and Ft. Sumter. Fishing may be a good excuse to spend the day here, but there are many pleasant distractions like the passing boats and wildlife—don't forget to check your line every now and then. There is no entry fee, but you will have to search for a metered parking spot or enter one of the nearby garages for a charge. The park and pier are open daily year round from 6 AM to midnight. No facilities are available, but an easy stroll down Vendue Range leads to restaurants and shopping on East Bay Street. (See our Kidstuff and Parks and Recreation chapters for more on Waterfront Park.)

The Battery
E. Battery at Murray Blvd., Charleston
(843) 724-7321
The seawall at White Point Gardens is a historic spot that has served as a promenade for Charlestonians for a couple of hundred years. This tip of the Peninsula is where the Ashley and Cooper Rivers meet,

as Charlestonians are fond of saying, to form the Atlantic Ocean. The confluence of the rivers here can make for some good fishing too, so drop a line anywhere along the 1.5-mile waterfront access. The Battery is open year round and, with any luck, parking is found alongside.

Pitt Street Bridge
End of Pitt St., Mt. Pleasant
(843) 849-2022
At the end of Pitt Street—on the Intracoastal Waterway overlooking Charleston Harbor—is the old Pitt Street Bridge. The half-mile bridge is the former trolley car causeway, now closed to traffic, which used to connect Mt. Pleasant and Sullivan's Island. It's a good place to fish and a great spot for watching waterway boat traffic. The town of Mount Pleasant provides year-round access to the bridge at no fee.

Breach Inlet Bridge
S.C. Hwy. 703, Sullivan's Island,
Isle of Palms
This bridge connecting Sullivan's Island and the Isle of Palms is almost never without some anglers. Because of the nar-

row inlet connecting the ocean with the creeks and waterway behind the islands, the currents are very strong, and swimming in the area is prohibited. But these currents can make for some lively fishing, as the fish are funneled through with the changing tides. Free parking is nearby on either side of the bridge, and the bridge's catwalks on both sides are open year round.

Fishing Tournaments

Almost year round (with the exception of the coldest winter months), a fishing tournament of some description can be found, usually benefiting conservation groups and charities in the Trident area. Some of the bigger ones offer large purses and prizes in the thousands of dollars. Competition can be pretty stiff, but the changing seas and good old-fashioned luck often come into play and ... anything can happen. If you are serious about getting into the competitive sportfishing tournament circuit, here are a few of the major ones to check out. For a more complete listing of the year's saltwater fishing tournaments held in South Carolina, pick up the brochure from the South Carolina Department of Natural Resources Marine Resources Division at area bait and tackle shops, or write to SCDNR, P.O. Box 12559, Charleston, SC 29422.

Bohicket Marina
Invitational Billfish Tournament
1880 Andell Bluff Blvd., Johns Island
(843) 768-1280, (843) 768-3461

One of the six tourneys in the Governor's Cup Series, the Bohicket Invitational is one of the major tournaments in the area. Held in mid-May, this one brings in the big boys competing for serious money; first prize for the largest marlin garners $7,500. Placing here can lead to even bigger prizes in the Governor's Cup competition. This tag-and-release tourney also awards $500 for the largest wahoo, dolphin, and tuna and the best female and youth angler. Get your crew, sportfishing yacht, and checkbook ready for an entry fee of $1,500 and a sportin' good time. It's called an invitational, but anyone can join in the fun.

Charleston Trident Fishing Tournament
861 Riverland Dr., Charleston
(843) 762-8023, (843) 795-4FUN

For 32 years the Charleston County Park and Recreation Commission, area businesses, and individuals have co-sponsored this tournament, which covers the fishing season from March 1 through October 31. Competitors enter catches on entry blanks after weighing in at official weigh stations. Points are amassed for classes of eligible fish in both saltwater and freshwater divisions. Awards and certificates are given for outstanding saltwater and freshwater anglers, outstanding lady and youth (16 and younger) anglers, outstanding light-tackle and fly rod, ecology, and more. There are also awards for the largest fish caught in various categories. The competition is restricted to the waters of Berkeley, Charleston, and Dorchester Counties and boats leaving from and returning to the waters between the South Santee and South Edisto Rivers.

Fishing for Miracles
King Mackerel Tournament
P.O. Box 13586, Charleston,
SC 29422
(843) 766-0011

Another of the South Carolina King Mackerel Governor's Cup Series tournaments in the area, the 8th Annual Fishing for Miracles event is one of our favorite summertime competitions. Held in mid-August, this tournament is one of the largest fishing tournaments in South Carolina. Its proceeds benefit the Medical University of South Carolina Children's Hospital and the Coastal Conservation Association of South Carolina. There are some terrific prizes (first place could net you as much as $25,000), and it is all based out of The Charleston Harbor Marina Resort just across the bridge in Mt. Pleasant. To get involved, contact the tournament committee by calling or writing. The boat entry fee in 2001 was $265 prior to August 1 and $315 after that date. See our Annual Events chapter for more on this tournament.

Off shore fishing is a favorite pursuit of Lowcountry anglers. Arrange-ments for charters can be made at many of the local marinas.
PHOTO: THOMAS P. FORD

James Island Yacht Club King
Mackerel, Wahoo & Dolphin
Tournament
P.O. Box 12840, Charleston, SC 29422
(843) 795-6060

Held in late May, this tournament is one of the area's popular competitions (many of which offer less pressure than the billfish ones) with an emphasis on having a good time. Locals and visitors compete for cash and prizes, with a boat entry fee of $125 per species or $300 for all three species. First-, second-, and third-place prizes are awarded for the heaviest king mackerel, wahoo, and dolphin with the biggest fish in each category paying from $5,550 to $6,000. Other non-cash awards go for the outstanding catch by a James Island Yacht Club member, outstanding

female angler, outstanding youth angler (14 and younger), and a tag-and-release award. This tournament is one of the six in the new South Carolina King Mackerel Governor's Cup Series.

South Carolina
Governor's Cup Billfishing Series
P.O. Box 12559, Charleston, SC 29422
(843) 762-5025

The Governor's Cup is an annual, umbrella tournament that encompasses six billfish competitions along coastal South Carolina each spring and summer. Anglers and boats participate by entering two or more member events in the series and either landing or tagging and releasing billfish to accumulate points. More points are given for tagged and released fish, encouraging conservation of marine resources. A perpetual trophy is inscribed with the names of the winners in the categories of Outstanding Billfish, Outstanding Boat, and Outstanding Billfish Conservation. The tournament series runs from May through July and has included area events such as the Isle of Palms Marina tournament, Charleston Harbor Marina Resort, and the Bohicket Marina Invitational Billfish Tournament. The Governor's Cup is an official program of the South Carolina Department of Natural Resources in cooperation with the South Carolina Department of Parks, Recreation, and Tourism. North Carolina and Georgia have a Governor's Cup, too, and the three states compete in a shootout at the end of the year. For more information write to the address above.

Hunting and Fishing Outfitters

The Lowcountry is loaded when it comes to terrific stores that stock all the stuff you'll need to bag your limit or catch a mess of fish for cooking. Here are a handful of our favorite outdoor goods suppliers.

Barton & Burwell
47 South Windermere Blvd., Charleston
(843) 766-3220

Serious anglers know the inventory at Barton & Burwell Fishing Supplies like they know the back creeks of the Lowcountry. Any and everything for the sport of fishing is here to be found. They carry tackle and supplies for inshore, nearshore, offshore, and blue water fishing with brand names such as Star Rods, Penn Reels, Shimano, Daiwa, Cape Fear, and Islander and Pakula lures. Clothing lines include Columbia, Woolrich, and Tarpon Wear, and monogramming and embroidery of hats and shirts is now available, too. Custom rod building is another plus at Barton & Burwell as well as the biggest rod and reel repair department in the area.

> ### Insiders' Tip
> Anglers in privately owned boats need to remember that it is unlawful to fish within 150 feet of commercial fishing piers extending into the Atlantic Ocean.

Buck 'N Bass
1040 Anna Knapp Blvd., Mt. Pleasant
(843) 971-9900

Buck 'N Bass is a great East Cooper source for hunting and fishing supplies. Look here for dove stools and chairs, tree stands, snake boots, chaps, and ammo. For anglers the shop has inshore and offshore tackle and fly fishing equipment too. They carry clothing for men, women, and children from Filson, LaCrosse, Browning, Mossy Oak, and Lewis Creek. The PSE Archery, Shannon's Bug Tamer, White Flyer Skeet, and Winchester supplies are other drawing cards to the store that claims: "From heads to tails, we've got it all."

Carolina Rod & Gun, Inc.
1319 Savannah Hwy., Charleston
(843) 571-7972

In their big, newly expanded store, Carolina Rod & Gun has a large selection of sporting firearms, archery supplies, and outdoor clothing. A full-line Browning dealer, this shop also carries Benelli, Smith & Wesson, Glock, and Ruger too. Two gunsmiths are also on hand for all gunsmith service and repairs.

Their archery department is well known here in the Lowcountry for their inventory, including Browning, Darton, and PSE bows. Sporting optics from Swarovski, Leica, and Schmidt & Bender provide a wide range of binoculars and scopes. Outdoor clothing by Beretta, Boyt, and Bob Allen as well as shoes and boots from LaCrosse and Chippewa complete your hunting gear.

Haddrell's Point
Tackle & Hunting Supply Center
885 Coleman Blvd., Mt. Pleasant
(843) 881-3644

Haddrell's Point offers a complete line of inshore and offshore fishing equipment for the novice to the serious angler. It is one of a few local stores carrying a full line of saltwater and freshwater fly-fishing gear. Sage and G-Loomis rods, Star Rods, and Abel reels are a few of the brands the center carries, and it is the only Shimano warranty station in South Carolina. They handle warranty work for Penn Reels too. Haddrell's also sells hunting accessories for turkey, duck, and deer hunters with clothing from Columbia, Oak Country, and Kahala. Check this place out and talk with the friendly, knowledgeable staff for sales assistance, education, and instruction on hunting and fishing pursuits.

Luden's
78 Alexander St., Charleston
(843) 723-7829

Whether you are gearing up for hunting season, setting out on a harbor cruise, or just want to look the part at a Lowcountry regatta or oyster roast, Luden's is a good source for clothing, gear, and quality marine supplies. Some of the popular clothing lines include Henry Lloyd, Pendleton, Filson, Woolrich, Barbour, Columbia, and Sperry Topsider. Marine supply brands include Richie, Marinco, Harken, Seadog, Perko, and Racor.

It's also the place for safety equipment, compasses, gas tanks, sextants, and charts. It has more in-stock topo maps than any other South Carolina dealer. Luden's is the Lowcountry's authorized Orvis dealer, selling fly rods and flies, fly-tying materials, and Battenkill luggage. Special orders are welcome here. Enjoy the free parking (a rarity downtown) to spend lots of time browsing their location just off East Bay Street. (Also see Luden's in our Shopping chapter.)

Spectator Sports

When most people in the Lowcountry think of sports, they think of grabbing their equipment and getting involved directly in a game of tennis, a round of golf, a dip in the swimming pool, and other activities. However, neither visitors nor locals should overlook the excellent professional, amateur, and collegiate spectator sports available for our enjoyment.

There's nothing like taking off for a day at the stadium to watch the great American sport of baseball, and Charleston's own RiverDogs provide an action-packed brand of play. There's also the option of cheering for the big-name professionals who regularly show up at area golf and tennis matches. And who among us doesn't enjoy an autumn afternoon spent cheering on the college football team, even if our own college days are but a dim, gilded memory.

Tennis, steeplechase, sailing regattas, soccer, ice hockey . . . you name it—if it translates into action, it can probably be found somewhere in the Lowcountry. So take some time off from your own sports regimen to sit and watch the following folks in action. You'll probably find yourself screaming "hey batter, batter, batter!" right along with the best of 'em!

Charleston's own RiverDogs give baseball fans close contact with local heroes.
PHOTO: COURTESY OF MT. PLEASANT RECREATION DEPARTMENT

Baseball

Charleston RiverDogs
360 Fishburne St., Charleston
(843) 723-7241,
(843) 577-DOGS (Ticket Office)

Our minor league team, reborn the Charleston RiverDogs in 1994, is a Class A farm team for the Tampa Bay Devil Rays. The RiverDogs' season runs April through August. Locals turn out regularly and appreciate exciting baseball while enjoying the antics of Charlie the River-Dog, the giant, costumed mascot who plays to the stands and brings out the kid in everyone. After 57 years at College Park, Charleston baseball moved to a new park. Home, as of 1997, is the 5,900-seat Joseph P. Riley Jr. Park on the banks of the Ashley River. This downtown location is next to Brittlebank Park, Stoney Field, and Lockwood Drive. General admission seats are $4 with a range of prices up to $8 for box seats. Watch for special, reduced-admission games and promotions such as fireworks displays after Friday night games and pre-game concerts throughout spring and summer. Plenty of parking is available adjacent to the ballpark for $2.50.

Equestrian

Charleston Cup Steeplechase
5304 Stono Ferry Course, Hollywood
(843) 766-6208

In mid-November, Stono Ferry and the South Carolina Jockey Club host Charleston's horse race: The Charleston Cup Steeplechase. The fun actually begins the night before at the black-tie gala and continues in earnest the next day around the oval track. Gates open at 9 AM, and races begin at 1:30 PM. General admission tickets are $12 in advance or $15 at the gate; reserved infield parking is $100 or $200 for the best locations on the front row. (Call the number above or see our Annual Events chapter for more information.)

Football

Charleston Swamp Foxes
North Charleston Coliseum,
5001 Coliseum Dr., North Charleston
(843) 744-1232

Lowcountry football fans have a new outlet to carry them over until fall. Charleston's Arena Football League 2 franchise, the Charleston Swamp Foxes, made their debut in spring 2000. The Swamp Foxes and 15 other start-up teams are charter members of af2, a regional offshoot of the larger Arena Football League. The new team plays minor league, indoor football at the North Charleston Coliseum. The season runs April through July and promises to be fast-paced and high-scoring with combined team scores of 80 to 100 points. The Swamp Fox name has a historical context referring to General Francis Marion, known as "the Swamp Fox," as he outmaneuvered the British in South Carolina during the American Revolutionary War. The new team hopes to make its own history here. Take the family for football entertainment with a new twist. Added treats may include face painting, a jump castle, and a live country band. Season ticket packages are available and single tickets range in cost from $7.50 to $26.50 with discounts available for children, seniors 60+, military personnel with I.D., and groups. Parking is $4. Call the number above or write to Charleston Swamp Foxes, P.O. Box 80027, Charleston, SC 29416 for more information.

Golf

Rice Planters Amateur Golf Championship
Snee Farm Country Club, U.S. Hwy. 17 N., Mt. Pleasant
(843) 884-8571, (843) 884-2600

Since 1972, Snee Farm Country Club has hosted the Rice Planters Amateur Golf Championship, recently ranked by Golf Week magazine and Titleist as tied for ninth in the top amateur golf events in the world. This tournament attracts top collegiate golfers, seasoned talent from across the United States and terrific international amateur players. Past champions have included current pros Tom Lehman, Scott Hoch, Stewart Cink, Andy Bean, Hal Sutton, and Allen Doyle. Held Fourth of July week, this event is open to the public at no charge. Call Snee Farm for more information.

Ice Hockey

South Carolina Stingrays
3107 Firestone Rd., North Charleston
(843) 744-2248, (843) 554-6060 (Ticketmaster)

The North Charleston Coliseum reverberates with very vocal ice hockey fans who pack in to watch the Stingrays do their thing each season from October through March (even later if we make the playoffs). The team's loyal fans turn out in the red, white, and blue team colors and average more than 7,400 in attendance for each home game. The Stingrays, affiliated with the NHL's Buffalo Sabres, are in their seventh year in the East Coast Hockey League, moving into the Eastern Division after winning the Southern Division a couple of seasons ago. In 1997 they ascended to the top of the heap by winning the ECHL Championship and the Kelly Cup. Again in 2001 they won this title. During intermissions, mascots Cool Ray and Li'l Puck keep the kids enter-

tained. And when the frozen stuff has melted, the children come out to enroll for in-line hockey camps scheduled all summer long. The excitement never fades with the hockey crowd, so call for more schedule and ticket information. Tickets range from $6.75 to $13.50 for adults, with a $1 discount for children younger than 12. Coliseum parking costs $4.

Intercollegiate Sports

With several institutions of higher education in the area, opportunities for checking out college sporting events are abundant. The most popular are, of course, football, baseball, and basketball, but you can also find soccer, track and field, and other events if you are interested.

The College of Charleston's Cougars made it to the Trans-America Athletic Conference championships in previous seasons and in 1997 made some major noise by knocking off regional power Maryland in the NCAA tourney. The College of Charleston now joins The Citadel as a member of the Southern Conference. Coach John Kresse with more than 500 Cougar wins to his credit was recently inducted into the South Carolina Athletic Hall of Fame. He is as popular for his youth basketball camps as for his college record.

In 2001 The Citadel Bulldogs won the Southern Conference Baseball Championship. This tournament is held in Charleston and affords collegiate baseball fans an opportunity to see some of the best teams in action.

Charleston Southern also cut the rug at the NCAA's Big Dance in '97. Citadel football fans recently have been gloating as one of their own, alumnus Travis Jervey, played for the 1998 NFC and the 1997 Super Bowl champions, the Green Bay Packers. So if you'd like to get up close to this college talent and competition while it's happening, get tickets by contacting The Citadel, (843) 953-5121, the College of Charleston, (843) 953-5479, and Charleston Southern University, (843) 863-7213.

Running

Cooper River Bridge Run and Walk
45 Courtenay Dr., Charleston
(843) 792-0345

Just because you don't feel up to walking or running over the infamous second span, don't give up on the 10-kilometer (6.2-mile) Cooper River Bridge Run. Each March or April (usually the weekend before Easter), you can be a spectator or a volunteer and get your own thrill from the collective energy of it all. Hit the streets and cheer the participants onward—hundreds of like-minded folks will be right out there with you. For more information, call the Medical University of South Carolina Wellness Center at the number above. (For more on the festivities, see our Annual Events chapter.)

Sailboat Racing

With the popularity of the Around Alone (formerly the BOC Challenge), the solo sailor around-the-world yacht race, hosted by Charleston in 1994–95 and 1998–99, sailboat racing events have sprung up in this area. The Charleston Ocean Racing Association, established in 1967, holds 35 to 40 sailing events year round in Charleston Harbor and offshore waters, promoting sailing and assisting members in obtaining competent crews and desirable berths. Also a Charleston to Bermuda Race sailed its third competition from Charleston Harbor in May 2001.

Local regattas are popular events too, particularly in the warmer months. From the Carolina Yacht Club and Charleston Yacht Club regattas to those hosted by the Hobcaw, James Island, and Sea Island clubs, there are races throughout the summer. A schedule is set in January and posted in the area yacht clubs. Spectators enjoy watching these races, free of charge, from The Battery or from the grounds of the club hosting the event. Children are welcome and may even start asking about those Charleston Yacht Club Summer Youth Sailing Program lessons (see Insiders' Tip in this chapter). Call the sailing department at the College of Charleston (which, by the way, traditionally has a fine sailing team) at (843) 953-5549 for more information about non-credit community sailing classes or sailing association memberships.

Charleston Race Week '02
Charleston Ocean Racing Association
P.O. Box 123, Charleston, SC 29402
(843) 722-0823

The Charleston Ocean Racing Association (CORA) presents the seventh annual Charleston Race Week at the end of April. Race Week is comprised of The Palmetto Cup regatta, an inshore competition for sailboats 22 feet and above, selected one-design regattas, and a Thursday evening harbor race. The Charleston Race Week Cup and overall Race Week winners are determined based on cumulative scoring results. More than 80 boats competed in 2001, and a good time was had by all.

Charleston to Bermuda Race
(843) 722-0823

Alternating years with the Bermuda to Newport Race, the Charleston to Bermuda Race leaves our city in May 2003. The 771-mile race is hosted on the receiving end by the Royal Bermuda Yacht Club (formed in 1844), and the finish line is off the St. David's Lighthouse in Bermuda. The 30-foot and larger sailboats are entered in either a double-handed class (two crew) or the fully crewed class with a minimum of four. Hundreds of spectators lined the Waterfront Park and The Battery as well as watched from more than 100 spectator boats as the sailors set out on this challenge in May 2001.

Soccer

Charleston Battery
Blackbaud Stadium,
990 Daniel Island Dr., Charleston
(843) 971-GOAL (4625)

In 1993, a professional men's soccer league team, the Charleston Battery, was formed, joining the United Systems of

Independent Soccer Leagues. After placing at the top of the Atlantic Division in '94 and '95, the team advanced to the USISL finals in 1996, and won the league championship in a thriller: a 3-2 match decided in a shootout. In 1997 the Battery changed to the new Division II A-League (one notch below Major League Soccer) and in 2000 won the Atlantic Division Championship. You can catch all the action at the new $4.5 million soccer-specific Blackbaud Stadium on Daniel Island (just off I-526 between the Cooper and Wando Rivers). The new facility provides fun for the whole family with an expansive kids' "Fun Zone" and the Three Lions Pub. The games run April through August. Charleston Battery tickets range from $6 bleacher seats to $12 club seats Kids younger than 4 are admitted free. Parking is $3 per car.

Stock Car Racing

Summerville Speedway
1896 Central Ave., Summerville
(843) 873-3438

Fans of stock car racing will find this local track a hot spot on weekend nights from April through October. Complete with lighted track and grandstand seating, the speedway is on Central Avenue in Summerville. Regularly scheduled events include NASCAR Dash division racing as well as weekly races for late-model stocks, super stocks, and two other four-cylinder divisions. Ticket prices for regular events are $15 for adults and $3 for children 8 to 12. Kids younger than 8 are admitted free. Call for race schedules and additional information.

Tennis

Family Circle Cup
Daniel Island Tennis Centre,
161 Seven Farms Dr., Daniel Island,
Charleston
(843) 534-2400, (800) 677-2293

Spectator tennis took a major leap forward in the Charleston area with the

> ## Insiders' Tip
>
> For the past 40 years, children have learned to sail in the Charleston Yacht Club Summer Youth Sailing Program. If you have kids ages 7 to 17, this may be just what you're looking for to add a little excitement to their lives. Parents do not have to belong to the club, but nonmember participants pay slightly more than members--$300, compared with $250. Six three-week sessions are offered each summer. For more information, write to the Summer Youth Sailing Program, Charleston Yacht Club, P.O. Box 20474, Charleston, SC 29413.

announcement of a relocation of the Family Circle Cup to our city after a long-time run in Hilton Head, SC. As many as 100,000 tennis fans have attended the nine-day, Women's Tennis Association Tier I event. A new $9-million tennis complex for the tournament was built within the new Town Centre Park in the planned community of Daniel Island. (See our Neighborhoods chapter for more on Daniel Island.) It served up an inaugural venue for this competition that attracts many of the top seeds in women's tennis. Some of the past competitors were Conchita Martinez, Monica Seles, Arantxa Sanchez-Vicario, Mary Pierce, and champion, Jennifer Capriati. Held in mid-April, the Family Circle Cup is a hot ticket in Charleston's busy spring tourism events. Ticket prices range from $20 for qualifying matches up to $60 for the finals. Call the number above or write to Family Circle Cup for more information.

Care Alliance Health Services
Pro Tennis Classic
Mt. Pleasant Tennis Complex,
889 Whipple Rd., Mt. Pleasant
(843) 856-2162
An important stop for aspiring tennis players in the U.S. Women's Tennis Association's satellite circuit events is the Pro Tennis Classic. Players from all over the world, ranking between 100 to 600, come to compete for $25,000 in prize money and valuable computer points. As a futures-level event, players who win a match here gain points that allow them to advance to tournaments such as Wimbledon and the U.S. Open. Held the second week in June each year, here's your chance to see the rising stars of women's tennis. Daily matches are from 10 AM to 5 PM with the finals at 1 PM on Sunday. There is no admission charge so bring your lawn chair and take in some intensely competitive, tournament-level tennis.

Neighborhoods

There was a time when living in Charleston meant hanging your hat somewhere on the Peninsula.

Somewhere in the quarter-century between the world wars, all that started to change. Mind you, Charleston is and always will be largely defined by the geographic boundaries of the Peninsula and the charming old houses that exist in the prestigious neighborhood referred to as "below (meaning south of) Broad (Street)." Living in one of those grand old houses will always be part of the quintessential Charleston lifestyle. Earthquakes, storms, fires, and wars have worked their woes and done their best to alter that reality. But an address Below Broad will always be a prestigious one in Charleston.

Meanwhile, it's also true that thousands upon thousands of other certified Charlestonians are thriving in other neighborhoods—living full, complete, happy, and productive lives.

We'll start this description of Charleston's neighborhoods with some of the spectacular statistics surrounding real estate Below Broad. This includes the soaring values that have been asked and paid there since Charleston encountered tourism and the nation's growing fascination with historic preservation.

For better or worse, there's apparently a hot and heavy national market for Below-Broad property and the prestige of owning it. In 1998 a famous mansion Below Broad known as the Sword Gate House on Legare Street, sold for $4.2 million. An out-of-town buyer paid that record price (so far) for residential property on the Charleston Peninsula.

Despite this kind of transaction, properties Below Broad are selling in the $600,000 to $1 million price range. And thanks to the efforts of our preservation-minded groups, institutions, and individuals, there are several other historic neighborhoods on the Peninsula where residential properties are a little more affordable. According to the Charleston Trident Association of Realtors (Multiple Listing Service), the average selling price range of a single family residential house on the Peninsula during the first half of 2000 (including new and previously owned homes) was $250,000 to $600,000.

Naturally, real estate prices fluctuate greatly in different areas. And in a market as attractive as Greater Charleston, many homes and condominiums sell quickly and never make it to the Multiple Listing Service. But wherever real estate sales are a matter of public record, we've based our information on neighborhood home values on real numbers. Ask a real estate professional for more complete guidance.

Although the historic area south of Broad Street is considered the quintessential Charlestonian neighborhood, several other locales north of Broad (between Broad and Calhoun Streets) are now looked at very favorably too. The French Quarter—so-named for the French Huguenots who once lived and worked there—includes the area around Philadelphia Alley, State, Queen, and Chalmers Streets and is a mixture of commercial and residential buildings with inns, offices, restaurants, bars, and shops. Even the theatrical entity known as The Footlight Players (see our chapter on The Arts) coexists with busy families in this bustling cosmopolitan atmosphere.

Because the French Quarter is a small neighborhood of only a few square blocks, we're only talking about 40 town houses or so. Behind their relatively common facades, they vary in size, configuration, and building date. However, a late-18th-century to mid-

19th-century, two-bedroom, two-bath home might average $600,000.

Ansonborough is one of Charleston's more famous examples of institutionally inspired restoration. In the early 1970s many architecturally significant homes in this neighborhood were in grievous disrepair. The Historic Charleston Foundation initiated a program that effectively and expediently changed the economic course of the entire area. A decade later, Ansonborough was one of the city's more sought-after neighborhoods, and it still is today. The advent of the new South Carolina Aquarium and the associated redevelopment along the western bank of the Cooper River just across East Bay Street from Ansonborough has added even more attractiveness to this downtown neighborhood. A typical 1830s house in Ansonborough with three bedrooms and two to three baths can sell in the $650,000 range.

Mazyck-Wraggborough includes the blocks between Calhoun Street and The Charleston Museum. Here you'll find an interesting mix of restored houses, beautiful churches, and light industry. Major historic anchors in this neighborhood include the Aiken-Rhett House, operated by the Historic Charleston Foundation, The Charleston Museum and its neighboring house museum, the Joseph Manigault House. (See the House Museums section of our Attractions chapter.) In this neighborhood, a three-bedroom, two-and-a-half-bath house would sell for about $300,000.

The area around the Medical University of South Carolina, the College of Charleston, Colonial Lake, and all points in between is Harleston Village. Here you'll find an eclectic mix of bed and breakfast inns, condos, town houses, stately 18th- and 19th-century properties, and even a couple of high-rise apartment buildings. Two-bedroom rental houses are in the $1,000- to $1,300-per-month range. One-bedroom condos sell for about $155,000. But an average selling price for a three-bedroom, two-and-a-half-bath home is in the $375,000 to $450,000 range.

Radcliffeborough is the area north of Calhoun Street, from the medical complexes

One of the 13 cobblestone streets made mostly of ships' ballast stones. PHOTO: FLETCHER NEWBERN

east to Mazyck-Wraggborough. Ashley Hall, an independent school for girls, is situated here on a 4-acre campus that includes the historic (c. 1816) Mcbee House. There are several other fully restored mansions nearby plus rental properties, and many fixer-uppers can still be found in this area. Two-bedroom apartment rentals in Radcliffeborough average $800 a month. A two-bedroom, two-and-a-half-bath home recently sold for $359,000.

East Cooper

Many neighborhoods east of the Cooper River—which include those in Mt. Pleasant, Sullivan's Island, and the Isle of Palms—are experiencing unprecedented growth. According to the Metro Chamber of Commerce Center for Business Research, Mt. Pleasant led the tri-county area with 1,610 new residential permits in 1999. The main corridor of growth seems to be along U.S. Highway 17 N. to S.C. Highway 41.

All this projected growth will undoubtedly have a major impact on the real estate market east of the Cooper. However, recent figures from the Charleston Trident Association of Realtors (MLS) for the average East Cooper residence (south of S.C. Highway 41) was a very respectable $238,593.

Another major growth area is the southern end of the Isle of Palms. The IOP Connector, linking the island to the Mark Clark Expressway and Interstate 26, has fueled a flurry of new construction at both the southern tip of the Isle of Palms and at Wild Dunes resort. In 2000 the average Wild Dunes residence was in the $450,000 range.

For newcomers who want a short list of lifestyle options, East Cooper offers a wide variety. There's the charm and quaintness of the Old Village in Mt. Pleasant. There are a number of older, established neighborhoods where families flourish—some of Mt. Pleasant's best are listed below. East Cooper's newer neighborhoods tend to offer several

Downtown Charleston neighborhoods can be an eclectic mix of 18th-, 19th-, and 20th-century homes.
PHOTO: COURTESY OF CHARLESTON AREA CONVENTION AND VISITORS BUREAU

levels of home ownership to more easily accommodate first-time buyers as well as the upwardly mobile movers and shakers. And, of course, East Cooper's beach communities are always popular with laid-back folk and the second-home crowd.

Established Neighborhoods

Creekside

Just off U.S. 17 N., Creekside is an established community and home to the Charleston Tennis Club. Residents have access to this facility with its courts and swimming pool. Winding streets and moderately upscale homes are handsomely individual. Many have a nice view of Shem Creek. An average four-bedroom, two-and-a-half-bathroom home in Creekside would be priced in the $335,000 bracket.

> **Insiders' Tip**
>
> New players on the real estate stage who fall in love with the proverbial historic fixer-upper can find solace in the Resource Center at The Preservation Society of Charleston. Therein lies a wealth of information on preservation and restoration techniques scripted by those who've performed that role in the recent past. This can be a major help in saving you time or money (or both).

The Groves

Between Coleman Boulevard and U.S. 17 N. is The Groves. This neighborhood is one of few established Mt. Pleasant neighborhoods convenient to downtown Charleston. It consists of mostly one- or one-and-a-half-story brick homes built in the 1950s and 1960s. In this family neighborhood with a nice park for the children, you'll also enjoy the quiet streets for bike rides and leisurely strolls. A three-bedroom, two-and-a-half-bath ranch in The Groves might sell for about $200,000.

Hobcaw

Off Mathis Ferry Road is Hobcaw, a large, established subdivision. Hobcaw has homes in many price ranges and is popular with longtime residents as well as young couples with children. Public records show recent sales ranging from $230,000 to $750,000, with the average three-bedroom, two-and-a-half-bath home selling for $400,000. Proximity to the Hobcaw Yacht Club, with its outdoor swimming pool and other recreational facilities, is an appealing feature. Some houses are on the water and these, of course, tend to be the priciest.

Old Village

This Mt. Pleasant neighborhood is one of the most appealing in the Trident area. Many of the restored antebellum homes are situated on large lots, while others are clustered along the tree-lined streets to form a village setting. Many houses were built in the last quarter-century, some even in this decade. Though certainly a real estate target for young, affluent professionals, the Old Village has retained much of the unpretentious, casual charm it was known for a hundred years ago. An average home in the Old Village is in the $440,000 range.

Snee Farm

Just south of where Long Point Road intersects U.S. 17 is Snee Farm, a large, established community with a country club. The golf course, tennis facilities, and the clubhouse are in great demand, and homes range in style from ranch to Georgian Colonial. Old oaks and gum trees soften the skyline and enhance a very attractive neighborhood. Here a three-bedroom, two-and-a-half-bath home sells for about $190,000.

New Neighborhoods

A quick glance at the map will tell you the East Cooper area, especially Mt. Pleasant, is ripe for growth. Charleston's annexation of Daniel Island is a prime example; the corridor along S.C. Highway 41 is another. Look to these areas for some of the Lowcountry's best new communities.

Daniel Island

If you've harbored a dream to sail into new territory, Daniel Island may give you that chance. Annexed as part of the city of Charleston but located east of the Cooper River, you're just minutes from downtown or North Charleston via Interstate 526. Daniel Island and its 20 miles of virgin waterfront on the Cooper and Wando Rivers are being developed into a town with public parks, residential neighborhoods, a town center with a waterfront park, and a corporate complex with 2 million square feet of office space. Ultimately, between 4,000 and 7,000 homesites are planned there. Residents are proud of the new Blackbaud Stadium, home of The Charleston Battery, a professional soccer team (see our Spectator Sports chapter). One of Daniel Island's new assets is the recently opened private high school, Bishop England, which moved from downtown. It now sprawls on a 40-acre campus (see our Education chapter). Another new educational facility, this one a public school, is the 74,000-sq.-ft. elementary school, Hanahan Elementary, which houses over 900 students.

Many new families are living on Daniel Island now. Homes in one phase of new "Charleston single houses" are selling in the $200,000 range. More upscale, custom-built homes with four-bedroom, three-bath floor plans sell for $400,000 and more. It's reasonable to expect this rapid development to continue throughout the next decade and a half.

Dunes West

A catalyst for the building boom off S.C. 41 is Dunes West. This golf course community also offers swimming and tennis in a beautiful, woodland and waterway setting. Many of these homeowners enjoy terrific views of the golf course and surrounding waterways. The upscale, 2,011-acre private development was well under way by the mid-1980s, and complete build-out is scheduled for sometime after the year 2011. The variety of housing options in Dunes West is an unfinished story; major tracts of the vast acreage are still on the drawing board. For now the price of a three-bedroom, two-and-a-half-bath home near the golf course is in the vicinity of $300,000.

I'On

One of the newer planned communities on Mathis Ferry Road, I'On is known for its family-friendly feel with wide sidewalks, parks, lakes, and trees. The homes are designed with a nod to traditional Lowcountry architecture—reminiscent of downtown Charleston neighborhoods and Mt. Pleasant's Old Village. The new I'On Club houses upscale amenities for residents which include tennis and pool facilities, a community dock and a boat ramp on Hobcaw Creek. Homesites in I'On are priced from $47,000 up. Completed homes there start in the $250,000 range.

Long Point

North of the Snee Farm Country Club community, just off U.S. 17, is Long Point. Beautiful views of the marsh are among this neighborhood's best features. These upscale, newly constructed homes are nestled amidst mature gum and pine trees. Nearby are tennis and basketball courts, a soccer field, and Palmetto Islands County Park. (See our Parks and Recreation chapter.) Prices here range from $125,000 to $615,000, with an average four-bedroom, two-and-a-half-bath place going for $220,000.

East Cooper Beaches

Sullivan's Island, Isle of Palms, Wild Dunes, and Dewees Island all have beautiful ocean or Intracoastal Waterway vistas. These upscale communities are among the Lowcountry's most popular. Land and real estate values are priced accordingly.

Dewees Island

Billed as "Charleston's Only Private Island," Dewees is being developed carefully as an environmentally protected enclave. Modern homes are nestled discreetly amongst the island's vegetation, and a limited number of others are planned. Dewees' developers are hoping to preserve the natural integrity of this barrier island while they create a quiet, isolated upscale community. Bear in mind you must be willing to make your way to

Charleston's famous Rainbow Row may borrow its colors from the Caribbean, but its architecture is purely 18th-century Charleston. PHOTO: COURTESY OF CHARLESTON AREA CONVENTION AND VISITORS BUREAU

Dewees by boat—no bridge is available and none is planned. Most of the real estate activity on the island is new construction. Homesites in this unique community range from $375,000 to $1.1 million, and the few resale homes there have ranged in price from $480,000 to $1,175,000.

Isle of Palms

This beach community has an inviting, sandy beach and access to the creeks along the back of the island. In most cases, renovation after 1989's Hurricane Hugo has enhanced the real estate values here. Bigger and better houses, built high on stilts, will hopefully avoid future water damage. There are still many wonderful old beach houses, however, that have defied a century's worth of storms and tourism's relentless intervention.

The commute to peninsular Charleston from Isle of Palms is about a half-hour. Large beachfront homes (as in six bedrooms and four baths) can soar as high as $3.3 million. Condos sell for $150,000 and higher. The average three-bedroom, two-and-a-half-bath home fetches about $300,000 to $400,000.

Sullivan's Island

There are no official subdivisions on Sullivan's Island, a laid-back beach community that's about a 20-minute commute from downtown Charleston. Rather, the location of property is described by its proximity to the water or local landmarks ("front beach" or "near Fort Moultrie," for example). This was the 19th-century summer community for many Below-Broad families of that time as well as today. The heightened real estate values of this historic island have encouraged more full-time residents. The current values range from $130,000 for a three-bedroom, two-bath house to $2.9 million for a four-bedroom, four-and-a-half-bath home on the beach front. The average price for a three-bedroom, two-and-a-half-bath home is $860,000.

Wild Dunes

Just 15 miles from Charleston proper, Wild Dunes is a separate community at the north end of the Isle of Palms. This luxury resort has conference facilities, vacation rentals, villa accommodations, and homesites for sale. Homes here can go as high as $3.3 million for a four-bedroom, four-and-a-half-bath house, or as low as $185,000 for a more modest two-bedroom, two-bath place. (See our Boating and Watersports chapter for information on Wild Dunes Yacht Harbor facilities.)

North Charleston

Although the city of North Charleston is largely outside the scope of this book, we'd be remiss if we didn't say there are many viable neighborhoods here that are both family oriented and affordable. According to the Charleston Trident Association of Realtors (Multiple Listing Service), the average selling price of a North Charleston home was $77,565 in 2000. That figure just surpassed the 1993 average of $60,279 in the last year. A decline in prices took place after the 1993 closure of the North Charleston-based Navy facility, but now appears to be rebounding.

There's a notion (often an unfair one) among some Charlestonians that North Charleston is a good place to work but not a good place to live. It is mostly a city of main corridors where people clip through at the speed limit, noticing all the business and industry but not the residential neighborhoods. The city is determined to remedy this perception with the encouragement of upscale neighborhoods such as Coosaw Creek, Whitehall, and Yeamans Hall. Newer options seem to appear on the city planner's drawing board with increasing regularity.

West Ashley

Since 1960, the population in the West Ashley area has doubled. That fact alone speaks volumes about the neighborhoods in this part of the Lowcountry. The growth was accelerated by a major city of Charleston annexation in 1979. Many of these new residents have chosen apartments and subdivisions built since 1980.

West Ashley seems to thrive on the myriad of small stores and businesses that line the major traffic arteries (S.C. Highways 171, 61, and 7, plus U.S. 17 S.). Tucked behind these throughways are many neighborhoods that house families of every ilk and category. The Trident Association of Realtors (MLS) average price for a West Ashley home in 2000 was about $173,369. Some of the better-known neighborhoods in this section of Charleston follow.

Established Neighborhoods

Byrnes Downs

Barely a mile from the Ashley River Bridge along U.S. 17 is one of Charleston's first major subdivisions, Byrnes Downs. It was built after World War II and named after James Byrnes, a South Carolina-born U.S. secretary of state. These small brick homes are popular with many first-home buyers who enjoy the advantage of being so close to the city. A recent average sales price for one of these trendy starter places was $165,000.

The Crescent

Folly Road and the Intracoastal Waterway border the Crescent. Described once as "the country, only five minutes from town," this highly desirable old neighborhood built in the 1950s and 1960s consists of established homes and yards with wonderful old trees. Generations of children have fed the resident ducks that inhabit the twin lakes, and all age groups take advantage of the quiet streets for walks and bike rides. A four-bedroom, three-and-a-half-bath home sells in the $750,000 range.

Parkshore I, II, III, IV

The Parkshore family of subdivisions is bordered by S.C. Hwy. 7 and the Ashley River. These are newer executive homes with large lots and some availability remaining. Many have marsh views and some have docks. Residents love the access to a community center within the Parkshore complex with its pool, park, and tennis courts. Most of these houses are three- and four-bedroom places with two-and-a-half to three-and-a-half baths. These homes recently ranged in price from $150,000 to $240,000, with an average home going for about $195,000.

Shadowmoss

Shadowmoss is a mid-priced, country-club community. It started in the 1970s and has been growing ever since. Many different builders have contributed to the development's housing mix, so there's something for every pocketbook here. Shadowmoss was designed around an 18-hole golf course and pool complex (see our Golf chapter). Residents enjoy community clubs and events and can make use of the on-site facilities. Real estate values range from $104,000 to $294,000, but an average three-bedroom, two-bath home might bring $155,000.

James, Johns, and Folly Islands, Kiawah, and Seabrook

The islands west of the Ashley River, connected by a series of bridges, are a diverse and intriguing group. When the James Island Expressway (S.C. Highway 30) opened in 1993, it made these islands prime targets for developers.

Already densely populated, James Island has spectacular views of the Charleston Harbor and Peninsula and has many neighborhoods housing people who work throughout the Trident area. Much of Johns Island is still rural. Bohicket Road, the main highway through the island, has been widened in part near the resorts of Kiawah and Seabrook.

New neighborhoods along this road are only a matter of time. Low-key Folly Beach is a casual, year-round island community with an eclectic mix of new construction and rustic old beach houses from Folly's days of yore. Real estate offerings include front beach, marsh and river, along with inland houses and lots. The average home price for a James Island home in 2000, according to the Charleston Trident Realtors, was $184,335. On outer James Island and on Folly Beach the average was $359,409. Johns Island homes ranged from $173,580 all the way up to $7.5 million for a Kiawah resort home.

James Island

Country Club of Charleston

Across the Wappoo Bridge off Folly Road is Country Club of Charleston (sometimes called Country Club I). This older, established community with beautiful homes and well-kept lawns is one of the area's most desirable addresses. The private club, pool, and golf course are obvious assets, and the proximity to the Peninsula is another plus. Homes on the

Strollers along East Battery admire the gracious homes and peek into the manicured gardens beyond the gates.

PHOTO: COURTESY OF CHARLESTON AREA CONVENTION AND VISITORS BUREAU

Neighborhoods / 359

waterway are priced in the $850,000 range for four bedrooms and three-and-a-half baths. Properties off the water sell in the $300,000 range for four bedrooms and two baths.

Parrot Creek

There is much to see in Parrot Creek. These newer houses and lots are large and beautifully landscaped—some fronting on deep water or marsh. Composed of mostly two-story homes on half-acre lots, Parrot Creek offers architectural variety and desirable extras such as wide porches to catch those prevailing breezes. A three-bedroom, three-and-a-half-bath home recently sold for $500,000. The average sale price is about $340,000.

Riverland Terrace

Riverland Terrace, off Maybank Highway, is an established neighborhood with origins dating back to the 1920s. Today, you'll find a conglomeration of sizes, styles, and prices. There are interesting rehab possibilities as well as extraordinary turnkey dwellings throughout. Young people have been drawn to this area in recent years because of its tranquillity and, in some instances, its affordability. The few houses on the waterway command the highest prices, while smaller houses in the middle of the neighborhood can be had for less. A three-bedroom, two-bath home might sell for as low as $117,000; a four-bedroom, two-bath house might be as high as $350,000. The average price for a home that's not on the waterway would be about $200,000.

Headquarters Island Plantation

Across the Stono River from James Island are Johns Island and Headquarters Island Plantation. Incredibly, this spacious development on the vast open marsh is only 4.5 miles from downtown Charleston. This upscale, planned community is close to restaurants, shopping, and championship golf, but has the feel and openness of a far more distant setting. Property values for a four-bedroom, three-and-a-half-bath home reach $419,000. The low end of the price spectrum is about $172,000 for some three-bedroom, three-bath places.

Folly Beach

Real estate on this small resort island has exploded in price over the past several years. Articles describe the island as "the edge of America" with tongue only slightly in cheek. Like Key West in the 1970s, Folly is attracting a chic and mixed crowd who choose digs that range from dilapidated rental properties to impressive, dramatic, and upscale homes. Most properties fall somewhere in between. Many artists and dedicated surfers can still be found on Folly, but the buying trend is moving toward the beach-loving executive types. The average three-bedroom beach home was $391,000 in 2000.

> **Insiders' Tip**
> Many of Charleston's downtown neighborhoods have very active membership associations that serve both social and economic (and sometimes even political) purposes. They have parties, sponsor tours, and work to govern future development. They also represent the neighborhood when resolving issues such as parking variances and utility construction.

Sunset Point

Near the west end of Folly, Sunset Point is an attractive newer subdivision. It is divided into six sections—some are a block from the beach, others front the marsh and deep water of Folly River. Prices here are in the $300,000 range.

Kiawah and Seabrook

These famous resort islands need no introduction here (see our Area Overviews, Golf, and History chapters). The residents of these islands are among the wealthiest in Charleston County, according to the latest figures from the Center for Business Research. Real Estate on these barrier islands is blazing to new heights.

Kiawah

With 10 miles of beach and 10,000 acres of forest, marshes, creeks, and rivers, Kiawah is a world-class destination where you'll find some of the nation's most interesting resort architecture. Although the houses blend unobtrusively into the environment, they are by no means uniform. Palatial residences with creative use of glass and materials make the most of spectacular views from ocean to lagoon, and there is a consistency in landscaping throughout. In 2000, the average Kiawah home was $1.3 million, a dramatic increase over 1998's $116,644.

A variety of wildlife abounds, and the athletic facilities and social activities also lure homeowners. At your disposal are more than 18 miles of paved bike paths, a 20-station fitness trail, golf, tennis, swimming, and a 21-acre park and pool complex. Kiawah also has an active vacation rental program, which contributes to the real estate's value.

Seabrook

Bordered by the North Edisto, Bohicket, and Kiawah Rivers and the Atlantic Ocean, Seabrook Island is awash in spectacular water views. Kiawah's smaller next-door neighbor has more than 3 miles of beach and 2,200 private residential acres. The demographic makeup is similar to Kiawah, with Seabrook being another upscale island community with a wide assortment of real estate options and amenities. More residential by nature than the other resort communities in the area, Seabrook incorporated as a town in 1987. There is a complete sports and recreation program, including a well-maintained equestrian center with aesthetically pleasing trail and beach rides. The average home price on Seabrook increased from $247,052 in 1998 to $557,899 in 2000. Seabrook, like Kiawah, also has a wide range of prices from $190,000 up to $1.3 million.

Charleston's beautiful architecture enchants visitors to this city. PHOTO: COURTESY OF CHARLESTON AREA CONVENTION AND VISITORS BUREAU

Real Estate and Rentals

Real Estate
Companies
Apartment Rentals

When it comes to real estate, one thing should be crystal clear, especially if you've scanned our Neighborhoods chapter: Greater Charleston has it all. You'll find everything—antebellum mansions, resort homes, luxury town houses, beachfront condominiums, suburban dwellings, planned communities, starter homes, affordable apartments, and even, every once in a while, a fine old plantation. In fact, the very abundance and diversity of Lowcountry real estate sometimes stun visitors and newcomers.

If you are new to the area and have turned to the Charleston Metro Chamber of Commerce, 81 Mary Street, (843) 577-2510, for any of its excellent visitor information, you might want to ask for its free list of area member real estate agencies too. This will give you a handy overview of the residential realtors as well as the commercial and industrial specialists who are currently chamber members and working here in the Lowcountry.

One of the best resources for specific real estate information in Greater Charleston is the Charleston Trident Association of Realtors, 5300 International Boulevard, Suite C-105, North Charleston, SC 29418, (843) 760-9400. In 1999, there were 1,800 member Realtors working throughout Charleston, Dorchester, and Berkeley counties. And the association can easily recommend a professional to help you find the home that's right for you.

If you are more interested in simply renting, we also offer useful information on renting an apartment in and around Charleston.

The real estate companies we selected to highlight in this guide are among the best in the area. Of course, there are other excellent companies, but space limitations won't allow a more comprehensive listing here. Another simple option in addition to the chamber and the Charleston Trident Association of Realtors: You may want to check the Yellow Pages to find a real estate firm that specializes in an area that's of particular interest to you.

Real Estate Companies

Naturally, choosing a real estate company is a very personal matter. Because it is such an important decision, be sure to find an agent who truly understands your priorities. Sometimes that's easier said than done.

An agent who specializes in investment properties may not understand why you want to see only pre-Revolutionary houses, or why an otherwise acceptable house won't do because your grandmother's furniture won't fit in the dining room. By the same token, an agent with a reputation for handling plantations and historic properties may not grasp the needs of a first-time buyer or the advantages of one school system over another. You can find agents who are such specialists if you ask the right questions. Be sure to be specific about your needs.

In general, the agents in the Greater Charleston area are well versed in the needs of a broad-spectrum market. And with computerized multiple-listing services, almost all agents can show you any house or property you might be interested in seeing. As with any business relationship, some frank discussions early on about your price range and what you're looking for can help avoid wasting your time and patience. Just remember that open communication with your real estate agent is the first key to finding the right home. And again, more information on the feel and price ranges in various Charleston-area neighborhoods can be found in our Neighborhoods chapter.

Downtown Charleston Properties

Residential real estate in downtown Charleston is a very specialized market. You're looking at properties with historic and aesthetic values that often override the considerations of ordinary shelter. And then there's that awesome specter of restoration to consider—whether it's something already accomplished at someone's great expense or it's something you feel you want to tackle yourself. These variables affect property values enormously. There are special tax strategies and things such as "facade easements" to learn about, which can actually make owning a home in the Historic District a little more affordable. Pricing is also affected by something called "comparables"—that's the price recently paid for a comparable house in the same neighborhood. That can change monthly or even (gasp!) weekly.

Sound complicated? It is, so it's best to get some help from people who deal with this on a daily basis. Here are some of the companies with plenty of experience selling residential real estate in downtown Charleston.

Disher, Hamrick & Myers
196 King St., 480 East Bay St.
(843) 577-4115, (800) 577-4118
This company has 15 full-time agents whose primary focus is on historic properties in downtown Charleston. It is the leading brokerage firm in the Historic District. The staff has more than 80 years of aggregate experience in the market. Many of these individuals are downtown residents who have been through the

restoration process themselves, giving them a perspective that clients find invaluable.

Historic Charleston Properties
67 Broad St.
(843) 853-3000
Begun in 1997, this fledgling real estate company came on fast and strong in the Charleston market—earning $18 million in sales their first year. The company now has five agents whose focus is on up scale residential properties and discreet, personalized service.

Lane & Smythe Real Estate, LLC.
9 Broad St.
(843) 577-2900
This firm, founded in 1999, has agents with 35 years of combined service in the real estate industry dealing in historic properties. It is proudly owned and operated by women who are skilled at presenting a total point of view, including the female perspective, in relocating to the Charleston area.

Pate Properties, Inc.
960 Morrison Dr., Ste. 200
(843) 577-3193
This closely held company, with more than 20 years' experience in the market, has a fantastic track record for handling

downtown residential real estate, small investment properties, and property management. The owner is one of the city's few buyer representatives, sanctioned by the National Association of Realtors.

Poston & Co. Real Estate
25 Cumberland St.
(843) 853-5300
Marketing mostly residential real estate in the upscale residential neighborhoods of downtown Charleston, West Ashley, James Island, Mt. Pleasant, and Daniel Island, this firm has been in business for over a decade. In 1997, their sales exceeded $61 million. They focus on residential sales and relocation services, including the marketing and sale of existing homes, new construction, and residential lots. They also offer property management services.

Arthur Ravenel Real Estate Co.
635 East Bay St.
(843) 723-7847
Ravenel is a small, family-owned company that has been in business since 1945. Its experienced agents can help you with purchases of historic downtown properties, waterfront properties, and commercial real estate.

Daniel Ravenel Real Estate Co.
33 Broad St.
(843) 723-7150, (800) 382-2279
This is a full-service independent agency with deep roots in the community. With offices in downtown Charleston, the agency provides customized residential, commercial, and waterfront real estate services throughout the Lowcountry—from The Battery to the beaches.

Joseph P. Riley Realty
13 Broad St.
(843) 723-3700
This downtown real estate firm has been around since 1937, when it was founded by the father of longtime Charleston Mayor Joseph P. Riley Jr. Agents associated with this firm have a knowledgeable perspective on the changing values of Charleston's residential real estate.

Although relatively small in size, the firm also has listings for local island properties and North Carolina mountain retreats.

Tri-County Real Estate Companies

In addition to the independent real estate companies that specialize in historic properties or beach homes, the giant franchise networks are established here. These companies are eager to meet your real estate needs and offer comprehensive, one-stop real estate service—whether you're moving across the country or across town. Look for names such as Century 21, Gallery of Homes, Better Homes & Gardens, Coldwell Banker, RE/MAX, and EPA.

In fact, we're seeing an ongoing trend among some of the older, larger, independent real estate companies toward joining these nationwide franchise networks. The idea here is that there's strength in numbers—that teamwork and standardization lead to better efficiency and greater success.

The Beach Company
211 King St., Ste. 300
(843) 722-2615
Founded in 1945, this is the largest full-service real estate company in Charleston. In addition to residential sales and property management, they handle acquisition, development, construction services, and commercial brokerage.

RE/MAX Realtors
37 Broad St.
(843) 577-5400
824 Johnnie Dodds Blvd., Mt. Pleasant
(843) 881-9925
632 St. Andrews Blvd., West Ashley
(843) 571-5220
8761 Dorchester Rd., N. Charleston
(843) 767-7777
The former Max Hill Co., with well over 25 years of experience in the local real estate market, joined the RE/MAX network several years ago. Today about 27 fully trained and qualified agents work out of the four independently owned Lowcountry offices.

Prudential Carolina Real Estate
43-B Broad St.
  (843) 577-0001
Ashley River Rd.
  (843) 571-74
706 Orleans Rd. (West Ashley)
  (843) 556-5800
3040 Hwy. 17 N. Mt. Pleasant
  (843) 266-5000
195 W. Coleman
  (843) 884-1800
790 Johnnie Dodds Blvd., Mt. Pleasant
  (843) 884-1622
452 Folly Rd., Charleston
  (843) 795-7810
125 Wappoo Creek Dr., James Island
  (843) 795-5000
3714-K Betsy Kerrison Pkwy., Johns Island
  (843) 768-4880
1400 Palm Blvd., Isle of Palms
  (843) 886-8110
567 Crowfield Blvd., North Charleston
  (843) 797-7799

7951 Dorchester Rd., North Charleston
  (843) 552-2905
1320 N. Main St., Summerville
  (843) 873-0722
1825 Old Trolley Rd., Summerville
  (843) 871-9000
Relocation Services,
  4024 Salt Pointe Pkwy.
  (843) 202-2030, (800) 476-1929

Clearly, this company takes an aggressive stance in the local real estate market with a wide-reaching array of regional offices throughout the greater Charleston area. They also serve newcomers with a full-time staff in their Relocation Office. The relocation staff can help with school applications, tax forms, tuition fees, handicapped-accessibility, and even career assistance. The relocation agent then refers you to a handpicked agent in one of the local offices.

Apartment Rentals

There are many apartment and town house complexes in Greater Charleston, the majority of which are in West Ashley, Mt. Pleasant, North Charleston, and the Ladson, Summerville, and Hanahan areas. Amenities vary wildly, with some including furnishings, balconies, fireplaces, ceiling fans, carpeting, or window treatments. Some apartment complexes have clubhouses, pools, and sports facilities; others have playgrounds or, especially downtown, reserved parking. Monthly rents range from $400 to $1,235 (more for luxury town houses and properties on the historic Peninsula), but the average hovers in the $750 to $800 range.

Lease agreements are usually for 6 or 12 months, although short-term leases, some with military-transfer clauses, are available. Security deposits also vary but are half to a full month's rent. Many places allow pets, but some complexes have size limits, and most require a deposit or a fee.

Apartment seekers will find these three free real estate publications helpful: *Apartment Finder Blue Book*, *Charleston Apartment Guide*, and *Rental Guide of Charleston*. Look for these pick-'em-up publications wherever newspapers are sold and at restaurants, sports facilities, and all information centers. Or you may want to write or call for a current issue and do some apartment shopping before you arrive.

Apartment Directories

Apartment Finder Blue Book
310 Broad St.
(843) 577-7882

This magazine-format booklet of apartment options is published four times a year. It is colorful and includes Greater Charleston neighborhoods from downtown through North Charleston to Hanahan, Ladson, Goose Creek, and Summerville. West Ashley and East Cooper neighborhoods are included, as well. Detailed maps help readers get acclimated to the various residential areas and transportation routes. And a handy comparison chart reduces the advertising hype to bare facts and figures for finding the bottom line. Almost 160 pages in length, this is perhaps the most comprehensive apartment guide currently published in the Lowcountry. Distribution of this free publication is widespread. You can almost always find a kiosk or rack of them outside any area grocery store or post office. Some convenience stores have them next to where the newspapers are sold. Of course, the Charleston visitor center on Meeting Street always has an ample supply.

Charleston Apartment Guide
147 Wappoo Creek Dr., Ste. 504
(843) 795-9008

Formerly known as *An Apartment Guide to Charleston*, this revamped booklet is published two times a year. It is well organized with full-color photos, maps, and an easy-to-use color code for area neighborhoods from downtown to Moncks Corner. Sometimes hard to find, it is worth tracking down because of its comprehensiveness. One good bet is to look just outside area grocery stores and wherever newspapers are sold. Also, the Charleston Metro Chamber of Commerce always has copies on hand.

Rental Guide of Charleston
PMB-376, 164-D Market St.
(843) 270-5261

Here's another rental directory—a newcomer to the Charleston market—with full-color photos, maps, and a color-coded key to the various neighborhoods in the greater Charleston area. Easy to use and well organized, this one includes an especially well conceived section of "Senior" apartments. The publication is free and found in brightly colored kiosks at public places—wherever newspapers are sold. If you're not in town and looking for an apartment in this area, you can call for a free copy, (800) 277-7800.

Retirement

With its mild climate and natural beauty, the Trident area is an attractive retirement destination. The mature market represents over 30 percent of the adult population here, and that number is growing every year. There are numerous residential communities geared to different levels of independence and a growing array of services in the business sector that are tailored to the needs of those enjoying their golden years. Some stores such as Revco, Eckerd, Kerr Drug, Harris Teeter, Lowe's, Belk, and Waccamaw Home Superstore even run regular discounts for shoppers 60 or older.

The Charleston County Public Library system maintains a community information database that provides detailed listings of organizations and resources, many geared toward senior citizens. It is updated on a continual basis and can be accessed by contacting any of the 15 county libraries. A listing of the county libraries can be found in the blue pages of the phone book or within our Education chapter that follows. For more information about this useful resource, contact the Main Library at 68 Calhoun Street, (843) 805-6801.

Resources

CareAlliance Advantage/Senior Services
Roper Hospital, 316 Calhoun St., Charleston
(843) 724-2489

A senior services department at CareAlliance Health Services is set up to deal with age-specific health issues. The Advantage program is a membership program for people 50 years and older that provides discounts on selected hospital services. Monthly meetings are held for an Alzheimers's support group, Mall Walkers, and an AARP chapter with locations in Roper Downtown, Roper North, and Bon Secours-St. Francis hospitals. (For more on these CareAlliance hospitals, see our Healthcare chapter.) Other community programs are offered throughout the year on topics such as Parkinson's disease. Additional benefits include a no-cost discount prescription card, eyewear discounts, and insurance assistance. Social activities include fitness classes and travel opportunities. Advantage membership costs $15 per membership or $25 for spouses joining at the same time.

The Senior Resource Center is a clearinghouse of information about resources for seniors not only at CareAlliance Health Services but also throughout the greater Charleston area. Visitors will find a library full of senior-related topics. Internet access is available to provide more information. A dedicated phone line covers topics such as fitness programs, retirement planning, support groups, household safety, and continuing education. The Senior Resource Center is located in the Advantage Office on the 5th floor of Roper Hospital's Pettit Tower.

Center for Creative Retirement
College of Charleston Office of Continuing Education, 66 George St., Charleston
(843) 953-5488

There is ample opportunity for seniors to join umbrella service organizations such as the Center for Creative Retirement at the College of Charleston, which is an affiliate of the Elderhostel Institute Network. Classes are held at the St. Joseph Family Center, 1695 Wallenberg Boulevard in the West Ashley area, during fall, winter, and spring. Non-credit courses comprise educational seminars, tours, lectures, and discussion groups. Some past topics have included "History of Film," "Contemporary Cuba," "Latest Trends in Medication," "History of Huguenots in Charleston," and "Poetry of Emily Dickinson."

**Charleston Area
Senior Citizens Services Inc.
259 Meeting St., Charleston
(843) 722-4127**
This nonprofit agency serves older adults in the Tri-County area. Its information and assistance line operates from 8 AM to 4 PM Monday through Friday. The senior center offers a noon meal, programs, activities, and health education. For the homebound, home-delivered meals and transportation on the Peninsula are provided. The agency's major focuses, which are making a difference in our community, are sponsorship of the Foster Grandparent Program and a job-training program with subsidized employment for people 55 and older. The agency also operates a 77-unit housing complex for seniors.

**Charleston County Community Education
Charleston County School District,
75 Calhoun St., Charleston
(843) 937-6424**
For those who are ready to plunge into creative stimulation, an interesting option is the moderately priced Adult and Community Education Programs, sponsored jointly by the Charleston County School District and the Charleston County Park and Recreation Commission. Categories of classes encompass arts and crafts, business and vocational concerns, computers, culinary arts, fitness and health, language arts, sports, and special interests. Eleven community schools across Charleston County are the sites of the classroom instruction. Offerings run the gamut from one-night, $5 sessions to six-week classes with fees of up to $150. Pick up information on the quarterly programs from the county school district offices on Calhoun Street or at Charleston County libraries. Please note that the district does not mail out class schedules.

The Carolina Lowcountry "good life" attracts new retirees to the area every day.
PHOTO: COURTESY OF SOUTH CAROLINA AQUARIUM

The Citadel
171 Moultrie St., Charleston
(843) 953-5188
College of Charleston
66 George St., Charleston
(843) 953-5620

South Carolina resident seniors 60 or older who are eager for an intellectual challenge can take any of the wide array of courses offered (on a space-available basis) at these two outstanding Charleston schools. The cost is just $25 a semester at the College of Charleston and only a $15 registration fee at The Citadel. Another academic resource is the Senior Scholars Program, sponsored by The Citadel. For a $25-per-term fee, non-degree-seeking seniors become members and select lectures presented by Citadel faculty and staff and community leaders. Members are issued student ID cards allowing use of parking facilities, Daniel Library, computer labs, recreational facilities, and the college bookstore. Fall, spring, and summer term programs have covered such topics as "Lighthouses of South Carolina," "Charleston Gullah Connection," "Maritime Piloting in South Carolina," and "Everything Old is New Again: New Urban Legends." Social activities are offered as well. These include lectures, tours, picnics,

and dancing classes. Anyone who is retired or semi-retired can enroll by calling (843) 953-5089.

Shepherd's Center of Charleston
53 Meeting St., Charleston
(843) 722-2789
Shepherd's Center of West Ashley
1293 Orange Grove Rd., Charleston
(843) 763-8833
Shepherd's Center of East Cooper
1885 Rifle Range Rd., Mt. Pleasant
(843) 884-3143

All three facilities hold weekly meetings for a diverse program of lectures, workshops, and fellowship. Diverse topics covered have included "Noted S.C. Statesman, Ben Tillman," "A Visit to China," "The Myth of Aging...Care for Life," and "The Secrets of Indian Food." Bridge, garden, and plantation tours are offered as afternoon activities. The registration fee for the Charleston and West Ashley centers is $15, plus an annual $10 membership fee. East Cooper fees are $20, plus a $10 annual membership. Lunch is offered in between the morning and afternoon class periods for around $4. The Shepherd's Centers are interfaith senior centers with older adults organizing the programs for their peers.

Many retirees explore the saltmarsh ecology. PHOTO: COURTESY OF SOUTH CAROLINA AQUARIUM

Retirement Housing

Charleston offers retirement housing options ranging from resort living to private-patio or high-rise apartments to supervised care. The choice is yours, depending on the physical wants and needs of those involved, as well as budget. Note that we do not include the resort areas (Kiawah, Seabrook, and Wild Dunes) in this chapter. The resorts are upscale choices that are popular with many retirement-age residents, but they do not offer any provisions for assisted living. See our Hotels and Motels, Neighborhoods, and Real Estate and Rentals chapters for more specific information about resort properties and amenities. The following living arrangements for seniors in the Trident area are a sampling of what is available.

Retirement Apartments

Canterbury House
175 Market St. & 165 Market St.,
Charleston
(843) 723-5553

Those interested in relocating into an apartment building for seniors will find the Canterbury House an appealing option. The Episcopal Church-sponsored complex has added a new building in 2000 of 46 one-bedroom apartments to the original one of 204 apartments. The location on the Peninsula is within easy walking distance of shopping on King and Market Streets. The independent-liv-ing facility offers efficiencies, one-bedroom efficiencies, and one-bedroom apartments for seniors 62 years old and older whose income does not exceed $25,000 for an individual or $25,850 for a couple. To qualify for the new building, income cannot exceed $15,600 per year. Location and convenient parking make it handy for visitors and volunteers such as local musicians and children's choirs, who participate in special programs for residents. There is usually a lengthy waiting list for these apartments, so get your name on the list early if the Canterbury House is the place for you.

Insiders' Tip

For active retired business people who want to lend a helping hand to young entrepreneurs and their start-up businesses, there's The Service Corps of Retired Executives (SCORE). These counselors offer in-depth one-on-one consulting to help their clients plan, market, manage, and package their ideas. They can be reached at (843) 727-4778.

Retirement and Life-Care Communities

Bishop Gadsden Episcopal Retirement Community
1873 Camp Rd., Charleston
(843) 762-3300, (800) 373-2384

Affiliated with the Episcopal Church, Bishop Gadsden is on a 54-acre site on James Island. Members enjoy the benefits of group living in a lovely setting and are often entertained and enlightened with lectures or presentations by volunteers from Episcopal churches in the community. An assisted-living option is also available. A 1999 expansion added 215 apartments and individual homes to the existing facility, and further expansion plans are in the works. A full range of amenities includes a wellness center, pool, casual and formal dining, beauty parlor, banks, and convenience stores on the premises. Services such as skilled nursing and dementia care make Bishop Gadsden the only nonprofit life-care community in the state.

Cooper Hall Senior Living Community
937 Bowman Rd., Mt. Pleasant
(843) 884-6949

Several options are available at Cooper Hall, including apartments, lakefront villas, and assisted-living quarters. A 1999 $7.5-million expansion added to the full range of choices available here. Assisted-living options include studio, and one- or two-bedroom apartments with kitchens and private bathrooms. Laundry service, medical observation, a continental breakfast and two meals a day, and a full slate of recreational activities are offered with transportation into town. Those in retirement living may choose from standard or deluxe one- or two-bedroom apartments with amenities such as an indoor swimming pool, pharmacy, beauty salon, laundry facility, and bridge rooms. Another popular feature is that pets are allowed in villa living areas. There is a licensed nurse on call at all hours, and residents can order from the dining room menu.

The Elms of Charleston
9100 Elms Plantation Blvd., Charleston
(843) 572-5154, (800) 237-3460

The Elms is a beautifully landscaped, controlled-access community of custombuilt patio homes, duplexes, town houses, and condominiums. Next to Charleston Southern University and Trident Regional Medical Center, the amenities at the Elms are extensive and include tennis and croquet courts and an 8,000-square-foot club with a fitness center, swimming pool, exercise area, spa, and library. The Wannamaker County Park with walking trails borders the property. Shopping, dining, golf, and other cultural opportunities are minutes away. Management

maintains the yard and home exteriors. Assisted living and long-term care are in nearby facilities.

Franke Home at Seaside
1885 Rifle Range Rd., Mt. Pleasant
(843) 856-4700

This residential-care facility, operated by Lutheran Homes of South Carolina, is located in Mt. Pleasant, just one mile from the beach at the Isle of Palms. It offers private and companion rooms with some assistance available. A full-time staff of licensed practical nurses and certified nursing assistants provides quality medical attention. Fifty one- and two-bedroom apartments are options for independent living. Residents enjoy a wellness program, meals, housekeeping, and transportation. Emotional support is offered through family support groups, volunteer interaction, and a chapel program. A new 44-bed skilled nursing center was recently added to the community, and plans are underway for additional independent living cottages, patio homes, and apartments.

Park Place Assisted Living Community
601 Mathis Ferry Rd., Mt. Pleasant
(843) 884-8812

Opened in 2000, by Manorhouse Retirement Center, Inc., of Richmond, Virginia, Park Place offers 4 floor plans in room or suite choices. Varying levels of care are available from short-term and traditional assisted living to a program for Alzheimer's patients. The 69-unit facility offers licensed nursing care on-site 24 hours a day. Independent living is available here as well. Amenities include activity/exercise rooms, lounges, a library, outdoor patios, a housekeeping/linen service, and a beauty and barbershop. A full-time social director is on staff.

Presbyterian Home of South Carolina
201 W. Ninth North St., Summerville
(843) 873-2550

The independent living options at Presbyterian Home in nearby Summerville include 59 outside cottages, 20 efficiency apartments, and 17 two-bedroom apartments. There are also 120 residential rooms with private baths, and residents are served three meals a day. Assisted living is an option here. On site are a beauty shop, barber services, and entertainment such as field trips to the Spoleto Festival, Monday night movies, ceramics, painting, and exercise classes. Bible classes and chapel are conducted, and transportation to the doctor or shopping facilities is furnished. Licensed nurses run a 90-bed infirmary. Opened in 1958, this community gives priority to South Carolina resident Presbyterians.

Sandpiper Village
1224 Village Creek Lane, Mt. Pleasant
(843) 884-5735, (800) 732-6761
Locally owned and operated, Sandpiper is a campus-like community with independent living in one- and two-bedroom cottage-style homes. These attractive residences have front and rear entrances with convenient access to the Community Center. The Sandpiper Courtyard apartments offer assisted living. Meals, housekeeping, transportation to doctor appointments, and emergency call buttons are included. Daily activities and social events, bingo, bridge, arts and crafts, church services, a beauty and barbershop, swimming pool, and a library are available. Small pets are allowed.

Healthcare

Everyone is concerned about healthcare these days, and here in the Lowcountry we're very fortunate to have exceptional healthcare facilities offering high-quality professional services. Our hospitals provide comprehensive services ranging from state-of-the-art neonatal care to heart and liver transplants. Thanks to CareAlliance's Lifelink ground and air mobile intensive-care units and the Medical University of South Carolina's Meducare, a helicopter transport service that extends across a 150-mile radius, patients can be placed in the hands of professionals by the fastest route possible.

Walk-in Medical Centers

Visitors to Greater Charleston, and sometimes even locals, need a handy reference to the neighborhood medical clinics for those minor but often vacation-spoiling emergencies that can slow down the busy traveler. The following list contains some of the clinics that will see patients on short notice. Most clinics are open every day for extended hours, and no appointment is necessary.

Charleston

Emergicare
2049 Savannah Hwy.
(843) 571-4101

Peds Plus at Roper Hospital
316 Calhoun St.
(843) 724-2273

Mt. Pleasant

Doctor's Care
631 Johnnie Dodds Blvd., Mt. Pleasant
(843) 881-0815

Peds Plus Mt. Pleasant
1051 Johnnie Dodds Blvd., Mt. Pleasant
(843) 849-9524

North Charleston

Doctor's Care
8091 Rivers Ave., North Charleston
(843) 572-7000

West Ashley

Doctor's Care
3424 Shelby Ray Ct.
(843) 556-5585

James and Johns Islands

James Island Medical Care
347 Folly Rd.
(843) 762-1440

Kiawah-Seabrook Medical Care
1003 Landfall Wy., Johns Island
(843) 768-4800

Dorchester County

Doctor's Care
10160 Dorchester Rd., Summerville
(843) 871-7900

Hospitals and Healthcare Facilities

Downtown Charleston

Charleston Memorial Hospital
326 Calhoun St.
(843) 577-0600

Charleston Memorial is dedicated to serving the needs of patients in Charleston County. This was the first area hospital to open a fully operational emergency room. Today Charleston Memorial's emergency facility treats more than 20,000 patients annually. The hospital has a general medical unit, an intensive care unit, and a pediatric episodic unit. Charleston Memorial provides 24-hour emergency service and limited outpatient services. The McClennan Banks Clinic for outpatient ambulatory care next door contains 86 examination rooms and provides laboratory, radiology, and diagnostic services on site. It also houses prenatal clinics with ultrasound and amniocentesis. Charleston Memorial Hospital provides workshops and seminars on health-related topics free of charge. Visiting hours are from 10 AM to 9 PM daily.

Medical University of South Carolina Medical Center
171 Ashley Ave.
(843) 792-2300

The MUSC Medical Center, a state-of-the-art teaching hospital, was named for the second year as one of the top 100 hospitals in the nation. This also is the heartbeat of the Medical University of South Carolina (see our Education chapter). This acute-care center, along with MUSC's outpatient clinic, serves not only patients from the Greater Charleston area, but also those attracted to it from all over the state and the nation. In addition to more than 50 certificate, baccalaureate, master's, and doctoral programs in virtually all areas of the health sciences, MUSC offers continuing education programs that help South Carolina's health professionals stay current with the latest medical treatments and procedures.

Under the umbrella of MUSC are several specialty facilities, including the Albert Florens Storm Eye Institute, MUSC Children's Hospital, MUSC Digestive Disease Center, MUSC Heart and Vascular Center, Hollings Cancer Center, MUSC Institute of Psychiatry and MUSC Transplant Center. Child Magazine recently named the Children's Hospital the 10th best children's hospital in the country. For more information on services, classes, physician appointments, or health information library topics, call the MUSC Health Connection number at (843) 792-1414 or (800) 424-MUSC. General visiting hours are from 10:30 AM to 8:30 PM daily, and 9 AM to 9 PM for the Pediatrics.

Ralph H. Johnson VA Medical Center
109 Bee St.
(843) 577-5011

This Department of Veterans Affairs medical center has 190 beds and 960 employees. The center provides acute medical, surgical, and psychiatric inpatient care plus primary and specialized outpatient care to veterans in a 13-county area of South Carolina. The VA Medical Center is affiliated with 50 different educational institutions but primarily works with MUSC, the main source of the center's paid resident staff. In fall 1996 the VA/MUSC Strom Thurmond Biomedical Research Center opened, providing a 42,000-square-foot location for the VA center's research staff. The hospital's 44 clinics work in a variety of health disciplines ranging from audiology to vascular surgery. Call the main switchboard at the number listed for additional information. Visiting hours are from 11 AM to 8:30 PM daily.

Roper Hospital
316 Calhoun St.
(843) 724-2000

With 453 beds and more than 2,000 employees, Roper Hospital is one of the Lowcountry's oldest and largest healthcare facilities. In 1998, Roper merged with Bon-Secours-St. Francis Xavier Hospital to form CareAlliance Health Services. Included in its services are several special units: Roper Heart Center, a complete cardiac care facility that addresses education, prevention, diagnosis, and treatment, including surgery and rehabilitation; Roper Cancer Center, offering compassionate care, state-of-the-art diagnostic and treatment services, and special resources for cancer patients and their families; and Roper's NeuroScience Center, providing the area's only acute stroke unit and specializing in neurological treatment including epilepsy monitoring and surgery with advanced microscopy, ultrasound, and laser technology. Women's and Children's Services at Roper include a resource center, family-centered maternity care, lifestyle services, diagnostic breast and osteoporosis services, plastic and reconstructive surgery, the *Bright Beginnings* newsletter, and Peds Plus after-hours urgent care for infants, children, and adolescents.

The Roper Rehabilitation Hospital is a 39-bed facility that focuses on rehabilitation and functional recovery. According to hospital statistics, patients who have been treated here consistently achieve higher levels of functional independence than the national norms. In addition to this inpatient facility, there are also outpatient rehabilitation services, such as physical therapy, occupational therapy, and speech therapy, available in Summerville, Goose Creek, and Walterboro. The direct line for the Rehabilitation Hospital is (843) 724-2800.

Roper has 9 diagnostic centers offering convenient access to lab, X-ray, and EKG services throughout the Trident area. To find the one nearest you, call (843) 402-2273 or (800) 868-4916. The centers are open from 8 AM until 5 PM Monday through Friday. Roper's downtown emergency room, (843) 724-2010, is open 24 hours a day with full-service emergency care. As a Heart and Stroke Emergency Network location, it also provides special-

ized heart care with its Chest Pain Observation Unit, which is next door to the E.R. The patient information desk can be reached at (843) 724-2111 and provides room numbers, or you may dial direct using 724, then 2, then the room number. General visiting hours are 9 AM to 9 PM.

East Cooper

Daniel Island Medical Center
900 Island Park Dr., Charleston
(843) 216-5100

Recently opened in the East Cooper neighborhood of Daniel Island, this medical facility is part of the Trident Health System. It offers medical imaging, (including mammography), lab collection, sports medicine, orthopedic rehabilitation, womens' health, cardiac rehabilitation, and diagnostic services. Several primary and specialty care physicians maintain offices on-site.

East Cooper Regional Medical Center
1200 Johnnie Dodds Blvd., Mt. Pleasant
(843) 881-0100

This hospital serves the communities east of the Cooper River but also draws patients from throughout the Lowcountry. East Cooper Regional Medical Center has 100 beds and about 500 employees. Recent renovations focused on improved

Physician Referral Services

Bon Secours-St. Francis/Roper Hospital,
(843) 402-2273, (800) 868-4916

Charleston County Medical Society,
(843) 577-3613

East Cooper Regional Medical Center,
(843) 881-0100, (800) 311-4803

Medical University of South Carolina,
(843) 792-1414

Trident HealthFinders,
(843) 797-3463

patient access. The hospital (formerly called East Cooper Community Hospital) has been in operation since 1986 and provides in-patient acute care and 24-hour emergency-room services. Additional special services include outpatient diagnostics, ICU/CCU, MRI, home health care, spinal care, ambulatory surgery, imaging, and OB/GYN. Call the main switchboard for patient information and room assignments. Visiting hours are from 9 AM to 9 PM daily.

North Charleston

Archdale Medical Center
5300 Archdale Blvd. (off Dorchester Rd.), Charleston Heights
(843) 552-8332

Opened in the fall of 2000, this is one of the newest facilities of the Trident Health System. The center offers primary and specialty care physician practices. Diagnostic services include mammography/X-ray, a lab collection site, and occupational and physical therapy.

Concentra Medical Center
8780 Rivers Ave., North Charleston
(843) 572-0810

A part of the Trident Health System, this facility offers a freestanding, comprehensive occupational medicine program serving more than 300 employers in Berkeley, Dorchester, and Charleston Counties since 1980. Services include post-offer physical examinations (when a prospective employee has been offered a job by a business pending the outcome of a physical exam), work injury treatment, drug and alcohol testing, and occupational injury and illness prevention programs. The physicians and staff are dedicated exclusively to the practice of occupational medicine.

HealthSouth Rehabilitation Hospital-Charleston
9181 Medcom St., Charleston
(843) 820-7777

Alabama-based HealthSouth opened Health South Rehabilitation Hospital in Charleston in 1994, one of 2,000 facilities in 50 states, Puerto Rico, Australia, and the United Kingdom. The full-service, 39-bed acute rehabilitation hospital spans patient care from injury or illness to maximum independence and function. Additional services include outpatient rehabilitation services, diagnostic imaging, outpatient surgery, and industrial rehabilitation. Their stated mission is "getting people back . . . to work . . . to play . . . to living." It is the only freestanding rehabilitation hospital in the Lowcountry and is accredited by the Joint Commission on the Accreditation of Healthcare Organizations (JCAHO).

Roper Emergency Services-Northwoods
7750 Northwoods Blvd., North Charleston
(843) 824-8733

Near Northwoods Mall, this facility offers full-service emergency care 24 hours a day. It also provides specialized cardiac care as a Heart and Stroke Emergency Network location with its Chest Pain Observation Unit.

Trident Medical Center
9330 Medical Plaza Dr.
(I-26 and S.C. Hwy. 78), Charleston
(843) 797-7000

The Trident Health System has 11 centers serving the healthcare needs of the Lowcountry by offering heart, cancer, women's health, sports medicine, skilled nursing, industrial medicine, surgery, home healthcare, and senior services. The Trident Medical Center is the largest facility in the Trident Health System with a 296-bed, acute-care hospital employing more than 2,000 workers. The center provides diagnostic and outpatient and inpatient surgical services, and the hospital provides 24-hour emergency services. Other specialties include ICU/CCU heart care, cardiac rehabilitation, OB/GYN, pediatrics, sports/industrial medicine, physical rehabilitation, and a cancer center. Trident Medical Center is in the process of a $28-million expansion and renovation adding 64,000 square feet to its facility and a 400-space parking deck to improve patient access. For patient information, call (843) 797-5200, then dial 4 plus the room number.

Trident Senior Health Center
2070 Northbrook Blvd., Ste. A-16,
Charleston
(843) 797-0416

Under the umbrella of the Trident Health System (see listing under Trident Medical Center), the Senior Health Center provides healthcare that meets the needs of residents age 65 and older. The center, which accepts Medicare assignments, is near Northwoods Mall. Staffed by a board-certified primary-care physician with advanced training in geriatric medi-

cine, the center also includes nurses, a geriatrician, and other healthcare professionals who are experienced in the special needs of the senior population. Primary medical care is provided for chronic illnesses such as heart disease, diabetes, and Alzheimer's. Trident Senior Health Center also takes a partnership role in wellness with monthly health education programs, health screenings, and a senior health library. Additional assistance is offered with insurance or billing questions as well as other social service needs.

Trident Surgery Center
9313 Medical Plaza Dr., Charleston
(843) 797-8992
Trident Eye Surgery Center
9297B Medical Plaza Dr., Charleston
(843) 824-5024

The Trident Surgery Center and Trident Eye Surgery Center specialize in same-day surgery performing about 500 procedures a month. The centers feature state-of-the-art medical equipment, four operating rooms, and 10 private recovery rooms. Affiliated with the Trident Health System, the Trident Surgery Center is the only surgery center in the Lowcountry accredited by the Accreditation Association for Ambulatory Health Care.

West Ashley

Bon Secours-St. Francis Hospital
2095 Henry Tecklenburg Dr., Charleston
(843) 402-1000, (843) 402-1010 (Healthline)

Bon Secours-St. Francis Hospital is the oldest Catholic hospital in South Carolina and the only one in Charleston. Its long history in this community goes back to 1882, when five sisters of Charity of Our Lady of Mercy opened a small, wood-framed building called the St. Francis Xavier Infirmary. A 1998 merger with Roper CareAlliance made Bon Secours-St. Francis Xavier Hospital part of CareAlliance Health Services. Then and now, the emphasis has been on a devotion to caring for the whole person—physically, spiritually, and emotionally.

The hospital relocated in December

1996 from its previous downtown address to a new facility west of the Ashley River. The new hospital focuses on several signature services including spine and sports medicine, women's, infants', and children's health services, digestive disorders and urological care, heart and stroke emergency network, and emergency services. The patient information and location number is (843) 402-1118, and Home Health Care services can be contacted at (843) 402-7000. (For information on Bon Secours' Senior Services, see our Retirement chapter.)

Medshares
29 Leinbach Dr., Ste. B-3, Charleston
(843) 766-2929
Medshares provides home care for both recovering, chronically ill, or disabled persons throughout Charleston, Berkeley, Dorchester, and Colleton Counties. Services include skilled nursing care, personal care, infusion therapy, medical social services, physical therapy, speech pathology, occupational therapy, respiratory therapy, home medical equipment, and hospice. Nationally, Medshares has more than 100 offices in 24 states.

Roper-St. Francis
Home Health Care, ProCare
1483 Tobias Gadson Blvd., Ste. 208,
Charleston
(843) 402-7000
Roper-St. Francis Home Health Care has two components: Home Health, and ProCare. Home Health provides home care by nurses, aides, medical social workers, and therapists. Services include skilled nursing, personal care, wound care, physical, speech and occupational therapy, and a centralized intake department. ProCare provides in-home private duty nurses, homemaker and companion services, and temporary staffing for healthcare facilities. Home Infusion IV therapies are located at 7 Amy Elsey Drive and can be reached at (843) 763-2600.

Roper West Ashley Surgery Center
18 Farmfield Ave., Charleston
(843) 763-3763
Opened in 1987, this West Ashley center performs more than 3,000 outpatient surgeries each year. Affiliated with the CareAlliance Health Services system, the Surgery Center provides general surgical services for adults and children.

Other Nearby Healthcare Facilities

Moncks Corner Medical Center
206 Rembert Dennis Blvd., Moncks Corner
(843) 761-8721,
(843) 577-9319 (Charleston phone no.)
This Trident Health System outpatient diagnostic and rehabilitation facility serves the residents of Berkeley County. The center sponsors a number of community wellness programs in addition to providing laboratory testing, physical rehabilitation, radiology, and mammography services. Physician services are available by appointment at this location as well.

Roper Berkeley Day Hospital
730 Stony Landing Rd., Moncks Corner
(843) 899-7700, (800) 846-7707
Roper Berkeley Day Hospital has Berkeley

County's only 24-hour emergency services department. The center also offers access to primary-care and specialty physicians as well as diagnostic services including laboratory testing, X-rays, mammography, CT scans, physical therapy, cardiopulmonary testing, endoscopy, and bronchoscopy.

St. George Diagnostic Center
217 Parler Ave., St. George
(843) 563-8452
Serving Dorchester County residents, this Trident Health System center features general diagnostic procedures such as X-ray and mammography, a laboratory drawing station, sports medicine, and rehabilitation services.

Summerville Medical Center
295 Midland Pkwy., Summerville
(843) 832-5000

The Summerville Center is a 94-bed, full-service facility with 24-hour emergency, general, medical, and surgical services, a heart center, intensive care and skilled nursing units, sports medicine and rehabilitation, and a sleep lab. It sponsors numerous wellness programs for the community in addition to providing medical imaging and X-rays, and diagnostic and physical rehabilitation services. The emergency room phone is (843) 832-5160. Summerville Medical Center/Downtown, 445 North Cedar Street, (843) 821-6085, serves town residents with general diagnostic services such as X-ray and mammography, and a laboratory drawing station.

Both Summerville Medical Centers are part of the Trident Health System.

Mental Health Centers

Charleston/Dorchester
Community Mental Health Center
960 Morrison Dr., Charleston
(843) 727-2118, adults;
(843) 740-6136, younger than 18
(843) 852-4127, Dorchester, younger than 18;
(843) 873-5063, Dorchester, all ages;
(843) 727-2086, after hours emergency

With children and adolescent programs serving Charleston and Dorchester County residents, the Community Mental Health Center offers a comprehensive program of general mental health services for adults, adolescents, and children. The staff provides assessment and ongoing treatment, and the facility is affiliated with the South Carolina Department of Mental Health. A crisis stabilization center is operated to provide an alternative to hospital admission with early crisis intervention. The center accepts Medicare, Medicaid, and private insurance. A sliding fee scale is offered, based on ability to pay.

Berkeley Community
Mental Health Center
403 Stony Landing Rd., Moncks Corner
(843) 761-8282, (888) 202-1381
(Charleston/Summerville)

This mental health center serves children, adolescents, and adults in Berkeley County with outpatient psychiatric services. The staff of 60+ includes three full-time psychiatrists. Day treatment programs, short- and long-term therapy, and specialized clinics on such topics as attention deficit hyperactivity disorder and family preservation are offered. Private insurance coverage is accepted with prior approval as well as Medicaid, Medicare, and the Civilian Health and Medical Program of the Uniformed Services. A sliding fee scale may be applied based on ability to pay. Transportation service is available for Berkeley County residents.

Palmetto Lowcountry Behavioral Health
2777 Speissegger Dr., Charleston
(843) 747-5830

Palmetto Lowcountry Behavioral Health offers 24-hour help, assessment, and referral for treatment of depression, anxiety, drug and alcohol abuse, and other emotional problems. Formerly Charter Charleston Behavioral Health System, Palmetto Lowcountry provides inpatient, outpatient, and partial services for children, adolescents, and adults at the above location.

MUSC Institute of Psychiatry
171 Ashley Ave., Charleston
(843) 792-9888

The Institute of Psychiatry at the Medical University of South Carolina serves not only as a center for professional education and psychiatric research, but also as a provider of state-of-the-art care for a full range of psychiatric problems. Nationally recognized psychiatrists, psychiatric nurses, social workers, psychologists, and researchers work together to offer personalized treatment to individuals and families. The programs are designed to help people of all ages meet the impact of behavioral, emotional, and substance abuse problems. The Institute of Psychiatry's services include Adult Services, the Center for Drug and Alcohol Programs, Geriatric Services (including an Alzheimer's Care Program), Youth Services, and Specialty Services. Specialty Services include the Eating Disorders Program, Crime Victims Research and Treatment Center, Weight Management Center, Tic and Tourette Disorders Services, and Attention Deficit Disorders Services. To receive a brochure on any of the services or to make an appointment, call the number previously listed.

Alternative Healthcare

Growing in popularity here in the Lowcountry and almost everywhere else are alternative healthcare practices such as chiropractic services, acupuncture, yoga, and holistic and homeopathic therapies. Here are some resources for those seeking new avenues toward well-being.

Acupuncture Works
647 St. Andrew Blvd., Charleston
(843) 769-7609

Trained in Asia, Gregg Smythe, DAc, is a national board-certified acupuncturist. Many receive effective relief from conditions such as back and neck pain, allergies, infertility, and incontinence. A native Charlestonian, Ms. Smythe returned to her hometown to practice this ancient Chinese treatment.

Alpha Care
435 Folly Rd., Charleston
(843) 762-7475
2 Carriage Ln., Charleston
(843) 556-7828

Alpha Care, open since 1994, has five licensed chiropractors and a total staff of 20 specializing in pain control, rehabilitation, family care, spinal injury care, plus full diagnostic and outpatient care.

Charleston Therapeutic Massage
310 Broad St., Ste. 8, Charleston
(843) 971-4141

Three licensed and certified massage therapists work here specializing in relaxation, sports and deep tissue massage, as well as craniosacral therapy. Charleston Therapeutic Massage offers corporate on-site chair massage at your location, too.

Cooper Spine Center
309 Coleman Blvd., Mt. Pleasant
(843) 884-8444

This center, with one licensed chiropractor, specializes in conservative chiropractic treatment of lower back pain, headaches, pinched nerves, scoliosis, and other difficult disorders of the back and neck. Sports and work injuries as well as auto accident injuries have been treated here since the center opened in 1983.

Island Chiropractic Centre
3546 Maybank Hwy., Johns Island
(843) 559-9111

Island Chiropractic is run by a certified

Insiders' Tip

Radio listeners can hear a licensed therapist weekly on What's on Your Mind? with Dr. Linda Austin of the MUSC Institute of Psychiatry staff. Her call-in format gives listeners an opportunity to ask questions about mental health topics in a comfortable atmosphere of anonymity. The broadcast is heard on South Carolina Educational Radio (89.3 FM) every Friday from noon to 1 PM.

Emergency and Healthcare Numbers

AIDS Hotline,
(800) 342-2437

Al-Anon/Al-Ateen,
(843) 762-6999

Alcohol & Drug
Abuse Hotline,
(800) 252-6465

Alcoholics Anonymous,
(843) 723-9633,
(843) 554-2998 (daytime)

American Cancer Society,
(843) 744-1922

American Heart Association,
Lowcountry Regional Office,
(843) 853-1597

American Lung Association of
South Carolina, Coast Branch,
(843) 556-8451

American Medical Association,
(312) 464-5000

American Red Cross,
Carolina Lowcountry Chapter,
(843) 744-8021

Berkeley County Health
Department,
(843) 719-4600,
(843) 723-3800 (Charleston
line)

Berkeley County Rescue
Squad,
(843) 719-4295

Center for Patient Advocacy,
(800) 846-7444

Charleston County Health
Department,
(843) 724-5800

Charleston County
Volunteer Rescue Squad,
(843) 745-4000

Child Abuse Hotline,
(800) 422-4453

Coastal Crisis,
(843) 724-1212

Compassionate Friends,
Charleston Chapter,
(843) 884-2589

Dorchester County
Health Department,
(843) 873-1241

Elderlink, Inc.,
Trident Area Agency
on Aging,
(843) 745-1710

Elder Support Line,
City of Charleston Police
Department,
(843) 724-7180

Family Services,
(843) 744-1348, (800) 232-6489

Grief and Loss Center of
South Carolina,
(843) 722-8371

Hospice for the Carolinas,
(800) 662-8859,
(803) 791-4220 (SC number)

Hotline,
(843) 744-HELP
(800) 922-2283

Juvenile Diabetes Foundation,
(843) 763-1973

Coastal Carolina Alzheimer's
Chapter,
(843) 571-2641,
(800) 860-1444

Lowcountry Children's Center,
(843) 723-3600

March of Dimes/
Birth Defects Foundation,
Lowcountry Division,
(843) 571-1776
MUSC Health Connection,
(843) 792-1414

Muscular Dystrophy
Association,
(843) 556-3654

Multiple Sclerosis Society,
South Carolina Chapter,
(800) 922-7591

Narcotics Anonymous,
(843) 852-3001

National Foundation for
Depressive Illness,
(800) 248-4344

National
Mental Health Association,
(800) 969-6642

People Against Rape,
(843) 722-7273,
(800) 241-7273 (hotline)

Poison Control Hotline,
(800) 922-1117

Roper Diabetes
Treatment Center,
(843) 724-2412

Runaway Hotline,
(800) 621-4000

STD Hotline,
(800) 227-8922

Teenline,
(843) 747-TEEN,
(800) 273-8255

sports physician with post-doctoral certification in X-ray interpretation, pain management, impairment ratings, CPR, and first aid. The staff of eight has been treating area patients at this location since 1987.

Island Therapy Group
2201 Middle St., Sullivan's Island
(843) 883-9497

A staff of eight licensed certified massage therapists provide services including

Swedish, deep tissue and sports massage, craniosacral and neuromuscular therapy, and reflexology.

Marti Chitwood, RD, CDE
738-B St. Andrews Blvd., Charleston
(843) 556-2123

With a background in dietary therapy and healthful nutrition, Marti Chitwood is a good resource of holistic nutritional advice. Her approach considers the whole person, including lifestyle, emotions, attitudes, beliefs, and symptoms.

To Your Health/The Charleston Yoga Center
1731 Savannah Hwy., Charleston
(843) 556-8060, (843) 556-9002

Certified therapist Lynn Meffert offers shiatsu acupressure therapy for those "in the flow." The Charleston Yoga Center has a full schedule of yoga classes at all levels. T'ai chi is offered as well.

Other Services

Grief and Loss Center of South Carolina
150 Wentworth St., Charleston
(843) 722-8371

The nonprofit Grief and Loss Center of South Carolina operates within the McAlister-Smith Funeral Home and serves as a clearinghouse of grief counseling and support programs for men, women, children, and adolescents in the community. A current list of grief services is maintained here. The center sponsors community and professional workshops including an annual Grief Conference in the fall.

Hospice of Charleston Inc.
3896 Leeds Ave., North Charleston
(843) 529-3100, (800) 617-6152

Licensed as both a hospice and home health agency, Hospice of Charleston has served the residents of Charleston, Dorchester, and Berkeley Counties since 1981. It provides medical, emotional, and spiritual care to terminally ill people and their families, with a staff of 50 full-time professionals and 150 trained volunteers. Grief recovery workshops are co-sponsored with

area hospitals that meet once a week for six weeks. Stepping Stones is a one-day seminar for teens from 12 years up who have experienced a loss through death. Twice a year Shannon's Hope Camp (at Camp St. Christopher on Seabrook Island) is held for bereaved children. The camp involves the children in fun activities such as music, drawing, and arts and crafts designed to help them work out their grief. Each November Hospice of Charleston sponsors the Candlelight Memorial Ceremony at Colonial Lake in downtown Charleston. For a $10 donation to Hospice, luminaries are lit surrounding the edge of the lake in memory of lost loved ones. A short program and music add to the remembrance ceremony. For more information on Hospice of Charleston programs, call the listed number.

Hospice Health Services Inc.
1 Carriage Ln., Ste. F, Charleston
(843) 852-2177, (800) 494-0418, 24 hours

Serving Charleston, Berkeley, Dorchester, Colleton, and Beaufort counties, Hospice

Health Services provides interdisciplinary care for the terminally ill in their own homes. Providers are licensed to serve by the state and are Medicare-certified and accredited by the Joint Commission on Accreditation of Healthcare Organizations. Periodic educational and support programs are offered. Annual memorial services are held to provide rituals for grieving persons.

Coastal Carolina Chapter,
The Alzheimer's Association
1941 Savage Rd., Ste. 4-D, Charleston
(843) 571-2641, (800) 860-1444

Coastal Carolina is a voluntary health, nonprofit organization dedicated to providing services and support to persons and families affected by Alzheimer's disease. An estimated 61,000 South Carolinians are afflicted with Alzheimer's. The Coastal Carolina Chapter offers educational seminars, workshops, and literature. Other services include support groups, a help line, and referral information. They are also an advocacy group and publish a quarterly newsletter for their membership.

Lowcountry AIDS Services
1501 Manley Ave., North Charleston
(843) 747-2273

Founded in 1985, Palmetto AIDS Life Support Services of South Carolina (PALSS), evolved into a statewide, community-based service agency now called Lowcountry AIDS Services (LAS). Lowcountry AIDS provides case management, counseling, and direct volunteer support to men, women, and children with HIV or AIDS in three counties—Charleston, Berkeley, and Dorchester. In addition to the practical and emotional support, this nonprofit social service agency works to educate and acts as an advocacy, resource, and referral agency for HIV/AIDS-infected people and their families. LAS is supported by the Community Foundation, Trident United Way, and private donations. (For information on LAS's Dining With Friends celebration, look under May in our Annual Events chapter.)

Palmetto Health Hospice
1815 Old Trolley Rd., Ste. 109,
Summerville
(843) 821-4011, (800) 775-1392

Formerly Hospice Home Care Resources, Palmetto Health Hospice was the first Medicare-licensed hospice in South Carolina. Serving 21 counties in South Carolina, Palmetto Health Hospice specializes in providing comprehensive compassionate care to terminally ill patients and their families in their home of choice. Organized as a nonprofit charity, care is based on need, not the ability or inability to pay. Their Pathfinders Support Group helps adults who have experienced a loss through death. The Group meets the third Tuesday of the month at 6 PM. Brett's Rainbow is a free camp for grieving children, ages 6 through 16. For more information on services, contact Palmetto Health Hospice at the numbers listed.

Education

Public Schools
Home Schooling
Private Schools
Colleges and
  Universities
Charleston County
  Library System

As in most communities its size, the academic options in Greater Charleston are greatly varied. Newcomers to the area with school-age children need to know specific details about the public and private schooling options and make their educational decisions accordingly. Sometimes this information is closely guarded (especially when the news isn't particularly good), but be diligent in your quest for detail. Finding good schools and good teachers is obviously extremely important.

If you're new to the city, one of your first sources of information about schools in your residential area should be your Realtor. Ask about the area schools' comparative test scores, student-teacher ratios, college placement percentages, and athletic options. Don't hesitate to ask about any recorded incidents of violence. Another resource with reliable information is your county school district office. Addresses and phone numbers for offices in Charleston, Dorchester, and Berkeley Counties are listed in this chapter.

Public Schools

Records from the first general public school system in the Lowcountry date back to 1856. Today, separate public school systems are in place in Charleston, Berkeley and Dorchester Counties. More than 90,000 students in kindergarten through 12th grade are enrolled at more than 136 schools in four school districts—Berkeley County, Charleston County, Dorchester II, and Dorchester IV.

The school year runs 180 days from the end of August or early September until the end of May or early June. All children entering first grade must present a birth certificate and must be 6 years old by September 1. Those entering South Carolina schools for the first time must show a vaccination certificate. School bus service is available for students who live more than a half-mile from their assigned school.

Among the area's educational options are seven schools serving children with special needs, 11 magnet schools for academically gifted students, and a special South Carolina-mandated program in each district for children with high test scores and strong academic potential.

Charleston County School District
75 Calhoun St., Charleston
(843) 937-6300

The Charleston County School District operates 78 schools in a 1,000-square-mile area along the South Carolina coast. About 45,000 students attend these schools. The county school system, governed by a nine-member board of trustees, is divided into eight constituent school districts, each one administered by an area superintendent. These eight districts, in turn, have elected school boards of various sizes that are responsible for establishing the attendance zones for local schools. The district employs 2,500 teachers and maintains an average pupil-teacher ratio of 16-to-1.

The district has been a trailblazer for the magnet school concept, with 11 locations—Buist Academy, Ashley River Creative Arts Elementary, Charleston Progressive Elementary, St. Andrews Elementary School of Math and Science, Charlestowne Academy, Montessori Community School, Jennie Moore Elementary, Norman C. Toole Military Magnet Middle School, Charleston County School of the

Arts, Garrett Academy of Technology and the Academic Magnet High School. These special schools serve a student population that is academically or artistically gifted. Located on the Peninsula, in West Ashley, and in North Charleston, they draw students from surrounding neighborhoods as well as areas spread throughout the district. Magnet school educational programs provide an alternative curriculum that integrates resources from the community, higher education, the arts, business, and technology. Call (843) 937-6407 for qualification information, as magnet schools can differ in entrance requirements.

SAIL–Students Actively Interested in Learning–is a state-mandated program in place in the Charleston County public school system. Offerings are innovative and challenging, designed to stimulate the academically talented students who are accepted into the program. Creative, critical problem-solving skills make up the focus of the curriculum content through programs such as the Academic Bowl and Odyssey of the Mind competitions, Advanced Placement courses, and a mentor program for grades 8 through 10. For more information on SAIL, call the supervisor at (843) 937-6477.

Special education programs for students with emotional, mental, or physical handicaps are available through the school district as well.

More than 8,000 students participate in a variety of summer programs ranging in scope from academic enhancement to cultural enrichment. The summer SPACE program (School for the Performing Arts and Creative Expression) serves about 300 talented students at Goodwin Elementary School. In a three-week session running mid-June through the end of the month, students, recommended by their teachers, study music, drama, art, or dance. Students enter at a 4th-grade level and are eligible to attend each year through the 7th grade. The number for inquiring about the program is (843) 937-6474.

All totaled, Charleston County administers 46 public elementary schools, 18 middle schools, 13 high schools, and one vocational school. Relying on the phone book for numbers to reach specific offices for the different constituent school districts can be confusing, so we have compiled a list of important contacts in various Charleston County areas for easy reference.

Districts 1 and 2 (Mt. Pleasant)
(843) 849-2878

District 3 (James Island),
(843) 762-2780

District 4 (North Charleston)
(843) 745-7150

District 9 (Johns Island)
(843) 762-2780

District 10 (West Ashley)
(843) 763-1500

District 20 (Charleston)
(843) 937-6598

District 23 (Edisto, Ravenel)
(843) 889-2291

Berkeley County School District
229 Main St., Moncks Corner
(843) 899-8600,
(843) 723-4627 (in Charleston)

Berkeley County School District is the third largest in the state, with 35 schools and one vocational facility serving nearly 27,000 students. The northern end of Berkeley County is rural and sparsely populated, while the area from Moncks Corner to Hanahan is suburban.

The curriculum is designed to meet the educational needs of all students, regardless of their academic achievement level. Accelerated students benefit from classes tailored to their advanced abilities. Call Anne Godbee at (843) 723-4627 extension 8640 for information on the ACE program (Academic and Creative Enrichment), Berkeley County's counterpart to Charleston County's SAIL program. Average students receive a steady diet of core courses designed to prepare them for the challenges posed by college and postgraduate jobs.

Remedial education is available for students requiring special attention. Special education programs are targeted to children with disabilities ranging from those who are visually impaired to the educable mentally retarded. All Berkeley County schools offer support personnel and services to students, including guidance counselors, psychologists, and speech therapists.

The breakdown shows Berkeley County administering 16 elementary, 12 intermediate and middle schools, six high schools, and one alternative school.

Dorchester County School District II
102 Greenwave Blvd., Summerville
(843) 873-2901

District II in Dorchester County has been designated one of the fastest-growing public school districts in the state. A study conducted for the school district by The Citadel indicated that 95 percent of the residential growth projected for Dorchester County by the year 2000 would occur in District II, the greater Summerville area. In addition, 98 percent of this growth was projected for the eastern or Oakbrook section of Summerville, where school enrollment bears this out by jumping from 10,106 in 1979-80 to 15,707 in 2000-2001.

District II operates 16 schools, specializing in extracurricular activities for students in kindergarten through grade 12. Students graduating from Summerville High School have consistently scored above the state norms on the Scholastic Aptitude Test. District II seniors received more than $3.8 million in academic and athletic scholarships during the 1996-97 school year. The January 1996 issue of *Money* magazine listed Dorchester District II among the top 100 school districts in the nation, based on high student achievement in a location with a moderate cost of living and proximity to a major metropolitan area.

GATE (Gifted and Talented Education) is Dorchester II's state-mandated program for those students who qualify for special enrichment and academic challenges. Debbie Call at (843) 873-2901 can provide more information on the qualifications needed to participate. Project Opportunity, an alternative program for young people in District II high schools, is a special counseling and basic skills program aimed at lowering the dropout rate. This program is conducted at an off-campus site—during the 1999-00 school year at Givhans Community School—during regular school hours.

Based on high achievement in standardized testing, District II has several schools that earned "deregulation status" from the state for updating school curricula, allowing greater innovation in teaching methods, and meeting the increasingly complex needs of young people. There are eight elementary schools, four middle schools, and two high schools in Dorchester District II. The Givhans Community School and Rollings School of the Arts complete the list of schools in this district.

Dorchester County School District IV
500 Ridge St., St. George
(843) 563-4535

Dorchester District IV serves the outer region of Dorchester County and, with only about 2,500 students, is one of the smallest districts in the state. The district boasts one of the best pupil-teacher ratios in South Carolina, with one instructor for every 16 students. Setting high standards for its faculty, the district provides incentives for the professional growth and advancement of its teachers and administrators through in-service training programs and membership in the Salkehatchie Consortium, which provides graduate courses at no cost to teachers.

The district's curriculum is designed for students looking to enter the work force after high school as well as students heading for college. District IV maintains three elementary schools, two middle schools, and two high schools.

Home Schooling

Parents who wish to teach their children at home can do so and should contact the school system in their county for specific guidelines and assistance. Standards are strict, so the number of home-schooled students fluctuates. Call John Raffaelle at (843) 937-6510 to find out more about home schooling in Charleston County. In Berkeley County, call Shirley Ford at (843) 723-4627 extension 5056; in Dorchester County, call Bali Cuthbert at (843) 873-2901.

Private Schools

There is an excellent selection of over 100 independent schools in the area, ranging from parochial to all-girl. Some offer financial aid, and most sponsor open houses on campus for visitors. A good source for more information on private educational options in the Lowcountry is the Tri-County Admissions Council, which publishes an informational brochure complete with locator map, phone numbers, and important facts about member schools. A copy of this publication is available from local Realtors or the Charleston Metro Chamber of Commerce. Write for a copy at P.O. Box 39612, Charleston, SC 29407. For contacts at nonmember schools, check the telephone directory. The following list of private schools is a sampling of what is available in the Greater Charleston area.

Addlestone Hebrew Academy
1639 Raoul Wallenberg Blvd., Charleston
(843) 571-1105

Addlestone accepts children from 18 months through grade 8 and provides secular as well as religious training. Conversational Hebrew classes are offered along with a full curriculum in the elementary grades.

Ashley Hall
172 Rutledge Ave., Charleston
(843) 722-4088

Founded in 1909, Ashley Hall is a college preparatory day school dedicated to educating girls from ages 2 through grade 12. It remains the only all-girl independent school in the state. A full 100 percent of the school's graduates are accepted by colleges and universities across the nation. The school's early childhood program also admits boys ages 2 to 4.

Lord Berkeley Academy
See listing for St. John's below.

Bishop England High School
363 Seven Farms Dr., Charleston
(843) 849-9599

Bishop England High School is a Catholic, coeducational secondary school operated under the auspices of the Diocese of Charleston. Grouping by academic ability is a unique feature of the school, whereby students of similar abilities are placed together for concentrated instruction. In summer 1998 the school relocated from its downtown campus to a state-of-the-art high school on a 40-acre

Insiders' Tip

It's another one of those perfectly Southern traditions the Lowcountry is famous for: At graduation exercises each spring at Ashley Hall, college-bound girls descend the spiral staircase at McBee House (c. 1816) in long white dresses with armloads of red roses.

site on Daniel Island. (See our Neighbor-hoods chapter for more on Daniel Island.)

Catholic Schools
1662 Ingram Rd., Charleston
(843) 402-9115
A full academic curriculum with all basic disciplines is offered at all six Lowcountry Catholic elementary, middle, and high schools, in addition to the study of religion and Christian values. The schools are Blessed Sacrament, Christ Our King-Stella Maris, Divine Redeemer, Nativity School, St. John's School and The Charleston Catholic School, Summerville Catholic School, and Bishop England (see previous listing). For more information, contact the Catholic schools office at the address listed above.

Charles Towne Montessori School
56 Leinbach Dr., Charleston
(843) 571-1140
Situated on a five-acre wooded campus in West Ashley, Charles Towne Montessori accepts children from 12 months to 14 years old. The school offers a learning environment in keeping with Montessori principles, encouraging creative expression in all aspects of a child's development. There is a studio program for the arts as well as an after-school sports program.

Charleston Day School
15 Archdale St., Charleston
(843) 722-7791
Charleston Day School is a coed day school enrolling about 185 students in grades 1 through 8. Graduates go on to local secondary schools and a variety of preparatory schools around the country.

First Baptist Church School
48 Meeting St., Charleston
(843) 722-6646
First Baptist Church School, established in 1949, offers a college preparatory education in a Christian setting for children ages 4 through grade 12. The academic curriculum is enriched by Bible study and extracurricular activities.

Mason Preparatory School
56 Halsey Blvd., Charleston
(843) 723-0664
The mission of Mason Preparatory School is to provide a solid academic foundation to students in grades 1 through 8. In addition to a well-rounded curriculum, a wide variety of after-school activities is offered.

Northside Christian School
7800 Northside Dr., North Charleston
(843) 797-2690
Northside is a Christian school offering a complete educational program for students ages 3 through grade 12. In addition to general, college preparatory, and Advanced Placement instruction, a fifth-quarter summer program is also available.

Palmetto Academy
913 Wappoo Rd., Charleston
(843) 571-7740
Palmetto Academy has small classes emphasizing the basics in both general and college preparatory courses for students in grades 9 through 12. The school offers help for children with attention deficit disorder as well as those who need more direct attention from teachers.

Pinewood Preparatory School
1114 Old Orangeburg Rd., Summerville
(843) 873-1643
This coeducational, college preparatory day school enrolls 500 students in preschool through grade 12. It offers a full developmental preschool starting at ages 4, a kindergarten program, and a challenging academic program for all students. A full athletic program as well as extracurricular activities such as art and music studies, student literary productions, and special interest clubs is available.

Porter Gaud School
300 Albemarle Rd., Charleston
(843) 402-4771 (Lower School),
(843) 402-4775 (Middle/Upper Schools)
Episcopal-affiliated Porter-Gaud is a coeducational, college preparatory school

Lowcountry students have a lot to smile about. PHOTO: COURTESY OF ASHLEY HALL

with students in grades 1 through 12. All of its graduates go on to four-year colleges. In addition to its strong academic program, participation in a wide variety of sports and extracurricular activities is encouraged at all grade levels of this school on a West Ashley campus.

Archibald Rutledge Academy
1011 Old Cemetery Rd., McClellanville
(843) 887-3323

The Archibald Rutledge Academy, named for the South Carolina poet laureate, offers full college preparatory and general curricula for students in kindergarten through grade 12. The school's small classes and updated facilities, as well as an emphasis on surrounding ecological and cultural resources, are important features.

St. John's Christian Academy
204 W. Main St., Moncks Corner
(843) 761-8539

St. John's (formerly known as Lord Berkeley Academy) is a coeducational, college preparatory day school for students ages 3 through grade 12. In addition to academics, St. John's offers extracurricular activities such as athletics and service clubs.

St. Paul's Country Day School
5139 Gibson Rd., Hollywood
(843) 889-2702

St. Paul's Country Day School provides academic instruction in a nondenominational Christian atmosphere. Students ages 4 through grade 12 attend classes on a 10-acre consolidated campus.

Sea Island Academy
2024 Academy Dr., Johns Island
(843) 559-5506

Sea Island Academy, on a 30-acre site in the middle of Johns Island, offers a college preparatory curriculum stressing the fundamentals in all academic disciplines. The school accepts qualified students ages 4 through grade 12.

Trident Academy
1455 Wakendaw Rd., Mt. Pleasant
(843) 884-7046

Trident Academy serves children ages 5 through grade 12 who have been diagnosed with learning disabilities. The basic philosophy at Trident is to teach students to compensate for their differences in learning, allowing them to mainstream as quickly as possible.

Colleges and Universities

Higher education has been a priority in the Lowcountry since the founding of the College of Charleston in 1770. Today there are many academic institutions of advanced learning with expansive, formal campuses and wide-ranging course offerings. In addition, there are junior colleges, business colleges, branches of out-of-state colleges and universities and even a culinary institute in the Trident area. Major institutions with strong ties to Greater Charleston are described below.

Charleston Southern University
9200 University Blvd., North Charleston
(843) 863-7000

When it was founded in 1964, Charleston Southern was called Baptist College—the only church-affiliated college in the area. Now elevated to university status and ranked as the second-largest church-affiliated university in the state, it offers 28 undergraduate degrees as well as masters degrees in business administration, education, and criminal justice. The student body has grown from an enrollment of 528 to more than 2,500. Sponsored by the South Carolina Baptist Convention, Charleston Southern University remains committed to its mission of "promoting academic excellence in a Christian environment."

The Citadel
171 Moultrie St., Charleston
(843) 953-5000

Recently ranked by *U.S. News and World Report* as one of the South's best colleges, The Citadel is a state-supported military college with an enrollment of 1,700 cadets. The 150-year, all-male tradition of the school was challenged in court, and the college accepted its first female cadets in fall 1996 with more entering every year.

With a formal campus and regimented activities, The Citadel combines academic requirements with military training in the areas of discipline, responsiveness, and leadership. Students select from 26 baccalaureate degree programs and must complete eight semesters of Air Force, Army, Navy, or Marine ROTC training, but they are not required to accept military commissions. Some undergraduate and a wide selection of graduate courses—including those leading to masters degrees in business administration and education—are offered through the College of Graduate and Professional Studies.

The Citadel Archives contain some very impressive collections: In 1966 Gen. Mark W. Clark, president emeritus of The Citadel, donated his personal, military, and official papers covering his career as commander of the Fifth Army in World War II, the Austrian Occupation, and the Korean War. Other notable collections include the Civil War letters of Gen. Ellison Capers (Citadel class of 1857) and the papers of Pulitzer Prize-winning historian Bruce Catton.

College of Charleston
University of Charleston
66 George St., Charleston
(843) 953-5507

Recognized as the first municipal college in the United States and the oldest institution of higher learning in South Carolina, the College of Charleston (founded in 1770) offers 43 undergraduate majors. This thriving academic institution provides a liberal arts education to 11,500 undergraduate and graduate students. The graduate studies program is now called the University of Charleston and offers degrees in such areas as education, marine biology, and public administration. The student-faculty ratio is 18-to-1, and 82 percent of the 420 faculty members hold doctorates or the highest degree in their field. For the second year in a row, the college was named "a top-rated college with the lowest costs" by America's 100 Best College Buys 1999 survey book.

Three original buildings made up the College of Charleston for nearly 200 years. Now more than 100 buildings—from historic structures to high-tech classrooms—constitute the campus in the heart of historic downtown Charleston. Within this setting the college showcases beautiful landscaping, with botanical displays for every season.

Johnson & Wales University
701 East Bay St., Charleston
(843) 727-3000, (800) 868-1522

Enrolling a dedicated group of students who will enter the food service industry, Johnson & Wales is a nationally recognized culinary school. The Charleston campus is one of three locations around the country offering associate and bachelors degrees in food service, hospitality, and travel-tourism management. Established in 1984, the local campus is known as "the Hospitality University of the South."

Enrollment consists of 1,450 students from 42 states and 8 foreign countries. The school places an amazing 98 percent of graduates within 60 days of graduation. It also offers fascinating short courses in the culinary arts that are open to the community at large.

Medical University of South Carolina
171 Ashley Ave., Charleston
(843) 792-2300

The oldest medical school in the South, MUSC was founded in 1824 and now is at the center of the largest medical complex in the state. The MUSC campus consists of 80 buildings covering 50 acres in downtown Charleston. The university includes six colleges—medicine, nursing, health-related professions, pharmacy, dental medicine, and graduate studies. Student enrollment is 2,300, with a teaching staff of 1,200 full-time and 1,250 part-time faculty. The university coordinates statewide training of more than 800 interns and residents. Patient care is provided within the Medical University of South Carolina Medical Center (see our Healthcare chapter), and faculty research is encouraged through facilities, funds, and administrative support provided by MUSC. MUSC is joining Johns Hopkins, Duke, the University of Kentucky, Case Western Reserve, Washington University, and University of Maryland to increase public awareness of its academic and clinical opportunities for medical students.

Trident Technical College
7000 Rivers Ave., North Charleston
(843) 574-6111
Trident Technical College is part of the state system and offers two-year programs for a variety of technical degrees. Trident Technical College also offers continuing education courses and customized training for business, industry, and government, helping to promote economic development in Charleston, Berkeley, and Dorchester counties.
Merging with Palmer College (a private business college in downtown Charleston) in 1973, adding its Berkeley campus near Moncks Corner, and expanding its main campus in North Charleston gave Trident Tech a three-campus network. The newest addition is the Complex for Industrial and Economic Development adjacent to the main campus.

The three campuses together serve around 10,000 undergraduate students, and 20,000 take continuing education classes each year. More than 90 associate degree, diploma, and certificate programs are offered. The curriculum includes programs in arts and sciences; business; health sciences; nursing; public service; hospitality and tourism; community, family, and child services; and industrial and engineering technology. Classes are offered days, evenings, and weekends.

Charleston County Library System

Twelve years in the making (since the public bond referendum for expansion of the library system and construction of a new main library), the new downtown branch of the Charleston County Public Library opened in the spring of 1998. The new library building on Calhoun Street is almost 2½ times larger than its previous location on King Street. The old 200,000-volume library now has 300,000 books with the capacity for 570,000. The handsome edifice is a three-level structure with ground-level covered parking offering the first hour free with library validation. The first floor contains cataloging, circulation desks, fiction, large print, and young adult books and audiovisual materials. Expanded children's services include a youth services librarian and a children's story room. Conference rooms and a larger auditorium are available for public use.

The top floor houses the reference desk and materials, periodicals, nonfiction books, and the South Carolina Room. Banks of computers are available for research and general word processing by library patrons. Check it out along with any of the other branch locations:

Main Library
68 Calhoun St., Charleston
(843) 805-6801

Cooper River Memorial Library
3503 Rivers Ave., North Charleston
(843) 744-2489

John L. Dart Library
1067 King St., Charleston
(843) 722-7550

Dorchester Road Regional Branch Library
6325 Dorchester Rd., North Charleston
(843) 552-6466

Edisto Island Library
Thomas Hall, S.C. Hwy. 174, Edisto Island
(843) 869-2355

Folly Beach Library
55 Center St., Folly Beach
(843) 588-2001

Hollywood/St. Paul's Library
5151 Town Council Dr., Hollywood
(843) 889-3300

James Island Library
1248 Camp Rd., James Island
(843) 795-6679

McClellanville Library
222 Baker St., McClellanville
(843) 887-3699

Mt. Pleasant Regional Branch Library
1133 Mathis Ferry Rd., Mt. Pleasant
(843) 849-6161

Otranto Road Regional Branch Library
2261 Otranto Rd., Charleston
(843) 572-4094

Edgar Allan Poe Library
1921 I'on Ave., Sullivan's Island
(843) 883-3914

St. Andrews Parish Regional Branch
Library
1735 N. Woodmere Dr., Charleston
(843) 766-2546

Village Library
430 Whilden St., Mt. Pleasant
(843) 884-9741

West Ashley Library
45 Windermere Blvd., Charleston
(843) 766-6635

Childcare

Where to Start

Mother's Morning Out

An International
   Option

Resources and
   Support Groups

Parenting Classes

Because many Charleston-area families are now of the single- or two-career, working-parent varieties, there is a real need in the Lowcountry for full-time childcare facilities—reputable establishments that provide quality care for children from the early morning until after regular work hours.

The options that are out there for full-day, extended-hour centers are easy to obtain. The phone book and the local social services office are two good places to start. In this chapter, we provide some helpful hints to assist you in your search for this type of care provider, but we have concentrated on alternative care options and harder-to-find services and support groups.

Where to Start

South Carolina licenses day-care centers only if they maintain standards in areas such as cleanliness, acceptable childcare-giver ratios, and adequate space-per-child allotments. Call the local office of the South Carolina Department of Social Services at (843) 740-0780 or (800) 260-0211 to request more detailed information about this process. We encourage parents to investigate some of the options, listen for word-of-mouth tips and read the classified section of the daily newspaper, *The Post and Courier*, for additional possibilities.

Before you make a decision about where to take your child, make sure the operation's license is up-to-date and the implemented programs fit your preference in terms of structure or freedom. Nose around the playground and check out the general atmosphere, but remember that this is real life and kids will be kids. You could stumble upon a bad day for everyone at a good day-care or early childhood center. But overall you should expect a day-care center to take care of your child in a way similar to a babysitter and an early childhood center to teach your child according to his age of development. Choose a center that allows drop-ins from parents; then do so regularly to ensure the center meets your standards.

There seem to be more centers in West Ashley and in other parts of Greater Charleston than on the Peninsula, and we hear parents complaining about that fact all the time. Mt. Pleasant residents have convenient access to several good childcare facilities. Often there are waiting lists at these establishments, so it would be a good idea to think ahead and get your name on a few. We recommend you schedule visits during the center's working hours, so you will have a chance to observe the children, the care providers, and the facilities on a normal day.

The following listings will give you a rundown on some childcare resources that can help guide you in your search for the most compatible solution for you and your child's needs. We have created a category with alternatives to traditional day-care centers, such as au pair care and drop-in sitting services. While these are not total childcare solutions, they are wonderful babysitting options and, in the case of the latter, may offer classes, birthday party possibilities, and the like. Samplings of some parent support groups and children's classes are included as well. Omitted are private, business-affiliated childcare operations run strictly for the children of employees, as they are closed to the public.

Childcare Alternatives

Drop-in Services

There are some establishments that allow parents to drop off their children for several hours of babysitting or a short class. These are not schools or substitutes for them but rather a great alternative to traditional babysitting. Most ask that you call ahead for reservations, as they will not take more children than they have space to house or adults to supervise. Another plus: Parents are not committed by contract to enroll kids for any specific number of days.

Building Blocks
1901 Ashley River Rd., Charleston
(843) 769-6082

Operated in Magnolia Park Shopping Center by creative and certified teachers, Building Blocks offers drop-in (call ahead, though) babysitting and much more. Children love the staff as well as the story hour, jumpnastics, arts and crafts classes, and science programs. Saturday night babysitting is available until midnight, and the facility (complete with soft gymnastic equipment) can be rented for parties. Building Blocks accepts children starting at age two. Monday through Thursday hours are 9 AM to 5 PM; Friday hours are 9 AM to 7 PM. Prices start at $5 an hour. Call for more information about registration.

> ## Insiders' Tip
> If you are a visitor to the Charleston area or a local parent, Lowcountry Kidsitters Inc. offers a babysitting referral service. Contact the Kidsitters at (843) 881-1862 for details on scheduling a responsible sitter to watch the kids in your hotel room or your home on your next evening out.

Roper Learning Center
182 Rutledge Ave., Charleston
(843) 722-2027

This downtown learning center accepts children from 6 weeks to 5 years old on a full-time, part-time, or drop-in basis. Children are divided into age groups allowing them to interact with others on similar development levels. Constructive play activities in many areas such as art, drama, literature, science, cooking, music, and social science, along with field trips, round out the experience. There are optional on-site activities such as jumpnastics and ballet. Hours are 6:30 AM to 7 PM.

Mothers Morning Out

Local Area Churches

Depending upon the age of the children, Mothers Morning Out programs are offered throughout Lowcountry churches two or three mornings a week. They usually take newborns through preschool and kindergarten ages. You do not necessarily have to be a member of the church to enroll your child, but church members are given first priority.

An International Option

If you are able to provide lodging and would enjoy a cultural exchange experience to enhance your child's learning environment, you might consider contacting an au pair placement service. AuPair Care, at (800) 4AUPAIR, can help put you in touch with a live-in nanny. This service arranges for English-speaking European au pairs between ages 18 and 26 to come to the United States for a year. Host families supply lodging, meals, and a salary in return for 45 hours of childcare a week.

Unlike employees, au pairs usually end up becoming much like family members, sharing meals and social occasions. A local community counselor is on hand to help the year go smoothly for both the au pair and the family. The folks we know who have used au pairs say it is a fun way to help solve the childcare problem and broaden their children's vision of world boundaries.

Resources and Support Groups

In 1994 the Peer Partnership for Civic Change selected Charleston as one of 14 communities around the country to receive a grant to participate in a community-building initiative.

The Charleston Civic Forum was formed as a result of this special funding. The Forum was composed of a group of concerned citizens working to promote community discussions, to encourage collaboration among existing community organizations and to make Charleston a better place for its children, youth, and families.

In 1995, The Charleston Civic Forum held small discussion groups to identify priority issues affecting children, youth, and families. Based on this information, two issues were selected for further study in 1996 and '97: improving race relations in the community and building civic capacity through community activism. Since then, several goals have been accomplished. A consensus of recommendations concerning race relations, improving public schools, and volunteerism in the nonprofit sector was developed. Seed support was established for creating the Mayor's Office on Children, Youth, and Families. (See subsequent listing.) A permanent, half-time researcher on Greater Charleston community issues was hired in partnership with the University of Charleston. (See our Education chapter for more on the University of Charleston.) Another partnership with Youth Service Charleston has funded dozens of community service groups and led to the development of a diverse new generation of young philanthropic leaders for the community.

The staff of the institute produced a resource directory, Services and Resources for Families, Youth, and Children in the Charleston Area, in the spring of 1995. The directory lists more than 800 different organizations under subject categories such as education, childcare, counseling, community service and civic organizations, hospital and medical associations, parenting, recreation, and support groups. The directory is available for reference at the Charleston County Library and public school guidance counseling offices.

Family Services Inc.
4925 Lacross Rd., Ste. 215,
North Charleston
(843) 744-1348, (800) 232-6489
Family Services, founded in 1888, is a private, nonprofit organization offering a full range of services designed to meet the needs of Trident-area families in the home, workplace, and community. The counseling staff is composed of social workers, marriage and family therapists, educational specialists, and budget and debt management counselors. Education and assistance are offered through seminars and workshops focusing on stress management, parenting, divorce adjustment, and self esteem. Family Services groups have addressed anger management, helping children cope with divorce, and family violence intervention. For more information on sessions, fees, and the complete range of services, call one of the listed numbers.

Home Alone
American Red Cross, 5290 Rivers Ave.,
Ste. 409, North Charleston
(843) 744-8021, ext. 318
The American Red Cross sponsors this training program for latchkey children—

those who go home from school to an empty house because both parents are at work. Groups of children and parents are taught how to best handle this situation, which has become commonplace in today's two-wage-earner and single-parent families. Sessions are scheduled as requested by calling the listed number. The fee is $1 per student for groups of up to 25 kids. The one-hour course includes a movie, *Alone and Home*, plus activity books and emergency phone number stickers.

Hotline, Inc.
P.O. Box 71583,
North Charleston, SC 29415
(843) 747-3007 (office), (843) 744-HELP,
(843) 747-TEEN, (800) 922-2283,
(800) 273-8255

Hotline provides a caring ear with information and referral services 24 hours a day to anyone in crisis or facing a problem. A Teenline is available for middle and high school students for discussing problems and concerns with others their own age. Educational programs and support groups are offered on a confidential and free basis. In addition to these services, Hotline compiles a frequently updated volume, the Tri-County Resource Directory, with cross-referenced listings of community organizations to assist families. The directory is available at the Charleston County Library Reference Department, or you may purchase a copy for $30 (or $34.50 with tax and shipping) by calling the office number. Proceeds go to Hotline.

Life Management Center
90 Alexander St., Charleston
(843) 577-2277

The Life Management Center helps people with learning differences, such as attention deficit disorder, as well as their families. Its services include individualized academic instruction, coaching, and time management and organizational strategies. Seminars, consultations, support groups, and referral services round out this valuable resource aimed at creating success for children and adults.

Lowcountry Child Care Association
137 Keenan Ave., Goose Creek
(843) 572-2690

The Lowcountry Child Care Association's purpose is to promote, educate, and support family and group day-care providers. The association also provides parents with referral information about family and group day-care homes registered and licensed through the South Carolina Department of Social Services. Requests for information should be faxed to the number above.

Mayor's Commission for Children,
Youth and Families
Office of Children's Services,
80 Broad St., Charleston
(843) 965-4190

This group serves as a clearinghouse for information about resources available to children, youth, and their families in the Trident area. The commission meets quarterly September through June. The office provides free listing information such as *A Guide to Services for Families*, published by the March of Dimes and the South Carolina Department of Health and Environmental Control. The guide contains phone numbers of area organizations involved in day care, youth services, mentoring programs, infant and child health, parenting, and support groups. Contact the March of Dimes directly to obtain this publication at (843) 571-1776.

MOMS Club
All Saints Lutheran Church,
2107 N. Highway 17, Mt. Pleasant
(843) 971-9751
James Island Recreation Complex,
1088 Quail Drive, Charleston
(843) 763-8624

The MOMS Clubs of Mt. Pleasant and Charleston were started as chapters of the national support group for mothers who stay at home with their children or work part-time. The group's broad range of activities includes special programs for mothers, play groups for children, and get-togethers for the whole family. Recent guest speakers presented talks on subjects such as college savings plans and children's dental care. The Mt. Pleasant MOMS Club meets every other Friday from 10 AM to noon at All Saints Lutheran Church. The Charleston Club meets every other Wednesday from 10:30 AM to 12:30 PM at the James Island Recreation Complex. There is a one-time fee of $20. Children are always welcome at the meetings.

Parenting Classes

Exchange Club Parent /
Child Resource Center
5055 Lackawanna Blvd., North Charleston
(843) 747-1339

This parenting class focuses on families with children from early childhood through teens. The weekly classes use the S.T.E.P. model—Systematic Training for Effective Parenting. Some of the topics covered include understanding behavior, self-esteem, communication skills, developing responsibility, effective discipline, and nurturing social development. Classes are held by child age groups Tuesdays, Wednesdays, and Thursdays in North Charleston. Additional classes are held on Wednesdays in Summerville and Thursday on Johns Island. Call for times and registration information. The fee is $70 for the six-week series.

Parents and Children Together (PACT)
P.O. Box 675, Charleston, SC 29402
(843) 769-5799

PACT is an educational and support program for parents of children ages six months to three years. The program is made up of three components: parent education, parent-child interaction, and early childhood education. The 10-week course meets once a week with fees ranging from $25 to $150. Sessions are held at area churches downtown, East Cooper, West Ashley, and North Charleston. Call the number above for a schedule and more information.

Sibling Class
Roper Hospital, 316 Calhoun St.,
Bon Secours St. Francis Xavier Hospital,
2095 Henry Tecklenburg Drive, Charleston
(843) 402-2273

This sibling class is a fun way to help children prepare for their new role as big brother or sister. Games, a short film, refreshments, and a trip to see the babies in the nursery are all part of this class. It meets one Saturday morning at Roper Hospital or one Thursday evening at St. Francis each month, and parents should schedule attendance during the last month of pregnancy. The class is free and is designed for children ages three and older. Call the number above to register.

Insiders' Tip

The Lowcountry Parent is the Charleston area's parenting magazine full of good tips and information on education, family-oriented businesses, health and fitness, plus a calendar of family fun events. Pick up a free copy monthly and learn about preschools, camps, time management, birthday party planning, and other parent-helpful topics. You'll find *The Lowcountry Parent* at branch libraries, schools, healthcare offices, and local businesses, or call (843) 795-2818.

Worship

Charleston has been called the Holy City for at least a couple of hundred years. Newcomers may at first be put aback by the reference, thinking it borrows too heavily against the true Jerusalem, but no such slight is intended. Instead, it's an old reference to Charleston's early tradition of religious freedom. Early on, that fact was demonstrated in the obvious proliferation of various church steeples in the city's skyline.

Apparently, early sailors enroute to Charleston first saw church spires on the horizon as they approached the Carolina coast. This may be where the term originated. Whatever its genesis, today that distinctive skyline is protected by Charleston law. One of the preservation ordinances passed by the city government many years ago was that no new building on the Peninsula could be taller than the steeple of St. Philip's Episcopal Church. State and federal buildings are exempt from such laws, mind you, so the medical university and Veterans Administration hospitals loom like Goliaths on the upper Peninsula. One or two other tall buildings squeaked in before the height law was enacted. But generally speaking, Charleston's historic Peninsula will never be blighted by unsightly skyscrapers. It will remain the Holy City—by law.

Many of the church buildings in the Holy City are of particular architectural significance. Note that those are described in detail in our Attractions chapter under the subtitle Historic Churches.

Charleston has every right to some kind of badge denoting its longstanding religious tradition. There's plenty of it, and religious diversification (some would say tolerance) has been a part of the city's heritage for a long, long time. A document called The Fundamental Constitutions of Carolina, penned in 1669, demonstrates this tradition:

"Therefore, any Seven or more Persons agreeing in any Religion, shall constitute a Church or Profession, to which they shall give Some name, to distinguish it from others . . . No Man of any other Church or Profession shall disturb or molest any Religious Assembly . . . It shall be lawful for Slaves as all others, to enter them selves, and be of what Church or Profession any of them shall think best, and therefore be as fully Members as any Freeman . . . No Person whatsoever, shall disturb, molest or persecute another for his speculative Opinions in Religion, or his Way of Worship."

Into this somewhat idealistic ecclesiastical atmosphere streamed many divergent groups who would eventually call Charleston and its surrounding countryside home. The procession began as early as 1680, making this city one of the settings where the concept of separation of church and state evolved. This, of course, became one of the new nation's most treasured principles.

It may not be enough to point out that religious tolerance is a Charleston tradition. It's worth adding that religious diversification is, in fact, another of Charleston's remarkable survivors. Not only did many of the church edifices outlast the earthquakes, wars, hurricanes, and fires, their congregations did as well. So did their religious thought.

The first English settlers brought their Anglican tradition, and derivatives of that church still dominate the Lowcountry worship scene today. But early on, there were French Huguenots, Scottish Covenanters, Independents or Congregationalists, Jews, Baptists, and Quakers whose congregations are still well represented in the Lowcountry today.

Close-up

Lowcountry Chapels of Ease

The actual author of the term "chapel of ease" may be lost to the mists of time. However, when England's House of Commons created the Church Act of 1706, its purpose was very clear. England was adamant in its desire to establish its own official church as the dominant and official religion of the New World. Religion, after all, was power.

As distant and primitive as the colonies were at this early date, it was all too easy for upstart congregations and religious factions to take hold in the far-flung colonies. Thus, a tax was levied on skins and furs imported from the colonies in order to fund 10 Anglican parishes with churches (chapels of ease) and parsonages conveniently located at various points in the wilderness. This allowed England to get a jump on any other form of government that might be evolving at the time.

In other words, the Church of England wanted to make it "easy" for settlers (and wealthy plantation owners) to have access to a "proper" house of worship. The chapels' convenient presence also made it much more likely that wealthy planter families would patronize the establishment and generously tithe to the Mother Church.

Amazingly, some of these lovely little chapels survive in the Lowcountry. Unlike many early colonial dwelling houses that were made of wood, these religious "houses" were built to last—constructed of substantial materials (brick, slate, and sometimes tabby). Scattered as they are through the countryside, many of them escaped the destructive influence of urbanization. And as a result, they stand today as tangible evidence of the Lowcountry's important early religious tradition.

One famous Lowcountry chapel of ease is Pompion Hill, built c. 1763 for planter families living along the east branch of the Cooper River. Locals call this little Georgian masterpiece "Pumpkin Hill." PHOTO: JOHN W. MEFFERT

One of the easiest to find may be Christ Episcopal Church, first constructed in 1707, the year after the imposition of the Church Act tax. It's on U.S. Highway 17, about 8 miles north of the Cooper River bridges (see our Lowcountry Daytrips chapter to learn more about this quaint little church). Unlike most of the old country chapels of ease, this one houses an active Christian congregation today.

But as for the name ascribed to these chapels, there remains an honest question: For whom was the "ease" really intended? Was it the isolated colonists or the Church of England?

The small symmetrical building with its jerkinheaded roof is Strawberry Chapel, c. 1725, a chapel of ease built in St. John's Parish along the Cooper River. PHOTO: JOHN W. MEFFERT

By most standards, today's religious climate in Greater Charleston would have to be called "traditional" . . . maybe even "conservative." But the city's early acceptance of religious diversity is still alive and well. A wide range of choices is available here—whatever your spiritual path.

For instance, the Seventh-day Adventists have a church on upper King Street. And the Scientologists have a congregation in North Charleston. There's a Quaker Society of Friends, a Greek Orthodox congregation, as well as a group from the Church of Jesus Christ of Latter-day Saints and a very strong Catholic archdiocese, too.

The Nation of Islam has a representation in the north area as well as the Buddhists. There are a Unity congregation and Unitarian Universalist church. There's a very strong presence of African Methodist Episcopal churches as well as a proliferation of Baptist congregations of many different designations scattered throughout the Lowcountry.

You'll find Christian Scientists, Charismatics, Evangelicals, and

The French Huguenot Church at the corner of Church and Queen Streets is one of the city's finer examples of Gothic Revival architecture. The city—a walker's delight—provides a fascinating architectural study. PHOTO: FLETCHER NEWBERN

Full Gospel congregations in addition to the mainstream Methodist, Christian, Presbyterian, and Lutheran groups. Charleston's Jewish community is one of the country's earliest, and it has a strong presence in the community today. And the interdenominational churches and nondenominational churches appeal to those without formal ties to any given group.

Not far from Charleston is the monastery called Mepkin Abbey, where 30 Cistercian monks live the simple contemplative life of work, study, and prayer.

At this writing, the Yellow Pages contain almost 10 pages of church listings. Newcomers and visitors alike can easily find a number of worship options to explore. Also, the Saturday edition of *The Post and Courier* features a Religious Services page that lists the upcoming Sunday's church options, along with officiating clergy members and sermon topics.

Media

As a result of relaxed federal ownership rules, the shift toward consolidation in media has swept across the nation's print and broadcast industries, and the Charleston market has been no exception. Local, privately owned Evening Post Publishing Co., publisher of Charleston's daily newspaper, *The Post and Courier*, has expanded its holdings across the media spectrum. The company owns thirteen television stations in Texas, Montana, Colorado, Idaho, Arizona, Louisiana, and Kentucky and six newspapers in South Carolina, three in North Carolina, and one in Argentina.

This national trend is evident in the local radio and television businesses also. In recent years Covington, Kentucky-based Jacor Communications Inc. and New York-based Wicks Broadcast Group purchased radio stations in the Charleston market. More switches took place in 1999 as Clear Channel Communications of San Antonio, Texas, bought up Jacor's four stations while adding an AM talk radio format station. Four of these five stations consistently rank highly in the Arbitron ratings. Citadel Communications of Tempe, Arizona, gobbled up the Wicks Group's eight stations in a move to grow its eastern expansion. This purchase of combined listenership is said to reach about 40 percent of the Charleston market.

Overall, the radio market is young and trendy in its tastes, and the local stations respond accordingly. There are numerous choices on the dial in the Charleston area, and formats change frequently as a result of the fierce competition among the national broadcast groups and the independent stations. One constant, however, is a large following for Christian, "family" radio in the Lowcountry.

Sinclair Broadcast Group of Baltimore, Maryland, has boosted its television holdings in mid-size markets with aggressive expansions. Locally, the group has purchased two stations, WTAT-TV (Fox Network) and WMMP-TV (UPN). Sinclair, one of the country's biggest broadcasting companies, owns or provides programming to 61 TV stations in 40 markets. Recent purchases have increased the company's reach to 25.0 percent of U.S. television households.

The Greater Charleston area ranks 104th among the nation's television markets. There are affiliates for all three major television networks, plus Fox Broadcasting, the Public Broadcasting System and an affiliate of the United Paramount Network (UPN). The larger cable television providers are Comcast Cablevision, serving the Greater Charleston area, (843) 554-4100; U.S. Cable Coastal Properties in Johns Island, Folly Beach, Kiawah/Seabrook and Wild Dunes, (843) 559-2424; and Time-Warner, (843) 871-7000, in the Summerville and Georgetown areas. Be sure to check in your specific area since new cable, internet, and mobile communications providers are starting up across the Lowcountry.

Newspapers

Daily

Post and Courier
134 Columbus St., Charleston
(843) 577-7111

As the oldest daily newspaper in the South, *The Post and Courier* is published by Evening Post Publishing. Today's newspaper is actually the combination of two of the town's longtime daily papers. *The News and Courier*, founded in 1803, and

The Evening Post, founded in 1894, merged as *The Post and Courier* on October 1, 1991. Although for years the morning and evening papers maintained separate editorial staffs, they shared a common publishing plant still in use today. In 1990 the latest of several plant expansions took place, and another 10-unit press was installed, doubling press capacity. Additionally, computerization has advanced production to state-of-the-art, full-page pagination.

Weekly neighborhood sections are published every Thursday and provide local news to the communities comprising the Trident area. Daily paid circulation is 108,927; the number for Sunday is 120,620.

Through the years, the staff has won numerous Associated Press awards and has been recognized for excellence by the Society for Professional Journalists. Editorially conservative, *The Post and Courier* gives the liberal point of view a nod on its op-ed page. However, the best airing of liberal opinion in the Lowcountry market will be found on the broadcast television stations.

Weekly

Airlift Dispatch (USAF)
102 East Hill Blvd., Ste. 223,
Charleston AFB
(843) 963-5536

With 7,500 copies printed each week, this exclusive Charleston Air Force Base newspaper is published 50 weeks per year (excluding the two Fridays after Christmas). The paper covers base and military news. The *Dispatch* is distributed to 1,052 on-base private residences and to 60 pickup points throughout the base.

Berkeley Independent
320 E. Main St., Moncks Corner
(843) 761-6397

The *Berkeley Independent* is a community-based weekly appearing on Wednesdays. Circulation is 11,500, which is the largest paid distribution of any weekly in South Carolina. The *Independent* covers the economic, recreational, school, and entertainment news in Moncks Corner and surrounding, fast-growing Berkeley County.

The Catalyst (MUSC Newspaper)
171 Ashley Ave., Charleston
(843) 792-3622

Published weekly, with 7,500 free copies distributed every Thursday evening, this tabloid is the Medical University of South Carolina's faculty and staff newspaper. Text and editorial content are produced by MUSC's public relations department. This publication reaches the highest concentration of degree-holding professionals in South Carolina. Dealing with issues of the medical community (including grants, awards, educational news, nursing, and medical breakthroughs), *The Catalyst* is highly respected among members of the medical profession.

The Chronicle
1109 King St., Charleston
(843) 723-2785

This African-American-oriented weekly is published on Wednesdays. Paid circulation is 2,490; total market coverage, 6,000. Covering the Greater Charleston area, *The Chronicle* deals with issues related to African Americans, including news on schools, religion, business, and politics.

Goose Creek Gazette
205 N. Goose Creek Blvd., Unit 12-A,
Goose Creek
(843) 572-0511

The *Goose Creek Gazette* covers news of Goose Creek and Berkeley County and is published on Wednesdays. Paid circulation is 3,900 with a total circulation of 5,000. The Gazette focuses on business and industry news due to the explosive industrial growth in the county over the last several years. Local features also cover school and church news.

Hanahan News
1924 E. Montague Ave., North Charleston
(843) 747-5773
This community-oriented weekly covers news of Hanahan, Goose Creek, and part of Berkeley County. It is published on Wednesdays. Circulation is 15,200. Church, school and local news are covered.

The Journal
1558 Ben Sawyer Blvd., Mt. Pleasant
(843) 849-1778
The Journal carries community news for Charleston's West Ashley area, James Island, Johns Island, Kiawah, Seabrook, and Folly Beach. It is published every Thursday. Paid circulation and rack sales are 4,000.

Moultrie News
1558 Ben Sawyer Blvd., Mt. Pleasant
(843) 849-1778
This is a free weekly carrying community news for Mt. Pleasant, Sullivan's Island, and Isle of Palms. Published on Wednesdays, its total market coverage is 17,500.

North Charleston News
1924 E. Montague Ave., North Charleston
(843) 744-8000
The *North Charleston News* covers local news of the North Charleston area and is distributed free. It's published on Wednesdays in conjunction with the *Hanahan News*. Total circulation is 6,200.

Summerville Journal Scene
104 E. Doty Ave., Summerville
(843) 873-9424
This community paper is published on Wednesday and Friday with comprehensive coverage of the Summerville area and Dorchester County. National wire reports are interspersed with local news and features. The paid circulation is 9,500.

Tabloids

The tabloid press in Greater Charleston is on the upswing, with several special-inter-est newspapers holding sway against the longtime survivors in this highly competitive advertising market.

Carolina Arts
P.O. Drawer 427, Bonneau, SC 29431
(843) 825-3408
Published by Shoestring Publishing Co., this is a free monthly publication distributed throughout the Carolinas as a voice for the local arts scene. The writers take on difficult and controversial subjects (such as arts funding) and do extensive background research. Reviews of local arts offerings and gallery profiles are standard fare, and you'll find a comprehensive calendar of each state's arts exhibitions, shows and special events. The publication was formerly known as *Charleston Arts*, which appeared in the Lowcountry from 1987 to 1994, and as *South Carolina Arts*, from 1995 to 1996.

Charleston City Paper
689 King St., Charleston
(843) 577-5304
This alternative, weekly entertainment and review tabloid is a voice for Charleston's way-cool crowd. It is the successor to *Upwith*, which the Jones Street Publishers took over in 1997. The owners renamed the tab and have picked up the following of the college and young adult set. Look for reviews of the local club scene, movies, dining, and commentary on the area arts in general. *City Paper* circulation is 30,000, and copies are found in area restaurants and cafés, clothing stores, and college campus locations.

Charleston Navy Shoreline
Naval Weapons Station Charleston,
2316 Red Bank Rd., Ste. 100, Goose Creek
(843) 764-4094
Published every other Friday, this tab is the official publication of the Charleston Naval Weapons Station. Started in June 2000, it covers the Navy news for the government and civilian employees in Charleston. Its 7,500 circulation is distributed free on base and to all base housing.

Charleston Regional Business Journal
145 Market St., Charleston
(843) 723-7702

Tapping into the success of business journal tabloids around the country, *Charleston Regional Business Journal*, published by Setcom Inc., was launched in 1995. After a year of providing in-depth business news coverage on a monthly basis, the publication doubled its frequency to twice a month in 1997. It is distributed free to area businesses with five or more employees, or it may be purchased by subscription. The circulation is 7,600.

East Cooper Monthly
1013 Chuck Dawley Blvd., Mt. Pleasant
(843) 881-1481

Launched in late 1997, *East Cooper Monthly*, published by Media Services, Inc., is a lampoon-style tab written to the swarms of young professionals with families living in East Cooper. Features cover the beaches, athletic events, education, local media news, and history with a twist. A dining guide and a calendar of events focusing on Mt. Pleasant, Sullivan's Island, and Isle of Palms activities are included in this newspaper, which is published every month. A circulation of 15,000 issues is distributed free at area newsstands, racks, and airport kiosks.

Island Life
1413 Captain Sams' Rd., Seabrook Island
(843) 768-4404

This monthly tabloid is delivered to seven sea islands in the Lowcountry: Edisto, Folly Beach, James Island, Johns Island, Kiawah, Seabrook, and Wadmalaw. It's also distributed in the downtown Charleston area and wherever books and newspapers are sold. Total circulation is 5,000 copies. Editorial content includes community news, entertainment, natural history, and political articles.

Skirt!
4552 King St., Charleston
(843) 958-0027

This trendy monthly tabloid, launched in 1994, is dedicated to, but not always exclusively about, women. It presents what's happening as viewed from the female perspective. Top-notch writers and smart, contemporary graphics make this idea really work. News, features, and regular columnists deal with local and national trends, political issues, creative arts, motherhood, and relationships—all delivered with a little cheek. In fact, *Skirt!* has dubbed itself "the monthly newspaper with an attitude." Total circulation is 22,000 and the tab is a free pickup available throughout the Lowcountry.

Periodicals

Best Read Guide Charleston
139-B Market St., Charleston
(843) 853-4074

Best Read Guide Charleston is the local edition of the tour and travel, digest-size publication currently in 38 markets around the country. Morris Communications Corporation publishes 600,000 books monthly in the Charleston market featuring the attractions and entertainment available here. Color-coded pages make it easy to find children's activities, golf course listings, a calendar of events, dining, tours, lodging, and maps. It is spiced up with short editorial features on local folklore, historical spots, nature trips, and other points of interest. The publication is a free pick-up in hotels, motels, restaurants, retail outlets, and visitor centers.

Charleston Magazine
782 Johnnie Dodds Blvd., Ste. C,
Mt. Pleasant
(843) 971-9811

Charleston Magazine provides Charleston residents and visitors a lively, informative, entertaining, and sophisticated resource about our Peninsula and outlying districts on a bi-monthly basis. Colorful features are offered on homes, gardens and architecture, dining, health and fitness, arts and entertainment, travel and style. Profiles of the region's most provocative and influential personalities, essays and opinion columns tackle some of the tougher issues and concerns facing Lowcountry residents. Published by Gulfstream Communications, *Charleston Magazine* has a circulation of 25,000 and is available on newsstands or by subscription.

Gateway to Historic Charleston
20 Burns Ln., Charleston
(843) 722-3969
Gateway to Historic Charleston, in its 45th year, annually distributes 600,000 free copies to area hotels, motels, restaurants, galleries, and information centers. Issued every three months, this pocket-size publication is a handy guide to sightseeing, dining, shopping, and cooking. It contains a three-month calendar of events, a centerfold map of the Greater Charleston area and a Peninsula street map.

Television

Three major cable providers serve the Greater Charleston area, so network channel numbers vary in different towns. Comcast Cable serves Charleston; Time-Warner serves Summerville and Georgetown; and U.S. Cable provides programming for Johns Island, Folly Beach, Kiawah, Seabrook, Wild Dunes, Awendaw, Edisto Beach, and the Hollywood-Ravenel area. The following is a list of local affiliates, with the channel numbers where each can be found in different area locales.

WCBD, Channel 2 (NBC)—Comcast (Channel 3); Time-Warner (2); U.S. Cable (3, except Channel 2 in Wild Dunes).
WCIV, Channel 4 (ABC)—Comcast (8); Time-Warner (4); U.S. Cable (4).
WCSC, Channel 5 (CBS)—Comcast (9); Time-Warner (5); U.S. Cable (5).

WITV, Channel 7 (PBS)—Comcast (11); Time-Warner (11, except 7 in Summerville); U.S. Cable (11, except 7 in Wild Dunes).
WTAT, Channel 24 (FOX)—Comcast (6); Time-Warner (6 in Summerville, 3 in Georgetown); U.S. Cable (6).
WMMP, Channel 36 (UPN)—Comcast (13); Time-Warner (13 in Summerville, 8 in Georgetown); U.S. Cable (13).

Radio

Here is a fairly comprehensive list of the current radio station options arranged by format. Remember, radio stations are after the listener's attention, which is a moving target. Formats practically change with the weather. Your best bet is to use your radio dial and go exploring.

Country
WEZL 103.5 FM
WNKT 107.5 FM

News/Talk
WSC 730 AM
WTMA 1250 AM

Oldies
WXLY 102.5 FM
WCOO 105.3 FM (Groovin' Oldies)

Public Radio
WSCI 89.3 FM

Rhythm and Blues
WPAL 100.9 FM

Urban
WWWZ 93.3 FM
WSSP 94.3 FM
WWBZ 98.9 FM
WMGL 101.7 FM (Adult Urban/Soft Soul)

Rock
WSSX 95.1 FM (Contemporary Hits)
WAVF 96.1 FM (Alternative)
WYBB 98.1 FM
WLLC-FM 100.5 (New Rock/Alternative)
WRFQ 104.5 FM (Rock Classics)

Sports
WTMZ 910 AM
WQSC 1340 AM
WQNT 1450 AM

Adult Contemporary
WSUY 96.9 FM

Christian, Gospel, Family
WFCH 88.5 FM
WYFH 90.7 FM
WKCL 91.5 FM
WJNI 106.3 FM
WQIZ 810 AM
WMCJ 950 AM
WAZS 980 AM (Country/Southern Gospel)
WXTC 1390 AM
WZJY 1480 AM

Military

Throughout our country's wars, both domestic and foreign, the strategic location of Charleston's port and the
energy of the city's defenders have both played important roles. Volumes have been written on the subject, movies have been made, and there's no small amount of high drama,
colorful characters, genuine courage, and even a bit of Nazi intrigue involved.

For most of the Cold War years, the Greater Charleston area served as the U.S. Navy's
third-largest home port and the country's largest submarine base. North Charleston is
currently home to the U.S. Air Force's 437th Airlift Wing. And the Marines, the Army,
and Coast Guard still work to underscore the military's presence in this area.

But how do Charlestonians feel about the military?

Many of Greater Charleston's proudest citizens are former military people who have
chosen to retire here. More former personnel from Charleston's military past return to
the Lowcountry every year. Their loyalty to the military is unquestioned. But the real
answer as to how they feel may be best illustrated by Charleston's fierce patriotism during the anxious days in 1991 preceding Operation Desert Storm in the Gulf War. As ten-
sions mounted in the Persian Gulf, Charlestonians watched quietly as ship after ship
from the Navy base slid slowly past the port facilities, under the Cooper River bridges,
out into Charleston Harbor and into the pages of history. These weren't ships from some
faraway port. These were men and women from here at home—Charleston's own fathers
and mothers, sons, and daughters.

Commuters on their way to work, tourists en route to the beaches, lovers strolling in
Waterfront Park—almost everyone who saw the ships heading out—felt a pull on the heart.

But such a scene is hardly new in this old port city. Generations of Charleston-based
military families have watched the same heart-rending parade head out into the Atlantic.
And while the individual soldiers, sailors, and the vessels may have changed, the deep
feeling of pride in many patriotic Charlestonians, native or adopted, has not.

Historically, the importance of Charleston to the military defense of our country is
almost impossible to calculate. On the other hand, the importance of the military to
Charleston is a matter of clear and impressive economic record.

Even though the Charleston Navy base and shipyard were officially closed in 1996,
the Lowcountry's military presence still packs plenty of economic heat. According to statistics released by the Charleston Air Force Base Economic Impact Analysis for 2000,
their input (alone) pumped nearly $390 million into the Greater Charleston economy.

Air Force manpower figures are slightly down (from 7,595 in 1999 to 7,298 in 2000)—
mostly because the number of planes and crews assigned to the base is lower.
Charleston's older fleet of C-141s was being phased out over the last year, and the last
one departed the base in July 2000. However, fourteen additional C-17 transport aircraft
with accompanying support crews are expected to join the current fleet of 40 C-17s.
Across-the-board pay raises for remaining military personnel and civilian employees
brought the current Charleston Air Force Base payroll to $135.7 million in 2000. Expen-
ditures for Air Force construction projects are another big ticket item—$49.8 million in
2000. The base's total expenditures for year 2000 were $178.8 million.

When those Air Force payroll dollars are combined with those of the 700 Coast
Guard personnel stationed in Charleston, the total economic impact is staggering.

Despite the crepe-hanging predictions that rang toll at the time of the Navy base-closure hearings in Washington, the military only dropped to third place among the top-ranking economic engines in the Lowcountry. This dependable portion of the area's economic pie had always worked to keep the Lowcountry relatively insulated against national recessionary trends.

Gone, but Not Forgotten: United States Naval Base, Charleston

As many of the Lowcountry's proud military retirees are quick to point out, Charleston used to be "a Navy town." And only a few years ago, the economic security blanket the U.S. Navy provided Charleston for generations started to unravel almost overnight.

In the spring of 1993, the March 13 headline in *The Post and Courier* shouted, "A Direct Hit!" In Washington, the Defense Base Closure and Realignment Commission had announced the names of the U.S. military installations under consideration for closure or "realignment" in response to the end of the Cold War. It was part of the government's all-out effort to curb the nation's suffocating deficit. With that announcement, the 200-year-long journey of Charleston and the United States Navy veered onto a new course. In May 1993 the final hearings were held, and Charleston's arguments to sweep back the tide were unsuccessful. The official announcement came in June: Both the Charleston Navy base and the Charleston shipyard were casualties.

The history of the Navy's official presence in Charleston only dates back to 1900—although there were Naval battles in and off Charleston's waters since the American Revolution. That year the 56th Congress authorized the establishment of a new Navy yard on the west bank of the Cooper River. A site comprised of three antebellum plantations about 6 miles north of the Custom House was selected, and surveying began in early 1902.

In 1909, the dry dock was the first project to be completed, followed by the red brick buildings and the main power plant. With a work force of some 300 civilians, the first ship was placed in dry dock, and work began on vessels of the American fleet in 1910. By 1915, 800 were employed at the yard.

During World War I, a naval training center was established at the yard, and there was a considerable expansion of facilities, land area, and work force. Employment soared to 6,500 personnel by November 1918. But after the war, the work force was gradually reduced, and only minor vessels were sent to Charleston for repairs. By 1922, the future of the Navy yard had become uncertain.

The beginning of a second surge of activity for the yard came in 1933. A large government-ordered work load created the need for more facilities and a much larger work force. These men and women formed the nucleus of the group that would soon meet the demands of shipbuilding and repair work during World War II. More expansion included what is now known as the south yard, the Naval Air Station, and the Noisette Creek Area.

During the war, Navy yard employees built some 200 vessels of various classes including destroyers, destroyer escorts, tank-landing ships, amphibious landing ships, and destroyer tenders. There was also much battle damage repair work to be done. Civilian employment at the yard peaked in 1943 with almost 26,000 employees sharing the work load in three shifts daily.

Meanwhile, the Sixth Naval District (which included South Carolina, most of North Carolina and Florida, plus Alabama, Tennessee, Mississippi, Louisiana, and Texas) was responsible for the protection of the sea lanes and convoy routes along 540 miles of coastline on the eastern seaboard.

The record for reported submarine contacts in coastal waters off the United States was set in April 1943, with 35 hostile contacts investigated. Unbeknownst to most people living in the Lowcountry at the time, the busiest area for antisubmarine patrols was right off the coast of Charleston. As a result of an intensive defense strategy, only three American ships were torpedoed off the Carolinas and Georgia coasts after May 1942.

Just before the outbreak of World War II, the naval complex had again been enlarged with the establishment of the Charleston Naval Ammunition Depot. It was 20 miles from downtown on the west bank of the Cooper River, set on land that had once made up five plantations in the Goose Creek area of St. James Parish. Throughout the war, the depot was receiving, storing, reworking, and issuing vast amounts of ammunition.

On November 30, 1945, the U.S. Naval Base, Charleston, was officially established, and the old Navy yard became the Charleston Naval Shipyard, a component of the base.

The ammunition depot was placed in "partial maintenance" status in 1950 during the Korean War, and that status was upgraded to active in 1952. In 1954, an additional tract known as the Liberty Hall Annex was acquired for further expansion. In another area on the Navy yard property, the Marine Barracks, Charleston, was established in March 1959.

During the 1950s, the Naval Shipyard became the major overhaul facility on the East Coast for submarines as well as the outfitter for new ships constructed for the Navy in private shipyards in the district. New piers, barracks, and buildings for mine warfare ships and personnel were started in 1956. Later, Charleston became home port for combatant ships and submarines of the Atlantic fleet. The Naval Ammunition Depot was renamed the Naval Weapons Station in 1965, and by 1990 the station covered 16,344 acres.

The Gulf War provided a major test of Charleston's continuing naval presence and

The U.S. Naval Base at Charleston. PHOTO: COURTESY OF CHARLESTON AREA NATIONAL PARK SERVICE

strategic importance, and by all accounts, the Lowcountry representatives in the conflict passed with flying colors.

And as dark a cloud as the 1993 news of the closures was to the entire Trident area, the story turned out to have a silver lining. First, Congress passed an economic growth package that one local member of the House says could eventually foster up to 132,000 jobs in South Carolina. A large percentage of those opportunities might eventually come here in the Lowcountry.

Also, the base closure commission chose not to close Charleston's NAVELEX facility, its Naval Electronics Engineering Command, but to expand it. That has brought hundreds of high-tech jobs into the area.

Topping it all off, the Department of Defense added to the good news by naming Charleston as the site for a small civilian departmental payroll center called the Defense Finance Accounting System, which was in place by late 1995.

Another agency that bloomed in the vacancy of Charleston's former Navy base is the NOAA Coastal Services Center (National Oceanic and Atmospheric Administration) at 2234 S. Hobson Avenue. This division of the U.S. Department of Commerce fosters and sustains the environmental and economic well-being of the coast by linking people, technology, and information.

The Coastal Services Center employs about 100 people with experience in many disciplines and organizations related to the conservation and management of coastal resources. Planners, geographic information specialists, marine scientists, oceanographers, natural resource scientists, physicists, and ecologists are represented. They work with private industry, state coastal programs, local, county, and state planning offices, NASA, the Central Intelligence Agency, and various divisions of NOAA, the parent organization. For more information, call (843) 740-1272 or (800) 789-2234.

Charleston Air Force Base

The 3,500 acres of North Charleston that serve as home for the Charleston Air Force Base are about 16 miles from downtown, nestled between Interstate 26 and Dorchester Road (S.C. Highway 642). The main gate is off Dorchester, but there is easy access from I-26 via Aviation Avenue and the Rivers Avenue base gate.

The base is not open to the public, but visitors may be cleared for admittance onto the base by base residents or employees. Both gates are manned around the clock by security police, and government or military identification is required to gain access. If you need more information about gaining access to the base, call the Security Police Law Enforcement desk at (843) 566-3600.

Base History

As the popularity of flying grew, air operations in Charleston began in 1928 on a small field north of the city at what later became Charleston Municipal Airport. During those first years, the airfield was used primarily by commercial and private aircraft. In 1931, the city floated bonds and sold stock for the purchase of 432 acres at a cost of $25,000 and established the area's first municipally sanctioned airport. In 1935, a Work Projects Administration group was given the job of modernizing the airfield, and, with a $313,000 grant, a new 3,500-foot paved runway with modern lighting was completed and another runway started.

The day after the Japanese attacked Pearl Harbor, the Eastern Defense Command met in New York City and made immediate plans for the defense of the East Coast. Those plans included the establishment of military operations at existing municipal airports up and down the coast. Thus, in December 1941, the Army Air Corps took full control of the field in Charleston for coastal operations.

In early 1942, the first flights from the newly designated Charleston Army Air Field consisted mostly of antisubmarine missions. As the year wore on, operations expanded to include the training of B-17 Flying Fortress and B-24 Liberator combat crews and their support crews bound for the European theater of war. At the same time, the airfield was being used by commercial aircraft. This was a successful early example of the "joint-use" concept that is still in place here today.

Joint-use operations continued until 1946, when the military portion of the airfield was closed and officially returned to the city. By war's end, the airfield consisted of 2,050 acres and had received $12 million in improvements. Military operations were re-established in 1952, when the city of Charleston and the Air Force agreed to establish a troop carrier base and, once again, allow joint use of the runways.

The Troop Carrier Wing became the host unit under the Tactical Air Command. The base was transferred to the Military Air Transportation Service (MATS) on March 1, 1956. The Air Transport Wing (ATW) was activated in 1954 and became the host unit until 1966.

On January 8 of that year, the Air Force revamped all MATS units and their missions. MATS became the Military Airlift Command and the ATW was discontinued.

It was Air Force policy at the time to renumber active duty units using the same numerical designations as those units showing distinguished service during World War II. When the 437th Military Airlift Wing was activated, it was assigned to Charleston Air Force Base. Personnel and equipment formerly assigned to the 1608th ATW were reassigned to the 437th MAW.

In October 1991, the 437th MAW was redesigned to the present-day 437th Airlift Wing as part of an Air Force-wide reorganization effort.

Air Park Tours

Currently on static (that's the military term for "permanent") display at the Charleston AFB are four aircraft that (with prior arrangement) can be toured by groups of 20 to 40 accompanied by an Air Force-qualified guide. Included are a Douglas C-47 (DC-3) Skytrain, a Lockheed C-121 Constellation, a Douglas C-124 Globemaster, and a Lockheed C-141 Starlifter. To arrange a guided group tour of the air park, contact the 437th Airlift Wing public affairs office at (843) 566-5608.

Lodging

There are about 167 temporary quarters (lodging) on base available to active duty and retired military personnel and their dependents plus Department of Defense employees. While priority is given to those on official government orders, military, and Department of Defense personnel traveling for leisure may make reservations 24 hours prior to their arrival date. There are 69 single rooms with private baths, 40 rooms with shared baths, 36 family units (with 2 to 4 bedrooms), and 12 "distinguished visitor" suites which may be reserved by any of these ranks: chiefs, master sergeants, colonels, and above. For more information, call (843) 963-3806 or (843) 963-8000.

Special Events

Charleston Air Force Base is host to several special events throughout the year. One is the annual Air Expo air show held in May (see our Annual Events chapter). This free air show features a military air demonstration team, such as the U.S. Air Force Thunderbirds or the U.S. Navy Blue Angels. Several dozen military aircraft of various shapes, sizes, and uses are displayed to go along with demonstrations by military police, working dogs, and air rescue crews. Crowds in the neighborhood of 70,000 come to these shows every year. You'll find ample free parking plus food and souvenir concessions on site.

For more information on this and other special events at Charleston Air Force Base, call (843) 963-5608.

Index

healthcare
alternative, 381, 383
emergency numbers, 382
hospices, 383-84
hospitals, 375-79
mental health centers, 380-81
surrounding areas, 379-80
walk-in care, 374
HealthSouth Rehabilitation Hospital-Charleston, 377
Helen S. Martin Antiques, 149
Henry's, 71
Hertz Rent A Car, 21, 24
Heyward-Washington House, 160-61
High Cotton, 45-46
Hilton Charleston Harbor Resort, 88-89
Historic Charleston Foundation, 129, 197-99
Historic Charleston Foundation Museum Shop and
Bookstore, 126-27
Historic Charleston Foundation's Festival of Houses
and Gardens, 243-44
Historic Charleston Properties, 364
Historic Charleston Reproductions Shop, 118
history
Civil War, 28
cultural and economical development, 29
Folly Beach, 36
Isle of Palms, 31-32
James Island, 34-35
Johns Island, 35-36
Kiawah Island, 36-37
Mt. Pleasant, 30-31
North Charleston, 32, 34
overview, 27-28
Seabrook Island, 37-38
Sullivan's Island, 31
through the '90s, 30
hockey, 347
Holiday Festival of Lights, 254
Holiday Inn Express & Suites, 90
Holiday Inn Historic District, 86
Holiday Inn/Mt. Pleasant, 89
Holiday Inn Riverview, 91
Holiday Traditions Inc., 118-19
Home Alone, 397-98
Hominy Grill, 46
Hoover Watches & Jewels, 149
Hopsewee Plantation, 279-80
horseback riding, 301-2
Horse & Cart Cafe, 72
Hospice Health Service Inc., 383-84
Hospice of Charleston Inc., 383
hospices, 383-84
hospitals, 375-79
hotels and motels, 83-84
Charleston, 84-88
Charleston International Airport, 94-96
East Cooper, 88-89
Folly Beach, 92
Kiawah and Seabrook Islands, 93-94
West Ashley, 90-91
Hotline, Inc., 398
Hot Wheels Skating Center Inc., 305

house museums, 158-63
House of Versailles, 129
Hungryneck Antique Mall, 149
hunting, 331-33, 343-44
Hyams Landscaping and Garden Center, 139
Hyman's Seafood Company, 46-47

I

ice hockey, 347
Idlewild, 54-55
IMAX Theatre Charleston, 80, 189-90
Indigo, 133
Indigo Books, 138-39
Indigo Inn, 108
Ingham, 192
In Good Taste, 140
inns, 97-99, 105-10, 112
International Piano Series, 231-32
International Taekwon-Do Center, 302
Island Bike and Surf Shop, 26
Island Chiropractic Centre, 381-83
Island Life, 406
Island Realty, 114
Islands West, 114
Island Therapy Group, 383
Isle of Palms
bars and nightclubs, 76-77
history, 31-32
overview, 7
parks, 293-94
restaurants, 60-61
Isle of Palms Connector, 20
Isle of Palms County Park, 293
Isle of Palms Marina, 321
Isle of Palms Marina Charters, 337
Isle of Palms Recreation Department, 293

J

J. Bistro, 55
Jack Patla Co., 150
Jack's Café, 47
James Island
history, 34-35
neighborhoods, 359-61
nightlife
bars and nightclubs, 77
movie theaters, 80
overview, 9-10
parks, 294-95
restaurants, 66-69
walk-in care, 374
James Island Antiques, 150
James Island County Park, 258-59, 294-95, 299, 326
James Island County Park Dock, 338, 340
James Island Expressway, 20
James Island Recreational Complex, 330
James Island Yacht Club King Mackerel, Wahoo &
Dolphin Tournament, 342
January events, 241-42
Jasmine, 47
Jasmine House, The, 108
Jasmine Porch, The, 67

McCrady's Tavern, 48
McKevlin's Surf Shop, 329
McLeod Plantation, 205
media
    newspapers
        daily, 403-4
        tabloids, 405-6
        weekly, 404-5
    periodicals, 406-7
    radio, 407-8
    television, 407
Medical University of South Carolina, 375, 392-93
Mediterranean Delicatessen & Café, 62
Medshares, 379
Meeting Street, 125-30
Meeting Street Inn, 109
Mellow Mushroom, 48
Melting Pot, 62
Melvin's Southern BBQ & Ribs, 56
mental health centers, 380-81
Mercury Air Center, 22
Mercury Air J.Z.I., 22-23
Merrill Benfield Interior Design & Decorative Accessories, 145
Metropolitan Deluxe, 130
Middleton Inn, 109-10
Middleton Outdoor Program, 326
Middleton Place, 169-71, 259-60
Middleton Riding and Hunt Stables, 301
Mike's Bikes, 26
military, 409-10
    Charleston Air Force Base, 412-14
    United States Naval Base, 410-12
Millennium Music, 137
Mills House Hotel, 72, 87
minigolf, 303
Mistral, 49
Mitchell's on the Market, 72
Miyabi Japanese Steak House, 62
MOJA Arts Festival, 223, 251
Mole Hole of Charleston, The, 130
MOMS Club, 398-99
Moncks Corner Medical Center, 379
Monday Night Concert Series, 232
Moore House Antiques, 150
Morris Island, 175-76, 206-7
Moultrie News, 405
Moultrie Playground, 303
movie theaters
    Charleston, 79-80
    James Island, 80
Mt. Pleasant
    bars and nightclubs, 74-75
    healthcare, 374
    history, 30-31
    overview, 6
    parks, 292-93
    restaurants, 54-59
Mt. Pleasant Children's Day Festival, 252-53
Mullet Hall Equestrian Center, 301-2
MUSC Institute of Psychiatry, 380-81
museums, 158-63, 181, 183, 185-94

Music Farm, 72-73
music venues, 82-83
Mustard Seed, 56-57
My Tho, 49

N

Nancy's, 124
Nathaniel Russell House, 161
National Car Rental, 21, 24
neighborhoods, 351-53
    East Cooper, 353-57
    James Island, 359-61
    Kiawah and Seabrook Islands, 361
    North Charleston, 357-58
    West Ashley, 358-59
newspapers
    daily, 403-4
    tabloids, 405-6
    weekly, 404-5
Nice Ice Fine Jewelers, 130
nightclubs
    Charleston, 70-74
    James and Johns Islands, 77
    Mt. Pleasant, 74-75
    Sullivan's Island and Isle of Palms, 75-76
    West Ashley, 76-77
nightlife, 70-71
    bars and nightclubs
        Charleston, 70-74
        James and Johns Islands, 77
        Mt. Pleasant, 74-75
        Sullivan's Island and Isle of Palms, 75-76
        West Ashley, 76-77
    coffeehouses, 77-78
    comedy clubs, 79
    concert information and venues, 81-82
    dinner cruises, 78-79
    movie theaters
        Charleston, 79-80
        James Island, 80
Niko's Café, 57
Nina Liu and Friends, 238
Noah's Nook, 130
Norma May International, 120
North Area Taxi, 24
North Charleston
    healthcare
        hospitals, 377-78
        walk-in care, 374
    history, 32, 34
    overview, 7-8
North Charleston Arts Festival, 248
North Charleston Coliseum, 81, 224
North Charleston Cultural Arts Program, 223
North Charleston News, 405
North Charleston Performing Arts Center, 81
Northside Christian School, 389
November events, 253-54
Number Six Ambrose Alley, 103

O

Oak Plantation Campground, 300

About the Authors

J. Michael McLaughlin

J. Michael McLaughlin has been living in and writing about the Lowcountry for the past 20 years. During that time, his interests in history, architecture, and the legendary Charleston lifestyle have led him into countless adventures.

His writing has found its way into numerous regional and national magazines and his freelance work as an advertising and public relations consultant has captured national marketing awards.

Michael was raised on a farm in Indiana, but he's quick to point out it was in southern Indiana, and "in Charleston, that makes a big difference." He graduated from Indiana University in 1967 with a B.S. degree in business-journalism, aiming for a Madison Avenue career in advertising. Instead, his first writing job turned out to be in Vietnam, where, as a war correspondent, he won a Bronze Star for his coverage of the 101st Airborne Division during the ill-fated 1968 Tet Offensive.

After a decade back home in Indiana as an award-winning writer-producer for several Midwestern ad agencies, he joined the writers' colony in Key West, Florida. And that's where he was living when 1979's Hurricane David forced him to evacuate the island and he discovered Charleston. Since then, he's considered himself "a born-again Southerner," writing about Charleston and the Lowcountry's charming, if idiosyncratic, ways.

Lee Davis Todman

Lee Davis Todman was raised in Charleston and returned to her beloved city in 1987 after pursuing her education and a nine-year stint away in "the real world." Lee received a journalism degree from the University of Georgia in 1976 and did graduate work there in public relations. In 1979 she began her career in Atlanta, working for several ad agencies, among them J. Walter Thompson USA, where she was a senior media planner.

The pull of the ocean and the traditions of her childhood proved too strong to abandon for long, though: "Who says you can't go home again? Being away from Charleston only sharpened my focus on the city's enduring appeal." Since returning, Lee has worked as a freelance advertising and marketing consultant on local and regional accounts, creating and implementing many award-winning campaigns. She enjoys the challenge of assisting area businesses in expressing themselves through marketing efforts in local, regional, and national media.

Succumbing to the allure of the Historic District, Lee has undertaken the renovation of an old house (c. 1803) in the downtown Peninsula area, and it has proved to be both a test of her endurance and a labor of love. But it provides the perfect setting from which to ponder the timeless beauty and vitality of old Charleston.